CURRENT BOOKS IN THE SERIES:

THE EVOLUTION AND MANAGEMENT OF STATE OWNED ENTERPRISES

YAIR AHARONI

Tel Aviv University

BALLINGER PUBLISHING COMPANY

Cambridge, Massachusetts

A Subsidiary of Harper & Row, Publishers, Inc.

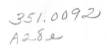

Manufactured in the United States of America.
10987654321

Library of Congress Cataloging-in-Publication Data

Aharoni, Yair.
  The evolution and management of state owned enterprises.

  Bibliography: p.
  Includes index.
  1. Government business enterprises.   I. Title.
HD3850.A46   1986   351.009′2   86–91539
ISBN 0–88730–164–9

Credits:
Grateful acknowledgement is made to the following for permission to reprint previously published materials:
1. *The Columbia Journal of World Business* for extracts from Yair Aharoni, "The State Owned Enterprise as a Competitor in International Markets" in Vol. XV, No. 1, Spring 1980, pp. 14–22.
2. *Cambridge University Press* for extracts from Yair Aharoni, "State-owned Enterprise: An Agent, Without a Principal" in Leroy Jones (ed.) ENTERPRISE IN LESS-DEVELOPED COUNTRIES, pp. 67–76.
3. *The Leon Recanati Faculty of Management*, Tel Aviv University for granting permission to reprint the requested material.
4. CIRIEC, Universite de Liege for extracts from A. Phatak (1969), "Governmental Interference and Management Problems of Public Sector Firms," *Annals of Public and Cooperative Economy*, Vol. 40, No. 3 (July-September), pp. 337–350.
5. *World Bank* for tables from the World Development Report and extracts from Mary Shirley, *Managing State-owned Enterprises*, Staff Working Paper No. 577 (Washington, D.C.: The World Bank, 1983).
6. *International Monetary Fund*, Washington, D.C. for extracts and tables from Peter Short (1984), "The Role of Public Enterprises: An International Statistical Comparison." IMF Occassional Staff Paper.

CONTENTS

PREFACE

Since the end of World War II, the SOE sector in all market economy countries has grown in size, increased in relative importance and diversified in activity. Many of these enterprises have expanded internationally, both by export operations and by foreign investments. They appear to have grown because of a shift in public opinion. The trend of establishing SOEs accelerated during World War II and mainly in the period after it. With time SOEs have come to control a large share of the GNP of many countries and are now to be found in all sorts of industries. They were established to maintain employment in declining industries, to foster the development of high-technology industries, to merge weak and diffused local firms, to prevent acquisition of local firms by large MNEs, to invest in industries for which private capital was not available and, mainly for ideological and political reasons, to exercise control over the national economy. They were also established to replace government departments.

The tremendous increase in government activities and its expansion to areas that may be considered competitive with private enterprise represent a major change in the operating of the free enterprise system. The state has become an economic actor in its own right and makes resource allocation decisions for the good of its citizens—or some of them. One result has been near-obliteration of the traditional distinction between private and public sectors (see, e.g., Smith, 1975, p. 8). Another has been the burgeoning use of hybrid organizations, namely, state-owned enterprises (SOEs). For a long time, the theory behind the creation of many SOEs, at least in English-speaking countries, has been based on Herbert Morrison's ideas (1933); these enterprises were expected to be commercial concerns delivering profits to the state instead of to capitalists. They were to be not only autonomous from political interference but also accountable to the public, represented by its elected officials. The SOE was to have an "arm's length relationship with government." It was to secure "a combination of public ownership, public accountability, and business management for public ends" (Morrison, 1933, p. 149). Experience, however, proved an arm's length relationship to be wishful thinking because ministers were unable to resist intervention. With time the point of view that the SOE should be used to implement any government policy has become widely held—less in theory but very much in practice. Most governments feel that the very fact that the government acts not only as a shareholder but also as a banker of SOEs imposes on them obligations toward the nation. The SOE is considered to be a tool for a variety of government policies and even a vehicle for political patronage.

The multiple goals by which an SOE is judged means that accountability is lost. Since objectives are unclear and ever changing, management can always blame losses on the various other policies it was asked to pursue. Management may also choose to pursue additional objectives, and this variation from policy is hard to detect. The problems of controlling the SOE are exacerbated, and the relations between managers and government become very unclear. Often, the results are that SOEs are not responsive to prescribed goals, and in many cases, the goals are not prescribed at all. Quite often, SOEs were asked to pursue objectives helpful to a government minister for political reasons. Carrying out such activities through an SOE has the dubious advantage of not subjecting them to rigid parliamentary scrutiny, and their costs are buried as being a result of ostensibly inefficient operations in the firm. This state of affairs had led to loss of public money and has weakened initiative and morale within SOEs.

SOEs are one of the many tools used by governments to fulfill their expanded roles. The definition of SOEs, and their shares in the economy are discussed in Chapter 1. Since SOEs are owned by the state, they operate in a political environment. Private shareholders are assumed to want profits. State shareholders may want different things from different firms, in different countries or at different times. SOEs are, therefore, heterogeneous. The relationships of SOEs to government and the environment in which they operate and the many preconceived notions about them are discussed in Chapter 2.

The heterogeneity of experience with nationalization or the creation of SOEs suggests that there were many reasons for state ownership, some of them peculiar to a certain country. The origins of SOEs and the different motivations for their creation and continued existence are the topic of Chapter 3. Still, all SOEs appear to have encountered certain common problems and share certain identifying features, almost irrespective of the causes that brought them into being. Every SOE is expected to direct its operations on the basis of two somewhat contradictory orientations: being publicly owned, it is required to pursue social goals in the public interest. These goals may be to alter income distribution, to generate employment, to bring in foreign currency, to be a model employer, to promote new technologies or to create employment in laggard regions. At the same time, it is expected to be oriented to the achievement of strict economic goals: to be profitable and to attempt to achieve efficient operations and allocation of resources. Questions related to goals are the topic of Chapter 4.

When SOEs are profitable, they become an important source of capital accumulation. Whether these funds become available for other enterprises depends on organization and control procedures. In practice, most SOEs are not net providers of funds. Their record, if measured in terms of profitability, is rather dismal; most SOEs constitute a chronic burden on the public treasury. Profitability is only a partial and inadequate measure of SOEs' performance. After all, they were created to achieve national goals, not profitability. Many economists believe that "pricing of publicly supplied goods is the primary vehicle for embedding public enterprises adequately into a market economy" (Bös, 1981, p. 1). The questions of performance, efficiency and effectiveness and their measurement as well as a comparative analysis of these variables between SOEs and privately owned enterprises are addressed in Chapter 5.

Private firms, although they may be constrained by government regulations, are expected to seek profits. The task of state-owned firms is different. Instead of private gain, SOEs are supposed to seek social reward. A profit-making SOE need not be performing in the interests of society. How is the state to ensure that the SOE indeed seeks to improve social welfare?

SOEs, being publicly owned, are expected to be accountable to the public, as represented in democratic societies by the legislature. They have, therefore, to reconcile the business requirements of operating and financial flexibility and prompt reaction to a changing environment with the need to assure public accountability and consistency with government policy. These enterprises, being publicly owned, are also expected to disclose publicly details of operations and financial conditions; but, being business enterprises, they must enjoy the freedom to maintain a minimum degree of business secrecy. It would seem that all SOEs strive to achieve a considerable measure of autonomy and make a conscious move to achieve this goal. The central question faced by SOEs is how to preserve the advantages of independent operation through a distinctive entity, an enterprise, while being responsive to government and accountable to bodies that represent the state, the taxpayers and the political process. Some governments have coped with the problem of multiple goals by denying their validity (e.g., Chile or Pakistan). Others did not make any attempt to separate ministerial responsibilities from those of SOEs—often at a high price of efficiency loss and a lack of any sense of direction, frictions and resentments. The French government attempted to solve the problem by negotiating program contracts with its SOEs. Others—Canada, e.g.—attempted commercialization, "thus enabling management of government-owned business corporations to operate with less reference to government and with a greater degree of discretion in decision-making" (Sexty, 1980, p. 377). The relationships between governments and SOEs is a major determinant of the efficiency of their operations. It is not easy to achieve trust, continuity, and accountability. Elaborate regulations and detailed controls may choke managerial initiative, hobble activities, impair flexibility and reduce innovation. The challenge, therefore, is to design a method of social control that ensures adequate accountability, without the detailed and multiferous controls that may hamper managerial efficiency or cause too many resources to be diverted either to the controls or to ways to circumvent them. The manner, scope, character and mode of the interactions between governments and SOEs are the subjects of Chapter 6.

Parallel with the tremendous growth of SOEs, a major shift is discernible in the officially proclaimed attitudes of governments toward these enterprises. In one country after another, laws have been introduced and reports written, urging these enterprises to earn a return for the taxpayers and behave in a businesslike fashion. Although these official declarations are not always followed in practice, there has been a move toward more aggressive profit-seeking behavior by SOEs, making them direct competitors of private firms. The more they compete, the more SOEs are expected to behave like private enterprises. Such competition is often perceived as immoral and predatory. The relationships between SOEs and their counterparts in the private sector as well as the need for special rules of conduct for SOEs are analyzed in Chapter 7.

In discussing the pros and cons of state ownership of enterprises or the achievement of public goals through nationalization, these enterprises are usually treated as uniform rational organizational units, attempting to maximize the achievement of their prescribed goals. The managers who coordinate and direct the pursuit of organizational goals are either ignored or implicitly assumed to be totally committed to these goals. However, organizations are not monolithic entities, and managers have a strong impact on the organizational goals actually pursued. The implications of variables such as managerial recruitment or managers' attitudes and their quest for autonomy are discussed in Chapter 8.

Unconstrained government action may result in a significant reduction of independent decision-makers in the society. Moreover, the total weight of the government on the economy and on citizens is viewed by many as having reached threatening proportions. Many economists see SOEs as a necessary evil, are hesitant to add to the responsibilities of governments and search for alternatives, including privatization. Problems of privatization are discussed in Chapter 9.

Since the 1960s, SOEs have been playing an increasing role in international trade and investment. The world in the 1980s is very different from that analyzed by Ricardo. In industries such as oil, petrochemicals, metals, automobiles, airlines, aerospace, shipping, shipbuilding, banking and agriculture, a growing percentage of international trade and production is carried out by SOEs or in government-to-government deals. As they pursue their national goals, governments use SOEs in ways that are regarded as injurious and unfair to the economic interests of other governments. The incidence of such cases seems to be increasing, generating a potential source of political friction of some consequence among advanced industrialized societies.

The implications of this new trend are not completely understood, but some of the contours of a theory to account for the presence of SOEs are beginning to come into view. The role of SOEs in the international arena and its implications for a more general analysis of the political economy is the subject of Chapter 10.

SOEs are a very heterogeneous group, varying both within and across countries. Some of them behave very much like a private enterprise operating in the same products and markets. Others, such as the French theater, the Austrian opera or the Mexican social security administration, share more of the characteristics of a traditional government unit and are beyond the scope of this book. Others, like most development banks, are essentially instruments of the government, transmitting governmentally supplied, subsidized, and often guaranteed credit to individuals chosen by government and for purposes determined by the bureaucracy.

In sum, state ownership is neither a panaca nor the only explanatory variable of behavior. Nationalizing the means of production does not change the necessity of management and does not necessarily lead to nationalization of the way managers think. Managing SOEs in today's complex world is an extremely difficult task. This task is more difficult than in private enterprises because of the necessity for catering to the needs of diverse publics. The problem of goal multiplicity is not easily solved. Managers must have enough rewards and discretion to make such a task meaningful rather than impossible.

To understand SOEs, a contingency theory is needed. In Chapter 11 the variables that seem to explain managerial behavior in SOEs are discussed. These firms are an emanation and extension of the state, and their behavior cannot be understood without understanding the role of the state and the groups that control its apparatus. Understanding the institutional setting and the perceptions of the different players will provide, it is hoped, a better picture of how decisions in the real world are reached and what are the magnitudes of different phenomena. This model may also suggest some of the contours of a theory of SOEs.

Yair Aharoni

ACKNOWLEDGEMENTS

Israel provides the researcher an ideal laboratory on the management of different sectors in the economy. I became interested in this topic in 1963, when I first compared the work of the boards of directors in the three sectors of our economy. Since then, I was fortunate to be a consultant to government, Parliament and enterprises—and learnt a good deal about the management and evolution of SOEs. My work with these different groups convinced me of the need to carefully examine the role of ideology, as well as to distinguish between myths and realities. This book summarizes lessons I have learnt from many managers, politicians, friends and colleagues, too many to be mentioned individually.

In 1978, I was invited to Harvard Graduate School of Business Administration to study state-owned enterprises. The time spent interacting with the members of the Boston Area Public Enterprises Group mainly provided intellectual support, stimulation and insights. In addition, I had the opportunity to observe management processes in action by working as a consultant to the Bolivian government and by working with groups of managers who came to Harvard for workshops on SOE management. I am sincerely grateful to my colleagues in Tel Aviv University and in BAPEG for the opportunity to learn from each other.

Ed Epstein, a long time friend, encouraged me to write the book and Bill Roberts was always eager to lend a hand during its production. I am deeply indebted to Christian Koenig, Leroy Jones, Ravi Ramamurti, Brian Levi and Zvi Adar for contributing ideas and suggestions and for providing penetrating insights. Christian Koenig and Eli Segev were especially helpful in critiquing drafts of several chapters. Raymond Vernon provided stimulation and useful ideas in the formulative stages of the project.

The task of putting the book together was made less onerous due to the help of many secretaries in the U.S. and Israel who struggled through piles of difficult handwritten pages. Most of this work was carried out by Dafna Baskin, Nava Ovadia and Diana Rubanenko who typed quickly and accurately many drafts of the book, meeting impossible deadlines with work of superb quality. Gerda Kestler and Shirley Gassner also provided excellent editorial assistance. Shira Bareli managed to check many obscure references and contributed as a research assistant in many other ways.

In writing the book, I used several of my previous publications on the topic. I am grateful to Gomeh publications for allowing me to use part of my Hebrew book on SOEs, to the Israel Institute of Business Research for providing support to several works comparing state and private enterprises, to Columbia Journal of World Business and to Cambridge University Press for allowing me the use of previous publications.

Writing such an ambitious work has taken a heavy toll on family life. To my wife, Nili and my daughters, Maia and Orna go that special thanks of love for bearing with me through many agonies. Their support, tolerance and encouragement during these years providing a loving home life, has made the task so much more enjoyable.

CHAPTER 1
An Overview

INTRODUCTION

State-owned enterprises (SOEs) are becoming quantitatively as well as qualitatively more important in the economies of developed as well as developing countries. The state has come to own or participate in an increasingly large number of trading bodies. The ubiquitous presence of SOEs across a broad ideological spectrum, their rapid expansion and increased significance, and the wide-ranging implications of their performance for achieving economic, political and social objectives have generated a great deal of interest in the methods they use to set priorities for resource allocation and in the way these enterprises are managed to achieve their objectives.

SOEs are an ancient phenomenon, with a history that stretches back thousands of years. In Renaissance times mining and metallurgy in several countries were dominated by SOEs. France's Maisons Royales produced many articles, the most famous of which were Saint Gobain glass, Sèvres porcelain and Gobelin tapestries, and many countries used fiscal monopolies and operated the postal services. In the nineteenth century SOEs were created to build railroads, construct canals and run municipal gas and water undertakings and telephone systems. In countries such as Belgium and Canada, SOEs have come to play a major role in pursuing nation-building objectives: forging a unified and integrated nation from the widely dispersed and diverse peoples and regions was a reason for governmental provision of certain services–notably, rail transportation. Nevertheless, SOEs were a minor phenomenon until World War I.

Since the 1930s the share of mixed economies controlled by SOEs has been on the rise and it accelerated after World War II. Until the 1950s, such enterprises were concentrated mainly in fiscal monopolies, monopolistic public utility-type industries (such as port authorities, railroads, bus transportation, water or electricity) or in direct services to government (such as a government printing office), or they were acquired to ensure that the commanding heights of the economy remained in public hands and subject to government direction. In some countries, like Italy, SOEs were also created to salvage private firms that were going under. In Spain, INI was created in 1941 to help develop the industrial sector. Although Turkey, Japan, Germany and Mexico also established SOEs in the manufacturing sectors in the 1930s, the proliferation of SOEs in that sector is a relatively recent phenomenon. In many developing countries—notably in Africa—industry itself is of recent origin.

From 1946 to 1970, an increasing number of LDCs (less developed countries) gained independence, and seventy-five new nations joined the United Nations, sixty-one of them from Africa, Asia and Latin America. Some of the LDCs reserved certain sectors exclusively for SOEs, as industrial policy enunciations show in India, Bangladesh or Trinidad and Tobago. In the 1950s and 1960s many governments in the developing countries, anxious to accelerate the rate of growth of their economies, created SOEs as part of their national programs of import-substituting industrialization. They also used SOEs to achieve control of major industries, previously owned by foreign investors—in particular, when these firms were considered symbols of political and social repression and economic domination. In the same period, developed countries created SOEs to promote high-technology industries, to develop certain regions of the country or to direct long-term credit for purposes deemed of national importance.

In the late 1960s and early 1970s, developing countries (and Canadian provinces) expropriated foreign-owned properties on a massive scale, especially in oil and minerals, and developed countries created SOEs to avoid selling domestic firms to foreign nations. Governments have also created SOEs to increase capital formation, to augment the information government has on private business operations or to influence output and pricing decisions in crucial sectors of the economy. The share of financial institutions in SOEs' value added has increased in nearly all countries. SOEs have been used to protect workers against the risk of unemployment and to save private entrepreneurs in declining industries who are suffering from losses. Thus the hard coal industries in the United Kingdom, Canada, France, Italy, Spain and West Germany were brought under state ownership or control to avoid closure: three-quarters of the Swedish shipbuilding industry was brought under government control. In many more cases, governments decided to bail out firms to avoid the political repercussions of lost jobs, despite the heavy drain on the public purse.

Existing SOEs, anxious to expand their operations, despite the heavy drain on the public purse, have created subsidiaries or acquired more business firms at home or abroad. In France, the Mitterrand government nationalized in early 1982 thirty-six major private banks, and six large multinational industrial concerns, and bought control stakes in three other companies.

In the 1960s and 1970s, the tendency to move business or trading operations from the government to specially created legal entities has grown. The operation of the post office is a well known example: a monopoly on the delivery of mail has been a governmental prerogative for many years. Many of these organizations were moved out of the general government budget by the creation of special government corporations that were supposed to be more autonomous. By the beginning of the 1980s, SOEs had come to occupy an important place in their respective economies. Although some SOEs, in the United Kingdom or Japan, for example, have been privatized and others have shed thousands of workers and reduced their size, as in coal, steel, ship-building and other declining industries, there has been an explosive growth of state ownership and a major expansion of the scope of activities of SOEs.

The tremendous recent surge of SOEs—the growth of the activities and importance of these enterprises in many economies—has increased interest in topics such as: What are the forces generating the rise of SOEs and the consequences of their emergence for national and international political and economic structures? What is the role of management and that of the board of directors in such a firm? How and by what standards is its management recruited? What are its objectives, and what are the criteria of performance measurement in such a firm? What are the relations between state-owned and privately owned firms? Are SOEs granted special rights? Are they restricted by special duties? To what extent should they be free from government interference in their business? How should pricing, financing and investment decisions be reached? Are they entitled to carry on activities subsidiary to their main functions in direct competition with the private sector? Are there systematic differences in behavior between SOEs and privately owned enterprises? What variables explain differences in performance between SOEs and privately owned enterprises and within SOEs in different countries or different industries? What adaptations in institutional arrangements, decision rules, control structure and other parameters can improve the performance of SOEs should there be a reversal of the trend, reducing the role of SOEs in the future, as several countries seem to aspire to in the mid-eighties.

This book examines these questions. It focuses on the structure, operations, performance, conduct and control issues and management problems of the SOE sector in various countries. It seeks to identify the variables in which the behavior of SOEs is different from that of privately owned firms, the causes of these differences and their consequences.

The analysis is restricted to mixed economies and excludes SOEs in centrally planned economies. Therefore, the performance of the state sector can, and should, be compared to that of the private sector in the same country. The preponderant share of attention on SOEs has been of late on those of developing countries in recognition of their extensive role as agents of hastening the process of economic development. Throughout, the term SOE is synonymous with *public enterprise, government enterprise, public corpora-*

tion, nationalized industry, state trading organization or *parastatal organization*. These various terms are used in the literature but seem less appropriate: *public* assumes that the government is answerable to the population, while *government enterprise* implies that the enterprise is owned by the government, not the state. *Parastatal organization* is used mainly in Africa.

State ownership has been argued on the grounds of ideology, political power, economic reasoning, social structure and administrative considerations. Ideology involves a belief in the superiority of public over private ownership or control, particularly of the commanding heights of economy. Political power considerations may lead to advancing the interests of certain groups and frustrating others, or consolidating the political power of the ruling party. Economic reasoning may produce a pragmatic response to economic problems, such as the need to eliminate, reduce or control a monopoly or to ensure an adequate supply of essential goods and services at reasonable prices when excessive financial and technical risks deter private sector investment or in cases where the private sector is not able to deliver what the government feels is required in the public interest. Social explanations emphasize the need to substitute absent or weak entrepreneurial strata.

Administrative considerations may result in transferring services such as post and telecommunication, credit, pension guarantee and transportation from government bureaucracy to more autonomous SOE status.

State ownership of means of production can evoke strong feelings. To some, it is a panacea and a part of socialist dreams of a new society, a means of eliminating the evils of poverty and exploitation that are seen as a result of private pursuit of profits. Others believe that enterprises managed by the state can better serve the public interest than enterprises operating in the private sector. Conversely, many see SOEs as a part of the trend toward more bureaucratization of life in modern society and less choice to individuals. To them, SOEs lend to inefficient resource allocation, a retarded creativity and prevent individuals from making choices that are beneficial to society by leading to efficient production. SOEs are sometimes seen as faithful instruments of policy, be it political vote gathering, stabilization policies or prodding the inefficient and fostering growth. SOEs are also seen as the capture of state policy by private interests. They are sometimes believed to be captured by their managers, who manipulate the state and buccaneer the SOEs. According to this point of view, managerial autonomy of SOEs results in "subversion of broader public policies" (Feigenbaum, 1982, p. 117).

These different points of view stem partly from different ideological beliefs, partly from differences in professional outlook. Economists tend to assume that the main target of SOEs is the optimal allocation of resources. "This allocative approach covers the question of the optimal size of the sector of public enterprises as compared with private enterprises; of the optimal structure of the sector of public enterprises themselves; and of the optimal input/output relation of every individual public enterprise" (Bös, 1981, p. 94).

Political scientists emphasize the role of SOEs in distribution of power, as vote-gathering mechanisms and highlight the benefits stemming from SOEs to different interest groups. They are also worried that the proliferation of governmental activities at the margins of the state effectively independent from core institutions means less accountability and a way to "escape the rules designed to curb favoritism in government departments" (Sharkansky, 1979, p. 11). SOEs are also organizations whose inner workings are influenced by their relationships with their environment. With time, these organizations become autonomous, and their managers, like managers of privately owned firms, seek to control their environment and to achieve autonomy by making conscious moves to become less and less subject to government whims. The evolution of the relationships between SOEs and their controllers is of major importance in understanding the managerial behavior of these enterprises.

Understanding SOEs requires a multidisciplinary perspective and cross-country analysis of how they behave and mainly why. Political scientists, as well as politicians, need to be aware of the extent to which SOEs can be counted on for the implementation of industrial planning aims. Policymakers need to know how and when SOEs truly react to their directives. SOE managers are badly in need of a descriptive theory of how strategy is formed, and private sector managers competing with SOEs need a framework to understand and predict the behavior of SOEs.

The existing polar paradigms of the market and planned economies do little to explain either behavior or performance of SOEs. The performance of an SOE and its managerial behavior are jointly determined by cultural variables, political considerations, the familiar industrial structure variables (such as the degree of competition in the market, technology, barriers to entry), the size of the firms and their importance to the national economy, control procedures, the objectives sought and the goal congruence among actors participating in and affecting many decision processes, as well as their power. Thus, ownership is only one of several explanatory variables of managerial behavior and performance of firms. SOEs work in an environment of bureaucratic, political, managerial and economic constraints, which engender behavior that diverges substantially from theoretical norms.

Until recently, the analysis of SOEs has been largely the province of lawyers and economists. Lawyers delved into legal differences stemming from the different legal structures of these enterprises. Economists used the tools of welfare economics to account for the existence of SOEs and mainly to propose rules of behavior once the enterprise is in operation. They have been concerned with questions such as optimal or second-best pricing and investment rules for public enterprises, social cost–benefit analysis and efficiency and performance measurement. Both professions share a common presumption that organizations are rational actors, instrumentally oriented to pursue some predetermined objectives.

Unfortunately, debates on SOEs have tended to run ahead of reliable data. In many countries no systematic body of data exists on spending, debts, savings, outputs, exports, imports or profits of SOEs. The data that do exist are often based on different accounting standards or even on intentional accounting obscurantism; information on transfers between government and SOEs or on conflicts between SOE managers and their controllers is either unavailable or difficult to obtain.

Incredible as this may sound, there is still no officially agreed way of defining the size of the SOE sector, mainly because there is no agreed official definition of that sector. To be sure, there have been many efforts, among others by the United Nations, the EEC and European Center for Public Enterprises (known by its French acronym CEEP) to define what is and what is not a SOE. However, like many terms in popular usage, it has benefited from a certain ambiguity.

DEFINITION OF SOES

As a first approximation, SOEs are identified by three characteristics. First, SOEs are classified as a part of the *public* sector. Therefore, they must be owned by the government. Second, the SOE is an *enterprise* and, therefore, must be engaged in the production of goods and services for sale. This function distinguishes SOEs from other public sector activities that are more in the nature of public goods (such as defense, police or courts) and are therefore unsuitable for sale to users. Third, sales revenues of SOEs should bear some relation to cost. Therefore, a public hospital charging a flat fee from its patients irrespective of treatment is not an SOE. A subsidized transportation sevice that differentiates its prices according to customers is. SOEs are predominantly of business character, and at least potentially self-sustaining and get their revenue through the sale of goods they either purchased or produced without much regard to the way they are legally organized. Our discussion thus includes those SOEs that supply their services against a fee paid by the users of the service and are intended to cover costs, whether or not they are separately incorporated.

Each part of this definition is somewhat problematic. "Public," in most studies of the topic, refers to those enterprises in which the state—either directly or indirectly—has a controlling interest, usually defined as 50 percent or more of the voting shares. The Indian Company Act of 1976 (Section 617) defines SOE as one "in which no less than 51 percent of paid-up share capital is held by the Central Government or any State government or governments or partly by the Central Government and partly by one or more State governments." Note that ownership by another SOE is not taken into account in counting the 51 percent. State control, however, may be exercised with less than 50 percent of the voting shares. In Germany, e.g., the government denationalized some of the large industrial undertakings inherited from the Third Reich and, as a result, does not have a controlling interest in any of them. However, since most of the shares are widely dispersed, the remaining large blocks held by the government are sufficient to influence the strategy of these firms.

Ownership does not always mean control, and in fact, control can be achieved without ownership. The government may control a firm through the dependence on the government. Thus, if the firm's only client is the state, it will have less discretion over its behavior than if it had a large number of customers. In the United States, most firms manufacturing weaponry are privately owned, but the Pentagon's acquisition rules determine the firm's bookkeeping system and its way of calculating costs. (For details of the managerial ramifications of the U.S. Defense Department's *modus operandi*, see Melman, 1970. Weidenbaum, 1974.) At the same time, the government may decide as a conscious policy (which this writer thinks is a good policy) to allow enterprises it owns maximum autonomy. Then there are dozens of cases in which managers of SOEs flatly refused a government order, request or suggestion and remained firmly the managers of the firm (see Chapter 8). In many countries the number of wholly owned SOEs is large and they are not really controlled by the government.

The boundary lines between public and private are often hard to establish for different reasons. The shipbuilding industry suffered a severe crisis in the late 1970s as the yards competed fiercely for a share of the rapidly declining demand. Some governments rescued private firms and guaranteed continued employment through nationalization (e.g., Sweden and the United Kingdom). Others granted large subsidies to the private firms on the condition that they would not significantly curtail employment. The German government increased the amount of aid to less-developed countries (LDCs) that agreed to purchase German-built ships. The French government implemented a scheme of assistance which provides subsidies of approximately 25 percent of the contract price to shipbuilders to save jobs (and votes). Government bailed out ailing firms by nationalizing them or it forced existing SOEs to acquire them or cajoled private banks to give the firm credit.

Miller and Ferrara proposed three criteria for the inclusion of an enterprise in the public sector: (1) Who are the owners? (2) Where does it receive its financing? (3) How much control is exercised by the government? They maintain that ownership is the least significant criterion (in Friedmann, 1974). The ownership criterion by itself is of limited usefulness in gauging the impact of the public sector on the operations of the market or on the behavior of the private sector. First, some SOEs operate in competitive market conditions, and their behavior is indistinguishable from that of private sector enterprises. Second, the very existence of SOEs may have changed the amount of information government has on the industry. Third, governments have other means to influence the behavior of private firms. According to Jay,

[T]he modern pope-emperor argument still continues in Britain: to nationalize or not to nationalize? A glance across the Atlantic ought

*to make clear that a modern government can leave this sort of dis-
cussion to the academic schools—as long as the government continues to collect its taxes and places large contracts with industry
it has all the control it wants as long as it chooses to use it. (1968,
p. 50).*

To be sure, when the firm is privately owned, the decisions are still technically made by the private owners according to what the individual sees as best
for him/herself. In Spain, e.g., 80 percent of electric utilities were in private
hands. The government regulated electricity rates at a level that would be
adequate to allow the firms to expand to meet future demands. The utilities,
however, chose to use the profits differently, and the expansion for which the
consumers paid did not take place because the subsidies did not induce the
firms to follow the government's wishes (Baumol, 1980, p. 136). In a way the
firms were myopic since the result of their behavior was that they were
nationalized.

In reality, there is a continuum of activities. Governments do not have
to own firms to control their activities or to finance them. The government
can and does create property rights and restrict others without any ownership
rights but through the use of licenses, grants, subsidies, loans without interest,
guarantees or long-term advances on contracts and procurements. On the
other hand, government does not always control the SOEs it owns. The widespread belief that SOEs are, by definition, an instrument of the government
is not always true in reality. As one example, France established a second
national oil company—Elf—because its existing oil company—Compagnie
Française des Pétroles—was reluctant to search for oil in the then-French
Sahara (Feigenbaum, 1985, p. 60).

Some countries created organizations that are not counted as SOEs to
circumvent certain legal restrictions. In the United States, e.g., government
corporations are subject to the Government Corporation Control Act of 1945
(Public Law 248, 79th Congress, Ch. 5577). Subsequent to the enactment of
this legislation, many firms were established by the government under different legal arrangements and are known as "Government Sponsored Enterprises." Their ownership is private, and they are not subject to the budgetary
control provisions of the Government Corporation Control Act of 1945. Yet,
in the words of Comptroller General Elmer Staats, they were "created to fill
the gap between what the private sector has been able to deliver and what the
government felt was required in the public interest" (in Smith, 1975, p. 60).
In all these cases, the firm was chartered by the federal government and is
supervised by a government agency. Although it is privately owned, some of
its directors are nominated by the president. If exclusion from budget is a
criterion, such exclusion was granted in 1974 to two newly established wholly
owned government corporations: the Federal Financing Bank and the Pension Benefit Guarantee Corporation. Musolf and Seidman feel that "legal
status as a private corporation may carry considerable weight when such a

corporation has financial independence to back it up" (1980, p. 126). They also note that "some of the newer 'for profit' corporations, however, *also* lack independence from government financing. The National Railroad Passenger Corporation (AMTRAK) and Consolidated Rail Corporation (CONRAIL) will be remembered far into the future for their vast and costly tax-supported expenditures" (pp. 125–126). In other cases, the government guaranteed loans to private corporations—well-known examples are the loans to Lockheed Corporation and Chrysler Corporation. According to Lee Iacocca, Chrysler's chief executive officer, "loan guarantees, I soon learned, are as American as apple pie . . . In fact, a total of $409 billion in loans and loan guarantees was outstanding when we made our $1 billion request" (Iacocca, 1984, P. 199).

"In the new political economy," says Bruce Smith, "the traditional distinction between the public and private sectors has become nearly obliterated through the flow of public funds to universities, industry, nonprofit institutions, voluntary hospitals, social welfare agencies, and other quasi-public entities" (Smith, 1975, p. 8).

It is sometimes suggested that *public* should be defined in terms of who makes the decisions. If the decision-making power rests with the government, the enterprise should be defined as an SOE (e.g., Ramanadham, 1984b, pp. 9–12). Indeed, when the EEC issued, on 25 June 1980, its directive on the financial relations between member states and public undertakings, it defined a *public undertaking* as "a body over which the public authorities may exercise, directly or indirectly, a dominant influence by virtue of their ownership of it, their financial participation in it, or the rules which govern it" (Article 2. See also Brothwood, 1981, p. 208).

Thus, the two aspects of the "publicness" of an enterprise are the extent of public ownership of the means of production and the control of the firms' internal decision-making process by public bodies. Both are present in varying mixtures in different types of enterprises in a mixed economy. There are cases where public control on the firm's decision-making process may be exercised without any government equity. Conversely, the government might own capital but leave the control of the firm's internal decision-making process with workers (as in Yugoslavia), managers (as is the case in many SOEs) or with private partners.

Definitional problems arise also in delineating the specifics of enterprise versus other activities. First, many business activities are carried out directly by the government through its budget, like the state monopoly imports of meat in Israel. Second, integral parts of the government have separate budgets; e.g., the post and telephone services in the Federal Republic of Germany or the railroads in Italy. Third, in some countries, the national opera, theaters or the social security system are classified as SOEs, while in others they are classified as part of the government. Hospitals are seen either as business enterprises or as social services. A precise definition of *business character* is elusive.

When the government is dealing with the public as a business rather than as a sovereign, it usually creates an autonomous legal entity: sometimes incorporated under the general Corporation Act, sometimes under a specific Act for Government Companies (as in Argentina or Israel), sometimes according to a special act for each corporation (as in the nationalized industries in the United Kingdom and, following it, in many of the previous British colonies). The French used statutory form mainly for public utilities and other monopolies. In other cases, such as Italy, Austria, Ghana, Zambia, Spain or Sweden until 1982, a government-owned holding company is the legal owner of the shares in these firms. The espoused purpose of these legal forms is to free the enterprise from the rules and regulations of the government that are expected to prevent flexibility and to reduce operating efficiency. It is also hoped to achieve some sort of separation of activities of government as a ruler of the country and its ownership of economic units engaged in production, exchange and distribution. Again, some of these firms are sometimes considered the only SOEs, while others are shown in the official statistics as belonging to the private sector. In quite a few cases, firms were nationalized but the legal form used meant that they are included in the statistics of the private sector. The most recent examples are the effective nationalization of Continental Illinois Bank in the United States and Johnson Matthey Bankers, the U.K. bullion company.

In contrast, the form of an SOE was sometimes used for the creation of an organization that was never expected to be autonomous or to sell its products in the market. In Israel, for example, on March 31, 1984 181 organizations were legally defined as falling under the Government Companies Act. Of these, only 42 and 64 subsidiary enterprises are defined by the Government Companies Authority as "business corporation." The rest include, e.g., agricultural schools, a school for sea cadets, theater buildings, a hotel management training school, education funds or research institutions. At the same time, some very large business enterprises such as the military industries, the agricultural marketing boards, the railroads, the port authority, the airport authority, the land authority (which owns most of the land in the country) or the government's extensive direct import activities are not legally defined as *government companies*. Excluded, too, are enterprises owned by municipalities. The State Comptroller's Law in Israel defines enterprises subject to state audit much more broadly. It includes under the audit of the Comptroller also all enterprises or subsidiaries thereof that receive government aid. Thus, the bus transportation system is not state owned but is a cooperative. Because it receives subsidies, it is subject to the state comptroller's audit, and since 1968, subsidiaries of SOEs can also be included under his audit. Likewise, the Act establishing the Tanzania Audit Corporation in 1968, which was empowered to audit all parastatals, defined this term in a much broader way than the Presidential Standing Committee on Parastatal Organizations.

Quite often the government uses an SOE to prevent the costs of a certain subsidy from appearing in the budget. When a government wants to save a sick firm, it can do so by a direct subsidy from the budget. Alternatively, it could aid it by restricting foreign competition or by nationalizing the firm. These are two ways whereby the increasing costs to the consumer will not appear in the budget. "The invisible government" (Aharoni, 1981a) seems to have grown in the last few decades more than the visible part of the government, and some of this growth has caused a surge in the size of SOEs. In other cases certain non-enterprise activities were organized autonomously in order to ensure freedom from civil service rigidity. Thus, in the case of Tema Development Corporation in Ghana, the Minister stated among the reasons for setting up this activity as a corporation the need "to provide enough staff for the planning and building of a town" which under staffed government departments could not shoulder. The minister felt that development of the town under the many departments of the government would make delays inevitable and coordination difficult (Pozen, 1976, pp. 123–124). In Puerto Rico, of the 13 SOEs created in the 1960s, "only two were intended to be self-supporting from the sale of goods and services. In the United States, the Inter-American Foundation, Legal Services Corporation, National Bank Foundation . . . differ from traditional government activities in legal but not in basic function" (Seidman, 1983, p. 65). These SOEs "drain away from the departments the most challenging and innovative programs and the most ambitious and talented personnel" (*Ibid*, p. 66).

To distinguish more clearly between enterprises used for purposes such as a district school or a charitable organization and those enterprises that produce and sell industrial, commercial or financial goods and services to the public, most definitions of SOEs add that the revenues of such an enterprise should be more or less related to its output. Some would go as far as to require that a majority, or a substantial portion, of costs should be covered by the enterprise's resources. Unfortunately, in the case of some very large and important SOEs, such a requirement is tenuous. In railroads and coal mining, SOEs do *not* cover their costs, but rely on extremely large subsidies. For example, in 1983 the French Railroad financed only 55 percent of its costs from revenues and received the rest in government subsidies. AMTRAK in the U.S. barely covered 60 percent of its expenses, and the Italian railroads only 20 percent (*The Economist*, Aug. 24, 1985, p. 33). Certain students of SOEs also add the requirement that at least some degree of operational autonomy should be in the hands of managers of these enterprises rather than in those of ministerial authorities. Obviously the operationalization of this part of the definition is not very easy (for an extended discussion of SOEs definitions, see Fernandes and Sicherl, 1981).

According to the definitions proposed by the United Nations (1968) the public sector is composed of units supplying general government services, business operations of the state and SOEs. The business enterprises supply their services for a fee but are part of the government and are subject to the civil service regulations, and their revenues and expenses are part of the budget. They have much less autonomy than statutory authorities that were created by special law, while state-owned companies operate under general company law. Although legally and managerially these are important distinctions, all these enterprises are SOEs by our definition irrespective of the legal form.

In many countries different laws define SOEs differently, and the official statistics do not include all SOEs. In Thailand the Budgetary Procedure Act of 1959 provides a slightly different definition than the one appearing in the National Economic Development Board Act, also of 1959, and both definitions seem to exclude the post office. In Mexico, the national lottery and the Social Security Institute are included in the SOE sector. In other countries they are not. Belgium includes public hospitals, while other countries do not. However, most countries include broadcasting services. France after 1974 includes in its statistics for SOEs only eight such SOEs engaged in energy, transport and communications. Sudan excludes state-owned corporations; Malawi excludes departmental enterprises. As a result, the quality of the official statistics leaves a lot to be desired. In fact, many countries neither collect nor consolidate information on SOEs, including Brazil which has over 560 such firms (Shirley, 1983, p. 4). Any set of published figures has to be checked for the definitions and must be treated with care. For example, in Mexico, the census data for 1970 indicated that SOEs produced 8.2 percent of the national manufacturing output. The Secretaria de Patrimono Nacional figure for the same year was 4.9 percent (Peres, in Ramanadham, 1984, p. 29). In fact, there are no comprehensive statistics on the share of the enterprises owned by different organs of the state in various economies.

Certain countries publish statistics only for the SOEs owned or controlled by the national government, sometimes excluding enterprises operated by the military or those whose accounts are part of the budget. However, many firms are owned by provincial states, local governments or municipalities. German statistics include only SOEs in which at least 50 percent of equity is state owned, thus excluding firms such as VEBA or Volkswagen, which is 20 percent owned by the federal government of Germany and 20 percent by the state of Lower Saxony. Turkey does not include regional and local government owned enterprises, while Italy includes municipally owned enterprises in the private sector. Local authorities also participate in the share capital of private firms. In France, the sponsoring ministries require that the local authority will own at least 10 percent of the voting shares. In the United Kingdom no such minimum exists. In all countries, statistics about the size of such participation do not exist in any usable form.

Subsidiaries of SOEs are sometimes excluded from statistics of the sector (on Korea, see Jones, 1975, Chapter 2). The French statistics, e.g., do not include subsidiaries of SOEs in the figures for public enterprises. However, much of the increase in the activities of SOEs has been through subsidiaries and their subsidiaries. Thus, France does not include the close to 100 subsidiaries of its Institut de Développement Industriel. In 1975, the annual register (*Nomenclature*) included 500 companies not subject to the audit of the Verification Committee. The *Nomenclature* includes neither subsidiaries of subsidiaries, nor shareholdings of the banks and other financial institutions of the public sector of firms whose activities are primarily outside France. In 1962, the Verification Committee estimated that the number of firms in which the state had less than 30 percent ownership was about equal to those in which it exceeded 30 percent. A study by Hanni Gresh (1975) of the French Mnistry of Economy and Finance noted that the number of government-held shares in the financial statements of the SOEs was often more than twice the number shown in the *Nomenclature*. The size of the SOE sector is far greater than can be implied from the official statistics of the countries or the statistics published by the CEEP. The ramifications of SOE activity in firms officially listed as private is far reaching. As one example, the French financial institution, Société Centrale Immobiliére de la Caisse des Depôts et Consignations, alone controls 40 firms (although most of them are real estate firms, managing buildings).

All in all, despite a lot of interest in the operations of SOEs and the wealth of data on scattered industries and firms, "it is extremely difficult to determine the share of public ownership of production in most countries" (Pryor, 1970, p. 166). Pryor contacted almost every central statistical office in Western Europe but found that the comparability of the data is doubtful and that a comprehensive, comparative analysis of the scope and significance of the SOE sector is most difficult. Pryor finally used what he called the "nationalization ratio," defined as the ratio of the labor force in state-owned institutions to the total economically active population in the economy. Pryor also included public institutions that do not market their output, like the armed forces, in the numerator of the ratio. This led him to the surprising finding that the nationalization ratio for the U.S. economy is 15 percent, only 2 percent lower than that of France and 6 percent higher than West Germany's.

CLASSIFICATION OF SOES

Lawyers classify SOEs according to their legal structure, dividing them into: (1) those that remain a government department, receiving funds as part of the general budget and employing civil servants, such as the post office in many countries; (2) those that were established by enacting a special law; and (3) those that are incorporated under the general incorporation laws of the country.

Theoretically, the latter two types of organization enjoy more autonomy. However, governments have been known to have little difficulty in making their presence known in government companies too. In some countries, the president of the country is the chairman of the board of the government company, such as in Zambia, and certain Canadian provinces. In many countries, the board of directors is composed mainly of government officials. In the Federal Republic of Germany, directors serving in the supervisory boards (Aufsichtsträte) include not only civil servants and ministers, but also members of parliament. In all cases, even in the case of a government department, the SOE may or may not be socially accountable, depending upon the extent to which the government represents the long-term interests of the nation rather than some other interests. Some countries are composed of a vast web of tribes, each of which is bitterly resented by others of different faith or language. The government in these cases does not necessarily represent the social interests of the entire country. Bureaucrats in many of these countries have treated managers of SOEs like schoolchildren and have not allowed them very much discretion in decision-making.

The legal form seems to be less important in maintaining the autonomy of the SOE than one might think by reading some of the theoretical literature. From the point of view of strategy, autonomy and managerial behavior, it seems more useful to delineate the following types of enterprises: natural monopolies, fiscal monopolies, other monopolies, so-called lame ducks, administrators and competitors.

Natural monopolies are usually in the infrastructure area and subject to strict regulation even when privately owned. These SOEs do not usually have any discretion over whether to supply services to any individual, and the consumers do not have much choice in choosing the supplier of the services: if they want electricity, they must buy it from the only firm that supplies it or turn to an alternative form of energy (or communication, transportation and so on). Because of their characteristics, their investment and pricing decisions are enormously important, and economists have developed a rich literature on the criteria for their decisions.

Fiscal monopolies are granted by the state as a means to raise revenue through the sale at high monopoly prices of goods for which the demand is highly inelastic (tobacco and liquor are two well-known examples) or through monopolistic procurement rights (as in the case of agricultural marketing boards).

Other monopolies are SOEs enjoying monopoly privileges that are not natural monopolies. These include fertilizer and steel manufacturers in Indonesia, domestic airlines, or match manufacturers in Bolivia, or "natural champions," such as the Brazilian Embraer.

"Lame ducks" are firms that became SOEs because they could not continue operations profitably under private ownership. The government decided

to bail out firms to save employment or because of other possible political repercussions.

Administrators are, at least from an economic point of view, part of the government. They were legally organized as a separate unit for any one of a number of reasons. Many of them are not enterprises in the sense defined earlier. Thus, the U.S. National Park Service, certain schools in Israel, hospitals in some countries or the opera in Austria are separate legal entities but are not enterprises. From an economic point of view, these SOEs are part of government administration.

Competitors are SOEs that compete against private firms in the same industry, either in the domestic market or internationally or both. Many countries do not include these firms in their official statistics as a part of the public sector. However, they constitute an important and growing part of the SOE sector. Unlike natural monopolies, consumers neither have to purchase their products nor do these firms have to sell. They operate in the high-technology fields such as aerospace, biotechnology, computers and electronics, and in minerals, automobiles, and other manufacturing sectors, as well as in construction, tourism and services. These enterprises have become a major tool of governments both in fostering new and growing sunrise industries and in slowing down the decline of senescent activities; some of them are multinationals. These are also the SOEs seen by U.S. commentators as a threat to the U.S. international competitive position or world hegemony. These are also the cases in which differences are found in the degree of government ownership in different countries.

A full taxonomy of SOEs should also include the following:

Degree of state ownership: Certain SOEs are 100 percent owned by the state; in others the government entered into joint ventures with private investors. In some of these cases the government has a majority holding and in others, a minority. Clearly, however, once the government has entered into a partnership with private investors, it has to take into account the point of view of the partners. These partners may be one owner, a single corporation or diffused owners, as in the case of the German SOEs and, more recently, some of the British. In some cases the joint owners are different governmental bodies such as the federal and state governments. In these cases the manager faces the complications of managing with more than one representative of the owners, but together the different organs of the government may have full control. In general, the degree of autonomy of management is greater in joint ventures than when the government is the sole owner.

Market environment: The SOE may operate under monopoly, oligopoly, large number of competitors or as part of a government portfolio.

Nature of emergence: SOEs were sometimes created *de novo*, while in other cases they were private organizations that were nationalized. In the latter case, the circumstances leading to nationalization are extremely important. For example, did the old cadre of managers remain with the company or did they leave? Was it nationalized to rescue it?

Mix of objectives: Some enterprises have clear commercial objectives and no others. Other SOEs were created to achieve social goals and are expected at most to break even. Most SOEs face multiple and conflicting objectives.

Importance of the enterprise to the country: This factor is composed first of the extent of coverage of the activity: Is the SOE a monopoly? Does it control a major part of the industry's output, or is it one of many competitors? A second point of importance is the area in which the SOE operates. Certainly the investment activities of an electricity firm are more closely scrutinized by the government, by private sector business-people and by the citizens, than those of a hotel SOE. A third ingredient of importance is the size of the enterprise relative to the whole of the public sector. The larger the enterprise, the greater its importance and, therefore, the closer the scrutiny to which it is subjected but also the more power its management has. Importance may have different magnitudes and mean different things for various stakeholders. Thus, an SOE with many customers, like the subway system, has to be much more sensitive to complaints of these consumers. A fourth variable is the degree of importance of exports versus local markets. The position of SOEs on these different scales will affect the degree of autonomy enjoyed by the management. It may also affect its cost/price position, financial viability and the degree of social accountability demanded from it.

Despite all the caveats mentioned, a good deal of information is available on the scope of activities of SOEs and their relative importance in various economies and different industries in terms of measures such as employment, investment, value added and output. Although an uninhibited international comparison is somewhat dangerous, an impression at least of the relative size and scope of activities of SOEs within and between countries may be obtained: the principal SOEs in terms of size and resources are easy to identify. In Mexico, e.g., there are currently about 1,000 SOEs as defined by the Mexican authorities. However, five of these SOEs (PEMEX in oil, Federal Electricity, PERTIMEX in fertilizers, the national railway company, and the food marketing agency CONASUPO) invested $14,260 million out of total public investment of $16,640 million for 1981 (Philip in Ramanadham, 1984a, p. 30).

In the Federal Republic of Germany, the Federal Government owns nearly 1,000 firms, and there are a few thousand Länder- and municipal-owned enterprises. However, about half of the employees in the SOEs in which the State holds 50 percent or more of the shares are employed by the German Federal Railways and the Post Office. When firms with less than 50 percent holdings are included, there are again a few very large firms or holding companies.

SOEs comprise a large segment of the economy in most mixed economies. In the industrial market economies, the contribution of SOEs to GNP in 1980 was about 10 percent (Short, 1984). The contribution of SOEs to the GNP in 1976, according to official statistics, was 22 percent in Austria, 25 percent in Italy (CEEP, 1978, p. 293, 223) and more than 11 percent in the United Kingdom (Redwood, 1981, p. 16). In the Federal Republic of Germany, SOEs contributed 11.9 percent of the value added and in France, 12.7 percent (CEEP, 1978, p. 59, 177). In Sweden at the end of the 1960s, the gross sales of SOEs in the industrial sector was 8.4 percent of the entire mining and manufacturing sector. In 1976, it was 13.2 percent, and in 1982, the comparative figure was 23.4 percent. When public utilities are included, the percentages were 17.7, 22 and 33.9, respectively.

Employment in the nonfinancial SOEs rose from 5 percent of employment in Sweden in 1968 to 7.5 percent in 1982. At the same time, the share of employment accounted for by industrial SOEs (excluding public utilities) rose from 4 percent to 17 percent (Carlson, 1984, p. 2). In all these cases, for reasons already explained, the percentage is an underestimate.

Figure 1.1 shows that for many countries with different levels of GDP per capita, non-financial SOEs'share of GDP is around 10 percent, at least as the share is defined in official statistics. For developing countries for which data are available, the average has risen from 7 percent at the beginning of the 1970s to about 10 percent by the end of the decade. Most countries are grouped in the 7 to 15 percent range, but there are variations from as low as 2 to 3 percent in the Philippines and Nepal to as high as 38 percent in Guyana and Zambia, 64 percent in Hungary, excluding cooperatives, which produce another 17 percent, and 66 percent in Algeria.

In all these countries, the share of SOE investment in total national investments is significantly higher than these figures, reaching about 25 percent. For the EEC countries as a whole, SOEs generated 12 percent of the GNP and invested 24 percent of investments, excluding agriculture (CEEP, 1978).

In most of the developing countries for which data are available, SOEs account for at least a quarter of total gross fixed capital formation and, in a few cases, significantly more (see Table 1.2). These figures understate the weight of SOEs in modern sectors of the economy. SOEs are often responsible for producing and distributing major exports of foodstuffs. They dominate domestic credit markets, particularly in small economies, because of their borrowing privileges; in the late 1970s, SOEs were responsible for 40 percent or more of domestic credit outstanding in Benin, Guinea, Bolivia, Burma,

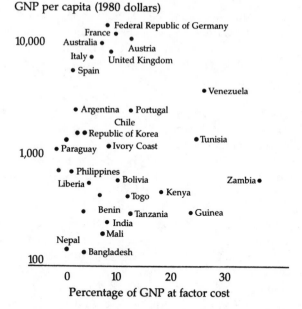

Figure 1.1   Nonfinancial SOEs' share of GDP

NOTE: This figure shows that, for many countries with different levels of GNP per capita,
SOEs' share of GDP is close to 10 percent.
SOURCE: World Bank; (1983).

Table 1.1   Nonfinancial SOE shares in GDP at factor cost (percentages)

Industrialized Countries			
France (1983)	17.0[ag]	Italy (1978)	7.5[a]
Austria (1978–79)	14.5[a]	Ireland (1982)	8.0
United Kingdom (1978–81)	10.9[d]	Denmark (1974)	6.3
Fed. Rep. of Germany (1979)	1.0[f]	Spain (1979)	4.1[a]
Australia (1978)	9.4[e]	Netherlands (1971–73)	3.6

Developing Countries			
Algeria (1978)	66.0	Portugal (1976)	9.7
Hungary (1980)	63.5[b]	Kenya (1970–73)	8.7
Zambia (1972)	37.8	Argentina (1975)	8.6
Guyana (1978–80)	37.2	Benin (1976)	7.6[a]
Nicaragua (1980)	36.0	Sierra Leone (1979)	7.6
Egypt (1977)	31.4	Mexico (1978)	7.4[c]
Venezuela (1978–80)	27.5[a]	Botswana (1978–79)	7.3[a]
Tunisia (1978–79)	25.4	Liberia (1977)	6.8
Guinea (1979)	25.0[a]	Korea (1974–77)	6.4
Senegal (1974)	19.9[a]	Greece (1979)	6.1

(cont.)

Developing Countries *(cont.)*			
Chile (1982)	17.7	Pakistan (1974–75)	6.0
Tanzania (1974–77)	12.3	Bangladesh (1974)	5.7
Bolivia (1974–77)	12.1[a]	Mali (1978)	5.2[a]
Togo (1980)	11.8	Turkey (1978–80)	5.0[a]
Ivory Coast (1979)	10.5[a]	Thailand (1970–73)	3.6
India (1978)	10.3	Paraguay (1978–80)	3.1[a]
Sri Lanka (1974)	9.9	Nepal (1978–79)	3.0
Mali (1978)	9.4[c]	Philippines (1974–77)	1.7

[a]Share in GDP at market cost.
[b]Excludes cooperatives.
[c]Major enterprises only.
[d]Includes financial enterprises.
[e]Includes some local enterprises.
[f]Includes only sues, in which at least 50 percent of voting rights are publicly owned.
[g]Includes only the eight largest SOES engaged in energy, transport and communication.
COVERAGE: Where possible the figures are for majority owned, national enterprises whose output is sold and is of a type where revenue is expected to cover a substantial part of costs.
SOURCES: Mary M. Shirley, "Managing State-Owned Enterprises," World Bank Staff Working Paper, No. 577, p. 95.

Table 1.2   National nonfinancial SOE shares in gross fixed capital formation (percentage)

Industrialized Countries			
Norway (1978–80)	22.2	France (1978–81)	12.1
Austria (1978–79)	19.2	Ireland (1978)	11.8
United Kingdom (1978–81)	17.0	Sweden (1978–80)	11.4
Spain (1978–80)	15.6	Japan (1978–80)	11.4[a]
Italy (1979–80)	15.2	Germany (1978–79)	10.8
Belgium (1978–79)	13.1	United States (1978)	4.4[a]
Netherlands (1978)	12.6[a]	Canada (1978–80)	2.7

Developing Countries			
Algeria (1978–81)	67.6	Sierre Leone (1979)	19.6
Zambia (1979–80)	61.2	Argentina (1978–80)	19.6[b]
Burma (1978–80)	60.6	Costa Rica (1977–79)	19.6
Egypt (1976–79)	47.8	Uruguay (1978–80)	18.3
Pakistan (1978–81)	44.6	Senegal (1974)	17.9
Bolivia (1974–77)	40.9	Kenya (1978–79)	17.3
Ivory Coast (1979)	39.5	Tanzania (1978–79)	16.3
Gambia (1978–80)	37.9	Peru (1978–79)	14.8
Mauritania (1978–79)	37.2	Honduras (1978–79)	14.6
Ethiopia (1978–80)	36.5	Mauritius (1977–79)	14.4

(cont.)

Developing Countries (cont.)			
Venezuela (1978–80)	36.3	Liberia (1977)	14.1
Tunisia (1980–81)	35.8	Guatemala (1978–80)	13.3
Guyana (1978–80)	35.1	Chile (1978–80)	12.9[b]
India (1978)	33.7	Thailand (1978–79)	12.8
Portugal (1978–80)	33.2[a,e]	Haiti (1978–80)	12.4[a,b]
Bahamas (1978–79)	31.6	Philippines (1978)	10.9[a]
Bangladesh (1974)	31.0	Greece (1979)	8.7[a]
Mexico (1978)	29.4	Dominican Republic (1978–79)	8.4[b]
Sri Lanka (1978)	28.4	Dominica (1978–79)	7.8
Panama	27.7[a]	Botswana (1978–79)	7.7
Turkey	27.5[f]	Mali (1978)	7.6[b]
Jamaica (1978–80)	24.8[a, b]	St. Lucia (1978–79)	6.7
Brazil (1980)	22.8	Paraguay (1978–80)	6.5
Korea (1978–80)	22.8[a]	Malta (1978–80)	6.3[c]
Malawi (1978)	21.2	Colombia (1978–80)	5.6
Weighted Average[d]			
Industrial countries	11.1		
Developing countries	27.0		

[a]Share in gross capital formation (including stocks).
[b]Major enterprises only.
[c]Excluding industrial enterprises.
[d]Weighted average for 1974–77 using gross fixed capital formation at market prices.
[e]Includes financial enterprises.
[f]State economic enterprises only.
SOURCES: Mary M. Shirley, "Managing State-Owned Enterprises," World Bank Staff Working Paper, No. 577, p. 96.

Table 1.3   Nonfinancial SOE shares of nonagricultural and public sector employment (percent)

	Nonagricultural Employment	Public Sector Employment
Australia (1980)	2.8	10.4
Belgium (1980)	7.5	23.0
Canada (1981)	3.3	20.3
Denmark (1981)	2.6	9.4
Germany (1980)	4.2	21.3
Iceland (1980)	2.8	16.2
Ireland (1978)	8.8	32.9
Italy (1980)	2.5	12.6
Japan (1980)	1.6	15.6
Netherlands (1980)	1.1	5.6

(cont.)

	Nonagricultural Employment	Public Sector Employment
(cont.)		
New Zealand (1981)	6.9	19.0
Sweden (1979)	3.4	10.1
United Kingdom (1980)	8.5	27.6
United States (1981)	0.7	3.6
Africa		
Benin (1979)	37.1	42.7
Kenya (1980)	8.4	21.5
Liberia (1982)	6.9	11.5
Mauritius (1980)	14.2	26.9
Senegal (1976)	12.9	28.2
Swaziland (1982)	1.8	7.5
Tanzania (1978)	31.9	40.8
Zambia (1980)	36.5	45.0
Latin America		
Argentina (1981)	4.5	19.7
Bahamas (1978)	16.0	13.9
Barbados (1981)	24.1	n.a.
Guatemala (1981)	15.9	5.6
Jamaica (1980)	23.4	n.a.
Panama (1979)	19.3	34.9
St. Lucia (1981)	28.3	n.a.
Asia		
India (1977)	17.7	24.5
Korea (1981)	2.5	15.8
Philippines (1979)	14.0	52.6
Sri Lanka (1980)	28.7	63.0
North Africa		
Egypt (1979)	10.3	26.0

SOURCE: Mary M. Shirley, "Managing State-Owned Enterprises," World Bank Staff Working Paper, No. 577, p. 97.

Gambia, Indonesia, Mali, Senegal, and Bangladesh (Table 1.3). The share of total gross investment of SOEs outside agriculture has been more than 75 percent in Bangladesh, Mexico and Bolivia, close to 50 percent in India and Turkey and around 25 to 33 percent in Korea, Brazil and Taiwan (Gillis, 1980, p. 255).

In many cases, SOEs were created as joint ventures with private owners and have often spread their activities outside the boundaries of the nation-state. Further, SOEs dominate a variety of strategic sectors of the economy:

energy, public transportation, communication and sometimes forestry, iron, steel and financial institutions. Moreover, these enterprises are producers of basic goods and services that are widely used by other industries. They are also important—and sometimes monopsonistic—customers. In the United Kingdom, e.g., the total plant and machinery purchases of six large nationalized industries accounted for approximately one-third of total U.K. industries expenditure in plant and equipment. These purchases were concentrated in a small range of capital goods such as power-generating transmission and distribution equipment, mining machinery and telecommunications equipment.

In some developing countries such as China, Korea and Laos, the public industrial sector identifies itself almost entirely with state-owned industry. In Mongolia the public sector accounts for 97.4 percent of total manufacturing output; in Iraq, People's Democratic Republic of Yemen, Syria, Egypt, Bangladesh, Somalia and Pakistan, it accounts for more than two-thirds of total manufacturing investment (UNIDO, 1983, p. 47).

The contribution of national nonfinancial SOEs in developing countries to value added increased from 6.3 percent in the early 1970s to about 10 percent in 1980. The SOE share of investment has also grown, from about 20 percent in the early 1970s to more than 30 percent by the late 1970s (Shirley, 1983, p. 6). Figure 1.2 indicates the sectoral value added attributed to SOEs.

Figure 1.3 lists twenty-five developing countries in descending order of 1980 GNP per capita and the share of SOEs of value added in manufacturing. In seven of these countries (Romania, Hungary, Syria, Tunisia, Egypt, Burma and Ethiopia, the share of SOEs in value added in manufacturing exceeded 50 percent.

SOEs also play a large role in foreign trade activities of many countries. For example, they account for 44 percent of Mexico's exports and 24 percent of its imports, 87 percent of Peru's exports and 27 percent of its imports. In other countries the role of SOEs has been much less important. In 1977, they accounted for 2 percent of the exports and 9 percent of the imports for Uruguay and 1 percent of the exports and 11 percent of imports for Argentina (Saulniers, 1980, p. 2). In India they accounted for 64 percent of imports but only 1 percent of exports (Narain, 1980, p. 38). For certain international commodities, however, the state trading organization's role is predominant. Ninety-five percent of the international trade in wheat involves SOEs on either the import or export sides, and in mineral trading public enterprises

Figure 1.2   SOEs' share of GDP by sector ▶

NOTE: The blocks indicate the range of sectorial value added attributed to SOEs. The color and height of the blocks indicate percentage shares. Developed countries are shown first, followed by developing countries grouped by region.
aEnterprises with more than twenty employees.
bGross output.
SOURCES: UNIDO; World Bank (1983); Peter Short (1984).

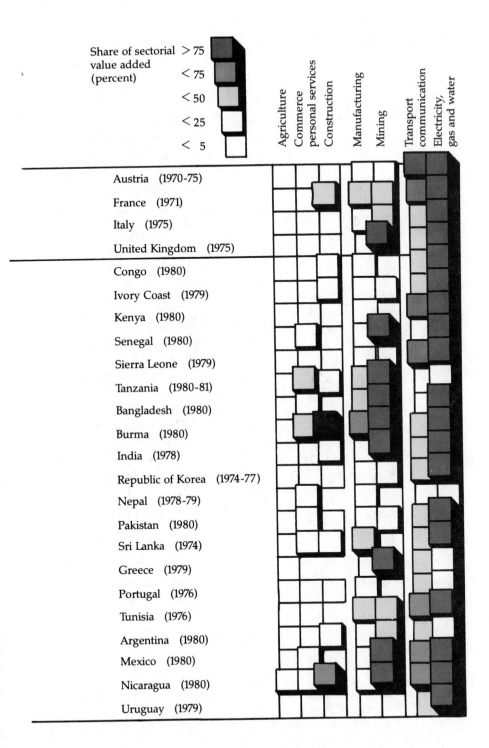

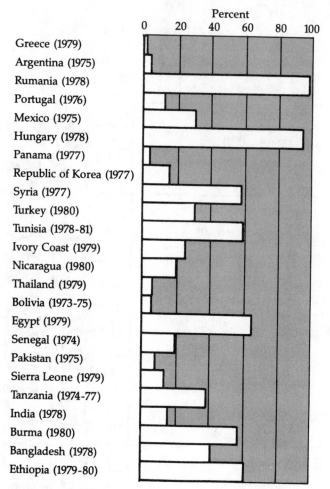

Figure 1.3   SOEs' share of value added in manufacturing

NOTE: The twenty-four developing countries shown are listed in descending order of 1980
GNP[a] per capita. The length of the bars indicates the percentage of the countries'
manufacturing value added attributed to nonfinancial SOEs.
 [a]Includes mining.

SOURCES: UNIDO; World Bank; (1983).

handle about 22 percent of the volume (Kostecky, 1982). SOEs today control
more than 70 percent of the oil production in the world (Noreng, in Kostecky,
1982), 45 percent of Western world capacity in bauxite, and their share in
copper increased from 2.5 percent of world total in 1960 to 43 percent by
1970 (Prain, 1975). They also control 40 percent of the world's iron.

The highest share of public ownership in most countries is in utilities
and infrastructure (transportation, communications and energy). In all coun-

tries postal services are a state owned monopoly. Electricity is dominantly private only in Japan, Sweden, Spain, the United States and Belgium. Railways are almost always state-owned, but Canada, Japan and the United States have a significant share of railroads in the private sector. Car manufacturing is state owned, at least for some part of the production, in Austria, the United Kingdom, France, West Germany, Holland, Spain, Italy and many LDCs. The presence of SOEs in other sectors is significant, although less predominant. SOEs' presence in agricultural production is the lowest of any sector: 1.8 percent in India and 0.2 percent in Korea (Jones et al., 1982). Nevertheless, SOEs have enormous influence on the input and output sides of agriculture because of the prevalence of monopsonistic agricultural marketing boards. In all, the share of the SOE sector in LDCs is between 7 and 15 percent of the GNP. These enterprises have a very high share in large-scale mining, and a large part of the natural resources industries is operated by SOEs (Short, 1984, p. 125) but a very low share in agriculture. Therefore, some of the variance is explained by the industrial structure of the country (Pryor, in Shepherd, 1976; Jones and Mason in Jones et al., 1982).

SOEs also constitute a major source of employment. In seven sub-Saharan African nations the SOEs accounted for 40 to 74 percent of all wage employment (World Bank, 1981, p. 40); in Kenya, parastatals provided almost 50 percent of the public sector employment (Republic of Kenya, 1979, p. 50, Table 5.5). In Benin, Tanzania and Zambia, nonfinancial state firms employ more than 30 percent of the nonagricultural labor force. The corresponding figures for Sri Lanka and Barbados were 29 and 24 percent (Shirley, 1983, p. 6), while in Argentina in 1975 the SOEs accounted for 8.4 percent of total employment (Boneo, 1981, p. 16), in Korea, 2.5 percent and in Swaziland, 1.8 percent (Shirley, 1983, p. 18). In the EEC, the proportion of SOEs salary earnings was 10 percent of the total for the industrial and commercial sector (CEEP, 1978).

The very low percent of SOEs participation in agriculture has often been noted (for example, Jones and Mason in Jones *et al.*, 1982). Austin shows, however, that "while SOEs play a relatively small part in farm production, they assume many, much larger roles at other points in the food sector, through which they significantly influence agricultural production" (1984, p. 14). Austin investigated SOEs share in various food-related functions from production inputs (fertilizers, other agrochemicals, seeds, water, energy, equipment, credit) to wholesaling and retailing. He shows that developing countries make more intensive use of SOEs than the industrialized OECD countries. However, all countries show high SOEs activities in credit, export marketing and transportation. (See also Chapter 10.)

The "world" average of SOE shares in GDP at factor cost, according to official statistics, is 9.4, and in gross fixed capital formation, 13.4. When the United States is excluded, the average share exceeds 16.5 percent. There are broad similarities in the shares of SOEs in different countries, especially in output. Most SOEs are capital intensive, and their share in employment is

Table 1.4   Nonfinancial SOE share in total domestic credit at year's end

Country	Year	Percent	Country	Year	Percent
Indonesia	1980	91.5	Sudan	1981	22.5
Guinea	1980	87.1	Togo	1979	22.4
Burma	1980	76.4	Guyana	1981	20.7
Benin	1980	54.2	Ghana	1980	20.7
Gambia	1981	40.5	Yemen Arab Republic	1980	18.5
Bolivia	1977	40.3	Turkey	1981	16.5
Bangladesh	1981	39.3	Haiti	1981	15.6
Senegal	1978	38.7	Pakistan	1981	15
Mali	1978	37.9	Malawi	1981	14.7
Somalia	1981	37.9	Egypt	1981	13.9
Niger	1980	32.4	Peru	1981	11.8
Ivory Coast	1979	29	Mauritania	1980	7.9
Upper Volta	1978	27.8	Jamaica	1981	7.2
Portugal	1980	24.1	Greece	1979	6.8

SOURCE: Shirley, 1983, p. 15.

lower than that in output. The share of SOEs has been growing, but mainly in developing countries. In these countries, the share of SOEs rose by 4.5 percentage points between the late 1960s and the end of the 1970s, and the share in investment increased by 10.5 percentage points (Short, 1984). Again, these figures are an underestimate. In the mid-1980s, however, several countries privatized some of their SOEs (See Chapter 9).

In many countries, SOEs are the key foreign exchange earners and tax revenue generators. This is true for the oil exporting nations (Mexico, Venezuela and the Arab nations) as well as for other commodity exporters. In the late 1970s, the Ivory Coast, Madagascar, and Malawi obtained from the surpluses of their agricultural marketing boards over one quarter of their total tax revenues (Boneo, 1981, p. 40). Within the LDC economies the SOEs are often very large and dominant enterprises by both domestic and international standards; in India 51 SOEs account for 80 percent of total assets and 70 percent of total net sales of its 101 corporate giants. Tata, the largest privately owned firm, is 13th on the list, and of the top 25 largest firms in terms of total assets, 22 were SOEs (Narain, 1980, pp. 37–38). In Brazil the 10 largest companies in 1978 were SOEs, as were the 7 largest manufacturers in India, the 5 largest enterprises in Mexico (Jones et al., 1982), the 9 largest domestic firms in Indonesia (Gillis, 1980, p. 254) and 12 of the largest 16 Korean enterprises in 1970s (Jones, 1975, p. 200). In fact, SOEs rank among the largest companies in the world, and 25 of the 50 largest European enterprises are wholly or partially state owned.

By any yardstick, the growth rate of SOEs is impressive. In Bangladesh, Nepal, India and Pakistan, the state-owned sector has grown at roughly twice that of the economy as a whole (Ramamurti, 1982, p. 10). Between 1958 and 1976, the sales and assets of SOEs in the *Fortune* list of the top 100 non-U.S. corporations grew at compounded rates of 20.3 percent and 23.2 percent, respectively, while the corresponding figures for private firms in the same list were 11.3 percent and 12.2 percent (Lamont, 1979, p. 255).

The rapid growth of the SOEs has required considerable capital: nonfinancial SOEs commonly absorb about one-third of domestic credit (Shirley, 1983, p. 15). In addition, these firms have become major borrowers in the international capital markets. In 1978 new Eurocurrency loans to the developing country SOEs passed $12 billion, which constituted almost a third of total LDC commercial borrowings and 12 percent of total lending from the market to developed and developing nations (*The Economist*, December 30, 1978). In 1980, nonfinancial SOEs' share of all Eurocurrency borrowing increased to 28 percent (World Bank, 1981), and from 1976 to 1983, SOEs raised over $10 billion through new bond issues in foreign markets (Morgan Guarantee Trust, in Vernon, 1984, p. 40). These borrowings, with their concomitant debt-servicing obligations, clearly carry significant implications for the balance of payments of the developing nations. They have been a prime factor in the build-up of large stocks of foreign debts in Brazil, Indonesia, Peru, Zaire and Zambia since the 1970s.

Another indicator of the importance of the SOEs may be seen from an analysis of *Fortune's* 1969 listing of the 200 largest industrial firms outside the United States. The list included 20 SOEs (3 of which were not defined as SOEs by *Fortune* Magazine). Twelve firms that appeared on the list were nationalized later. Only 5 of the 200 lost money, and 4 of them were SOEs, 2 were German, 3 were British, 5 were French, 3 were Italian and 1 was Dutch. Only 4 were from Third World countries, 3 of which were national oil companies and 1 was in minerals. In 1984, 27 SOEs were among the largest 100, while 83 SOEs, of which 23 were from LDCs, were among the largest five hundred industrial corporations outside the U.S.A. (*Fortune*, August 19, 1985). The recent U. K. privatizations, such as British Aerospace, ICL and Britoil were included in the private sector. In 1979 the list of the 50 largest banks included 4 French SOEs, 5 Italian and 1 German. In 1984, 26 of the 100 largest commercial banks in the world were SOEs (*Fortune*, August 19, 1985).

In 1962, in a compilation covering 483 largest enterprises of the world's market economies only 14 SOEs appeared, accounting for 2.4 percent of sales of this group. In 1978, the list contained 37 such enterprises, covering 7.8 percent of aggregate sales of this group (U.N.C.T.C., 1983, pp. 50-52).

It is also clear that there are significant differences in the size of the total SOE sector in some countries. Thus, while most countries cluster around 7-15 percent share in GDP, in Ghana, Nicaragua and Zimbabwe, the figures are almost quadruple the 10 percent world average, and for Venezuela, Tunisia, Guinea, Chile and Senegal about double the average (Table 1.1 above). There are even more significant differences in the scope of SOEs activities in different sectors; thus, food retailing activities are high in certain Latin American countries and in India. Fertilizer production is state-owned in LDCs, but not in OECD; commercial banks are state owned in some countries and private (but regulated) in others. Although the term SOE is not very well defined, and many cases exist in which it is hard to decide whether a certain enterprise does or does not belong to that sector, it is clear that most governments do own and control a significant number of SOEs and that the share of these enterprises out of GNP is substantial. We should therefore come back now to the question: why public enterprises?

EXPLANATIONS FOR THE SIZE AND STRUCTURE OF THE PUBLIC SECTOR

It was shown above that political considerations, economic reasoning and technological changes combined to expand the role of the state and the degree of its intervention in the economy. Changes in market conditions and increased concentrations made intervention necessary. Shift in public opinion and newly gained independence made intervention mandatory. Yet, the need for more state intervention does not explain the choice of instrument. A government can achieve the goals it wants by regulating private firms, taxing them, subsidizing or cajoling them. It is not obvious that a SOE competing in the market would behave differently and make decisions different from those of a privately owned competitor nor is it obvious that a price-regulated, privately owned monopoly would behave differently from a state-owned monopoly. One difference may be said to be in the distribution of surplus: privately owned firms can distribute their surplus in any way they like, while in SOEs the surplus accrues to the public treasury. Again, life is not that simple: theoretically at least, the government can impose a 100 percent tax on the privately created surplus and may not be able to allocate a surplus of a SOE, whose management may keep this surplus for whatever it sees as the most pressing need of the enterprise. Of course, governments do not impose 100 percent taxes, but the oil firms certainly pay most of their profits as royalties to the government. In France, as early as 1928, oil was regulated by quotas. In order to develop a national refining capacity, the French government imposed import controls on crude oil, and awarded twenty-year licenses for the import of crudes to eleven companies. In order to qualify, these companies had to undertake obligations to maintain compulsory "reserve stocks," to accept requests from the government of "contracts of national interests," to manufacture products required by the army, and to use French ships for 66 percent of the imports. Companies were not allowed to be net importers of finished products, thus providing a further incentive to local refining. In the United States and Canada, privately owned railroads were built largely because of government subsidies and land grants.

State ownership and management of certain units producing certain goods and services for sale is one of several possible tools used by government in its attempt to direct the economy, to achieve a higher level of efficiency or more equitable distribution of resources among income levels or regions, or to achieve other goals it considers to be important. The choice of the appropriate tool is partially a function of ideology, partially of political expedience, partially of historical inertia and, to some extent, a result of economic calculation of costs and benefits associated with its use.

Does the rationale for choosing the SOE firm lie in "bounded rationality" of the decision process? (Kostecky, as quoted in Austin 1984, pp. 9-10). State ownership has to do with the power to allocate resources (and profits) of a particular product or service. In this sense, the reason for state ownership is said to be ideological. In India, the Industrial Policy Statement of December 1977 explained the predominant role the public is expected to play as follows:

> *Apart from socialising the means of production in strategic areas, public sector provides a countervailing power to the growth of large houses and large enterprises in the private sector. There will be an expanding role for the public sector in several fields. Not only will it be the producer of important and strategic goods of basic nature, but it will also be used effectively as a stabilising force for maintaining essential supplies for the consumer. The public sector will be charged with the responsibility of encouraging the development of a wide range of ancillary industries, and contribute to the growth of decentralised production by making available its expertise in technology and management to small scale and cottage industry sectors.*

As shown earlier, however, the share of SOEs in GDP is about the same in many countries of the world, irrespective of ideological predilection. These ideological predilections must therefore be reinforced by other factors. One way to look at these issues is to examine them in normative terms, analyzing the reasons for governmental intervention and the explanations for the use of regulation, taxation or direct ownership. Normative analysis, by its very nature, must be based on some ideological or other norms such as the economic theory of public choice or market failure.

One normative reason for state ownership is that markets do not perform perfectly—either because of insufficient information or because they do not take into account indirect benefits or losses (or so called externalities). Nor can markets handle natural monopolies or public goods.

The "old" type of SOEs were indeed confined to mainly public utilities—post and telecommunications, gas, electricity, railways, water, street lighting or sewage systems. Most of these services are natural monopolies, i.e., services in which the size of efficient operation is very large in relation to the size of the market, or in which duplication of facilities would involve public inconvenience. Natural monopolies are by definition areas of economic activity in which the restraints of competition are neither available nor socially desirable, and many countries chose to operate SOEs in such cases. Other countries, however, choose to regulate privately owned firms, or to use contracts by a public authority with private operators for the supply of the service. These different institutional choices are important and relevant in determining economic outcomes, and the choice of the instrument in each case cannot be explained only by economic theory. The choice of the different institutions depends on desired outcomes. What is desired is different in different societies and is not necessarily based on the marginal conditions of Pareto efficiency.

Unfortunately, neoclassical economic theory tends to ignore cultural and political differences, as well as the diversity of historical backgrounds, social factors and institutional requisites. Development economists often argue that state ownership is preferable in countries that were late in industrialization, facing a greater number of development gaps and lacking indigenous entrepreneurs to mobilize domestic resources (Gerschenkron, 1962). Therefore, the SOE sector is expected to be larger in manufacturing, the lower the level of economic development. At a higher level of economic development, SOEs would be used more extensively in public utilities. It is also argued sometimes that the more open the economy, the more vulnerable it is to external factors. To avoid instability and protect their populations from adverse implication of international trade, the government intervenes (Cameron, 1978).

The Keynesian revolution added two instruments for the management of the economy: direct governmental expenditures and monetary and fiscal stimulants of demand. Governments also used so called national champions to achieve their goals. In the 1960s, governments created SOEs mainly to supply long-term financing for investments with long-term horizons. In addition, it was felt that structural inadequacies and other deficient market mechanisms may mean that the economy will not respond to Keynesian stimuli of demand, and direct intervention at the level of the firm and through SOEs is required. This point of view was articulated by Pasquale Saraceno in Italy and by other European economists, like François Perroux in France. Many of the new policies were premised on a confident optimism that the most intractable and daunting problems would yield to the resolute assault of committed and enthusiastic persons, applying superior intelligence and analytical minds. At the end of the seventies, many of these programs had visibly failed, and hopes were turned to new innovations.

One result of governmental use of policy tools is various degrees of dependence on government. The government also needs the business to achieve its aims, and so the situation is one of mutual dependence. In the 1950s, a government could create a state of mutual dependence, offering tariffs and other protections to private firms that followed its desires and instructions. It could, therefore, achieve its goals by aiding private firms.

The increased free international trade, the opening of the EEC, and the growing tendency of multinationalization of production left the government feeling impotent. This bolstered the case for SOEs to meet the new challenges. The international obligations of governments reduced the possibility for creating mutual dependence and the private firms in many countries have become less dependent on government, as they had enough retained earnings or other sources of funds. Large firms are much less limited by market forces. Their managements are responsible to nothing other than what Berle (1969, p. 90) termed "the corporate conscience". If these firms are not dependent on government, SOEs may be seen as a better solution.

The most complete welfare economic analysis of the reasons for state ownership is that of Jones and Mason. They stress economic structure and focus on

> [a] rational decision-making entity exclusively concerned with max-imizing economic welfare through a choice among a wide variety of centralized and decentralized institutions . . . Benefits can be had from government intervention where market failures lead a profit-maximizing private producer to behavior incompatible with social-welfare maximization . . . Public enterprise is . . . one among many tools available for achieving the government's goals, and the choice of this tool is a function of the costs and benefits associated with its use as compared to those of other institutional forms" [Jones and Mason, in Jones, et al., 1982, p. 24].

To them, the correct question is whether a given enterprise will contribute more to national economic welfare under private or state management. Therefore, an SOE should exist if two conditions are fulfilled. First, the national benefits should exceed the costs. Second, these net benefits are greater for SOE as compared to alternative institutional forms such as regulated private enterprise, taxed/subsidized private enterprise, unrestricted private enterprise and no enterprise (e.g., relying on imports). The benefits of state management of enterprises are due to the removal of market failures (e.g., monopoly caused by decreasing cost technology and external effects), which would accrue under private operation. These benefits must be set against the costs of public operation that are due to organizational failures of public operation (e.g., centralized administration creating inadequate incentives and excessive controls, resulting in production with excess costs and intertemporal delays) plus costs incurred at the enterprise level in providing information, bargaining and designing means of circumventing the intervention mechanism.

Their perspective led Jones and Mason (in Jones, et al., 1982) to suggest that the benefits from an SOE are liable to be particularly large when the alternative is no enterprise (due to inadequate private entrepreneurial capacity), private monopoly, oligopoly or where there are significant externalities. These circumstances are particularly likely for sectors in which firms are capital-intensive and large in scale relative to both product and factor markets, employ modern technology, are centralized, produce standardized, easily marked products or high-rent natural resource exports and generate substantial forward linkages; this prediction is consistent with available evidence on the size and structure of SOEs in many developing countries. It may also be noted that in many developing countries, large family groups control existing industries and exert political power as a result. They can thus reduce entry unless the government creates firms.

Conversely, costs of public relative to private operations are liable to be high for activities that are small scale, decentralized, produce nonstandardized products and sell in highly changing or highly competitive markets. Indeed, the USSR's greatest problems with public production have been in agriculture, where private plots, accounting for only 3 percent of the agricultural land, produce over 30 percent of output. Even giant investor owned firms tend to use independent retail distributors and subcontractors: the cost of monitoring all these enterprises is too high to be internalized within the firm. Jones and Mason feel it was completely predictable in Pakistan that the nationalization of thousands of rice and flour mills and cotton-ginning mills would create major difficulties and organizational costs of keeping managers operating in the public interest rather than their own. Indeed, these were the first (and only) sectors to be denationalized, as their theory would predict (see Chapter 9).

However, there is little evidence to suggest that vote-maximizing politicians establish SOEs to maximize social welfare, at least as this term is defined by economists. The vast literature of case studies on SOEs in different countries seem to show that governments have established SOEs for many different reasons (see Chapter 3).

Politicians, guided by vote-maximizing or satisfying behavior, tend to allocate resources where the political benefits are highest. They therefore lean toward preserving employment and protecting ailing firms. Although the growing social and redistributional ambitions have been straining resources badly needed for industrial restructuring, political reason dictated the need to help these ailing firms, often by nationalizing them. In other cases, private firms defaulted on their government's loans and surrendered their assets to the government.

When the problem is normative, the answer is shaped by the observer's viewpoint. Industrial policy, the acid test of which is government willingness to discriminate between private firms operating in the market, embodies appeals to ideological values such as planning and freedom. In this case, economic (or at least neoclassical economic) arguments begin to break down in the face of political priorities. Politicians enunciate such policies, but they are vulnerable hostages to economic fortune, often acting under pressure of events. Whatever one's ideological belief on these questions, it is clear that economic activities are taking place within nation-states, which differ from each other in the nature of their political and social institutions. These institutions are the legacy of past history as well as culture, language and many other attributes.

REGULATION AND OWNERSHIP: POLITICAL-ECONOMIC EXPLANATION

An alternative explanation for when government would prefer state ownership to other policy tools must be embedded in a theory of a political economy of the state. The focus of such an explanation is on political contests for control over resources. It recognizes that state ownership is not necessarily an island of socialist production. In fact, it may be the result of power exercised by large private firms. For example, electricity SOEs almost always subsidize private industry. SOEs may be the result of a continuous political bargaining among interest groups, state bureaucracy and political parties. Neo-Marxists such as Miliband (1969) or Offe (1972) argued that a welfare state cannot effect a socialist transformation under liberal democracies because of the existence of a fundamental imbalance between labor and capital's economic and social power. Some of them see SOEs as serving the interests of the dominant capitalist class. In developing countries, the balance between conflict and cooperation among the state, multinational enterprises and private local firms and differences among them in their access to resources required for production may explain the creation of SOEs (Evans, 1979; Ahmad in Jones, 1982). Freeman claims that "the state must assume the role of entrepreneur or continue to rely on foreign entrepreneurship to promote economic growth" (Freeman, 1982, p. 92). The key to understanding entrepreneurial policies in developing countries according to him, "lies in the state's participation in a "triple alliance"—a pact between state, local, and multinational capital for the pursuit of dependent development. State entrepreneurship is one of the principal means by which the public authority, for its part, forges and maintains the triple alliance" (*Ibid*, p. 93).

He thus sees the growth of SOEs as a nationalist response of latecomers to the problem of industrialization. He modifies Gerschenkron's (1962) thesis by adding to it a political explanation, based on Evans' (1979) work on Brazil. Martinelli (in Vernon and Aharoni, 1981) shows that in periods of political consensus, SOEs were able to be instrumental in achieving economic development. Katzenstein (1984) shows that an ideology of social partnership allowed what he called "democratic corporatism." In Austria, "the nationalization of a large portion of the means of production was not so much an expression of the class struggle in a capitalistic society as an assertion of Austria's national independence in the conflict among nations" (Katzenstein, 1984, p. 49). In Austria, SOEs have weakened the power of the private business community.

If state ownership is a result of a political contest for power and control over resources, SOEs will still be concentrated in the same industries as predicted by Jones and Mason, but for entirely different reasons. In these firms, it is easier to have slack than in small-size firms in industries in which competition is vigorous. Slack is of course needed to allow political contests for control. In fact, there are greater opportunities for slack in SOEs than there may be in private enterprises. Since the flow of funds of the SOEs is not part of the government budget, allocation of invisible resources is allowed (Aharoni, 1981a). This invisibility is crucial for the SOEs to achieve objectives the government does not necessarily want to make public, such as subsidizing certain sectors of the economy by lower prices or diverting funds to certain groups and to a specific region, to help certain constituents or to employ certain persons.

Theoretically, the size of the largesse conferred through SOEs is limited since if these firms distribute too much of it, they will lose and these losses will have to be covered by financial allocation from the budget. Two things have to be remembered, however: first, to the extent that demands for distribution of largesse will indeed result in losses, these losses will be seen by the public as being the result of inefficient operations of the SOEs. It is not very easy to trace the losses back to the use of the SOEs for the achievement of all sorts of policies or allocations. Second, many of the policies may not result in recorded losses. In fact, an SOE can increase the slack available for distribution without necessarily showing losses. The SOE can cross-subsidize the losses from profit-making activities. In other cases, the SOE may allow its fixed costs to deteriorate without asking for additional funds, and SOEs can also neglect or deepen in the short run maintenance of plant and equipment. Zambian copper mines, e.g., have cut their costs to "limit the fall in declared profits or to reduce emergent losses" (Radetzki, 1983, p. 155).

In all these cases the possibility for creating slack and invisibly distributing it among different constituents is a powerful device that only SOEs possess. SOEs base their profit and loss statements on the conventions of accounting. They do not record what the economist would term *opportunity cost*. Therefore, SOEs can have slack, or in the economy lingo, cause inefficiencies, without recording any of these as costs. For example, Gillis (1977, p. 34) reports that in both Bolivia and Indonesia, energy consumption is markedly underpriced relative to world prices, and investment decisions in extractive and processing industries are heavily influenced by the availability of low-cost energy. The low cost of energy is not registered as an expense of the oil firms. In fact, it is not shown anywhere. The mining and processing firms may increase their slack by the difference between the cost of oil to them and the world price of oil. They may, e.g., use such slack to grant their work force higher wages, or for any other use they (or the government) might decide. In theory, the government may even police a reluctant manager by the threat of increasing the price of oil to the enterprise if he does not follow instructions. The practice of pricing certain inputs or outputs at prices that are different than world prices is widespread. Thus, land can be used for different purposes. Housing construction firms may sell houses at lower than market price to designated groups or consumers, if they receive the land at less than market prices or if they are allowed greater density of building.

In Canada until 1983, the so-called "crow's nest" agreement ensured that grain farmers paid railroads only 0.5 cents per ton-mile (*The Economist*, August 24, 1985, p. 32). Pressures by the farmers' lobbies led to lower-cost credit through state-owned banks. Electricity can be sold at different prices to different customers, and the same is true for transportation, telephone and postal services. SOE may give their customers subsidized loans and receive loans from the government at a subsidized rate; they may receive from the government equity with the understanding that dividends will not be expected, and so on. In all these cases, SOEs do not necessarily use these privileges to compete in a predatory way against private enterprise. Instead, they are used to achieve a myriad of goals desired by the power coalition that decides on the resource allocation in the firm. Most of the decisions in these areas are taken in closed cloisters without public knowledge. However, the availability of such a powerful tool for distribution of largesse and achieving all sorts of short-term goals is too important for politicians, and it is hard to assume that they will not attempt to use it to achieve political and social goals. True, these uses have long-term consequences in terms of the efficiency of the enterprises, but in governments long-term goals are often less important than, say, winning the next election.

One can give many examples of such allocative inefficiencies in terms of both input and output prices. One way to make the point is to show that in many cases SOEs price their services below costs, at least for some customers. Several studies indicate that SOEs price output below cost of production. Hirschleifer, DeHaven and Milliman (1960, p. 111) found "that water rates—especially those of publicly owned systems—are characteristically far too low to recover a correctly calculated average cost." Bain, Caves and Margolis (1966) reported distortions of water allocation among classes of urban and agricultural customers. "The major distortion seems to lie in prices too low to reflect the long-run marginal costs of the typical system" (p. 361). Wallace concluded that "TVA rates are too low to reflect the cost of overall increases in power supply" (1967, p. 533). Gordon documents several examples of below-cost pricing in Canada. She feels that "The impetus for public ownership of utilities has often been based on misconception. One dubious belief was that there was a social advantage in having utilities financed by low-cost, government-backed borrowing" (1981, p. 44). Shapiro and Shelton (1981) constructed a formal model, based on the assumption that agencies attempt to maximize their budget. They assume that the budget of the agency (SOE) is based on two sources of revenues: revenue from the sale of output and per unit subsidies, both of which are determined by the legislative process. According to them, there are several reasons for underpricing: first, high prices tend to worsen the prognosis of project adoption. Officials have a lot to gain from the expansion of projects since expansion creates opportunities for increasing personnel. After the project is adopted, reluctance to raise prices continues since significant increases in prices will tend to create strong opposition among users—who are also citizens and voters who can, therefore, exert pressures on the legislature. Shapiro and Shelton assume that the pressures of the citizen would affect the managers of the SOEs directly. However, to get the same results it is enough to assume that the legislature would not allow the rise in prices, being motivated by the desire to be re-elected.

To the extent that this explanation is true, the alternative of a regulated investor-owned monopoly will not be preferred. Under Jones and Mason's (in Jones *et al.*, 1982) explanation, there are certainly some costs in the regulation of private enterprise, e.g., it may lead to excessive capital-intensive investment decisions (Averch and Johnson, 1962). Investor-owned utilities, however, must show profits after taxes. In contrast, state-owned utilities often provide their services in little better than break-even position. Ontario Hydro, Hydro Quebec and British Columbia Hydro supply their customers with electricity at less than real cost. They all have lower cost of capital because their debts are guaranteed by the governments of the respective provinces and show essentially no return on the large capital investments in their facilities (see, e.g., Gordon, 1981).

In many cases, SOEs were transferred from the general government to an independent entity. Welfare economists look at SOEs as rational actors actively pursuing efficient attainment of goals, but such transfers can hardly be explained in their terms. One reason is that business enterprises need flexibility that cannot be achieved within the government bureaucracy. Another is political. Thus, in the United States, "Congress determined that among the principal causes of the [post] office decline was the political influence to which the office had been subjected since 1792. To purge this political influence", (Priest, 1975, p. 68), the Postal Reorganization Act of 1970 established the postal services as an independent entity.

SOEs also provide politicians an opportunity to shift the responsibility for intractable problems the government is expected to handle onto different shoulders. "If all goes well later, the politicians can share in the glory. If all goes poorly, the politicians can point the finger at others who, after all, had independent responsibility for handling the problem" (Tierney, 1984, p. 78).

In other cases employees of the business organizations wanted to receive higher remuneration and pressed for the creation of a different legal entity, to escape the salary limitations and personnel ceilings of the civil service. Managers of these enterprises found themselves spending a lot of time bargaining for funds, and wanted to escape the limits of the budgets. Politicians often looked for methods to escape constitutional limits on public borrowings. They were also eager to find ways to finance activities outside the budget so they could claim a balanced or a reduced budget. All these forces combined to move more and more activities from the general government to "public authorities" or "public corporations." In the United States, the major force seems to have been the desire to circumvent public debt ceilings and constitutional limits on borrowing. Thus the state of Pennsylvania had 1,814 SOEs mainly because it imposed strict limitations on public borrowings (Walsh, 1978). In other countries the power of the workers demanding higher wages was a major cause. Very often, the official excuse used to create the new entities was that their creation would reduce political patronage and influence on their activities. This reduction rarely happened in practice, but the higher salaries or the escape from the budget did occur.

Musolf and Seidman quote a *Washington Post* estimate, according to which the number of people paid by the U.S. federal government is more than double the number listed on the official civilian payroll. They noted, dryly, "Manifestly, personnel ceilings control not the number of individuals working for the federal government, but the number formally listed as employees" (1980, p. 127).

In many countries where governments are composed of coalitions of different parties, the creation of separate SOEs was a means to reduce the control of the ministry of finance on the activities of other ministries. Using separate entities allowed the ministers to control the funds generated in the enterprises; it also allowed them more latitude in giving patronage, e.g., in jobs and in positions on the board of directors, or to give invisible largesse to certain constituents, like cheaper credit to farmers through a state-owned financial institution controlled by the ministry of agriculture. Many of these enterprises continued because of inertia, or were left as a corporate shell although their missions were transferred to another organization. In many countries, different ministries are like feudal barons, each with its own power base in certain SOEs. One result of this state of affairs has been that the responsibility for some important national affairs was transferred to SOEs: national oil firms, e.g., usually have more executives on their planning staff and more expertise than the ministry does and actually dictate the country's energy policy.

Many SOEs were created as statutory organizations, and in each case their creation had to be enacted by Parliament. With time, the ministers learned that it is easier and more expedient to use company law to incorporate a firm whose shares are owned by the government. Parliamentary laws may be changed during the process of legislation. Further, the law is much more rigid, while the establishment of an SOE under a company law allowed ministers much more maneuverability. Thus, more SOEs were created under private law as companies whose shares are held by the state or as subsidiaries of existing SOEs. These companies (and their subsidiaries) mushroomed, and the results were calls for more governmental control. Once such control was established, however, a new invisible legal form was found. We have already noted that the U.S. Congress enacted in 1945 the Government Corporation Act. Since then, SOEs became government sponsored. In Israel, the Government Companies Law gave a lot of power to the minister of finance to control SOEs. At least in one case, an authority belonging to a certain ministry was not made an SOE to avoid this power. In Argentina, the legislation of a strict Government Companies Act caused in practice a situation in which the law was circumvented (Barak Committee, 1970, p. 25). In India:

> Today, the state governments are generally inclined to form an enterprise and register it under the Cooperative Societies Act because a government company is subject to the oversight of the Registrar of Companies and the Company Law Board. . . . For a cooperative society, under the Registrar of Cooperatives, an officer of the state government, a rigorous compliance of provisions of law can be avoided. [Narain, 1982, p. 24]

Any SOE of whatever legal form reduces government dependence on the private sector to achieve national goals. It also allows the government to train managers and allows private individuals to reach managerial positions outside the often closed circle of family enterprises.

Independent government services may or may not be more efficient. They certainly allow more control over resources to their managers, more power to their employees and more invisible methods to pay largesse to different constituents and to dispense political patronage. SOEs "exist in a gray area on the margins of the state" (Sharkansky, 1979, p. 4). Their positioning enables politicians to claim they are free of blame if a project carried by the SOEs fails and to take credit for any success. The officially declared autonomy of these enterprises also allows governments to use them to carry out projects that might not win legislative approval, to give special favors to supporters or to help a particular region or group, to appoint the politically faithful or to help a certain interest group—all done invisibly and escaping the rules of equality applicable to government departments.

Once SOEs are operating, they may or may not be efficient. Again, economists design pricing and investment rules for such enterprises to ensure the achievement of social welfare. There is also a considerable body of systematic empirical works on the performance of private enterprises and SOEs in specific industries and specific settings, to be reviewed in Chapter 5. However, again, the analysis is based on specific assumptions and ideological precommitments that often preclude dispassionate analysis. Different persons have various views on the rationale for SOEs and therefore on the ways their performance should be evaluated.

The major problems of SOEs are related mainly to politics (who controls the SOEs? In whose interest are they managed?). Textbooks preach the virtues of keeping the income-generating SOE outside the realm of politics and free of political pressures. Managers are to be allowed to conduct the affairs of the business in accordance with policy guidelines formulated at the political level. This ideal picture turns out to be utopian, and government ministers tend to intervene. This intervention may result in management that is complacent, inward looking, inbred and amateur. Alternatively, the manager may enter the political game.

The relationships between SOE managers and their controllers also change with time. The SOE goes through an evolution, gaining with time more power for the managerial class. Although ownership is collective, decisions are made by individuals, who become what Djilas (1957) called "the new class": those having the control on means of production. We shall discuss this question inasmuch as it relates to control in Chapter 6, while the behavior of managers is discussed in Chapter 8.

A theory of SOEs in a democracy must be based on political economic arguments, the contours of which have been suggested earlier: SOEs add to the ability of those in power to achieve resource allocation in an invisible manner, partially by increasing the slack available. The slack is greater in capital-intensive; oligopolistic or monopolistic industries. The power characteristics are country-specific, and therefore, there may be differences in the specific industries that are state owned. At the same time, the characteristics that made state ownership attractive are industry-specific, leading to many similarities across countries

Therefore, most SOEs will be found in highly concentrated industries where competition is imperfect and leaves enough slack. The interests served by the slack may vary with time and with the age of the SOE: with time, managers of SOEs become an important class and acquire political power. They become less dependent on the state and can pursue more autonomous strategies. SOE managers, however, are very much aware of the limits of their power. If they step beyond these limits or if an improper behavior is disclosed, creating a scandal, they lose much of their power, and the pendulum swings sharply to more controls and reduced autonomy.

One interesting result of the invisibility argument is that countries may have good reasons to avoid publicizing the detailed transactions between SOEs and the government. Transparency of operations does not allow invisibility. Indeed, we saw earlier how difficult it is to get figures on the SOE sector and on its activities or even a central listing of their firms. The invisibility relates also to the legal form employed.

A significant part of the theory about SOEs has been written on socialist countries, of a command economy type. Under this model, the firm management has very little autonomy, and a central planning board decides on specific output goals. The firm management typically neither has to sell its output in the market nor has to decide on prices of various inputs. In the Oscar Lange version of market socialism, each firm has much more autonomy, but its investment decisions are usually based on the decisions of a central planning board. The focus of this book is on SOEs operating in a mixed economy; side by side or even in competition with private enterprises to which their performance may be compared. In these mixed economies, there are important differences in the political milieu; some of them are democracies, in which different political parties propose to the voter candidates for political leadership. Others are dictatorial regimes, attempting to achieve different goals. In a democracy, the political leaders attempt to be re-elected, which significantly influences their behavior. If the major goal of a government is indeed to be re-elected, one may assume that it will use all the resources it controls, including the SOEs, to achieve this goal. Therefore, the SOE's policies would be subjected to political influence. Before an election their managers will be asked to preserve and expand jobs, even through featherbedding or overhiring; they would not be allowed to lay off people; they would have to resist price increases to help the government control inflation or to develop certain regions. Given that politicians seek to win elections, the pressures on SOEs to avoid firing or increasing hiring would be greater the nearer the election date. More generally, government political intervention would tend to increase the nearer the time to elections but also as a function of general macroeconomic conditions; a government that suffers acute budgetary deficits would behave differently toward its SOEs than a government whose resources are less limited.

Another political consideration is the degree to which the government knows what it wants the SOEs to do. In some African countries, it is often said that the government wants to bring the SOEs under control but without any clear ideas as to the purposes for which such control might be exercised. Many would emphasize this factor as the one that undermines the performance of SOEs. Frank (in Ranis, 1971, p. 170) compared the performance of SOEs in Ghana, Nigeria and Uganda. The performance was best in Uganda, which at that time was the least politicized of the countries studied. He concluded that the political milieu was by far the most important determinant of economic efficiency. In Ghana, the policies of IDC have been left to be formulated by the firm with foreign experts. Research on different firms in Ghana revealed a similar disinterest in general policy. A World Bank study of Zambia states in part that, "In some cases policy guidelines simply do not exist, in others there are contradictory policies, and in still other cases guidelines exist only on paper and are dealt with quite differently in practice" (World Bank, 1977, p. 41). The authors of the report felt that there has to be a clearly articulated policy with guidelines for its implementation. Government has not provided such guidelines.

CONCLUSION

The expansion of the public sector led also to an increase in its business activities. SOEs have proliferated since World War II, and it is important to understand their role, reasons for creation and major characteristics and to explain variances among countries.

There are also differences among the major missions of enterprises in the same country. Some are expected to generate very high rates of profits and are used mainly as a tax agency—national lotteries being one example. Others are expected to cover their costs and still others have limited external revenue sources and are supported by the government for the majority of the funds they need while still others are allowed or even encouraged to tap debts from the private capital market. This spectrum of product/market diversity is important in understanding the behavior of these firms.

Therefore, to answer the question, where would public ownership prove socially advantageous and efficient? Other questions are raised: What is the impact of size (inefficient giants exist on both sides)? How much can one rely on idealism or social pressure? How can one prevent financial gains from monopoly while simultaneously rewarding efficiency? And mainly, who decides and what are the results of these decisions on patterns of work organization, location of firms, executive compensation, what is produced, in which quantities and by what technology, how are resources allocated and who gets what? SOEs operate in the fringe of government and are used as an invisible means to disperse largesse.

While there are many differences between SOEs and private firms, the major such difference relates to the environment. All managers reach decisions based on what they perceive to be the objectives of the firm, its product/market opportunities and the constraints imposed by the environment in which they operate. One major difference between SOEs and private enterprises, therefore, is the environment in which they operate. This environment is different for different SOEs, either because of differences in the system of government or the level of development or the market structure, or any of the above.

CHAPTER 2

Myths and Realities: The Curious Relationships of Governments and SOEs

INTRODUCTION

It is clear from our discussion in Chapter 1 that national ownership of enterprises is increasingly recognized as a new political and economic policy tool available to government for the purpose of directing the economy, achieving higher levels of efficiency, equalizing incomes, distributing resources among regions and achieving other goals a government considers important. Regardless of a country's size, political leaning or degree of development, its government is involved in business. Clearly, there is a need for a comprehensive understanding of the role and impact of SOEs and mainly of managerial behavior in these enterprises. "The key factor determining the efficiency of an enterprise," notes the World Bank, "is not whether it is publicly or privately owned, but how it is managed. In theory, it is possible to create the kind of incentives that will maximize efficiency under any type of ownership. But there is a great difference between what is theoretically feasible and what typically happens" (World Bank, 1983, p. 50). Whether an SOE is more or less wasteful of social resources depends on the quality of enterprise management. The behavior of an SOE is also a function of the specific environment in which it operates (and from which it receives its legitimacy) and mainly of relationship with the government.

If government allows financial discipline to relax by paying subsidies, management may not try very hard to secure change. As a result, it may become increasingly difficult for SOEs to close down unprofitable plants, to adjust manufacturing standards to more realistic levels or to introduce labor-saving techniques.

If economic conditions mean that the firm has to reduce outputs or reduce its labor force, the problem may become political. Many constituents will try to influence recruitment, salary structure, rewards and punishment and incentives decisions. In particular, when the enterprise is labor-intensive, local authorities will attempt to influence its location, not necessarily by the lure of attractive financial incentives but possibly by lobbying the central government.

The government is the final arbiter on all matters of policy and is expected, in theory, to give the management a clear direction on objectives. However, the government may disagree on the objectives to be pursued, find it difficult to articulate them or simply think it politically expedient not to define the objectives clearly. When under pressure for action in one area or another, government perceives the SOEs to be an integral part of the tools it has at its disposal. It may solve the problem of riots by the unemployed in a particular area by directing an SOE to build a plant there, as the Italian government did. It may also claim the SOE is independent if a failure is likely to reflect badly on it.

Mr. K.E. Adje, enumerating factors considered in locating projects (Commonwealth Secretariat, 1978b, p. 60), candidly says, "In selecting public enterprise, strict economic criteria may be compromised if the social or personal benefits far outweigh the purely economic gains. Benefits such as:

> equitable distribution of projects in the country (the score-board approach—which region, district, constituency got what and when and whose turn is it this time)
>
> various promises made by leaders to constituencies or on special occasions . . .
>
> technical aid requirements or preconditions dictated by donor countries or agencies
>
> ability of salesmen to convince and sell projects, machinery, equipment, etc., etc.
>
> how much bribe (kick-back) is paid or received and by whom given or taken . . .
>
> a lot of fortuitous incidences, involving timing, personalities, and location of project, e.g., the accidental working together of two schoolmates ("old-boyism"); projects presented to catch votes just before elections; proposal coming from a friendly country.

Managers who obediently do all they are told may find that these directives are immediately followed by a howl of anguish about the losses of the SOEs and cries that private enterprise is so much more efficient. Every month, certainly each time a minister changes, managers may find that the objectives and priorities have been changed. To be as efficient as a private enterprise, they may want to make a long-term plan and warn that unless certain steps are taken now, a shortage will be developed for the product or better products will replace it several years hence. They may then find that the minister thinks in terms of the period until the next election, which is much shorter than the enterprise's time horizon. Why should a minister care about a shortage in 10 years if elections are 3 months ahead? Managers may also learn that certain decisions are not made and certain priorities shift before the elections. They may feel the development of the business is profitable and can even prove it by very convincing economists' reports. However, they cannot go to the financial markets of every country and get a loan, and it is a rare event that they can get equity. Thus, managers have to queue with their investment program in line with the social security, the defense needs and all other priorities and claims of a complex government.

The reader may feel by now that the manager of the SOE is a helpless pawn moved by many political players. Not so. The managers learned how to affect the environment and have become one of the political actors in this complex jigsaw puzzle of combined economic rationality (enterprise, remember?), political fights for power (public, after all) and interest group pressures. The SOE is a part of an open system and is far from operating at arm's length from the political system. The SOE itself is a source of enormous power, and managers who learn how to use this power well actively gain more autonomy. A resourceful SOE manager does not see the government as a source of frustrations and constraints but as a source of opportunities and intelligence and a resource to be used to gain access to political power and establishing an independent power base. They "learn to accept and manipulate levers of power in the government and refuse to view their business and regulatory environment as unalterable by them" (Khandwalla, 1984, p. 183).

The problems are myriad: e.g., numerous, conflicting and ambiguous objectives, fluctuating in their order of priority from government to government or from year to year; inadequate measures for judging performance, coupled with extreme oscillations in governments' attitudes toward control of SOEs and to their pricing policies and financing; lack of precise knowledge how to reconcile autonomy with public accountability; to which one may add sometimes lack of competent managers or even good accountants; bureaucratic style of management and incentives that are not linked to performance. Little wonder that most descriptions of SOEs in different countries prescribe that these firms should be subjected to market discipline or that the best cure for them is to sell them to private investors. These may be very good solutions. However, SOEs have been created in the first place because of market failures or the existence of externalities. It is not easy to make them work in a market when the market does not exist.

An increasing proportion of manufacturing output is controlled today by a decreasing proportion of giant corporations. This fact has considerable implications for business behavior and government policy. The choice is often between the visible private hand and the visible government one, not between visible and invisible hands (see Chandler, 1977; Hannah, 1976). Private corporations, too, are essentially political constructs (Berle and Means, 1968, p. xxvii); social goals cannot easily be made operational, and state ownership is often the only feasible alternative to foreign domination. Further, the assumption that organizations are rational single undivided entities working to achieve (or even maximize) their prescribed objectives has long been shown to be an inaccurate depiction of the real world. Organizations may be more accurately described as an aggregation of semi-autonomous entities, more or less knit together by agreed procedures which constrain the range of possible action.

Thus when the government is in business, the picture is extremely complex, but also extremely interesting. Unfortunately, differences of opinion about the value and uses of SOEs are often based on preconceptions and myths. Folklore is often mistaken for fact, and experience in one country is generalized as if other countries are the same.

When problems of SOEs and their relationships with the environment are discussed, strongly held views and preconceived notions are often encountered. To be able to offer as dispassionate discussion as possible of such a value-laden issue, it may be useful to first enumerate some of these myths and analyze them carefully on the basis of existing evidence before moving to unfold the different aspects of this complicated picture.

MYTHS AND REALITIES

State Ownership Is a Panacea for the Ills of the Capitalist System

For many persons the idea of state ownership of means of production is an ideological question. It is seen either as a panacea for all perceived ills of the capitalist system or as an encroachment of the rights of individuals.

For the socialists, state ownership of the means of production is a goal in itself. Socialists were convinced that the legal status of property is a crucial determinant of the use of that property. They were repelled by what they perceived as "the waste and inefficiency involved in the abandonment of British industry to a jostling crowd of separate employers with their minds bent, not on service to the community, but by the very law of their being, only on the utmost possible profiteering" (in Kelf-Cohen, 1969, p. 18). Capitalism for them meant a dance around the golden calf—oppression of workers and a wrong distribution of wealth and power. State ownership was seen as an ideal despite strong hostility to the state as an employer. The state was deemed as representing the community, not as a political power.

The transfer of the means of production was believed to create automatically a just economic system and an ideal society based on cooperation, equality and mutual collaboration. It was also believed to eliminate worker alienation, create harmonious relations, emancipate oppressed groups and liberate frustrated energies. Democratic control over the means of production was expected also to create more efficiency and economic growth. For many, nationalization defined socialism and was an end in itself. Others saw it as a means for achieving social justice and a classless society. To be sure, some revisionist Socialists argued that: "individual property rights no longer constitute the essential basis of economic and social power. . . . Today, with active ownership converted into passive shareholding, control has passed elsewhere, and much of the traditional socialist–capitalist dispute is irrelevant" [Crosland, 1953, p. 38]. Crosland (1956) argues that the basic socialist objective is equality and that public ownership may or may not be the means to that end. The Webbs (1920) abhorred national monopolies that would give too much power to the state and preferred workers or municipal ownership of the means of production. However, most socialists continue to see nationalization as a means to "put a stop to any further large-scale exploitation of our workers and peasants through the private ownership of the means of production and exchange" (Julius N. Nyerere, quoted in Ramanadham, 1984b, p. 117).

In France the nationalization of forty-one banks in February 1982 was seen as a way to reform the economy. The nationalization, according to the explanation for the Nationalization Act 82-155 of February 11, 1982, had three goals: "By law to vest in the nation the power to create money; to enable the banking system to respond to regional needs; and to facilitate changes in habits, attitudes and strategy to enable the institutions better to serve the country's objectives" (Dupont-Fauville, 1983, pp. 32–33).

State ownership was later also seen as a way "to render accountable to the public the power of those increasingly anonymous, unidentifiable, often faceless, more often soulless corporations, national and multinational" (Harold Wilson, in Epstein, 1977, p. 285). Socialists believed—naively as it turned out—that one needs simply to transfer wealth-producing assets from the private to the public sector and that this move would lead to a revolution in industrial democracy, placing the workers in a new position of trust, responsibility and involvement, reducing the costs to the consumer and creating greater equality among individuals. The reality, however, was very different, and the anticipation that state ownership will wipe out all problems perceived to be created by the greed of the capitalist system was certainly exaggerated. The anticipation that nationalization would redistribute property was not realized. First, as Hugh Gaitskell argued in a Fabian tract (1956), compensation had to be paid to the previous owners. Second, many of the nationalizations put in public hands lame ducks—firms that were in such a desperate state that the government would have been obliged to intervene to help them anyway, or to let them go bankrupt. In these cases, the private owners of the firms might have been worse off if the firm would not have been nationalized.

SOEs also do not have a very good record as a tool for income redistribution. In fact, in many cases the SOEs aid the rich more than they help the poor. Baer and Figueroa, in a paper presented at the Second BAPEG Conference (1980), showed that SOEs did not generate equality of income distribution: in Peru the deficits of SOEs caused regressive impact on income distribution, while in Brazil SOEs concentrated on achieving economic growth, ignoring income distribution considerations.

Large segments of the poor gain subsidies from SOEs that supply electricity, food, water, or bus transportation, but these subsidies are enjoyed by the rich more than by the poor. As one example, in Indonesia, "for each dollar of kerosene subsidy, 20 percent goes to the poor and 80 percent to the well-off and the relatively well-off" (Gillis, 1980, p. 284).

SOEs were also expected to mobilize savings, augment governmental revenue and contribute to macroeconomic stability. The consolidated SOE sector accounts, if such consolidation exists, however, typically show big losses or meager profits. SOEs did generate savings but not enough to cover their investment requirements (see Chapter 5). Attempts to use SOEs to plan the economy foundered because of computing difficulty: by one estimate, the Soviet government assigns 8 million prices. Computations of the impact of such a large number of figures is impossible even with today's computer capacity. More important, the task of drawing up the necessary equations for a model of the whole economy is formidable, subject to error and beyond today's professional competence (see Balinky et al., 1967). Moreover, property is not comprised only of physical units. Much of it is in the form of human capital such as education, brains and human ability to plan, direct, manage and control enterprises. As a result, nationalization of physical units turned out to be a partial answer to social or economic problems: the brains and the willingness to cooperate could not be nationalized.

"Ideology," claims Feigenbaum, "is in a sense the secret weapon of the private sector in keeping the state at bay, or at least in minimizing state incursions . . . the ideological sinews . . . inhibit [the state] from solving the problems of advanced capitalism. Neither the private sector nor the state capitalist sector seems to have an incentive structure that promises an easy solution to the problems of energy reindustrialization, and inflation" (1985, p. 171). Strong states, Feigenbaum argues, become weak states because they are captured by the managers and by the idealization of the market (1985, pp. 173-4). Nationalization of physical resources does not necessarily change human behavior. As to workers alienation, it was certainly not reduced by state ownership. The heightened expectations of the workers may have meant that the alienation is even greater in SOEs than under private ownership. Workers' control of factories certainly does not reduce conflicts between consumers and producers. As Sloman reminds us, "No one in the Labour Movement would agree that the hospitals should be run for the benefit of the doctors" (1978, p. 117). In many cases, instead of revolution in industrial relations, labor relations in SOEs have vaneourous character. Each union in the public sector jealously guards its status relationships to each other. If one union is able to change the relationships or get different differentials, the other will attempt to win the same settlement, to restore differentials and to gain pay parity with other workers. Some of the unpleasant confrontations between government, management and the work force have been in SOEs. A pervasive feeling of disorientation, outraged and more rigid unions, intensely competing for better settlement, and rancorous labor relations are often the characteristics of SOEs. Changes in government policies cause low morale and alienation that sometimes run from the front line to the very top ranks. Day-to-day decisions often create unintended consequences, and managers often behave in an uncontrollable way.

A second argument advanced for state ownership was full employment for the workers. This argument sounds feebler given the other tools the government has to achieve this lofty goal. Moreover, most SOEs tend to warp investment choices toward capital-intensive projects and have not demonstrated notable success in job creation.

SOEs have, however, been required to preserve jobs threatened by the demise of sick private firms. In many of the declining industries, the governments were later faced with the politically unpleasant task of allowing these firms to shed workers. In some countries, one may argue that the government allowed SOEs more autonomy to avoid getting involved in this task. At least one observer feels this way about Sweden: "the politicians wanted to be protected from blame for unpopular commercial decisions and wanted to avoid the role of hostage to local employment problems" (Eliason and Ysander in Hindley, 1983, p. 170). As we shall see in Chapter 9, avoidance of political embarrassment was also a cause of privatization.

In France, nationalization of coal "implied a chastisement of the leaders of the old order; the demand for nationalization represented the widespread condemnation of the trusts" (Holter, 1982, p. 35).

> Yet the nationalization ultimately served the general needs of French business. By nationalizing certain industries, the state took steps to revive a faltering capitalist economy. In this role, the state functioned both as a crisis solver and a regulator between capitalist interests. . . . For the business community, the net result of the nationalization seemed to vindicate the state's action. After five years under the nationalized regime, the backward industry of 1944 emerged as a model of productivity in the early 1950s. (Holter, 1982, p. 37)

The state shifted "from reform and integration to accumulation and rationalization" (Holter, 1982, p. 38). It moved from production at any cost to production at a lower cost. Management was given sole power of decision on dismissals, and the size of the labor force was reduced.

To the socialists, nationalization also meant transfer of power from irresponsible private owners to more responsible public owners. Gaitskell claims that this argument is less forceful today. "The power of employers over workers is nowadays very severely limited by the trade unions" (1956, p. 11). In monopolies, "it must be admitted that demands for nationalisation and workers' control are sometimes associated with the desire of a little group of workers to get more for themselves; if not at the expense of the shareholders, then at a cost to the rest of the community" (p. 12). Such attitudes were not anticipated by socialist writers who naively assumed that state ownership would create harmonious relations and attempts by individuals to give more to the community as a whole.

Nationalization of the means of production is sometimes assumed to be the equivalent of control in the public interest (Holland, 1972, 1975; Stoffaës and Victorri, 1977). In many cases, however, the private managerial class has been replaced by a new class of managers. As Simonnot observed about state-owned banks, "Monetary developments since nationalization leave the impression that these banks have behaved more like barons than agents of the State" (1975, pp. 166–167). State ownership was also advocated as a way to protect the consumers against monopolies. Here again, the implicit assumption is that a monopoly sanctioned by government or by a parliamentary act ceases to behave like a monopoly. How this miraculous transformation of behavior can occur is usually not explained. In short, state ownership did not turn out to be in practice the best way to achieve either higher production, greater efficiency or less alienation of workers.

State ownership was also assumed to create a system more sensitive to the avoidance of the ills of externalities like pollution. Very few studies have been made to date on this important question, but there is ground to believe that SOEs are not more socially responsible than their private-sector counterparts. Roberts (1975) conducted one of the few studies of this question, comparing the behavior of three pairs of electricity generation firms in North America. Some of these companies have done more than what is formally required, while others have refused to abide by environmental regulations, sought exemptions to them or worked strenuously for their relaxation (Roberts, 1975). The TVA, e. g., "has been committed to the notion that it should minimize power costs. As a result, electrostatic precipitators to remove fly ash were designed to minimize cost and they worked very poorly" (p. 410). Roberts concluded that "because the categories 'public' and 'private' include organizations that exhibit a wide (and overlapping) set of internal features and external circumstances, that distinction contains little predictive information about behavioral differences" (p. 423).

As Epstein points out, "with regard to broader social issues such as consumer satisfaction with goods and services, labour relations, industrial democracy and worker's participation, and environmental protection" (1977, p. 284), the record of British SOEs "has not been conspicuously superior" to that of private enterprise, and "public ownership *per se* does not resolve the issue of social responsibility" (p. 310). Thus, state ownership did not fulfill the utopian dreams of its socialist advocates. Many of them believe today that the way to achieve their goals of greater social and economic equality is to gain more political power and control the legislature.

State Ownership Means Creeping Socialism

On the other side of the political spectrum are those that see any state ownership as wrong, unjust and unjustified. To them, the very existence of an SOE is a manifestation of "creeping socialism," to use President Eisenhower's phrase regarding the TVA. They believe SOEs are highly inefficient, almost by definition, and are an encroachment on the freedom of the private businessperson to carry out his or her affairs. According to the free enterprise believers, large-scale state ownership centralizes power, creates a monolithic society and reduces dissent. According to Friedman and Friedman:

> [n]ationalized industries proved so inefficient and generated such large losses in Britain, Sweden, France, and the United States that only a few die-hard Marxists today regard further nationalizations as desirable. The illusion that nationalization increases productive efficiency, once widely shared, is gone. Additional nationalization does occur—passenger railroad service and some freight service in the United States, Leyland Motors in Great Britain, steel in Sweden. But it occurs for very different reasons—because consumers wish to retain services subsidized by the government when market conditions call for their curtailment or because workers in unprofitable industries fear unemployment. Even the supporters of such nationalization regard it as at best a necessary evil. [1980, p. 95]

However, anecdotal evidence about the comparative efficiency of privately and publicly owned firms, reviewed in Chapter 5, shows that it is very difficult to generalize that SOEs are inherently less efficient or, for that matter, less innovative than private firms. After all, some firms found themselves in the public sector because those who made the decisions made the wrong decisions and were rescued by nationalizing them.

It is often claimed that state ownership reduces adaptability to a changing environment. However, as Lawrence and Dyer (1983) documented, many private U.S. firms failed to maintain their competitive vitality. There must be more to performance, adaptability and innovation than just ownership. To be sure, the laborious machinery of government, constricted with elaborate checks and balances to avoid the perils of corruption and to ensure democratic rights, is not often vigorous enough to run an entrepreneurial activity. But when managerial responsibility is left to those experienced in exercising it, while retaining control over policy and strategy as well as full monitoring power, many SOEs have shown at least equal if not more vitality than large privately owned business enterprises. The performance of the SOEs in most

LDCs is certainly not very good and is often disastrous. Whether the faults are of ownership, government control or bad management remains to be analyzed. A corollary of such a belief is that the more socialist a government is, the greater is the share of SOEs out of GNP. Another corollary is that non-socialist governments will tend to denationalize and certainly would not create more SOEs.

State Ownership Is Based on Ideology

Ideological beliefs have indeed been an important reason for the creation of SOEs, but SOEs exist in all countries—socialist or not. The share of SOEs is certainly higher in the communist world. Outside these countries, however, both the share of the SOEs out of GNP and their distribution by industries is very similar in countries with totally different ideological beliefs, such as South Korea and India. Moreover, Sweden nationalized more firms in the short period in which it was governed by a conservative Flåden government than it did in the previous 30 years in which it was dominated by a Socialist government, and right-of-center parties in Canada have created more Provincial Crown Corporations than the Socialist party. Seventy-two percent of all the Provincial Crown Corporations have been created since 1960—more because of changes since then in public demands from government than because of ideology (Vining, 1983, p. 46). The Conservative British government in the 1970s was responsible for the nationalization of firms such as Rolls Royce and British Leyland, and the socialist-dominated coalition in Israel sold more SOEs to the private sector than the Liberal government that followed it. The latter promised to dismantle the state-owned sector but sold very few firms, while at the same time it nationalized more firms than it denationalized.

It is popularly held that the United States never nationalized firms and had no SOEs. Some would add except the TVA, of course. For many, the government corporation has become a symbol of an institution that endangers the so-called American way of life. However, the U.S. government did create many SOEs, many of which were sold later.

Historically, the first U.S. SOE was created when the United States acquired the assets of the French Panama Canal Company in 1904, acquiring thereby the Panama Railroad Company. During World War I, the U.S. government found it necessary to construct and operate a merchant fleet, to lend money and to enter into commercial activities such as the sale of sugar and grain. In all these cases, the government dealt with the public, not as a sovereign but as an entrepreneur. To operate as an entrepreneur, there was a need to achieve managerial discretion in areas such as procurement, contracts and personnel. Without such autonomy, governmental business activities were doomed to failure. As a result, all SOEs have achieved a high degree of autonomy from the myriad regulations faced by public sector management and were expected to operate on a self-sustaining basis and to be managed by an independent board of directors.

The number and scope of activities of the SOEs in the United States have grown tremendously since the first of them was established. The public authority created by the British to operate the London docks in 1909 was the model for the creation in 1921 of the Port Authority of New York and New Jersey, as the authority is now known. Between 1933 and 1945, the number of SOEs and the scope of their activities increased in response to changing needs. The depression era of the 1930s brought about the creation of the Commodity Credit Corporation, the Reconstruction Finance Corporation (RFC), the TVA, the Federal Deposit Insurance Corporation, the Regional Agricultural Credit Corporation, the U.S. Housing Authority, Home Owners Loan Corporation, as well as thousands of SOEs at the state level, many of which were aided by Federal subsidies or by the purchase of their bonds by the federally owned RFC and later by the Public Works Administration. During World War II, RFC created subsidiaries that produced and distributed petroleum, rubber, metals and other defense supplies. The Defense Plant Corporation alone owned more than 2,000 plants. By 1945, 58 SOEs held combined assets of $30 billion. Based on the recommendations of the second Hoover commission, most of these were liquidated or privatized after the war (Walsh, 1978, pp. 30–31). At the state level, however, the number of SOEs continued to increase. This proliferation came about to avoid constitutional debt limits, to take advantage of federal aids and subsidies and to avoid the need for voters' approval of additional state loans. As one example, between 1938 and 1965, public housing and publicly aided construction in New York City accounted for almost 50 percent of new units completed (Morris, 1980, p. 18). These enterprises are sometimes fiscal monopolies, selling liquor or providing gambling opportunities. Sometimes they are legal monopolies, such as the Post Office service. In other cases, they operate side by side with privately owned firms, as in the case of electricity generation or the operation of forest lands. All these enterprises have been created as a pragmatic response to a particular need, and "there are hundreds of remarkably efficient and innovative public enterprises in the United States" (Shepherd, 1976, p. 116). Today, according to Walsh, about 7,000 SOEs are operating in the United States (1978). This number does not include thousands of state and local enterprises not organized as authorities and tens of thousands of municipal owned enterprises.

Other prevalent preconceived notions abound about SOEs. Careful examination reveals that these notions are sometimes true, sometimes not. It is questionable whether the reason is ownership as opposed to some other variable such as the degree of competition, the legal status of the enterprise, cultural differences, decision-makers' characteristics and abilities and mainly the relationships with external controllers that is different in different countries and for different SOEs.

SOEs Cannot Reduce the Size of Their Work Force

It is often alleged that SOEs are the employers of last resort, that their militant unions will not accept reduction of the work force; instead, they use their political muscle and get the minister to intervene on their behalf.

The NCB in the United Kingdom was created by the Coal Industry Nationalization Act of 1946 (9 & 10 GEO 6 ch. 59). The mine workers union is considered both strong and militant. Given these factors and the monopoly status of the NCB, the reader may be surprised to learn that employment in the firm was reduced from 765,000 in 1958 to 401,700 in 1968, 287,000 in 1978, 235,000 in 1979 (Pryke, 1981) and 178,800 in 1984.

Coal presented in 1947 90 percent of all the fuel consumed in the United Kingdom, and the output consumed was 190 million tons. In 1957, NCB produced 220 million tons (Redwood, 1980, p. 52). In 1968, production went down to 158.7 million tons, in 1978 it was 106.9 million tons and in 1984, less than 100 million tons. This reduction in production was necessitated by the decline in demand caused largely by the availability of cheaper sources of energy. The government tried to help the coal industry by imposing a tax on fuel oil that was equivalent to about 40 percent of the delivered pretax price. It also forced the electricity industry—also state-owned—to pay dearly for locally produced coal. However, the same government allowed British Rail to transform itself to diesel-operated locomotives, reducing its consumption of coal by 10 million tons. It also accepted the initiative of British Gas to move from the use of coal to that of naphtha.

This is to argue neither that the British NCB is an efficient operator nor that all inefficient collieries were closed. In fact, unprofitable pits are still kept in operation. Pryke (1981, p. 68) suggests that during 1978 to 1979 there were sixty collieries in the central coal fields that failed to earn sufficient revenues and that employed 65,000 workers. In addition, there were at the same period around fifty-five unprofitable pits in Scotland, Wales and the other outlying coal fields that employed 50,000 workers. Mr. Bill Robinson of the London Business School estimated that to break even—cross-subsidizing unprofitable pits by profitable ones—the NCB should reduce its employment to 140,000 in 1984 to 1985, almost 40,000 fewer than at this writing. If all unprofitable pits are closed, Mr. Robinson estimates that the number of NCB employees should be 60,000 (quoted in *The Economist*, December 15, 1984, p. 31). In March 1983, there were 23,400 miners in South Wales and 16,900 in Scotland. Since then, the NCB has closed twelve pits, with a reduction of jobs of 16,000 (in 1982 to 1983 it had seven closures and reduced the work force by 10,200).

Hardly an issue of *The Economist* fails to print some news item about the NCB, often moaning about the need to close more pits. The rate of redundancies may not have been fast enough, and the NCB certainly loses large sums of money (£485 million in 1984, up from a £206.8 million loss a year before). According to the NEDO study of U.K. nationalized industries (1976), however, the rate of decline of employment in the NCB was 5.9 percent per annum for the period 1960 to 1975, and the rate of decline of output was 4.3 percent. To be sure, the NCB did better in the 1960s. Then, the annual rate of decline in employment was 6.8 and in output, 3.5 percent. Output per capita thus increased per annum in the 1960s by 3.6 percent and for the 15-year period, 1960 to 1975, by only 1.7 percent. Moreover, real staff cost per employee when 1968 = 100 was 156.2 compared to 128.9 for all manufacturing. Not everything has been rosy in the NCB garden, but the point is not to analyze this specific firm but to show that SOEs did shed a very large percentage of their employees when they were required to do so and did not behave as employment maximizers.

It is also important to inquire whether the size of the employment is a function of the state ownership; that is, had the coalfields been owned by private investors would they have reduced employment more? Unfortunately, a hypothetical question like this cannot be answered unequivocally, but the experience in other countries, where coal is not state-owned, may give us some indication. According to Pryke (1981), the only two countries in Europe that have shown large gains in productivity between 1968 and 1979 were Poland and the USSR.

Returning to the employment question: For the period 1960 to 1975, total manufacturing employment in the United Kingdom went down at the rate of 0.7 percent per annum and for the period 1968 to 1975, at 1.6 percent per annum. During that period (1960 to 1975), the rate per annum of reduction in employment was 5.5 percent for British Rail, 2.5 percent for British Steel (1968–1975), 1.6 percent for electricity, 3.4 percent for the National Bus Company (1970 to 1975) and 6.5 percent for the National Freight Corporation (1969 to 1975). The only two SOEs that increased employment were British Airways (3.6 percent per annum) and the postal services (0.1 percent for posts, 2.1 percent for telecommunications).

To avoid any misunderstandings, the performance of the nationalized industries in the United Kingdom was very unimpressive in the 1970s. The pretax rate of return on capital employed was either negative or a maximum of 2 percent and has always been much lower than that of industrial and commercial companies in the United Kingdom (Redwood and Hatch, 1982, p. 18). At this point we deal with the employment maintenance hypothesis, not with performance in general. Monsen and Walters (1979) hypothesized that SOE managers maximize growth and employment. I would suggest instead that SOE managers are influenced in their behavior by what their controllers expect them to do. In certain cases it means maximizing employment, in other cases, reducing it.

To be sure, governments, especially those of the left, find it extremely difficult to allow massive reduction of labor force. As Dudley (1979) points out, the inevitable closure of older steelmaking plants to make way for the development of large coastal works highlighted the Labour party dilemma of how to preserve the British Steel Company's strategy, while at the same time protecting the interests of workers threatened with redundancy (Second Report of the Committee of Scottish Affairs, as quoted in Grant, 1982, p. 92). Tony Benn set up a review committee in effect to stop plants being closed. Only a quarter of the proposed closures in terms of job loss were carried out (Cockerill, 1980, p. 139).

Nor are these problems faced only by Labour government. In 1985, Mrs. Thatcher agreed to postpone for three years the closure of the Ravenscraig and Llanwern steel plants that British Steel Company wanted to close because they suffered heavy losses. These two plants "stayed at work while striking miners picketed" (*The Economist*, Aug. 10, 1985). Apparently in recognition of their cooperation, the workers were able to save their jobs, at a cost of continued losses to BSC.

As another example, Turkey went through a crisis as a result of which the army took control in 1980. At that time, Turkey had a large SOE sector, largely the heritage of Mustafa Kemal who believed that the shortage of private capital left him no option but to industrialize Turkey through SOEs. Most of these SOEs later degenerated; they were inefficient, overemployed and loss-ridden. During 1977 to 1979, Turkish SOEs averaged net losses equivalent to 3.9 percent of GDP (World Bank, 1983, p. 74). Since then, according to an *Economist* survey of Turkey, the SOEs' "wage bill as a percentage of their total expenditures has declined in every year since 1978. Their subsidies have been cut and they have been given more freedom to raise prices" (*The Economist*, Turkey Survey, November 3, 1984, p. 14).

In the United States during the late 1970s and early 1980s, Conrail abandoned one-seventh of its lines, which had been producing only 1.6 percent of the company's operating revenues. It pared the labor force from over 100,000 to 60,000 employees (*Fortune*, August, 23, 1982, p. 7). Since 1981, Conrail halved its labor force and won large wage concessions from its employees and recorded its first profit in that year. In 1984, it was able to reach an operating profit of nearly $500 million and was offered for sale to private investors (*The Economist*, February 16, 1985, pp. 48–49).

SOEs are alleged to regard their labor force as a fixed cost. They are said not to have any discretion in laying off workers. Instead, they are alleged to be expected to increase employment or at least to maintain it. Therefore, *ceteris paribus*, an SOE might be expected to have more employees per unit of output than its private counterpart.

An alternative hypothesis is that state ownership is an efficient means for reducing employment in declining industries in a world in which politics and economics are inexorably bound. In the post–World War II era governments have become responsible for the maintenance of full employment. One consequence has been attempts to save lame ducks and bolster declining industries to save jobs. When a large employer is rescued, the government has essentially two choices. One is nationalizing the firm; another is to aid it by less visible methods like tariff protection or by forcing banks to extend credit. In the first case, the recurring losses of the enterprise (if the losses are indeed recurring) have to be covered by annual capital appropriations from the government budget. The SOE management has to come to the legislature, to ask for such an appropriation. The sorry state of affairs of the corporation and the cost to the country are publicly debated, and the public is enraged. Since nationalization means that the power of the private owners is eliminated, they do not lobby for additional help. The coalition of workers and capitalists is broken. The legislature presses for cuts, and so does the ministry of finance. Labor may attempt to resist but often sees no alternative and has to agree to a reduction in the work force.

Under state ownership, the pressures to reduce the size of the labor force are stronger, and the coalition for the continuation of the employment weaker than when invisible methods like tariff protection, voluntary curbs on imports or other orderly marketing arrangements are used. In the latter case, the costs to the consumers are not registered anywhere. The coalition demanding continuation of the aid is much more powerful because it includes also the owners of the firms. Since costs to the consumer are not recorded, they are not continuously shown in public and do not have to be voted annually by the legislature. Therefore, there is less scrutiny and less pressure for reducing the subsidies and no built-in mechanism for reviewing them. Thus, in the United States, President Kennedy aided the textile industry by invisible methods. The immediate result has been increased employment in the industry: it employed 863,000 in 1963 and 1.18 million in 1973 (Kurth, 1980). In contrast, when Congress created AMTRAK, "it provided for the passenger rail corporation to receive an infusion of Federal cash each year until the system became self-supporting" (Tierney, 1984, p. 83). AMTRAK's deficits meant that its management had to plead its case before Congress every year in order to obtain funds. The first result was that Congress "agreed to remove some of the political baggage burdening AMTRAK since its birth" (*Ibid.*, p. 84), allowing the firm to close unprofitable lines. Since then, "the modest and declining subsidy accorded to AMTRAK has become a symbol of Federal waste" (*The Economist*, August 24, 1985, p. 34). It might well be that the feeling that SOEs cannot trim the size of employment results from the fact that the fight for such trimming is conducted openly and is therefore known to the public. When a government helps an industry as a result of silent lobbying, the public is generally unaware that aid was given, and certainly do not know the extent of that aid.

This is not to say that governments are always able to maintain an efficient size of labor force in its SOEs. The argument is much weaker: it is that invisible methods of aid would cost more in public funds and would reduce employment in declining industries less than when the firm is state-owned.

Of course, if subsidies to a private firm are granted visibly, for example directly per employee, they are also visible to the legislature.

In SOEs the government might also decide to avoid a big reduction in the labor force by moving the existing labor force to different occupations. This is essentially what Austria has been doing. Its state-owned steel firm, Voest Alpine, reduced the size of employment in steel but moved the workers to new occupations in new businesses—from oil trading to electronics. Crude steel and raw materials, 52 percent of the firm's sales in 1974, were only 22 percent of the total in 1983 (*The Economist*, December 15, 1984, pp. 69–70). The Japanese railroad, saddled with enormous overemployment, diversified its activities to create gainful employment for those redundant employees.

It should be reiterated that this argument related to the visibility of the aid, not strictly to the ownership. Thus, in many cases SOEs have been used as a means to aid an industry or a firm without the need to go to the legislature. In France, the Interministerial Council for Restructuring Industry (CIRI) is responsible for mobilizing state-owned banks to stem the rise of unemployment. However, similar calls are made by government officials to private banks in Germany and the United Kingdom. Zysman (1983) argues "that structural differences in national financial system contribute to the differing capacities of governments to intervene in the industrial economy" (p. 285). According to him:

> [The] concept of the state as marketplace player is quite distinct from the concept of public ownership. The distinction between public and private ownership does not identify the degree of control the government executive will have on a corporation's affairs . . . discretion in the provision of industrial finance—in the selective allocation of credit—is necessary for the state to enter continuously into the industrial life of private companies and to influence their strategies in the way that a rival or partner would [p. 76].

SOEs Are Rational Actors Serving the Interest of the Country

Another myth often found is that the country as a whole works as one rational actor to achieve certain agreed and shared national objectives. SOEs are portrayed as docile rational actors attempting to achieve predetermined ends set up by the government that controls them completely. Lamont, e.g., claims, "State enterprise capitalism means marshalling all the nation-state's resources and the talent to enable the nation-state to compete better in the world market" (1979, p. 193).

The reality of the SOEs is much more complicated. First, nation-states rarely reach consensus on national objectives. Second, conflicts between

SOEs and their governments as well as between SOEs and other SOEs are abundant. To be sure, most of these conflicts are not publicized and are either solved in closed camera or a compromise is reached outside the glare of the television cameras and the press. Still, enough anecdotal evidence exists to document the prevalence of such conflicts. The behavior of SOEs is better explained as a result of contests for control over resources rather than as an outcome of pressures for efficient attainment of national or other objectives.

A related myth often found in the literature is that the government is responsible for the strategy of the SOE and does not intervene in operating decisions, while the management of the company enjoys full autonomy on all operating problems. In fact, most governments do not give their SOEs strategic directions. At the same time they frequently intervene in the operating decisions of the firm. In many cases, the concept of an autonomous SOE is a misnomer.

Why is it that governments cannot refrain from interfering in the affairs of these SOEs? The reasons are different in different countries. In all of them, the government feels that since in the final analysis it will have to cover the losses of these enterprises, to the extent that such losses occur, it has both the right and the duty to direct and control their affairs. More fundamentally, governments feel that SOEs are instruments of the state and can be used to achieve all sorts of short-term goals for the government.

In a democracy, the legislature and government officials try to cater to the wishes of the voters. At least in SOEs that are very, very visible and important to the public at large, such as transportation, electricity, water or telephone, there will be strong pressures to reduce the prices paid for the service. Governments intervene in SOEs because they think in political terms, thus making the SOE one of their instruments to achieve political goals.

Theoretically, the board of directors is expected to shield the SOE from these political interventions. In reality in most countries, the members of the board of directors are each appointed to represent a certain group of constituents and see themselves as the guardians of the right of these specific groups. In many countries, board members are civil servants, who perceive their role as getting enough information on the SOE to be passed on to the minister or as representing the ministry to the SOE. In many SOEs, the board of directors appears to have become an interministerial coordinating committee. This situation creates what Sir Peter Parker, ex-chairman of British Rail, referred to as "government by nudge and fudge." To them, the government is a portfolio, in which the SOEs are certain subsidiaries. Their activities should be closely monitored to achieve the best results for the economy as a whole.

In many cases, the SOEs have more power and more expertise than the ministries, and it is sometimes hard to tell whether the government bureaucracy controls its SOEs or vice versa. In West Africa, the financial resources of the marketing board, both on current and capital accounts, exceeds those of the West African government. The major Austrian state-owned banks are vast empires, powerful because the government needs to get funds from them.

SOEs Receive Special Treatment from the Government

One of the most widely held myths is that SOEs receive special privileges from their government and therefore are unfair competitors. In particular, SOEs are alleged to enjoy the following advantages: they are not required to earn profits or dividends; they receive lower investment and export financing costs; they pay lower or no domestic taxes; they receive purchasing and sales preferences from their governments and they are favored by international information reporting, trade and burden of proof regulations (see, e.g., Nielsen, 1982; Lamont, 1979; Monsen and Walters, 1983).

SOE managers would argue almost exactly the opposite. As they see it, they are subject to many more controls that take an inordinate amount of their time; they have to reveal business secrets to their competitors as a part of the parliamentary accountability requirements; they are subject to too many audits that cost them time, money and revelation of business secrets. We shall discuss these questions in the context of the domestic environment in Chapter 7 and in the international competitive environment in Chapter 10.

SOEs Are by Definition Not Profitable, Loss-Ridden and a Burden on the Public Purse

Since managers of SOEs are alleged to be less interested in profits than in the achievement of an easier life-style, it follows that SOEs cannot be profitable. Indeed, the record of SOEs as far as return on investment is concerned is not very good, as the figures presented in Chapter 5 reveal. As a group, SOEs in most countries certainly constitute a burden on the national purse.

The relevant question, however, is whether SOEs are not profitable because they are state-owned. The answer to this question is much less straightforward. First, many SOEs are natural monopolies, and the economists' prescription for these firms is to price their products at a price equal to marginal costs. In this case, social welfare considerations mean that SOEs should not be profitable and even that they should receive subsidies. At any rate, the pricing policies of these firms are a function of their natural monopoly status, not that of state ownership. The SOEs may also be profitable because they enjoy monopoly privileges and protection from imports. The question, therefore, is whether or not those SOEs that compete against private enterprises are profitable and whether or not they are more or less efficient than private firms similarly situated. The facts are that some of these firms are indeed very profitable. Well-known examples are the national oil firms. Firms such as the

Swedish tobacco firms have also been innovative and very successful in their exports: the Swedish tobacco firms captured 9 percent of the U.S. market for tobacco as a result of its innovation of a new pipe tobacco.

Other firms have been known to lose a lot of money. However, in many cases these firms were nationalized because of these losses. British Leyland, e.g., did not lose money because it was state owned; rather, it became state-owned because it lost money. The same is true for many other firms. This does not mean that SOEs are more efficient than their private sector coun-terparts. A World Bank study (1981) has pinpointed the high inefficiency of SOEs in sub-Saharan Africa as a cause for slow economic growth. The point, however, is that SOEs may be inefficient not because of their ownership but because of reasons ranging from lack of experience (as in the case of some of the mineral firms in Zaire or Zambia or manufacturing firms in Africa), to too high and too detailed government intervention (as was the case in India), special demands on them of achieving social goals or because they have been used as a political tool. In many cases, the losses of SOEs are caused by their use for invisible subsidies.

SOEs Are Not Required to Pay Taxes

This allegation is often heard and is true for some countries but not for most. In the United States, Canada, South Africa, Brazil and El Salvador, Colum-bia until the later tax reform, among others, SOEs are exempt from corpo-ration or other forms of income taxation. However, in many other countries the taxes they are paying are exactly equal to those paid by a private enterprise similarly situated. In fact, governments feel that the uniform application of income taxes to their enterprises has the advantage of forcing the managers to distribute some of the profits to the government. In contrast to dividends that may or may not be paid, there is a certainty of control over that part of the profits that is paid as income taxes.

In some countries SOEs are subject to the same corporation taxes under the same rules as any private enterprise. This is the situation in the United Kingdom, the Federal Republic of Germany, France and Spain, as well as in many less-developed countries such as Sri Lanka, the Philippines, India or Tanzania. To be sure, in some of these countries taxation is levied only on operations resulting from profits from industrial and commercial activities. In the U.K. income of firms owned by local government bodies such as munic-ipalities is not subject to taxation and local public utilities in France do not pay taxes. All in all the actual practice on taxation of SOEs is different in different countries.

Whether or not an SOE is subject to taxes depends also on its legal status. When an SOE has no separate legal personality and its staff is consid-ered government employees, as in the case of many railroads or postal ser-vices, there are no taxes. Still, in the Federal Republic of Germany, the Federal Post Office must deliver annually 6.6 percent of its revenue to the Federal Government (Sector 21 of the Post Administration Act). In the Federal Republic of Germany, the Credit Agency for Reconstruction (Kreditanstalt für Wiederaufbau) "has the same fiscal privileges as the German Federal Bank (Deutsche Bundesbank); it pays no taxes on property (Vermogensteuer), no corporation tax (Korperschaftsteuer), and no turnover tax (Gewerbesteuer)" (Keyser and Windle, 1978, Part III, P. 42).

SOEs Are Not Allowed to Diversify

As in the case of income taxation, there is a diversity among countries in their treatment of the ability of SOEs to diversify. Noel Capon hastily concluded, on the basis of a very small sample of countries or of firms, that SOEs are not allowed to diversify and are therefore not concerned with fundamental choices of product–market combinations because they are not, by law, allowed to move their business. Thus, he claims:

> Many factors make it less likely that state-owned enterprises are as diversified as private corporations. They typically have narrow mission definitions, often constrained by statute, and based on products or technology (e.g., steel, railroads, coal, gas, electricity, postal service). By contrast, large private corporations today have broader mission definitions such as being energy companies (coal, oil, gas) or serving the needs of middle-income consumers (with many product lines based on many technologies). When state-owned corporations try to diversify, private enterprise may raise the spectre of unfair competition and cause them to desist, especially if current operations are unprofitable. While private corporations may acquire businesses to obtain cash or reduce risk, for government portfolio elements these concerns are minimized. Government may constrain state-owned enterprises from acquiring private businesses independently, and government acquisition of private companies is more difficult than a share transfer in the private sector. Since state-owned corporations can only acquire whereas private corporations can both acquire and be acquired, potential diversification is less. Finally, most governments prefer a portfolio of independent entities rather than a supernational enterprise with vast concentrations of power.
>
> To the extent that state-owned enterprises extend their business horizons, they are more likely to focus on highly related activities, such as an airline acquiring holiday hotels or a postal service incorporating telephone and telegraphic service, than less related activities.
>
> Proposition 3: State owned corporations are less diverse in the markets they serve, the technologies they employ and the products and services they produce than are private corporations [1981, pp. 14–15].

However, many SOEs are highly diversified. Witness cases such as IRI in Italy, the NEB in the United Kingdom until it was dismantled in 1981, Statsförtag in Sweden until 1982, ÖIAG in Austria and many others. Some SOEs diversified even without the consent of their governments. Pertamina, Indonesia's state-owned oil firm, provides the classic example. Flush with resources from a booming oil market, it was able to break away from government control and to diversify into ventures as disparate as iron and steel, vacation resorts, insurance and airlines. By the time control of the firm was regained in 1976, it had run up debts of $10.5 billions (Gillis, 1977, p. 15). ENI, the Italian state-owned oil firm, armed with funds and expertise, also diversified in many directions. It has interests in oil and gas exploration, production, transportation, refining and marketing, nuclear energy, chemicals, mechanical engineering, pipeline construction, and an assortment of other activities.

In the Federal Republic of Germany, the permission of the Minister of Finance has to be sought before shares are bought or sold (however, in federal industrial private law companies, diversification is much less restricted and the Federal Ministers do not have seats on the supervisory boards (Aufsichtsträte). (Keyser and Windle, 1978, Part III, p. 79). Salzgitter Ag. or Volkswagenwerk are quite diversified firms.

The notion that SOEs cannot diversify may be based on the situation in the United Kingdom, where the major nationalized industries are single business, mainly monopolistic, enterprises: coal, gas, electricity, rail and so on. Even in the United Kingdom, however, there is some diversity, sometimes due to historical reasons; that is, those diverse activities were already being carried out by the private firms before nationalization. In the case of the U.K. Central Electricity Generating Board, 5 percent of net output consists of domestic appliances, and 3 percent of net output is in electrical contracting; the British Gas Corporation's sales of appliances and its installation/contracting work consists of 6 percent of net output. Seven percent of the net output of the NCB is in bricks and distribution of appliances and building materials, while 14 percent of British Rail's net output is generated by repair and construction of locomotives and rolling stock, shipping and hovercraft, hotels and rail catering (NEDO, 1976, Appendix Volume, pp. 18–28). Moreover, many countries organize all the SOEs under one or several diversified holding companies. We already mentioned some examples in the developed countries, but this system is even more prevalent in the developing nations. Some examples are the National Development Corporation in Tanzania; the Industrial Development Corporation in Uganda; Guyana State Corporation in Guyana; Pernas in Malaysia; Indeco, Mindeco, Findeco and Rudeco in Zambia; Indu Peru in Peru; Temasek Holdings in Singapore and the now defunct Corporacion de Emprecases Nacionales of Argentina. The degree of diversification of SOEs is, to a large extent, again, a question of contest for power.

When the private sector is strong, it opposes diversification seen as unfair competition (see Chapter 7). At the same time, diversification allows more invisible cross-subsidies. In Sweden Statsförtag subsidized the ailing firms it was forced to acquire with profits of other firms. In many cases, the government forced diversification to give invisible aid to a private firm.

SOEs Will Never Be Bankrupt

One strongly held belief is that "just as state-owned companies need not earn profits to prosper, neither do their losses lead to bankruptcy. Judging by the evidence, state ownership usually confers immortality on an enterprise" (Monsen and Walters, 1983, p. 112). Other authors make an even more unequivocal statement, claiming that SOEs will never be allowed to default and that their management is assured of new financial infusions. They are a savior of last resort (Gillis, 1980; Radetzki, 1985).

It is true that some large SOEs do not go bankrupt. By the same token, no government since the 1970s has allowed any large firms, either public or private, to go bankrupt. At the same time, SOEs were allowed to go bankrupt. Several dozen of the U.K. NEB-sponsored firms were closed or allowed to declare bankruptcy, and the Scottish Development Agency closed Stonefield Vehicles (Grant, 1982, p. 279). Several state-owned coalfields and railway lines have been closed in the United Kingdom since 1970, accounting in the former case for 15 to 20 percent of the reported increase in productivity over this period (Sheahan, in Shepherd, 1976, p. 138). In Italy, EGAM (Ente Gistione Aziende Mineraria e Mettallurgiche) was founded in 1958 and started operations in 1971. It had to manage a group of managerially weak, technologically obsolete and financially precarious firms. At the time of transfer to the new holding firm, these companies showed losses of 72 billion lire and had debts of 391.3 billion lire. Up to March 1977, EGAM's accumulated losses were 512.6 billion lire, and its debts, mainly short-term, were twice that amount (125 percent of the turnover). The company was dissolved in March 1977, and its fifty companies were distributed between IRI and ENI, causing the vice-chairman of ENI to resign in protest. In this case, the subsidiary companies continued to operate under state ownership. Still, the holding was dissolved and the managers lost their jobs. In other cases, the parent company continued, but the subsidiaries were dissolved, as in the case of NEB cited earlier. Finsider, in Italy, closed several inefficient steel plants and laid off workers.

There are many other cases in which SOEs were allowed to go bankrupt or to cease operations. In Israel there were at least a dozen such cases, including manufacturing firms, a copper mine, a plantation firm and several export trading firms. The Ivory Coast has closed sixteen firms since 1980, and Brazil closed ten SOEs in 1980 (Shirley, 1983, p. 55). In Singapore, according to Tan Chwee Huat (in Reddy, 1983, p. 261), "The guiding principle of these government enterprises is that they must operate on business lines and compete with other firms on equal terms. They are expected to make profits, and if they do not come up to expectations, they are allowed to go bankrupt." More relevant to our discussion, from the point of view of its managers, a firm does not have to go bankrupt. It is enough that the manager is sacked, which leads us to the next myth.

Managers of SOEs Have Longer Tenure

Related to the belief that SOEs are not allowed to go bankrupt is the assertion that their top managers are assured long tenure: "Security of tenure for the top management in publicly owned enterprises is not absolute, but typically much greater than in private corporations" (Radetzki, 1985, p. 25). The reason for this assertion is partially based on property rights theory. Based on the theorem that individuals behave to further their interests, it is assumed that SOE managers are risk averse; since they do not have equity shares or similar stakes in the enterprise in the same sense as a private owner, and since their pecuniary gain is not directly related to profits, SOE managers would tend to opt for an easier life, avoid errors of commission in contrast to errors of omission, thus avoiding visible disaster and demotion or dismissal. Longer tenure of office gives also a higher lifetime income (Davies, 1981, p. 115). It is further argued that the formal conditions in the public service guarantee job security and that there is a greater difficulty in measuring performance and, therefore, establishing managerial failures.

In contrast, Shirley reports, "the managers of SOEs typically have a high rate of turnover in developing countries, partly because of shortages as competent people are shifted around to head troubled SOEs, and partly because of political changes" (1983, p. 50). Based on World Bank files, she reports that in Liberia "the average tenure of SOE general managers in the 1970s was less than two years" (p. 50). In many countries SOE managers change with each change of the political regime, at the discretion of the controlling ministers. In India, e.g.,

> The frequent changes of top-management personnel are [sic] another disturbing phenomenon. For instance in Mysore Iron and Steel Ltd., there were three managing directors between June 1970 and June 1973; in the Mysore Urban Developing Corporation Ltd., there were three chairmen and three managing directors between December 1970 and 1972. In A.P. Agro Industries Corporation Ltd., there were two managing directors between June 15, 1971 and June 28, 1971; in Leather Industries Development Corporation of Andhra Pradesh there were four managing directors between April 1977 and November 1978. [Narain, 1982, p. 145]

These changes in tenure, one should note, are caused by failure to establish the right political contacts, not only by failure to do the economic job. If the tenure of an incumbent is very short, he or she does not have either to understand the industry or to make real contributions for its efficient running. Often, the manager does not intend to make any changes that would disturb anybody. He or she knows his or her tenure is too short to do that.

Regarding risk, a distinction must be made between risk to the manager and risk to the enterprise. The less the traceability of a decision to the action of the manager, the less the personal risk, even though the risk to the enterprise may be great. Risk-averse managers may insure themselves by receiving approval for their actions before taking them. Risk sharing increases the dangers of moral hazards in the behavior of individual managers since it reduces the traceability of decisions and outcomes to individuals (Adar and Aharoni, 1980).

In theory, SOEs are the ultimate vehicle for distributing risks across the entire population. Therefore, SOEs should be risk-neutral (Arrow and Lind, 1970). In practice, the risk to the manager depends on whether or not responsibility is traceable. Whether or not, and to what degree, responsibility is traceable depends on the system design. For example, the use of new and untested technology usually entails high project risk. From the point of view of the SOE manager, a success means promotion and prestige, but a failure may be regarded as an act of God. Conversely, the risk of system failure may be very low, but the risk to the manager is usually much higher because of the publicity of such a failure. In an electricity-generating firm, e.g., the expected value of lost income resulting from a temporary system failure may be very low. Still, the managers of the firm may choose to install backup generating capacity to avoid such incidents. The problem, therefore, is how to make innovation an acceptable risk not only to managers but also to their controllers. Diskin (1980) found in the case of Israel that managers of SOEs take higher risks than those in private firms when the risks are taken for a national objective and the manager feels that the board of directors does not demand profitability.

SOEs Cannot Attract Innovative Managers

Observers usually take it for granted that the public and private sectors have different goals, modes of operations, incentives, control methods and sources for management recruitment and that there is an inescapable contradiction between creativity and innovation on the one hand and the public sector on the other hand. Innovation and creativity need flexibility and organic organization (Burns and Stalker, 1961). Public sector organizations typically operate under a Weberian bureaucratic systems, appropriate to stable and predictable environments. The uncertainty inherent in many changes and innovations runs against the need for machine bureaucracy.

Bureaucratic organizations and innovations, to borrow a phrase from Levine, are "strange bedfellows" (1983, p. 235). In a study of entrepreneurial activities in the USSR, Levine found seven characteristics of bureaucratic organizations that hinder innovation: strict hierachy of authority, narrowly specialized units, striving for stability, risk aversion, measurability of performance and reward structure, role of slack, competition and bankruptcy.

One reason for lack of innovation in the Soviet system, according to Levine (1983), is information degradation: any proposal has to be passed through the ranks, and any level can veto it. This point, in addition to the vast difference in technical knowledge between ministers and the people in the field, impedes communications and degrades the information flow on its long way from the innovator to the granter of approval. It takes a number of approvals to adopt an innovation but only one veto to kill it.

The system is organized in narrowly specified units, and the interest of the ministry in meeting its targets and obligations is stronger than its interest in meeting the overall goals of the economy. The narrowly defined specific units do not reward innovation and impede a close linkage between R&D and production—an essential prerequisite for innovation to be successful. Furthermore, bureaucrats cherish routine, repetitive methods that allow stability. They resist new approaches that threaten to upset the routine and standardized procedures of work. Performance of subordinates tends to be based on quantifiable measures, while innovation needs an environment that does not unduly penalize failure. Managers resist innovations and try to keep the targets low. In addition, the central planning authority applies extreme pressure, not leaving enough slack time for alertness to opportunities. Finally, the risk of bankruptcy does not exist: "The state will bail out a firm that is losing money through grants, subsidies, emergency credits, and allowed higher prices and the firm will continue to operate" (Levine, 1983, p. 254).

Soviet enterprise managers, according to Levine (1983), have little incentive to experiment with the new. Since this year's performance is next year's target, and since implementing new processes may interrupt current schedules, nibbling away at possible bonuses from above-target production, and since, if innovation fails, the risk to the manager of lost status is very high, innovation is discouraged and the replacement of old technology by a new one fails to occur.

Most of Levine's analysis is applicable to any public sector in the world as well as to any large, bureaucratic organization whose future existence is important for the achievement of state goals—be they employment or national pride. Given the past behavior of governments in bailing out large business firms in the private sector, it is unclear whether the managers of all large firms do not feel that the state will bail them out.

Certain public sector characteristics that impede innovation are peculiar to it. A private firm can work on a new program in relatively complete secrecy, while the work of the public sector is carried out under the glare of the press

(Bower, 1983). In addition, many innovations are destructive to some interest groups that resist their introduction. The public sector is expected to take into account these views and pressures much more than the private sector does.

Also unique to the public sector is the salience of public accountability. Public accountability in a democracy calls for openly declared facts and open debate of them by laypersons and their elected representatives. Accountability means that every decision must be documented, explained and approved by different echelons. It is not feasible under accountability rules simply to say: "I believe the need exists for a new product." One has to document one's beliefs, prove them to one's superiors and explain them to the state's auditing arm. Although accountability is extremely important, it might dampen creativity and innovation, at least when real major breakthroughs are contemplated. Moreover, by the very nature of the democratic process, elected officials tend to have a short time horizon, looking for tangible results before the next elections. They can rarely afford the time or trouble to master the complexity of the situation. While the civil service provides substantial continuity, the pressure for quick-fix solutions is strong and again works against major innovation, which, by its very nature, requires a long time for conception, development and implementation. Innovation is impeded as a result of organizational form and the incentive structure associated with it.

Despite these examples, many SOEs demonstrate their ability to innovate and to allow entrepreneurs to flourish. In the public utilities field, British Gas was totally dependent on coal. It arranged with considerable enterprise the importation of liquefied methane from Algeria. It also adopted an ICI invention and produced gas from naphtha with low capital and operating costs. This move allowed British Gas to scrap carbonization plants: between 1963 and 1969 British Gas eliminated about half its carbonization plants, increasing at the same time sales from 2.9 billion therms to 4.4 billion and output per equivalent worker by 43 percent (Pryke, 1981). A famous innovation is the basic oxygen process, invented by the Austrian SOE, Voest-Alpine (and named LD technique after the sites of two plants, Linz and Donawitz). The airbus is another example of a very successful introduction of new technology and innovative design by an SOE. SOEs also innovated in computer designs (ICL in the United Kingdom) or in chips manufacturing (INMOS) as well as in many military applications.

In addition, entrepreneurs flourish in SOEs all over the world. Enrico Mattei turned the fledgling AGIP, for sale by the Italian government, into the giant ENI, turning Italy from an oil-short country to one with energy surplus and innovating new contracts between the oil-producing countries and the oil distributors, and forced what he called "the seven sisters" to follow in his footsteps. Ozires Silva headed a new organization that designed, developed and built a Brazilian turboprop transport plane. Al Schwimmer did the same in Israel. Robert Moses, who began his career in the state of New York in 1924 as the head of Long Island State Park Commission, was instrumental in creating many public enterprises over the next 44 years of his career, as were Pierre Lefaucheux, who, against government wishes, developed an inexpensive popular car in Renault and Pierre Dreyfus who made the company a multinational. Many more managers of SOEs have been successful entrepreneurs and innovators (see Chapter 8).

The entrepreneurs and innovators in the public sector are not motivated by pecuniary gain; rather, they are driven by power, glory, prestige, the satisfaction of serving their country and mainly a high need for achievement. A common feature of SOEs in mixed economies is a squeezing of pay scales. Workers are overpaid and managers are underpaid. The ratio of the net compensation (including all cash payments plus compensation in kind such as housing and transportation, but after taxes) of the lowest paid worker to the highest paid manager in the United States and the USSR is 1:15 to 1:20. In most SOEs it is much lower. Still, to use Hirschman (1970) terms, even though managers may voice complaints, they are loyal enough to continue instead of exercising their exit option.

There are at least three reasons why different managers are willing to accept lower incomes to manage SOEs. Some may derive satisfaction from serving the public rather than private interests. Others want to run large, modern capital-intensive enterprises, which in many countries are mainly state owned, and where large-scale activities are not public they are often in the hands of family groups where promotion opportunities for outsiders are severely limited. Third, to the extent that opportunities for promotion exist outside the public sector, the manager may perceive him- or herself as being constantly evaluated within a national market for managers where alternative job opportunities are traded. If the innovative manager is interested in the present value of his or her earnings, he or she does not succumb to the temptation of an easy life. If indeed the last two explanations are the major reasons that attract the innovative managers, too much control may not only stifle initiative but also cause managers to go elsewhere.

Since entrepreneurs believe outcomes are contingent on their own actions, they do not like to have risk-averse partners or controllers who would veto new ideas. Therefore, an SOE may lose its ability to innovate if its activities are subject to close scrutiny, leading managers to share risks by committee decision-making structure. Professional managers become extremely frustrated when their efforts are blocked by what they see as unnecessary bureaucratic interference that keeps them from managing their enterprise in an innovative manner.

To be sure, some of these public entrepreneurs, such as Moses of New York or Kenneth Abeyaickrama (who left a lucrative job as president of Unilever's subsidiary in Sri Lanka to turn around the ailing State Timber Corporation), were independently wealthy. There were also those, such as Ibnu Sutowo of Pertamina, the Indonesian oil company, or Louis Tonti of the New Jersey Highway Authority, who were found guilty of using their position to gain personal profits (Ramamurti, 1985a). These cases, however, are quite rare. SOE managers innovated and built empires because of a high need for achievement. They may have been attracted by the possibilities of taking high project risks.

Some discussions of entrepreneurship have viewed the process as being embedded in a competitive free market system (Kirzner, 1973). In this century, entrepreneurs have changed the course of very large organizations, both private and public. Hage and Aiken (1970), summarizing the existing literature on innovation, found that seven properties tend to encourage the generation and acceptance of innovations in products and services: a high rate of professional specialists, decentralization, low formalization, low stratification, absence of high-volume production, relatively low emphasis on cost reduction and high job satisfaction. Organizations must be fluid rather than rigid, dynamic rather than static, and have organic structure (Burns and Stalker, 1961). This view of the organization has ramifications for their design, control and performance evaluation.

Innovations may enhance the power of managers, who understand the new technology, relative to government controllers. Their professional knowledge enables these managers to control the resource allocation function. Finally, success is due not only to the entrepreneurial drive of an individual but also to the availability of alternative public enterprise decision centers. Under the right system design, SOEs can be innovative, they can pick winners and allow entrepreneurs to flourish (see Chapters 6 and 8).

The Alternative to SOEs Is a Free Market

Many of the other allegations and myths discussed here are derived from the basic belief that if SOEs did not exist, the market mechanism would flourish and that the alternative to state ownership is atomistic competition of a large number of firms in the market. The real alternative to most SOEs, however, is not atomistic competition but a monopoly, oligopoly, cartel or government-subsidized and heavily protected privately owned firm.

For most economists a smoothly functioning market is the ideal in which allocative efficiency can be achieved. Any divergence from perfect markets is dubbed *failure*, *imperfect* or a similar pejorative term. State ownership should be used ony if markets are unable to work efficiently because of monopoly, high risk or imperfect information and if market failure costs are greater than the costs of organization failure (Jones and Mason, in Jones *et al.*, 1982).

Today, however, market failure is almost the rule rather than the exception. The share of large firms in GNP has been growing. Western economies today are dominated by giant, often multinational firms, most of which are managed by professional managers and owned by passive shareholders. In fact, some of the largest hierarchical organizations are not governmental but private business enterprises. In the United States, e.g., the largest employer, as of August 1984, is the Department of Defense, with 1,074,239 civilian employees including branches of the various armed forces (excluding the armed forces themselves). However, the largest organizations are not other branches of government but General Motors, employing about 691,000 employees. The Ford Motor Company, with 380,000 employees, is larger than any government department except defense and the postal service (that employed 684,364 employees), and so is IBM with 369,545, Mobil with 178,100 or Exxon with 156,000 employees. The U.S. Health and Human Services Department employs 147,730 people (*Fortune*, April 30, 1984, pp. 274–322; U.S. Office of Personnel Management, Monthly Release of Federal Civilian Workforce Statistics Employment and Trends as of August 1984).

If industrial corporations are compared with state and municipal governments, sixteen of the twenty largest organizations—when size is measured by output—are investor-owned corporations. Thus, bureaucratic organizations are not confined to the public sector. The vast resources of these firms are not controlled by their diffused owners. Although these owners admittedly can sell their shares if they so desire, they have no effective way to monitor the behavior of the managers or even to replace them. Economic power is concentrated in the hands of the managers of a few hundred large firms. These firms have tremendous impact not only on economic matters but also on society and community life. The opening or closing of a major plant in a small town changes not only the economic future of the town but also its social and cultural life. Big firms have a pivotal importance in determining priorities of resource allocation; they have power over the prices, products and distribution of scarce goods. Their sheer size often creates barriers to entry for new rivals. They have enormous impact on the character and performance of other social institutions, on the use of natural resources, over regional developments and over life-styles. They largely determine the technologies used in society. Finally, large firms have enormous power over government policymaking, lobbying for institutional arrangement—from trade barriers to subsidies—to their benefit.

In small countries the alternative to a state-owned monopoly is a private one both because the size of the market is small and because many of the industries are controlled by a few large firms. Economists also ignore the possibility of state ownership as resulting from the interplay of sociopolitical forces and quest for power. However, polity and economy cannot be divorced. SOEs are capable of generating surplus that is used and distributed according to the political power of different groups. The control over the SOEs can be in the hands not only of government but also of managers. Since contending social forces are different in different countries, and evolving over time, behavior of SOEs is also different: they may operate mainly as a means to supply products and services below cost to certain interest groups, or to achieve other goals—and these goals are largely a result of the interplay of social forces in the polity. If SOEs are an emanation and extension of the state, their behavior cannot be understood without understanding the role of the state and the beliefs and attitudes of the groups that control its apparatus. To be sure, the degree of intervention depends also on culture and on power of different actors. These power relations evolve with time: when an SOE is established, government has more power. The expertise and experience gained by managers usually allows them to accumulate more power and achieve more autonomy. We shall develop the different parts of this taxonomy as we proceed. At this stage it is important to realize that SOEs are different along many dimensions.

CONCLUSION

Clearly, there are many points of view on SOEs, many of which are based on ideological beliefs and values, and some on a limited base of knowledge or preconceived notions, as well as misconceptions and unrealistic ideas on how SOEs operate. SOEs vary in their specific legal powers and constraints, although they commonly enjoy more latitude than traditional government departments. The widespread use of SOEs increase the diversity. However, they are still seen as "creeping socialism" or a panacea. Because of the diversity, many commonly-held beliefs about SOEs are not always true and many of the expectations attendant to their creation were inflated or were not fulfilled. While an SOE with unassailable autonomy does not exist, these firms are not always an instrument of government. No SOE exists "whose actual operations reflect the full measure of political isolation and managerial autonomy portrayed in either the theoretical literature or the rhetoric accompanying the organization's creation" (Tierney, 1984, p. 85). Still, the more financially independent these firms are, the more their operations are inconspicuous or incomprehensible to the general public, the more they control information and the more they are able to recruit professional managers—better and more permanent than the Ministry, the less are the differences between them and investor-owned firms. Ministries are not always strong enough to impose policies on reluctant SOEs, and their managers may enjoy more autonomy than officially prescribed.

Hopefully this book will make some small contribution to clearing some of these issues. It may be as well to start by looking at the origins of the different SOEs and the variety of reasons for their creation in different industries and in different countries: these different origins are important in understanding the actual relationship between governments and SOEs.

CHAPTER 3
Origins of State-Owned Enterprises

INTRODUCTION

As stated in Chapter 1, state ownership has been argued on the grounds of ideology, political power, economic reasoning, social structure and administrative convenience. Although elements of each of these explanations can be documented through the history of state ownership in different countries, none gives the total picture of the complex reality.

How can one explain, e.g., the existence of state-owned book shops in Sweden, hotels in Spain, Portugal, Sweden, the United Kingdom, India and France or funeral services in Austria, car insurance in Canada, travel agencies in Germany and theaters in France? If economic reasoning were the only factor, why is it that some railroads are privately owned and that most of the electricity supply in Belgium is privately owned? Why are some steel firms state-owned and others not? Why is Renault state-owned and Peugeot a private enterprise, or why is Alfa Romeo state-owned and Fiat private? Political considerations are certainly important, and class struggle over the surplus generated by the public sector may explain some SOEs' policies, such as cross-subsidization of certain sectors or pressures for the redistribution of income. However, this goal can be achieved effectively by taxation rather than state ownership, as the experience of the Scandinavian countries demonstrates.

The answer may be found in the ways countries differ in their cultural heritage, the traditional role of government in society, the degree of congruence between public goals and private business interests, economic structure, the characteristics of the political power struggle and the availability of endogenous entrepreneurs. The reasons SOEs operate in certain economic fields today are also a function of the stage of economic development, historical events, political reactions to crises and different sources of support for a variety of political moods, caused by changing environment, circumstances,

72

expectations and lifestyles. One way to understand the operations of SOEs and their impact on the economy is to trace their origins and, more important, their evolution. The original rationale is often forgotten with time, and the official pronouncements then made do not always reflect the true reasons for the establishment of the enterprise. However, today's policies are, partially at least, a result of past commitments, institutions and decisions that are maintained because of inertia.

Today, almost all railroads are state-owned. The obvious and simple economic explanation for this is that railroads are capital-intensive, heavily concentrated industries, requiring a very high initial capital investment, which private entrepreneurs would find difficult to raise. Nevertheless, very few railroads were originally constructed by government, although most were nationalized later, often to save the system from bankruptcy. Moreover, many other industries—basic chemicals and petroleum, e.g., have the same characteristics, and they are not always state-owned. Oil firms are now mostly state-owned, but most of them were nationalized only in the 1970s. In the U.S., a bill in 1974 to create a U.S. state-owned oil firm that would have competed with the investor-owned oil industry failed in the Senate (Vogel, 1982b, p. 22). Goodermote and Mancke (1983) concluded that "Americans have benefited from their government's decisions not to create a national oil company" (p. 78).

To some degree, railroads might be thought of as a natural monopoly. Even Adam Smith, writing before the railroad age, conceded that roads and bridges were appropriate public sector operations, and the railroads may be seen in a similar light. As late as 1933, however, it was estimated that only 38 percent of the world's railway mileage was under state ownership. Private ownership predominated in North America, South America and Africa, while state ownership predominated in Europe, Asia and the South Pacific (Thomson, 1938, p. 874). A short survey of the history of railroads in different countries may give the reader an idea of the diversity of the origins of state ownership as well as its evolution.

EXAMPLE OF ORIGINS: RAILROADS

The rapid expansion of the railroads and the associated technologies, like steam engines, occurred in the early nineteenth century. Concurrently, other technologies—chemical production, telegraph, gas industry and steel ship-building—also evolved. In the United Kingdom, the major industrial nation of that time, the costs of the Napoleonic wars brought about an increase in the size of the government and saw the extremely unpopular introduction of an income tax system. This was also the period when influential thinkers such as John Stuart Mill and Herbert Spencer preached a limited role of government, and indeed, the tendency was to limit the role of government to that of protector. In 1860, Gladstone expressed his concern in his budget speech that U.K. national wealth had grown by only 16.5 percent between 1853 and 1859, whereas public expenditures had increased by 58 percent. "I may at once venture to state frankly that I am not satisfied with the state of public expenditure and the rapid rate of its growth. I trust, therefore, that we mean in a great degree to retreat our steps" (in Klein, 1976, p. 410). Indeed, the railroads in the United Kingdom were financed through the private capital market although all new lines had to be authorized by an act of Parliament and safety regulations were enforced by a newly created Government Railways Department (1840). Since then, many people have advocated nationalization of the railroads, citing the more efficient systems operated by civil servants in other countries. Several parliamentary commissions looked into the question, but the railways were finally nationalized only in 1947, when according to Aldcroft (1968): "Some form of public ownership or control was largely inevitable whatever the political party in power at the time" (p. 106). It is true that during both world wars the railway system was transferred to the hands of a royal commission and shareholders were compensated. However, in 1919 the railways were privatized after they were compulsorily amalgamated into four companies.

In other developed countries, the story was very different. The United States, too, strongly adheres to the free enterprise ideology. Nevertheless, by 1873, about $350 million of state and federal funds plus many millions of acres in land grants and aid in the form of services of public officials and property, materials, tax exemptions, grants of right of way and other privileges had been pumped into the canal, river and railroads systems. In a study of expenditures on railroads in the South, Heath estimates that based on the total value of the railroads in the 1860 census, 55 percent of the investment in that area was made by federal, state, county and municipal governments (Heath, 1950). State-owned or supervised canals and then railways were the chief mode of transportation in the United States. Hibbard (1939, p. 267) has pointed out that land grants were "a major part of the whole episode of conscious development of the nation through public action" since it was believed that private action was likely to be too uncertain and too slow. The federal government also financed surveys, largely by the army, of possible railroad routes (Hill, 1951). Despite this vast government aid, more than 100 private railway companies were bankrupt by 1874. The government also built and managed railroads directly: Pennsylvania started its state-owned and operated railroad in 1823. This venture tottered and started again in 1846 with most of the stocks held by public agencies from Philadelphia and Allegheny. However, it eventually fell, to become a part of what later became the Pennsylvania Railroad.

The 525-mile Alaska railroad was built by the federal government and was completed in 1923. Despite perennial deficits, the federal government never seriously considered abandoning the railroads. On January 14, 1983, President Reagan signed the Alaska Railroad Transfer Act, whereby the Federal Railroad Administration was authorized to sell the railroad and all its holdings to the state of Alaska. For some time, Alaska refused to purchase the line. However, in the face of implicit threats that the federal government would shut down the railroad, Alaska agreed to a state takeover, creating a public authority known as the Alaska Railroad Corporation to manage and operate it (*The New York Times*, January 5, 1985, p. 17).

As the railroads grew into the United State's first big business, the efficacy of market competition as a regulatory mechanism was brought into question. The railroads often exhibited tendencies toward frenzied finance, corporate arrogance and discriminatory pricing practices that, however logically they might flow from the economics of railroading, nevertheless appeared to violate basic notions of fairness. And underlying the entire railroad problem was the political incongruity of a democratic society in the role of servant to one of its industries (McCraw, 1980, p. 796).

As a consensus on the need for federal regulation developed, the operations and pricing of the railroads were made subject to regulation by state bodies and, since 1887, by the Interstate Commerce Commission (ICC), although their ownership remained in private hands. As in the United Kingdom during World War I, the railroad system was nationalized by the establishment of the Railroads War Board in April 1917 but was handed back to private ownership in 1920. Later, the development of an extensive highway system and the emergence of new forms of transportation—trucks, cars, airplanes and modern barges—created new competition. In addition, the dispersal of manufacturing plants around the country brought points of production closer to points of consumption, thereby decreasing transport distances. In the northeast in particular, a decline in the steel industry and decreased demands for coal led to dramatic reductions in overall rail traffic. Attempts to raise prices were blocked, proposals to cut operations on money-losing branch lines were turned down by the ICC and efforts to cut running costs were frustrated as labor unions objected to changes in work rules.

The highest passenger volume in U.S. railroads was reached in 1920, when they carried about 1.27 billion passengers a total of 27.4 billion passenger miles (*The Economist*, August 4, 1984, p. 29). Since then, volume has gone almost continuously downhill. By 1933, passenger travel was no more than a third of its 1920 level. In 1970, under a Republican administration, it was decided to bring together the problematic passenger services of the various railways under one federally financed authority—the National Railroad Passenger Corporation (AMTRAK). To make the company a legally private for-profit, mixed-ownership government corporation, some of its common stock was sold to private railroads, but its loans are guaranteed by government. Its early deficits were colossal, and Congress encouraged cost- and staff-cutting measures, demanding that it must earn 50 percent of its annual costs by 1982. AMTRAK barely did so, and since then, the size of the subsidy it receives has been declining.

In the early 1970s, railroads of the Northeast Corridor of the United States collapsed or were sliding into bankruptcy. The largest, Penn Central, filed for bankruptcy in 1970. Private institutions had failed to uncover a profitable plan for reorganizing the failing railroads, and liquidation threatened to be extremely disruptive to U.S. markets. The court-appointed trustees soon gave up hope of any profitable reorganization and, in 1973, recommended to the courts that Penn Central's assets be sold, preferably, but not necessarily, for rail use by another railroad company. The ICC balked at this proposal, however, stating that liquidation of the country's largest railroad was neither in the public interest nor in accordance with the objectives of Section 77 of the Federal Bankruptcy Act.

Based on the ideology of the United States, the solution was the Regional Rail Reorganization Act of 1973. Through this law Congress created a tripartite organization to restructure insolvent northeastern railroads into a new railroad. One member of the tripartite was the U.S. Railway Association (USRA), legally a nonprofit, federally chartered mixed-ownership corporation with responsibility for planning and directing the reorganization of insolvent railroads. The second was the Consolidated Rail Corporation (Conrail), a newly created entity with responsibility for operating the new railroad system. The third member was the Rail Services Planning Office, a federal agency with responsibility for reviewing USRA proposals for reorganization. Conrail is an SOE in every way except its legal status. The USRA received government appropriations to purchase its debentures and series of preferred stocks. Tough management brought Conrail back to profits, partially because the number of employees was cut by over half. In 1985, negotiations were in process on the privatization of Conrail.

In Belgium, the railroads were built by the government as a part of its effort to unite the new state, created in 1830. The Belgian railroad system, publicly owned since 1836 and managed by civil servants, has been for many years the most profitable in Europe.

In Germany, Bismarck aspired to unite the country under Prussia, to catch up with other Western nations economically and to pursue a warlike foreign policy. An efficient railroad system, geared to military needs was clearly indispensable to the achievement of these objectives. Thus, Prussia bought the few existing private lines in 1848, and the system of state-owned railroads expanded all over Germany.

In France, the construction of the railroads was delayed by the lack of private enterprise capital and the hesitance of Louis Philippe's government to take the construction and operation of the system into the hands of the state. The more efficient German railroad system was certainly a factor in the conquest of France in 1870. Still, the French railroad system became state-owned only when the socialists formed the government in 1937.

In India, railway construction started after an agreement was reached in 1849 between the U.K. government, the East India Company and other private promoters. According to the agreement, the promoters would raise the capital for construction and manage the railways for 99 years and were given the right to hand over the enterprise to the government of India at any time on one year's prior notice. If they did so, they would receive back their capital expenditure in full. The government agreed to underwrite losses, guaranteeing the promoters 5 percent return on the invested capital. It also had the right to regulate modes of operation and fare policies and an option to buy the system after 25 years. In fact, the railways suffered losses between 1850 and 1900, and the government paid the promoters to cover the guaranteed return on the investment. This guarantee system was a disincentive for efficiency: the railways were not developed and complaints of poor service mounted. British traders, suffering from the bad service, pressed the government to take action, and in 1920, the Acworth committee recommended state management. At the time, the state already owned 73 percent of the total mileage but operated only 21 percent of it. In 1923, the East Indian Railways were purchased by the government, but it took more than 20 years to complete the entire process. The railways are now managed by a semi-autonomous railway board, established in 1905 (Narain, 1980, pp. 76–77, 113).

In Australia, railway projects were initiated by private entrepreneurs in New South Wales (1849) and in Victoria just before gold was discovered. As the private sector entrepreneurs turned their attention to the more profitable gold, the government gradually accepted financial responsibility for the railways and, in 1854, ownership of the assets. Since then the Australian railroad (and telegraph) systems have been constructed and operated by the colonial government. It is interesting that even though government policies of rapid construction "deliberately operated to limit profit, one of the striking features . . . is that railway enterprise in the hands of government was profitable" (Butlin, in Aitken, 1959, p. 40). By the 1870s the social consensus was that state-owned and operated railroads were needed to foster general economic growth and that railroads should limit, although not disregard, profits (p. 42).

In Canada, early financing and construction of railroads followed a different pattern. The initial promotion and construction were usually the work of private entrepreneurs. However, the Guarantee Act, passed by the Canadian legislature in 1849, provided government guarantees for half the bonds issued by any railroad over 75 miles in length, provided that half the line had already been built. In 1851, the provisions of the act were restricted to three major lines under construction—the Northern, the Great Western and the St. Lawrence and Atlantic. Land was also granted to facilitate railroad construction.

In 1867, following the British North America Act and the beginning of the Confederation, the new political situation made the federal government responsible, among other things, for the construction of a transcontinental railroad connecting Nova Scotia and New Brunswick. When it joined the Confederation, British Columbia was assured that a transcontinental railroad would be started within 2 years and concluded 10 years after this province joined the Dominion. The principal railroad of the time—the Grand Trunk—was willing to construct the line but only through the traffic-producing United States south of the Great Lakes. The Canadian government, unable to accept the proposition that part of the railroad be constructed outside Canada, started to build sections of the line within the limits of its resources. Years passed, and only in 1880 did a group of private entrepreneurs consent to construct the railroad from central Canada to the Pacific. They were to receive from the government $25 million in cash and 25 million acres of land. The government further agreed to grant the line a 20-year monopoly, to finish construction of all sections under contract and to give them as well as the already completed sections free of charge to the new company. The Canadian Pacific Railroad was finished in 1885 (Innis, 1923). The cost of transcontinental expansion in Canada was "borne originally by the government but finally by consumers in high freight rates and high tariffs" (Aitken, 1959, p. 102).

While the Canadian Pacific dominated the west and the Grand Trunk dominated central Canada, the new federal state assumed both the assets and liabilities of the railway-building effort of New Brunswick and Nova Scotia. In fact, every province except Saskatchewan has owned a railway at some time or other, and British Columbia, Ontario and Alberta still do. At the beginning of the twentieth century, the Canadian Northern Railway, based in Manitoba, attempted to become a transcontinental line. Aided by both federal and provincial governments, its lines reached Montreal, Toronto and Vancouver. The Grand Trunk was able to persuade the government to construct a third transcontinental route, to be leased to its subsidiary, the Grand Trunk Pacific. According to Grant Stevenson:

> The response of Sir Robert Borden's government to this unhappy situation led in a series of steps towards Canadian National Railways. When the Grand Trunk reneged on its promise to lease the National Transcontinental, the latter, which had almost no traffic, was added to the Intercolonial system, more recently dubbed the Canadian Government Railways. Next a Royal Commission was appointed, which recommended nationalization of the Canadian Northern, Grand Trunk, and Grand Trunk Pacific. The impecunious Canadian Northern was nationalized almost immediately, and without visible dissent, in August 1917. The Grand Trunk, traditionally an ally of the Liberal Party, was spared until a Union government could be formed. Even then it proved truculent in adversity, and the

necessary legislation was not adopted until November 1919 . . .
Meanwhile the Grand Trunk Pacific had been taken over under the
authority of the War Measures Act in March 1919, after its parent
firm had ordered it to cease operations.

Unlike some other state enterprises, therefore, Canadian National
. . . arose from a number of decisions taken by different governments
for different reasons over a period of years . . . The Canadian North-
ern was taken over because further loans to it would have been po-
litically unpopular, while its bankruptcy would have threatened the
Canadian Bank of Commerce. The National Transcontinental was
simply left in the government's hands, while the Grand Trunk Pacific
was taken over to save it from destruction at the hands of its parent.
The Grand Trunk itself was nationalized because its lines in central
Canada were needed to make the other properties into a viable sys-
tem [in Tupper and Doern, 1981, p. 321].

In Brazil, the imperial government stimulated private construction through
guarantees of profits, duty exemptions, subsidies and monopoly route concessions. In several cases, the government had to bail these firms out, and by
1889, 34 percent of Brazil's tracks were owned and operated by the government. The burden of profit guarantees became onerous, and the government
reluctantly nationalized 12 more foreign companies in 1901. (In 1898, one
third of the budget was used in payment of profit guarantees.) It "became
apparent that it would be cheaper to nationalize the foreign lines rather than
to continue the profit remittance policy" (Trebat, 1983, p. 40).

The anti-trust sentiment has grown mainly against the foreign-owned
Brazil Railroad, founded in 1907 and operating by 1915, 40 percent of all of
the country's rail miles. Foreign control of most of the railroads was also seen
as endangering the country's national defense. Because of its financial difficulties, the Brazilian government suspended guarantee payments. Partially in
consequence, the Brazil Railroad fell into receivership in 1915.

Aroused nationalism led to changed attitudes on the proper role of the
State. In 1920, Brazil nationalized its fishing waters, restricted federal loans
to steel mills to Brazilian-owned companies and required telegraph operators
to be Brazilian citizens. The federal government took over additional railroad
lines from unsuccessful private companies. In 1930, it owned and operated
59 percent of the railroads, states operated 9 percent, and private firms the
remaining 32 percent (Topik, 1979, p. 337).

In several countries, railroads were nationalized. For example, Bismarck
nationalized the German railways for military reasons, and France did so for
ideological reasons. Italy nationalized its railroads in 1907 with the unification of the state. The British nationalized their railroads only in 1947, to a
large extent because the system was almost bankrupt. In Argentina, the railroad was nationalized in the 1880s, in Mexico, in 1909 and, in Brazil, gradually since 1901. These events were sometimes sparked by the desire "to ab-

sorb socialism into a liberal capitalist framework" (Posner and Woolf, 1976, p. 19) but mainly because the railroads had to be supported by the state to avoid their bankruptcy. In Latin America, most railroads (and other utilities) were foreign-owned, and their nationalization was perceived as a means to reduce foreign domination. Since the railroads were foreign owned, the nationalization was not resisted by the private endogenous business community (for the history of Mexico, see Powell, 1921, p. 173; Pletcher, 1958, pp. 305–306, on electricity, see Wionczek, 1964; on Brazil, see Tendler, 1968, pp. 78–79, Topik, 1979).

In many cases, the original reasons for state ownership of the railroads are not necessarily identical to the objectives pursued today. With time, the military importance of the railroads, their salience as a vehicle of economic development and the possibilities inherent in them for invisibly subsidizing private business interests were discovered. Today, most railroads in the world are state-owned, and they are heavily dependent on government for investment funds and operating subsidies. In 1983, e.g., subsidies as a percent of operating costs were 80 percent in Italy, 25 percent in Belgium, about half in Denmark and Holland. They were more than 40 percent in France, Austria, Japan and the Federal Republic of Germany, and about 35 percent in Norway, Ireland and Great Britain (*The Economist*, August 24, 1985, p. 33). AMTRAK in the U.S. barely covered 60 percent of its expenses. In Latin America the losses are also very high, as we show in Chapter 5. These figures underestimate the level of subsidies since they do not show the allocation for capital investments. Railroads often maintain networks and pursue structures that create these losses and are in some countries at least, employers of last resort. In Japan, the railroad is said to employ many more persons than are needed for efficient operations mainly because it has been used as an employer of war veterans. Finally, this section is not intended as a detailed history of the origins of railroads; rather, it is intended to show how shifting public opinion and mainly shifts in the relative power of different actors affected state ownership as well as the degree of autonomy of management.

Railroads have been managed by governments and were not seen as inherently inefficient because of the type of ownership. It may well be that until the beginning of the century, before the rise of the large private corporation, government was seen as the only large organization capable of managing such a system. Most railroads were run by civil servants and their finances were controlled by the government. With time, some railroads became legally independent, but a mere change of legal status was not a magic wand that avoided political interference, low fares and continued operations of losing lines.

Changes of regime have often led to changes in the role of SOEs. One example is that of Germany.

GERMANY: CHANGING POLITICAL AND IDEOLOGICAL INFLUENCES

Government ownership of enterprises in Germany may be traced back to the last quarter of the nineteenth century, a period of dramatic takeoff of the German economy. In 1878, the German Reichsbank was formed, and several more state banks followed. In 1880, as already shown, several railways came under state ownership. The Länder (state) railroads were transferred to the Reich in 1920, and the Reich railways became organizationally independent in 1924. The Prussian state followed an interventionist policy, nationalizing the coal mines, increasing its potassium mine holdings in 1905 and purchasing the Hibernia Mining Corporation in 1917. Bismarck established the Imperial Post and Telegraph, and the Imperial Bank subsidized shipbuilding. He also created the first National Health System with the concomitant aims of improving the physical condition of army recruits and neutralizing socialist attacks.

The Bismarck era pioneered the state organizations necessary for World War I, and the war brought about a major expansion of the SOE sector. In 1914 the Deutsches Bundespost became the first and only public enterprise of the first German Reich. During World War I, the Reich developed several plants for the exploitation of nitrogen and aluminum and associated energy supply corporations. [These enterprises are now under the Associated Industries Joint Stock Corporation, Vereinigte Industrie-Unternehmungen Aktiengessellschaft (VIAG), created in 1923 by the Weimar Republic.] In 1923 Prussia consolidated most of its mining operations and foundry works into the Preussag AG and in 1927 merged its energy supply corporations into a Prussian electric company. In 1929, all state-owned energy supply firms and mines were combined into one holding company, VEBA [Vereinigte Elektrizitats and Bergwerks-AG (the Associated Energy Supply and Mining Works Corporation)]. During the time of the national socialist regime, the Reichswerke Hermann Göring was created to exploit the iron ore deposits of Salzgitter, and a military vehicle manufacturing firm, Volkswagenwerk, was founded. The national socialist regime also nationalized many Jewish-owned enterprises, passing some of them to private hands. During this period, the influence of the state was all-encompassing, and the economy operated increasingly under central direction.

Perhaps as a reaction to the Nazi period, the period after World War II in Germany, unlike in France and the United Kingdom, was not one of nationalization, although the German Constitution of May 23, 1949, did transfer the Reich and Prussian enterprises to the federal government and the then French administration of the Saar transferred the Saarbergwerke to Federal (76 percent) and state (24 percent) governments in 1957.

During the ensuing lengthy period of debate between the federal government and the states on government ownership of enterprises, the official policy of the federal government was to establish a so-called social market economy, according to which competition would be the means of securing prosperity, obviating poverty and business collusion. Transportation and public utility services were required by law to be operated on collective economy principles, but moves were made to privatize all industrial holdings. Such denationalization was included in official government plans as early as 1953, and social denationalization was one of the major issues in the 1957 elections. The Christian Democratic party (CDU) viewed industrial SOEs as inherently bad and connected them with the Nazi period. To be sure, immediately after World War II, both the CDU and the social democrats (SPD) advocated nationalization of basic industry as a means of permanently containing the economic power of the larger industrialists who had condoned the rise of national socialism. Nevertheless, the CDU adopted the principles of social market economy in the 1949 election campaign, and even the SPD formally abandoned its ideological commitment to extensive nationalization in 1959.

The federal holdings in Preussag AG were reduced to 17 percent in 1959. The shares were widely distributed among 200,000 shareholders, but 22 percent were purchased by state-owned VEBA. Sales of shares were limited to persons having a maximum income of DM16,000 per annum. In the case of Volkswagenwerk, the then Christian federal democratic government and the government of Lower Saxony, unable to agree on total denationalization, each took 20 percent of the shares (Thimm, 1976, p. 94), and the remaining 60 percent were sold in 1961 to 1.2 million private individuals. In 1965, the majority of the shares in VEBA, the largest industrial concern in the Federal Republic, were disposed of, in the form of so-called people's capitalism, to more than 2.6 million persons. This issue was not a success and share prices slumped after the sale, leaving the government with 44 percent ownership. The official aim of these actions was to promote savings and the widest possible distribution of shares among the population.

The official statistics in the Federal Republic of Germany include only those enterprises in which the government owns more than 50 percent of the voting shares, excluding, therefore, some very large enterprises. Still, the share of SOEs according to official statistics is almost as high as in the United Kingdom (Short, 1984, table. 1, pp. 16-117). The large state holdings grew by a process of diversification. In 1976 the Monopolies Commission found that the government was the most important shareholder in the top 100 firms in Germany (Monsen and Walters, 1983, p. 12). In addition, many SOEs operate at the Länder and the municipal level. Thus, the German Länder of Bremen owned 26 percent of VFW-Fokker, and 43 percent of Messerschmitt-Boelkow-Blohm (MBB) is owned by Bavaria and Hamburg (both these firms are in aerospace and participate in Airbus Industrie) (Monsen and Walters, 1979, p. 163; later, VFW has broken its alliance with Fokker).

Keyser and Windle (1978, Part III) identified in 1975 885 SOEs in which the federal government owned directly or indirectly at least 25 percent of the equity. They included also Ruhrkohle AG, reporting that 14 percent of its equity is owned by VEBA AG, 11 percent by Salzgitter AG and 13 percent by Gelensberg AG. Gelensberg AG also owns 25 percent in Ruhrgas AG. These two firms are usually not considered SOEs "since their public share-holdings are in a minority and remote" (Keyser and Windle, 1978, Part III, p. 10). They also report on many Länder SOEs, controlling, e.g., 24 percent of all banking, 10 percent of insurance and dozens of industrial enterprises. In addition, there were thousands of municipally-owned enterprises: 680 for the production and distribution of gas, water and heating, 160 transport enterprises, 649 municipal savings banks as well as port authorities.

Municipally owned enterprises began to develop in the second half of the nineteenth century with the development of water systems and then gas and electricity. Thus, the Berlin Elektrizitatswerke was found in 1885. The municipalities extended their operations to manufacturing, commercial activities, housing and banking. This expansion was checked by the 1931 economic crises, and the German Municipal Order of 1935 first stipulated the provisions under which a municipality was allowed to establish a business. This is now part of new municipal orders of the Länder written after World War II.

Through its financial institutions, with which it has strong symbiotic relationships, the German government has a strong influence on private enterprise. Rescues of large private firms such as Krupp in 1967, the coal industry in 1968 or AEG Telefunken in 1982 were all bank-led. However, the federal and Länder governments provided loan guarantees and subsidies, and the economic minister took an active part in the rescue negotiations. The federal government has majority holdings in five state-owned banks. Other banks are owned by the Länder and the municipalities.

Since the mid-1970s, the German government increasingly intervened in the economy through financial assistance, tax concessions and direct participation in business and commerce. State ownership is still seen as a remnant of the Nazi period, so other means of intervention are preferred and SOEs are allowed a relatively high degree of autonomy. As a senior West German civil servant observed:

> Industrial enterprises of the federal government find themselves, in our economic system, in competition with other enterprises, both German and foreign. They must, therefore, like their competitors be managed on commercial principles. These give absolute priority to the maximization of profits. Without profits, there can be no investment, and, without investment, no guarantee of employment. . . . We refrain deliberately from impairing the freedom of decision of the enterprises so that the directing boards shall have the full responsibility for the results of the enterprises' activities. [Cited by Garner, in Reddy, 1983, p. 10]

Thus, because of its history, the Federal Republic of Germany allows its SOEs a large degree of autonomy. The same is true in Austria although for different historical reasons.

AUSTRIA: PRAGMATISM OR POLITICS?

Austria today has the highest share of state ownership in its GNP of all Western developed democracies, a phenomenon which appears to derive from a strong monarchical past, a strong labor movement and the country's history. In the Hapsburg Austro-Hungarian monarchy the state already played an important role in the development of infrastructure, like railroads, and supporting industrialization. It also established fiscal monopolies in salt and tobacco and built arsenal workshops for military purposes. The social democrats, coming to power after World War I, attempted to nationalize big business but failed. During the depression of the 1930s, the government had to aid the large banks to prevent them and the manufacturing firms they owned from failing, and the municipalities established or expanded gas and electricity supplies and transportation systems as well as building companies and retail enterprises.

Massive German investments and procurements for the German war machine started in Austria mainly after the banking system collapsed in 1929. After the Anschluss in 1938, German investments intensified, and during the Nazi incorporation of Austria in Hitler's Germany, many enterprises came under the control of state-owned or private German trusts. The Nazis constructed on Austrian territory important new industries, such as the steel works in Linz, later part of Vereinigte Österreichische Stahlwerke (VOEST). VOEST integrated with the Alpine Montan Company to become VOEST-Alpine.

By the end of World War II, "Austria had found itself with a set of ownerless enterprises that had belonged to either the government of greater Germany or to private owners who had fled or died" (Lauterbach, 1985, p. 61). The Nazi-owned enterprises and banks were seized by the Allied forces, and much of whatever installations and equipment had not been destroyed were sequestered by the Soviet occupation forces. Forty-four of the seventy key industrial enterprises and hundreds of smaller ones were taken over by the Soviets, being designated as formerly German property. An attempt by the Austrian provisional government to nationalize key industries was vetoed by the Russians in 1945. They remained under Soviet control until 1955 but were administered and financed by the Austrian government. The consensus at the time was that recovery necessitated state ownership. In July 1946, key enterprises in coal, oil, transport, iron ore, heavy engineering, steel and non-ferrous metals, aluminum, chemicals and electrical equipment were nationalized, as were three banks including the two largest that controlled a myriad of firms. The Soviets protested, but because of a change in the Allied Treaty of Control, they could no longer prevent the nationalization, except in Soviet-occupied regions. Electricity was nationalized in 1947, but this law involved mainly reorganization between federal and Länder authorities. When the USSR withdrew in 1955, it relinquished its grip on hundreds of Austrian enterprises that moved to state ownership, mainly oil fields, refineries and machine building. Some of the refineries had to be returned to their original foreign owners (Shell and Mobil Oil) because of pressure from the U.S. and U.K. governments.

During this critical time, many managers of large firms fled, ownership of many enterprises was in doubt and the need for planning was agreed upon by both socialists and conservatives. "Thus, the nationalization of a large portion of the means of production was not so much an expression of the class struggle in a capitalist society as an assertion of Austria's national independence in the conflict among nations" (Katzenstein, 1984, p. 49).

The two large political parties in Austria have persistently disagreed on the role of the SOE sector in the economy. The conservative OVP [Austrian People's party (Österreichische Volkspartei)] has traditionally argued for a limited role of the SOE sector while the SPO [Socialist party of Austria (Sozialistische Partie Österreichs)] maintains that a planned and market economy are complementary. The conservatives proposed partial denationalization in 1956 and, in an attempt to create a stronger middle class, issued nonvoting shares in the large banks, to which the public responded with indifference. Experiments in denationalization came to an end after the socialists strengthened their electoral power in the 1959 elections.

The boards of all SOEs are staffed with politically appointed figures, chosen by the coalition partners according to the *Proportz*, a system that was legally sanctioned in 1956 and, according to the impartial UN Economic Commission, provides for greater independence from government control than in other countries with much smaller public sectors (United Nations, 1959, Ch. 5, p. 35). Organizational changes in the SOE sector have come about as a result of the changing balance of power between the two major parties, with the coalition agreements between them even including matters such as nomination of supervisory board members and executives. Although the Austrian government has made a "serious attempt to keep the conduct of undertakings which form part of the public parsimony under some kind of political surveillance" (Shonfield, 1965, p. 195), in practice, state power has been largely neutralized by the conflicts and stalemates between the two major parties, and managers of SOEs, particularly the profitable ones, have for pragmatic reasons been allowed much more autonomy. Further, since the only way the state is able to influence the SOEs is by exercising its rights as a shareholder, and since each decision about an SOE at its annual shareholders' meeting has to be made unanimously by the cabinet (a ponderous process), government intervention is very much restrained.

Nevertheless, the SOE sector has been an important factor in the stabilization of the Austrian economy, although this may be due in large part to the national belief in social partnership rather than class conflict and the realization that one has to produce to distribute. The centralized interest groups maintain voluntary, informal and continuous political bargaining and demonstrate a penchant for compromise. Bruising confrontations that thwart policymaking are thereby avoided.

In January 1970, SOEs were put under the aegis of a holding company, Austrian Corporation for Industrial Administration—ÖIAG (Österreïchische Industrieverwaltungs-AG), to facilitate overall coordination and as a compromise on several issues between the socialists and the conservatives. This holding company also retains key elements of the *Proportz* system. For example, its supervisory board is not elected by the annual meeting of its shareholders. Instead, fifteen members are nominated by the political parties according to their strength in Parliament, and three members are nominated by the government. This arrangement grants the ÖVP a substantial representation of its interests while assuring the SPÖ of a working majority. In the 1970s the ÖVP controlled appointments to 61 of 136 positions available on the supervisory boards of the nationalized firms under the control of the ÖIAG. Five of 10 chairmanships and 18 of 27 directorships were also held by managers with close ties to the ÖVP. The SPÖ controls virtually all other positions. "The allegiance of these politically appointed managers to their respective parties varies from case to case," writes Andrlik, "even though practically all are members of party suborganizations that unite them within an informal club-like atmosphere" (1983, p. 190).

The partisan neutralization of the power of the state bureaucracy is also evident in its relations with Austria's state-owned banks, which have been "singularly negligent in lending their services to the public sector" (Langer, 1964). The bank managers were able to keep government at arm's length and run their industrial empires largely according to market criteria, to some extent as a result of their partial reprivatization between 1956 and 1959 but mainly as a consequence of the government's insatiable need for credit. The Austrian Proportz has ruled here too; the Creditanstalt Bankverein is considered black while the Österreichische Landerbank is seen as red. The two large banks represent 64 percent of Austrian corporate banking. They also control a greater number of industrial and commercial enterprises (Lauterbach, 1985, p. 63).

At present, about 30 percent of all persons employed in industry are employed directly or indirectly in SOEs. SOEs are also the largest industrial enterprises, occupying in 1975 the first seven places on the list of largest industrial enterprises in Austria (Van der Bellen, 1981, pp. 75–76). Among Austria's fifty largest corporations, SOEs account for more than two-thirds, private firms for little more than 10 percent and foreign firms for about 15 percent of the total. Austria's fifty largest firms account for more then half the country's industrial production. The government owns the two largest commercial banks, the two largest insurance companies and a host of other financial institutions. The banks own, directly and indirectly, a large number of subsidiaries. "Calculating the extent of the banks' ownership and control of industry is as much a pastime in Austria as are guesses about the hidden assets of the three largest banks in Switzerland. By most accounts Austria's nationalized commercial banks own about 10 percent of the nominal capital of all joint stock companies, and their subsidiaries have about 60,000 employees" (Katzenstein, 1984, p. 51). Banks, while falling short of ownership, also have at their disposal a variety of instruments that enhance their dominant position in Austria's economic life. They have a lot of information about firms and often have representatives in the board of directors. Municipal and provincial governments in Austria own savings banks and other financial enterprises and the city of Vienna owns a sizeable network of enterprises including gas, electricity, water, construction, public transportation, insurance, storage facilities and funeral services. Thus, the SOE sector is a result of the feudal and monarchical past and the economic disruption at the end of World War II, followed by the interruption of national existence for seven years. Its behavior can be understood by the power structure of the public authorities, and by the social structure and beliefs. This social partnership and political consensus was also maintained in Italy but was broken in the 1970s, with disastrous results for the efficiency of the SOEs.

ITALY: STATE OWNERSHIP AS A SOLUTION TO A CRISIS

The origin of the state-owned sector in Italy may be traced to the fifteenth century when the first publicly owned banks (e.g., Monte dei Paschi di Siena) were established in 1472. With the unification of the states into one nation under the house of Savoy in the nineteenth century, the new entity took over activities such as iron ore mining, navy arsenals, army factories, salt extraction and refining, railways, tobacco manufacturing and thermal resorts. At the end of the nineteenth century, the law regulated and declared public the social security agencies that had previously been private. In 1911, INA (Instituto Nazionale delle Assicurazioni) was formed; it was to have a monopoly over all insurance. Although the monopoly was never realized, INA continues as a public sector enterprise. Postal and telephone services were also part of the SOE sector at the beginning of this century, as well as several state fiscal monopolies in quinine, bananas, cigarette paper, tobacco, matches and salt. Italy has never had a pronounced *laissez faire* policy, and the public and private sectors have always been intimately linked. Nevertheless, the major surge of state ownership came about not as a result of socialist ideology but because of the failure of the banking system.

The first great industrial swing, mainly in producer goods sectors and power production, started only in 1896 and was confined for the most part to the north. The south remained miserably poor and regarded itself as a conquered nation. Even the north was quite backward compared to other Western European countries, with inept education, lack of personal security and poor communication combining to produce high levels of emigration. Because capital accumulation was lacking, the major burden of financing this rapid industrial expansion fell on the banks.

The newfound relationships of the industrial firms with the banks was to a large extent, as Gerschenkron (1962) describes it, that of master and servant. The banks usually acquired the role of a sole surveyor of credit of the client firm or group. With time, the relations with the client firm deepened: the banks purchased more industrial shares in an effort to protect their position and maintain stock prices in the fledgling and highly volatile stock market. As a result, the banks' fortunes became more and more dependent on that of the industrial firms: the capital locked up in industry was mainly depositors' funds and far exceeded the bank's equity base. The banks also purchased their own shares heavily on the stock exchange through subsidiary firms, thus further increasing their vulnerability.

This structure, not surprisingly, foundered during the depression of 1907, and the Bank of Italy had to intervene directly to save a major bank and a group of steel companies. Italy's defeat in World War I left the country ready for revolution, and in 1919 Fascism emerged from the founding meeting in San Sepulcro. The Fascist regime advocated an almost religious ideology of state control, coupled with capitalism in the service of society. De Stefani, the first Fascist minister of finance, carried out a very conservative reform, abolishing the excess profit tax, reducing public spending and restoring the telephone system to private ownership. Import restrictions and tariff barriers were widely used to invigorate the domestic economy. All the same, however, large-scale direct state intervention was quickly forthcoming. In 1921, the bankruptcy of Ansaldo and Ilva, two of the largest Italian steel industrial companies, brought down the Banca Italiana di Sconto. To save the bank, the Italian government set up, under the direct jurisdiction of the Bank of Italy, an Autonomous Bureau for Industrial Advance (renamed in 1926 "Liquidation Institute"). This was the first move leading later to the creation of SOEs to help the private sector (for details, see Posner and Woolf, 1967, p. 22; Einaudi, Bye and Rossi, 1955).

The Fascist concept of the state as the central part of life called for the establishment of numerous public agencies, including not only economic enterprises but also trade unions and cultural institutions. In 1926, AGIP (Azienda Generale Italiana Petrole) was founded to encourage oil exploration and the development of the oil industry. In 1933 Azienda Carboni Italiana (ACAI) was formed to place coal under national control and Azienda Minerale Metallici (AMMI) to exploit Italian mineral resources.

In 1931, to stave off the danger of imminent collapse of the financial system, brought on by the considerable problems of reconstruction following World War I and aggravated by the crash of 1929, the government created the Instituto Mobiliare Italiano (IMI) to grant emergency support to firms in difficulties and thereby also the three large banks that controlled them. Shortly afterward, in 1933, as a continuation of these emergency measures, the Instituto per la Ricostruzione Industriale (IRI) was set up as a temporary public agency to provide long-term funds. At that time, the three major banks faced bankruptcy and the Bank of Italy was in difficulties, partly because of the loans made by its special credit unit. The major task of IRI was to acquire all the shares and the credit the banks held in industrial enterprises, thus saving the financial system from collapsing by transferring the losses to the state. Since it was assumed that these industrial concerns would be reconstructed and then returned to private hands, IRI did not change their legal status but left them as separate limited companies.

In the first 2 years of the reorganization process, divestments realized 37 percent of total assets received. It was soon found that the remaining private-sector firms were too small and too weak financially to acquire the firms offered for sale by IRI, and the Fascist government refused to sell these companies to foreign owners. In June 1937, IRI became a permanent holding company for manufacturing businesses, mainly because the continuing depression limited the prospects for denationalization. IRI was given the new purpose of providing the efficient administration according to unitary principles of the shareholdings it owned in accordance with the regime's directives on economic policy.

This situation continues to the present day, and what started not as a national political decision but as a temporary emergency measure and perhaps the most absentminded act of nationalization in history, was the beginning of what has become known as the "IRI formula." Largely because of the special circumstances of its creation, IRI operates under private law. It is partially financed by a fund provided by the treasury—a capital endowment that can be compared to the equity capital of a private firm. Increases in the endowment fund depend on parliamentary votes in the same way that increases in shareholders' equity depend on shareholders' votes. IRI also has recourse to the capital market to issue bonds.

By 1938, the managers of IRI reorganized their holdings into what are essentially their present-day divisions. Their ambition was to reconstruct the firms and turn them into models of management and entrepreneurship for the private sector to follow.

During World War II many of IRI's enterprises were destroyed. Private firms were offered the possibility of taking over the destroyed iron plants, but none of them was willing to take on the task. This gave IRI its final legitimization as a necessary ingredient of the Italian economic structure although not without public debate, disputes and tensions. Luckily for its future, IRI was not considered a direct offspring of Fascism and therefore did not meet with the opprobrium due institutions connected with that regime. Still, parties of the left wanted to see more nationalizations of industries rather than a continuation of the IRI formula. Some of the Christian democrats felt IRI should be privatized, and most of them felt "It had become the duty of the state to manage this patrimony in the best possible way and either keep it or dispose of it, in whole or part, sooner or later, according to its convenience" (Meniehella, governor of the Bank of Italy, in Einaudi, Bye and Rossi, 1955, p. 199).

The Giacchi Commission was appointed to inquire into IRI's record from its establishment. A further report was published in 1956 by Professor Pasquale Saraceno. Since 1956, the pressures for breaking up or transforming IRI have been negligible. "IRI's establishment as a meaningfully permanent institution dates from 1956 rather than from the statute granting it permanent status twenty years earlier" (Holland, 1972, p. 65).

Since then, IRI has diversified into new sectors—mainly in services. In 1960 it was given the major responsibility for completing the national highways (autostradas). In 1968 it diversified into food, acquiring Motta and then, in 1970, Alemagna to preempt a takeover of these firms by U.S. multinationals.

Only in the 1950s did IRI develop an ideology that legitimized its existence. This ideology, according to Professor Saraceno 1962), advocates macroeconomic planning as a guideline to state policy and intervention in certain key firms and sectors. He sees such planning as a solution to monopolistic tendencies, structural inadequacies and other deficiencies that make Keynesian aggregate demand measures inadequate. Intervention is needed to obviate the stagnation and underconsumption that may result from market economy principles, while yet avoiding the limits to political freedom characteristic of East European state planning.

IRI's management structure has become a source of envy to and sometimes imitation by socialists in other Western European countries. But the origins of the system had nothing to do with ideological beliefs and arose out of pragmatic realism. In fact, only in 1980, for the first time in about 50 years, was the minister of state shareholdings a socialist.

IRI is only one of many SOEs in Italy, which may be classified into three distinct legal and administrative forms: the public economic agencies, the autonomous administration and the state shareholders.

> Public economic agencies (Enti Pubblici Economici) operate at national and local levels. Economically, the most important of these agencies offer various types of health and life insurance. Public economic agencies also include the Bank of Italy, several other financial institutions, state pawnshops, the state electricity firm, ENEL, created as a result of the nationalization of the electricity firms in Italy in 1962; the State Agency for Intervention in the Agricultural Markets (AIMA); the ag-

ricultural development agencies; the National Rice Agency, and the port authorities.

The autonomous administrations (Aziende Autònome) enjoy a somewhat greater degree of autonomy. The major autonomous administrations are the state railways, the post and telegraph, state-owned agriculture and forests, and the fiscal monopolies. The latter are being abolished. The banana monopoly was abolished in October 1964, the quinine, cigarette paper and salt monopolies in 1973, and the saccharin in July 1980. As a result of EEC regulations the tobacco and matches monopolies are losing their monopoly position.

The state shareholding system started with the official creation of IRI. These holdings were put under the control of a special minister for state shareholdings and a ministerial committee by law number 1589 on December 22, 1956. This committee was dissolved in 1967, and its functions transferred to the Interministerial Committee for Economic Programming (CIPE). The aggregate of the state shareholding system developed over time into a large, politically powerful and financially weak public enterprise system.

Other major holding companies, apart from IRI, are described briefly in the following.

1. Ente Nazionale Idrocarburi (ENI) was created in 1953 to coordinate the exploration, extraction and refining of natural gas and petroleum. It grew rapidly in the first decade of its operations, expanding into the chemical sector with the acquisition of ANIC in 1954. In the same year the company entered the nuclear energy field with the acquisition of a private sector firm and, in 1962, began its penetration of the textile industry when it was forced to acquire Lanerossi. More on ENI later in this chapter.

2. Ente Autonomo di Gestione per le Aziende Minerarie e Metallurgiche (EGAM) was founded in 1958 and started operations in 1971, when the shares of the first metallurgical mining companies it was expected to operate were transferred to it. Since then, it has been dissolved.

3. Ente Autonomo di Gestione per la Aziende Termali (EAGAT) was established in 1958 to manage the fourteen state-owned spas.

4. Ente Autonomo di Gestione per il Cinema (EAGC) was established in 1958 to manage the two movie-making companies, Cinecittà and Instituto Luce, and the distribution firm Italnoleggio.

5. Ente Partecipazioni e Finanziamento Industria Manifatturiera (EFIM) was established in 1962 to take over the light engineering group from the original 1947 FIM (Fondo per l'Industria Meccanica).

6. Gestioni e Partecipazioni Industriale (GEPI) was established in 1971 to restore ailing private enterprises to self-sufficiency and thereby relieved

IRI and ENI of unremitting political pressures to acquire these sick firms. Although it was founded as a financial agency rather than a state holding company, in practice, it faced enormous pressures to rescue firms by a takeover, a role supported by the risk-averse private sector.

Until the mid-1960s, the major state-owned holding companies—IRI and ENI—were one of the main forces behind the industrial expansion. Firms were merged, expanded and liquidated, new sectors were promoted and the firms were profitable. During the 1960s for some of the SOEs—notably, ENI—"expansion at any cost became an end in itself, independent of content and motivation" (Prodi, in Vernon, 1974, p. 59), and "public industry was in no way penalized for its management errors . . . Extended periods of losses were being tolerated even in areas in which these losses did not have any economic justification, and thus without exposing the managers to a process of evaluation and dismissal" (p. 59).

From the 1970s, the degree of governmental intervention increased. Since 1957, all state holding companies have been obliged to direct 40 percent of their total investments and 60 percent of new investments to the underdeveloped Mezzogiorno—the southern part of the country. Since 1971 these percentages have been increased to 60 and 80 percent, respectively. State holding companies were also used as a direct instrument of counter-cyclical policy; their investments were accelerated during the 1970s to prevent a recession in Italy. A major task of these firms has become the rescue of dozens of ailing private firms to avoid bankruptcy or to keep them from being acquired by a multinational enterprise (MNE). IRI became a paddling pond for lame ducks and grew in size and inefficiency. IRI was also used to circumvent the government bureaucracy, building and maintaining the Italian highway network and constructing low-cost housing projects. From 1970, SOEs in Italy recorded negative returns of increasing magnitude: since 1970 IRI has shown positive returns only in one year, ENI in two and EFIM in none. These losses materially increased the public sector's borrowing requirements. By the end of 1984 national debt was equal to 92 percent of GDP (*The Economist*, "Italy Survey", Sept. 14, 1985, p. 7). By 1980, the state holding companies employed 1.7 million Italian workers—a quarter of the labor force (*The Economist*, "Italy Survey," July 28, 1983, p. 37). IRI alone employs 490,000 in its companies, has sales of L48.9 trillion, equivalent to 7 percent of Italy's GDP. By the end of 1985, its accumulated losses since 1979 will be more than L17 trillion. Its losses in 1985 were L1.55 trillion, down from L2.7 trillion in 1984 and L3.2 trillion in 1983 (*The Economist*, "Italy Survey," September 14, 1985, p. 20).

Faced with a crisis of large magnitude, the Italian government appointed experienced economic managers—namely, Professor Romano Prodi to head IRI and Mr. Franco Reviglio to head ENI—making a break in a long tradition of political appointments for these jobs. Both men are committed to bringing their respective firms back to profitability even at the cost of shedding workers and despite the rumpus caused by attempts to close loss-making enterprises. They also attempt to sell off non-strategic firms either to private industrialists or through the stock market (see Chapter 9).

CANADA; NATION BUILDING

Unlike its neighbor, the Canadian government has traditionally played an important role in the country's development. It financed, built and operated several canals, several commissions were formed as early as 1852 and 1858 to administer harbor facilities in Quebec, and its role in the development of the railroad system has already been described. SOEs, first in transportation, then in 1932 in broadcasting and in 1937 in air transportation, were perceived to be necessary to unite the large and sparsely populated country, to head off pressures of integration with the United States and, later, to avoid its domination. The Canadian Wheat Board was formed in 1935 to market in an orderly manner grain grown in Western Canada for the interprovincial and export trade. During World War II, concerns about national unity merged with those of national defense, and 32 more SOEs were created to cope with the procurement, production and distribution problems of the war effort.

SOEs were established to obtain materials such as wool, silk, nylon, kapok, Sitka spruce and natural rubber; to produce munitions, optical glass and radar equipment; to supervise chemical, explosives and synthetic rubber plants; to administer naval shipbuilding yards and a cargo ship container program; to allocate, distribute, salvage and recondition machine tools and gauges; to develop housing projects; to supervise the development of new oil wells and to mine and process radium and uranium. A number of these ventures have survived—notably, the Polysar Limited (as the company is now called), a producer of synthetic rubber, and Eldorado Nuclear, which mined and refined uranium and for a time became a purchasing agent for all uranium produced in Canada.

In the provinces, business interests pressured for cheap sources of power, resulting in the creation of Ontario Hydro in 1906, followed later by the creation of state-owned electricity firms in most other provinces. In some of these provinces, the demands of the sparsely populated rural areas for cheap electricity brought about government involvement. In Nova Scotia, the SOE supplied electricity only to the rural areas of the province from 1919. It did not take over the private-sector firm dealing with urban power distribution until 1972. For the same reasons, the three prairie provinces entered the telephone field.

After World War II, Canadian governments at all levels responded to public demands for more services by entering into more SOEs to bail out firms, to boost regional development and to encourage risky endeavors. The number of federally and province-owned enterprises grew from 86 in 1958 to

156 in 1977. One hundred thirty-five of these enterprises coexist with private sector firms in the same field (Gordon, 1981, p. 11). In the same period, the percentage of total assets of federally owned SOEs in transportation went down from 65 percent in 1958 to 21 percent in 1978, while the share in finance, real estate and insurance increased from 20 percent to 54 percent of total assets. In 1974, the government entered the field of aircraft production and, through the Canadian Development Corporation, owns a variety of manufacturing firms. In 1975, Canada created its own national oil company, Petro Canada, to ensure Canadian ownership of the foreign-dominated oil and gas fields.

The provinces created at the same time several development agencies, giving loans to industrial firms. Some of them also bailed out firms and thus found themselves producers of plywood and pulp and owners of sawmills (British Columbia). The provinces are also heavily involved in housing and in providing automobile insurance to assure universal coverage at reduced costs. Alberta acquired in 1974 ownership of Pacific Western Airlines. Other provincial SOEs include forest products (Saskatchewan); steel (Quebec) and numerous others. In 1975, Canadian SOEs' share of business activities was 5 percent of total sales, 9 percent of profits and 19 percent of assets. In 1980, the share went up to 7 percent of sales, 9 percent of profits and 21 percent of assets. It is estimated that by 1985, the share will reach 10 percent of sales, 11 percent of profits and 25 percent of assets (McCready, 1977, p. 331).

Motivated as it was by the desire to build the nation, to increase equality in rural areas and to reduce foreign domination, Canada resembles most of today's developing countries in the rationale for establishing SOEs. In LDCs, the state owns not only public utilities and financial institutions but also firms engaged in agriculture, tourism, industry, housing, films, retailing (including bowling centers and supermarkets), engineering companies, commodity development, regional development as well as travel bureaus and hotels. In most of these countries, political elites felt a moral obligation to constrain *laissez faire* for the common good. In order to achieve economic growth, governments stepped in to alleviate problems of capital scarcity, to achieve economies of scale, or to reduce the role of foreigners as well as that of certain ethnic groups, such as Asian minorities in Africa or non-French in Quebec. Governments were also induced to undertake activities to achieve positive externalities—that is, benefits to society in cases when private gains were not sufficient incentives (e.g., transportation).

HISTORICAL ANTECEDENTS

A study of the history of government involvement proves fallacious the notion that most state ownership in Europe and LDCs is a result of waves of nationalizations by socialist governments, particularly after World War II. A more realistic view is that capitalism is a relatively recent phenomenon. SOEs were common in the ancient world. Joseph, in biblical times, is said to have created huge government operated warehouses in the seven good years; the Egyptians also manufactured the wax they used for mummification. "The Athenian State made a handsome profit from the silver mines of Laurium" (Kelf-Cohen, 1969, p. 15). Rome had a state monopoly on corn in 189 A.D., "supported by the riches and power of the minister" (Gibbon, 1952, p. 122. For other examples see Silver, 1983), and the Byzantine emperors made 500 percent profits on their silk-manufacturing facilities between the sixth and the eleventh centuries. The origins of other SOEs can be traced back many centuries. Some SOEs were originally created by a king or a prince, as in France and Austria, to produce porcelain or, more often, to raise revenues through the creation of a fiscal monopoly. Governments have always played a crucial role in the beginning stages of industrialization, and this is true also for the United States and Canada as well as for the latecomers to industrialization, such as Germany or Japan in the nineteenth century. Several European countries did nationalize certain enterprises immediately after World War II, but this was either the culmination of trends that can be traced at least to the beginning of the century or a direct result of the war.

Social and political realities are grounded in changing property relationships. The feudal relationships of lord and vassal collapsed with the growth of multiple autonomous centers of power. Representatives of the towns, the clergy and the nobility sought to share power with the ruler over issues in the public realm, such as taxation.

Passions of human beings have also been important for the creation of SOEs. States are run by people, not by machines. Between the sixteenth and the eighteenth century, many countries were ruled by absolutist regimes. The dynamic property of the State, as well as beliefs about its primacy in social life are important in understanding the origins of SOEs. In France, for example, "the statist tradition has a venerable intellectual lineage, and has the value of historical acceptability, if not transhistoric presciption" (Feigenbaum, 1985, p. 4). France has continued to cherish the guild organization of the pre-Revolutionary period.

Classical economics was based on the philosphical supposition that the pursuit of individual interest will in itself produce the best good for society. The state is expected to provide the impartial institutional and physical structures for the market to function. The state was therefore expected to build infrastructures and this role was often interpreted quite broadly by states that were late in industrialization (Gerschenkron, 1962, pp. 5-30).

In contrast to classical liberalism (and command socialism), certain countries were influenced by the belief in what Stepan calls "the organist-statist approach to the state"—"a body of ideas running through Aristotle, Roman Law, medieval natural law and into contemporary Catholic social philosophy" (Stepan, 1978, p. 27). Under this set of beliefs, the role of the State is much more central and normatively legitimate. The liberal state is rejected as leading to "abuses and antagonism between classes, and because the State does not play its normally proper role [of] pursuing the common good" (*Ibid.*, p. 32). In the organic-statist tradition, the state is clearly interventionist and strong. "The goal of stable, organically integrated society might entail radical change in basic structures" (p. 34)—from land reform to SOEs established to achieve rapid structural change. This tradition has been influential in Latin America, as well as in Nazi Germany and Fascist Italy. In many LDCs military aspirations combined with development aspirations and led to an increasing role of SOEs. The larger the SOE sector the more it recruited ambitious managers. These managers used accumulated profits to further extend public ownership—both by growth and by diversification. Such a growth was seen as a way to maintain a first-rate staff (Trebat, 1983, p. 34).

THE NEED FOR FUNDS: FISCAL MONOPOLIES

One reason for state control has always been the need for revenues, which has led to the creation of monopolistic enterprises intended to generate high revenues in industrial branches with low demand elasticity. One such enterprise, created by Colbert in France in 1674, was SEITA, the government monopoly on tobacco, cigarettes and matches. This, and other SOEs he created, such as the Gobelin tapestry and Sèvres porcelain, are still in operation. State-owned tobacco monopolies have operated in Japan since 1906, in Sweden since 1914 and in Austria and Thailand. There have been state monopolies for tea and caviar (Iran), playing cards (Greece), quinine (Italy), sugar (Japan, Italy), salt (Austria, Italy, Japan) and matches (France and Italy). Alcohol has often been used as a state fiscal monopoly, as it is in Sweden since 1914, many states in the United States and Canada and in Germany, France, Italy and Thailand.

National lotteries and state betting agencies are another type of SOE used mainly to raise revenue. Most countries see any form of vice as immoral and therefore illegal, but they are willing to operate state lotteries and betting agencies for collecting revenues. Sweden, e.g., established its betting agency in 1934 and its national lottery in 1938. The same reason is sometimes given for state ownership of retail stores that sell alcohol.

The state need for funds also led to ownership of mines. The coal mines of the Saar were taken over by the prince of Hesse-Nassau in the eighteenth century and were run for fiscal reasons. In the nineteenth century, the Prussian state-operated lead mining and smelting and coal mines and created the iron industry of Upper Silesia although mining operations were nationalized for other reasons, too. In modern times, many LDCs have nationalized the major revenue-producing mines (see Chapter 10). In many LDCs, foreign trade monopolies are state-owned, a tendency that may sometimes be traced to the mercantilistic period. The intricacies of foreign trade, the wide fluctuations of commodity prices and the state needs for funds led to the creation of state-owned monopolies for all export activities (e.g., Burma or Egypt) or for a certain commodity (oil), as well as for certain imports (Chapter 10). In Brazil, e.g., *autarguias* were set up in the 1930s "to control the production and sale of coffee, sugar, pinewood, and other primary products" (Trebat, 1983, p. 41).

Revenue-producing enterprises may also be used to redistribute income, as in the case of the Korean fertilizer industry, for which the planning board determines both the transfer price from producer to distributor and the distribution price to the farmers as a part of the overall agricultural strategy (UNIDO, 1983, p. 41). Another example is that of CONASUPO (Compania Nacional de Subsistencias Populares) in Mexico, a vertically integrated food and staple goods company designed to redistribute income through efficient retailing for low-income families. Similar SOEs operate in Chile, India, Jamaica, Guatamala, Brazil and Venezuela.

SOEs have often been created with the rationale of generating surpluses for the government. This savings mobilization argument is often heard in LDCs that are facing difficulties in generating investment finances (Gillis, 1980, p. 260). Unfortunately, in many cases the results have not fulfilled these expectations.

A new breed of SOE, created partially at least to generate revenues for governments, is the marketing board. For example, in the late 1970s surpluses generated by agricultural exports accounted for more than a quarter of the revenue in Ivory Coast, Madagascar, and Malawi (World Bank, 1981, p. 40). In the developed countries, agricultural marketing boards are producer controlled, oriented to advancing farmers' interests. In LDCs, they were initiated by government and operate as a central and compulsory marketing authority, through which all crop exports must be channeled (Hoos, 1979). In many cases marketing boards are used to transfer funds from the farmers for the development of manufacturing. In African and Asian countries growers are paid prices substantially below those received in the world market, and accumulated surpluses are used for other purposes.

In Ghana, for example, where cocoa accounts for over 60 percent of total exports, the Ghana Cocoa Marketing Board, established in 1947, has a monopoly on cocoa exports. In time, its aims of ensuring long-term price stabilization for growers and stimulating the activities of small growers became secondary to its function as a tax collection agency. Since 1965, it has not been allowed to hold reserves. The government share of sales revenues, merely 3 percent in 1947 to 1948, reached 30 to 40 percent in the mid-1950s and soared to 60 percent in 1978-9. This combined farmers' earnings became a residual. As a result (and with overvalued exchange rates) 1979 producers' prices were half their 1963 level, which naturally caused a drastic drop in production of cocoa and encouraged smuggling, resulting in an almost 80 percent fall in cocoa exports from 1965 to 1979 (World Bank, 1983, p. 77).

Cocoa production has fallen from 500,000 tons in 1965 to less than 200,000 tons in 1984. Producers, reacting to lower prices, move to other crops or smuggle the cocoa to the Ivory Coast and Togo where they receive higher prices and are paid in convertible CFA francs with which they can buy goods Ghana has stopped importing.

DEFENSE AND SECURITY

The need to protect society and its vital strategic interests has always been a reason for state control. After the decline of feudalism the notion of state control of strategically important resources emerged. Of the 193 ships of the British fleet that defeated the Armada, 163 were privately owned vessels that served the navy in return for trading privileges. During Cromwell's time government-controlled shipbuilding was instituted, although in earlier periods a certain number of ships were built by British kings, mainly for prestige.

Harbors, docks and canal systems have been very important in the defense of certain countries. The French Revolutionary government nationalized the inland water canals, and they have remained state-operated ever since. In the United States, concern with inland water transport developed because of various wars. Albert Gallatin, then Secretary of the Treasury, proposed in 1808 Federal development of the Chesapeake and Delaware Canal, and the War of 1812 proved him right. The Chesapeake and Delaware Canal was finally taken under public ownership in 1919. Since then, the strategically important waterways system has been the direct responsibility of government and today is run for the most part by the U.S. Army Corps of Engineers. The National Defense Act of June 1916 (Section 124) also directed that nitrate plants, needed for the supply of explosives, "shall be constructed and operated solely by the Government and not in conjunction with any other industry or enterprise carried out by private capital."

In the United Kingdom provision of a navigable thoroughfare between the North Sea and the Atlantic was to a large extent spurred by the threat of French privateers to the coastal trade during the Napoleonic wars. It is now under the control of the British Waterways Board, together with the other state-owned inland waterways. The establishment of this board was first recommended in 1906 by the Royal Commission on the Internal Waterway System. The commission observed that the establishment of state-owned infrastructure operations would by their very existence increase economic growth. The recommendation of the commission to nationalize the waterway system was, however, not carried out.

The strategic importance of the waterway system was a major consideration in the creation of one of the few federally owned enterprises in the United States—the TVA. The Tennessee River is an important inland means of navigation. It flows for 1,200 miles to join the Ohio River, and at Mussel

Shoals it descends in a series of rapids. Starting in 1889, more than 100 bills were introduced in Congress proposing improvement of navigation on the Tennessee River and harnessing the energy at Mussel Shoals to produce electricity. One such bill, in 1903, reached President Theodore Roosevelt but was vetoed. Authorization was, however, given to build the Hales Bar Dam just below Chattanooga, and this became the first source of hydroelectric power on the Tennessee River. Frank Washburn, president of American Cyanamid, was also president of the Mussel Shoals Hydroelectric Company, which applied for congressional authorization to build a dam to create hydroelectric power for the manufacturing of nitrates needed during World War I. When the war was over the dam was still unfinished, and the Harding administration proposed selling the dam and nitrate plant to private investors. Henry Ford bid $5 million for the project, which had cost up to then $150 million. Senator Norris, a Republican from Nebraska, was able to block the sale of the project to private investors and it was reluctantly finished by the government with taxpayers' money (Hubbard, 1961, Lowitt, 1971).

Immediately after his inauguration, President Franklin D. Roosevelt proposed setting up a TVA to carry out the Mussel Shoals development and much more. On May 18, 1933, the TVA was founded in the Tennessee Valley Act. It was charged with the broadest duty of planning for the proper use, conservation and development of the natural resources of the Tennessee River drainage basin and its adjoining territories "in the interest of the national defense and for agricultural and industrial development, and to improve navigation" (Ch. 32, Sec. 1, 48 Stat. 58).

In the case of the TVA, strategic considerations were interpreted very broadly, as they were in the cases in which national oil companies were created. In Japan, during the early years of the Meiji era (1868–1912), state entrepreneurial activities were motivated by the desire to enhance the country's military and economic power. Since private entrepreneurs familiar with Western commercial practices and technologies were few, the state took the lead, creating many economic enterprises and staffing them with Western experts. Most of these enterprises were sold to private Japanese citizens in the 1880s to relieve budgetary difficulties, but others were created when they were perceived as needed for military purposes. The Japanese state founded the first modern steelworks in 1901, nationalized the main-line railways in 1906 and subsidized the shipbuilding industry during the 1890s. By 1913, SOEs provided 12 percent of total factory employment. By 1930, however, this ratio had declined to 4 percent (Allen, in Maunder, 1979, p. 21). Prior to World War II, strategic considerations again led to the nationalization of electricity and steel. These industries were denationalized by the U.S. Occupation Authority.

Energy supply has long been seen as strategically important and has now become a permanent political issue. As early as 1899, Shell tried to convince the United Kingdom's Royal Navy to switch from coal to oil. Marcus Samuel, the founder of Shell, "even offered (in June 1902) to put government representatives on the Board of Shell to guarantee its concern for the national interest" (Sampson, 1976, p. 59). The admirals resisted, reluctant to replace the secure supply of U.K. coal with uncertain foreign imports. The navy finally converted to oil in 1910 but, still suspicious of Shell, used the newly discovered Burma oil. When Winston Churchill was appointed first lord of the admiralty, he, too, was urged to collaborate with Shell, but he preferred another prospect. To ensure supply to the navy, Churchill announced that the British government had acquired 51 percent of the Anglo-Persian Oil Company (today, British Petroleum). As Churchill said, "we must become the owners, or at any rate the controllers, at the source of at least a proportion of the supply of natural oil which we require" (in Sampson, 1976, p. 66). Although this was not announced at the time, the agreement called for the nomination by the government of two directors with power of veto. Churchill agreed in 1914 (and the agreement has been honored ever since) that this veto would be exercised only on questions of foreign or military policy or on matters bearing directly on admiralty concerns. Apparently, because of this lack of formal control of British Petroleum the firm is not seen by the U.K. government as an SOE (see Pliatzky, 1982).

Davenport and Cooke argued at the time that government ownership meant "pitting the British State against the nationals of other states, not only in producing but in consuming countries" (1923, p. 57). They also argued that the U.K. example would encourage nationalistic oil policies in other countries. On that score, they were certainly right. The French created their own national oil company (Compagnie Française des Pétroles) in the 1920s, and so did Argentina [Yacimientos Petroliferos Fiscales (YPF)]. Italy created AGIP, which later became the foundation of ENI (Zakariya, 1978). During the 1970s, national oil companies mushroomed (see Chapter 10).

In several countries, the military elite's concern about the nexus between internal security and national development increased the SOE sector. Military regimes promoted agrarian reforms. They saw capitalism as contributing to a "state of inconceivable misery of the masses" that "are the principal causes of the expansion of communism" (in Stepan, 1978, p. 143). Strategic considerations were broadly interpreted to need "a more active role of the State in restructuring economic and social systems (Ibid., p. 143). The national security concerns of the armed forces led not only to the nationalization of oil firms (as in Peru) but also to the creation of food marketing SOEs, nuclear energy firms (such as NUCLEBRAS in Brazil) and to the establishment of aerospace manufacturing in Brazil (Ramamurti, 1982; Sarathy, 1985).

In some countries, strategic importance and military needs have been more narrowly interpreted as the erection of armament factories. In Norway, e.g., three of the largest SOEs are an ammunition company, an arms manufacturer and a shipyard—all established as important elements of national defense. In wartime, expediency called for control of more business activities;

the railroads, as we have seen, were put under government control during wars, and the United States Defense Plant Corporation owned more than 2,000 factories. In Sweden during World War II, several SOEs were created to ensure the domestic supply of raw materials and energy. The army often operates its own enterprises, not only armament factories but also department stores for military personnel and their families.

IDEOLOGY

In socialist ideology, state ownership is an end in itself, and the transfer of ownership of wealth-producing assets from the private to the public (or workers') sector of the economy is a prerequisite for a better world and for social justice, and a necessary condition for a true democracy. Specifically, it is believed that state ownership would create greater equality among individuals, that removal of profits would give a substantial advantage to consumers, and that elimination of competition would reduce the vicissitudes of business cycles and eliminate the waste and extravagance of activities such as advertising. At the other ideological extreme, any government intervention in the workings of economic markets is perceived to be wrong and evil and leading to an excessive and dangerous concentration of power. Moreover, government is assumed to be both corruptible and incapable of running business activities efficiently. Chapter 2 shows that both these ideas are not necessarily true, but belief still influences behavior.

Thus, in the 1930s the French Socialist party called for state ownership of certain firms to break the so-called *mur d'argent* (wall of money). According to socialist beliefs, these firms had unduly strong influence on government affairs. When the Socialist party came into power in May 1936, it nationalized the Bank of France, the railroads and certain military equipment producers. After 1945 the French carried out another series of nationalizations, and when the Left wing came into power in the 1981 elections, six big industrial corporations and sixty six banks were nationalized in February 1982. The parties of the Right in Germany bitterly opposed public ownership of enterprises and in the late 1950s wanted to denationalize the existing SOEs by selling them to the public.

Careful analysis of the history of state ownership, purporting to stem from ideological beliefs, often shows other causes. Socialists argue that certain sectors of the economy are of strategic importance and generate linkages significant to economic growth. These so-called commanding heights are typically basic industries such as steel, electricity, coal, banking or heavy engineering. Immediately after World War II, the commanding-heights argument was used to justify nationalization in the United Kingdom and India and later in Pakistan during the Bhutto administration. In fact, in most cases these commanding heights turned out to be sinking sands. In practice, state ownership often "meant the servicing of mainly private enterprise by public enterprise" (Holland, in Vernon, 1974, p. 25) and saving the newly nationalized firms from bankruptcy. As another example, the Socialist-dominated government of Saskatchewan nationalized the potash works, and the Quebec government, after the election of the left-of-center Parti Québéçois in 1976, took over the asbestos mines. In the first case, the reason was

> less a sense of commitment to public ownership than a sense of outrage at corporate ploys intended to vitiate government endeavours to influence the pace of potash development and to maximize its revenues that convinced the Cabinet to proceed with the take overs . . . the government's loss of control over potash development and expected revenues due to the escalation of conflict with the industry provoked a more radical solution. [Laux and Molot, in Tupper and Doern, 1981, 193-194]

In the case of the asbestos industry, the official rationale was to "gain full advantage from its position as first world producer and exporter" (Fournier, in Tupper and Doern, 1981, p. 358). It was not a manifestation of socialist ideals but rather a means to "strengthen the economic clout of the state and its managers" (p. 364).

In certain developing countries, ideological reasons were important. The belief that government control over the commanding heights of the economy is a necessary condition for establishing socialism is explicitly stated in the 1948 and 1956 Industrial Policy Resolutions in India, in which certain industries are declared as exclusively reserved for public ownership. Tanzania also created many SOEs because of socialist ideology, and so did several other African countries (e.g., Benin, Zambia) as well as Sri Lanka and Pakistan. Figures presented by Shirley (1983, p. 97) indicate that at a very low level of development, ideology might be more important than it is at higher levels of development. African countries ruled by socialist leaders (Tanzania, Benin, Zambia) employed at the beginning of the 1980s 30 percent of the nonagricultural employees in the SOE sector, while the comparative figure in countries ruled by different ideologies, such as Kenya, Liberia or Swaziland, was 10 percent. However, India has a similar size of SOE sector employment as the Philippines and the size of the SOE sector under liberal and conservative governments in the Federal Republic of Germany is about the same as that of Sweden (Short, 1984).

Public ownership of essential infrastructure is advocated sometimes to help the poor and the underprivileged, to redistribute income or to supply goods or services at less than market price. Public transportation is one example; telephone and electricity supply to rural areas is another. In addition, many advocate state ownership of pharmaceutical firms in Europe, not only because of the alleged excessive prices charged by them but also because these prices are paid mainly by the state-owned national health system. In other cases—notably, in defense-related firms—R&D is financed by the state, which is, in any case, their major or only customer. It is sometimes argued that, since all risks are borne in these cases by the taxpayers, they should also reap the benefits. According to this line of reasoning, the bigger the government, the greater the need for SOEs to supply the increasing purchases of the government. Indeed, most governments own enterprises that supply them with printing and publishing services, clothing for the army or military stores. Another side of the argument is that the larger the government outlays on goods and services, the greater the need to use private suppliers. The substantial increase in acquisition of resources by government is said to reduce the efficiency of their use, diminish private-sector profitability (e.g., Randall, 1978) and affect the costs of production factors like labor (see Chapter 9).

A different ideology of sorts claims that natural resources belong to the nation as a whole and should be state-owned. In Sweden, e.g., the Forestry Agency was created in the mid-nineteenth century. In extractive industries, although the state's role historically has been to collect rent on the production capacity of often privately held resources (Klapp, 1982), sovereignty over national territory has been perceived as calling for state ownership. As early as the twelfth century, the king of Castille reserved the mines in his land for the exclusive use of the Crown, and on December 9, 1526, King Charles I of Spain declared that all mineral deposits in territories discovered by Spain would belong to the Crown. Sweden acquired 50 percent of the stock in the LKAB mining company as early as 1907. The rationale for this act was that the state should take direct responsibility for the exploitation of the country's national resources (Carlsson, 1984, p. 3).

State ownership of natural resources may be explained as a desire to demonstrate self-reliance and freedom from foreign domination. Host countries renegotiate terms they (or their colonial predecessors) had offered to induce foreign firms to make the initial investments. Sometimes, as in the case of Liberia's ore mines, government has received ownership rights as a result. More often, however, nationalization has been the outcome despite problems of barriers to entry. In the mid-1970s, the frequency of foreign-owned divestiture in LDCs rose to about 5 times the rate that had prevailed in prior years (Kobrin, 1980, p. 74, see also Chapter 10). Governments have also established SOEs to search for minerals. In 1958 the Indian government established a National Mineral Development Corporation, and the state-owned South African Iron and Steel Corporation has long held mining options on the iron ore deposits in the northern Cape Province.

Oil today is 70 percent controlled by SOEs. The objectives of the national oil companies, according to Grayson (1981), are threefold: to reduce dependence on the oil MNEs, to enable the government to develop the specific understanding necessary to check the MNEs' activities and to assure inexpensive and reliable crude supplies. In some cases, the government also wanted to protect the state's existing petrochemical industry by backward integration into oil. Grayson's reasoning also explains the origins of other energy-related SOEs: the coal industry before oil, natural gas and electricity later and atomic energy today.

Decolonization arguments apply not only to mineral resources but also to manufacturing industries. Both Socialist and non-Socialist governments have nationalized industries previously owned by colonial industrial interests:

> This rationale accounts for perhaps three-quarters of the nearly 200 central-government-owned enterprises now operating in Indonesia, primarily expropriated from Dutch interests in 1957 (and British interests in 1972), for a large number of Egyptian SOEs created in 1957 when Nasser, after the Suez war, nationalized important foreign firms, and for a significant share of public enterprises in Ghana and Algeria. This rationale has also been important in Peru, Mexico and Chile, where nationalization was undertaken in response to what was perceived as economic neocolonialism from the North rather than from the former colonial occupying power (Gillis, 1980, p. 263. On Algeria, see also Causey, 1984, pp. 158-163).

Third World countries usually nationalized an enterprise as soon as foreign owners were seen as dispensable, taking advantage of the weakened bargaining position of the foreign owners whose large capital outlays had become sunk cost. In this way, railroads and then the electricity system were the earliest to be nationalized. In the case of mining and the oil fields, despite the Hispanic tradition that soil rights are the inalienable property of the sovereign, nationalization was delayed until the country had acquired the necessary and more sophisticated production and marketing expertise. In the few cases in which, because of strong political pressures, the government nationalized too early (as with Bolivia's oil wells in 1937, Iran in the 1950s or Africa later), the consequences were costly (Vernon, 1979). The tendency to hold nationalization until the government felt secure about its capacity to manage the foreign-owned properties was graphically stated by Singapore's Prime Minister Lee Kuan Yew in a television interview in 1965:

> If you are going to have a planned economy, take over everything, plan your economy before you have got your technicians and your technocrats, how do you do it unless you have a really big power who says, "Look, let me help you and train these men for you?" Whereas if you take a more pragmatic approach and say "Well, all right, let us build up these skills and this capacity for industrial production, half socialist, half capitalist, and let the future be decided by the next generation." I think you will make better progress. We haven't driven out the capitalists in Singapore. We are doing fairly well. But we have redistributed the benefits of industrial and economic activity in Singapore in a much fairer way. In an under-developed situation where you have no managerial or technological class, the State ownership of all basic industries simply does not make sense. [In Pillai, 1983, p. 32]

In the United Kingdom in 1946 the Labour government nationalized the Bank of England as well as the coal industry, creating the National Coal Board (NCB). In the same year, the Labour Government created three independent state-owned companies: British Overseas Airways Corporation (BOAC), British European Airways (BEA) and British South American Airways. (Although the relevant Act creating BOAC was passed in 1939, the outbreak of war prevented its execution (Webb, 1973, p. 4).) In 1947, several transport industries, including the railroads, were nationalized, and the gas industry became state-owned in 1948. The major part of the iron and steel industry was nationalized in 1949 (the steel industry was later denationalized by the Conservative government beginning in 1953 and then renationalized in a different form by the Labour government in 1964 to 1967). However, observers of the British scene unanimously agree that it is highly unlikely that had a Conservative government been elected in 1945, it would have behaved differently.

REDUCING FOREIGN DOMINATION

In Latin America, where the fear of *dependencia* is often voiced, SOEs have been created to reduce the dominance of foreign owners. In other cases, foreign-owned enterprises were nationalized to eliminate potential sources of opposition. Nasser nationalized foreign-owned firms after the Suez War in 1956 to eliminate the economic base of political opponents to his government (O'Brien, 1966, p. 214). Consolidation of political power is often stressed as a motivation of nationalization, although Evans, e.g., claims symbiosis between the foreign-owned MNEs and SOEs, supporting capitalist interests (1977, 1979). As already shown, nationalization of foreign interests after independence has been a recurring theme in Asia and Africa.

SOEs have been established in the absence of private domestic entrepreneurs to initiate a program of economic growth and industrialization and avoid foreign dominance. In some countries, local entrepreneurs were mainly confined to clearly defined racial minorities and were resented by the racial majority. In countries such as Malaysia or East Africa, SOEs were established to provide *bumiputra* (sons of the soils) with opportunities to build up managerial skills.

State ownership to reduce dependence on foreigners has also been resorted to in more developed countries. IRI in Italy has often been called to acquire a firm to avert its sale to foreigners. The Canadian government explicitly attempted to reduce foreign domination in important sectors of the economy by creating its own firms: Petrocan in oil, the Potash Corporation of Saskatchewan and primarily the Canadian Development Corporation (CDC), created by the Canadian government in 1971 in order to develop and maintain strong Canadian-controlled and managed private sector.

France vetoed General Electric's proposal to acquire 20 percent of Bull (for this and other examples on France, see Michalet, in Vernon, 1974, pp. 105-125). Many countries created state-owned national champions in computers, aerospace and nuclear power to ensure that MNEs did not dominate these particular industries (Hochmuth, 1979). The Australian Resource Development Bank was established in 1968, and later, the Australian Industry Development Corporation was formed to reduce the dominance of U.S. companies in mining and manufacturing industries.

NATURAL MONOPOLIES AND OTHER INFRASTRUCTURES

We have discussed historical origins of SOEs, in which politics, ideology, strategic needs and considerations, social beliefs and economic rationality mingled. One case in which SOEs may be said to have originated in pure economic pragmatism is that of natural monopolies. Although its precise meaning may be debated (Kahn, 1970, pp. 119-126), the term *natural monopoly* refers in general to a unique relationship between market size and technology of supply. A natural monopoly is characterized by an output vector that can be produced more cheaply by a single producer than by any combination of smaller firms. Technically, such a cost function is called subadditivity. In a case of a firm producing more than a single product, economies of scale are neither necessary nor sufficient for subadditivity (for a mathematical proof, see Baumol, Panzar and Willig, 1982, pp. 170-189). If a natural monopoly exists, rival firms may engage in an intense and ruinous price competition, and each firm will produce at lower than the optimal scale, increasing the cost of the service. Often, duplication of service is a waste. Since technology dictates that competition is not a feasible solution, the choice is between regulation and ownership. The government may grant an exclusive franchise to a private firm, and regulate its operations. Alternatively, the government may act as a monopoly, producing and supplying the service. If the cost of regulation is higher than the costs associated with ownership, a national government will prefer ownership.

The overriding motives for state ownership have been the need to render necessary and important services efficiently and the concern that private owners might abuse the monopoly power inherent in these services. Further, in many cases the provision of these services was possible only by exercising the public authority's power of interfering with existing property rights. Eminent domain is often essential, and the government is sometimes reluctant to surrender this power to a private firm.

The oldest of these SOEs is the postal service, which has been a monopoly of kings and the state for a long time and is state-owned today all over the world. In Sweden, e.g., the Post Office was created as early as 1636. Even in the United States, the Postal Act of 1845 put private services out of business and to this day outlaws private delivery of letters (Priest, 1975). The Postal

Reorganization Act of 1970 (39 U.S.C. & 101 *et seg.* 84 Sta 3) made postal services an independent SOE. Similar laws to grant more autonomy to these services by shifting them from a government department to an autonomous enterprise have been passed in other countries, like the United Kingdom. In most countries, largely for historical reasons, the postal services also operate a savings bank and other financial services for small-scale depositors. In Austria and Switzerland, it also operates bus transportation services mainly to remote areas.

State ownership of infrastructure services came about gradually. Initially, one of the major motives was to provide necessary services efficiently to all parts of the country, and another was to achieve strategic dominance and to help in creating a unified country. Originally, at least in some countries, the prevailing wish was to encourage competition, and several enterprises operated in the same area. It was soon discovered that this system, rather than erecting a more efficient service, duplicated capital expenditures and made the service worse. In the United Kingdom by the mid-nineteenth century, monopoly rights had been granted for each enterprise in its designated area, and they were regulated or were owned by municipalities. In time it was realized that the municipal scale of some of these enterprises was too costly and hindered technological progress, but only in the 1920s did national public enterprise emerge, first with the creation of the Central Electricity Generating Board in 1926. In Brazil, the early impetus for the construction of basic public utilities was provided by foreign capital, but the State guaranteed a minimum rate of return. Getulio Vargas, Brazilian president, believed that SOEs should operate only at the generation end of the production process in contrast to retail distribution that was seen as presenting more opportunities for corruption (Tendler, 1968). Largely because of popular resentment, the foreign owned firms were not allowed the minimum rate they needed for expansion of their facilities. The result has been an increasing role for SOEs. The last remaining private electric utility was acquired by ELECTROBRÃS only in 1978 (Trebat, 1983, p. 59).

Today, most infrastructure services are state-owned: the postal service all over the world, almost all the railroads and public transportation as well as electricity, water and gas. In a few countries the industries are regulated by central government but are owned by municipalities or private investors. The mere size of some of these enterprises, both in terms of labor and capital expenditures needed, makes them extremely important. In the United Kingdom in 1977, the British Central Electricity Generating Board alone invested 4 percent of total gross domestic capital formation, excluding housing, and employed 0.7 percent of the work force. The postal services employed 0.8 percent of the work force and telecommunications 1.0 percent, while British Rail employed 0.9 percent. These firms invested 0.1, 4.2 and 1.3 percent, respectively, of total gross domestic capital formation, excluding housing (Pryke, 1981, p. 2). The price setting of these monopolies is of unique importance to both households and businesses. In France, the services supplied by the public corporations account for about 10 percent of the consumers' basket; since wages were tied to the consumers' price index, a policy of manipulating these prices as an anti-inflationary weapon was at least attempted. In Finland, programs in these sectors may have been canceled, postponed, launched or speeded up according to the countercyclical objective laid down in the unemployment law, even though changes for the pattern of investments from the technical factors determining them may have led to waste.

Infrastructure industries are characterized by their relative lack of autonomy when compared with other SOEs, their large work forces and their recurring needs for huge investments. Another characteristic of these industries is the tendency to create cross-subsidization: long-distance telephone calls cross-subsidize local services, and mail from dense urban areas is used to cross-subsidize delivery in less-populated areas or for printed matter. The same is true for electricity or public transportation.

Electricity production and distribution has become state-owned in most countries of the world, with Belgium, Japan and Sweden being notable exceptions. In India ownership of electricity is at the state government level. In the United States, with the exception of TVA, electricity is supplied by state-owned (Nebraska, New York) or municipal-owned (Los Angeles) authorities or by investor-owned firms. The TVA alone generates 10 percent of the electric power produced in the United States (Wolf, in Moore, 1967, p. 82). In Canada, too, electricity is supplied at the state level (Hydro Quebec, e.g.) or by private firms. In the Federal Republic of Germany, only 16.7 percent of electricity production capacity appears in official reports as being owned by the central government. An additional 45 percent of the electricity industry, however, is in the hands of VEBA (44 percent federally owned), Vereinigte Elekrizitatswerke Westfalen AG (87.9 percent owned by public institutions) and Rheinisch-Westfalisches Elektrizitatswerk AG (30 percent jointly owned by states and municipalities).

Nuclear power generation is the responsibility of the state-owned electricity firms, although R&D is typically carried out by separate state agencies, as in France and the United Kingdom. Japan, India and Brazil also have state-owned suppliers of atomic energy. Italy's AGIP Nucleare is 100 percent owned by ENI and other nuclear firms (SAIGE, MIRA, PMN), by IRI.

Gas production and distribution is also state-owned in many countries. In the Federal Republic of Germany and in Austria, gas, water and electricity are often combined in one municipal enterprise. SOEs often also control pipeline transportation (United Kingdom, Germany, France) and hydroelectric power (Canada, Scotland, France). Water production and distribution, one of the oldest of SOEs, is usually municipally owned; the first one in the United States commenced operations in Boston in 1652 (Lanier, 1976). The reasons for public ownership were, first, the belief that matters of public health should not be left to the private sector and, second, the large initial investment requirements and the anticipated low return on the investment, which discouraged private-sector suppliers. Furthermore, the provision of the service was sometimes used as an implicit tax device, and finally, fire protection needs called for a significant excess distribution capacity, the cost of which could be spread out over all users. According to Eutsler, property owners supported public ownership since otherwise the cost of fire protection would be borne by them (1939, p. 276). In most countries, privately owned water suppliers are confined only to smaller communities.

The advent of the telegraph in the mid-nineteenth century proved extremely important both for the expansion of trade and the control of empires. Today telephone services are sometimes organized as a part of the government department responsible for post, telephones and telegraphs, as in Switzerland, Kuwait, Iraq and Burma; sometimes these three are combined in a quasi-autonomous SOE, as in the United Kingdom before 1981, Rhodesia, Kenya, Uganda, Tanzania and Chad. In some cases the telephones are separated from the postal services but are a government department, as in Norway, Uruguay and Bangladesh, or a separate SOE, as in the U.K. after 1981, Sweden, Iraq and Nepal. In other cases telephone services are jointly financed by government and private investors (Mexico, Peru), or some telephone services are state-owned and others are privately owned (Canada, Portugal, Laos). Finally, in certain cases (United States, Jamaica, the Dominican Republic, the United Arab Emirates) the telephones are privately owned but government regulated. Some international telecommunications services are separately administered by other SOEs; as in France or Italy. Radio and television, although often state-owned or state-licensed and -franchised, do not qualify as SOEs under our definition. All in all, despite differences in terms of size, regime, ideology and historical evolution, almost all public utilities in the world are state-owned today. Despite this similarity, many differences can be found in the *timing* of the creation of these SOEs. These differences are mainly the result of the political power of private firms, foreign enterprises and the government.

COMPENSATING FOR THE PRIVATE SECTOR'S INABILITY TO SUPPLY NEEDED RESOURCES

Lord Delborne, Joseph Chamberlain's secretary, in describing the strategic importance of the telegraph in 1899, gave a more general reason for state ownership:

> *With progressive development of society the tendency is to enlarge the functions and widen the sphere of action of the central government . . . where the desired end is difficult to attain through private enterprises where the result of entrusting such powers or services to pri-*

vate enterprise would be detrimental to the public interest through
their being in that event necessarily conducted for the benefit of the
undertakers rather than of the public. [In Welsh, 1982, p. 25]

Indeed, the argument that public ownership is needed to build an infrastructure has been expanded of late to include all cases in which profit-
guided investments are less than socially optimal. Lord Kaldor (in Baumol,
1980, pp. 5-6) describes several such instances. First, since the profitability
associated with a project is based on expectations, when the uncertainty is
large, private investors tend to use highly discounted rates of return like, e.g.,
with industries resulting from new technologies. Second, in many cases the
market does not operate efficiently or perfectly. One of the several reasons for
market failure is that private entrepreneurs take into account only the profits
accruing to them, with little regard for benefits to society that may be created,
such as increased employment or transfer of labor to more productive occupations (or, in economist's language, the existence of external economies).
Third, additional investments may cause economic growth and, therefore,
additional income. These indirect, or what Kaldor terms "criss-cross," effects
are not taken into account in the calculations of the private businessperson.
Further, in many LDCs that gained political independence in the 1950s and
1960s, strenuous efforts have been made not only to achieve development but
also to better the economic situation of national ethnic groups.

Based on such arguments, state ownership has been extended to many
areas, from high technology industries to any case in which investments were
rejected by private businesspeople. Keeping up with the rapidly increasing
costs and complexity of the technology underlying industries such as aircraft,
aerospace, nuclear energy, computers, telecommunications and microelec-
tronics was beyond the means of private-sector companies in most countries.
Reluctant, nevertheless, for reasons of national prestige, to forfeit all progress
in these areas to the United States and the USSR, European countries have
sought ways to remain abreast of the two superpowers in both development
and production of high-technology products. J.J. Servan Schreiber, in his best
seller *Le Défi Americain* (1968), portrays the fragmented European industries
as unable to cope with the U.S. giants. Often the reaction to the American
challenge was the establishment of SOEs. This served to merge weak and
diffused local firms and ensure that technological know-how would be maintained and enhanced. France, Germany, Spain and the United Kingdom
have also created joint transnational SOEs like Airbus Industrie to share the
costs and risks involved and to counteract the U.S. MNE threat. At least
some of these cases raise the question: Can the government spot investment
opportunities and pick winners not noticed or acted on by private individuals?
Whatever the answer to this question, public ownership has been accepted
not only for strategic or natural monopolistic reasons but also for investing

when the private sector does not pick the winners or to sustain industries that are considered essential but do not meet the profit criteria of the market.

In developing countries, because of the magnitude of the investment required, the risk involved or the long gestation period, private entrepreneurs refrain from investing. The government becomes the sole entrepreneur capable of mobilizing the resources for many industrial investments. The reason most SOEs in developing countries initiated and organized new sectors seems to be a special sort of market failure: a very weak and risk-averse private sector with very little entrepreneurial drive. Economic growth is likely to be slow when entrepreneurs are few, since most businesspeople are not accustomed to taking risks and expect a relatively high rate of return. The state preferred usually "to expand into the 'empty spaces': steel, petroleum, iron ore" (Trebat, 1983, p. 64). To be sure, the record is not very successful, and there have been many cases in which it turned out that the caution of the private sector regarding economic viability was justified while government was mistaken, but still it may be said that public entrepreneurs filled a vital hiatus. In certain newly independent countries it was necessary also to replace the many and key foreign nationals who fled after the fall of the old regime opposing independence or to train indigenous entrepreneurs to replace Chinese or Indians. Also, in countries in which the small market size has led to many industrial firms becoming monopolies or oligopolies, state ownership has been perceived as necessary to avoid concentration of private economic power. These criteria, of course, are extremely broad, and can justify state ownership of almost any enterprise.

FINANCING DEVELOPMENT AND CONTROLLING FINANCIAL INSTITUTIONS

The first notable public bank was created by the city of Amsterdam as early as 1609, to limit abuse of the currency. "Similar institutions were soon established in Rotterdam, Delft and the then important trading town of Middlebourg" (Galbraith, 1975, p. 16). The bank's affairs were wound up in 1819, as a result of too many loans granted to the City government and to the Dutch East India Company. Since then, governments learned more about the intricacies of finance—and what banks can do with and to money. They introduced a variety of regulations on banks' reserves and on their right to issue notes. They also own and control central banks as guardians of the money supply, as well as the financial concerns of the government. The Bank of England was founded in 1694, the Banque de France in 1800, in 1875 the former Bank of Prussia became the Reichsbank, and other countries have acquired similar institutions. These banks were nationalized mainly in the mid-1940s. The American colonies were the pioneers in the issue of government paper money—used to pay for military operations. Still, in almost all countries, all banking and issuing of currency were in private hands.

Cycles of panic and epidemics of bank failures caused citizens' demands for government protection. In the United States, the Federal Deposit Insurance Corporation was charted in 1933 to insure deposits. In other countries, central banks were nationalized (as in England in 1946) and in still others e.g.—France—the commercial banks and insurance firms were nationalized in the 1940s. The banking sector of Portugal was nationalized on March 14, 1975, and the insurance industry, a day later. In India, life insurance has been nationalized since 1956 and general insurance since 1973. In almost all other countries, with the glaring exceptions of the United Kingdom, the United States and Switzerland and to a lesser extent Canada and Japan, most financial institutions are state-owned or at least state-controlled and -directed. In many cases, banks became state-owned in order to bail them out, as in the case of the Banco de Brazil in 1905 (Topik, 1979) or in Italy.

The Chileans and the Italians were among the first to experiment with state-owned special-purpose credit institutions. Italy established the first of these institutions in 1929, and Chile created CORFO in 1939; since then, state involvement in the supply of funds by loans from state-owned financial institutions has been widespread, mainly where the capital market proved to be inefficient or nonexistent. This has led, naturally, to an increase in governmental power and control, e.g., by provision of subsidized loans with attendant goal-oriented conditions. Juggling the flow of loans and the rate of interest charged for different purposes is a powerful device for influencing behavior. The institutional suppliers of funds have a critical control on many business firms. They often advise them, influence their policies, intervene in their management and set the level of risk they are willing to tolerate in the investments and the operating policies of the clients. They also have access to confidential information. For all these reasons, control of financial institutions is often seen as thrifty use of state capital and management. At the same time, their operations may have retarded the development of a more efficient capital market, thereby influencing other factor markets and affecting the structure and performance of the business sector.

Japan may be the best known example of the control and direction of economic development through financial institutions. The major source of finance after World War II was the government-owned Reconstruction Finance Bank. A number of other state-owned financial institutions were set up to furnish loans at a subsidized rate of interest to industries the government regarded as important to future development and therefore deserving of special assistance. The Central Bank developed the use of preferential rates of interest and so-called window controls, achieving an enormous leverage over the policy of private firms.

Essentially the same methods have been used in almost all countries. Public control of financial institutions is said to enable a government to direct the flow of funds in the economy to areas of its choice. All LDCs and most industrialized countries have used development banks to achieve economic resurgence after the war or to implement their economic growth objectives. Even the United States has resorted to development banks, not only at the time the RFC operated but also through the Export-Import Bank, the Federal National Mortgage Association, the Small Business Administration and the Agricultural banks. The largest insurance agency in the United States is the Social Security Administration. In all countries, there are SOEs supplying long-term finance to agriculture and housing—and in most of them also for manufacturing. The World Bank made loans on credit to more than 70 such development finance companies in more than 40 countries (Su, 1982, p. 47).

PUBLIC DEMANDS

In the last few decades, SOEs have been created mainly as a result of a shift in public opinion regarding the appropriate role of the state in economic affairs. The extent and character of the shift have varied from one country to the next, but typically, the management of the economy, to achieve growth, prevent unemployment or promote regional development, is perceived as the responsibility of government. The public demand for a larger role of government meant, as already discussed, more intervention in the working of the market economies. Governments have also found it necessary to slow down and control the inevitable process of economic adjustment, which, left unchecked to market forces, would have created politically intolerable high unemployment and unacceptable human hardship. Socializing the capitalists' losses, by establishing SOEs and acquiring ailing, bankrupt or even abandoned firms, has become the task of government in its efforts to mitigate the social and political consequences of the closing down of larger firms.

A persistent and pervasive issue on the political agenda of the 1970s in most countries has been the problem of whether or not to bail out firms in jeopardy—and if so, how? Strict credit control, the oil crisis, as well as competition of the newly industrialized countries (NICs), have forced many firms into liquidation in the last few decades. Governments have responded in two directions: On the one hand, they have bowed to calls for relief, at least to those firms with a high level of employment, and on the other hand, they have made efforts to facilitate positive adjustment by retraining and fostering the development of new technologies and new industries. In both cases, SOEs have often been created and existing SOEs used to achieve these goals. In Sweden and Italy the major holding companies of SOEs were forced to accept the role of wet nurse to governmental reconstruction of bankrupt companies, designed to solve shortrun employment problems, in the hope of getting them back on their feet. Many of those who claim government intervention—and certainly ownership—to be destructive, call for such intervention when a large employer faces imminent collapse or threatened closure of a major plant or when a sector or a region faces decline.

Governments, even those ideologically inclined to the right, find it extremely difficult to ignore pressures and silently witness battles for industrial survival or commercial plunder. The unacceptability of certain consequences of social Darwinism ("natural selection") meant increasing attempts by government to bail out firms in trouble and many countries established special SOEs to administer such help. In fact, in the six years of Sweden's bourgeois government (1976 to 1982), the SOE sector increased more than it did in four decades of Social Democratic governments, as the Swedish government felt compelled to salvage failing firms by nationalizing. The United Kingdom under Conservative as well as Labour governments, bailed out lame ducks by bringing them under state ownership. The same story may be repeated for developing countries. Thus, India aided 103 sick textile undertakings in 1972, Bolivia rescued cement plants and bicycle manufacturers, and many Mexican SOEs resulted from the bail-outs of floundering private enterprises. The Argentine SOE sector "grew rapidly in the 1960s and 1970s for precisely these reasons" (Trebat, 1983, p. 65). Sometimes, nationalization of firms in a fragmented, ailing industry has led to a takeover of the entire industry by the state—e.g., coal in the United Kingdom or aerospace in France (Robson, 1962, pp. 29-32; Hanson, 1963, pp. 67-70; Keyser and Windle, 1978, Part 4, pp. 125, 144).

The reaction to the problems of declining industries or firms in crisis is not necessarily nationalization. Whole industries and specific firms have been helped by tariff protection and quotas or through subsidies, loans and grants. The United States, as an example, rarely resorted to nationalization. It aided firms such as Douglas, Lockheed or Chrysler mainly through government guarantees of loans, approved on an *ad hoc* basis. Since the RFC was abolished in the early 1950s, the federal government has not had a flexible instrument for crisis intervention.

Crises have beset not only the declining sectors such as steel (United Kingdom, Germany, Sweden, Belgium, France), shipbuilding (United Kingdom, Sweden, Italy) and textiles (India, Italy, Sweden, Belgium) or tractors (International Harvester, Massey Ferguson) but also growth-sector firms such as aerospace (Lockheed in the United States, Rolls Royce in the United Kingdom), computers (ICL in the United Kingdom, Machine Bull in France, Sweden) and electronics (AEG Telefunken). Many of these firms were aided directly by government. Other rescue operations were carried out by SOEs or by institutions such as the Economic and Social Development Fund (FDES) or the IDI in France. Private capital was usually reluctant to join such rescue operations. If it did, it was only after the loans were guaranteed by governments, as in the case of the Canadian-based multinational tractor manufacturer, Massey Ferguson, in 1981. The CDC refused the government's request to rescue Massey, and apparently, CDC enjoyed enough autonomy to make its refusal stick.

In some cases, government assistance—by one means or another—is deemed essential to prevent collapse of the whole financial structure. Thus, a concern for the exposure of the banking system and the impact on confidence in volatile financial markets has been another reason for nationalization. In July 1984, the Federal Deposit Insurance Company (FDIC) announced its takeover of Continental Illinois Company, the eighth largest bank holding company in the United States. FDIC committed $4.5 billion—and said it would spend whatever it took—to prop up the bank. The FDIC decision was made after an earlier announcement on May 17, 1984, that it would guarantee all the bank's deposits, including those above the statutory limit of $100,000, failed to stop the cash from flowing out. Before bailing out the bank, FDIC embarked on a search for a private buyer, but those who showed any interest expected the bank to be cleared of any bad loans. According to Hector, "Viewed politically, the idea of FDIC shelling out billions of dollars so that such investors could earn fat returns was almost ludicrous" (1984, p. 136). Even though the government has financial control and is able to veto the bank's policies and fire its directors, FDIC chief William M. Isaac insisted, on announcing the rescue plan, "This is not a nationalization." His reasoning was that the FDIC did not use taxpayers' money for the bailout. Ideology, after all, is important!

STRONG PERSONALITIES

Sometimes, the major reason for the growth of the SOE sector is the strong conviction of a leader. One example is that of the growth of AGIP into ENI. As mentioned, AGIP was founded in 1926 to conduct exploration and refining activities of oil at home and abroad. In 1945 the Italian government tried to divest the firm, but no one wanted to buy it, perhaps because it was a "dumping ground for worn-out politicians, hacks and superannuated civil servants" (Votaw, 1964, pp. 8-9). Enrico Mattei, who became the manager pending sale, had other ideas. He started an active search for oil and gas, discovered some in 1946 and more in 1949 and, without bothering to ask for permission or instructions, immediately launched large-scale pipeline construction activities. He charged high prices and, at least according to Votaw (1964, pp. 25-29, 34-44) understated in the published financial statements both revenues and investment expenditures (see also Frankel, 1966).

On February 10, 1953, Enrico Mattei created ENI as a holding company of several SOEs operating the petroleum sector. His vision was to free the Italian market from foreign domination and break into the oligopoly he scornfully termed "the seven sisters." Using the large cash flows of the gas monopoly from the Cortemaggiore in the Po Valley, he had almost complete freedom of decision. The lack of strong political guidance from the Italian government enabled Mattei to exercise political power and strongly influence Italian foreign policy, at least in energy matters. Mattei reinforced his power by acquiring an advertising agency, a news service and a Milan paper, *Il Giorno*, which he used to pit his point of view against political adversaries.

Mattei's political power is often described as legendary. He negotiated joint exploration and production agreements; he gave the producing country 75 percent royalties and forced the multinational oil companies to follow his precedent; he introduced many government-to-government deals (and preferred such deals) but was in fact the representative of Italy in such negotiations. Even Mattei had prices to pay, however. For example, in 1956 ENI was forced by the Italian government to acquire a bankrupt engineering firm, Nuovo Pignone, and in 1961 it was obliged to bail out the Lanerossi, a textile firm, and absorb substantial losses for many years. He also had to pay the price of giving up his seat in the Chamber of Deputies when a law forbidding MPs to hold positions in SOEs was passed, with the explicit intention of limiting Mattei's power. Indeed, Mattei was often accused of wielding too much unbridled power, and many opponents tried to curb him. A law, passed in 1957, preventing ENI from entering further joint ventures with private enterprises, was repealed after Mattei's death on October 27, 1962. However, Mattei had a vision that ENI would be the dominant enterprise in the Italian market and the largest oil concern, and during his term ENI had indeed become a major integrated oil company on a world scale. During this period it trebled its turnover, doubled gas production and pipeline network, and quadrupled the size of its employment. ENI grew rapidly in the first decade of its operations, expanding into the chemical sector with the acquisition of ANIC and to the nuclear energy field with the acquisition of a private-sector firm, both in 1954. In 1962, ENI was forced to diversify into the textile industry with the acquisition of Lanerossi.

After Mattei, Boldtini became president and Cefis, vice-president. Cefis stepped in as a CEO in 1967, continuing Mattei's strategy and enjoying much freedom. In 1972, Cefis bought 13 percent of the largest chemical firm, Montedison, after failing to gain its cooperation in the petrochemical field. This move met a lot of opposition, but Cefis was able to get it through. He resigned in 1971 to become Montedison's president, and since his term, no president of ENI has had the political power to act independent of the state. In 1979, Socialist Giorgio Mazzanti was nominated ENI's CEO. His appointment lasted less than a year: he was mentioned in a case of commissions paid to ENI officials as a part of a deal between Italy and Saudi Arabia. His replacement resigned "one day before he was scheduled to assume the position . . . allegedly because of increasing governmental interference into ENI's affairs. Thus, the chaotic Italian political situation finally was transferred, in full, onto ENI" (Grayson, 1981, p. 123).

The impact of the strong will of a public entrepreneur on the growth of SOEs has been evident also, e.g., in state oil firms and in the Port Authority of New York (Walsh, 1978). Some of these entrepreneurs also expanded SOEs beyond the border of the state, acquiring firms in other countries (see Chapter 10). Other SOEs, once created, have expanded into related areas. Diversification of existing enterprises, using their retained earnings, has been a major reason for growth of the SOE sector in many countries. PERTAMINA in Indonesia embarked on a wide diversification program: petrochemicals (1971-1978), liquefied natural gas (1973), a hotel chain, an aviation company, an insurance firm, steel company, fertilizers, and even a restaurant in New York (Fabrikant, 1975; Lipsky, 1978). Canadian National Railways owns trucking services, hotels, telecommunications, real estate and consulting services.

Diversification activities of SOEs were called by Mr. Edouard Bonnefous, chairman of the French Senate's commission inquiry into nationalized industry, a "process of creeping nationalization." According to him, the number of state-owned parent companies in France has decreased in 20 years from 170 to 130, but their subsidiaries have grown from 266 to 650 (Bonnefous, 1977).

Finally, since SOEs enjoy more autonomy than other governmental institutions, pressures have mounted to move activities from existing government departments to SOE status (see Seidman, in Smith, 1975, pp. 83-108; Musolf and Seidman, 1980). Much of the growth in scope and scale of SOEs in the future may be expected to result from such spin-offs. One may also expect more of the SOEs to be competitive and not fitting the classic British mold of a nationalized industry: 100 percent state-owned, aiming toward zero profits and drawing capital only from the Treasury.

OTHER FACTORS

According to Friedmann and Garner, "In most cases public corporations have been established in response to practical needs, and they have often been successful in ideologically uncongenial surroundings" (1970, p. 306). Pragmatism, however "is usually an excuse for an explanation which remains to be given" (Reg Whitaker, in Tupper and Doern, 1981, p. 11). Some of the pragmatic reasons include *political retaliation*: Renault and Gnome de Rhône in France were nationalized as a punitive measure for alleged collaboration with the Nazi occupation forces; Norway nationalized ASU, an aluminum-smelting firm, and Norsk Hydro in the 1940s as a confiscation of German property. In Nicaragua after the 1979 revolution, the properties of the ousted Somoza group were nationalized (Austin, Fox and Kruger, 1985). LDCs nationalized certain firms in a drive to get rid of foreigners who were associated with, and carried the stigma of, colonialism. The government has also invested for reasons of *national prestige*. The Conservative government in the United Kingdom helped establish Imperial Airways and 15 years later nationalized it, creating the British Overseas Airways Corporation in 1939. Today, almost all countries of the world operate their own state-owned national airline because of national pride and prestige.

Other reasons given are essentially to the national economy, like atomic energy in Japan or France, protecting domestic industry, improving productivity, preserving declining industries, promoting national champions in high technology, steering economic growth, fostering structural change, and short-term economic stabilization.

There may even be other reasons. For example, certain electricity firms in Canada were nationalized to avoid federal income taxes: Privately owned electric utilities pay federal income taxes, while Crown corporations do not. In the campaign for the nationalization of electricity in Quebec, proponents estimated that the federal tax exceeded $20 million. British Columbia also nationalized the private electricity utility in 1961, and Premier W.A.C. Bennett announced that he took over the company because the federal government refused either to eliminate the income tax on the utility or to give its full proceeds to the British Columbia government. To be sure, the Canadian federal government began in 1966 to rebate to provincial governments 95 percent of the proceeds of income tax on electric utilities "in order to eliminate the bias in favor of provincial takeovers" (Gordon, 1981, p. 35). Still Nova Scotia took over the private electricity firm in that province in 1972.

INSTITUTIONAL REQUISITES

Another reason for state ownership has been the use of the proceeds of foreign aid. The World Bank "viewed existing governmental departments as either too inefficient or too corrupt (or both) to execute large-scale projects effectively even with the active assistance of technical experts from the Bank . . . State-owned enterprises became the preferred channel" (Gillis, 1980, p. 265). The World Bank also insisted on government guarantees to its loans, and governments were reluctant to guarantee loans to private enterprises. A Danish loan, tying high-priced procurement to Denmark, was not used by the Nepal private sector. Instead, a state-owned Nepalese livestock company came into being to take this loan (Ramanadham, 1984b, p. 83). In other cases, SOEs were created to help consumers: e.g., Sweden created state-owned restaurants in the 1940s. Several countries created SOEs to seek price stability of basic food stuff, mainly for low-income groups. Mexico's CONASUPO operates a chain of 14,000 stores mainly around Mexico, and the Food Corporation of India supplies a network of Fair Price Shops in which the retail price to the consumer is determined by the government. In the United States, as shown in Chapter 2, SOEs were created to circumvent constitutional limits on a state's debt.

In some countries, SOEs were created to help boost exports or to reduce imports. One typical case is that of an export guarantee against a political risk, e.g. Another is the creation of a state-owned reinsurance firm to reduce the foreign-exchange costs of insurance: Private firms may tend to reinsure in the major financial centers and to avoid the risk of participation in reinsurance of foreign insurance firms. The government may then decide to create a state-owned reinsurance firm, often forcing the companies to reinsure through such a firm to reduce the reliance on foreign reinsurance. Thus, Brazil created the Instituto de Resseguros de Brazil, which was 51 percent state-owned by the private insurance firm and 49 percent owned by the private reinsurance firms, and Korea founded the Korean Reinsurance Corporation. In many cases, state ownership came about not by design but as a result of a default on a loan received from the government or from a state-owned financial institution. When the private firm could not repay the loan, the government had to take possession of the firm.

CONCLUSION

SOEs used to be thought of as originating from ideological belief in public ownership or from the need to generate revenue or to regulate a natural monopoly, mainly when market demand is small relative to economies of scale. More and more, as the scope of governmental activities has grown, SOEs have been created for motivations of different sorts. These include:

> Initiation of new activities because of the belief that private-sector supply of entrepreneurs, initiative or capital or of willingness to take risks is inadequate;
> Savings mobilization and development financing;
> Control of strategically important industries and increasing competitiveness vis-à-vis large foreign firms;
> Creation of new jobs and rescue of failing firms to save existing jobs;
> Creation of a pacesetter to invigorate competition and to increase knowledge of the government bureaucracy about the inner workings of the industry (electricity, oil, insurance);
> Administrative convenience: donor's preferences or transferring services such as housing for the needy, postal distribution or supply of funds from the government to a more autonomous type of SOE, allowing flexibility in changing priorities or simply undertaking special functions of the public sector more autonomously;
> Ensuring perceived sovereignty and reduction of dependence on MNEs.

In addition, some believe, although the evidence is contradictory, that SOE status may modify the power structure within the firm and in society. It was believed that SOEs would pay special attention to social harms that the private firm ignores—from aid to the elderly and low-income groups (housing to the poor) to corrective structural disequilibrium (shrinking railroads), concern for pollution and other externalities, and more equality for workers. They were seen as potent tools for generating surplus and mobilizing resources for socioeconomic development.

The SOE sector has grown both by design, because of governmental initiative, and unintentionally—as a result of a crisis in which nationalization was forced on the government or because of the powerful personality of an empire-building public entrepreneur. It grew sometimes as a result of nationalization but more often through the initiation of new activities. The origins are diverse and cannot easily be explained solely by economic rationale, social structure, political motives or ideological predilection. Motives are usually mixed and the declared reasons are not necessarily the real motives. Some of the SOEs created in time of war or economic dislocation were later dissolved; some were not, finding new objectives and new roles.

SOEs may be found in almost all sectors of the economy although, for reasons explained, the probability of their existence is lower in agriculture production and small-scale retailing activities. The postal services seem to be the only case in which all countries of the world have a monopolistic SOE, albeit under different organizational forms. In most other cases, SOEs operate side by side with private firms. The newly created developing countries preferred state ownership, apparently not only for good economic reasons but also because they considered economic self-reliance a vital component of political independence. With no savings and a low per capita income, the only way seen for growth was massive public injection of funds. In some countries, the SOEs were intended to reduce income disparities. The unintended consequence was very often subsidization of the upper middle class. SOEs have been used to avert unemployment, to resuscitate private firms or to inject competition—as in the Indian decision to build state-owned hotels to bring down soaring hotel prices in Delhi.

History tells us that, once established, an SOE may change and adapt, and its role may alter with time, with changing environment and changing governments. The original motivation for state ownership and the expectations held by governments may or may not guide the firm's management or its controllers over time. Organizations tend to have a life of their own, based on standard operating procedures and the influences of strong individuals. Assessment of the evolution of these enterprises is often as important to understanding their role today as an understanding of their origins.

The major problem of an SOE is its hybrid nature. Public administration scholars claim it is not accountable enough. Entrepreneurs find it is too bureaucratic because of the public accountability. The way these enterprises should be managed or when should they be divested to the private sector continues to baffle researchers and practitioners. Governments have long wavered between extremes in many things related to these enterprises—a desire to promote these firms and a deep reluctance to let them loose. They have oscillated between social goals, political objectives and economic missions, unable to agree on their priorities. As a result, SOEs face conflicting goals, with an unspecified trade-off between the multiple goals and a high level of expectations from politicians and the public. To assess the performance of SOEs, we have to understand how these goals are agreed on and articulated.

CHAPTER 4
Objectives

INTRODUCTION

Formal organizations can be characterized as being directed toward attaining specific goals (Parsons, 1960, p. 17). The managers of organizations are charged with realizing the goals of these organizations. Well-defined organizational goals serve as clear-cut criteria to guide the managers' behavior and give direction to their decisions. These criteria can also serve as a touchstone for examining the organization's achievements and as a basis for the legitimacy of the organization's existence and activity. Indeed, the major reason that one can assume *a priori* that differences exist between private firms and SOEs is that these enterprises are owned by different groups that have different objectives and that created the firms to achieve different goals.

Privately owned enterprises, at least according to conventional wisdom, are expected to be managed toward one goal: long-term profits for their shareholders. Private shareholders may be assumed to be a uniform group whose goal is to maximize profits. Even if they do not, this is their personal decision. SOEs are expected to steer their operations to achieve the goals of their owners—namely, the citizens of the country. In contrast to the private firm's situation, this is not a uniform group and their goals are many, ambiguous, ill defined and even conflicting. To many observers, SOEs are by definition expected to achieve broader goals than private firms. Profitability is seen as one goal but certainly not the most important one.

SOEs are hybrids, largely influenced by the political environment while also attempting to influence it. Their management must also take into consideration the expectations and conflicting demands of the public and various interest groups within it. As one example, Sexty (1979, p. 11, quoted in: Gordon, 1981, pp. 158-180) found in a case study on the Canadian Cellulose Company Limited, an enterprise 81 percent owned by the government of

British Columbia, that the corporation was confronted by a series of demands after being taken over by the government. For example, roads leased by the corporation from Indian reserves were closed as a tactic to force the provincial government to negotiate the Indian claims. A sit-in occurred at an associated company in Belgium, Papetéries de Gastushe, when the decision was made to liquidate the company, and Canadian diplomats were asked to mediate on the workers' behalf to prevent closure.

What are the implications of this hybrid form for the behavior of SOEs? The most important one is that the issue of goal formulation should have a central role in any theory of SOEs behavior (Levy, 1985). Choksi (1979, pp. 172-181) lists 25 objectives SOEs are expected to achieve. How are these objectives and the trade-offs among them decided and communicated?

There are at least three points of view on the ways goals should be assigned to SOEs. The first looks at SOEs as an instrument of government. The government, therefore, should assign goals to each SOE. Assuming the government represents the national interest, the goals assigned to SOEs would be to maximize social benefits. Alternatively, the government may be interested in vote maximization, or some other maximand. To ensure the achievement of the goals, a set of incentives must be designed to align as far as possible the interests of the manager with the goals of the government.

A second point of view stresses that SOEs should maximize efficiency. In some cases, e.g., when they are natural monopolies, they should not be expected to achieve profits. In others, i.e. fiscal monopolies, they should maximize profits. The difference between SOEs and private enterprises, from this viewpoint, is in the distribution of surplus. This belief is shared by many economists and by most managers of SOEs. With the growing recognition that SOE's deficits create a fiscal burden on the state, the demand that SOEs should be measured by efficiency (and compensated for the performance of social goals) is increasingly heard.

A third point of view is that the goal of SOEs should be to serve different interest groups—mainly, consumers and workers. Thus, France has union, consumer and government representatives on the boards of directors of its SOEs (although these representatives are nominated by the government). In the United Kingdom the National Economic Development Council (NEDO) proposed, in its 1976 report, a two-tier board system with a board selected by the interest groups, leaving the government the right to approve or disapprove. In its 1978 White Paper the government rejected the idea, claiming that "the government is the sole shareholder of the nationalized industries and their principal banker." When workers' directors were nominated to the board (as in British Steel or in some industries in Israel), they had very little effect on the decision-making process. Those proposing interest-group representation were unable to demonstrate how conflicts of interest are to be resolved.

These different points of view are rarely discussed explicitly, and different recommendations on the way SOEs should be managed are a result of different ideological points of view on the goals these organizations are to pursue. Further, a fundamental problem often ignored is how trade-offs among goals are resolved. For example, should British Rail construct and operate unprofitable lines for defense or strategic reasons? Should it deliberately maintain excess wagon capacity so that important loads that must meet ships at ports will get there on time? Should the Post Office incur losses by running post offices in far-flung places that generate very little business? Should the Post Office plan to reduce employment, as part of a voluntary reduction of its services, at a time of serious unemployment? and so on (Nove, 1973, Chapter 1). Different financial objectives may conflict, such as when the SOE is required to export to earn foreign exchange at a time of domestic shortage or to lower the quality of products as a result of employing relatively less-skilled workers from economically backward regions.

These multiple goals may sometimes be complementary. In other cases they may be independent or contradictory. How can one reach trade-offs between balance of payments impact, net addition to real GNP, environmental pollution, employment, tax revenues, profitability, inflationary effect, power to a certain minister, innovation, long-term stabilization of prices for users of the product and sellers of the outputs and increased managerial positions for local managers of a certain race? Attaining various goals may benefit one group and injure another, make a contribution in the short run but be damaging in the long run or vice versa.

In reality, the basic *raison d'être* of SOEs is never solved; they remain both an instrument of government to achieve short-term policies, designed to cater to conflicting interest groups, and are expected to be an efficient producer of economic goods at the same time they are used as a vehicle for political patronage. Governments have strong political motives to keep objectives fuzzy and ill defined and to refuse any quantification of trade-offs. When priorities are not defined and goals are set out in a vague and generalized manner, the managers may enjoy wide latitude to define goals as they like, but this may also lead to conflicts between the management and various stakeholders.

But without clearly defined objectives it is extremely difficult to pin down what SOE managers are expected to achieve or to measure their performance. If different stakeholders expect an SOE to go in different directions that are conflicting and inconsistent, then whose objectives are actually pursued? How are conflicts among goals reconciled?

WHOSE OBJECTIVES SHOULD BE PURSUED?

For quite some time organizational theory followed the lead of economic theory, assuming that the goals of the organization are those of its owners. If the organization is viewed as one individual, acting rationally to achieve prescribed goals (Allison, 1971), there is no difficulty seeing whose goals the firm serves. When product and financial markets are competitive and efficient, organizations are small, environments are stable and certain and limitations of human cognition do not present any problem; the goal of maximizing profits for the owners is equal to that of maximizing their wealth. This simplistic view of the world has come under considerable attack, and the profit-maximization hypothesis has been shown to be an inaccurate description of behavior, at least for the large firms (Baumol, 1959; Marris, 1964; Galbraith, 1967).

First, since the seminal work of Berle and Means (1932), it was recognized that, at least in certain large organizations, ownership is diffused and control has moved to a self-perpetuating group of managers. If managers control the firm, whose goals do they pursue? Second, the firm was viewed by some as society's instrument, attempting to achieve desirable social goals, "profit being the secondary goal" (Sales, 1972, p. 234). Third, once uncertainty is recognized, the goal of profit maximization "becomes an empirically irrelevant tautology" (Papandreou, 1952, p. 208). Further, profit maximization assumes impossible demands on human cognition: managers possess only limited knowledge on future demand and competition, as well as incomplete, and often doubtful, information on actual and future organizational costs. Uncertainty and limited human cognition do not allow managers to maximize profitability, even if they would have wanted to.

Fourth, in real life, external influence may be exercised over a firm by many actors. As a result, any large firm has to attend to a multiplicity of goals. Papandreou (1952) assumed that, although goal formation is a function of the influence of many external actors, the chief executive officer ("the peak coordinator") is "performing the integrating function" by formulating "a consistent preference system" (p. 211). However, external powers may use different methods to influence an organization and to cause a change in its goal structure (Richards, 1978). These efforts include stressing social norms, imposing specific official constraints, mounting pressure campaigns, enjoying direct access to decisions and to the firm and having board of directors membership. Once it is recognized that the organization faces conflicting pressures for multiple goals, the questions of how organizational goals are produced, how to make sure that the goals pursued are legitimate, and the way organizations deal with conflicting pressures and reconcile conflicting goals become important. Drucker (1954, 1974) suggested that managers pursue surrogate goals such as market standing, innovation, productivity, physical and financial resources, profitability, manager performance and development, worker performance and attitude and public responsibility.

Simon (1964) suggested that the assumption of maximization should be dropped and that all goals should be treated as a set of constraints. Referring to managerial decision-making and to the process whereby goals to be pursued are determined, Simon concluded that it is basically a matter of analytic (or linguistic) convenience whether constraints are treated symmetrically or some of them are referred to asymmetrically as goals. Similarly, Eilon (1971) discussed constraints versus goals, concluding that "all constraints are, therefore, expressions of goals." (p. 295) Richards (1978) suggested that there are three ways to relate to organizational goals: a single goal under multiple constraints, multiple constraints or multiple goals (see also Bilky, 1973). One possibility is to assume minimum or threshold levels of goals in several areas, treating them as constraints, and managing the one remaining goal given the constraints. Another is that "all goals taken together define a space of acceptable solutions" (Cyert and March, 1963, p. 10). Goals are not given in advance but are a series of independent constraints arising from a continuous bargaining/learning process and power interplay among many actors in the dominant coalition (Cyert and March, 1963, p. 28).

Drawing the boundaries in an organizational coalition once and for all is impossible. Many of these constraints cannot be reconciled, but slack enables the organization to survive despite inconsistencies in its participants' goals. Goal incongruence is solved by sequentially attending to different goals, "first doing the one and then the other" (Cyert and March, 1963, p. 118).

Thompson and McEwen observed, "Goals appear to grow out of interaction, both within the organization and between the organization and its environment" (1958, pp. 28–29). The size of the coalition, claims Thompson, increases with the sources of uncertainty in the environment. He adds, "The more dynamic the technology and test environment, the more rapid the political processes in the organization and the more frequent the changes in organizational goals" (1967, pp. 128–129). Organizations may respond to external pressures in myriad ways, from outright resistance, through theoretical support, attempts to influence the environment toward goals sought by the organization, compliance and internal change, to advocacy of social or environmental cause (Richards, 1978). In all cases, organizations attempt "to avoid becoming subservient to elements of the . . . environment" (Thompson, 1967, p. 32).

To Georgiou (1973) organizations are purely political arenas. The organization is not endowed with personality. Rather, it is "an arbitrarily defined focus of interest" (p. 304) and a "marketplace in which incentives are exchanged" (p. 306). Crozier and Friedberg (1977) define the power of individuals as depending on the uncertainty to which they can put others, and argue that, just as actors play a game of power within the organization—restricting outputs or disrupting operations—organizations play a game of power with their environment.

Pfeffer and Salancik (1978, p. 133) view organizational adoption of external values as a process of legitimization. A corporation can only survive if it develops goals and operations perceived as legitimate by the large society. Following Parsons (1956) and Maurer (1971), Pfeffer and Salancik (1978) suggest that legitimacy is bound up with social norms and values. Since it is a conferred status, it is controlled by the environment. They suspected the organization should attend to the goals of a dominant segment of the environment to achieve legitimization. Still, according to them: "It is not clear by what process social collectives come to judge an activity or an organization as being legitimate or illegitimate" (p. 194).

Personal values and attitudes of top management are known to significantly influence the course followed by enterprises. Top management often confuses its *personal* goals and those of its enterprise. According to Jay:

> *The self-interest of individuals must be harnessed to the good of the state, or the corporation. It is easy enough at the lower levels. . . . But at higher management levels it can be very difficult as it becomes progressively easier for people to invert the process, to pursue their own interests while deftly harnessing the good of the corporation to them by subtle sophistries.* [1968, pp. 218–219]

These theoretical developments raise many pertinent questions: Are organizations instruments of some actors, be it owners, society or stakeholders, who impose goals on the organization, or are they a political arena in which groups and individuals vie for power, and goals are the outcome? Does it make sense to talk about organizational goals or should the organization be seen simply as a collection of its actors? If so, who are the actors and what is the game?

If organizational goals are simply the result of power play among the internal members of the organization, difficult questions are raised about the legitimacy of the large business corporation (and the SOE) today. A central debate in the last few decades has been on this very question: Who should control the giant business corporation, and in whose interests should it be run?

If the organization is run for the benefit of specific owners, legitimacy is achieved by a chain of authority from the owners to the managers. Legitimacy is less clear once the corporation is controlled by the managers. At the same time, the corporation has gained an enormous economic power over the prices, products and distribution of scarce resources. Corporations today also have power over the character and performance of other social institutions, over the technology used in society, over the use of natural resources and over government policymaking (Epstein, 1973, 1974). This powerful institution, according to many views, is too important to be controlled by a self-perpetuating management enjoying "power without property" (Madden, 1977, p. 65).

Hundreds of papers have been published with opposing and contradictory points of view regarding social responsibility. Many proposed more regulation of the affairs of the corporation while others believe that "there is one and only one social responsibility of business—to use its resources and engage in activities designed to increase its profits so long as it stays within the rules of the game" (Friedman, 1962, p. 133).

Whatever is the preferred point of view, two major problems remain to be explicitly confronted: How do all personal goals, values and aspirations translate into organizational actions, and how does the organization deal with multiple goals? If goals are independent variables, and the organization is an instrument, how can one use incentives, socialization or any other control devices to create a system reasonably approximating whatever results the proponents of different roles of the corporation (or the SOE) would like to see pursued; that is, assuming that individuals have personal goals and aspirations that are not equal to those expected from the organization, how can we assure that the organization will pursue the goals expected of it? These questions are relevant to any organization but crucial to understanding the behavior of SOEs.

SHAREHOLDERS WITHOUT SHARES

Private firms are owned by individuals who may buy or sell ownership rights at some price. Most large business organizations work toward achieving a number of goals that may conflict with one another and whose attainment may have contradictory ramifications. However, in private firms, long-term return on resources employed is perceived as the primary goal guiding their behavior. Further, competition forces firms either to remain profitable or go out of business. SOEs are ultimately owned by all citizens of a country and are financed from the general pool of funds mobilized by the government through taxes or other means. As such, SOEs are expected to achieve a multiplicity of goals and to satisfy a variety of expectations. Many of them are also not subject to the discipline of the market. However, the SOE "shareholders" do not hold any shares that can be traded in the market. Therefore, no market mechanism allows them to signal their views on the performance of the enterprise, and they cannot take part in a proxy fight for a takeover bid. Today, the citizens of a country do not have even the minimal influence enjoyed by shareholders of an investor-owned corporation.

Olson (1965, p. 165) concluded that "large or latent groups have no tendency voluntarily to act to further their common interest." No one member of a large group benefits by expending an effort to organize it, and apathy is the natural strategy for such large, dispersed groups. What happens, then, when power is widely dispersed among apathetic citizen-shareholders? One hypothesis is that the power in the firm moves to the managers. As Thompson (1967, p. 40) hypothesized, "when power is widely distributed, an *inner circle* emerges to conduct coalition business." In this sense, an SOE is not different from a widely held U.S. private firm, in which the shareholders are so unorganized, ill informed and dispersed that the top management controls even the selection of directors.

A more realistic hypothesis is that ministers behave like the owners of a closely held company, having strong influence. Ministers can use their power to hire and fire directors and managers to impose their point of view. But the state is not a person, not even a single organization. It acts through a variety of ministers, legislators and civil servants who are agents of the general public. These different agents invariably seek different objectives, and interministerial conflicts are normal. These conflicts affect the process of goal specifications of SOEs. One government official, concerned with foreign affairs, may see the interest of the state as reducing dependence on imported technology and therefore seek an increase in the SOE's R&D budget. The minister of labor may see the state's role as maximizing employment, and thus favor more labor-intensive procedures for the SOE. The finance minister may view him- or herself as *the* shareholder and want the firm to pay higher dividends. Yet another minister, whose agency buys the firm's output, may seek to reduce its prices.

These competing representatives cannot be considered the only principal of the firm whose interests are well defined. Consequently, no perfect contract can structure managers' incentives so that their interests will match the principal's goals. These goals are rarely, if ever, stated explicitly, and trade-offs among them are not agreed. Instead, different agents give the enterprise conflicting, parallel commands, which turns SOEs into political arenas, expected to achieve traditional economic goals in the marketplace, as well as all sorts of social goals such as helping the poor, increasing employment, redistributing income and developing laggard regions. SOEs are also expected to be a model employer, to function as a pacesetter for growth in some sectors; to regulate and maintain price stability in specific markets; to promote exports or to substitute imports; to invest in an anticyclical manner to stabilize fluctuations in the economy. They are also expected to achieve political goals such as securing preferential access to vital raw materials, borrowing abroad to help the balance of payments and freeing the home country from foreign political and economic domination by avoidance of perceived domination by foreign multinationals, development of new technologies or enhancement of the glory of the state but also to provide sinecures to friends of ministers and supporters of their party.

Goal conflicts among state agents are sometimes solved by formally assigning two or more of these objectives to an SOE. At other times conflicting commands are faced by SOEs because several external agents of society, right or wrong, view SOEs as legitimate tools for achieving overall national goals. Thus, the principal (the populace) is represented by a loose coalition of agents: the President of the country, sponsoring minister, the treasury, the civil servants, other ministers and the Parliament. Their decisions are influenced by all sorts of interest groups—consumers, labor unions and others—that claim at least some right to participate in the process of goal formulation. Even countries with a decentralized framework of control have a continuous flow of *ex ante* intervention in various decisions.

If the SOE is a joint venture owned in partnership with private interests, these problems become even more complicated. Eckel and Vining suggested that mixed enterprises reduce the monitoring costs required to raise the private return to the maximum level consistent with existing social return (in Stanbury and Thompson, 1982, p. 216). This hypothesis assumes that government cannot impose additional social or political requirements on mixed enterprises. The reality of the situation is much more complex (see Chapter 7).

Can the principal be assumed to be a collective term for a coalition of ministers, interest groups, civil servants, trade unions and Parliament members? Even such an assumption does not seem to hold since SOE managers try to influence the process of goal specification, often resist the imposition of certain goals and claim the right to participate in the formulation of goals.

LEGITIMACY OF GOALS AND STRATEGIES

There are four major explanations of why SOE managers can resist certain goals imposed on them by various government agencies. The first is the difference between managers' self-interest and that of other state agents. This is by now a well-theorized phenomenon in both large diffused ownership corporations and in SOEs. The notion that professional managers single-mindedly operate the firm to maximize profits was long ago rejected. It was replaced by behavioral or managerial theories developed by Baumol (1959), Simon (1959), Cyert and March (1963), Marris (1964) or Williamson (1970). This difference in self-interests is also at the root of the agent-principal problem and the view of the firm as a set of contracts. Alchian and Demsetz (1972) and Jensen and Meckling (1976) are two well-known examples of this view.

Second, SOE managers can afford to resist certain goals because it is difficult to measure managerial performance. In a private firm, managerial performance is scrutinized by the board of directors, which in turn is viewed as a market-induced institution. In an SOE, managerial performance cannot be gauged because there are many conflicting and ill-defined objectives. Moreover, in many countries, the control structure is not clearly defined, and the board cannot discipline or replace a manager, at least not without a lengthy negotiation with a sponsoring minister and other agents. Therefore, although a market for the services of managers does exist (Fama, 1980), and although managers may be dismissed, the policing of managers is much more difficult than in the private sector. Ambitious managers may be able to achieve more discretion than private-sector managers. Less-ambitious managers, faced with conflicting goals and restrictions, may simply choose to defer to governmental constraints. In extreme cases, managers may develop what Phatak (1969) called the "don't rock the boat" syndrome, whereby they avoid changes that may alienate any powerful groups.

Third, many managers consider themselves to be the trustees of the real interests of the state at least as much as the government employees or the politicians. Managers sometimes bring to their job the same set of values and ideologies that belongs to the rest of the business world. As they see it, the intervention of various government ministries to achieve noneconomic goals is an encroachment on their prerogatives as the trustees of the economic interests of the firm. SOE managers would probably argue that if the government, for social reasons, wants an enterprise to deviate from its economic mission, it should compensate the enterprise for the economic losses incurred. Such a point of view has been presented independently by public committees on SOEs in different countries. The Nora Commission in France (1967), the 1967 White Paper on nationalized industries of the United Kingdom, the Israeli Government Companies Law, the Statsförtag law in Sweden and the Privy Council report on Crown corporations in Canada are some well-known examples that are discussed later.

Managers of large corporations accept the legitimacy of the shareholders' interests although they may not always pursue those interests. SOE managers may question the legitimacy of demands from government, not only because they try to maximize their utility but also because they perceive the real goals of the amorphous principal—the state—to be different. Here lies the major difference between SOEs and large private corporations with diffused ownership. SOE management feels it has as legitimate a claim to goal specification as other agents.

Aberbach, Putnam and Rockman, (1981) see the clash between professional administrators and politicians as "the axial problem of modern society" (p. 238). Professional administrators are "endurance runners" seeking technically appropriate solutions, whereas politicians are "sprinters," defining problems in terms of political advantage (pp. 240-244). Politicians are guided by short-term political considerations. Coronel (1983) who was an executive of an SOE in Venezuela, sees the main weakness of a professional politician as "that of sacrificing the public interest to self-interest or to the interests of a small group or tribe" (p. 260). Managers see it as their legitimate right—even their duty to the real interest of the state—to attempt to avoid what they see as a wrong government order, get around it or procrastinate. In certain cases, managers may bring their case before the public by leaking information to the press or applying to the president or prime minister to repeal a sponsoring minister's decision. Professional managers must satisfy themselves that they have done the best they could. They are their main judges on excellence and honesty. However, managers who perceive goals imposed by government as illegitimate and against the public interest may also attempt to achieve their own brand of illegitimate goals, be it a kickback, a receipt of a bribe, or the selling of jobs. (For some examples in the case of PEMEX, the Mexican oil firm, see Coronel, 1983, p. 245.)

Fourth, managers of SOEs often enjoy their own brand of political power. They can buy the right to act in a certain way by dispensing largesse or by doing small favors to ministers and other leaders. The formal controllers may prove unable to control the SOEs, and ambitious managers may grasp power, working a divided and convoluted government unit to achieve the goals they see as important. Some SOE managers are as independent as nineteenth century robber barons, even leading the state into serious problems without involving key government officials. Some of them have direct contact with the head of the state, and they ignore the minister in charge of their enterprise. Others are even more independent. They see power and autonomy as legitimate, based on the ideology that SOEs should respond only to market forces (Feigenbaum, 1985).

An SOE should be viewed not only as a set of contracts among factors of production but also as a coalition, whose members include the managers, the board of directors, government ministers, civil servants, labor unions, members of Parliament and others. The principal of the property rights theory does not exist. Instead, there are different members of internal and external coalitions. The goal formulation process is the result of a contest for power among the various agents of the state. Therefore, one needs to analyze and conceptualize the various sources of power for managers of SOEs in the power game. This might include information, expertise, direct command over vast resources, an independent reputation for competence (which can be translated into a threat-of-resignation weapon) and countervailing political contacts. Managers of SOEs seem to spend more time than their private-sector counterparts in managing the environment, aiming at coopting the controlling agencies or assuring their allegiance. The outcome of this fight for power—i.e., the strategic choices made—can be predicted only in terms of contingency theory (see Chapter 11).

Briefly, the ability of SOE managers to choose the strategy they prefer and the objectives they see as most relevant is a joint function of personality, the legal and institutional environment in which they operate, the time devoted to control, and the expertise of those monitoring them. Experience shows that management can dictate goals; the bigger the firm is, the more independent it is of the government (by generating its own funds), the more technical the information needed to operate the enterprise and the more expertise concentrated in management at the firm level. In addition, management enjoys more discretion in its strategic choices when it operates internationally (by being at least partially outside the domain of government control), the more customers and product lines it has and the freer it is to choose its customers, product lines and suppliers. Finally, the degree of goal congruence is a crucial variable. The more legitimate the demands of government agencies in the eyes of the managers, the more they will abide by those demands (Aharoni, 1981c).

The complex relationships between the SOE and its environment cannot be solved by an optimal contract since the optimality characteristics are ill defined. Different agents of the state, including the managers of the enterprise and their controllers as well as other constituents, look for ways to reach some quasi-resolution of conflicts, often by ill defining the objectives of the enterprise or by official requirements to achieve multiple and conflicting goals: The way the coalition of forces is structured bars the definition of precise goals. However, even though conflicts cannot always be solved, they can be brought into the open to force decision-makers to confront several concrete choices. The agents can be forced to argue on choices to be made—and therefore implicitly on the goals—if an independent goal audit is introduced, embodied in a broader comprehensive audit, as an integral part of the institutional design. Note that since goals are formulated as a result of interaction in a coalition, different institutional designs may change membership in the coalition and the relative power of different coalition members.

In some cases, sponsoring ministers control the SOE as a part of a coalition agreement among the parties creating the government. They then see SOEs as their feudal property.

Thus, in Italy in 1979, the coalition agreement stipulated the nomination of a Christian Democrat to chair IRI, a Social Democrat as a chairman of EFIM, and a Socialist as a chairman of ENI. In many cases, goals expected from SOEs are changing with a change of government—or of a minister. If one believes SOEs should respond to changing social goals, these shifts are legitimate. Certainly, however, the need to start afresh a learning process with each new regime reduces the efficiency in which SOEs can operate. To quote Lord Beeching, the former chairman of British Rail "Management does not have the freedom to optimize its own performance in pursuit of a single objective, or even, in pursuit of a number of stable and compatible ones" (in Coronel, 1983, p. 248).

In other cases, the salience of the SOE to the country is so great that its goals are directly dictated by the head of state. In the case of CODELCO, a Chilean state-owned copper mines firm, e.g., the firm is the major foreign exchange earner, and final decisions on its strategy are reached by President Pinochet (*The Economist*, December 22, 1984). In most oil-producing countries, the board includes several ministers and major strategic decisions are made by the Cabinet or by the head of state. The state bureaucracy often perceives the national oil companies as "states within the state" (Grayson, 1981; Philip, 1982; Feigenbaum 1985; Noreng in Vernon and Aharoni, 1981).

In summary, SOEs' goals are independent variables that stem from the contest for power of individuals in a political arena, not dependent variables, being the instrument of one or more groups that impose goals on it. The organizational goals can be inferred from the action of the organization. Organizational goals are not simply declarations of intent, and an unimplemented strategy cannot be considered a strategy. Top management of organizations has very strong views about the goals it would like to pursue. These goals are not necessarily identical to the perception of managers of the goals that others with strong influence on the organization in the dominant environment would like pursued. The managers, therefore, face a dilemma: which goals are they going to pursue—those they believe are the right ones, or those they feel are demanded from them by environmental forces, or can they pursue different goals at different times? These conflicts are reconciled on the basis of the power of different actors, and the result is the goals actually pursued. The goals pursued by the organization are rarely the same as formally published goals or the manifestation of an official declaration. In an SOE published goals are often meant for public relations, and both managers and controllers understand that these are *not* the goals to be pursued.

PUBLISHED AND ACTUAL GOALS

Most SOEs have officially declared objectives. These formal objectives laid out in statutes, memoranda of incorporation, official published government documents or declarations are usually very broad, vague, not easily made operational and not necessarily a guide to actual action. Objectives pursued by SOEs may change over time, but formal objectives may be static.

A distinction is sometimes made between missions and objectives. The first are stable over a relatively long time. The latter are defined in more concrete and specific terms and refer to "a desire or needed results to be achieved in a specified time" (Steiner, 1969, p. 150). Formal missions of even private enterprises are often vaguely worded because "developing a suitable network of business aims is extremely complex" (Steiner, 1969, p. 141). It is difficult to encompass in a single sentence the fundamental aims of the organization. Vagueness prevails in SOEs because it is deliberately designed both to leave room for future interpretation and because certain goals to be pursued are never officially stated.

The kinds of vague missions laid out for SOEs in the statutes may be illustrated by several examples from different acts. The Nationalization Act of 1946 in the United Kingdom defines the mission of the NCB as follows:

> [M]aking the supply of coal available of such qualities and sizes, and in such quantities and at such prices, as may seem to them best calculated to further the public interest in all respects, including the avoidance of any undue or unreasonable preference or advantage. (In Ezra, 1974, p. 21)

Paragraph 30 of the White Paper on steel nationalization (1965) defines the mission of the British Steel Corporation thus:

> [T]o promote the efficient and economic supply of iron and steel products in such quantities and at such prices as may seem to them best calculated to meet the reasonable demands of customers and to further the public's interest.

On the difficulties of translating such statements into more detailed working objectives, a CEO of the NCB said the following:

> There are clearly great difficulties in constructing a clear and practical objective from such terms of reference. First and foremost, perhaps, is the difficulty of deciding what constitutes the public interest; and there is also the continuing question of the conflict between financial and other aims. [Ezra, 1973, p. 13]

The statutes also explicitly entrust the SOEs concerned with responsibility to decide what goals would best achieve a balance between divergent aims. "The Coal Industry Nationalization Act gave the Board no guidance how to run its affairs" (Kelf-Cohen, 1969, p. 43).

In some cases the Nationalization Act lays out also what the SOE shall not do. These statements, as the following illustrations show, are relatively unambiguous. For instance, in the case of the British Airports Authority, the act says that "BAA shall not provide any navigational services—except with the consent of the Minister" and that "it may not discontinue the use of any of its airports without the Minister's consent" (in Turner, 1976). In the case of British Airways, "The Civil Aviation Act, 1971, establishes the general functions and powers of the Board *without, however, defining its purpose.* The Act specifies certain limitations of activities—it says, for example, that we may not manufacture airframes and aero-engines" (Wheatcroft, 1973/74, p. 26).

The official missions may also be multiple and contradictory. State marketing boards, i.e., have "the contradictory objectives of providing farmers with reasonable prices for agricultural produce, presenting consumers with *best* prices, keeping a certain number of people on the payroll and living within a budgetary provision" (Commonwealth Secretariat, 1978b, p. 17; see also World Bank, 1983). They are also expected to shield consumers from scarcities and high fixed prices while simultaneously protecting farmers' income, insulating consumers from fluctuations in world prices and raising fiscal revenues.

The Telephone Organization of Thailand has the statutory objectives of "carrying out and promoting telephone activities for the benefit of the state and the public and carrying out the business in connection with telephone activities and other business incidental, pertaining or beneficial to telephone activities." The mission does not define pricing or quality. The 1980 annual report of the Telephone Organization of Thailand states the following principles:

1.   To improve and promote the telephone system with an emphasis on quality, rendering quick, efficient and reliable service to the public;
2.   To expand plants and increase quantity in order to meet the demands of the public;

3. To try to minimize hindrances and inconveniences in telephone usage;
4. To charge reasonable fees for services rendered. [p. 10]

These stated missions may or may not be a guide to action. Often, the missions as stated in the memorandum of incorporation are intended to avoid future problems of *ultra vires* and are therefore worded to include many possibilities. Thus, Thai Air, in its annual report for 1980/1981, lists thirteen objectives of the airline, including, among others:

> To set up aircraft manufacturing and maintenance plants and with components, along with all tools and equipment.

> To undertake matters related to airports, flying stations, aircraft fuelling and lubrication, runways, hangars, components and service stations, and all other undertakings related to aviation.

> To enter into limited partnership with the limited partnerships, or as shareholders in any companies, when it is obvious that the objectives of the limited partnerships or firms are in accordance or similar with the company's objectives.

> To export or import goods for commercial purpose.

> To carry out any undertakings which promote the company's businesses.

> To lend money, and/or giving the limited companies engaged in aeronautical businesses in which the company holds shares to borrow money from the company, including the company's staff who can borrow money as welfare.

> To undertake business related to hotels, restaurants and other concerned businesses which promote the company's businesses. [p. 46]

Further, missions of SOEs may change over time, and the changes are only rarely acknowledged. When IRI was established in Italy in 1933, it was regarded as a temporary body whose "function was to reorganize its holdings in certain sectors with a view to selling them back to private enterprise" (Posner and Woolf, 1967, p. 23). A year or two later it was evident that IRI had come to stay, and in 1936, IRI was "granted a permanent status as the administrator of state owned securities" (Martinelli, in Vernon and Aharoni, 1981, p. 87). The final change came only in 1956 (Holland, 1972). Even in this case, there were many additional changes in the firm's missions.

It was also used "to help finance political parties and campaigns" (Grassini in Vernon and Aharoni, 1981, p. 75). In 1974, a law was passed prohibiting enterprises holding 20 percent or more state shares from contributing to political parties. However, "rumours suggest that indirect financing continue[s] despite the 1974 ruling" (*Ibid*, p. 25). (See Chapter 3 for details.)

The corporate shell of an SOE has been used in different times to achieve different objectives. As one example from Germany, Industrieverwal-tungsgesellschaft was established in 1916 to manage the Kaiser's state-owned industries. This firm later took over the Nazi arms industry, and today it manages office buildings.

In other cases, there is no formal change in the objectives, although in practice, the emphasis on various objectives may change or a new interpretation may be given to an existing vague objective. These changes may follow shifts in the party in power, changes in the minister or in the CEO of the SOE or changing economic conditions. The original reason for the creation of the SOE is often forgotten. For example, an Israeli SOE was created to construct shopping centers in development regions. Its management decided to tap funds for this objective by constructing and selling apartment buildings in the cities. Today it is one of the largest construction firms in the country. Formal objectives may also be declared but are understood not to be taken into account. Riggs (1964) argues that elections, legislatures and governments in Asia, Africa and Latin America were patterned after forms observed in Europe and North America, but the Third World varieties perform differently, often with masked dictatorship or corruption behind the facades of Western democracy. What Riggs termed "formalism" is often true for SOEs. Formal objectives are not followed, and there are strong political motives for keeping them fuzzy. In countries such as the United Kingdom or Australia, there is a general respect for the law, orderly procedures and professional norms. Formal objectives in these countries may be more of a concern than in other countries, where the law is not necessarily a guide for action.

FORMAL, ESPOUSED AND PURSUED OBJECTIVES

It is clear from this discussion that formal objectives are different from those espoused and pursued. Considering the NCB once again, its vaguely worded formal objective was seen by its CEO in the following way:

> [N]otwithstanding the difficulty of drawing up long-term objectives in these circumstances [i.e., given only vaguely worded statutory aims], this task has to be done. So far as the NCB is concerned, we plan our strategies on the basis of making the largest possible contribution to the long-term energy needs of the country at an economic cost. [Ezra, 1973, p. 13]

This statement could be considered to constitute the espoused objective (Argyris and Schön, 1978). The objective(s) actually pursued by the NCB, however, may have been different and can be determined by studying the directions taken by the organization.

Thus, the espoused objectives of U.K. SOEs have been stated to be that of autonomous commercial operations. In practice, the U.K. government has behaved differently. Again and again it has intervened to achieve social or political objectives. Its decisions seem to be based on a theory that commercial orientation is not intended, that financial viability is sometimes (but not always) a constraint to be satisfied while one or more social objectives are maximized. SOEs were forced to freeze prices to combat inflation. Government has also seen nationalization as a politically popular way to fight unemployment and has resuscitated firms by massive infusions of state funds.

Electricity is one example. The Herbert Commission (1956) forcefully said the electricity industry "should have one duty and one duty alone: to supply electricity to those who will meet the costs of it and do so at the lowest possible expenditure of resources consistent with the maintenance of employment standards at the level of the best private firms" (para. 507). In fact, the electricity firm subsidizes British Coal: some 75 percent of NCB's output is taken by the CEGB (two-thirds) and British Steel (roughly one-third). "The average pithead cost of British Coal is more than double the extraction cost of strip-mined coal in the United States and Australia" (Hindley in Roll, 1982, p. 189). Clearly, CEGB is being used to subsidize coal. Moreover, "the domestic consumer has been receiving his electricity on favourable terms as compared with the industrial consumer" (Kelf–Cohen, 1969, p. 114).

Conflicts on objectives between SOE managers and their controllers are widespread. These cases are rarely publicized, and most of the conflicts are debated and solved in private. Some cases, however, are documented.

The history of the NEB, e.g., illustrates the ambiguous political contexts in which objectives of SOEs are pursued and is therefore outlined in some detail. The conventional form of nationalization in the United Kingdom was the creation of an SOE by act of Parliament. These SOEs were to be autonomous and managed by an independent board of directors. As it turned out, these firms were less autonomous than the law called for. The disillusionment with this conventional form led to a search for new methods. The idea of a state holding company attracted support from all sides of the political spectrum, albeit for different reasons. Socialists became interested in the Italian experience with such organizations, which appeared to be the political means to achieve socialist transformation without being hindered by the necessity of getting parliamentary approval. A Fabian pamphlet (Posner and Pryke, 1966) studied the idea, and later Holland (1972) published a book on the Italian state holding system. Holland saw this system as providing "governments with a concrete example of what otherwise appeared difficult or impossible to achieve—state enterprises as efficient and dynamic as leading private enterprise groups, yet still directly serving the ends of government economic policy and the interests of society as a whole" (p. 1). Holland and Pryke played at that time a key role in the Labour party's industrial policy thinking (Hatfield, 1978, pp. 99-106). For the Liberals, the IRI formula was seen as allowing SOEs to operate according to commercial considerations, more so than public corporations. Deaglio (1966) published for the Liberal Institute of Economic Affairs a favorable account of the Italian state holding system. In 1970 the Swedish government followed the Italian example, establishing Statsförtag, and Austria moved in the same direction, transferring in 1970, its vast state-held enterprise under the umbrella of ÖIAG. In the same year, the French IDI came into being.

The British followed, when the 1975 Industry Act created the NEB in "an attempt to combine the advantages of public-sector financial resources and the private sector's entrepreneurial approach to decision making" (Committee on Public Accounts, 1977–1978, p. 150). The NEB, according to the 1974 White Paper leading to its creation, was to operate directly to create employment. Following its creation, the guidelines for its operations were issued by Eric Varley, the industry secretary, after extensive consultations with the private sector interests. These guidelines included some restrictions on strategy. For example, NEB was to dispose of any interest in a newspaper or magazine that it acquired (or at least not to influence editorial functions). The 1975 act required the NEB to promote industrial democracy in its subsidiaries, but these requirements had little effect in practice. In contrast to the original intention of commercial considerations, the guidelines "required the NEB to make appropriate arrangements with their subsidiaries, to the satisfaction of the Government, to ensure that management in these undertakings is playing its part in furthering government policies in this field" (1976, Paragraph 29).

While Labour's left wingers hoped the NEB would spearhead the U.K. economy to socialism (Coates, 1980), Harold Wilson, then prime minister, noted: "Contrary to the revolutionary hopes which surrounded the NEB when it was conceived in Opposition days, Eric Varley's department . . . ensured that it would not operate like an industrial rogue elephant. It had to operate within the existing rules governing the provision of industrial finance" (Wilson, 1979, pp. 141–142). Lord Ryder, the first full-time chairman who was drawn from the private sector, stressed that "Although funded from public sources, the NEB has to exercise a commercial judgement in the same way as any other business" (NEB Annual Report, 1976, p. 3). Ryder's successor, Sir Leslie Murphy, announced that "the strong commercial flavour which Lord Ryder imparted to the NEB will continue (NEB Annual Report, 1977, p. 4), and its former planning director has stated, "The NEB is not playing and could not play an overwhelming role in determining the development of British industry. The claims that have never been made for it have never been made by it. The idea that the NEB could or even should regenerate British industry is absurd and it has never accepted the extension of public ownership as an end in itself" (Marks, 1980, p. 12). Hatfield (1978) reports "there was a need to build the holding company up to such an extent that the Conservatives would find it impossible to unscramble it if they were returned in the next general election but one" (p. 100). He quotes Pryke "if the holding company is already making a contribution to solving the regional problems, its liquidation will be politically unpopular" (p. 100).

Each one of the statements gives different weight to commercial considerations, employment goals, development of industry objectives or the possible conflicts with private firms. The NEB did face conflicts with both government and private-sector interests; namely, its decision to acquire Fairey Aviation defeated a bid from a private firm and raised a storm of opposition in the city, and the closure of one of the subsidiaries in one area of high unemployment was not exactly in fulfillment of government's desires.

The actual financial performance of the NEB was not as good as expected. It was required to achieve a return on capital employed at historic cost of 15.2 percent before interest and taxes. Excluding British Leyland and Rolls Royce, its return on capital employed was 11.8 percent in 1976, 11.4 percent in 1977, 11.3 percent in 1978 and 4.8 percent in 1979. It was soon required to acquire from government some lame ducks, nationalized to avoid their collapse. These were British Leyland, Rolls Royce, Alfred Herbert and Cambridge Instruments. The preoccupation with these firms crippled NEB's finances. The transfer of these companies, however, was perceived at the time as making it harder for an incoming Conservative government to dismantle NEB and the board "avoided public controversies [and attempted not to] indulge in a political free-for-all" (Marks, 1980, p. 6).

When the Conservatives did come into power in 1979, they changed NEB's objectives. For example, the 1975 act made the NEB responsible for "extending public ownership into profitable areas of manufacturing industry." The 1980 act replaced that goal with one of "prompting the private ownership of interests in industrial undertakings by the disposal of securities and other property held by the board, and any of its subsidiaries." In addition, British Leyland and Rolls Royce were transferred to the industry department. Sir Leslie Murphy, NEB chairman, publicly criticized Rolls Royce's financial controls. Sir Kenneth Keith of Rolls Royce disagreed. Sir Keith Joseph, the industry secretary, decided to move Rolls Royce to the direct control of the industry department. The entire NEB board resigned in protest, and the resignation was accepted. In December 1980, following the resignation of the new chairman, Sir Arthur Knight, former chairman of Courtaulds, Sir Frederick Wood became chairman. He was also chairman of the National Research and Development Corporation and immediately took steps to merge the two corporations (for details, see Grant, 1982).

This short account of NEB's history shows how objectives may change not only with changing governments but also with different chairmen. It also shows that government ministers feel they cannot refrain from intervention. While it is understandable that ministers were very involved in the affairs of firms as large as British Leyland and Rolls Royce, they were also involved in lesser affairs. As one example, INMOS, one of NEB's subsidiaries, created a research center and production unit in Colorado Springs. It took Mrs. Thatcher's government six months to provide £25 million for the continuation of the project in July 1980. At the same time, INMOS agreed to construct its first factory in South Wales, as the government demanded, instead of Bristol, its preferred location. Thus, NEB's objectives were often dictated by what was politically tolerable, not by commercial considerations.

Certainly, published or even espoused objectives were not necessarily the objectives pursued. SOEs are vulnerable to all sorts of external forces, and their external boundaries are "more permeable than those of private firms, leading any number of factions of society to assume they have a claim on its resources" (Levy, 1985, p. 7). Again, the goals pursued are a result of a power play among different actors. These goals may or may not be those of efficient use of resources. As Green noted:

> If, for example, a public works program is primarily designed to maximize bribes to ministers and civil servants, no analysis which does not take account of the fact will be fully satisfactory. Take account of need not, of course, mean approve of. However, criticism of such a system as not minimizing costs or maximizing useful road–bridges–ferries is simply evading the primary problem. [1977, p. 94]

The goals SOEs pursue are as diverse as the interests of their various stakeholders and depend on the dominance of various groups. Note also that the goals pursued are a result of an interaction between the organization and its relevant environment. Environmental influences are important in the goal-setting mechanisms and in achieving legitimization. Before exploring this point of view, some alternatives should be considered.

NATIONAL OBJECTIVES, NATIONAL PLANNING AND SOEs

SOEs are often said to be created to "pursue whatever national objectives are defined by Parliament" (Canada Privy Council Office, 1977, p. 22). A draft legislature contained in the Canadian Privy Council Report sees SOEs as instruments. It states:

> It is hereby declared that every Crown corporation is constituted an instrument for advancing the national interests of Canada and that in order to best advance those national interests it is the duty of the directors of every Crown corporation when managing the Crown corporation to take into consideration the national interests of Canada as well as the interests of the Crown corporation and, within the scope of their powers and the powers of the Crown corporations, to pursue those corporate policies that best advance such national interests. (Ibid, p. 50)

The problem, again, is how to define national objectives, who defines them and how they can be translated into operational terms. One theoretical possibility is that national objectives are defined for each SOE by Parliament in the enabling act. There are several problems with this approach. First, not all SOEs are created by Parliament. Second, the enabling act cannot forecast all possible future changes. Third, Parliament may or may not have the required power or will to enforce its point of view. Robson (1962, pp. 181–183) observes that formal discussions or debates in Parliament on SOEs have seldom been of a strategic nature. Finally, not all countries have a democratic parliamentary regime.

Another possibility to cut through the confusion and conflicts that typify democratic governments' efforts to articulate national objectives is by using the national plan. National planning in one form or another is widespread in both developed and developing countries today, the major exception being the United States. Theoretically, the national plan can give directives to SOEs or at least the SOEs' objectives will be strongly influenced by the plans. After all, while governments can say "no" to the private sector only through regulatory mechanisms or offer incentives and apply pressure on them to act in desired ways, they can (at least in theory) force SOEs to act positively toward desired goals. Therefore, while national plans may be viewed by private firms merely as one external source of information for drawing up their strategic plans (except, perhaps, in the case of private firms heavily dependent on government for survival and growth), in the case of SOEs national plans may lay out the boundaries of an SOE's long-range plan. In some countries, national plans spell out what the SOEs should be doing over the next 5- or 10-year period, although they sometimes say only what an SOE should not do.

National plans, however, are usually not very flexible (probably updated only once every few years) because of the elaborate exercise involved in preparing them and not very comprehensive (covering mainly production targets for future years, major investment proposals of SOEs, etc.). Moreover, in an open economy, severe constraints are placed on the ability of planners to specify targets. Strategic plans of SOEs, conversely, would have to be more flexible, comprehensive and detailed, and their objectives might change with time.

National plans have been used as targets mainly for projects vital to the economy. If an SOE is a monopoly in a major strategically important industry, a national plan can be used to target its operations.

National plans do not explore in detail the country's production activities. Governments often lack the expertise to direct the SOEs and sometimes refrain from giving such guidance for political reasons. The national plans are usually written after a great deal of consultation and are less a directive of government than a consensus of the major political factions of the country. National plans are often prepared with the active help of the SOE concerned that possesses much of the information and expertise required. Very often the experts on industries such as nuclear power, oil, electricity or airlines are employees of the SOE, and the government delegates to them the power of deciding on national objectives. In Italy, according to Prodi, the SOEs "have developed a relationship with the Ministry of Public Holdings that might be called 'patronage without political purpose'" (in Vernon, 1974, p. 61). They "have played the role of ghost writer to the Ministry" (p. 62).

In Austria, according to Shonfield, "the managers of the [SOEs] run things pretty much their own way so long as they make sure to respond demonstratively every now and then to the distant bark of the parliamentary watch-dog tethered to his post" (1965, p. 195). In the developing countries, the bureaucracy and the ministers do not possess the necessary knowledge to understand the technical aspects of SOEs' operation and cannot direct these enterprises. The same problems beset developed countries, too.

A national plan is a technique. It cannot solve the problems of conflicting multiple objectives because it is also based on compromise and negotiations among contending centers of power.

One way for the SOE and the government to formulate goals explicitly is by working out a strategy through an interaction between SOE management and civil servants. Tucker (1974) a senior civil servant in the British government suggests that, by discussing the underlying assumptions of the plan before it is completed and presented, government "may have a useful input to feed into the total picture" (p. 66). In the corporate plan itself, government checks whether the objectives "are consistent with the government's general policy for that sector of industry . . . what options have been examined for achieving these objectives. Are the options selected by the industry . . . likely to carry out an economic penalty for the nation as a whole . . . Will some adjustment of timing or pattern remove this disadvantage without significant adverse effects for the industry" (p. 65). Above all, where will the plan "take the industry, physically and financially"? (p. 66).

Strategic planners generally believe that the process of deliberation on the plan results in a better understanding between the SOE and the government. They also recognize, however, that the SOE has more power because of its control of the information. Chambers (1984) notes that planning could be interpreted as forecasts or promises. The first "brings together a range of views about the future, exposes any disagreements or inconsistency of assumption" (p. 36). The second "consists of building up a structure of interlocking commitments." (p. 36) He argues that "corporate planning is actually perceived as a relatively banal activity" (p. 48). Corporate planning is seen as a process of informing, making forecasts and increasing the level of understanding. Rees (1984) notes that control constraints "are the outcome of a process of discussion and negotiation" (p. 109). The strategic plan is prepared by the SOE with only one assumed future state of the world. The plan undergoes an appraisal process in which its internal consistency and plausibility are discussed. The SOE seeks to manipulate the process by choosing information to be presented. The government is "a very passive participant in the process" (p. 123).

Tucker (1974) feels that government lacks information to meaningfully criticize or evaluate many technical or economic aspects of plans proposed by some SOEs. He also notes that civil servants lack in-depth familiarity with the industry and do not have the competence to evaluate several aspects of the plans drawn up by SOEs. Further, SOEs are generally committed to their corporate plans by the time they reach government for comments. There is a fundamental difference in the time perspectives of planning between SOE managers and the government. (Ministers hold office usually for only 2 or 3 years.) Finally, fundamental differences in values between SOE managers and civil servants make the interaction on strategic matters more difficult. Disagreement is seldom open and is "rarely resolved in rational discussion of priorities" (NEDO, 1976, p. 24).

OTHER PROPOSED SOLUTIONS FOR MULTIPLE OBJECTIVES

It is widely recognized that the reality in SOEs is a far cry from the Morrison principles: governments do not give the SOEs clear directions, refuse to spell out objectives or to quantify its trade-offs and intervene in operational details. One consequence of this state of affairs is the impossibility of pinning down managers and monitoring the performance of the SOE. The pursuit of non-economic goals is often used as an excuse for poor performance. This problem is fully recognized and is discussed in the voluminous literature as well as by many government-appointed public committees in developed and developing countries. The World Bank, too, called for the design of a "system that holds management accountable for results while giving it the power to achieve them" (World Bank, 1983, p. 78).

One solution to the problem is to assume that SOEs should carry out only commercial objectives on which they will be judged. The Nora Committee, which investigated French SOEs in 1966, observed:

The essential vocation of public enterprises is therefore to satisfy their market at the lowest cost for them and for the collectivity (1967, p. 95).

Ideas of this sort have been put forward in different countries. In Canada several SOEs were mandated to operate on a commercial basis. The legal status of Air Canada, e.g., was changed by the Air Canada Act of 1977. The act officially changed the airline's mission from the provision of essential public service at break-even to a profit-seeking, commercially oriented enterprise. Sweden created a holding company whose goal was formulated "under a profitability requirement, to attain the greatest possible expansion." The same trend can be seen in other countries, too. In some of them government credits are given to SOEs that are required to transfer subsidies to specific groups. Food-marketing SOEs such as the Food Corporation of India or CONASUPO of Mexico receive credit to offset the inevitable losses due to buying high (to subsidize farmers) and selling low (to subsidize consumers). Nicaragua's agricultural SOEs are implementing an accounting and statistical control system (Sistema Uniforme de Control Administrativo) that segregates social activities (such as housing and health care) from productive operations (Austin, 1983).

One solution, therefore, is to make the SOEs responsible only for the achievement of narrow economic goals, like profits, and to forbid by law any type of intervention of government ministers or civil services, requesting any other behavior. Under such a system, the enterprise's management receives full autonomy, its board of directors is recruited for its business abilities and no one else receives any information or is allowed to intervene in the way the enterprise is being managed. If the enterprise is loss-ridden, it is left to go bankrupt. Under this kind of institutional arrangement, the SOE may not achieve certain national goals like increased employment, and there is no guarantee that it will be successful even in the narrow economic sense. However, its management is motivated to achieve only economic goals, and its workers know that the government will not be forthcoming with additional funds if the enterprise employs too many persons or pays too high salaries. Therefore, the probability of economic success is high. Of course, government ministers may attempt to press management to achieve noneconomic goals, and Parliament members may ask special favors, but if the legal arrangement requires only profit seeking, such interventions may be rejected by the managers. A system may even be designed in which the government minister will not have the power to fire a director without the consent of the majority of the board members, and the management will be recruited, judged and sacked if necessary by the board.

If the objectives of SOEs are only commercial, their performance can be monitored. However, SOEs are, after all, different from private enterprise. For SOEs to function as tools to achieve certain national or social goals, they must be compensated in full for the costs of such deviations from pure economic behavior. The amount of compensation is subject to negotiations, and management does not have to pursue the noneconomic goal unless it is fully compensated. To use an example borrowed from the Nora Commission report in France (1967), railroad management should determine the costs of abnormally low fares or of the continuation of lines that run at deficits for social and regional reasons. Then, the relevant ministries concerned with social problems or regional development should show that such objectives cannot be realized more effectively by other means. As in any case of cost–benefit analysis, various possible trade-offs must be compared. If it is then decided that railroad subsidy is the best method, it should be used. However, the cost of the constraint must be incorporated into the budget of the ministry responsible for that activity (Nora Commission, 1967).

The suggested scheme has several theoretical advantages: Economic and social costs of activities will be properly recorded, these activities will be available for public scrutiny, the national interest will be decided by those entrusted by the public to do so and the management of the SOE will know which criteria are used to judge it in its operations. However, there is a multitude of practical problems in following the compensation approach, reimbursing firms for activities undertaken in the national interest. The following lists some of these problems:

1. Identifying which activity is of noneconomic nature is difficult. Every large organization cross-subsidizes some activities because it is felt that these activities are necessary for the profitability of the organization. Thus, an airline may decide it is worthwhile to lose on certain short-haul lines because they serve as feeders of passengers for long flights. If a subsidy is offered, an airline may always claim that the short lines are losing in the national interest of serving one community or another. The distinction in this and many other cases is not easy to make.

2. It is almost impossible to allocate costs in a way that compensates for the marginal costs of the noneconomic activities.

3. Some noneconomic activities are shared by all enterprises as a burden imposed by government. An example is the Canadian language legislation or an antipollution legislation. Should these activities be compensated for?

4. Compensation schemes entail another danger: since it is not easy to calculate the costs of achieving noneconomic goals, management may develop skills of extracting higher compensation rather than devote its energy to the pursuit of efficiency.

If SOEs are to function as instruments of overall national development, two provisions can be added: the right of ministers to issue written directives to SOEs to adopt certain strategies or policies in the broader national interest, usually with compensation, and the annual corporate planning exercise in which SOEs interact closely with state authorities on matters of objectives and strategies. In practice, ministers do not like to commit themselves to written directives. Instead, they prefer informal means to get SOEs to do what they want without either taking the responsibility for issuing written instructions or compensating the enterprises for losses they may incur in the process of following the informal directives (e.g., NEDO, 1976, pp. 35–36). Ministers also use various other means of influence. In the case of Air Canada, in late 1978, "the government, evidently without consulting Air Canada's board, named Bryce Mackasey—a long-time Liberal politician who had just been defeated at the polls—Chairman of the airline" (Gordon, 1981, p. 30). Mackasey advocated that the aircraft selection process—the single most important decision determining the efficiency and profitability of an airline—"would be submitted to a group in Ottawa that would either approve or reject it, depending on how much business the purchase would bring to Canadian aircraft plants" (pp. 80–81).

In Sweden also directors and top managers were appointed partly on a political basis rather than on purely professional competence. Statsförtag was forced to take over several companies in deep financial trouble, mainly in textiles and steel. (The Swedish government also bailed out its private shipbuilding industry by taking into state ownership all but one of the large Swedish shipyards. These firms were not made part of Statsförtag. Instead, a separate firm, Svenska Varv, was created for this purpose.) Statsförtag used the profits of firms like LKAB to finance its newly acquired loss-ridden firms but had also to increase its external borrowing. According to the firm's projections, its equity would have been reduced to such an extent that it would be bankrupt in 1983 or 1984 because of the financial needs of the subsidiaries and the servicing of the external debt. In 1982 the group was broken into several industry-specific holding companies. Experience shows, however, that commercialization proposals are not very realistic. Politicians do not cease to be politicians, and the ability to influence the SOEs is too important for them. They can circumvent law by nominating managers whom they can influence without giving them an official directive. Even in a democracy like the United Kingdom, according to Hanson (1963), "Lack of ease about the prevalent or 'old boy' relationship between Minister and Board and about the consequent difficulty of assigning clear responsibility for policy decisions has been frequently expressed ever since the early days of post-war nationalization" (p. 281). Regarding the negotiations of the annual corporate planning exercise, the major problem here is the differences in time horizon between government and SOEs and the differences of opinion about the salience of certain goals. Further, as already noted, SOE managers do not always agree that governmental directives are made for the public interest. They therefore do not comply that easily or willingly with government directives that do not fit well with their own strategies. Musolf says:

> Commentators on mixed economies sometimes overstate the authority of the government in directing public enterprise to follow a national plan . . . Hopes may be falsely raised by the assertion that "if the commodity is to be produced by a public enterprise, or by a public-private partnership, the targets tell officials what they are supposed to do. . . ." As Mason has emphasized, "even in countries which have extensive nationalized industries, these are usually under the control of managements that enjoy most of the freedom of action of private enterprises. [1972, p. 15]

Musolf argues that there is evidence that, in some cases, SOEs may be less responsive to governmental wishes than giant private enterprises (1972, p. 17). Most of the conflicts about goals and strategy are not published, but in certain instances the conflict has been fierce enough to reach the press. An example of an SOE resisting a policy directive from the government (on the grounds that its public ownership responsibilities endanger its competitiveness objectives) is Air France's refusal to buy French-made Caravelles in preference to Boeing aircraft. Air France was eventually allowed to lease the Boeings until it could receive airbuses. Air New Zealand, in contrast, was forced to buy Rolls Royce engines instead of the General Electric engines it preferred for its new fleet.

Another example is the dissenting point of view expressed by the NCB (U.K.) in its annual report (1967–1968) to the policy conclusions reached by the government in its White Paper on fuel policy (Cmnd. 3438) (see Tivey, 1973). Other examples are the CDC's refusal to help Massey Ferguson; BOAC's refusal to purchase the Concorde or the conflicts in the NEB enumerated earlier. In some cases, the CEO resigned, as did Egidio Egidi, who was scheduled to be the president of ENI in 1980, because he disagreed with a government-backed plan for ENI to divest some of its chemical holdings or Sir William Barlow, chairman of the British Post Office, who resigned in the same year over a disagreement on government-imposed external financial limits.

Other solutions sought were to install a different organ of control, to make sure that the ministries would develop the strategy and allow the SOEs autonomy. In the United Kingdom, the Select Committee of Nationalised Industries proposed the establishment of a ministry of state shareholdings. The NEDO report suggested a buffer of a different sort: a policy council. NEDO proposed a German-type two-tier board. The policy council would be composed of representatives of unions, government and management and would be in charge of defining strategy. Both proposals were rejected by the U.K. government.

Another method to tackle the problem of goals was proposed by the Nora Committee in France. According to this idea, the government should negotiate an explicit and detailed contract between each SOE and the administration. The contract was to become an agreement on goals, targets and measures of performance. Several such contracts were signed between 1971 and 1973 (for a detailed summary see Anastassopoulos, 1980, pp. 131–163). A second round of contracts was attempted in 1978 to 1979 and a third round of "plan contracts" was negotiated since 1982. The Senegalese government also attempted a similar arrangement, negotiating contract plans with several SOEs since 1980.

The experience in using the contract plan has been mixed in the first two French contracts because the provisions for revisions were found inadequate to cope with the unexpected 1973 oil shock and subsequent stagflation.

Later attempts to negotiate contracts were initially opposed by the bureau-cracy, which disliked the degree of pricing freedom given the SOEs by the contracts. Still, the contracts forced both SOE managers and controllers to articulate medium-term goals, to compare more systematically the cost of social services, for which compensation was negotiated by the French railways and by the Senegalese bus company, and political goals (Air France negoti-ated compensation for having to operate the Caravelle IIIs and split operations between the two Paris airports). In some cases, the negotiations led to cuts in social costs in Senegal, resulting in a cutback of air services to certain remote areas. The negotiations and the reviews of the contracts also forced the parties to discuss objectives and strategy and make them transparent. Still, the con-tracts were not a panacea to the problem and did not help when conditions changed drastically. The process of the negotiations is also lengthy and time consuming, and contracts were agreed only with a few large SOEs (see also Chapter 8).

In sum, the problem of multiple objectives under conditions of uncer-tainty and change has not been fully solved. Clearly, the goals pursued by SOEs are not identical to the published goals. It is also usually agreed that SOEs' managers sometimes attempt to define objectives on their own, break-ing loose from government. Martinelli (in Vernon and Aharoni, 1981) ob-served that SOEs can achieve goals of industrial development if a broad po-litical consensus exists and less so when the national political process becomes fragmented, again illustrating the importance of the environment.

Actually, goals pursued are a result of a process of interaction among various actors. Many SOEs operate in relatively stabler economic environ-ments than private firms (because of their monopoly position or control over the market or government protection and backing), but their political and social environments are more dynamic than those of private firms. They are subject to greater external influence in objective-setting, the process is con-siderably more political and the objectives are more fluid and unstable than in private enterprises. Goals pursued are partially determined by the percep-tion of the environment.

ENVIRONMENTAL INFLUENCE ON GOALS

The crucial need for a good organization–environment fit is recognized today by social scientists studying a whole gamut of organizations and coming from different disciplines such as industrial economics, business history, decision theory, organizational behavior, business and society, as well as political sci-ence. In some studies, policymakers are portrayed as unable to understand their environments; therefore, they prefer to introduce marginal changes and rely on environmental feedback to correct mistakes. In their descriptions of the interrelationships between organizational behavior and environments, some posit that managers can and should adapt to environmental changes and may even be able to shape them (Pfeffer and Salancik, 1978). Others view the manager as a helpless pawn and the organization's survival as a combination of luck and random error (Aldrich, 1979). All agree that whether the process involves organizational submission to environmental constraints and forces or positive organizational proaction to change environments or both, the objective is compatibility between the organization and its environment. To assure its survival, an organization must continuously scan the subenvironments on which it is dependent to ensure a continuation of its fit (Aguilar, 1967).

Certain characteristics of organizations affect the degree of freedom management has to change its environment as opposed to adapting to it (Child, 1972). Thus, a very small business firm may not be as able to change the environment as a large one, but it may find it easier to select a new environment than a large organization would. More relevant to us, a private business firm is less constrained by laws and regulations concerning its missions than a government bureau, and an SOE falls between these extremes. Often, SOEs are less able to change their environment or to move to another environment than privately owned firms. The environment of SOEs is different at least in the following:

Expectations of labor, consumers, customers, suppliers and the public;
Sources and structure of funds;
Cabinet as a final arbiter in all matters of policy;
The way foreign aid donors influence policies;
Effect of view, opinions and recommendations of Parliament;
Operation under a blaze of publicity resulting, in many cases, in a business problem becoming a political issue.

Organizations can function effectively only when a balance is achieved between the contributions and inducements of different participants (Barnard, 1938). Contributions depend not only on financial incentives but also on social background and, therefore, norms and ideological proclivities. Participants include not only the managers but also many other actors in the environment, including owners, customers, suppliers, and others willing to spend time to gain influence in the organization's various publics. Therefore, to understand the goals SOEs actually attempt to pursue, one has to understand who the different players are in the power and influence game from which decisions and actions emerge; what their means of influence are, and how these affect results and what the goals are which they attempt to achieve. Organizational goals can be deduced from behavior. The combination of these factors may enable us to understand how and why organizations in different sectors behave and what the differences are among them, as well as differences among various types of SOEs.

PROCESS MODEL OF GOALS

Organizations whose goals cannot be connected operationally with actions use subgoals that can be so connected. When a problem arises, organizations tend to search for a satisfactory solution to the problem as they perceive it. Under these conditions, well articulated in the writings of Simon (1979) and others, a theory that purports to describe the real world must have a model of process. Further, responses to environmental events and pressures depend on the specific decision process that the firm employs. The decision process, in turn, is at least partially a function of institutional and legal arrangements that prescribe the roles of the various participants.

Decisions are based on and substantiated by premises or propositions from which they are derived. However, the problems perceived by the decision-makers, the alternatives they weigh and the consequences they forsee all are affected to a large degree by the social system within which they operate. The manner in which a problem is defined and the type of problems on which one's attention is focused depends on one's definition of one's role and on one's interpersonal relations with other individuals in the system. When an investigation is made, it must be borne in mind that, although facts are universal, the interpretation of facts is personal and is dominated by concepts, beliefs, and the ideas one brings to the analysis. The interpretation is shifted and changed by continuous reciprocal influences among various participants in the system. Implications of alternatives from premises are achieved by "objective relations between propositions" (Cohen and Nagel, 1934) measurable by objective standards. They are also largely inferred from one's value premises, measured by one's personal yardstick and influenced by one's environment, interpersonal relations and background and experience.

Neither are problems defined once and for all. As Beer (1959) has stated, normal human behavior consists of what he terms "ubiquitous feedback," or continual referral of results back to problems leading to these results. This produces a continuing series of checks that often lead to redefinition of the problem. Very often human beings—in particular, business executives or government officials—have neither the time nor the inclination for lengthy investigation. They shortcut the analysis by accepting the plausible as true and rejecting the uncongenial as false. What is considered plausible, however, depends again on values and social influences.

To consider the decision-maker as a person sitting in an ivory tower, devoting all his or her time, energy and thought to a deliberate, orderly process of plan and search, is a very misleading notion. One should keep in mind not only the changing environment but also the continuing stream of other activities—sometimes quite remote ones—that will influence the outcome of any decision.

The environment is nonstationary, nor is it, as most theories assume, passive. Cyert and March (1963), e.g., argue that forces in the environment supply alternatives; that is, not only are searchers looking for alternatives but also alternatives are looking for a problem. Thus, when a worker was killed by a crane load, proposals for a crane control device were advocated by the environment, although no link had been established between the old control device and the accident.

A dynamic theory of goal-setting must, therefore, see the decision as part of a complicated social process. The dynamic, ongoing stream of activities in an organization, its history and its relations to other organizations and groups in the society influence the problems considered as well as the way they are solved. People in organizations do not stop operating when a specific decision is contemplated. They act continuously, making many small choices under pressure of time. In this process, members of an organization do not respond to every stimulus. The forces leading somebody in the organization to focus attention on certain problems are, therefore, of crucial importance.

To the extent that these hypotheses are correct, the outcome of any decision process can be partially controlled by a different design of the roles of different actors. In the specific case of SOEs, changes in the design of the system are at least a possible avenue for a change in managerial behavior if it is agreed that performance evaluation is an unattainable ideal. The Bergsonian solution (Bergson, 1978) of the agency cost problem through monetary rewards and incentives may be in theory a better solution. (See also Miller and Murell, 1979, James *et al* 1979.) However, to be effective such a scheme means that the government should know the utility functions of all SOE managers and that the costs of implementing such a scheme could easily exceed the benefits. Further, the size of the monetary incentives may be so high that they cause havoc in the total salary system of the public sector, not to mention the social unrest that would result. Again, a change in institutional arrangements may be less than optimal, but its benefits may exceed the costs and the results might be far better in practice than if we continue to look for first or second best solutions.

If decision-making is viewed as emerging from a continuous social process, composed of many small acts and carried out by different people at divergent points in time, then changes in the rules of the game of the institutional system in which decisions are made should cause different outcomes of the decisions. Analysis of interrelations among different parts of the system may lead to a design of a better system of interactions between government and SOEs. The major parts that might be changed through institutional or legal arrangements are (1) the structure in which the activities take place, (2) the participants in the process and their role in the structure, (3) the interactions among the various participants and (4) the information available to the participants both through past experience and through acquisition of additional data.

Prescribing the participants in the decision process is, therefore, one way to change outcomes and goals actually pursued. As one example, if the directors of the enterprise are government civil servants, the enterprise might behave differently and choose a different strategy than if the directors are re-cruited from independent businesspeople. Goal formulation can also be affected by the prescription of the information to be generated in the system before a decision can be made. For example, the enterprise may be required to present detailed budgets. Further, the decision-making process might be influenced by requirements of initiation of debates. For example, the board of directors might be required to discuss the corporation's strategy, its labor relations or its contribution to social goals at least once a year. The very discussion of these topics necessitates preparations and calls for conclusions based on an open debate, as the French and Senegalese experience with contracts demonstrated.

An institution can constructively deal with the incompatible purposes of its members in some combination of four ways:

1. Reduce the discretion to pursue conflicting purposes through monitoring;
2. Reduce the incentives to pursue conflicting purposes through rewards and penalties;
3. Reduce conflicting purposes through education and persuasion;
4. Drop the fiction of common purpose, acknowledge and embrace conflict, and legitimize open bargaining under rules that promote efficient agreements.

Governments (and many SOEs), however, manage conflicting interests by wishing it away. It is driven below the surface of public discourse, where bargaining is harder to track and to pursue efficiently. As a result, disagreements over objectives are sometimes settled through debates about factual forecasts, knowledge is withheld or manipulated and bargaining subverts learning. Therefore, the process by which goals are chosen is based on different power configurations, and these configurations evolve with time.

POWER CONFIGURATIONS AND THE EVOLUTION OF GOAL FORMULATION

Mintzberg (1983) provides a set of hypotheses on the relationship between the influencers in what he terms "the Internal and External Coalition." These different combinations create what he refers to as "configurations" of power. The external influencers are the owners, the associates (suppliers, clients, partners, competitors), the employee associations and the publics. The co-alition of external influence might be dominators, in which either one voice or a consensus dominates the external influencers; divided, in which external power is divided among many external influencers, or passive, in which the power of each external influencer is diffused until a point is reached in which the external coalition becomes passive. In the first case, "management knows where the real power lies, and is careful to stay within bounds acceptable to the key influencer" (Mintzberg, 1983, p. 97). In the second, the organization is pushed in different directions, and the board of directors becomes "a battle-ground for control" (p. 101). A divided external coalition also tends to polit-icize the internal coalition. When the external coalition is passive, power passes into the internal coalition (p. 104).

In the internal coalition, Mintzberg identifies five systems: personalized, in which the personal control system rules; the bureaucratic, in which au-thority is maintained primarily by standardization of work processes and of outputs (1983, p. 236); ideologic, with tight integration around organizational goals; professional, in which the system of expertise dominates, and the po-liticized, in which power rests in politics.

Of all possible combinations of power configurations, Mintzberg selects six as the most likely. These are reproduced in Table 4.1. In the first case (instrument), the organization is dependent on the environment for key re-sources, external power is focused and organized and the goals are clear and operational. The tight control exercised by the dominant coalition makes the internal coalition bureaucratic. The board of directors is either a control de-vice or a facade. The organization acts as an instrument to execute the wishes of an external influencer. This external power is focused and organized, nor-mally around a critical dependence. Typically, such an organization operates in a stable environment with mass outputs. Mintzberg hypothesizes that this type may be found in subsidiaries of other organizations, closely held business corporations, fire departments and post offices and coercive organizations like custodial prisons. In SOEs this type will be found in railroads, postal services, fiscal monopolies, as well as most SOEs in the first years of operation.

This rational model of the organization as an instrument is the model implicitly assumed in many discussions of SOEs. It is assumed that the firm was nationalized (or created) for a clear purpose, that its goals are prescribed by a strong external influencer (the government). This would create a bu-reaucratic organization geared to achieve the prescribed objectives, and the

Table 4.1   Combinations of internal and external coalitions and power configurations for each combination

External Coalition	Internal Coalition	Power Configurations
Dominators	Bureaucratic	Instrument
Passive	Bureaucratic	Closed system
Passive	Personalized	Autocracy
Passive	Ideologic	Missionary
Passive	Professional	Meritocracy
Divided	Politicized	Political arena

SOURCE: Henry Mintzberg, *Power In and Around Organizations* (Englewood Cliffs, N.J.: Prentice-Hall) 1983, p. 307).

autonomy required in theory is restricted to the means needed to achieve these objectives. The autonomy should be restricted to the minimum commensurate with commercial objectives. This point of view is shared by writers from all types of political affiliations, most of which perceive the SOEs as an instrument of national economic policy.

Of course, the evolution of organizations should be explicitly taken into account. An instrument may change because of a diffusion of the external influencers, breakdown of consensus (compare to Martinelli, in Vernon and Aharoni, 1981), as well as success and growth of the organization. Since the government is not monolithic, it is also possible that the SOE will become an instrument of different ministers sequentially.

In many cases, an SOE will become a closed system: the external co-alition being passive, power resides in the internal coalition. The board of directors becomes a facade. Insiders are motivated by utilitarian goals and recognize that their rewards are tied to the organization's success. To ensure the passiveness of the external coalition, the organization attempts to control its environment. Mintzberg predicts that such an organization will be found mainly in larger, mature organizations operating in stable environments, when owners are dispersed and unorganized or firms are ignored by the external influencers because of their small size (Mintzberg, 1983, Chapter 19). An SOE becomes a closed system if the external influencers are diffused or if the surveillance of its performance becomes more difficult. Since surveillance takes energy, it is sometimes not done and nonoperational goals emerge. In other cases, surveillance is difficult because of the technical nature of the SOE and its control of the information. In each of these cases, "insiders . . . given half the chance . . . will happily seize the power from the outsiders" (p. 475). Some examples are large oil firms or electricity generating SOEs.

Thus, managers of SOEs may be assumed to resent external control. They will attempt to make it less effective or more costly or both. This may lead to confrontation, and the relationship between the SOE and the con-trollers will become what Mintzberg calls "the political arena." With time, SOE management may learn to gain more power and to become a closed system. However, if insiders exploit their power in ways perceived to be ille-gitimate, a crisis may develop, the internal coalition will lose power and the organization will return to become an instrument.

Again, goal formulation is a process in which different actors interact. Managers continuously seek to break loose from dependence on government by attempting to make controls more costly or less effective.

Managers of SOEs often feel that the national interest argument has been abused. As they see it, many of their problems stem from the fact that governments have shirked the task of clearly defining the economic and social objectives of each of these enterprises. In fact, there are substantial differences of orientation with regard to goals between SOE managers and their superiors in the government, with the managers stressing economic more than social goals, while the government ministers tend to use their enterprises to attain social and political goals as well (for some empirical evidence see Dornstein, 1976; Aharoni, 1984).

When managers perceive their goals to be different from those of their superiors, they may oppose the use of the company to achieve short-term political and/or economic goals. However, managers with backgrounds as civil servants tend to refrain from rocking the boat; that is, they tend to argue less with ministers or to take action that will lead to conflict with political forces. The ability of the manager to break loose from controls is also a function of the salience of the issue to the controllers.

Managers would have a different approach toward the goals of one sector or another only when it seemed to them that the legitimacy of the sector was under attack (Aharoni and Lachman, 1982). Under any other circumstances, the fact of belonging to one sector or another does not necessarily lead to identification with the sector's goals.

If indeed there are discrepancies between the goals the managers would like to pursue and the goals they perceive to be important to the controllers, we have the classic problem of control: how to make the managers behave according to the goals the controllers would like them to pursue. SOE managers perceive themselves as better custodians of the national interest than their politically influenced controllers. Studies carried out in different countries clearly show that managers of SOEs believe they should pursue economic goals and that one of their major missions is to protect the destiny of the firm against politicians who want to gain short-term political benefits by instructing the firm to follow lines of action that the managers believe are against the best interests of the nation. This again creates conflicts. The way these conflicts are resolved is different at different stages in the evolution of the relationships among the various actors.

Hafsi (1981) analyzed the strategic decision-making process of several SOEs. He found an evolution, or a life cycle of government–SOE relationships, from cooperation to confrontation to autonomy. To Hafsi, the process is based on interaction between the core process (decision-making within the firm) and the boundary process (in government). With time, these processes tend to be separated from each other. SOEs gain autonomy by having access to resources other than the state's and by the costs of surveillance and enforcement. Autonomous SOEs define their own goals. Still, as Ferrario (1978) argues, SOEs will always depend to some extent on the state. Their "management will be faced with constraints of a nature extraneous to the business logic, but internal to the organization because of ownership of the state" (p. 233). Ferrario calls the managerially perceived organizational dependence on these extraneous factors "allodependence."

Stressing that goal formulation and autonomy comprise a process does not imply a deterministic evolution in which time is the only exogenous factor: SOEs, like any other organization, attempt to manage their environment in different ways, and the degree of success in doing so depends on several rational, political and organizational variables. One such variable is the ability of the SOEs to internalize—anticipate or dictate government's preferences. Others are the interface between the internal and the external coalitions and the structure of the markets in which the SOE operates. This last variable includes the extent of competition, complexity and uncertainty of the market environment, as well as the relative importance of exports versus production for local markets. The organizational goals pursued depend on the interaction of all these variables.

The analysis of the problem of goals means that seeking universal rules for performance evaluation may not be a viable approach to the problem of effective management of SOEs. Instead, the building blocks of the system design and the effect of different relationships among them should be investigated. Within the system, the impact of variables such as the organizational devices, administrative procedures, managerial recruitment and information flows should be explored. To quote Pfeffer and Salancik: "Prescriptions for effective organization design depend on one's view of organizations, how they operate, what their principal problems are, and how they are managed" (1977, p. 15). Indeed, Murthy goes so far as to suggest that a "rational hierachical 'first goal, then plan' model appears inappropriate for the management of most public enterprises in mixed economies of less developed countries" (1981, p. 107). He calls for a "supportive and collaborative relationship between the enterprise and its control system" (p. 99). He argues that without a collaborative process of learning and iterative adjustment of behavior and goals on the part of both the SOE and its controllers, SOE management is likely to find itself locked in endemic conflict with its direct controllers and other external parties affected by enterprise actions. Goals in this view are a result of collaboration between SOE management and its controllers, a continuous learning of all concerned and more effective flow of information.

Better knowledge of the decision-making process can lead to better results, and an emphasis on system design is at least as important as the economist's kit of tools on performance evaluation. Different processes may be designed contingent on the type of decision to be reached or the type of the enterprise in which the decision is being made and the size of the enterprise. Thus, the strategy of a competitive firm might be decided on differently from that of a public utility or strategically essential enterprise. By the same token, decisions on dividends or the creation of a subsidiary may be based on a different process and involve different actors than decisions on products to be sold or the wages of the employees.

Whatever the virtues of one or another design, SOE objectives are usually vague, conflicting, multiple and likely to be unstable. When ill-defined goals are accompanied by arms length control and financial interdependence in noncompetitive markets, the SOE management may define its goals in accordance with its personal goals. Conversely, if the SOE is financially dependent and closely controlled and if no agreement on goals among different actors is reached, its management will have little independent ability to set the course for its SOEs; the goals pursued will fluctuate according to external pressures of contending interest groups and their balance of power. Ramamurti (1982) has described this situation as leading to a downward spiral. India's Heavy Engineering Corporation (HEC) was continually beholden to government for financial support because the demand for its production was never high enough to enable full-capacity operations. The firm became vulnerable to conflicting demands of unions, politicians and the bureaucracy. Its most competent staff left, frustrated by their inability to make autonomous decisions. As of 1977, HEC was too politically entangled to be shut down and too weak managerially to achieve any strategic goals. It continued to show heavy losses with no apparent predetermined social goal.

Since the state as an owner usually stands behind the SOE's borrowings and makes up any losses and since most SOEs enjoy monopoly power, a genuine arm's length policy is a contradiction in terms. Governments feel they have to intervene. At the same time, they refuse to define goals. Thus, the formulations of goals, the relation between SOEs and their environment, the incentives used and the methods of measuring performance are linked and embedded within an evolutionary process.

CONCLUSION

These findings amount at first sight to a bewildering array of generalizations. Several things, however, are clear. First, in any industry at a given point in time, stakeholders of SOEs have greater expectations than stakeholders of private firms; e.g., workers expect better pay and perks for a given amount of work and better working conditions and security; customers expect prompt, high-quality and reliable products or services at low prices regardless of actual costs; suppliers expect to receive steadily growing business at remunerative prices; society expects SOEs to be responsive to all kinds of social problems and to maintain higher ethical standards. Further, objectives of SOEs are perceived differently by different actors: ministers, bureaucrats in different wings of government, parliamentarians, employees, SOE managers and different sectors of the public.

Second, as owner, the government has far greater say in setting the objectives and policies of SOEs than do shareholders in most large private firms. Ownership is seldom concentrated in one person in large private firms the way it is in SOEs (the minister). In fact, ministers have more direct control over SOEs (not only in appointments but also in issuing directives) than do shareholders of private firms. They also have greater access to additional information than shareholders or other stakeholders of private firms.

Third, objectives of SOEs are not clearly defined in formal documents such as acts of Parliament or the memoranda of association, and formal objectives are not equal to those pursued. There is a divergence between formally stated objectives, espoused objectives and pursued objectives.

Fourth, objectives of SOEs are rarely clearly stated (in writing) by ministers. SOEs have multiple objectives in addition to profits, including transferring power to the state, acting as an instrument for curbing inflation by discriminatory price restrictions, subsidizing private interest, maintaining jobs, improving or modernizing an industry in terms of its organization or capital investment, coordinating competing services, stimulating economic growth, protecting the public against exploitation by private monopolies, rescuing industries in danger of collapse and providing political patronage. No trade-off among objectives is explicitly specified, and objectives change over time. Goals, therefore, emerge from a process, depend on power configuration and change over time.

Fifth, parliamentary debates on SOEs seldom deal with strategic issues (Robson, 1962, pp. 181–183). The government, too, does not conduct systematic strategic reviews of SOEs. Strategic reviews by government are not usually prompted by regular, annual planning exercises; it appears that more often these are caused by a financial crisis (e.g., British Rail), a technical crisis (electricity industry in the United Kingdom; NEDO, 1976, p. 27), an ethical crisis (Israeli Government Companies Act and the Estey inquiry into Air Canada and the Atomic Energy of Canada Ltd.) or an economic crisis, as in Brazil. Political pressure, impinging on SOEs' objectives and strategies, increases just before and just after elections.

Sixth, SOE managers do not simply accept directives imposed from the top by government if these directives are strongly in conflict with the goals they perceive as important. SOE managers use ambiguities in objectives to increase their discretion not only in operations but also in strategies and objectives. Influence of top managers on external controllers is an important determinant of the degree of autonomy of SOEs on strategic matters. The amount of influence of top managers increases with longevity of service, direct access to politicians in power, strong support from employees, extended relations with influential political circles, proven managerial competence and strong personality and financial conditions of the firm. Profitable and financially self-sufficient SOEs enjoy greater autonomy in strategic planning than unprofitable ones or those that are not commercially viable. SOE managers also try to withhold information from bureaucrats or to provide information selectively and use foreign operations to increase their discretion.

Seventh, government officers lack the competence and information to question or criticize meaningfully the strategic plans of SOEs except in terms of the plan's basic assumptions about the rate of growth of the economy, demand for end products, assumptions about other sectors of the economy and alternative uses for the enterprise's surplus resources. Governments spend more time regulating or supervising the behavior of an SOE to ensure adherence to policies and rules than on creative strategic planning. In addition, there are fundamental differences in values between SOE managers and government officers and a lack of trust between them. Strategic planning in SOEs is considerably complicated by a lack of assurance of continuity of objectives and policies on the part of government.

Finally, the goal formulation process may change even though no specific prescriptions are being made for any specific case, the outcomes of the decision are not dictated and shadow prices are not prescribed (although they might be). This process can be achieved by different procedures by which the decisions should be made, the type of information various individuals should receive before a decision is made as well as the participants in the decision-making process and their power to veto decisions. In real life situations, it is impossible to foresee all the decisions to be faced and have shadow prices for them. In a world of uncertainty many situations arise in which judgment may be used, and the accumulation of these decisions affects goals. The degree to which the goal formulation can be changed depends on the political structure and its ability to adapt itself. If politicians do not want to waste more resources than needed for the maximization of the votes, goal formulation processes can be managed by explicit bargaining among the various actors to establish a clearer framework and to renegotiate when the agreement is threatened by unforeseen developments. If governments are willing to eschew *ad hoc* interference, then SOEs can accept performance targets.

CHAPTER 5

Measuring the Performance of State-Owned Enterprises

INTRODUCTION

Are SOEs more or less efficient than private enterprises? If SOEs are less efficient, what are the systematic determinants of this difference? The efficiency of SOEs is an important issue since greater efficiency of the SOEs is a pure gain to the economy rather than a transfer. The larger the share of SOEs in the economy, the more salient is the gain from increased efficiency. Jones (1981c), assuming that there is room for at least 5 percent overall improvement in efficiency, has calculated the resulting efficiency bonus. For example, a 5 percent increase in SOE sector efficiency was about 1 percent of GDP in 1980/81 in Pakistan. If these additional funds were transferred to the government, it would provide revenue equal to 53 percent of direct taxes, or 82 percent of all foreign grant assistance. Stated differently, this efficiency bonus would be enough to finance a 46 percent increase in total government expenditures on education.

Using the same calculations, in Egypt, e.g., such an increase in SOE efficiency is equal to an increase of about 5 percent of GDP, and if these additional funds were transferred to the government, they would provide revenue equal to 75 percent of all direct taxes, or enough to triple governmental expenditure on education. A 5 percent increase in SOE efficiency amounts to 1.7 percent of GDP in South Korea (Jones, 1981c); almost 2 percent of GDP in Turkey, or 10 percent of tax revenue; 1.5 percent of GDP in Tanzania, enough to finance all its spending on health; 1.4 percent of GDP in Bolivia, 14 percent of its tax revenue, and 2.2 percent of GDP in Mali, twice the expenditure on health (World Bank, 1983, p. 75). A 5 percent increase in turnover of Zambia's manufacturing holding company would free resources equal to almost 90 percent of the country's expenditures on education (Shirley, 1983, p. 17).

The assumption of a 5 percent increase in overall efficiency implies improved capital utilization as well as more efficient use of intermediate inputs and labor. Jones (1981c) argues that this gain in efficiency may be attained by installing an appropriate signaling system that will guide managers to act in the interest of society as a whole. Such a system, according to Jones, is composed of two major components. The first is a *performance evaluation* system in which national goals are translated into explicit enterprise objectives and quantified in a performance criterion. The second is an *incentive system* in which managerial welfare is linked to national welfare by a pecuniary or non-pecuniary bonus system based on achievement of particular target values of the criterion variables.

In reality, signaling systems of SOEs are usually woefully inappropriate and inadequate, creating negative and unintentional results. Problems in the signaling system stem from several inherent characteristics of SOEs, discussed in Chapter 4. These enterprises are hybrids, expected to achieve multiple economic, social and political goals without any clear and agreed on trade-offs among them. SOEs have plural principals, or different control organs, with different perceptions of what the priorities in achieving different goals should be. The ambiguity caused by the plethora of goals and the plural principals allows both controllers and managers to pursue objectives they see as important and makes an objective performance evaluation extremely difficult, if not impossible. If goals cannot be specified, there is no way to judge performance.

The problem is compounded by the fact that an SOE can be evaluated by numerous possible criteria of success. The success of the firm can be rated by measuring its internal efficiency. Alternatively, the SOE may be judged by its contribution to goals such as social welfare, economic growth, employment creation, social equity or workers' satisfaction. Differences of opinion about goals to be pursued may lead to different evaluation of SOEs' performance.

The efficiency of private firms and SOEs may be compared on several levels. First, efficiency of socialist countries and capitalist countries may be compared. If socialist countries have established a more efficient mode of production, this will affect the macro results for the economy as a whole. Second, efficiency of the SOE sector in a mixed economy may be measured. Third, and more relevant to this book, the efficiency of SOEs and privately owned firms in a similar setting within a mixed economy may be compared. Finally, it is necessary to establish the reasons for whatever systematic differences in efficiency are found. Before attending to these tasks, however, it is necessary to define terms such as *efficiency* or *performance* in order to have agreed-upon criteria for performance measurement.

THE ECONOMIST'S CRITERIA FOR PERFORMANCE

Economists focus mainly on efficiency as a criterion for performance. There are basically three types of efficiency. Internal efficiency is defined as the ratio of outputs (the products) to the inputs (resources used in production). If the firm can create more outputs with the same inputs or the same outputs with less inputs, it increases efficiency. In neoclassical economic theory, the concern is with allocative efficiency, and the firm is expected to be always efficient in the sense defined here—namely, to be on the production frontier. Under certain assumptions about the technology of production and the preferences of individuals, the market price mechanism works in achieving the efficiency conditions in which marginal cost is equal to price and Pareto optimum is achieved. Allocative efficiency requires, of course, that the social costs of producing a given level of output desired by consumers be at a minimum. The second type of efficiency is *dynamic efficiency:* measuring the rate of change of output per unit of input. Thus, an economy is *production-efficient* if the supply of any good or service cannot be increased without reducing the supply of some other good, including all possibilities of foreign trade. Allocative efficiency requires also that it is impossible to make anyone better off without making someone worse off; in addition to production efficiency, all final consumers must have exhausted all possibilities of mutually beneficial exchange.

Leibenstein (1966) pointed out, quite correctly, that firms do not always operate under these conditions. As a result of motivational factors within the firm, motivational factors from external sources and nonmarket input efficiency, firms may be what he termed *x-inefficient*.

The degree of x-inefficiency may be defined as the difference between maximum and actual effectiveness in the utilization of inputs. The theory of x-efficiency is more akin to managerial theories because it assumes that effort of individuals is a discretionary variable, that no identity of interests exists between the firm and individuals, that rationality is selective and that individual motivation is a significant variable.

Most observers believe that x-inefficiency is more prevalent in SOEs; that is, they are less efficient than they could have been if all possible variations of individual and collective motivational structures had been exhausted. In Pakistan, the Chamber of Commerce and Industry claimed, "Briefly, the taken over industries are caught in the whirlwind of spiraling costs and expenses, pinpointing the gross negligence in controlling and checking them" (1979, p. 27, quoted in Jones, 1981c, p. II-5).

One way for SOEs to be efficient is to guide them along the commercial principles discussed in Chapter 4. If SOEs operate in perfectly competitive markets, the ubiquitous competitive process will lead each SOE to an efficient use of resources. In fact, under perfect competition conditions, with many buyers and sellers and perfect and costless information, managers do not have any discretion. In real life, managers do have discretion, markets are less than perfect and uncertainty is ubiquitous. Still, many economists would argue that the bulk of the services to society of non-monopolist SOEs comes through their commercial activities. Therefore, their performance must be evaluated like private enterprises, and their managers should be compensated according to their success in achieving the measures agreed on. It is also argued that a lack of commercial discipline is dangerous. As one student of SOEs put it: "If the public comes to regard the railways or any other nation- alized industry as a special service which can and should be subsidized year after year from the taxpayers' money, then there will not be the slightest pros- pect of achieving financial solvency. . . . a concerted attempt to scotch this pernicious idea should be made" (Robson, 1962, p. 288).

A more realistic situation for many SOEs is that of *monopoly*. In this case, a profit-maximizing firm knows that the more it sells, the more it drives the price down. It will prefer to restrict output to the point where its marginal revenue equals marginal costs. At that point, prices are higher than marginal cost. This means inefficient use of resources and reducing consumers' welfare.

Economists expect SOEs to maximize social welfare, not profits. It fol- lows that one must have a definition of welfare from which the behavior of the enterprise must be determined and its performance assessed. This behav- ior is operationally defined by economists in terms of the prices to be charged by the enterprise and guidelines for investment decisions. As Bös (1981) ar- gues, "pricing of publicly supplied goods is the primary vehicle for embedding public enterprises adequately into a market economy" (p. 1). Welfare is de- fined, in terms of the theory of benefit–cost analysis, as the difference between social benefits and social costs. Social benefits are equal to the benefit to the SOE, measured by its revenues plus the consumer surplus.* Consumer sur- plus is measured in the benefit–cost analysis by the consumers' willingness to pay. Empirically, it is not very easy to calculate willingness to pay—and there- fore consumers' surplus—and the analysis is fraught with many difficult the- oretical questions such as the empirical estimates of external effects, intangi- bles, the choice of optional rate of time preference or rate of opportunity costs. Therefore, before continuing, it is important to estimate the size of the wel- fare losses. Technically, the question is that of the quantitative importance of allocative efficiency measured by the difference between marginal cost pricing and that of profit maximization.

---

*There is a debate among economists about whether one should use the Marshallian consumer surplus or the Hicksian consumer surplus. In the first, individual income is held constant. In the second, individual utilities are held constant. Since individual utilities cannot be measured empirically, applied economists tend to use Marshallian concepts, in an attempt to measure the area under the market demand curve.

Economists have attempted to measure the welfare losses resulting from resource misallocation because of monopolistic structure and conduct. Harberger (1954), by making a number of simplifying assumptions, estimated these losses in the U.S. manufacturing sector to be less than 0.1 percent of GNP. Several other empirical studies confirmed these results (Schwartzman, 1960; Worcester, 1973). At least two others, however (Kamerschen, 1966; Cowling and Mueller, 1978), estimated that the welfare losses were in the range of 4 to 7 percent, and Harberger's results were criticized on various grounds (Bergson, 1973; Cowling and Mueller, 1978). Most writers on this subject assess welfare losses from monopoly by summing a series of partial equilibrium estimates. Kay (1983), using a general equilibrium framework, found that the size of welfare loss depends on the weight given consumption because the consumer buys the consumption goods but sells labor. More fundamentally, he found the bounds within which welfare losses to lie to be very wide. He concluded that "there is sufficient rationale for anti-trust policies. The test of the utility of the fire brigade is not whether fire losses are large but whether they would be large if fire proceeded unchecked" (Kay, 1983, p. 331).

Whether or not welfare loss is significant, one would certainly like to avoid it in the case of SOEs. The loss of the efficient allocation merits cannot be rectified by imposing financial targets or profit-limit rules. These rules are not necessary or sufficient to guide allocation toward efficient patterns. In this case, economists developed the so-called marginal cost pricing rule: efficient allocation requires that the monopolist public utility should price its output at marginal costs. Any deviations of price from marginal cost must entail some welfare loss. Unfortunately, marginal costs are extremely hard to define and measure because there are differences between short-run and long-run marginal costs, marginal costs are different for each gradation of time horizon and it is extremely difficult to allocate joint costs (e.g., among bus lines) or to compare marginal costs of different technologies (coal and oil in electricity generation) (see Nelson, 1964; Shanks, 1963, pp. 56–71). Thus, given present knowledge, a good portion of the theoretical solution is not amenable to practical application (see, e.g., Nove, 1973, Turvey, 1971).

Even if marginal costs can be calculated—e.g., for the peakload in electricity—the marginal cost pricing rule means that the SOE will lose; since costs are declining, marginal costs are less than average cost. These losses may be covered by cross subsidization among different units or by subsidies from the treasury. Even if we neglect the practical problems involved, direct subsidies have to be paid ultimately through taxes, and taxation may have its own distortion effects on efficiency. A host of alternative pricing rules, including two-part and multipart tariffs, has been developed in response to the recognition that adherence to marginal cost pricing sometimes yields operating deficits (Turvey, 1971; Reed, 1973).

Further, marginal cost pricing may not lead to allocation efficiency. Remember that the rationale for this method was that other sectors of the economy are perfectly competitive and charge marginal costs. However, if prices exceed marginal costs in other parts of the economy, using marginal cost pricing for the monopoly may not be justified. This situation leads to the theory of second best (Lipsey and Lancaster, 1956/1957), since elimination of distortions in one market might not advance welfare if distortions.existed elsewhere in the system. Any deviation of an SOE's prices from marginal cost can be interpreted as an implicit subsidy or tax. Therefore, SOEs' pricing rules are a special case of the design of a set of optimal taxes on all sectors (Atkinson and Stiglitz, 1980; Diamond and Mirrless, 1971).

Finally, prices and costs may misrepresent true social costs and benefits since they do not take into account externalities. If cost is reduced by discharging pollution into rivers or corrosive wastes into the air, then marginal cost pricing is socially undesirable. Therefore, many would advocate adjusting all costs and prices to take account of external effects and then using marginal cost pricing. In many cases, other public policies that absorb or offset the repercussions directly are preferable. For example, a bus line may help the aged. One possibility is to maintain the line with cross subsidies. Another is to aid the aged directly. Once we get into this area, we have to find an effective allocation of all governmental programs to decide on proper measures for SOE behavior and the means of assessing their performance since SOEs are not necessarily the only, or the best, alternative for achieving national goals. In most countries, SOEs are exposed to all sorts of political pressures, bureaucracies are not able to calculate all possible effects of policies and the ready access to subsidies may erode managerial incentives to achieve efficiency. Therefore, it is often argued, it is more practical to achieve social ends through other policies and to judge SOEs by their ability to generate surplus.

Financial statements must be corrected to reflect differences between private and public relevant profits. To arrive at social profits, a series of adjustments has to be made. Thus, if wages are valued above their marginal product in an alternative employment, the opportunity cost of labor is used. If unskilled labor has been hired from the pool of unemployed, this opportunity cost is zero. Another adjustment is made for the costs of borrowed funds. SOEs may have received these funds at subsidized rates, not at the market rate. Adjustments are made also for imports and exports, if the exchange rate is overvalued. Other types of adjustment are for government-set prices, taxes paid to government, subsidies received, for the effect of underpriced SOEs produced goods for reason of redistribution of income and for the effect of regional imbalances. More generally, a public manager is expected to look for the interests of all citizens of the country. The manager, therefore, has to be judged by public profits, or social benefits less social costs.

Economists have developed an impressive analytical artillery to calculate the public profits. Their solution rests on the foundation of a set of preferences provided by government. These preferences set out the goals of society and the rate at which one goal is appropriately traded off against another. The preference set can be used to generate socially optimal shadow prices that embody the social opportunity cost of society's resources. Using the social rate of discount, the relative social profitability of alternative operations can be calculated. Activities that are unprofitable when measured in private (market) prices may prove appropriate when evaluated on the basis of social (shadow) prices. Indeed, Handoussa (1980) showed for Egypt that social profits were positive and higher than accounting profits. Of course, not the government directly but the manager (the agent of the state) is charged with the realization of social welfare through the SOE, and as the theory of agency cost highlights, the private interests of the enterprise manager need not be served best by operating the SOE according to the criteria prescribed by the state. Here, too, economic theory offers an analytical answer. With knowledge of both private preferences of the manager and the preferences of society, government can tailor managerial incentives. With appropriate incentives the objectives of the manager can be made identical to those of society.

Unfortunately, in the real world the shadow price prescriptions of economists founder on the rock of uncertainty. Setting accurate shadow prices requires complete information of the social opportunity cost of resource utilization, and such information is unavailable. Moreover, firms do not operate in a neoclassical world; rather, they have a certain size and are therefore managed hierarchically. Much of the available information on costs to the enterprise is collected at the firm's level, and such information is not always presented to the government decision-makers. Decision-makers are not characterized by omniscience; rather, the typical government executive—in the LDCs in particular—is overburdened with too many responsibilities and does not have the time to learn even available information or reflect on its significance. Further, social planning includes decisions that will affect future generations, and trade-offs between the present and the future have to be embodied in the social discount rate. The future, however, is unknown. Projects such as building a nuclear generator or exploring for oil are fraught with uncertainty and extremely hard to quantify, and, as Wells (1973) pointed out, engineers have a different notion of efficiency.

The difficulties in implementing the economist's solutions to performance evaluation do not end with problems of uncertainty, high costs of information or its unavailability at any price and the difficulties in allocating precious time of overburdened government officials. In oligopolistic markets, private firms are likely to adjust their behavior in response to any initiatives by SOEs (Jones and Vogelsang, 1982). In some cases, governments might use the threat of entry into hitherto privately controlled oligopolistic sectors of industry to improve market performance. In addition to these well-known problems, as already shown, making coherent social choices is extraordinarily difficult, not only because the environment is suffused with ambiguity but also, mainly, because of power struggles. In responding to political demands,

SOE managers may choose their high-priority clientèle, excuse the lack of compliance with political demands by citing technical requirements or simply refuse to conform.

Economists have also developed techniques of project appraisal to help SOEs determine the social efficiency of their investment plans and to enable governments to evaluate the social efficiency of establishing new SOEs and the performance of existing ones (Little and Mirrlees, 1974). However, in practice it is extremely difficult to make operational the socially optimal behavior criteria. As Scherer (1980) notes, in particular when SOEs operate in sectors:

> [R]ichly interconnected with other sectors . . . the general solutions [of second best analysis] are so complex that it may be impossible to deduce unambiguously even the direction in which particular controlled prices should be adjusted in order to improve resource allocations. . . . no central authority could conceivably obtain the masses of information on demand elasticities, cross elasticities, cost functions and prices needed to devise fully articulated, second-best pricing policies for even a single major industry. [Pp. 27–28]

In summary, economists devoted most of their attention in analyzing SOEs to the derivation of optimal and efficient pricing and investment rules. Much less economic analysis is available on how costs could be minimized. Most economic analysis of pricing and investment implicitly assumes that monitoring costs are zero. In fact, those with the greatest knowledge of the ways by which costs can be reduced are on the employees and managers of the SOEs. The gains of efficiency, however, accrue to all taxpayers and consumers, and employees may even lose by greater efficiency. Given the asymmetry of goals and of information, the problem of achieving cost minimizing is insoluble.

If managers are offered incentives, they can meet targets and get incentives based on profits simply by raising prices. Rees (1968) has suggested linking managerial rewards to the SOEs' profit, but also to improve pricing rules to prevent managers from abusing their monopoly power. However, to calculate prices "on the basis of expected marginal costs" (Rees, 1968, p. 272), again requires that the monitors will have information on the firm's cost structure. Bös (1978) suggested a system of minimization of Laspeyres price index, subject to profit constraint. An even more basic limitation of economists' solutions is that they are based on certain assumptions about the definition of social costs and social benefits that are not necessarily agreed to by all. Most important, governments' decisions with regard to SOEs, as shown in previous chapters, are not necessarily motivated by the goal of maximizing social welfare. For example, the distribution of power among different actors may be more important. Normative guidelines do not give us an idea as to what might be the actual behavior of governments and of SOEs. Moreover, a survey of the economic literature on SOEs would give the impression that we live in a certain world with perhaps some uncertainty as a special case. Some new theoretical developments introduced uncertainty, but assume that individual consumers are risk-neutral—an unpalatable assumption if uncertainty is recognized. Further, most analyses assume that welfare distribution is acceptable or has been optimized. All these difficulties led Nove (1973) to conclude that "commercial operation of nationalized industries raises a host of problems which are now, as a rule, swept under the carpet or ignored" (p. 132).

ORGANIZATIONAL EFFECTIVENESS AND VITALITY

Efficiency must be defined in terms of achievement of goals. Without clear cut and measurable goals it is impossible to measure performance. If goals are stated in static terms, their achievement allows repetition, learning and specialization and creates greater efficiency in production but may also hinder innovations and adaptation to changing market needs. Even operational efficiency may be difficult to achieve. Managers can be held responsible for the performance of their subordinates (and, thus, the enterprise) only if they have the power to hire/fire and reward/penalize them. In SOEs, appointments and the size of employment are often controlled by ministerial selection boards, and managers are neither allowed to appoint all subordinates nor always allowed to decide on the size of the labor force.

Performance evaluation thus involves a dilemma. The more operating routines are retained and repeated, the easier is the performance evaluation. However, very little innovation will occur, and very little novel activity will be available from which to select adaptive response when environmental circumstances change. The very attributes that make actions efficient limit the visibility of alternatives and prevent the intrusion of new ideas or different perspectives, even when changes are required by changing environments. In an SOE, managers are often penalized more for one failure than they are rewarded for several successes.

One way to achieve organizational effectiveness is to guarantee that all the actors in the organization devote all their energies to performance and employ their knowledge creatively toward achieving the goals of the organization. Such an organization, according to Miller (1977), possesses "organizational vitality." Organizational vitality refers to the capability for future achievement in contrast to effectiveness, which measures past success. It may also be said that vitality ensures future effectiveness.

Organizational vitality depends on the existence of implemental capability, which is the totality of competence and skills required to accomplish an objective and motivation, that causes the individual to deal with the objective and carry it out with purposeful effort. In referring to the motivation of all those participating in the organization, we may speak of a suitable organizational climate.

One way to achieve a suitable organizational climate for ensuring the achievement of goals is the selection of managers according to their identification with the goals of one sector or another. All other things being equal, it is reasonable to assume that a manager who identifies with the sector's goals will achieve them far better than a manager who does not believe in them. As one example, Pierre Dreyfus, CEO of Renault, recites in his memoirs how Renault, at a time of a run on the French franc, at its own initiative, supported the currency by accelerating the conversion to francs of receipts in foreign currency (Dreyfus, 1977, p. 35). Unfortunately, those who believe in the right ideology are not necessarily the best and most effective managers. As one example, rapid Africanization meant that SOEs were managed by weak and inexperienced leaders. The political claims in this case had costs in terms of efficiency.

The greater the identification of managers and workers with their organization's goals and a consensus among all stakeholders on these goals, the less important it becomes that these goals be defined and quantifiable by outsiders: the unanimous agreement should lead to concerted efforts to achieve the goals, even if they are not sharply defined. Of course, the achievement of goals does not depend solely on ideological views, and all other things are not necessarily equal. No less important for the achievement of goals is the manager's implemental capability, competence in utilizing and employing optimally the resources at the organization's disposal and competence in getting a maximum of further resources required for the achievement of tasks.

The dominant characteristic of firms whose goals are conflicting and ambiguous is the tension created by the various actors' attempts to place emphasis on different goals. All those dealing with issues concerning the SOE agree that the central problem in monitoring such a firm stems from the inability to weigh various goals and frequently from the manager's perception that the goals of the political controllers are illegitimate, at least in terms of how the manager perceives the goals of the organization. Such a conflict returns us full circle to the question: How and by whom are the goals actually pursued by the organization formulated, and how can stakeholders' satisfaction with the organization's performance be ensured?

MEASURING EFFECTIVENESS

Efficiency measures gauge whether things are done right and effectiveness is purported to measure whether the right things are done. Thus, effectiveness has as much to do with missions and goals as with unit costs, productivity and resource conservation. It is, therefore, an elusive concept, not easily quantifiable. The criteria for evaluation may be subjective, based on value judgments and personal preferences. Further, organizational effectiveness encompasses a large number of criteria.

There are at least three ways to define organizational effectiveness (Cameron, 1980). The first is the inputs or resources method. According to Yuchtman and Seashore (1967), an organization is more effective insofar as it can obtain resources from the environment. To the extent that these resources exist, there is a clear connection between the inputs the organization receives and its products. Yuchtman and Seashore (1967) propose ten indexes for measuring organizational effectiveness according to the resources approach. Steers (1975, p. 549) listed fifteen criteria used by researchers in evaluating organizational effectiveness. Campbell (1976, pp. 36–38) listed thirty.

The second approach focuses on the organization's stakeholders or beneficiaries—individuals or groups whose participation is essential to the proper functioning of the organization—including workers, suppliers, customers and users. According to this point of view, organizational effectiveness is measured by the degree of satisfaction of different stakeholders. The effectiveness of the organization "derives from the management of demands, particularly the demands of interest groups upon which the organization depends for resources and support" (Pfeffer and Salancik, 1978, p. 2). One way to measure effectiveness, according to this point of view, is by the absence of criticism "for it means that no one views the operation of a particular program or organization as inimical to his own interests or goals and that some may even perceive it as beneficial" (Sapolsky, 1972, p. 232). According to this standard, Sapolsky suggests that the Polaris program was successful. This success "was not assured at its establishment" (p. 243).

> [It] depended upon the ability of its proponents to promote the Polaris. Competitors had to be eliminated; reviewing agencies had to be outmaneuvered; congressmen, admirals, newspapermen, and academicians had to be coopted. Politics is a system requirement. What distinguishes programs in government is not that some play politics and others do not, but rather, that some are better at it than others. [Sapolsky, 1972, p. 244]

A third approach views the organization as being effective if it functions without internal tensions. This approach focuses on the processes within the organization and examination of the meshing, coordination and cooperation among the organization's units and groupings, as well as the degree of communication among its various parts. This approach is akin to the human relations school of thought.

The differences between these approaches are quite substantial. An organization may be effective according to one approach and ineffective according to another. Some of the approaches also focus on one specific aspect of the organization's extremely complex structure. Thus, harmony within the organization does not necessarily guarantee achievement of goals and may even lead to decay. Technological innovation, e.g., often entails changes, tensions and conflicts.

SOCIALIST VERSUS CAPITALIST COUNTRIES: A COMPARISON OF THEIR EFFICIENCY

One way to understand the problems involved in measuring performance of SOEs is to ask the question, are socialist countries more or less efficient than capitalist ones? The discussion is intended only as an illustration of the difficulties in assessing relative efficiency in agreed terms and not as a comparison of different economic systems. Bergson (1968) one of the major researchers of this question, claims that there is no evidence to support the Marxist view that socialism is more efficient than capitalism. In fact, "Socialism, exemplified by the USSR, is markedly less efficient than capitalism, as exemplified by the U.S.A., though perhaps about as efficient as capitalism as exemplified by Italy" (Eckstein, 1971, p. 239). This conclusion was reached by comparing the static efficiency (output per unit of inputs at a given time) and concluding that it is worse for the USSR than for the United States, France and Germany and on par with Italy.

Bergson (1968) also compared what he termed the *dynamic efficiency,* or the rate of change of output per unit of inputs, and found that it is better in the USSR than in the United States and the United Kingdom but worse than that in Germany, France and Italy. These conclusions are based on calculations for the economy as a whole and assume that the only difference between the economies is the system. It is further assumed that each country faces constant or decreasing returns to scale, identical technology and homogeneous labor and capital. Of course, if in reality there is, e.g., a technology gap between the United States and the USSR, and the former is in fact using more advanced technology, it is possible that the USSR is more efficient but that this efficiency is more than offset by the technology gap. Further, the two countries differ in their historical and cultural heritage, not only in the system.

Theoretically, these problems can be solved by comparing the efficiency of the German Democratic Republic and the Federal Republic of Germany. These two countries may be said to be identical in most of the aforementioned respects, differing only in their economic systems. Several researchers have compared the performance of the two Germanies (Schnitzer, 1972; Gregory and Leptin, 1977). These studies show that the static efficiency of the Federal Republic of Germany has been higher throughout the postwar period. Comparison of the dynamic efficiency is more problematic, since it is sensitive to the year for which the comparison was made, and the data used is based on different national accounting systems. While the rate of growth of aggregate labor productivity for the period 1950 to 1958 was a third greater in the Democratic Republic than in the Federal Republic of Germany (Gregory and Leptin, 1977, p. 529), it was about equal for the period 1960 to 1973. It may well be that these differences are the result of differential wartime destruction in the two Germanies. More important for our discussion, these studies are based on a comparison, rooted in the tradition of neoclassical economics, between utilized inputs and the available level of outputs as measured in the national accounts. Marxism's major attack on capitalism, however, was not cast in these terms. The efficiency discussed in Marxist theory is the relationship between available inputs and the social utility of outputs. Capitalism, socialists would argue, is inefficient because it fails to utilize the available resources, allowing idle capacity as well as unemployment.

Further, socialists refer to the social utility of outputs. According to them, much of the capitalist outputs consist of social ills like hard drugs or waste like that caused by the frequent change of car models or by advertising. Baran and Sweezy, two Marxist economists, calculated that car model changes in the late 1950s were costing the United States 2.5 percent of its GNP every year (1968, p. 141). When they combined all they perceived as "surplus" or social wastes—military expenditures, real estate services, advertising, legal services, waste in distribution—they concluded that total surplus as a percentage of GNP in the United States was 56.1 percent in 1963 (p. 374).

The picture is further complicated by the fact that "efficiency depends predominantly on the stage of development, and so in reality is little affected by the social system" (Eckstein, 1971, p. 238). At the same time, Marxist economists would argue that the stage of development is not independent of the social system. Of course, the USSR also devotes some of its resources to the production of goods defined by Baran and Sweezy as not socially desirable, from military expenditures to vodka. In short, what is socially desirable is a value-laden question (e.g., is censorship a waste?) Ellman concludes:

> Neither the neoclassical hypothesis nor the Marxist hypothesis are [sic] corroborated by the evidence. Whether or not both, either, or neither, are considered to be definitely refuted depends on how precisely the hypotheses are formulated (e.g., do the hypotheses refer to some measure of central tendency or can they be refuted by a single observation?), which theory of economic growth one utilizes, which time period one considers, what proportion of the output of each system one judges to be waste, and on what the level of waste of resources outside and inside production is judged to be. . . . The two systems are equally good at producing tendentious arguments. [1979, p. 257]

When a term like *performance* is used, factors other than economic efficiency should be taken into account because one system may have more or less skewed income distribution than another (for the evidence on this point, see Bergson, 1984), the distribution of power may be different (state ownership may reduce the power of the private business firms) or workers may be happier in one system than they are in another. It is therefore extremely important to be crystal clear on how performance is measured. The major problem in measuring the performance of SOEs is similar to that analyzed previously: different persons would like the SOEs to achieve different goals. Therefore, they measure their performances differently.

THE FINANCIAL PERFORMANCE OF SOEs: PROFITS

Most studies of SOEs' performance measure the results of the operations of these firms by calculating accounting profits. Thus, a study of sixty-four SOEs in twenty-six countries in the 1960s measured flow of funds, investment ratios, surplus after investments and transfers (excluding loans from the government budget) as a percentage of current activity. The researchers found that when a normal depreciation (estimated by the authors to be 24 percent of activity as a whole) was included and subsidies excluded, these enterprises showed a loss equal to 16 percent of total activity (defined as operating revenues less operating expenses) (Gantt and Dutto, 1968). (By using this base, the authors avoided the problem of calculating current value of assets, an almost insurmountable difficulty in countries with high rates of inflation.) Some results of this study are reproduced in Table 5.1. All ratios are percentage of activity as defined here.

Despite low cash flows and operating deficits, SOEs' investments were high, amounting on the average to 74.3 percent of current activities of which two-thirds were the net investment and one-third was the renewal of assets. According to the capital/output ratios calculated by the writers, the SOEs they studied as a group increased their output by 5 percent a year, the fastest growth being in electricity (28.4 percent) and the smallest in railroads (0.1 percent).

Table 5–1 shows also the financial position of the firms after taking investment needs into account. On the average, for each monetary unit of current activity, the corporations needed an additional two-thirds of the unit to cover investment requirements. The largest needs are in electricity enterprises because of high growth. The railroads had low investment requirements but large operating deficits. About half of the external finances needed were provided by government transfers. Although differences were found among regions and industries, flow of funds as a percentage of activity was low, in particular in Latin American railways. The authors conclude that "government-owned enterprises, rather than serving as a focal point for collecting financial resources for their own investment or for other purposes, have generally placed a financial burden on parent governments" (Gantt and Dutton, 1968, p. 128).

Table 5.1 Indicators of performance of SOEs in LDCs by area and industry

Area and Indicators	Railways	Other Transport	Petroleum	Electricity	Communications	Other Industries	Overall Mean
				Industry			
Europe							
Flow of funds as percentage of activity	-20	-0.5	10.1	27.4	24.8	-12.4	0.7
Gross investment ratios as percentage of activity	17.7	14.8	24.1	49.3	20.3	162	80.7
Surplus after investment as percentage of activity	-37.7	-15.3	-14	-21.9	4.5	-174.4	-80
Transfer excluding loans from government budget	29.2	3.3	1.3	1	-8.1	74.6	33.2
Latin America							
Flow of funds as percentage of activity	-57.1	-3.8	43.3	21	26.7	-6.6	2.1
Gross investment ratios as percentage of activity	32.3	46.3	70	114.2	51.5	48.5	58.4
Surplus after investment as percentage of activity	-89.4	-50.2	-26.7	-93.2	-24.9	-55.1	56.3
Transfer excluding loans from government budget	90.6	44.5	-1.6	59.6	14.5	45.7	42.3

(cont.)

Area and Indicators	Industry						Overall Mean
	Railways	Other Transport	Petroleum	Electricity	Communications	Other Industries	
(cont.)							
Africa							
Flow of funds as percentage of activity	18.2	30.2	—	21.4	-27.3	31.7	19.5
Gross investment ratios as percentage of activity	26.8	24.7	—	100.9	13.8	449	80.6
Surplus after investment as percentage of activity	-8.6	5.5	—	-79.5	-41.1	-417.4	-61.1
Transfer excluding loans from government budget	0.6	-1.5	—	8.4	42.1	100.6	13.4
Asia							
Flow of funds as percentage of activity	16.6	14.5	—	37.7	-10.2	—	16.4
Gross investment ratios as percentage of activity	29.1	19.1	—	208.7	47.9	—	91.2
Surplus after investment as percentage of activity	-12.5	-4.5	—	-171.1	-58.1	—	-74.8
Transfer excluding loans from government budget	-0.1	6.4	—	56.1	58	—	34.8

Asia (cont.)

Overall Mean

Flow of funds as percentage of activity	−13.5	10.9	33.8	27.2	5.7	−6.3	8
Gross investment ratios as percentage of activity	27.5	30.1	56.9	129.2	37.7	131.7	74.3
Surplus after investment as percentage of activity	−41	−19.3	−23.1	−102	−32	−138.1	−66.3
Transfer excluding loans from government budget	35.3	17.8	−0.7	33.7	28.6	63.3	32.9

SOURCE: Gantt, Andrew H., and Guiseppe Dutto, 1968, "Financial Performances of Government-Owned Corporations in Less-Developed Countries," IMF Staff Papers 15:108, 111, 113, 115.

In a more recent International Monetary Fund (IMF) study, Short (1984) found that nonfinancial SOEs in twenty-four developing countries earned an average operating surplus before depreciation of about 1.3 percent of the GDP in 1977. The net budgetary burden (defined as government subsidies, transfers and net lending to SOEs, less dividends and interest payments to government) averaged more than 3 percent of GDP, of which current subsidies and transfers were 1.4 percent of GDP. In developed countries, for the same year, the budgetary burden of SOEs for seven countries averaged 2 percent of GDP (Short, 1984). The budgetary burden is partially the result of government policy but partially a result of losses and the inability of SOEs to generate funds for investment. The losses ultimately have to be paid by the taxpayers. Individual country studies also show a dismal picture of losses and self-financing close to nil. Shirley (1983, p. 12) shows that gross profits as a percentage of sales for Turkey's manufacturing SOEs was 1 percent in 1973, −4.7 percent in 1974, −10.3 percent in 1975, −23.2 percent in 1976, −20.3 percent in 1977, −16.6 percent in 1978 and −2 percent in 1979. In 1976, SOEs in Turkey required 1 percent more labor and 43.6 percent more capital per unit of output than private enterprises. In comparing these figures, readers should bear in mind that the average SOE in Turkey is about 50 percent more capital-intensive than a private enterprise. From 1965 to 1975 average labor productivity in Turkey rose by 9 percent per annum in the private sector and 7 percent in the SOEs. In 1979, average labor productivity was 30 percent higher in the private than in the state-owned manufacturing sectors (Shirley, 1983, p. 16). These poor results may have been caused by bureaucratic interference and the imposition of price ceilings on the output of SOEs that reduced their growth potential.

Frank found the performance of five African economies—Kenya, Tanzania, Nigeria, Ghana and Uganda—"hardly short of disasterous." He attributes this abysmal performance to bad management and to the fact that investment has been made "with political patronage in mind and to the benefit primarily of powerful political figures" (in Ranis, 1971, p. 97). Killick (in UNIDO, 1983), in a later survey of manufacturing firms in four African countries, found that they contributed little to economic growth, that they were a drain on public finance and that they discouraged the growth of private industry. The World Bank survey of sub-Saharan Africa reports, "Public enterprises have thus far caused serious fiscal burdens" (1981, p. 38). Gillis (1980, p. 267) observed that SOE savings in Korea, Uruguay, Pakistan and Indonesia represented 10 to 15 percent of gross investments. However, in each of the first three countries the SOEs were unable to generate enough funds to finance their investments. Diaz found that subsidies in Argentina, through the cheap operation of railroads and other SOEs, reached 3 percent of the GNP (in Ranis, 1971, pp. 218–219).

The profit record of most SOEs in other LDCs shows a similar dismal picture of many ill-conceived investments and huge capital needs. A report of an international workshop on financial profitability and losses of SOEs, held in Yugoslavia in June 1981, (Ahmed, 1982) shows that in many individual SOEs the financial losses are heavy:

> Bangladesh: "The overall financial picture of the public enterprises . . . shows substantial negative returns." [p. 23]
> Somalia: "The production enterprises run at a heavy loss." [p. 24]
> Tanzania: "The majority of the public enterprises are being run at heavy losses." [p. 24]
> Algeria: "The general picture of the financial situation of the Algerian public enterprises was one of losses." [p. 24]
> Sri Lanka: "A majority of public enterprises were making heavy financial losses." [p. 25]
> Thailand: "Though 'on an aggregate basis' public enterprises make profits, the size of the profit has been decreasing for the last few years." [p. 25]
> Tunisia: "In certain sectors such as mining, textiles and transportation, the enterprises are suffering financial losses." [p. 26]
> Jamaica: "By and large the public enterprises are being run at substantial losses." [p. 26]

For the aggregate of SOEs reported on in the conference, 70 percent operated at financial losses. In Nigeria, the average annual losses as a percent of sales of 44 SOEs studied for the period 1975-1979 was 55.1 percent. Only the SOEs in the service and in the finance and investment sectors were profitable, while agrobusiness SOEs lost on the average 70.9 percent of their sales revenue. Manufacturing firms lost on the average 4.2 percent of sales (Fubara, 1984, p. 10).

According to the World Bank, SOEs in Mexico, excluding state petroleum company, showed a net loss of 1.2 percent of GDP in 1980, and Senegal's SOEs recorded a deficit in 1977/1978 and again in 1979/1980 (1983, p. 74).

Ramandaham (1984b, p. 136) cites more examples:

> Zambia: "Parastatal performance was negative in terms of net profit in mining, tourism, agriculture and miscellaneous industry, and also, on the whole, in 1978." (Third National Development Plan, Lusaka), p. 416.
> Sudan: "The financial performance of the public sector enterprises registered deterioration" (over 1970/75). "The past record of financial performance of public enterprises clearly indicates that their net contribution to domestic capital formation has been minimal." [The Six Year Plan of Economic and Social Development 1977/78–1982/83, Vol. 1 (Khartoum, 1977) pp. 13 and 68.]

Table 5.2 shows profits and subsidies of SOEs in selected developing countries as a percentage of GDP at market prices. In all of them the return on investment is low and sometimes negative, and self-financing of investment is close to nil.

In some cases, the situation may be worse than Table 5–2 reveals. Thus Trebat (1983, p. 177) reports that Chile's SOE losses as percentage of net worth in 1978 were 3.12 percent and Mexico's SOEs' net losses as percentage of 1972-74 were 3.8 percent. On the other hand, in Brazil, the ratio of net profits to net worth was 11.4 percent in 1974 and 7.9 percent in 1978.

In Thailand, total deficits of SOEs are expected to double in the two years to end in September 1986 and to be equal to 3.5 percent of GNP (*The Economist*, December 21, 1985, p. 75).

In many cases, the losses wiped out the total equity several times. "The oldest and largest of Uganda's public enterprises, the Uganda Development Corporation, had an accumulated deficit of 128 million Uganda shillings, as compared with its total share capital of 159 million shillings, by the end of 1977. (It was 90 percent of the value of its fixed assets.) (Ramandaham, 1984b, p. 126). Table 5.3 indicates how high the accumulated deficits have been as a percentage of paid-up capital in certain Indian and Pakistani SOEs.

In Liberia, SOEs are experiencing acute cash flow problems and large operating losses. They have financed their losses largely through arrears in payment to the government and to other SOEs and increasing debts to sup-

Table 5.2   Profits and subsidies of SOEs in selected countries as a percentage of GDP at market prices

Country	After Tax Profit/Loss (−)		Current Subsidies	Gross Margin (Surplus/Deficit before Subsidies, Interest and Depreciation)
	Before Depreciation	After Depreciation[a]		
Industrialized Countries				
Australia (1974–1977)	1	—	n.a.	2.2
Canada (1978–1980)	1.1	0.4	n.a.	n.a.
France (1978–1981)[b]	1.2	n.a.	0.7	1.1
Italy (1978–1980)	− 0.3	− 2	n.a.	n.a.
Japan (1978–1980)	1	− 0.1	n.a.	n.a.
Netherlands (1978)	2.3	0.6	n.a.	n.a.
Norway (1977–1980)	0.8	n.a.	n.a.	n.a.
Developing Countries				
Africa				
Botswana (1978–1979)	1.7	0.9	n.a.	4.9
Ivory Coast (1978– 1979)	2.8	n.a.	n.a.	n.a.

(cont.)

Country	After Tax Profit/Loss (−)		Current Subsidies	Gross Margin (Surplus/Deficit before Subsidies, Interest and Depreciation)
	Before Depreciation	After Depreciation[a]		
Developing Countries *(cont.)*				
Malawi (1978)	2.9	1.5	0	n.a.
Mali (1978)[c]	− 2	− 3	n.a.	− 0.9
Senegal (1974)[d]	4.9 (0.0)	3.2 (− 1.4)	n.a.	n.a.
Tunisia (1978–1980)	3.4	0.6	n.a.	n.a.
Asia				
Burma (1978–1980)	1.7	n.a.	n.a.	n.a.
India (1978)	1.7	0.4	0.6	3.6
Korea (1978–1980)	2.1	n.a.	n.a.	n.a.
Thailand (1978–1980)	1.2	n.a.	0.1	n.a.
Europe, Middle East				
Portugal (1978–1980)	n.a.	n.a.	4.5	n.a.
Turkey (1978–1980)	0.8	− 0.1	2.7	− 1.4
Western Hemisphere				
Argentina (1976–1977)	2.1	n.a.	1	n.a.
Barbados (1978–1980)	0.3	n.a.	1.3	n.a.
Bolivia (1974–1977)	2.4	n.a.	0.1	8
Chile (1978–1980)[b]	1.5	n.a.	0.3	8.2
Columbia (1978–1980)	1	n.a.	0.3	1.5
Dominican Republic (1978–1979)[b]	0.3	n.a.	0.7	n.a.
Guatemala (1978–1980)	0.3	n.a.	0	0.5
Guyana (1978–1980)	6.5	n.a.	1.1	13.5
Jamaica (1978–1980)[b]	1.3	n.a.	1.2	n.a.
Mexico (1978)[b]	1.5	n.a.	0.9	4.9
Panama (1978–1979)	0.6	− 1.8	0.4	n.a.
Paraguay (1978–1980)	1.4	n.a.	0.1	2.2
Peru (1978–1979)	0.6	n.a.	0.1	n.a.
Uruguay (1978–1980)	2.3	n.a.	0.3	3.8

NOTE: Gross margin is sales revenue less operating expenditures excluding depreciation and interest. Profits equal gross margin plus current transfers and subsidies less interest, dividends, and taxes. These data are not fully comparable because of differences in the treatment of SOE taxes, subsidies and finance charges.

[a]At replacement cost for most countries. The basis of measurement for several African countries is unknown.

[b]Major enterprises only.

[c]Eight large enterprises only.

[d]Figures in parentheses exclude the phosphate company.

SOURCE: P. Short, 1984.

Table 5.3   Accumulated deficits of selected SOEs in India (1981–1982) and Pakistan (1980–1981)

Enterprise	Deficit as percentage of equity
India	
Indian Firebricks & Insulation Co. Ltd.	279
Bharat Coking Coal	191
Heavy Engineering Corporation Ltd.	170
Jessop Co. Ltd.	211
Mining & Allied Machinery Corp. Ltd.	240
Triveni Structurals Ltd.	156
Biecco Lawrie Ltd.	627
National Instruments Ltd.	667
Central Inland Water Transport Corp. Ltd.	353
Garden Reach Shipbuilders & Engineers Ltd.	123
Scooters Ltd.	604
Bharat Ophthalmic Glass Ltd.	259
Rehabilitation Industries Corp. Ltd.	627
Tannery & Footwear Corp. of India Ltd.	222
Banana & Fruit Development Corp. Ltd.	269
National Textile Corp. (Delhi, etc.) Ltd.	173
NTC (Maharashtra North) Ltd.	116
NTC (Maharashtra South) Ltd.	120
NTC (UP) Ltd.	228
NTC (W. Bengal, etc.) Ltd.	242
Elgin Mills Ltd.	317
Cotton Corp. of India Ltd.	269
Jute Corp. of India Ltd.	1,297
Hindustan Prefab Ltd.	129
Hindustan Steel Works Construction Ltd.	251
Engineering Projects (I) Ltd.	719
Pakistan	
Antibiotics Pr. Ltd.	363
Kurram Chemical Co. Ltd.	196
Pakdyes & Chemical Co. Ltd.	134
Pakistan PVC Ltd.	360
Ravi Rayon Ltd.	100
Ravi Engineering	495
National Fertilizer Marketing Ltd.	472
Bannu Sugar Mills	1,067
Utility Stores Corp.	167
Printing Corp. of Pakistan	264

SOURCE: V. V. Ramandadham (1984) *The Nature of Public Enterprise* (New York: St. Martin's Press) pp. 127–128.

pliers and local banks. In many LDCs, because of similar circumstances, the SOEs are vulnerable to court action by creditors. This situation often forces the government to inject more cash into the SOEs. The poor aggregate financial performance of the SOEs is damaging to the economy as a whole and is a growing burden to the treasury.

In Mexico, the only SOE to earn a substantial profit in the first 9 months of 1984 was PEMEX, the oil SOE (earning $2.38 billion). The rest lost $789 million between them, of which the federal electricity commission lost $550 million. In Argentina, the accumulated losses of the SOE sector in 1983 were estimated at $1.7 billion, or about 2 percent of GDP. Even the Argentinian oil company, YPF, managed to be probably the only loss-ridden oil company in the world (*The Economist*, February 16, 1985, p. 67). Capital-intensive mammoth projects in the SOE sector led to its growing indebtedness and reliance on governmental transfers. In Argentina, the total indebtedness of the SOE sector was $14.2 billion, or 23 percent of the GDP (*The Economist*, February 11, 1985, p. 67).

The financial performance of the SOEs in the developed countries may be seen from Table 5.4, showing net income (or loss) of the largest Western European SOEs for the selected years in the decade 1969–1984. Several interesting observations can be made. First, most oil companies are very profitable. Second, the largest losers are the declining industries (coal, steel). Third, British Aerospace, after privatization, is much more profitable than when it was an SOE, and than other SOEs in other industries.

Accounting profits are not a good measure of efficiency of SOEs since accounting conventions define "profits" in different and still acceptable ways. Many SOEs use historical cost accounting, and this gives unfair advantage to older firms with historically low depreciation charges. In fields such as energy, water or transportation, SOEs are natural monopolies that have declining average cost curves, profits being determined by government decisions, so that accounting profits may be the result of taking advantage of the monopoly power despite inefficient use of resources.

Other SOEs are not business enterprises and were not established for profit purposes. Others are established by the government to develop new technologies. Evaluating their activities by the criterion of profitability is most misleading. Frequently, private-sector firms were nationalized to prevent their going bankrupt. Serious rehabilitation efforts are required to make such companies profitable again. Here, too, profitability is not the only criterion. In other cases, SOEs serve as a tax instrument, and their high profits derive from the monopoly granted them, not from the efficiency with which they are managed. High profits may also result from inadequate maintenance. Then again, higher profits may simply reflect market imperfections, not efficiency.

Profitability is certainly not the sole index of managerial efficiency in an SOE. Profitability and cost minimization can be used as a criterion only if they are the avowed objectives of the enterprise. SOEs are also seen as instru-

Table 5.4 Net income (or loss) of the largest western European state-owned firms (in thousands of dollars)

Industry	Fortune 500 Rank 1984	1969	1974	1979	1983	1984
Metals and Heavy Engineering						
British Steel (UK)	88	(54,766)	170,455	(600,796)	(1,452,230)	(381,804)
Cockerill (Bel)	173	22,127	18,139	(122,423)	(658,907)	73,107
Halsider (It)	*	—	50,413	(309,730)	—	—
Salzgitter (Ger)	146	9,875	20,503	(1,997)	272,863	(153,279)
Svenska Varv (Swed)	*	—	—	98,724	61,961	—
Svenskt Stae (Swed)	343	—	—	(6,882)	3,962	24,164
VIAG (Ger)	239	—	23,684	25,325	31,684	37,993
VOEST-Alpine (Aust)	130	1,981	9,901	(29,124)	(2,062)	27,117
Sacilor (Fr)	110	—	24,385	(358,452)	(710,785)	(920,006)
Usinor (Fr)	105	16,176	29,041	—	(713,874)	(845,921)
British Shipbuilders (UK)	368	—	—	(124,573)	(213,718)	(346,053)
Valmet (Finland)	452	—	—	5,509	6,984	15,185
Preussag (Ger)	94	—	24,289	23,739	41,860	47,575
Motor Vehicles						
Alfa Romeo (It)	*	—	(89,432)	(109,920)	—	—
BL (UK)	100	46,769	(56,318)	(306,632)	(229,656)	107,516
Renault (Fr)	30	29,191	7,261	241,520	(206,769)	(1,435,861)
Volkswagenwerk (Ger)	16	126,904	(312,585)	371,534	(51,083)	85,916
SEAT (Sp)	427	—	6,463	(224,855)	(249,251)	(224,905)

Electric and Electronics					
CGE (Fr)	46	18,784	25,654	—	52,611	67,533
Thomson (Fr)	61	19,279	34,339	64,457	(140,776)	(2,402)
Norsk Hydro (Nor)	109	—	—	28,985	66,839	130,399
Bull (Fr)	321	—	—	—	(82,023)	55,921
ICL (UK)	*	—	—	71,284	59,772	—
Petroleum						
Britoil (UK)	242	—	—	28,859	217,226	226,245
BP (UK)	2	232,320	1,140,117	3,439,582	1,562,873	1,474,466
CFP-Total (Fr)	11	—	292,457	1,137,282	101,548	149,476
Elf-Aquitaine (Fr)	7	62,741	238,229	1,310,132	488,451	742,576
ENI (It)	3	16,800	(91,256)	89,040	(928,925)	(50,119)
OMV (Aust)	181	—	13,153	19,616	133	12,002
Saarbergwerke (Ger)	206	—	(10,157)	—	(81,067)	(28,777)
VEBA (Ger)	55	—	12,118	50,367	5,208	(21,011)
ENPETROL (Sp)	111	—	—	25,226	2,775	19,526
Statoil (Nor)	106	—	—	—	187,369	143,745
Neste (Fin)	80	—	3,056	30,560	11,121	11,763
PETROGAL (Port)	233	—	—	26,414	1,786	3,612
Hispanoil (Sp)	454	—	—	—	11,117	36,909
Butano (Sp)	*	—	—	(23,836)	(5,502)	—
Petroliber (Sp)	*	—	—	—	4,500	—

(cont.)

Industry	Fortune 500 Rank 1984	1969	1974	1979	1983	1984
(cont.)						
Mining and Chemicals						
National Coal Board (UK)	59	(21,314)	(315,777)	(37,671)	(185,498)	0
Charbonage de France (Fr)	295	(10,865)	(2,573)	18,249	(29,215)	(24,326)
DSM (Neth)	57	30,650	192,995	44,446	57,328	144,289
Enterprise Miniere et Chimique (Fr)	317	—	42,770	22,988	(16,829)	6,689
Montedison (It)	56	66,198	173,602	22,193	(211,882)	(47,218)
Saint-Gobain (Fr)	58	28,960	146,386	154,350	53,135	58,761
Ruhrkohle (Ger)	49	—	—	3,249	15,293	41,042
Rhone-Poulenc (Fr)	74	92,612	179,556	186,019	12,857	227,473
Pechiney (Fr)	120	60,367	154,589	233,124	(60,771)	62,398
Holding Companies						
IRI (It)	5				—	
Statsfortag Group (Swed)	348	—	16,869	45,000	35,060	7,008
EFIM (It)	198	—	—	—	(509,307)	(323,694)

Aerospace					
Aerospatiale (Fr)	180	8,876	(76,569)	1,956	(46,903)	37,969
British Aerospace (UK)	156	6,703	40,421	86,844	124,757	144,235
Messerschmidt-Bolkau-Blohm (Ger)	247	—	—	24,024	35,896	34,408
Rolls-Royce (UK)	265	10,140	—	(133,475)	(292,565)	26,711
SNECMA (Fr)	305	—	—	15,527	(7,077)	6,707
Avions Marcel Dassault-Breguet (Fr)	277	—	—	64,020	51,661	49,377
Matra (Fr)	316	—	—	47,108	4,463	7,838
Tobacco					
SEITA (Fr)	*	—	—	(55,532)	(14,396)	—
Tabacalera (Sp)	299	—	9,086	10,985	9,551	7,344

*not in Fortune 500 of 1984

—data not available

SOURCE: Fortune Directory of the 500 Largest Industrial Corporations Outside the U.S.—August 1970, pp. 143–150, August 1975, pp. 156–167, August 11, 1980, pp. 190–205, August 20, 1984, pp. 200–219, August 19, 1985, pp. 168–187.

ments for the execution of social and economic policies of the government, as tools for winning the next election, or as a means for distributing political patronage. They are also expected to be sensitive to the needs of people (Otter, 1984).

Since economies are riddled with market imperfections and distortions, financial profitability is not necessarily consistent with positive social surplus. Firms in oligopolistic industries control prices, they are sometimes protected by high tariff barriers and market prices for imports do not reflect their opportunity costs.

Lower profits or loss may point to indirect subsidy or to low controlled prices for an SOE's profits. At the same time, the government also determines many of the company's costs. The government may set wage ceilings, fix raw material costs, subsidize interest rates or give SOEs their investment funds at preferential rates. The company's profits are the outcome of policies regulating input and output prices, which the company does not set. In these cases the degree of profitability of such a firm cannot be used to indicate the level of efficiency with which it exploits its inputs. Thus, if a subsidy given to farmers is granted directly, an SOE making fertilizers may be profitable; if the same subsidy is given as a reduced price of fertilizers, the firm would show losses that are not necessarily a reflection of its efficiency. In Indonesia weaving SOEs were profitable because state ownership guaranteed a supply of raw materials, obtaining a quota of yarn (that was in short supply) and "virtually ensured the profitability of the recipient" (Hill, 1982, p. 1019). With the abolition of yarn quotas in 1966, the financial position of these SOEs gradually deteriorated.

Finally, SOE managers may hide profits or at least attempt to smooth them. As Grayson (1981) notes in the case of national oil companies (NOCs),

> If returns are too high, owner governments assume (1) that the NOC charges outrageous prices, (2) that it pays inadequate wages, (3) that it ignores some or most of its nonfinancial objectives, or (4) that it commits all three sins simultaneously. In fact, a national oil company's public position resembles that of the multinationals. The moment that ROI seems more than 'reasonable', governments and the news media begin to talk about 'excess' or 'windfall' profits. A very profitable NOC would lose some of its managerial independence— the government might ask it to undertake a new nonfinancial project, for instance. On the other hand, running the NOC at a loss would also erode managerial authority (Grayson, 1981, p. 254).

The burden of the social welfare programs is often used as an excuse for inefficiency. In fact, the major reason most economists insist on the separation of the economic and social tasks of these enterprises is to allow a better assessment of their performance. Today, unfortunately, it is impossible to relate SOEs' profitability or rate of self-financing to the ownership factor or to bad management. Losses could have been a result of resource diversion for various means; remember that in Mexico, most losses come from electricity, used to subsidize the private sector. These uses, in turn, created a budgetary burden but may also have reduced incentives for cost controls, resulting in greater losses and higher indebtedness. Some developing countries also face acute shortages of trained managers, engineers and foreign exchange.

The major reason for losses, however, is the political milieu in which SOEs operate. According to Ghai, SOEs in Africa are frequently used as a means of patronage and a source of wealth and power for political and administrative leaders.

> *The role of the State has therefore been to enable groups which have acquired control over the State apparatus to establish an economic basis for themselves . . . The distinction between the government and the enterprises tends to become blurred and the government has often a vested interest in hiding the inefficiency of enterprises (in Reddy, 1983, p. 182).*

On the other hand, in countries in which SOEs operate under control structures with less governmental interference, the financial results were much better (UNIDO, 1983), as Brazil, Chile, Peru, Thailand and Uruguay, more SOEs showed positive accounting profits than losses. The German or Austrian SOEs fared as well as private enterprises.

The financial results of SOEs are important insofar as they have an impact on the resource utilization of the country. However, these results are not necessarily an indicator of efficiency or performance. A comparative study of the relative performance of public and private manufacturing enterprises in India (Dholakia, 1978) found that although SOEs were not very profitable, they have shown much larger increases in total factor productivity. Over the 15-year period 1960–1975, the total factor productivity has increased by 89 percent in the SOEs and by only 3 percent in the private sector (p. M-8). "The severe criticism of the management of public enterprises solely on the ground of low profitabilty, may often turn out to be misleading inasmuch as it represents a partial view of the overall performance" (p. M-9). SOEs have been absorbing an increasing amount of scarce national resources and used these resources with "most rapidly increasing efficiency" (p. M-4). At the same time, Ramamurti (1985b, p.10) found that senior bureaucrats and selected journalists used as external evaluators of Indian SOEs "espouse one set of standards for judging performance but use a different set of standards (in which profitability plays a very important role) for *actually* judging performance (p. 18). His study shows that profits are a more important criterion for performance evaluation of SOEs in practice than they should be according to official policy or economic theory. Perhaps because SOEs are judged in practice by their accounting profitability, public perception is that SOEs are less efficient than private enterprises. Is that perception true? Can one discern systematic differences in behavior or results between private and state-owned firms? If such differences exist, what are the reasons?

COMPARING PRIVATE FIRMS AND SOEs

Theoretical Arguments

According to the proponents of the property rights school of thought, individuals respond to incentives, and the pattern of incentives at any time is influenced by the property rights structure. Individual managers are assumed to maximize their utility subject to the limits established by the existing organizational structure. They respond to incentives, and different property assignments have different effects on the penalty/reward system. Individual businesspersons in private enterprise are profit maximizers, who are attempting to achieve efficiency. When owners are not the managers, they incur costs in contracting, policing, negotiating and enforcing their property rights. Private property rights are exclusive and voluntarily transferable. In some cases, the government limits the individual owner's rights to change the form, place, substance or use of an asset. Thus, zoning laws put restrictions on the free use of land. Attenuation causes the market value of the assets to decrease.

In an SOE it is virtually impossible to transfer the ownership rights belonging to the state from one individual or group to another. Taxpayers who wish to change their portfolio of assets cannot sell their shares in an SOE. In theory, at least, they can change citizenship and move to another country in which the portfolio of assets held by the state is more to their liking. These taxpayers may, of course, cast their votes in the elections, attempting to change the preferences of the state and its policies. However, they do not have any easy or direct way to transfer their share of the property rights in any one of the SOEs. The inability to transfer ownership rights is said to mean that state ownership is inherently less efficient than private property.

First, it is argued that owners of a private firm have an incentive to monitor management behavior to ensure efficiency in the production of goods and services. In contrast, a taxpayer-owner of an SOE, being one of many diffused owners, does not have a similar incentive to scrutinize management. The greater the personal financial investment, the greater the interest in the operations of the firm. Owner-managers have the highest stake and, therefore, care more. If ownership is diffused and separate from management, the additional monitoring costs may make the firm less efficient. However, the owner can still motivate managers by linking their pecuniary compensation with the profits of the firm, allowing the managers to capture part of any monetary gains, e.g., through stock options. In an SOE the manager (and the government's bureaucrat) has no wealth invested in the firm and no rights to profit sharing. Lack of a link between the firm's economic performance and the manager's personal pecuniary gains, it is claimed, will have detrimental effects on efficiency.

Second, transferability of shares encourages specialization of ownership. According to Armen Alchian (1965, 1977), since owners of shares in a private firm can sell these shares in the capital market, shareowners will be those who find their highest valued use as an input. Others will simply exercise their exit right and sell the shares. Ownership, Peltzmann (1971) argued, can be viewed as a productive input that organizes managerial inputs and fulfills the functions of risk bearing. If a market for these rights is not available, as is the case in an SOE, the distribution of taxpayer-owners or even that of the government bureaucrats, acting as their agents, will not reflect their highest valued use as an input, at least not as frequently as in an investor-owned private enterprise.

This line of thinking is based on the axiomatic assumption that individuals operate to maximize their utility. In some of the theoretical presentations, this assumption is said to imply that utility includes both pecuniary and nonpecuniary gains (e.g., Furubotn and Pejovich, 1972, 1974). Under this configuration, one may hypothesize that SOE managers will be individuals who possess different utilities, valuing, e.g., prestige or power more than the additions to their wealth. In most studies, however, utility is equated with pecuniary gains. It is hypothesized that the more wealth the manager owns in a firm, and the more the manager's income is a function of this wealth by the linking of personal net monetary gains to the operational results of the firm, the higher the manager's incentives to invest more time, energy and efforts in ensuring organizational efficiency.

Berle and Means (1932) detected a growing tendency for the separation of ownership and control, at least in the United States. The separation of ownership and control means that diffused owners cannot really control management and that many large private firms are run by a self-perpetuating group of managers. As Dahrendorf correctly noted, a class theory based on the relationships between the owners of means of production and the workers "loses its analytical value as soon as legal ownership and factual control are separated" (1959, p. 136). Separation of ownership and control may reduce efficiency, and the manager may not single-mindedly pursue profits. Adam Smith certainly thought so: "The directors of such companies, however [are] the managers rather of other people's money than their own. Negligence and profusion, therefore, must always prevail, more or less, in the management of the affairs of such a company" (1937, p. 700).

One should, therefore, expect to find that the more dispersed the ownership, the lower the level of profits and efficiency. Pondy (1969) found that as ownership was separated from management, the ratio of administrative to operating personnel in forty-five manufacturing firms increased. His explanation for this finding is the "stronger preference for hierarchical expansion *per se*" of the professional manager (p. 57).

The vast literature on the separation of ownership from control has not reached any clear conclusions. There is considerable debate on the proportion of shares needed for effective control by the owners, as well as to whether shares held by one family or a pension fund should be counted as one. Certainly, concentrated ownership is not synonymous with the degree of involvement of the owners in the affairs of the corporation, and a pension fund, e.g., may not exercise its ownership rights in the same way as a private owner. Different researchers have used different approaches to these questions and have come out with different results. Berle and Means (1932) used 20 percent ownership as defining effective control, while Larner (1970), Palmer (1972) and Sheehan (1967) used 10 percent. Villajero (1962) used 5 percent and McEachern (1975) used 4 percent as sufficient control. Gordon (1945) added the shares held by what he termed "a small compact group of individuals," and Villajero (1962) included the holdings of investment companies and insurance firms in his measures of control. In view of these differences in definitions, Larner (1970) maintained that separation of ownership and control is growing, and Zeitlin (1974), using the same data, argued that there was no discernible trend.

Further, in most studies of the effects of ownership, the differences were not statistically significant. In some, the statistical techniques were defective, partly due to failure to control for government regulation. At any rate, the results did not resolve the questions. Some of these empirical studies support the hypothesis that individuals work more productively if they can appropriate the managerial gains of their work. Others do not. (For a summary see Nyman and Silberston, 1977. See also De Alessi, 1973; Gordon, 1945; Larner, 1966; McEachern, 1975, 1976; Jensen and Meckling, 1976, p. 305; Leibenstein, 1976, p. 44.) It stands to reason that additional factors, like the structure of the markets in which the enterprise operates, influence the profit rate. (See Demsetz, 1983.) In any event, it is clear that when a company is not run by its owner, there are likely to be agency costs.

Franchise agreements are a profitable device for reducing monitoring costs. Shelton (1967) compared two sets of franchises, one set operated by owner-managers and another by experienced managers employed by the parent company, motivated by bonuses that could be as high as a third of their salaries. His results show clearly that higher net returns are associated with owner-management. For example, the net revenue/sales ratio averaged 1.8 percent for franchise employees and 9.5 percent for owner-managers.

Even though it is difficult to monitor managerial behavior in a diffused ownership firm, it may be argued that managers in private firms receive bonuses and stock options that may be an incentive for seeking efficiency. The shareholders (as well as the capital market) may discipline the managers to behave in a profit-maximizing and efficient way (Stano, 1975). Thus, one major difference between private firms and SOEs is claimed to be in the incentive structures. Private enterprises "operate for profit and public ones must at least avoid losses" (Davies, 1981). A manager in an SOE does not increase his or her present monetary gain because of benefits that will accrue to the organization. Government controllers have even less personal monetary gain from increased efficiency of SOEs. Since shares are not transferable, private individuals are said to have no incentive to devote their time and energy to detect inefficient management in SOEs. They cannot use their resources to acquire the firm, apply their skills to reorganize it and, thus, appropriate gains to themselves. Even if an individual would be willing to reorganize such a firm, bearing all costs of implementing corrective actions, his or her personal gains in terms of lower taxes will be miniscule or even zero. In a private firm, even when ownership is diffused, managers always face the possibility that certain individuals, constantly searching for monetary gains, will take over a laggard firm. The very existence of those alert entrepreneurs puts pressures on managers to perform efficiently (Manne, 1965, p. 110). State ownership does not have a similar ingenious institutional device. Moreover, the government bureaucracy does not bear personal costs if firms are inefficient. They may also be constrained by a host of bureaucratic rules and regulations.

As a result of these factors, SOE managers are said to have no incentive to run efficient operations, and the monitoring system of their operations suffers from the same weakness. In fact, it may be argued that managers of SOEs have more opportunities to further their interests at the expense of the owners-taxpayers. They can insure themselves by employing larger staffs and more capital aids to assist them in decision making (De Alessi, 1974a). They can increase the size of the organization simply because larger size means higher salaries, more perquisites and higher budgets. To achieve high growth, they can use lower discount rates in evaluating investment opportunities, thus implementing larger projects, using more capital (De Alessi, 1969, 1974a, 1974b). They can monitor work less effectively (Davies, 1981) or simply opt for an easier life. In short, they will manage the firms less efficiently and take fewer risks than their private sector counterparts. Therefore, SOEs will use more labor and capital for a given output and will have lower profits, and their managers will enjoy more leisure than managers in privately owned firms similarly situated.

This explanation does not seem to be very convincing. Large business enterprises are very complex, and the decisions made by their managers involve a trade-off between short- and long-term considerations. In fact, many claim, the need to show quarterly results means that large private enterprises, at least in the United States, tend to develop myopic behavior, ignoring the long-term needs of the firm. Managers seeking to maximize their gains in an uncertain environment may decide to cut R&D costs or to minimize maintenance costs. Moreover, several studies point out that managers of private business enterprises attempt not to achieve efficiency but to maximize the growth of the firm (Baumol, 1959) or that they prefer to spend more on staff and perquisites (Williamson, 1964). Further, managers are not necessarily motivated by pecuniary incentives. They have been portrayed by Maccoby (1976) as gamesmen, playing the games of power and of prestige and attempting to win games, not because of their stock options but because of the rules of the game. No empirical evidence supports, however, the hypothesis that firms that have higher incentives are better and more efficiently managed. Further, in a democracy, the electorate can voice their concern about higher prices, putting pressure on Parliament to demand efficiency from SOEs.

The earlier quote from Davies (1981) suggests a totally different explanation—i.e., a difference in management's perception of the objectives to be pursued by the enterprise. Private-sector managers know they are expected to be efficient and to make profits. SOE managers perceive their role differently: they have to avoid losses, but they may see their major role as managing the environment rather than managing the business in an efficient way. Since SOEs have many stakeholders, all of whom have to be satisfied, the managers spend more of their time in public relations activities, in making explanations or in negotiations with external authorities. The more of the manager's extremely scarce time that is devoted to the management of the environment, the less time is left for the efficient management of the enterprise.

We have considered differences in behavior caused by behavior of managers and their controllers that is based on their different self-interest. Lindsay (1976, p. 1062) suggests another reason that leads him to believe that SOEs are inherently less efficient than private enterprises: customers of SOEs affect supply behavior, not only by their decisions in the market but also through political channels. This demand-based political influence is strongest when the enterprise supplies services that economists classify as public goods; i.e., those goods in which the consumption by one individual does not reduce the amount available to others. In these cases, one encounters problems like the familiar free rider problem observed by Olson (1965). When the SOE produces outputs of private goods to be sold in the market, no free riders exist. Still, taxpayers can and do pressure government to force SOEs to supply them goods at below market value because of an alleged or real social value of the output. For example, the government may instruct a railroad to maintain unprofitable services, not because of its market value but because it wants to help the elderly or simply because the constituents of the political representative of a certain town put pressure to maintain the service at prices that do not cover the cost. The market value of the consumption without any governmental intervention is simply the amount individuals are willing to pay for the services. If this value is below cost, the service will not be offered. When the service is supplied by government directly or by an SOE, political pressures may force its continuation at a loss. The loss, of course, is covered either by direct subsidy, by cross subsidization or by continuous losses of the SOE that are covered by governmental capital appropriation.

The same phenomenon is true also in the case of a private enterprise. In many market-oriented economies, government restrictions on economic activity are a pervasive fact of life. These restrictions give rise to rents in a variety of forms, and people often compete for the rents. This competition is for directly unproductive profit-seeking activities, e.g., through lobbying. As long as the cost of lobbying is lower than the expected benefits, rational profit maximizers will lobby in an attempt to get government subsidies or other forms of largesse. It is important to remember that the alternative to state ownership in many cases is regulation rather than a totally free market. In the case of water supplies, for example, there is a need to maintain a significant excess capacity for fire protection. Whether the additional cost of this protection is absorbed into the rates or paid by the property owners is a question decided by the regulators, not by the firm supplying the water—be it public or private.

Property rights theorists correctly point out that the very existence of private transferable property rights allows the flourishing of new entrepreneurs, eagerly looking for new opportunities. They also remind us that the threat of takeover bids may act as a constraint on managers. Still, in a mixed economy, a significant percentage of economic power is concentrated in the hands of the managers of a few hundred large firms. Many of them—in both private firms and SOEs—are motivated by considerations of power and achievement, not by personal pecuniary gains (see Chapter 8).

In many cases, the preservation of a nonprofitable service may generate a variety of external benefits, not captured by the accounting conventions. A government wishing to internalize these benefits may use public ownership or other means. Thus, "[t]he preservation of rail service avoids negative social and environmental impacts, such as air and noise pollution, increased traffic congestion and accidents, or increased risk from shipment of hazardous materials" (Fisher, 1982, p. 267). If business firms move away because of an abandonment of rail services, this factor may also increase the net fiscal burden on the state. Infant industry agreements, job preservations, or strategic considerations may lead a government to impose tariff restrictions. Potential entry of new companies may be deterred by minimum wage laws, health and safety regulations or environmental restrictions. In most of these cases, allocative efficiency is not the politician's ideal, and prospects of rents are created for both private firms and SOEs.

Another theoretical approach predicts SOEs to be less efficient than private enterprise for reasons of a different sort. The "public choice" school of thought is directed by the so-called theory of bureaucracy (Niskanen, 1971). Niskanen (1971) proposed that bureaucrats attempt to achieve more pay, power and prestige. Since in public bureaucracy there is no "bottom line," these "three p's" can be maximized by budget maximization. The coalition of bureaucrats and special interests pushes the budget to a higher level. According to this line of thinking, SOE managers attempt to maximize growth. De Alessi (1969) found some evidence that public managers use larger staff. They also use higher capital–labor ratios: the excess capital make productivity look higher to their monitors. This theory was tested mainly on public bureaucracies (for a summary, see Borcherding et al., 1982, pp. 136-145). However, it may be applied to SOEs, too.

EMPIRICAL EVIDENCE

Much of the debate on comparative efficiency of privately owned firms and SOEs is waged primarily on ideological grounds, generating much heat but very little light.

It is extremely difficult to compare efficiency in private enterprises and SOEs because it is not very easy to find two firms operating in the same country that are exactly comparable. Electric utilities in the United States are one exception described "as close to perfection in public–private comparability as any other imaginable real-world case" (Yunker, 1975, p. 66). California private electric utilities, however, have conceded that their costs are higher than state-owned electric firms but argued that their territories are more difficult to serve (Neuberg, 1977, p. 310, footnote). Different electric firms also have different input costs because one uses hydroelectric power and another coal or fuel or because the cost of capital to the SOE is lower: municipal firms in the U.S. can tap funds by issuing tax-exempt bonds. At the same time, it may be argued that differences in input costs are a result of absence of pressure on management to bargain.

Despite these difficulties, there is a growing number of studies comparing private enterprises and SOEs comparatively situated, i.e., cases in which both operate in the same country and the same environment. These studies were carried out mainly in the United States on electric power and refuse collection. There have been also a few studies in other countries.

Electricity and Telephone

Yunker (1975) estimated costs as a function of output and number of customers for 1969 on private and municipally owned firms producing 0.5 to 4 million megawatt hours per annum. He found that the costs of the public firms were lower but the results were not statistically significant. Further, Yunker did not control for input prices and for the different mixes of generation, transmission and distribution.

Meyer (1975) attempted to offset the problem of input prices by grouping the population geographically, assuming input prices vary regionally. He then chose a random sample of thirty firms in each ownership category. Real estate taxes, income taxes and interest costs were included in the general and administrative cost components but were excluded from the operating costs. He found for the years 1967, 1968, and 1969 that generating costs per megawatt hour declined with the size of the output and were lower for the SOEs. Transmission costs were also lower for SOEs and varied with the number of customers.

His study, however, was criticized on several methodological grounds, including the fact that he failed to exclude the cheaper federal hydroelectric plant (Meyer, 1975). Of course, if private plants burn fuel and a public firm uses hydropower, the cost difference is not necessarily a result of ownership. Meyer did, however, show that the cost coefficients are lower for SOEs. Wallace and Junk (1970) compared large private utilities with small municipalities. They found, not surprisingly, the former to be more efficient but mainly because of the economies of scale. When size and use of hydroelectric power was controlled for, municipal firms were found to be more efficient (Hellman, 1972; Yunker, 1975). Peltzmann (1971), however, attributed the difference to the tax-exempt status enjoyed by the municipalities. Spann (1977) concluded, on the basis of a different sample, that private firms adjusted for scale were no less efficient than municipal ones, and probably more so with respect to operating costs and investment per kwh.

Neuberg (1977) compared costs of distribution systems of 90 private and 75 municipal firms for 1972. He found the operating costs of public firms were 23 percent cheaper than private firms. This figure falls to 15 percent when capital costs are included.

Pescatrice and Trepani (1980) estimated simultaneously the cost and input demand functions and explored differences in generating technology, using generation data for the years 1965 and 1970 for 33 private firms and 23 municipal firms. They found SOEs minimize cost and have 24 (in 1965) to 33 (in 1970) percent lower per unit cost than their privately owned counterparts. Moreover, the rate of technical progress in SOEs was found to be considerably higher than in private firms.

Vaughn and Rives (1982) hypothesized that

> Ownership form can affect the firm's taste for price discrimination rather than its level of sales and output. At the same time, rate of return regulation (ROR) can affect the private firm's output decisions while not changing its taste for price discrimination. Finally the public firm's decisions may be affected if the firm cross-subsidies [sic]. [p. 385]

Therefore, the rate of return of SOEs may be lower, even though they are equally efficient.

The property rights theory would also predict that SOEs would charge lower prices that favor large users with much political power. Moore (1970) estimated profit-maximizing prices for sixty-two privately owned and twenty-seven municipally owned U.S. electric utilities. The prices charged by the latter were 10 to 22 percent below the profit-maximizing level, while those of private firms were between 0 and 5 percent below this level (see also Peltzman, 1971, Baldwin, 1975).

Mann and Seifried (1972) report for 128 U.S. municipally owned electric utilities that the rates are more cost related for domestic users than for commercial and industrial users and that industrial users reap most of the benefits. Jackson (1969) and Mann and Mikesell (1971) report that the price behavior of privately owned U.S. electric utilities is similarly cost related across different user categories. This evidence corroborates much anecdotal evidence from other countries that SOE electric firms are used to benefit large industrial users. It does not show, however, that these firms are more or less efficient. Gordon (1981) compared five state-owned and three investor-owned electricity firms in Canada. There were no fundamental differences among these firms. For example, all operated both in high-cost, remote areas and in lower-cost, heavily urbanized areas. They used different combinations of power sources and had different load factors. State-owned Hydro Quebec had the lowest cost (11.6 mills/kwh) and investor-owned Newfoundland Light and Power, the highest (393 mills/kwh). Hydro Quebec, however, had a high load factor and a high concentration of hydroelectric power, while Newfoundland Light and Power sells to a low-load residential service. A trend within utilities over the 1967 to 1976 period showed that all except one had a decreasing cost performance and that the SOEs had a better cost structure (Gordon, 1981, pp. 253–260).

Like the electric utilities, telephone companies operate in monopolistic environments, and the terms and conditions for these services are subject to the approval of a regulatory commission. A comparison of seven investor-owned and three state-owned telephone companies did not demonstrate major performance differences (Gordon, 1981, pp. 263–269): "When operating costs are totaled . . . investor-owned and government-owned telephone companies displayed very comparable performance" (p. 267). Bell-Canada has fewer employees per 1,000 telephones, apparently because of economies of scale.

It is also argued that price discrimination is a means for wealth maximization. SOE managers are reported to adopt fewer rate schedules than private managers. Peltzman (1971) hypothesized that the primary objective of SOE managers in public utilities is to maintain both their managerial tenure and political support for the firm; that is, managers would use the price mechanism to redistribute wealth within their political constituency, conferring benefits on voter-consumers, trading profits for political support. Therefore, there will be a tendency to average costs uniformly across classes; they will forego opportunities for price discrimination in the rate structure; prices will rise less frequently, and prices for nonvoters (consumers who are not residents of the community) will be higher than for resident-voters. The rate structure of those consumer groups that are more politically active or have lower costs of organizing will be lower regardless of the group's size or relative usage. Peltzman indeed found that the tariff structures of municipal electric utilities reflected less closely the costs of serving specific customer groups. He also found that privately owned firms engaged in greater price discrimination within customer groups and sell more output. De Alessi (1977) corroborated this hypothesis. He concluded that SOEs use less peak load pricing and that their rate structure is less complex than that of private firms. These results were corroborated by an international study of telephone rate structure. Littlechild (1983b) found that privately owned telephone systems are significantly more likely to use three or more time-of-day pricing periods for toll calls than SOEs. He also concluded that "separating a traditional PTT into its component postal and telephone business is unlikely to have much effect on telephone tariff policy unless the telephone business is also transferred to private ownership" (Littlechild, 1983b, p. 375).

Moore (1970) found evidence suggesting that municipal firms have greater capacity and built more plants at higher costs than private firms. He also reported that although fuel costs per kilowatt hour were not different for various ownership groups, operating costs per kilowatt hour were higher for municipally owned firms. De Alessi, in a summary of many studies, concluded that SOEs in electric power relative to privately owned firms charge lower prices, use less price discrimination, have more favoritism toward business relative to residential users and show less frequent rate changes, longer managerial tenure and less speed in adopting cost-reducing innovations (De Alessi, 1947a).

Blair (1976) also argues that rate structure in an SOE is particularly vulnerable to political influences. Prices will be based on subjective criteria such as "fair and equitable" and "less discriminatory."

In contrast, it should be noted that EDF in France has been a pioneer in the introduction of peak load pricing. The reason for the differences may be related more to the U.S. SOEs. Further, in many countries governments required uniform rates across customer groups and geographical areas for macroeconomic and social reasons. Whether the reasons for the rate structure are management inefficiency, electoral considerations or social welfare ideology cannot be deduced from these studies.

Foreman–Peck and Waterson (1985) focused on electricity generation in the United Kingdom, using data for 1937, when electricity in Britain was still generated by competing firms, selling their outputs to the national grid operated by the Central Electricity Board (CEB). At that time, CEB selected certain firms to supply it with electricity. They concluded that "the best municipal undertakings are on a par in static efficiency terms with the best companies and that they do not appear to show any biases towards the employment of particular factors of production" (p. 93). They also conclude "that in the absence of CEB regulation, the local authority sector would have been less efficient on average than the private sector" (p. 93).

Refuse Collection

In contrast to electricity, there are very small economies of scale in refuse (solid waste) collection. In the United States, refuse collection is sometimes performed by a municipal sanitation department, sometimes by private firms enjoying franchises to certain areas, or by competing firms. Most comparative studies in this area focus on the user charges levied, not on cost. Thus, Bennett and Johnson (1979) report on their home county of Fairfax, Virginia, that householders must contract with one of 29 competing firms or with the municipal solid waste division. The cost for municipal collection was $126.80 for one weekly collection, while the mean charges for private collectors was $85.76 with estimated standard deviation of $18.20 (p. 59). The authors do not explain the wide dispersion of prices charged by private collectors. They propose that these differentials are a result of the "transient nature of the population" (p. 61). The difference in user charges between private firms and the municipality is largely mitigated by the fact that municipal charges are deductible from both federal and state taxes.

Spann (1977), reviewing various activities including electric utilities and garbage collection concluded that, for the majority of the activities "private producers can provide the same services at the same or lower costs than can public producers" (p. 88).

The many studies of refuse collection often fail to take into account factors such as the volume and type of garbage, distance from disposal site and split between residential and commercial sites. Savas (1982) summarizes his and other studies, estimating municipal collection to be on the average 29 to 37 percent more costly than contract or franchise collection (pp. 93–94). This finding is attributed to the use of more persons to do the job, higher rates of absenteeism and the use of less productive vehicles (Spann, 1977, p. 82; Savas, 1979). Savas (1977a) also found that conventional municipal budgets understate the cost of the service by an average of 23 percent. Since the full costs are not revealed, municipalities tend to prefer their own refuse collection.

Hirsch (1965), however, found more significant differences between public and private cost of residential refuse collection in his study of 24 cities and municipalities in St. Louis and Missouri. Kemper and Quigley (1976) report, from an analysis of 101 Connecticut jurisdictions, that private collection appears to be 30 percent more expensive than municipal collection, which in turn appears to be about 25 percent more expensive than contract collection.

Kitchen (1976) studied 48 Canadian municipalities for 1979, each with a population in excess of 10,000. He found municipal collection is more costly than private collection.

Since most studies are based on user costs, differences in trucks used and other factors may influence the result. Still, most of the studies do point out that private refuse collection is cheaper.

Water

Other researchers in the United States compared the supply of water by municipal utilities and privately owned firms. Crain and Zardkoohi (1978) argued that a municipally owned water firm would tend to have more employees. They explained the propensity for increased employment as stemming from the desire to elevate the proportion of the population that supports the enterprise. They also report that the marginal product of labor was higher and the marginal product of capital lower for privately owned compared to municipally owned firms. In one case, a private firm became public and experienced a decline in output per employee of 40 percent. In another, a public firm became private and output per employee increased by 25 percent.

Mann (1979) compared 315 public and 56 private water utilities in the United States. The mean daily production of the publicly owned utilities was much larger than privately owned utilities, they experienced much greater maximum daily demand and per capita use, served more population that is less dense and rely more heavily on surface water sources as opposed to groundwater sources used by private firms. The publicly owned firms had much more debt costs and paid much less in taxes. They employed more employees per 10,000 population served but fewer per 1,000 customers served; this difference is apparently explained by the lower density. Both their monthly charges and their weighted annual labor cost per employee were lower, and they served fewer customers relative to the size of the population. Their operating cost per million gallons supplied was $198.50 compared to a mean of $203.09 for the private firms. Their total costs were higher because of the much higher debt charges (mean $64.10 compared to $36.46 for the private firms). In his regressions, Mann combined operating costs and debt charges, thus reaching the conclusion that total unit costs decrease, among other things, with private ownership (Mann, 1979, p. 22). He also claims that "one cannot assert unambiguously the sources of the [unit operating costs] differences. Regulatory environment may have a greater effect than ownership *per se*" (p. 25). Mann and Mikesell (1976) and Morgan (1977) showed that U.S. state/municipal suppliers of water are costlier by 15–20 percent than private suppliers.

Other Services

Scottsdale, Arizona, receives its fire protection under contract from a private company. A comparison of this city to three other Phoenix-area cities of comparable size, age and demographies demonstrated that Scottsdale ranked number one in speed of responses to alarms, and its average per capita cost for fire protection was $6.48 compared to $11.58 average in the three other cities (Poole, 1983, p. 109). Ahlbrandt (1973) compared Scottsdale to the Seattle area, showing Seattle municipal fire departments had 39 to 88 percent higher cost per capita.

Pashigian (1976) examined 58 U.S. bus transit systems, all of which had monopolies in their particular areas. He reports that private bus companies were more successful than municipally-owned companies in reducing the diversion of passengers from local transport to private autos. He also found that the convergence of urban transit systems from private to public ownership occurs earlier in cities where users have more voting strength. Blankart (1979) reports from Germany that municipal bus transport costs were higher per kilometer than the contract price paid to private bus operators for comparable services.

Borcherdring et al., (1982) summarized findings from more than fifty studies and in most of them SOEs had higher unit cost structures. The empirical evaluation of the reasons for the differences is fraught with many difficulties. No two firms are perfectly comparable, and even a single firm is not comparable over time. The size may be different and the distribution of clients and their density may not be identical.

Many studies rely on cost estimates for only one year, and have to make many assumptions. Certainly, the subject of comparing SOEs to private firms is in the embryonic stage.

Unfortunately, there are very few other studies comparing SOEs and private firms. Nunnenkamp (1981) compared the efficiency of SOEs and private firms in Taiwan. His analysis compares performance at the level of aggregate industries such as food, textile or basic metals—and therefore heterogeneous products and different types of these firms in the two sectors. Nunnenkamp found that in half the industries SOEs were less efficient. In general, he found "a lower technical efficiency in the public sector (although the differences between the various industries are considerable)" (p. 107). He also found SOEs had advantages in terms of economies of scale, but noted that "it is to be expected that SOEs' advantages will diminish with an increasing engagement of private enterprises in industries characterized by far reaching economies of scale" (p. 107). This study compares all manufacturing at the aggregate. It is thus highly influenced by factors such as type of product or firm's size.

The studies of electrical utilities in the United States do not provide support to the superiority of private ownership, although many researchers clearly have an ideological bias, attempting to substantiate such superiority (see De Alessi, 1980; Borcherding et al., 1982).

At least one study of short-line railroads in the U.S. (John Due, summarized in Fisher, 1982, p. 240) also shows that city-owned railroads had comparable cost of ton/miles of freight. Goodermote and Mancke (1983) report that the fears that the British National Oil Company (BNOC) will be inefficient "appear to be unfounded. As BNOC gained experience and territory it also earned grudging respect from the oil industry" (p. 70). In many cases, government policies dictate higher costs, e.g., when the SOE is required to use high-cost inputs (as in the case of coal sold to electricity producers in the United Kingdom or when more manpower is used for social reasons.) Whether or not such a policy is misguided is an important question, but it is not easy to isolate managerial efficiency in such cases.

Pryke (1971), one of the ardent believers in public ownership, studied the performance of the state-owned sector in the United Kingdom. In his first study (1971), he found the state-owned sector to perform better than the private sector and reported on very favorable productivity of the U.K. nationalized industries. In a follow-up study for the period since 1968, Pryke reversed his earlier conclusions, taking a much less favorable view of the subject. He believes his "views have changed because the facts have altered and because [he] know[s] more about the subject" (Pryke, 1981, p. vii). He found that the real return for the private industrial and commercial sector had fallen to 3 and 4 percent and that the average return of SOEs in the 1970s plummeted to about zero. Detailed comparisons of the state-owned British Airways and the private British Caledonian, state-owned cross-channel ferries and hovercraft services and the sale of gas and electric appliances by the state-owned firms indicated that state-owned firms performed less well than private enterprises. He sees the reasons for inefficiency as stemming mainly from the size of the SOEs and their monopoly power:

> The fact that the nationalised undertakings are so large and are in public ownership converts what would otherwise be a collection of local difficulties and decisions into a national problem about which pressure groups and trade unions become concerned and politicians adopt policies. Corner shops have been quietly closing for years, but if retailing had been nationalised there would have been a great outcry some years ago when it became known that the Shops Board had a ten-year plan to close many of its uneconomic local outlets, and the process would probably have been slowed down. If the Coal Board did not exist and the railways had not been nationalized the problems of closing down loss-making pits and withdrawing unprofitable rail services would be less formidable. Moreover, if the electricity industry has been less centralized, different utilities would have chosen different types of reactors and some of them at least would have made the right choice. The great advantage of decentralized decision-making is that bets are hedged, change is gradual and issues are not politicised. [Pryke, 1981, p. 265]

While I fully agree that many of the reasons given by Pryke for the politicization of the SOEs are because they are too centralized and mainly too subject to governmental political interference, I would question the effect of their size. Had the United Kingdom nationalized only one grocery shop, its board would have faced the same almost insurmountable problems in attempting to close it. The member of Parliament for the area would surely have demanded explanations in Parliament, and the government might have decided that the closure was not worth the political uproar. Had there been a coalition government in the United Kingdom, and the minster for that shop felt that he would lose power by the closure, the same thing would have happened. The problem, again, is not size but the institutional structure and processes.

Pryke's (1981) second point is well taken: had there been more than one electricity firm, they might have experimented with different reactors. However, if all these electricity firms had been state owned and tightly controlled by one minister of energy, the minister (or his or her staff) would have felt such experiments to be a waste of money. A committee of experts would have been nominated inside the ministry to repeat the staff work already done at the level of the different corporations. It is highly probable that such a committee would have found one reactor to be better than the others and forced all the enterprises to purchase it. If these enterprises were told in the past to freeze their prices as a part of the national government's anti-inflation measures, they would all be starved for cash and would have to crawl to the Treasury to ask for funds. The Treasury would then nominate another committee of experts and would recheck all the figures and work done at the enterprise level and at the ministry of energy level. Their decision would be the one the enterprises would have to adopt to obtain the necessary funds.

Gordon (1981) in Canada compared airlines, in addition to electricity and telephone utilities. Air Canada was relatively less efficient in using people and capital than were the privately owned U.S. carriers and Canadian Pacific Air. However, such a comparison "cannot be definitive because of the differences among airlines in routes flown" (p. 281). In steel, the state-owned Sidbec had a sales turnover broadly similar to the industry's but a low return, caused by its flat rolling mills operations running at low volumes (p. 287).

These studies compare firms that are heavily regulated. They thus combine a mixture of the effects of property rights with those of limited competition and regulation. In addition, except for the studies of Blankart and Pryke, they were all carried out in the United States or Canada.

IMPACT OF COMPETITION

Both socialist and capitalist economists accept that competing firms are more efficient than monopolies and that industrial structure has very important ramifications for efficiency. They also agree that "The differences between government monopolies and government firms with private competitors might be greater than the differences between government firms and private firms in competition with one another" (Peltzmann, 1971, p. 146). Still, it is possible that "the managers of political firms . . . are less constrained by market considerations . . . and find it easier to obtain subsidy and to mask bad management under the guise of fulfilling other 'social' costs. Government firms . . . can survive for long periods . . . [with] grossly inefficient management" (De Alessi, 1974a, p. 7). Therefore, even under competition, an SOE would be less efficient than a private firm. Conversely, "One would expect competition to exert some market pressure on government enterprises to hold down costs . . . and to eliminate some of the opportunities for directing behavior on the part of bureaucracies" (Spann, 1977, p. 75).

There are, however, very few cases in which the effects of property rights can be isolated from those of noncompetitive markets and regulation. One of the few cases studied is that of the Canadian railroad industry. In Canada, two large railroads of roughly equal size are in operation. One is the privately owned Canadian Pacific, which has spanned the North American continent since 1885. The other is the state-owned ("Crown corporation," as such firms are called in Canada) Canadian National. This firm has been a nationwide competitor of Canadian Pacific since 1923, when the government decided to take over and consolidate several failing railroads. The two railroads account for 90 percent of Canadian railway gross revenues. Since World War II, restrictions on their ability to compete for traffic have been removed.

Caves and Christensen (1980) measured the production efficiency of the two railroads using total factor productivity (TFP), or real output per unit of real resources expended, as a measure. They reported the following:

> *Contrary to what is predicted in the property rights literature, we find no evidence of inferior efficiency performance by the government-owned railroad. In fact, our evidence indicates that the CN [Canadian National] has achieved larger gains in productivity than the CP [Canadian Pacific] since 1956. In the late 1950s and early 1960s the CN had a level of productivity approximately 90 percent as high as the CP, but this gap has been closed. We conclude that in the case of Canadian railroads the beneficial effects of competition have been sufficient to overcome any tendency toward inefficiency resulting from public ownership. [Caves and Christensen, 1980, pp. 960–961]*

R.A. Daly and Co. Ltd., studied the same railroads for the period 1971 to 1976. Their analysis suggests that Canadian Pacific's railway operations were more efficient, but Canadian National has been closing the gap. Daly concluded, "By most measures utilized, CP appears to be the most efficient transporter, but its lower exposure to rail lines which must be operated in the public interest must be considered. Measures of labor efficiency indicate that [CN has tightened] its managerial control in recent years" (in Gordon, 1981, p. 278). Caves and Christensen concluded:

> *[T]hat public ownership is not inherently less efficient than private ownership—that the oft-noted inefficiency of government enterprises stems from their isolation from effective competition rather than their public ownership per se. Of course, our findings do not provide any evidence in favor of public ownership over private ownership. There*

may be criteria other than productive efficiency which provide the basis for preferring either public or private ownership, but that is another question. [1980, p. 974]

In a later publication, Caves and Christensen were joined with two other authors and continued their investigation, this time comparing the economic performance of U.S. with Canadian railroads. They concluded that the degree of economic regulation had a strong influence on the economic performance of the North American railroads. "When one controls for the influence of regulation, there is little indication that ownership form influences performance" (in Stanbury and Thompson, 1982, pp. 146–147). They observed no substantial differences in productivity growth rates between Canadian National and Canadian Pacific. The substantially less-regulated Canadian railroads had a distinctly better performance than the more regulated U.S. railroads in terms of productivity growth rates. The productivity levels of the two Canadian railroads and their growth rates exceeded that of all U.S. railroads except three small ones. They concluded that the

[S]pecific explanation for the superior economic performance of the two Canadian railroads must ultimately lie in the area of organizational design and control. . . . For example . . . as the Canadian railroads were deregulated the marketing organizations of those companies were radically altered . . . Canadian railroads have much more elaborate "costing" systems than those of their U.S. counterparts . . . perhaps the greatest costs associated with transportation regulation are not those associated simply with misallocation of traffic between modes . . . or expenses incurred in maintaining services that would not be provided in a competitive setting, but those associated with a lack of innovation. [In Stanbury and Thompson, 1982, pp. 147–148]

One of the most quoted papers on comparisons of state-owned and private firms is that of Davies (1971). He compared the performance of the two domestic Australian air carriers. The two were in the same country and the same line of business and were operating in the same lines. Both were regulated. Davies studied their performance for the 16-year period from 1958/1959 to 1973/1974. He concluded, "The evidence indicates that the private firm [Ansett Airlines], operating under the rules and customs associated with exchangeable private property rights, is more productive than the public enterprise [Trans-Australia Airlines] (1977, p. 226). William A. Jordan, however (in Stanbury and Thompson, 1982, pp. 161–199), claims that Davies used consolidated figures for Ansett and its four subsidiaries but that only one of these subsidiaries was similar to the state-owned Trans-Australia Airlines in providing interstate trunk operations. Based on a more detailed breakdown of the figures, Jordan claims:

[O]wnership is not a relevant factor in airline performance where regulatory monopolies exist. . . . the evidence regarding ownership does not necessarily apply to performance in a deregulated environment. Indeed, it could well be that the performance similarities among federally regulated airlines, regardless of ownership, are a common response to a dominant environment produced by a regulatory monopoly, and that performance differences due to ownership would develop with the removal of such regulation. For example, in the absence of regulation, would a government-owned airline respond in the same ways as a privately owned airline if it faced bankruptcy because of the competition of rival carriers? Might not the government-owned airline (supported by its employees and suppliers) turn to the government for subsidies (such as direct payments and low-interest loans) or for the allocation of an increased share of government traffic, rather than make the painful adjustments that a small, privately owned airline would tend to make in similar circumstances? If so, the performance of the government-owned airline would diverge from that of the privately owned airline. [p. 194]

Certain cases exist, to respond to the implicit question posed by Jordan, in which a state-owned airline had to take the same painful adjustment that a privately owned small airline does. El Al Airlines was literally allowed by the government to file for bankruptcy. Since December 1982, it has been operated and directed by a court-appointed receiver. Its new fleet of airplanes was acquired by the government and leased to it for operations. The firm made many painful changes in employment and work rules and installed many more cost-saving measures. The Sri Lanka airline was also allowed to be closed, and a new firm was immediately created to take some of its employees. To be sure, managers, employees and other interest groups did fight to receive subsidies. However, when they understood they would not receive these subsidies, they took draconic measures to become more competitive. The point is that managers of SOEs may be hypothesized to learn with time how to negotiate with their environment—in particular, the part in it that gives them the authority and the legitimacy. In fact, private firms also approached their respective governments demanding subsidies and aid. The U.S. steel firms have been doing that, and others attempted but were less successful.

Again, the emphasis is on the importance of the common response to a dominant environment produced by a regulatory monopoly. There, no differences have been found, either in the famous Australian case or in North America, that can be explained by ownership differences. The question, therefore, remains, are any differences caused by ownership in a nonregulatory environment?

Davies (1981) compared Australian private and state-owned banks. Seven large banks, each with an extensive network of branches, control 92 percent of assets and deposits of the Australian trading banks. Six are privately owned and one, the Commonwealth Trading Bank, is owned by the government. This bank and the Bank of New South Wales are the largest and are similar in size and other important characteristics. The banking legislation passed in the years 1956 to 1959 attempted to put state-owned and private commercial banks on equal footing so that the banks in both sectors operate under virtually identical legal constraints. Prior to 1955, private commercial banks were not allowed to own savings banks. Since then, each one of the major commercial banks has a saving bank subsidiary.

Davies (1981) hypothesized that a private bank will hold a higher proportion of its assets in loans while state-owned banks will hold a higher proportion of government securities, reflecting their risk aversion. Indeed, the private banks held a larger share of total investments in higher yielding but riskier nongovernment securities than the state-owned banks, and in every year except one, the ratio of loans to assets was higher for the private compared to the state-owned banks. In 10 of 11 years, the state-owned bank had a higher ratio of Australian public securities to total assets. No test of significance for the difference is provided.

A comparison of the state-owned Commonwealth with privately owned savings banks shows that the proportion of assets held in relatively riskless, low-yielding Australian public securities by the state-owned bank is larger than that of the private enterprise for all years except 1970 and 1971, when the ratios were identical for the two institutions. This is the only substantial piece of evidence that runs counter to the risk hypothesis (Davies, 1981, p. 127).

Davies (1981) further hypothesized that managers of state-owned banks will arrange their bank affairs so they can enjoy a less arduous life. Another hypothesis was that SOE managers would attempt to increase the size of the organization, "which in turn leads to correspondingly higher salary, as well as more power and prestige" (p. 129). Davies concluded that the state-owned bank had a higher ratio of expenses to net earnings and lower ratio of profits to assets, to expenses, to employees, to deposits and to capital.

In France, the three largest banks were nationalized immediately after World War II and most of the other financial institutions, in 1982. Following nationalization, chairmen of all banks were replaced by political appointees, loyal to the government line. Still, it is believed that nationalization was a complete waste of taxpayers' money. The newly appointed managers, according to *Institutional Investor*, "have been quick to identify with their new fiefdoms and, more surprisingly, have become quite vocal in defending their turf" (February 1983, p. 112). To be sure, the French government requires banks to maintain credits to sick companies at artificially low interest rates for a long time. However, *Euromoney* (July 1983, p. 66) quotes one bank manager in France: "Nationalization responded to certain political and economic objectives of the parties that took over power in France. . . . There was no economic reason to do it . . . and many Western governments, either with conservative or social democratic systems, are able to manage their economic goals through a private or semi-private banking system."

Finsinger (1983a) studied the performance of insurance markets in the Federal Republic of Germany and concluded that SOEs and mutual companies outperformed privately owned joint stock companies. Competition seems to be important in keeping SOEs efficient.

In some other cases, for historical or other reasons, SOEs were allowed to compete in the market. British Petroleum is one such example, and it does not seem that the firm is less efficient or gives its managers an easier life or better working conditions than the private oil multinationals. Monsen and Walters (1983) showed that SOEs are less profitable than private enterprises in Europe in areas like automobile production, but then in 1983, Peugeot's losses were greater than those of Renault's.

Primeaux (1975, 1977) reported that there are 49 cities with a population exceeding 25,000 in the United States where consumers can choose between more than one electric company. These cases are categorized as competitive. In a cross-sector regression equation designed to explain intercity variation, the competitive variable is used as a dummy variable and explains the cases of cities with relatively low rates. The duopolistic rivalry, according to Primeaux, causes efficiency that is greater than the loss of economies of scale.

Private competitive firms avoid any costs that would reduce their ability to compete. SOEs are often forced to carry additional costs because they are state owned. SOEs may be forced to operate on a scale that is prefixed by the size of the political unit, not by efficiency considerations (Spann, 1977). SOEs may be forced to deliver their services also to remote, sparsely populated areas.

Funkhauser and MacAvoy (1979) compared private firms and SOEs in Indonesia. In observing industries with both public and private firms, average profit margins for SOEs were 0.22 and for private firms −0.36. In fact, in all four samples used by the authors, SOEs had lower profit margins than private companies (p. 363). These results may be explained as stemming from the economist's prescription of optimal departures from marginal cost pricing (Baumol and Bradford, 1970). Baumol and Bradford, however, assume that SOEs add to consumer benefits by having lower profit margins, but the cost of production is assumed to be the same as in private firms. Funkhauser and Mac Avoy found that the reason was higher costs than the private firms. This higher cost was explained by them as "a 'tax' on operation to meet the requirements of local political organizations" (p. 367). SOEs' "goals are met by payments to factors [of production]—resulting in higher operating costs rather than by increased dividend payments" (p. 367).

Hill (1982), too, compared privately owned firms and SOEs in Indonesia. His sample included firms operating in a competitive environment: the weaving industry. According to him, government's goal in entering this industry was to reduce the dominance of Chinese entrepreneurs. His study shows that in 1976 there were 14 Indonesian weaving SOEs, operating 4,448 looms—or 318 looms on the average—as opposed to 75 looms in the average private firm. To get comparable data he chose only those firms operating fully automatic mechanized looms (M3) or semi-automatic looms (M2). His sample included 10 firms using technique M2—and in each category there were two SOEs. He then calculated the ratio of SOEs to private firms by technique.

For the fully automatic firms, the SOEs required 1.59 times the capital for a given value-added measured at market price (capital was measured as the replacement cost of all fixed assets). To find out how efficiently equipment is being used, the ratio of machinery output was calculated. This time SOEs reached 1.02 times capital compared to the private firms. The difference between these two measures show that SOEs had more capital invested in buildings and inventories.

By subtracting the labor costs from the value-added denominator, Hill (1982) obtained the capital/surplus ratio. Here, the ratio SOEs/private was 3.44. In other words, labor costs were much higher in the SOEs. Indeed, labor costs as a percent of total costs were 2.56 times higher in SOEs than in private firms, although wages were similar. Thus, SOEs employed many more workers. Finally labor hours per M^2 of cloth was 1.26 times higher in SOEs.

When semi-automatic equipment was used, all ratios were much higher per unit of value added; SOEs required 5.38 times capital, 1.66 times machinery. Capital surplus ratio was 18.01, labor hours per 1000 M^2 was 1.88, and labor cost as a percentage of total costs was 2.58. All in all, SOEs were found to require both more capital and more labor per unit of production. Still, all four SOEs covered their current expenditures from current revenues and one was "almost able to cover its full cost of production" (p. 1018).

Hill did not say how the four SOEs were chosen from the 14 operating in Indonesia. One of these SOEs, he reported had "aging machinery" (p. 1019). It had a sole agent who charged for the raw materials more than material prices and more than the selling price that he himself determined (p. 1019). Management was replaced and losses went down for three months from Rp 150 million to Rp 1.6 million.

Hill draws two implications from the above. First, "State enterprises are vulnerable for personal gains . . . [and] abuse. Secondly, the internal environment of government weaving mills may not be the major determinant of their performance. The quality of mill management is obviously very important" (p. 1019). One of the firms "had almost 12 month's stock of production on hand" (p. 1022) at a peak period of demand for cloth where three months is considered the upper limit in this industry. It is difficult to say how representative these SOEs were. Hill (1982) does mention two state-owned mills with significantly different results.

In another study of LDC, Victor Levy (1982) compared the allocational and technical efficiency of private and public firms in the chemical, mineral and food-processing industries in Iraq for 1962–1968 (1963–1968 for chemicals). In all three industries, SOEs were not using labor at its optimum amount: the value of marginal product of labor is above the wage rates. Instead, they were found to be overcapitalized. As to efficiency, SOEs were found on the whole to be "more efficient than private firms in the food and mineral industries" (p. 247) and no differences of efficiency were found in chemicals.

One advantage of competition from the professional manager's point of view is that the government and perhaps other stakeholders tend to reduce demands for achieving other social and political objectives when the firm faces direct competition in its spheres of activities. Governments tend to use SOEs to achieve these external objectives when the additional costs can be hidden from the public. One dubious advantage of subsidies to industrial users through the price mechanism of SOEs is that the subsidy is hidden— thus, it does not cause a public outcry. In fact, one way to interpret the property rights theory in terms of political economic argument is that government favors certain strong interest groups and uses SOEs to grant them more subsidies and more largesse. In Sri Lanka, e.g., the minister of industry called the managers of a U.S. MNE subsidiary, demanding that they curtail their output because their SOE competitor was inefficient and could not compete with them (*Financial Times*, October 10, 1984, Sri Lanka *Supplement*, p. 4).

Thus, an alternative explanation may be that government bureaucracies may allow more latitude and more discretion to managers of SOEs in a competitive environment; that is, when competition exists, one would expect government to allow the firm to pursue pure efficiency goals and demand from the managers less in terms of social goals. If this hypothesis is true, the problem with an SOE is not necessarily the nontransferability of shares but the institutional process of control. In fact, we know that the performance of the SOE sector in France, the United Kingdom or Italy has been deteriorating when measured in pure economic criteria of return on investment, profits or returns on assets in the 1960s and 1970s when government required these firms to freeze prices, bail out ailing firms, and in the case of Italy, direct increasing investments to the Mezzogiorno.

IRI, during the 1950s, enjoyed considerable autonomy, and all accounts analyzing its history seem to agree that in that period it was innovative, well managed and efficient. With time, however, it was required to direct its funds to the Mezzogiorno and to become the major rescuer of failing private firms (which preferred to be nationalized rather than to make the painful adjustment assumed as coming so naturally to a privately owned firm). As a result, it became inefficient, debt-ridden and a tremendous burden on the government budget. IRI's management tried to resist governmental pressures, and GEPI was created because IRI did not want to acquire more ailing firms. The U.K. nationalized industries suffered heavy losses because the government did not allow them to raise prices as an integral part of its attempt to combat inflation (NEDO, 1976; Daniels, 1977). In fact, it is extremely difficult for managers to maintain morale and lead the firm on the efficiency route when they are expected also to carry out and advocate to middle management other projects that are less acceptable to them. Managers also learn very fast how to lean on government once such behavior is legitimized.

However, since the French government reversed its earlier policies in 1983/1984 and insisted that its SOEs must be profitable or their managers would be sacked, the financial performance of these SOEs has dramatically changed. Péchiney, for example, posted a consolidated net for 1985 of FFr 750 million and FFr 550 for 1984, contrasted to a loss of FFr 4.46 billion in 1982 and 480 million in 1983. The turnaround has been attributed largely to the recovery plan instituted by George Besse, the group's chairman (*Financial Times*, February 19, 1986). Mr. Besse was named to head Régie Nationale des Usines Renault, replacing a chairman who had planned to shed jobs gently.

It seems, therefore, that efficiency differentials are the result of market structure and institutional controls as much as ownership type. SOEs operating in a competitive environment may be as efficient as privately owned firms. Competitive market pressures may be sufficient to yield productive efficiency even when shares are nontransferable.

Competition can be stimulated by institutional means, too. Tendler (1968) shows that, in the case of Brazil, competition for funds among different state-owned electricity generating firms "demonstrated a novel way of spurring performance in state enterprises" (p. 152). She notes:

> A traditional argument against state production is that such ventures are not exposed to the rigors of market competition. In the Brazilian electric power sector, the government went into a naturally monopolistic industry, but left alone the branch of the industry (distribution) that required supply by only one company. By taking on generation only, state power production could contain many companies. In lieu of competition in the product market, competition for financing could stimulate state enterprise to behave like competitive private enterprise. Although the performance of the Brazilian state power companies in many cases, and at many points, fell below the standards of efficiency suggested here, there is no doubt that the successful cases can be explained in part by the competitive atmosphere in which they had to exist. (p. 52).

In some cases, private enterprise seems to be more efficient (and certainly more profitable) because its operations are concentrated in the profitable parts of the business. In many cases, the SOE has to supply a certain service to all customers for the same price regardless of the costs. Public utilities often cross subsidize one part of their operations from the profits in other parts of the system. Parts could be either geographical, as when the rail service to a certain small community is cross subsidized by the profits from other lines, or based on time, such as when the bus or subway services in the peak rush hour are profitable and they subsidize the losing operations during other times of the day. In the telephone industry, long-distance phone call rates were fixed in a way that cross subsidized the local calls. Whether or not it is economically justifiable to use a cross-subsidization system is a point often discussed in the economic literature. It is argued by many that a system of differentiated prices that will take into account the real costs of operations district by district or hour by hour will be less costly to operate, more efficient, more equitable and fairer.

The argument for or against this type of differential pricing is not the subject of this book. The point, however, is that when such a system is not in operation, there is a strong incentive for a new entrant to the business to operate only part of the system at a lower cost, charging lower prices. Indeed, one argument for state ownership is that private operators will cream off the profitable work. In fact, the entry of private entrepreneurs in such cases may be beneficial: if cross subsidization is unavailable, consumers will have to pay the real cost of the service. To be sure, the criterion of willingness to pay assumes certain values; the elderly who need mobility to do their shopping or visit their children may not be able to pay. If government wants to subsidize certain services, however, it can do so openly through its budgets. The wider latitude to hide costs is not a good enough theoretical reason for using SOEs. In some countries, this wider latitude may even increase the opportunity for corruption (Levy, 1982).

POLITICS AND EFFICIENCY

Organizations are often seen as instruments for accomplishing complex tasks efficiently, with explicit, defined, and measurable goals. They are structured to achieve these goals and accomplish tasks effectively and efficiently. As shown in Chapter 4, SOEs have a multitude of goals and are required by different parts of government to stress different objectives. Government is not a single controller, speaking with one voice; it is a plethora of ministries, bureaus, agencies and departments pursuing a variety of conflicting goals. Managers are not innocent bystanders in this game. They, too, attempt to exert influence on their environment (Aharoni, 1982) and to coopt their controllers (Selznick, 1949). Corporations are essentially political constructs, and the manager's behavior may be governed by political more than by economic considerations.

Large corporations are managed not only by the top management but also by what Mintzberg (1983) called "the internal coalition"—that is, the full-time career managers of the firm. Chandler took the position that "career managers preferred policies that favored the long-term stability and growth of their enterprise to those that maximized current profits" (1977, p. 10). According to Baumol (1959), Roberts (1959) and Marris (1964), this preference is largely because of the association between size and managerial compensation and other perquisites. Professional managers tend to avoid controversy, criticism and risk. They are also, according to Monsen:

> [P]robably more responsive to pressures from the various constituent groups of the firm such as workers, consumers, suppliers, or stockholders, and the government. The professional manager is apt to respond to conflicting demands from these groups by balancing one off against the other or by utilizing compromise as an issue settling device. The owner-manager, who views each dollar given to workers, suppliers, consumers or the government as coming from his own pocket, is less likely to compromise. [1969, p. 48]

Since governmental impact on the economy has increased, the professional managers would be inclined to "shift their battleground from the firm level to the political level. Control of the government may then become the means for establishing 'control' of the firm" (Papandreou, 1952, p. 203). While state ownership may lead to politicization and inefficiency, there is much more to performance, innovation and efficient management than just ownership.

The first best requirement for efficiency is competition. However, many SOEs are monopolies. Privately owned monopolies have no reason to be more efficient than state-owned ones. They may capture the bodies that are supposed to regulate them. To the extent that pecuniary incentives and self-interest operate, they may merely mean that monopoly power will be exploited more fiercely. A privately owned monopoly may escape both political and market discipline. In other cases, SOEs are said to be less efficient because their management know losses are borne by the state. This fact, even if true, is not necessarily a function of ownership but that of certain institutional design. Governments are not required legally or otherwise to cover losses of SOEs instead of allowing them to go bankrupt!

To a large extent, efficiency depends on the design of the system, which as discussed in chapter 4, is composed of the rules of interactions of both the internal and external parts of the organization. Within the organization, resource-allocation decisions are influenced by the structure of tasks and authority, by the reward and punishment structure and by the values and beliefs of its internal coalition. Most decisions in the organization tend to reflect its past history and accumulated experience. Organizations, however, are also dependent on their environment and must ensure fit with the external environment to survive. Thus, competition can also be among different SOEs for funds from the government. Further, public policy and public outputs have many, very subtle dimensions. Internalization of externalities, well accepted by economists since Coase's (1937) seminal work, is true in SOEs, and even more so. Measuring efficiency is important, but the process of interaction of goals and means is even more important. Some of the higher costs of SOEs may be least-cost means to achieve certain social, political and redistributive goals. Some of the measured inefficiencies are in fact transfers to certain interest groups. Transfers through SOEs are politically preferable because they are invisible. Unfortunately, no test has yet been devised to measure the effectiveness of this method of transfer, and to separate these transfers and managerial effectiveness. It is almost impossible to separate what economists may see as waste from the political transfers in the form of higher wages or payments to other interest groups. It is also impossible to assess the extent to which government direct budget expenditures would have been increased if SOEs would not have been used to achieve these transfers with far less discrimination. Much more understanding of the process through which public production and provision is determined is needed (Aharoni, 1981b).

CONCLUSION

It is widely believed that SOEs are inherently less efficient than a private firm: first, the management of SOEs is not expected to achieve profits, and profit orientation is impaired by controlled prices, by political intervention in the SOE's strategy, marketing mix, financial policies, or appointment policies. Subsidization practices may weaken the SOEs' willingness to avoid inefficiencies. Most of the SOEs operate natural monopolies or so-called key industries, in which competition is restricted. For political reasons, SOEs may operate plants at suboptimal size. Finally, managers do not have sufficient incentives to avoid waste of resources.

The empirical evidence is much more ambiguous and lends only limited support to the hypothesis that SOEs are less efficient than private firms. The financial results of SOEs certainly show a dismal picture of losses. However, these losses may be a result of social and political demands on the enterprises. In terms of efficiency, these firms' performance is much less bleak. As efficient users of resources, they may have done as well as private firms producing the same product, in the same country.

SOEs' performance is affected by three sets of factors: First, objective factors such as input prices or the level of available infrastructure. Second, decisions made externally to the enterprises regarding its labor policies, investment and pricing. Third, the internal organization of the firm (McCawley, quoted in Hill, 1982, p. 1020). These three sets are obviously interrelated. Thus, the internal organization may suffer low morale because of decisions made externally to the enterprise. External influence also means that managers have to devote much time to the submission of reports and negotiations with controllers. If managers have little influence on input prices and on machinery used, they might resort to apathy. In most countries, SOEs have comparative disadvantages in terms of requirements to achieve noneconomic goals, to employ individuals of certain political affiliation or of certain tribes or to achieve a host of other social and political goals. The more they have to achieve these goals, the higher the probability that management will suffer from "widespread resentment, cynicism and loss of morale" (NEDO, 1976, p. 10).

In some countries, SOE managers are appointed, not because of their competence but because of their political or tribal affiliation and for the same reason they are not dismissed when they do not perform efficiently. To the extent that managers are indeed appointed because of political largesse, they owe their allegiance to the minister who appointed them and will follow his or her directions, not necessarily attempting to run efficient operations. This issue is discussed in Chapter 8.

Three things seem clear. First, poor monitoring, excessive intervention and attempts of civil servants to minimize managerial discretion lead to risk aversion, lack of initiative and waste. Second, the persistent tendency of government to use SOEs as conduits for dispensing subsidies or giving political patronage has been a major cause of losses and of inefficiency. Third, at least in some countries, a new managerial class has evolved, attempting to acquire more autonomy and increasing elbow room for independent action. These managers have different values then their private-sector counterparts but also deep-seated different outlooks and goals than the civil servants. In the eyes of their controllers, many SOE managers mirror private-sector behavior, taking advantage of opportunities for profitable growth and ignoring what civil servants see as the national interest. As SOE managers see it, their controllers do not understand the way business firms should be run. They are therefore unresponsive to central direction and resent any attempt to direct them in a way detrimental to the conduct of the firm with the same degree of business acumen displayed by firms in the private sector.

However, government is responsible to its citizens for the efficient conduct of its business and must, therefore, control the operations of the enterprises it owns. Let us turn to an analysis of how controls of SOEs operate in real life.

CHAPTER 6

The External Coalition:
Control and Accountability

INTRODUCTION

"Control" can be defined as the regulation of activities to ensure the attainment of goals efficiently and effectively. When goals are clearly stated, the control system is designed to reinforce the objectives by measuring the level of accomplishment and the costs. In public administration, control "is the set of measures taken by one body in connection with the activities of another body in order to ensure that the latter's actions are in conformity with the standards and principles laid down to govern that activity" (Stefani, 1981, p. 49).

In SOEs, the management of productive activities necessitates making immediate decisions under uncertainty. Therefore, controls cannot be directed to each separate action and its conformity with prescribed rules. Instead, the aggregate of management actions, judged according to expected results, are to be the subject of controls.

The literature on SOEs treats the question of controlling these enterprises as one of establishing organizational relationships that assure public accountability and consistency with government policy (Seidman, 1968, p. 156) without impairing the flexibility necessary for the effective conduct of an SOE.

This theory implicitly assumes pyramidal relations between government and its SOEs. The government, representing the public interest, sets up or at least approves, subject to parliamentary control, basic objectives, goals and major policies. The managers of the enterprises have full autonomy in operating decisions, that is, in choosing the means to implement the prescribed goals, and flexibility in the conduct of at least some aspects of their operations. At the same time, the managers must remain accountable to government for the results, for the effective utilization of resources put at their dis-

217

posal and the effective achievement of the goals with which they were entrusted.

Because of the need for autonomy, traditional governmental regulations and control have not worked for commercial-type enterprises. The decision to conduct some of the business of government in the form of a legal entity separate from more traditional civil service organization suggests at least a tacit recognition that efficient handling of the trading activities of these SOEs requires some special form of organization and control. Official proclamations declare the SOE should receive its own funds, hire its own staff and run the firm on a purely commercial basis, but be subject to government guidelines on pricing, investments and strategy. The challenge is to develop new types of relationships and controls that reflect the peculiar requirements of commercial and industrial undertakings. How can the government be assured that companies subject to only loose market and fiscal discipline will avoid waste or not depart from their original goals? How can managers manage effectively when they are subject to too strict controls?

The accumulated experience with SOEs shows that this challenge is difficult. As one authority in the field observed, "there is no difficulty in recognizing the *need* for a particular public enterprise. The difficulty lies in establishing it, financing it, providing it with personnel, giving it suitable organizational shape, assuring that it attains the maximum possible efficiency, subjecting it to adequate but not excessive controls, etc." (Hanson, 1965, p. 204).

Lack of consensus on goals is the major reason for confusion about the needed controls and for the absence of objective measures to gauge whether controls are adequate or excessive. Democratic states may want to have a coherent industrial strategy but often find it very hard to reach consensus on national goals. The very essence of democracy is the recognition of the legitimacy of rival points of view. Changes in the power structure, and certainly a change in the government in power, cause changes in the goals to be pursued.

The use of the corporate device was supposed to enable the state to have an agency operating under its own name rather than that of the state. However, ministers, Parliament and the civil service usually claim that the SOEs should be subservient to several interests of the state or that their programs must be coordinated with those of the government. In many cases, the intervention of ministers in the affairs of the SOEs has reduced accountability rather than increased it. For example, SOEs have been directed to finance programs in which the minister had special interest, without subjecting the programs to parliamentary scrutiny and the rigid control and auditing systems of the government.

The minimum cost of an arbitrary intervention by all sorts of controllers is the time and management attention it takes to file reports, answer the questions, petition for licenses and argue about priorities. Usually, the cost is higher: adversary relations develop, bureaucratic ineptitude stifles initiatives and innovation, regulations are circumvented and human energies are diverted to establish a secured political base rather than to manage the enterprise.

NEED FOR CONTROLS

After several decades of operations of many SOEs, there is still no coherent and agreed conceptual scheme to guide the controllers or an agreed definition who they should be. It is extremely difficult to judge whether SOEs are effective and efficient; very few of them face genuine domestic and international competition. Overemployment or appalling levels of service may be covered by subsidies (and therefore noticed and debated) or by higher charges or cross subsidization (and thus the costs to society are not usually known). Attempts to proxy market forces through pricing rules, investment criteria, required rate of return or external financing limits have failed. Because of past governmental pressures, bad managment, errors of judgment in carrying out large-scale investment or a combination of these factors, the real financial return from most of the huge investments of SOEs, are negative in some countries, zero in others and very low in the most successful cases. Governments attempted to rectify the situation by adding more controls. However, as Claude Albert Colliard noted: "the controls are multiple, confused, crossed, superimposed. They slow down decisions in the enterprises, spread and dilute responsibility, limit management's authority without, however, arriving at exemplary sanctions if, eventually, blame or errors are uncovered" (quoted by Cassesse, in Vernon and Aharoni, 1981). He concluded that in many cases, if there had been no controls, French SOEs would have had greater success than they had actually achieved.

Control may be seen as reducing the discretion of management. Managerial discretion is made possible because information on costs, efforts of the firms and the states of nature the SOE encounters are imperfect and asymmetrically distributed: managers possess more information than controllers. Managerial discretion is pursued because of noncongruence of goals. If information is perfect and goals are congruent, "the study and public control of SOE behavior become of no interest" (Koenig, 1985, p. 2).

Managerial discretion is made possible because information on costs, efforts of the firms and the states of nature the SOE encounters are imperfect and asymmetrically distributed: managers possess more information than controllers. Managerial discretion is pursued because of noncongruence of goals. If information is perfect and goals are congruent, "the study and public control of SOE behavior become of no interest" (Koenig, 1985, p. 2). Government officers wish to control the degree of discretion available to SOE managers for at least three different reasons with different motivational origins.

First, taxpayers own SOEs. By virtue of their ownership rights, they want public money to be used properly and effectively. Ministers are seen by the public (and see themselves) as the interpreters and protectors of taxpayers' interests and as such have reason to control SOEs to make sure that the national missions for which public money was invested in the SOE are fulfilled. The government is often also the banker of these enterprises and must protect its loans. Unless performance of SOEs is monitored and controlled, SOEs may become a drain on the public purse; they may be efficient but attempt to achieve objectives different from those desired. They may even become a source of political embarrassment. PERTAMINA in Indonesia concealed its disappointing performance for a long time, and its failures caused enormous foreign exchange problems in the country (Lipsky, 1978, pp. 1-41). A Canadian SOE caused a lot of embarrassment when it was found to have paid bribes.

The motivation of the state to exercise control over its SOEs goes beyond property rights and the desire to satisfy public expectations. As the contribution of SOEs to GNP increases, the dependence of the state on the outcomes of economic decisions (production, employment and investments) in the private sector is lessened as the contribution of SOEs to GNP increases, the less crucial becomes the economic performance of the private sector and the greater the perceived abilities of governments to control their social, political and economic destinies.

Further, it is never completely clear which course of action out of available alternatives would further public interest the most. Ministers tend to equate the interests of their constituencies with the public interest, controlling SOEs to protect and enhance those particular interests.

Finally, ministers are individuals with personal political interests and ambitions who attempt to channel SOE operations into directions that will further these interests. In some cases, governments act as if they do not want SOEs to be efficient. The control system has become a political game in which power is the important consideration. Controls may occasionally be designed to achieve personal gains for the controllers.

These different reasons for control mean that the legal distinctions have not been adhered to in practice: a minister has many ways of giving informal directives in particular if the SOE is dependent on the government for funds. They have also caused other problems from difficulties in recruiting managers willing to work in an environment in which their discretion is severely restricted to apathy to corruption, as well as too much risk taking. The record is easy to criticize and not too difficult to explain. Suggesting a workable alternative is more of a challenge and depends on one's point of view.

To this author, SOEs belong to the nation as a whole, not to the officials of the elected administration. Once this simple truism is recognized, it is clear that checks and balances are essential. The SOE should neither be an instrument of the government nor a tool for its managers to achieve independent political power. Both are trustees of the interests of the nation. When government ministers restate their priorities, it is very difficult for the managers of the SOEs, who can be removed unceremoniously by the ministers, to ignore this change. However, in a democracy, the managers should be able to bring their case to the attention of other ministers, members of parliament or the free press. If one accepts the idea that an SOE belongs to the nation as a whole, one may not necessarily look for compromise or for harmony. One would also conclude that if the electorate turns on one political party in favor of another, directors and managers of SOEs must not be replaced wholesale. Further, one would accept the right of management to resist what they see as unjustified government pressures in particular when these pressures are intended to achieve short-term political gains. In evaluating existing control methods, the legitimacy of these controls is an important issue.

The major problem in the institution of controls on SOEs is that both goals and controllers are multiple and ill defined. The first question to be dealt with, therefore, is that of the definition of the controllers, or more precisely, what Williamson termed "willful external control agent," defined by him as "any group outside the firm that attempts self-consciously to enforce what it regards as legitimate expectations" (1970, p. 173). We shall then consider what might be termed "macro level controls," treating the SOEs as a portfolio of units managed by governments.

At the micro level, a distinction is helpful among four different issues: first is the *organizational* aspect. Second is the *form* or the mechanism by which the control is implemented. Third is the *functional* problem: what are the functions or the types of decisions in which one would expect, require or allow intervention of a higher authority? A fourth, and related issue, is the *strength* of control. It is also important to distinguish between the formal (or legal) controls and the actual day-to-day practices, in which some formal controls may never be used while other informal channels might be utilized.

The control system is run by human beings, with different aspirations and desires. In many countries, they have much less expertise than the management of the SOE and much lower status. The SOEs may have more resources and much larger staff, while the controllers are fewer and overburdened. In theory, the design of the control system should take these problems into account; often, however, it does not. Many detailed controls are instituted, that must be handled by a tiny number of overworked controllers. Further, the control methods are and should be different for different SOEs. Differences in origin, size, importance to the country, industrial structure, strategy and organization structures entail differences in control.

This chapter analyzes common problems, dealing mainly with SOEs that are separate legal entities from the state and are not jointly owned with private shareholders. If these SOEs are registered under the general corporation law, the state—represented by the government as a shareholder—cannot operate formally except through annual or special shareholders' meetings and the minister cannot legally give instructions to the directors or the management. If the SOEs are created by a special act, as the public corporations were in the United Kingdom, then this act defines the right of the shareholders. The board of directors is the trustee of the enterprise. Its role in SOEs is discussed in Chapter 8.

Finally, the need for public accountability means that special organs need to be operated to control an SOE that would not have been operating to control a private firm. The state auditor general or parliamentary committees are examples to be discussed later.

How should the SOEs know the express wishes of elected officials? More important, when are these wishes legitimate? This question brings us again to the question of goals, already discussed, and to that of defining the controllers.

PRINCIPALS AND AGENTS: WHO ARE THE CONTROLLERS?

One way to look at the relationships between managers and owners of firms is in terms of the principal-agent theory. An agency relationship exists where one party, the agent, acts on behalf of another, the principal. Control of the agent is based on seeking contractual arrangements that will induce the agent to behave as if he or she were maximizing the welfare of the principal. In business firms, managers are contracted to act on behalf of (private or public) shareholders. As in all agency relationships, managers are assumed to act to maximize their personal interest. Therefore, a perfect contract would structure the managers' incentives to correspond exactly to the shareholders'. In real life situations, however, no contract is expected to meet this standard, and agency costs are more than the costs specified in the contract.

What are these additional costs? First, there are certain costs of detecting decisions that are incongruent with the shareholders' interests. In real life, monitoring costs are high because the principal (shareholder) does not have an independent source of information. In addition, under uncertainty, optimal decision-making depends on the risk preferences of managers and shareholders, which may not be identical. Moreover, to avoid replacement costs, shareholders may allow managers a certain amount of discretion.

These types of agency costs—distinct managers' interests, monitoring and detecting costs, replacement costs—as well as environmental variables such as uncertainty about strategy are likely to apply to SOEs. However, the agency costs cannot be conceptually defined in SOEs because the principal is not identifiable. The notion that the government, the president or the minister is the principal and the enterprise is the agent is misleading. Instead, the populace as a whole is the principal, with a variety of agents acting on its behalf. These agents include various government ministers, members of parliament, civil servants, managers of firms and all sorts of interest groups. As shown in Chapter 4, all these agents are in fact a coalition—a group working together who share some, but not all, goals. SOE shares are not traded in the market, and the populace does not have an effective voice in their direction and control. In some countries, the government is a coalition of different parties, in which ministries are assigned to member parties of the coalition to operate with a considerable degree of autonomy, almost like feudal barons. Even under a strong dictatorial leader, different ministers push for their point of view. Many issues are settled by compromise and thus never reach the head of state for adjudication. Further, government is only one of the willful external control agents that attempt to steer the behavior of the SOE to meet their preferred goals.

Thus, the question, who are the controllers?, does not have a simple, unequivocal answer. The source of legitimacy of the controllers is also unclear. From the point of view of the enterprise, the question should be rephrased: what is the external coalition?

THE EXTERNAL COALITION

The organization is a system linked with its external environment, influenced by the environment's demands and mandated to satisfy the desires of its stakeholders to survive (see Chapter 4). Like any other business enterprise, the SOEs are dependent on many environmental factors for their resources and support. Some of these—consumers, suppliers or financial institutions—are the same as in the private sector. The more the survival of the enterprise depends on its clients, the more resources the organization would devote to keeping potential clients informed about its activities and to receiving information about their expectations and desires. On the one hand, in a competitive environment in which the survival of the enterprise is not guaranteed by the government, the market controls the operations of the firm and maintains its efficiency. An electricity monopoly, on the other hand, is much more dependent on Parliament's decision on its rates and the ministry's decisions about its allocation of resources than on its clients' desires. In several cases, SOE electricity firms were even instructed to carry out campaigns to persuade their consumers to conserve energy.

Consumers expect SOEs to charge them lower prices. They also expect quality of service including safety, punctuality, frequency of service, information and cleanliness. Indeed, the U.K. Monopolies and Mergers commission observed in its report on the British Railways Board that the board is provided with "no specific formal targets or constraints on the quality of service expected of them" (1980, p. 32). The NEDO (1976) report noted that many sponsor departments "do not seem to have given prominence to the problem of relating prices to standards of service which customers require" (p. 31).

Domestic suppliers to SOEs often demand preferential treatment and priority over foreign suppliers, even if their prices are higher. Because they are state-owned, the enterprises are sometimes perceived as having to aid domestic industries. Labor in SOEs also has heightened expectations, demanding higher salaries, better working conditions and a much higher level of guarantees against shedding workers than in private firms. Financial institutions tend to perceive loans to SOEs as implicitly guaranteed by government.

In some cases, SOE managers may feel that the survival of the enterprise is guaranteed by the government, not by its profitability. They would thus perceive the need to ensure governmental support to be of paramount importance (see Chapter 2).

The real owners of the SOEs are the citizens of the country. However, certain strong influencers have the legal right to represent these owners and to control the enterprises. Although the owners are dispersed, their representatives are not. In practice, the major environmental factor that has to be reckoned with in terms of control is the government. In democracies, another such factor is the Parliament. The rest of this chapter, therefore, analyzes mainly the formal and informal controls imposed by governments on their SOEs. It also discusses problems of relationships between SOEs and Parliament.

We shall not deal with government control issues typical of all enterprise, like the impact of taxes on behavior. Also ignored are problems common to private and state-owned enterprises, like relations to customers. Not all control problems of SOEs are covered. Thus, problems of internal control within SOEs or honesty controls (designed to minimize corruption, nepotism or other forms of dishonesty) are not covered. The focus is on control problems specific to SOEs, and therefore, mainly to the ways and means by which governments attempt to control these enterprises. Since government is not a homogenous entity with a well-defined preference function, who precisely are the controllers is an extremely important question that will partially determine also the instruments of control and their form.

ORGANS OF CONTROL

In all countries of the world, at least four different organs control various aspects of the operations of the SOE: the government, the Parliament, the state comptroller (or auditor general) and the board of directors of the enterprise.

Theoretically, the governmental control could be executed by one of the following:

The government as a whole;

A sponsoring minister who is usually appointed according to the main economic function of the specific SOE;

A sponsoring minister, together with the minister of finance;
A special minister for state shareholdings.

Government as a Whole

Control by the government as a whole has the advantage that the government must first reconcile its differences as to the objectives sought and the directives to be given to the SOE. Only after the different points of view have been integrated should the government issue any directives or control the behavior of the SOE. Once the government as a whole reaches a decision, its directives will carry much weight, and managers of SOEs will find it difficult to work against them. Moreover, sponsoring ministers may represent sectorial interests and are sometimes seen as representing the point of view of the industry in the cabinet. To achieve an integrated point of view, the whole government has to deliberate and decide.

Governments, however, are burdened by many state issues, all of which are extremely important, and do not have the time or the inclination to reconcile differences among ministers regarding problems of SOEs. Governments do issue special directives to SOEs when they are perceived as extremely important or politically sensitive. Crossman (1976) in his memoirs gives a fascinating account of a debate in the U.K. government on the price of coal in August 1965. According to this account, the objections to the proposal of the NCB to raise coal prices ranged from the impact of the decision on the municipal elections that were being held, to income policy, to "could we risk the TUC blowing up in your faces at their Congress in September?" The government committee was split evenly on the issue, and when it came to the vote, "Fred's was the extra vote which gave us the seven to five majority for economic madness but for political sanity" (p. 303).

More generally, the government as a whole decides on matters that may have strong political repercussions. As one example, in Venezuela, the government as a whole decided in September 1982 to take the oil investment fund from its oil SOE and transfer it to the central bank (Coronel, 1983).

The government as a whole also decides on matters such as the creation of a new SOE (or suggestions of a bill to Parliament for the creation of an SOE) or on proposals for the sale, merger or voluntary bankruptcy of an SOE. The government may also make certain policy decisions with regard to the SOEs as a group, such as the recent decision of the U.K. government on a policy of privatization (see Chapter 9). At least in this case, the conventional wisdom that SOE managers would honor decisions of the whole government did not turn out to be the reality. Thus, Sir Dennis Rooke, chairman of British Gas, fought bitterly against the government's decision to privatize the retail stores owned by British Gas and won the fight.

Sectorial Sponsoring Ministers

The predominant organizational form in most countries is to nominate for each SOE a minister who is responsible for its control and is accountable to Parliament for the operations of the firm. This method fits easily with the usual sectorial structure of the government. Theoretically, a sponsoring minister can see the whole picture for the sector entrusted to him or her and thus eliminate unnecessary duplications. The sponsoring minister also has, at least in theory, a staff of civil servants who are experts in the affairs of the specific enterprise. Moreover, this minister has the authority to grant required licenses and should control the budget for the economic area for which he or she is responsible.

In the U.K. system, e.g., each one of the nationalized industries has a sponsoring minister. The sponsoring department has to approve a 5 year investment program for each of these enterprises. The approved investment program becomes part of the government's statement of its public expenditures programs, which are submitted to Parliament for approval. Each sponsoring ministry also receives a long-term (usually 5 years) corporate plan and approves the annual budget of the enterprise. The sponsoring minister is supposed to lay down policies to guide the operations of the industries but refrain from encroaching on the firm's autonomy on operating decisions. This minister is also accountable to Parliament on the affairs of the corporation (see Robson, 1969). The practice in the United Kingdom is very different from the theory. The Select Committee on Nationalised Industries, (SCNI), in its first report published in 1968, noted:

> Ministers have largely done the opposite of what Parliament intended. They were supposed to lay down policies—in particular for the whole of their sectors of the economy—which would guide the operations of the individual industries, but not to intervene in the management of the industries in implementing those policies. In practice, until recently, they have given the industries very little policy guidance but they have become closely involved in many aspects of management. (Vol. 1, paragraph 40)

In fact, in all countries of the world that have used a sponsoring minister, complaints abound that the minister intervenes directly in the day-to-day management of the enterprises under his or her supervision, giving management direct orders and putting pressures on the firm to follow these directives, using the different powers of the ministry, including procrastination in the approval of budgets, licenses and so on. These directives are not given in a formal way but through what the select committee report called "lunch table directives."

Two other problems of the system of a sponsoring minister should be mentioned. First, many SOEs could be put under the direction of different ministers, and it is not easy to choose the suitable sponsoring minister. Thus, a fertilizer manufacturer could be sponsored by the ministry of mines, or by the ministry of industry or, since it sells its total output to farmers—by the ministry of agriculture. These different ministers have different points of view and may give different directives to the enterprise. In many cases the enterprises have diversified, and their range of activities is much wider than the responsibility of one minister. PETROBRAS, the Brazilian state-owned oil firm, is not only in the field of oil exploration (ministry of mines and hydrocarbon) but also refining, production of fertilizers and petrochemicals, operations of a fleet of oil tankers, a distribution chain and exports.

Second, the sponsoring ministries are often said to be co-opted or captured by the enterprise with little will (or ability) to resist it, presenting the point of view of the enterprise in the government instead of controlling the enterprise. This claim often comes from the ministry of finance. As the bankers of the country, ministers of finance have to pay for SOEs' deficits and are notorious in their attempts to control the SOEs. They often fight other ministers who are willing to approve for their enterprises what the treasury sees as grandiose plans, taking too many of the scarce resources of the country. They call for closer scrutiny of SOEs and a tighter control of their financial affairs. Finance ministers question whether the government can continue to afford the luxury of supporting a cash-hungry SOE sector when they also impose limits on the right of the enterprise to raise funds from outside sources.

In the United Kingdom the treasury controls the SOEs by the so-called external financing limits (EFLs), the mechanism of which is explained later in this chapter. The treasury also decides on the required rate of return on assets. In certain cases it forced the enterprises to increase their prices (and in other cases, to freeze them). In 1984, Mr. Peter Rees, chief secretary at the British Treasury, asked for comments from the chairman of the nationalized industries on a proposed new statute that will further enhance the power of the treasury as well as reduce the threat of litigation against the government, which habitually demands from its enterprises a return on their assets although the enabling legislation required these same enterprises to break even. The proposed legislation gives government the right to interfere, abandoning formally the idea that the SOEs should be run at arm's length as commercial enterprises. It would give EFLs and financial targets primacy over an enterprise's other duties and would require the firms to surrender excess cash to the treasury rather than lend it with interest. Further, secretaries of state could dismiss boards if they did not agree with governmental policy (*The Economist*, September 22, 1984, pp. 26-30).

If indeed one wants all SOEs to be a portfolio of the government, then these firms should be managed like a private enterprise portfolio. Why not allow the Exchequer more controls? Some of the worst offenders, however, are the ministers of finance who caused nationwide natural monopolies, like railroads, to suffer from huge cash hemorrhages almost everywhere by freezing their prices.

The Sponsoring Minister Jointly with the Minister of Finance

Since the minister of finance holds the purse and is the person responsible for the preparation and the execution of the budget, he or she is expected to be the coordinator and integrator of governmental policies and responsible for the state's assets and the final allocation of governmental resources. As such, these ministers have a very important stake in and a great deal of power over the operations of the SOEs.

In recognition of this special status, the Government Companies Act in Israel put each SOE formally under the control of the minister of finance jointly with the sponsoring minister. It was assumed that the joint responsibility would neutralize pressures on the enterprise or the granting of unjustified preferences by the sponsoring minister. The two ministers have to agree between them on issues such as the nomination of directors (paragraph 18), approval of the board's chairman (Paragraph 25), receipt of reports from the chairman of the board (Paragraph 25), fixing the responsibilities the board of directors cannot delegate (Paragraph 30), demand for a debate in the board (Paragraph 32), decision on the budget and other reports (Paragraph 34), approval of the appointment of the managing director (Paragraph 37) and nomination of the state's representatives to the general assembly of shareholders' meetings (Paragraph 50). The sponsoring minister alone has only two legal authorities: receiving reports from the auditor of the firm (Paragraph 45) and from the directors (Paragraph 20).

A Ministry of State Holdings

If sponsoring ministries are captured by the firms, then a central body of control is needed. In some countries, these powers are granted to the ministry of finance. Italy established a special ministry for state holdings. The existence of a special ministry for state holdings may emphasize the importance of this sector. It is also said to allow more budgets and personnel for the control of the firms, to help integrate the whole sector, to create a coherent way of working for all SOEs and to avoid the problem of deciding who should be the sponsoring minister in those cases in which the enterprise operates in more than one economic field.

The major disadvantages of this method were enumerated in the U.K. government's response to the proposal of the SCNI to create such a ministry (Cmnd 4027, 1969). According to this White Paper, it would be a mistake to separate responsibility for efficiency from responsibility for the wider public interest. Further, each sponsoring minister is responsible for the economic well-being of both private and state-owned firms, and it would be a mistake to separate the two. Finally, the government said, such a special ministry would not reduce the political involvement of the ministers. In addition, it is clear that there would inevitably be conflict between the ministries that were sponsors for the SOEs and the new ministry (for an analysis, see Robson, 1969).

A special ministry for state holdings is used only in countries in which the SOE sector is organized under one or more holding companies (Puerto Rico, Philippines, Italy). Although the power of different ministries varies in different countries, in all countries public control of SOEs has taken the shape of ministerial control. These controls may therefore reflect the vested interests of the minister or a political party rather than the amorphous public interest.

In some cases, although the SOE is officially subject to the control of a sponsoring minister, the real controller in the eyes of the management is the president of the country, who is also the one nominating the managers. This is the case, e.g., in the national oil firms of Mexico or Brazil and in the holding companies of Zambia.

SOES AS A PORTFOLIO; MACROLEVEL CONSIDERATIONS

With the increasing importance of SOEs in most Western economies, their financial circumstances are seen by many observers as an integral part of public finance, not merely the problem of each SOE. Continuing deficits of SOEs are, in the final analysis, covered by the taxpayers and cause budget deficits. SOEs account for a large percentage of total capital formation, and these investments are often financed from the government budget, increasing the public debt. The macroeconomic impact of SOEs on parameters such as money supply, interest rates, inflation, balance of payments and their growing claims on government budgets have gradually become of interest.

The relationships between SOEs and government have been analyzed in terms of the financing requirements of these enterprises and, the forms of controls exercised on the use and release of these funds. However, the growth of the SOEs has created a major change in the character of the government budget. From the SOE's point of view, to the extent the firm needs outside financing, it is forced to take into consideration not only usual business variables but also questions such as the budgetary deficit of the country and the government's fiscal and income policy. From the government's point of view, slippages in the SOEs' performance create budgetary difficulties, partially because one of the first ways by which SOEs finance their deficits is nonpayment of loans and taxes or interest arrears to the government.

In most countries, the government budgetary process takes into account SOEs only inasmuch as these enterprises need funds. As a result, there is very little coordination of financing in different SOEs, which is in diametrical opposition to the situation in a large privately held multibusiness firm.

One way to look at the SOE sector as a whole is to assume that consensus can be reached on goals. If both the goals and the controllers who should monitor their execution can be agreed on, the SOE sector might be seen as part of a portfolio of the state, managed by the head of government in the same way a large U.S. multidivisional firm is managed by its CEO. In both cases, the problem of control is the same: what is the best way to ensure that the management of the firm will carry out the tasks it was entrusted to perform, and what is the system of rewards and punishment in case management did or did not fulfill these tasks? In both cases, the CEO does not know every decision made by the hundreds of executives under his or her command. The private firm is managed by dividing it into divisions and strategic business units (SBUs), allowing the manager of each SBU some discretion within the overall corporate strategy. In a parallel way, the president or the prime minister is a manager of a portfolio, and the government is the headquarters of a large multidivisional firm, with different SBUs (or SOEs) to manage.

The portfolio may be managed by allowing each manager a considerable amount of discretion, balancing the portfolio by controlling strategic decisions, allocating resources to the different units or taking money out through dividends. Viewed this way, the SOE may appear to have a very large amount of autonomy, but its strategic decisions really may be controlled from the top through the resource allocation process. To think through the theoretical ramifications for the management of such a portfolio, one has to have a theory of the state and its goals. As long as such a theory is unavailable, normative methods for resource allocation among different units in the portfolio cannot be proposed.

If the SOE sector is treated as a portfolio, one problem is the degree to which the government can and should move funds from one SOE to another. In a private firm, portfolio theory advocates transfer of funds from the non-growth-heavy cash-producing firms (the "cash cows") to finance the rapidly growing firms (the "stars") and to create opportunities for the new or the question marks. In SOEs, the government rarely transfers funds from one SOE to another on such considerations. When SOEs are controlled by sponsoring ministries, each ministry is interested in sheltering the funds from the treasury. In a holding company, cash cows finance the dogs rather than the stars. Statsförtag, e.g., financed its terminally ill enterprises from the cash generated by its profitable subsidiaries. In many countries when the enterprises are a part of the general government, cash transfers occur but in the opposite direction: growth firms are drained of funds to finance other activities. A case in point is the telephone services in many countries.

The effects of an efficient telephone system on economic life are indisputable, albeit immeasurable. Moreover, telephone service is usually a very profitable, even lucrative, business. However, in one country after another the same sad story is heard: perhaps because of inadequate forms of administration, perhaps for other reasons, there has been a lag in the introduction of new telephone equipment and in many countries the waiting line for the installation of a telephone is appalling. Funds generated by the telephone are used to finance the loss on the mail, other services or general government, resulting in delays and malfunctions of the telephone system.

In France, the government decided to raise telephone rates in order to make funds available for investment in the electronic industry. The opposition felt it was illegal to do it. For them the PTT is an annex to the state budget and raising telephone tariffs to reduce budget deficits is wrong. A major reason for transferring the telephones to a separate legal entity has been the attempt to save the funds generated by it for more investments and to avoid losses caused by unreasonable and shortsighted government requirements. Many economists claim that to provide resources for needed industrial restructuring, the expansion rate of social services has to be reduced. Instead of facing the question in this global form, many preferred a different solution: that of creating an SOE. This way, the funds generated by the business would be preserved for its expansion.

When the SOEs are legally organized as a private joint stock company, the government may not be able to force the board of directors to declare dividends. In some countries, the law specifically allows the government to demand dividends. This is the situation, e.g., in Israel. In Sri Lanka, specific legislation, allowing the enterprises to contribute money to the government, was passed. In contrast, in Korea no dividend is payable to the government under the legislation, and every SOE is allowed to maintain the surplus it has accumulated for further investment. In Venezuela, the oil industry investment fund was transferred to the central bank, despite protests of oil industry management and the main opposition party (Accion Democratica).

Politicians are said to be guided by vote-maximizing behavior and to allocate public funds where the political benefits are higher. Therefore, as SOE managers see it, the funds are better hidden from them. Central control of government is feared, not only because it reduces autonomy in operational decisions but also because of a basic fear that politicians do not necessarily represent the public interest.

CONSOLIDATED INFORMATION

One difference between a privately owned multidivisional organization and an SOE, is that in the case of a private firm, it is highly unlikely that top management would not have a list of all its subsidiaries. In many countries, the government does not even have a list of the enterprises it owns. In France, subsidiaries of SOEs have mushroomed and have escaped many of the formal controls. In Israel, until 1975, most SOEs were started using the legal means of creating a private joint stock company. As a result, every minister could and did establish SOEs, subject to very little, if any, formal control. Different ministers continued to create new enterprises in one way or another until the Law on Government Companies was passed in 1975. Up to the 1960s not even a central record existed of SOEs. A 1956 staff report on public authorities under New York noted, "Over the last fifty years the public authority device has grown into a significant element of government, and its area of operation has spread into a number of divergent fields" (State of New York, 1956, p. 3). The report also notes that "at present, the State government is operating in the dark with respect to much public authority activities" (p. xix) and that "only through extensive research was it possible to determine: (1) how many authorities have been created; (2) how many authorities are active in the State; (3) the status of those authorities which are now not active: and (4) the salient facts about those authorities which are currently active in the State" (pp. 5–6). Twenty-five years later, a thorough survey of state enterprises in the United States reached similar conclusions (Walsh, 1978, p. 353).

In Brazil until 1979, the government had no consolidated information on its hundreds of SOEs, which received transfers from government in many ways, most of them off budget. As a result, control was gradually eroded (Shirley, 1983, p. 22). The crisis brought about by this state of affairs caused the government to reverse its attitude toward SOEs' autonomy. In 1979 the government reacted to increasing inflationary pressures and a deteriorating balance of payments by centralizing controls in a new agency, the Special Secretariat for the Control of State Enterprises (SEST), which is empowered to monitor and approve the budgets of each of the 382 SOEs. Its prior approval is required for all domestic and foreign credit operations by an SOE. It also imposed enterprise-by-enterprise ceilings on imports and fuel consumption and intervened in salary and pension decisions.

As shown in Chapter 1, governments define SOEs differently. In many cases, the definition is so narrow that government does not have the true picture of its assets and potential liabilities. SOEs finance their investments not only from direct government transfer of funds but also from retained earnings, loans obtained abroad and from state-owned financial institutions, which are often guaranteed by governments. The heavy reliance on many extra budgeting operations by the government is often not recorded in any central fashion, and the operational results of SOEs are not consolidated. The result is not only lessened control on the economic and financial operations of the SOEs but even worse: an erosion of the ability of the government to control its financial flows and borrowing requirements.

Further, SOEs have started large investment projects without adequate concern for the needed funds. Governments have sometimes been surprised to discover that they have to transfer more funds to finish a large-scale project and to avoid defaults to contractors and suppliers. Large SOEs have created many subsidiaries at home or abroad, not always with governmental blessing or even knowledge. This situation often resulted in more contingent liabilities that turned out sometimes to be real ones. To avoid the political embarrassment of a bankrupt subsidiary abroad, governments again had to supply more finance in a hurry. Consequently, macroeconomic management was undermined, sometimes with devastating effects on the country's foreign exchange position or its monetary policy.

This problem has become more important with the growing claims on government budgets by SOEs. As one example, a third of all Peruvian foreign debt in the period 1976 to 1980 was incurred by the SOE sector. During 1980, SOEs were responsible for 91.5 percent of total domestic credit in Indonesia, 87 percent in Guinea, 76 percent in Burma and 54 percent in Benin (Short, 1984, Table 8, see also Shirley, 1983; Choksi, 1979). One result has often been an overreaction to the abuses and panicky introduction of a whole new set of controls, as in the Brazilian example described earlier.

Certainly, a minimum requirement of control is to have information. Even if the government prefers to leave its SOEs completely autonomous, it should have some idea who these enterprises are, what are they doing and what kinds of liabilities are they taking; otherwise, it may find itself faced with many surprises and its macroeconomic management undermined. The need for information is so obvious that its absence seems unbelievable.

It is well to remember, however, that more than seventy developing countries lack any accounting standards. Heller and Tait (1984) were "surprised and depressed" at the paucity of data on public sector employment and pay. There is also very little data on transfers between governments and SOEs. In the IMF *Government Statistical Yearbook of 1981*, useful data on transfers from SOEs to governments are limited to about thirty countries, and no data appear for any country on transfers from governments to SOEs. These problems are exacerbated by internal accounting obscurantism to mask poor performance (and, in some cases, to mask good performance to weaken labor's demands for higher wages or to continue receiving government's subsidies or to avoid government demands to aid ailing firms). The controllers are often a part of a power game and do not necessarily have the upper hand in this game. A report of the French parliament on the state oil firms even accused them of giving erroneous information (Schvartz, 1974). The complex system of cross subsidies also obscures the results and makes controls more difficult.

FORMS OF CONTROL

The mechanisms used by the external coalition to control the discretion of SOE managers can be categorized as motivational, cognitive, contextual and structural.

Motivational Mechanisms

The most direct method for one to constrain another individual's behavior is to make sure that the individual will be self-motivated to behave in the manner one desires. Through their power to appoint, promote, transfer or dismiss, directors and managers of SOEs, ministers can to a substantial degree ensure that loyal individuals are placed into these "discretionary roles" (Thompson, 1967), and the remaining individuals are thus motivated to implement the formal or informal directives of the ministers. Indeed, in many countries a change of government is followed by a massive change of directors in SOEs and often also of managers—to ensure loyal and obedient management. Sometimes, the minister (or the president) nominates him- or herself as a chair of the board and some close associates as directors. Thus, in Abu Dhabi and Saudi Arabia, the chairman of the board is a minister (but a two-thirds majority of the board can overrule him) (Zakariya, 1978, p. 493). Ministers are chairmen also in Venezuela and Zambia.

Managers and board members, therefore, know they have to please a minister or the president of the country as a necessary condition to the continuation of their job. A manager who is not known and trusted is replaced. A manager who does not look after the interests of the government in power, may be fired. Appointments typically reflect political leanings, party affiliation and personal loyalties (see Chapter 8).

Cognitive Mechanisms

The authority and power to issue formal and informal directives and to penalize their nonimplementation provides ministers with added control over the discretion of SOEs' top management. Most governments do not control their SOEs by issuing directives or publishing guidelines. Instead, they tend to intervene in the decisions of the firms. Government controls often deal with petty questions and are rarely related to a real attempt to think through the major strategic questions of the SOEs (Chambers, 1984) and, worse still, do not change in any material way the strategic directions of th SOEs or their efficiency.

Controls have grown on an *ad hoc* basis. When one kind of control seemed inadequate, another layer was added. The result has been a formidable array of controls, some of them working at cross purposes and none taking into account the administrative capacity (or lack of it) of the civil service. The system therefore causes many bottlenecks, overworked civil servants and frustrated managers. In many LDCs, the functional details that have to reach government monitors for approval are quite staggering. In Thailand, e.g., SOEs are controlled by a sponsoring department, the Bureau of the Budget, the Ministry of Finance and the National Economic and Social Development Board. These entities—sometimes all of them—approve investment plans, revenue budgets, prices, external financing proposals and pay. The Ministry of Finance has to approve bonuses, retirement age, welfare funds, study tours and even the treatment of certain transactions in the account. All appointments to the major SOEs, many investment programs and the final accounts after auditing have to be approved by the government as a whole (Garner, in Ramanadham, 1984a, p. 19). Even the electricity authority contracts with insulators need approval (p. 22). In Peru, travel out of the country by executives of SOEs must be approved by a presidential decree (Boneo, in Reddy, 1983, pp. 162–163).

In many cases SOE employees and managers receive better salaries than those prevailing in the government sector. Civil service commissioners claim that these higher salaries impede them from recruiting the best persons to the government and advocate equal treatment of the civil service and the SOEs. Indeed, in many countries, the salary structure of SOE employees has to be approved by a higher authority. In Uruguay, the National Office of the Civil Service must approve the hiring of new functionaries. In Argentina, acquisitions over a certain amount had to be approved by the Corporation of National Enterprises. In many countries, like Venezuela, certain financial credit operations need prior approval of the Council of Ministers.

In India, "the control exercised by the ministers often goes to fantastic lengths. Some of them have been known to have used informal guidance and pressure not merely on broad matters of policy but also in matters of detail, such as personnel management, labor relations, stores purchases policy, etc." (Das, 1966, p. 71). The Bureau of Public Enterprises (BPE) issues guidelines, instructions and advice on many matters of detail. Thus, the BPE advised in 1977 to 1978 "to exercise austerity in all entertainment and restrict the number of invitees to a minimum" and prescribed per capita limits on entertainment (Narain, 1980, p. 313) and even attempted to set standards for factory perimeter fencing (Shirley, 1983, p. 28) and so-called guidelines for the color of the paint of the cars. In one case, an SOE was called on to explain why it built quarters with a ceiling of 9 feet 6 inches instead of 9 feet 3 inches (Narain, 1982, pp. 22–23). In some extreme cases, the degree of intervention was so great and detailed that the management of the enterprise lost its autonomy completely—as in the case of the Damodar Valley Corporation. In many cases, "the controllers have failed effectively to lead; the controlled have refused to be led" (Cassese, in Vernon and Aharoni, 1981, p. 148).

A seminar on the control systems of SOEs in developing countries summarized the situation:

> While [executive and government controls] are essential for good management and are important tools which could be utilized by public authorities to ensure good performance, there is a danger and indeed some situations in developing countries where external controls tend to be excessive. Such excessive controls would be counterproductive as they would stifle initiative, entrepreneurship, risk-taking and managerial courage which are prerequisite for the running of the business organization. There is clearly a need to ensure that the control systems, while serving the purpose for which they are intended, do not reduce the autonomy of the enterprises. [Fernandes, 1979, p. 22]

The problem, however, is that the purposes for which the controls are intended are often related to the second and third reasons discussed when the question of why there should be controls was analyzed. In many cases in various countries, SOEs were instructed to pursue various policies for political gain for the party in power or, in some cases, for pecuniary gains for certain individuals.

A major cost of detailed control is delays. Much of the managers' time is spent in getting various approvals or licenses or asking for permission for quite routine operations, or finding ways to avoid the need for permission— sometimes by concealing the fact that an act was taken. On more important decisions, the delays are longer. For example, "it took five years to finalize the proposals of the Indian Airlines of the type of aircraft to be purchased. By that time it was not a current aircraft, spares and maintenance schedules were out of date, resulting in higher maintenance costs" (Narain, 1982, p. 16).

Contextual Mechanisms

The external environment of the SOEs includes suppliers, consumers and workers, and the enterprise must continuously adapt to changes in these environments. By controlling these components of the SOE's environment, or the SOE's input prices, the ministers can further control managers' discretion. Thus, the SOE may be required, as it is in many LDCs, to pay higher wages to preferred local suppliers or to sell its outputs at subsidized prices. These controls affect, among other things, the financing requirements of the SOE.

Structural Mechanisms

The most important *de facto* power ministers have to control SOEs is the power of the purse. Indeed, in many cases, the government restricts the ability of an SOE to tap funds from outside sources, forcing it to come to the government when funds are needed. This enhances the power of the ministry of finance over the sponsoring ministry. The minister of finance also controls the discretion of SOE top management by undercapitalizing the enterprises (Phatak, 1969), ensuring that the SOE's management must approach the ministries from time to time for debt financing. Each such interaction provides the ministers with an opportunity to channel the exercise of SOE top management's discretion in the direction they desire.

Present systems of control evolved with time, as a short history of the United Kingdom shows. When SOEs were first created, they were part of the government, operating under bureaucratic controls. With time, it became apparent that these controls were too tight, and the government adopted an almost *laissez faire* attitude, assuming that the "responsibility for efficient management rested with the board" (Chester, 1975, p. 961). Even at that period, there were interventions, mainly in delaying price rises or the choice of investment projects (Pryke, 1971, pp. 48, 201, 318). The increasing losses of the British Rail, the SOE's over optimistic forecasts and its deteriorating financial position (Aldcroft, 1968, p. 156) led the government to scrutinize all SOEs major projects (Hannah, 1982, p. 204). Controls were imposed because of the government's concern that public expenditure was getting out of control. It was declared (in the 1961 White Paper) that "the operation of the nationalized industries with an unduly low rate of return is sooner or later damaging to the economy as a whole" (p. 5). Instead of a requirement to break even, the 1961 White Paper introduced financial targets as a means of control. The result was price increases by the (monopolistic) SOEs. Investment projects were seldom vetoed. Foster (1971) found to his astonishment "that no railway investment project was turned down, in spite of . . . the widespread feeling, shared by many officials, that a very large slice of railway investment has been digging BR deeper into the red since the mid-fifties" (pp. 57–58).

In 1967, the financial targets were replaced by pricing policies and investment criteria. More important, SOEs were used as a tool for anti-inflation policies: these firms were restricted in raising prices (Pryke, 1981, pp. 259–261). It was also found that "the information which would be required for effective monitoring . . . is not usually requested from or provided by the corporations" (NEDO, 1976, p. 30). The reality was that political considerations of vote-seeking led to approval of huge investments and to restraint on prices, and the White Paper was not taken too seriously. Callaghan, the then Chancellor of the Exchequer, felt "I couldn't care less. I take no responsibility and took no part in composing it." (Crossman, 1976, Vol. 2, p. 524). In 1976, NEDO reported "a lack of trust and mutual understanding between those who run the nationalised industries and those in government . . . who are concerned with their affairs" (p. 8). In 1976, the EFL was introduced.

In the United Kingdom, nationalized industries are expected to limit their external borrowing to an amount allotted annually by the government. The EFL covers loans, grants and the issue of the so-called public dividend capital (PDC), a form of equity capital available to few enterprises. EFL is equal to the difference between total external borrowing in year 1 and total external borrowing in year 0; that is, EFL is equal to the capital investment plus increase in working capital minus internally generated funds from depreciation and after-tax profits.

The EFL is set 6 months before the beginning of the financial year as a result of negotiations between the SOE and the treasury. As a result of this system, the operations of SOEs are artificially restricted. When the government attempts to curb their borrowing requirements, SOEs with heavy needs for funds for capital investments may find themselves starved for cash. These limits may also damage the long-term competitive position of the SOE. A tight EFL may also involve deferring maintenance expenditures essential to the continuation of the business, attempts to increase prices to raise funds or reduction of services to the customers. By using EFLs, the government turns the SOEs into a surrogate tax collector: because of the low levels allowed for EFLs, monopoly firms are forced to raise their prices, and the money is used for government purposes. Finally, EFLs encourage window dressings in the balance sheet: SOEs may decide to delay certain obligations until a day after the year end to change the official amount of their EFL.

Those in favor of the EFL system argue that the system forces more efficiency in the SOEs, encouraging them to use working capital prudently, to avoid paying excessive wage demands and to impose a discipline analogous to that imposed by banks on private sector firms. While there are arguments for and against EFL, one point seems clear: this system means that the government looks at all its SOEs as a part of a total portfolio. Short-term budget requirements may affect the ability of the firms to invest funds. This shortage of funds has been one of the reasons for selling shares of SOEs in the private capital market.

If the state, as an owner, is a banker of last resort of SOEs, a system of looking at their total financial requirements is indispensable. However, a system of rationing based on total public sector requirements is not necessarily better than rationing by the prevailing rate of interest and equity yields. Certainly, for industries with attractive investment opportunities like the telephone industry, the latter is a better system.

Financial targets were largely based on haggling between the SOEs and the government departments. Fear of unpopularity led to increasing subsidies and more informal intervention. Throughout this period, actual control was not based only on legal prescriptions, but on political power and popularity considerations and on the Exchequer's needs to keep the budget within limits.

Most countries attempt to control the budgets of SOEs. The use of the budget as a control device has its problems. The government operates on an annual budget, while the enterprise must have a much longer time horizon to decide on its investment priorities. For example, the time horizon for the development of a new type of airplane or the erection of a new electricity generation facility is longer than a decade. Since the government works on an annual budget cycle, it is often reluctant to commit itself for a longer period of time, causing the SOE more uncertainty. SOEs also play what Hofstede (1968) called "the game of the budget": the enterprise presents a budget that is larger than its needs, assuming from past experience that it will be cut. The government knows that the budget is higher than needed and proposes a lower figure. The final outcome is that the budget is not a pure control device but is based on power play and compromises.

The budgets of SOEs are usually sent for approval to the sponsoring minister. In some countries, both revenue and capital budgets are sent for approval; in others, only capital budgets. When a holding company is in operation, such as in Italy or Korea, many of these approvals are done at the holding company level or by sector corporations, as in Bangladesh or Pakistan. In Portugal, the sponsoring ministry shows the finance minister only the relevant transfer of the current account, and in India, the financial advisor is associated with every stage of budget preparations. In most countries, no general guidelines are issued to SOEs on budget preparations, and the budget may be based on different assumptions—e.g., with regard to anticipated inflation rates. The wider linkages between the SOEs and the national economy tend to be ignored or to be concentrated only on things such as the EFL in the United Kingdom (and Korea) or on project financing (in Tanzania).

Controllers often assume that indirect methods of control may not be sufficient. They thus introduce more direct forms of control. Thus, SOEs have sometimes been directed to borrow abroad, not according to budgetary needs but because the government saw these borrowings as a source of foreign exchange generation. An enterprise may receive a direct order to invest in a certain laggard region, to carry out its short-term banking operations only through a certain bank (Peruvian enterprises, e.g., are required to deal only with the Banco de la Nacion; see Boneo, 1983, p. 19) or to freeze its prices.

More often, certain decisions are moved entirely from the enterprise and are made for it by higher authorities. These decisions may range from the creation of a subsidiary to approval of foreign travel by an SOE manager. Given the diversity of motivations of ministers to control the discretion of SOE managers and the diversity of control mechanisms the ministers have at their command, the most dominant problem of SOE management in nearly all countries appears to be one of overcontrol by the ministers and the legitimacy of those controls (Phatak, 1969; Maniatis, 1968; Aharoni, 1977; Coombes, 1971).

To explain actual control—and relationships between SOEs and government—a conceptual framework is needed that explains, among other things, the legitimacy of control. Warwick (1980) identifies six key transactions (control, oversight, interdependence, exchange, competition and conflict) among five key actors (controllers, managers, interest groups, competitors and allies). Hafsi (1981) proposed a life-cycle concept in which the SOE-government relationship develops from cooperative to distant to adversarial to autonomous. The official side of these relationships is manifested by the functional powers of the controllers.

FUNCTIONAL PROBLEM

The range of the statutory rights of ministers to intervene in functional areas is very wide. In Sri Lanka, the government can fix the salaries of employees in SOEs. In France, until the end of the 1960s, there were many controls: the ministry, the contrôleurs d'état as well as the state auditing arm, the court of accounts (Cour des Comptes, operating under the ministry of economy and finance) and the Commission de Vérification des Comptes des Entreprises Publiques (whose duties were transferred in 1976 to the Cour des Comptes). Many decisions of the SOEs required an *a priori* approval of the civil servants.

The decisions that formally need *a priori* approval are different in different countries. In most of them, formal ministerial power usually relates to the appointment of members of the board, capital expenditures, research programs, training and education, the form of accounts (with treasury approval), authorization to borrow (with treasury approval), mergers and acquisitions, financing, increases of share capital and approval of the budget. A United Nations publication (1973) proposed the apportionment of certain major control items shown in Table 6.1.

SOEs are, of course, also subject to indirect governmental controls. Like any other enterprise, they are affected by changing laws, tax structures and regulations.

STRENGTH OF CONTROLS

Two related issues are the strength of controls and sanctions imposed. A theoretical progressively stronger scale of controls may be envisaged, from the diffusion of information and publicity after the act to informal consultation before the act to *post factum* change to *a priori* approval. From this point of view, it is useful to differentiate, as the French do, between control before the act *(tutelle)* and after the act *(controle)*. In many LDCs, controls are strong but sanctions are weak, and there are no requirements of publicity. According to one interpretation:

> *The fundamental point in an examination of control systems is that no one in authority, either in the government or enterprise, wants true accountability of the public sector. The public sector has been used extensively as a form of patronage, as a device to channel resources to the ruling political party, to build the economic base of the political leaders . . . Occasionally, government may find a convenient scapegoat in a public enterprise for its own failures, and a new government may institute enquiries into the performance of public enterprises under the previous regime to expose the corruption*

Table 6.1   Suggested apportionment of control over public enterprises

Control Item	Agency	Qualifications
Appointment of board members	The minister concerned	
Appointment of chairperson and managing director	The minister concerned	Subject to cabinet approval

(cont.)

Control Item	Agency	Qualifications
(cont.)		
Revenue budgets	The board and the finance and administrative ministries	Subject to discussions with administrative ministry and finance ministry where subsidies are called for
Capital budgets	The minister concerned	Subject to finance ministry clearance and interministerial committee or cabinet guidelines and on the basis of project appraisal agencies' recommendations
Pricing policy	The minister concerned	Subject to an expert agency's recommendations, financial objectives determined for the enterprise and consultations with consumer councils
Fixing financial objectives	The minister concerned	Subject to finance ministry's concurrence and interministerial committee guidelines
Procurement of funds	The finance minister	In the case of long-term funds
Disposal of profits	The minister concerned	Subject to finance ministry advice
Declaration of dividend	The minister concerned	Subject to finance ministry concurrence
Accounting and audit	The act concerned	Specific, optional powers to audit
Reports	The act concerned	
Appointment of managerial staff	The board	Subject to ministerial or central public enterprise bureau guidelines
Salaries and wages	The board	Subject to ministerial or central public enterprise bureau guidelines
Incentive schemes	The board	Subject to ministerial or central public enterprise bureau guidelines
Purchase of stores	The board	Subject to ministerial or central public enterprise bureau guidelines
Approval of projects	The minister concerned	Subject to cabinet approval

> *of the previous regime. By and large, the government and the management have a common interest in hiding the reality of public enterprises.* [*Ghai, in Ramanadham, 1984a, p. 64*]

The least strong controls are needed when the market works, leaving no discretion to managers. In theory, an ideal control system would rely on the market, adjusted for social costs and benefits, compensating the SOE for achieving social goals imposed by government. Despite widespread adoption in academic literature, this scheme is hardly used. British Rail receives so-called public sector obligations (PSO) as a grant from the government because of the socially desirable but economically unprofitable services it provides, but the amount is based on negotiations between the firm's management and weary civil servants. Only recently did Mr. Bob Reid, the chairman of British Rail, agree to a 3-year reduction in the PSO, and the government approved that firm's plans to electrify the London to Edinburgh east coast mainline (*Financial Times*, October 10, 1984, p. 15). In 1974, Air France was able to negotiate compensation for being forced to shift its operations from Orly to the newly completed Charles de Gaulle Airport in Paris (Anastassopoulos, in Vernon and Aharoni, 1981, pp. 102–103). In most instances, however, undefined objectives with no clear trade-offs are seen by governments to be of political advantage. Compensation is based on implicit or explicit negotiations between the government and the SOEs, not on economic criteria.

RELATIONSHIPS BETWEEN THE CONTROLLERS AND THE CONTROLLED

The relationships between the controllers and the managers can be seen in at least three, not necessarily mutually exclusive, ways:

- As determined by rational decisions, clearly defined preferences, insight into alternatives and knowledge of methods to maximize expected utility;
- As determined by bargaining and conflict resolution between two competing organizations with different goals and interests, where no single organization can force a decision and where resources are decisive;
- As determined by response to events already taking place—that is, more or less passively adjusting to changing external conditions or to crisis situations.

In all cases, the controls are made by human beings, with limited cognitive abilities and with very few independent sources of information. In some cases controllers would like to work later in their career in the SOE and therefore do not want to antagonize its managers. In other cases, controllers are envious, believing the working conditions and the remunerations paid in the SOE are much better than other government salaries. In most countries, there is a basic psychological difference between the civil servants and the SOE managers, leading to lack of trust. Civil servants are used to universalistic, fixed procedures, rules and routines for defining a control domain. SOEs managers may have come from the private sector and are used to a different style of decision-making. (See, e.g., NEDO, 1976.)

In France, the Nora Committee (1967) found that the controllers were isolated from each other and were often captured by the controlled. All researchers on the French scene unanimously agreed that the many controlling bodies attempting to apply detailed controls resulted in less formal autonomy to the corporations but did not help to achieve much (Delion, 1963; Friedmann, 1974).

In many LDCs, the extreme scarcity of qualified civil servants causes more obstruction than control. Managers often blame their controllers for lack of understanding, procrastination and lack of trust (on Venezuela, see Coronel, 1983). Despite the ostensibly detailed controls, public entrepreneurs often act and then ask for permission. In some extreme cases, managers of SOEs have even dictated the foreign policy of the country. One well-known example is that of Enrico Mattei, ENI's president, discussed in Chapter 3.

The sponsoring ministry is often much weaker than the enterprise. State oil companies are portrayed as subject to little outside control and are able to influence their environment. These national oil companies—PETROBRAS in Brazil, PEMEX in Mexico, YPF in Argentina, PETRONAS in Malaysia, PETRONIN in Venezula or STATOIL in Norway—are very large and powerful, with many more planners and administrative personnel than the ministry. As a result, the national plans on energy are made in the enterprise, not in the ministry (for example, Richardson, 1981). One may argue that there is no *a priori* reason to believe that the interests of the country are represented better by a ministry than by a large SOE. Still, the enormous power of these large SOEs is often a source for concern. At least in some cases, presidents of such firms have used their power for the betterment of their personal wealth. A case in point is the Indonesian oil firm, PERTAMINA, whose president, Ibnu Sutowo, was found guilty of using his position for private gain (*Financial Times*, September 13, 1977, p. 14).

The problem of size and expertise residing more in the enterprise than in the sponsoring ministry is true also in many other cases. Empresa Embraer, the Brazilian producer of aircrafts, knows much more about its business than the civil service, which often uses the staff of the enterprise to prepare national plans or position papers for international negotiations. Sheahan argues that "the relationships of the EDF to national economic policy have been complex, and in the last few years disturbing. . . . the company has developed a great deal of power to influence national decisions involving issues of public welfare going well beyond commercial considerations" (in Shepherd, 1976, pp. 147–149).

Ministers are left in the position forecast for Dwight Eisenhower when Harry Truman, commenting on Eisenhower's possible succession to the presidency, said, "he'll sit here" (tapping his desk for emphasis), "and he'll say, 'Do this! Do that.' *And nothing will happen.* Poor Ike—it won't be a bit like the Army. He'll find it very frustrating" (Neustadt, 1960, p. 9).

The hodgepodge of directions, regulations, approvals and veto powers and the fragmentation of a host of controls have not really helped to ensure that SOEs are accountable to the public. Dynamic public entrepreneurs were able to build empires, co-opting the controllers and influencing them in many different ways. The more controls are imposed, the more SOE managers either ignore them or resort to apathy. The elaborate French system of control was not more effective than the rudimentary Italian control of a much weaker government. Large and profitable SOEs generating their own cash are in effect self-governing, while those SOEs that suffer from cash drain and have to come, hat in hands, to the civil service, lose much of their autonomy.

Ownership by the state of the means of production does not necessarily imply control over the internal decision-making of the firm. State ownership does make moot the question of the social and political legitimacy of an SOE. Since the property rights are vested in the state, the SOE is expected to include the public's welfare in its decision-making. Controllers and managers often disagree, however, on the definition of the public's welfare.

DIFFERENT CONTROLS FOR DIFFERENT SOES

Neither one organizational form nor one control system is well suited for all purposes. In enterprises subject to market competition, control systems are superfluous. Different SOEs operate in different environments and are expected to achieve different objectives. They therefore should have different control systems. SOEs that operate as government departments are subject to all its regulations concerning matters such as salaries, bidding requirements and financial accounting. As such, they operate under a Weberian bureaucratic system appropriate to stable and certain environments. This type of control may be appropriate for the Post Office. However, in SOEs that are expected to be innovative, the control system should be differently designed. For example, alternative decision centers should be allowed. Bhatt's (1982) analysis of the Indian Swaraj tractor is relevant here:

The tractor was designed in 1970. However, the central government was not willing to provide the resources for its production. The Mining and Allied Machinery Corporation (MAMC), an SOE that assisted in constructing the prototype, "was not willing to take the additional risk involved in the production of the new tractor" (Bhatt in Jones *et al.*, 1982, p. 31). Hindustan Machine Tools preferred a tractor of Czech design, suggested by Russian experts.

At this stage, the Punjab State Industrial Development Corporation, picked up the project. The tractor was then completed on schedule and at the cost envisioned. Except for a strike, full-capacity operation would have been reached in 3 years as planned; consumer acceptance and demand have been high and innovation continued, with two new models introduced in 4 years. In this case and many others, institutional pluralism substitutes for market competition in allowing innovation and in producing pressures for efficient outcomes. Further, an integral part of entrepreneurial decision making is the uncertainty inherent in many changes and innovations, and this runs against the needs of machine bureaucracy. Derogatory observations by controllers—sometimes after several years—do not encourage risk taking and innovation.

Lorsch and Allen (1973) have shown that the more diversity, the less likely it is that management will have the knowledge to understand detailed product/market issues. Therefore, their capacity to become involved in the substance of issues becomes very limited. In addition, their capacity to motivate through leadership will be limited by the fact that they lack the expertise that is one important basis for organizational power. Top management power is also limited by the resentment held by subordinate managers toward top management involvement in the substance of such issues. Meddling and interference is demotivating in the public as much as in the private sector.

Structures in which SOE managers are left to carry on the operating decisions will have very little variation in the decision-making and in tasks, but operating routines will be perfectly retained. If the SOE operates under uncertainty with high need for change and adaptation, it requires a great deal of variation and intrusion of other perspectives, not unity of direction. In a stabler environment, a different control is possible.

PROPOSALS FOR LEGAL REFORM

The perceived lack of control over SOEs led many observers to demand a change in the system. The U.K. SCNI proposed the establishment of a centralized, single ministry of nationalized industries. The NEDO report (1976) recommended a two-tier board, which was rejected by the government. [Incidentally, Morrison also rejected such an idea: "the board above and the board below, a sort of heaven and hell of . . . management" (1933, p. 217; see also p. 222).] In Italy, the Chiarelli Commission proposed in 1975 that "The power of ministers to intervene for the purpose of *ante facto* control be clarified by the issuance of specific authorizations, these to be made public" (cited in Stefani, 1981).

Others believe that the problem may be solved by enacting a special law for all SOEs. The problem, however, is that without a coherent conceptual scheme on the role of SOEs, agreed by all, it is difficult to see what the law will say. Further, a law applicable to a large public utility may impose too many restrictions on a small subsidiary managing real estate.

Legal prescriptions on the ways of controlling SOEs may or may not be followed in practice. In Israel, the law specifies that an enterprise has to get approval on its investments but not on leasing. Thus, some SOEs made large-scale leasing commitments to circumvent the need for approval. All in all, it is extremely difficult to enact laws that will anticipate the different needs of the future and all possible ways of peforming an economic act.

Sometimes, because the law did not anticipate certain situations, ministers found they could not force the corporation to do what they believed was needed in the public interest. When the U.K. government sought to sell parts of certain enterprises, it faced opposition by the board and, at least in some cases, had to give in, having no legal means to force its point of view. As a result, there are now recommendations for a change in the law. In India, in contrast, the president can issue such instructions and directions that may be necessary in regard to the conduct of business by the corporation.

PARLIAMENTARY CONTROL

One result of the growth in the size and scope of the public sector in democratic countries has been the decline of parliamentary control over the executive. The diminished status of the legislature is evident when the question of its relationships with SOEs and its control over them is analyzed. The problem of "accountability to Parliament" is even more difficult than accountability to government.

First, many SOEs were established to circumvent parliamentary control and the need to get approval for a budget appropriation. In most countries, the approval of the legislature was needed to establish a public corporation, but not necessarily for the acquisition of shares in a company or the establishment of a subsidiary. This freedom of the executive branch has been one of the main battles of the legislative, solved in different ways in different countries.

Second, the legislative receives a considerable amount of detailed information on SOEs from annual reports to answers to questions. In the U.K. SCNI has held dozens of meetings on each of the nationalized industries, in which thousands of questions were put by the committees (as one example, 3000 questions in the investigation of British Railways in 1960). According to Kelf–Cohen (1969), "Appearance before the Select Committee must be regarded as an occupational hazard of a chairman" (p. 172). Yet no experts are available to analyze all these data. In fact, legislators rarely possess the expertise to discuss strategic issues. Instead, according to an Acton Society Trust Report (1950):

An analysis of speeches shows that the content of each can generally be divided into four parts. Speakers tend to open with a number of miscellaneous formalities - congratulating or decrying previous speakers etc. Next they usually consider it necessary to establish that the troubles now besetting the industry derive from the past errors of the opposing party. After this the member comes to his own knowledge of the subject, recounting the experiences and reminiscences. Finally in the time left, the member addresses himself to the particular subject of the debate - the railway deficit, the man-power shortage in the coal mines, etc. This account is unjust to the best speeches; in the worst, the final and relevant part of the speech is omitted altogether (p. 20).

Third, and most important, if SOEs are to be autonomous, the legislative must be restricted in its supervisory functions. Managers complain, first, that information that is commercially secret when divulged to the Parliament is in the public domain and available to competitors. Second, the number of persons with the authority to take up management's time is excessive. Managers have to spend a lot of their time answering inquiries, being subject to cross examination in parliamentary committees or arguing with the civil servants. But in a democracy, the legislature, as a representative of the people, wants to get adequate information on the SOEs, particularly when these enterprises are subsidized from the public purse. Full accountability to the Parliament would require at least that that body receive annually a balance sheet, profit and loss statement and sources and uses of funds statement, as well as reports of the state auditor and follow-up on the results. In the U.K. the SCNI concluded in its report of July 1953 that a special committee was needed

which would offer the additional means of informing Parliament of the affairs of these industries, compatible with their statutory position and with constitutional propriety." However, [t]he nationalised industries were statutory bodies and had to work within the framework of the Acts which created them; without amending legislation, not even Parliament could enunciate doctrines not to be found in these Acts. In fact 'accountability to Parliament,' as we shall see, cuts clean across the tenor of those Acts (Kelf-Cohen, 1969, p. 160).

In India, a parliamentary Committee on Public Enterprises (CPU) was set up in 1964. It is expected to examine, in the context of autonomy and efficiency of the SOEs, whether their affairs are managed in accordance with sound business principles. The question of autonomy has proved to be a stumbling block to the operation of any such committee. Legislators would like to air their views about SOEs, but these views may be on matters considered by government and SOEs to be shielded from parliamentary accountability, under the rubric of "autonomy." In fact, it is not very clear in what sense SOEs are "accountable to Parliament." In Norway, for example, in view of the importance of oil, article 10 of Statoil's articles of association states that:

> *The Board shall submit to the General Meeting, ordinary or extraor-*
> *dinary, all matters which are presumed to involve significant politi-*
> *cal effects on the nation and its economy. (Richardson, 1981, p. 38).*
> *Article 10, taken literally, should mean that Statoil makes no moves*
> *of significance without prior political approval* (Ibid.).

Statoil submits its annual plan to the Ministry of Petroleum and Energy and the Ministry sends the plan to the Industry Committee of the Storing. Although the plan is 'proposed' to the Storing, "Statoil, by and large, gets what it wants in terms of the main investment programme" (Richardson, 1981, p. 45).

If the legislature does play a strong supervisory role, there are many duplications between its activities and those of the sponsoring ministry and the Ministry of Finance (on these problems in the U.K.; see Robson, 1962 pp. 162-183, Robson, 1969, Kelf–Cohen, 1969, ch. 7, Chester, 1958. On proposals of Hugh Molson for Parliamentary control, see *The Times*, in Hanson, 1963, pp. 311-316. On India, see Narain, 1980, Bhambhri, 1960 and Ramandham, 1981; on the United States, see, e.g., Seidman, 1952, 1954. See also Musolf, 1959.

The legislature has an important role to play when a new SOE is created, when more money is needed for an SOE, or when a report on the SOE is presented by the Comptroller and the Auditor General. In other cases, the legislature tends to deal with trifling questions. Conservative members extol the wonderful good old times before the firm was state owned and socialists "rejoice in the transformation of our railway system brought about overnight by nationalization" (Robson, 1962, p. 182). The legislature has many opportunities to discuss, commend or criticize the activities of the SOE. It rarely controls them and they are rarely accountable to it.

ACCOUNTABILITY

State control is called for as a means of ensuring that SOEs will be motivated to achieve in the most efficient manner objectives that the state, through its representatives, deem proper. As discussed, such control has been difficult—some say impossible—to achieve. There have been pendulum swings between more or less autonomy. To a large extent, the problem of control is inherent in the nature of the SOE—a hybrid of economic missions and political goals.

An alternative approach is to accord accountability a greater emphasis. Herbert Simon differentiates between what he refers to as "procedural rationality" and "substantive approaches" common in economics and other social science (Simon, 1978). The procedural, or process, approach to the problems of SOE direction and control has not been tried enough and may give a better solution. Basically, if management can take whatever actions it feels are justified in the circumstances, knowing at the same time that these actions will have to be justified, one can introduce enough flexibility to allow the management to take the actions if it is willing to accept the consequences.

"Accountability" means a responsibility or liability to reveal, explain and justify what one does—to account for one's action, to report on the actions and the results arising from the exercise of authority. Since managers of SOEs have the authority to exercise discretion over the use of public funds and to exercise economic power associated with diverse social consequences, they must be accountable for their decisions to the representatives of the public. This simple statement raises three related issues: accountability for what? to whom? and through which channels?

The manager is accountable presumably to the owners of the firm— namely, the public at large. Formal channels of accountability are usually prescribed—namely, to the Parliament, through the government or a specific minister within it. The accountability is made operational by reports to these bodies and by an independent audit. If accountability is interpreted to mean justification of each action and each decision, then managers would be paralyzed in their ability to take risks. Many decisions made under uncertainty may turn out to be wrong when more facts are known, which does not necessarily mean they were wrong given the information available when they were made. Still, since the manager is a trustee of public money, people may be enraged when his or her decisions turn out later to be wrong. The right answer to this question has not been found. Its solution needs to be more by ensuring public accountability through audits of the trade-offs.

The basic philosophy of private auditing is based on objective tests to verify compliance with certain accounting principles. The auditor determines values of certain actions using some objective rules and professional canons of care and validation. The major advantage of these rules and procedures is that one can develop a set of criteria that is generally applicable and use it to evaluate a limited and well-defined set of actions. A private external audit today concentrates on accounting procedures, internal controls, internal financial and operating reports, documentary support for different transactions, inventory controls and reporting systems, administration of property and equipment and compliance with legal and regulatory requirements. In addition, auditors promptly report on any irregularities that come to their attention during their examination. They are not conducting audits of their clients' objectives and effectiveness in achieving the objectives. Government auditors are more concerned with the economy, efficiency and effectiveness of government operations. These audits may or may not encompass SOE activities, but the trend is to subject SOEs to state audits.

One extreme is the United States. According to the Government Corporations Control Act of 1945, SOEs are subject to the audit of the General Accounting Office (GAO) in the same way as government departments. Another extreme is the United Kingdom, in which public corporations are audited by private auditors, and the Comptroller and Auditor General (C&AG) does not have access to their books. Since 1980, however, U.K. nationalized industries have been brought into the orbit of the Monopolies and Mergers Commission (MMC). The MMC carries out studies to determine whether the activities of these enterprises were in the public interest. In fact, the MMC has become the state auditor for these industries. In other countries such as India, Finland or Israel, both the state auditor and private auditors examine the accounts of the enterprise. This is also the situation in Canada since the new Auditor General Act came into effect on August 1, 1977. In almost all countries, the authority of the state auditor was expanded with time in two different ways, First, the number of enterprises subject to its examination was enlarged to include subsidiaries of SOEs. Second, the audit was extended to include efficiency. In Israel, the state comptroller is also allowed to demand that any SOE prepare an annual plan, including forecasts. Further, the comptroller is allowed to publish (and did publish) general instructions for private auditors on how to audit SOEs as well as the way the financial statements are to be prepared. The state auditor usually reports to the legislature. In some countries, the board of directors should give its comments to the report as well as suggest proposed changes if needed.

When the shareholders are the taxpayers as represented by their legislators, an auditor's expression of opinion on a set of financial statements is perceived as only a part of the work. The auditor is expected, in the words of the Canadian Auditor General Act, to "call attention to anything that he considers to be of significance and of a nature that should be brought to the attention of the House of Commons." This wording gives the auditor general a great deal of latitude in the way professional judgment is exercised. The act specifically requires the auditor general to report, *inter alia*, on cases where:

> [T]*he rules and procedures applied have been insufficient to safeguard and control public property; money has been expended other than for purposes for which it was appropriated by Parliament; money has been expended without due regard to economy or efficiency; or satisfactory procedures have not been established to measure and report the effectiveness of programs, where such procedures could appropriately and reasonably be implemented.*

Thus, the auditor general is expected to conduct a comprehensive audit, or "value-for-money-audit."

In Canada, the comprehensive audit comprises five closely interrelated components collectively referred to by the acronym FRAME. These are: financial controls, reporting, attest and authority, management controls and EDP controls.

The U.S. GAO includes in its audit not only financial auditing but also the following:

Compliance determines whether the entity has complied with laws and regulations that may have a material effect on the financial statements;

Economy and Efficiency determine (a) whether the entity is managing and utilizing its resources (such as personnel, property, space) economically and efficiently, (b) the causes of inefficiencies or uneconomical practices, and (c) whether the entity has complied with laws and regulations concerning matters of economy and efficiency;

Program results detemine (a) whether the desired results or benefits established by the legislature or other authorizing body are being achieved and (b) whether the agency has considered alternatives that might yield desired results at a lower cost (United States Comptroller General, 1981).

Similar systems are used in other countries.

Reviewing compliance, economy and efficiency and program results is highly desirable if better accountability of SOEs is sought. However, evaluating the performance of SOEs is much more complex. Management has to make continuous trade-offs among the different objectives it is expected to achieve. Further, missions and objectives are subject to alterations as needs, priorities, aspirations and resources change over time.

At the same time, the public needs to be reassured that SOE management is doing its job. To maintain public vigilance while allowing the required degree of freedom, I have suggested (Aharoni, 1982) a comprehensive audit of objectives, too. Such an audit should bring to light different trade-offs, understanding there is no objective way to determine the right objectives to be pursued or the right trade-offs. The elected representatives of the public must retain ultimate authority over any agency and the objectives it will pursue. The role of the comprehensive audit is to bring to light the different options and their costs, without impairing the ability of management to use its autonomous judgment in carrying out its missions.

When value judgments are involved, it is extremely difficult to prescribe precise regulations. Overemphasis on controls through regulations and standards may lead to too high emphasis on parameters that can be measured. However, many important variables defy accurate quantification or reduction to the legal language of a regulation. Moreover, the drive, enthusiasm, dedication and skills of managers are too important and must not be tampered with by too many detailed controls and regulations. Auditing may be a better alternative to detailed prescriptions of behavior. The managers thus remain free to make their strategic choices and are not obliged to conform to the letter to any standard. Instead, they are required to justify gross deviations as well as the choices they made.

True, a comprehensive audit of objectives refutes the assumption of objectivity, narrowly defined. There is no set of rules against which one can check an objective and no acceptable method for objectively identifying organizational goals. As a practical matter, the costs of the audit must be evaluated, as well as the availabilty of skilled persons to carry it out and the time taken up by managers in answering requests by auditors.

In addition, SOEs may be reluctant to reveal commercial information since full disclosure puts them in a position of comparative disadvantage by allowing them less commercial secrecy than their private sector counterparts. However, such an audit can help to establish a system of checks and balances at much lower cost to society than detailed controls (for more ideas on such a system, see Chapter 9).

Comprehensive state audits may be less effective than one might wish if the government controls the Parliament. Comprehensive state auditing may be even less effective in regimes where democratic institutions are less powerful and where checks and balances in the political systems are not adhered to. In such regimes, the government may not even allow such audit to be carried out.

Different individuals hold different points of view about the propriety of the objectives pursued, but the publication of comprehensive reports brings the conflict into the open. It also helps in discussing the propriety of objectives actually pursued. In an area where objectives are hard to agree on and their achievement difficult to control, a comprehensive audit, if available to the public, is of great importance.

CONCLUSION

After a few decades of experience with different legal methods and different control mechanisms in SOEs in various countries, it is clear that the problem of control does not have an easy solution. Control systems were not based on a systematic, internally consistent conceptual scheme. Instead, they have evolved, changed because of a change in economic conditions or because of a crisis. Countries have oscillated between reliance on autonomy to very detailed controls. Controls have also been directed mainly to the large and visible SOEs. The managers of these enterprises have continuously attempted to increase discretion. They have created subsidiaries that were not controlled and have co-opted, cajoled or hidden information. The atmosphere of control in most countries unfortunately, has been one of continuous confrontations rather than reconciliation and coordination. In certain cases, the controls have gone into almost ludicrous detail—from attempting to control trips abroad to regulating the size of the entertainment budget. The energies spent on these small battles could have been spent much more profitably by looking at strategic issues and trade-offs.

Worldwide experience with SOEs demonstrates that when government resorts to petty controls of personnel policies, details of purchasing and contracts, or other procedural controls, it is unable to attract dedicated, stable, innovative and talented executives. Executives who were capable of managing large programs efficiently are not prepared to be encumbered with what they consider petty controls. Managers with strong entrepreneurial drive act and then ask for permission (or don't ask at all) and the rest become apathetic. An able and resolute manager needs enough autonomy to do the job properly, and whims of politicians are not always the best guarantee that the public interest will prevail. Managers tend to keep the more aberrant politicians at bay to achieve the public interest as they see it. They act like medieval barons in simmering revolt against the monarchy. The ministry of finance usually seeks to tighten control, but the control is often executed by inexperienced young civil servants who have very little understanding of the intricacies of business.

Both the managers and the civil servants are unhappy with the situation—the first complaining that the controls are too rigid and do not make much sense, the latter anguishing that the SOEs do whatever they please, raising the banners of commercial efficiency and freedom. The controllers are very often too few and too uninformed and may also be jealous of the better salaries enjoyed in the SOEs. The problem, however, is not so much that it is very difficult to reconcile the public interest with commercial autonomy but mainly that the degree to which SOEs should be used as instruments of public policy is an unresolved issue, and the role of political parties in SOEs is not well understood. The trade-offs inherent in commanding the enterprises to pursue different lines of actions are not very clear. The price paid is that the managers develop a political orientation, thus managing the government more than they manage the enterprise.

Central control is necessary to obtain a general picture on the SOEs sector and to gather systematic information on performance. In practice, many governments do not even have a compilation of their SOEs names and status. Observers agree that controls of SOEs have been inefficient, *ad hoc* in nature and not necessarily in the enterprises' best interests. Public control over SOEs has become mainly ministerial control. Different governmental agencies intervene in different operating decisions of the SOEs, with very little coordination and even less control. The government takes all the time in the world to settle these matters, with consequent delays, and ministers have the authority to control but lack the norms by which to adjudge problems and the needed expertise.

As long as the legitimate objectives of SOEs are not agreed, there is no way to give a normative answer to whether or not the performance of a certain enterprise is socially desirable, and an ideal control system cannot be prescribed. However, individuals have an intuitive feeling of what is legitimate and what is in the public interest. In many cases, controls have been used to achieve parochial interests of parties and even individuals. Not all such controls may be considered legitimate. An independent audit of goals and objectives may, at least under some conditions, make the problem recognizable and thus partially solvable. At the very least, the decisions of management and other state agents may be subjected periodically to public scrutiny and subsequent adjustment. Without an open system of goal statement and auditing, state ownership may degenerate into a shift of power to a new managerial or bureaucratic class instead of achieving socially desirable objectives.

CHAPTER 7

The State-Owned Enterprise and Private Investors

INTRODUCTION

We have analyzed the relationships between SOEs and the external coalition. SOEs may also compete with private-sector firms for inputs such as capital and labor, and private firms may be barred from entering certain lucrative businesses reserved for SOEs. Government officials, who are also directors of SOEs in their role as regulators, may be recipients of confidential business information on private firms competing with the SOEs. Private-sector firms may see any kind of direct and indirect competition as unfair since they expect government to be a neutral umpire, not one of the players. The use of tax money collected from the private sector to finance SOEs that may compete with that sector is often seen as unfair.

The first issue to be addressed is to what extent the government should be free to establish SOEs even in competition with its private citizens. What should be the restrictions, in the event such restrictions are desirable, on its establishing an SOE? Once the SOE has been established, should its scope of activities be restricted, and how? Second, should SOEs receive special rights and privileges or should they carry out special duties? Third, what rules of government conduct should be applied to SOEs? Fourth, should special rules be applied to cases of joint ventures between government and private firms? Finally, how and by whom should the rules be made and enforced?

The basic rule in a democracy is Aristotle's celebrated principle of distributive justice: equals should be treated equally. To maintain this rule, "no privileges or immunities should be granted to public enterprises in comparison with private enterprises with which they compete directly or indirectly" (Friedmann, 1974, p. 390). An SOE "is not the Crown and has none of the immunities or privileges of the Crown. Its servants are not civil servants, and its property is not Crown property" (*Tamlin v. Hannaford*, 1950, I.K.B. 18,

255

24). As SOE managers see it, however, they often have more duties and are therefore entitled to certain privileges to compensate them for carrying out the additional burden. Moreover, an SOE that is expected to act like the government civil service is operating on unequal terms with a private firm that is not subject to these requirements.

If an SOE is allowed to operate exactly like a private firm, it may not always follow the elementary principles of natural justice. Worse still, its activities may embarrass the government. Thus "equality before the law" is an elusive concept.

MACRO-CONSIDERATIONS

Apart from ideological beliefs, private entrepreneurs may oppose the establishment and operations of SOEs mainly for 3 reasons. First, SOEs often enjoy monopoly privileges, not only in public utilities and fiscal monopolies but also, e.g., in fertilizers and steel manufacture in Indonesia, cocoa marketing in Bolivia and Ghana and domestic airline and international air services in most countries. Given the substantial market power available to SOEs, they constitute a high barrier to entry to some lucrative fields. Air Canada, e.g., was expected to pursue government-determined social policies, in return for which it received a high degree of government protection. To some extent, this high degree of protection allows the firm's management to build up strong constituents to help it maintain its monopoly position. Air Canada served high-cost domestic routes and, in return, received highly profitable transcontinental and international routes. When the Canadian government proposed to allow Air Canada's private competitor, Canadian Pacific Air, to expand its role, Air Canada's management stated publicly that transcontinental competition meant it would be forced to curtail unprofitable services. This announcement caused a wave of protests from organized groups, demanding assurances that the competition would not cause curtailment of the services they received, in those areas of Canada in which these unprofitable services were offered. As a result of the protests, the Conservative minister of transportation announced that "competition would be considered only if it did not cause major detrimental effects on existing operations" (Baldwin, 1975, p. 147), and Canadian Pacific Air was allowed only one flight a day between Vancouver and Montreal. In many cases, monopolistic SOEs cross-subsidize loss-ridden activities by higher rates charged on other activities. Private entrepreneurs are not allowed to compete on the lucrative activities— and resent this fact.

Second, despite their control over some of the largest revenue-earning activities, such as oil and mining, the poor aggregate performance of SOEs causes an increased fiscal burden. SOEs' losses are not necessarily a result of inept management or the insidious influence of corruption. Losses are largely due to price controls and other various responsibilities and the fact that SOEs are used as an invisible method to subsidize the private sector. Still, the losses have to be paid, either by higher taxes or by increased inflation. To the extent that SOEs are seen as the reason for these problems, they are resented. The large size of the SOE sector has other profound macroeconomic effects. Pryke, e.g., argues:

> Due to North Sea oil the pound is now very strong and it is difficult for British manufacturers to export or to meet competition from imports. In consequence workers are being thrown out of jobs and factories are being shut. This must, in part, be regarded as the price of maintaining unprofitable pits in operation and of preserving jobs in coal. If loss-making collieries were closed and more coal were imported the pound would (temporarily) weaken and our hard-pressed manufacturers would find it easier to compete. [1981, p. 67]

Third, SOEs, have a strong impact on resource markets. If SOEs borrow in the capital market, a crowding out effect is created, leading to high interest rates and tight credit and making it more difficult for private firms to borrow (Bennett and Sharpe, 1980, p. 186). SOEs, particularly in LDCs, are forced to pay much higher wages to their workers (and employ many more of them than needed). Killick observed that in Ghana, the wage bill as a percentage of value added was more than twice as high for SOEs as for private firms. Killick notes that the SOEs tended to be much more capital-intensive than their private-sector counterparts, a fact that should have resulted in a lower share of wages for SOEs (1978, p. 223). If SOEs pay higher wages to attract workers, then the private sector has to follow suit or will find it difficult to recruit employees.

Most governments grow in response to incessant demands for more services. Policymakers cannot deal with all these new demands and may be constrained by a strong private sector and by the reluctance of citizens to pay increased taxes. The creation of SOEs on what Sharkansky (1979) calls the "margins of the state" helps satisfy increasing and contrary demands without revealing the true size of the public sector. With time, the SOE managers become a strong interest group, reducing the power of both the private sector and the elected officials. The expansion of the SOE sector is more a result of the acquisition of power and the increasing autonomy of SOE managers. Occasionally, these managers undertake a venture to help private firms, but in many other cases, they compete with them. At the same time, the private sector benefits from SOEs' stimulation of investments, reduction of risks, stabilization of investments, operation of essential services at a loss and extension of credit to support and strengthen the private economy.

When price controls are used to mollify urban elites and to subsidize private firms, there is no reason for the private sector to oppose SOEs existence. However, a large and strong SOE sector means that government is much less dependent on the private sector to achieve economic growth because it has at its disposal a new means of implementing economic policy.

Most of the cases in which conflict and dispute developed over the expansion of SOEs were instances in which this expansion was perceived as reducing profit opportunities to the private sector because of direct or indirect competition.

The establishment of SOEs to compete directly with private firms to stimulate certain responses is also accepted and is not seen as opposing individual freedom or equality before the law.

> In short, whether in the garb of droit administraif or the prerogative jurisdiction of the higher courts in the common law world, the scope of legal remedies is essentially confined to the, on the whole exceptional, cases of the abuse of powers for alien purposes, or the excess of powers as clearly defined by statute. [p. 388] Friedmann, 1976

The question of competition among sectors is not so much a legal problem as a political one. A Socialist government may favor the expansion of SOEs while a Conservative government may have a different policy. The courts will be extremely reluctant to rule improper discrimination on questions of public policy.

Basically, state ownership has to do with who can and should have the power to allocate the profits of a particular activity. The relationship between SOEs and private enterprise depends on the power structure of the two sectors. In many countries, the power of the private sector is large enough and the dependence of the government on it to achieve its political, social and economic aims is great enough to enable this sector to avert any plans to increase the SOE sector if it so desires. In the United Kingdom, e.g., a publicity campaign launched by Tate and Lyle in 1950 and by ICI in 1955 were both very effective in deterring the government from nationalizing sugar in 1950 and chemicals in 1955. One has, therefore, to analyze two questions: How powerful is the private sector? When will the private sector oppose state ownership?

The first question is country-specific and is not dealt with here. As to the second, it may be assumed that utility-maximizing managers in the private sector will meet with unanimous approval any state activities that do not interfere with their ability to increase their wealth. State ownership is always welcome when it parcels out government power to various organized economic interests and allows them to receive more largesse. The private sector will also welcome the government's undertaking risky projects or opening up new technologies requiring high capital investment.

Nationalization of foreign ownership may also be welcome by the indigenous private sector. It has nothing to lose and some things to gain if the ownership of certain firms passes from the hand of foreign MNEs to that of the government. The latter may, e.g., increase the domestic procurement by the enterprise, thus benefitting local businesspeople. Private-sector enterprises in many countries would also welcome state-owned utilities, in particular if these utilities supply them power below cost. They even demand the creation of an SOE to rescue a private firm or when private firms default on their obligations. However, when the government enters into a field in direct competition with its private sector, then one may expect strong pressures on government to avoid the entry. If these pressures are unsuccessful, one may expect a close scrutiny by private sector interests to make sure the enterprise did not get any benefits that would be perceived as being unfair.

Private-sector interests may also resent their exclusion from certain economic fields reserved only to SOEs, as is the situation in India, or for distribution of refinery products in Greece. The two private refineries in this country may only sell their output for exports.

The relations of SOEs and private sector are relevant not only when the motivation for the creation of SOEs are discussed. Once created, SOEs may grow or contract over time, they may diversify or remain in the same field—and this evolution is also embedded in the balance of political power among sectors (see Sobhan, 1979). In many Asian and African countries, SOEs were established and expanded to create opportunities for certain ethnic or tribal groups reducing the power of the dominant Asian commercial class. In Indonesia, for example, the dominance of Chinese businesspersons in the private sector and the desire of government to promote indigenous managers was important. SOE establishment and growth threatens certain interests. An appreciation of the capacity of these interests to resist what they perceive as state encroachment and to mobilize themselves to limit it is important.

In Ghana, for example, the SOEs were established in the 1960s to consolidate the power of Nkrumah's Convention People's Party (CPP) (Pozen, 1972; Wilson, 1984). The opposition party, consolidating the interests of the established alliance of commercial and traditional elite, fought these expansions. In South Africa, the upwardly mobile challengers were the Boers and they used their political strength to create SOEs. These moves were opposed by the established wing of English-speaking bourgeoisie.

Thus, the capacity of private interests to resist what they perceive as state encroachment and to mobilize themselves to limit it is important. The relative power of the private sector is an important explanatory variable in understanding the size and operations of SOEs. A strong private sector means fewer SOEs, more restrictions on their diversification, and the use of existing SOEs to benefit the private sector. However, when political power is seized by an upwardly mobile group, SOEs may be used to seize also economic power in opposition to traditionally strong economic players—foreign investors, Asians, etc. Further, the more unified the political elite, the less politicized and the more efficient the SOEs (Levy, 1985; Martinelli in Vernon and Aharoni, 1981). When SOEs were used to seize power by a new political elite, this group may not have had enough skilled managers to staff the SOEs, and this will affect SOEs' performance negatively. Therefore, when political and economic powers are disassociated, SOEs' performance will be weakened (Dressang and Sharkansky, 1975; Wilson, 1984).

In any given economy or even any given industry, there are conflicting interests, some of which will have a stronger political voice than others. It is critical to define in each case *which* private interests are affected, what is their *strength*, and which type of firms *control the industry association*. Political factors may explain not only the size of SOEs and their rate of expansion, but also their areas of operations, pricing policies, and the demands of governments on them.

Thus, strong private sectors may want cheap electricity (Gordon, 1981). When consumer organizations are weak, SOEs may be used to benefit business firms more than consumers, and the state may be less constrained by political pressures to reduce these invisible subsidies than visible ones when macroeconomic considerations require a reduction in the government's budget.

Competition and Fairness Considerations

Competition is beneficial to consumers, and it would thus be desirable for the government to increase it. However, any attempt by government to establish an SOE in direct competition with existing private firms is accompanied by tension and dispute. Private enterprise managers always perceive such competition as unfair and as a distortion of market conditions. They look askance at using taxpayers funds to compete against these same taxpayers. They also claim that civil servants acting as directors of such SOEs may use information they received on the private firms to benefit the SOE and that the government may prefer the SOEs over private-sector enterprises in its procurement.

Indeed, it is difficult to draw the lines of fairness and equity between the sectors. The admittedly politically weak private sector in Israel accepted state ownership of natural resources, utilities and even path-breaking industrial enterprises. However, when the ministry of defense started an SOE to operate retail stores for army personnel and their families, the private merchants wanted these stores restricted to army camps only and periodically claimed that the ability of this SOE to compete stems from preferential treatments such as tax exemptions and contracts without bids.

In the United Kingdom both the gas and electric SOEs operate a network of retail shops. By the end of the 1970s there were 950 electricity and 930 gas shops. Until North Sea gas made gas competitive with other fuels, private entrepreneurs had shown little interest in the sale of gas appliances, apart from central heating systems. As a result British Gas came to dominate the retailing of most gas appliances: its market share was 90 percent of cookers, 85 to 95 percent of space heaters and 65 to 70 percent of water heaters, but only about

25 percent of central heating boilers. The electrical appliance industry, by contrast, has been dominated by private sector retailers who have continually complained about the trading activities of the Electricity Boards. Because of these complaints, a number of public commissions investigated the situation. In 1956, e.g., the Herbert Commission concluded:

> We have carefully considered the objections of the trading organisa-
> tions of the statutory powers accorded to the Electricity Boards
> against the background of the Board's practices and policies. We find
> on balance that the incursion of the Electricity Boards into the retail
> field is in the best interests of electricity consumers who undoubtedly
> benefit from competition between the Electricity Board and private
> traders and contractors. (para. 463)

A report from the SCNI in 1963 came to a similar conclusion, emphasizing the importance of the retailing side of Electricity Boards for monitoring and influencing demand to achieve a balanced load. In the 1980s, this view has changed, and the retail shops were declared unfair competition.

Privately owned firms in the U.K. produced around a quarter of the total steel production, weighted towards the finished end of the product spectrum. The private sector has been on guard lest BSC might try to diversify into the finished (and higher-value) end of the product range. It has portrayed the attitude of the government of BSC as "the judge, jury and hangman attitude" (Grant, 1982, p. 95). Broadway (1969) notes that SOEs in the U.K. were given what he terms "limitless powers . . . to move into new sectors of industry" (p. 70). SOEs, he complains, can move "into competition with private companies, and then have their losses guaranteed if they proved unsuccessful . . . in the process, efficient companies could suffer substantial loss through having to meet this financial competition" (pp. 71-72).

Whether or not government will overrule the claims of the private sector for equality or accept that SOEs competition is artificially financed is to a large extent an outgrowth of a particular constellation of power relationships. Sri Lanka's minister of industry "calmly asked Union Carbide to cut its battery output by 25 percent to protect a partially state-owned competitor. Such attitudes have meant that private and foreign companies largely confined their investments to quick-return ventures such as hotels (frozen because of the ethnic troubles), garments, real estate, and trading" (Financial Times, October 10, 1984, Supplement on Sri Lanka, p. 4). In Canada, the Supreme Court of Ontario has ruled that Uranium Canada, Ltd., and Eldorado Nuclear, Ltd., were immune from prosecution for conspiring to fix domestic prices in connection with an international uranium cartel. The court ruled that they were acting as agents of the federal government. Canadian SOEs are presently exempt from the Federal Combines Act (Canada's antitrust law) (Sexty, 1983, p. 31). In India, the Monopolies and Restrictive Trade Practice Act does not apply at all to SOE, (Ramanurti, 1982, p. 354).

In Israel, the government established in 1962 a state-owned insurance firm, Yuval.[1] According to its manager, Yuval was created to achieve the following aims: first, to execute the insurance business of the government and SOEs at lower premiums, benefitting the government by being a profitable SOE; second, to advise the government and the SOEs on insurance matters; third, to try to increase the capacity of the Israeli insurance market and to receive insurance business from abroad.

Two days after the new company was created, all the insurance companies in Israel announced they would oppose it any way they could. Further, the industry decided to refuse any competition or cooperation.

The insurance companies claimed they had agreed to government control, but it was understood, they said, that the government would never enter the insurance business on its own. Further, establishment of a state-owned insurance company signalled government encroachment into the private sector and intervention in free initiative.

Despite this protest, two private insurance companies, Sahar, and its subsidiary, Bohan, entered into a partnership agreement with Yuval. It was speculated that the reason was a desire of these companies to retaliate against the large insurance firms that controlled a big portion of the insurance companies' pool insuring government property until Yuval's establishment. After some months, other members of the association agreed to participate in Yuval, and the association began to accept the SOE as a *fait accompli*. It therefore agreed to be a partner in the company, on two conditions. First, the two existing contracts signed with Sahar and Bohan should be annulled. Second, all participation would be given to the association pool for allocation among the insurance companies according to a formula agreed on by these companies. Sahar and Bohan agreed to annul the partnership agreement they had signed with Yuval in return for a reallocation of shares of all insurance policies written through the insurance companies' pool.

In the meantime, the vice-comptroller of insurance in the government, Mr. Karniel was made vice-president of Yuval. In his official capacity this person knew all the foreign reinsurance contracts that were made by the insurance companies. Although the official declared he would never use the information he had received as a civil servant to compete against private insurance companies, these companies were concerned that the information could be used in promoting Yuval at their expense.

In some cases, government used SOEs to curb or reduce the influence or abuse of private power—in particular, when this power was concentrated in the hands of a small number of families. The Bhatto government in Pakistan nationalized many banks, insurance firms, industrial enterprises and

---

[1] The description is based on a case study copyright by the Leon Recanati Graduate School of Business Administration, Tel-Aviv University. Reproduced with permission.

agricultural interests to curb the power of the dominant twenty-two families. So did Allende in Chile in 1971 to 1973 (Gillis, 1980, p. 264).

When SOEs grow, their managers gain more power and become an interest group with its own political base, having an interest in furthering the growth of state ownership and expanding its scope, mainly through diversification of their operations (Freeman, 1982, Trebat, 1983). They constitute a distinct social group—distinguished from both government bureaucrats and private-sector managers. These managers attempt to gain more autonomy from government and may create alliances with private-sector interests to allow their expansion along certain lines. In Brazil, e.g. the SOE managers aligned themselves with the military and strengthened their position. These pressures result in a further increase of the role of SOEs. These expansions often mean that the state finds itself in lines of business it never intended to enter. The power of the managers is resented by the private sector and by the elected representatives of the public, who see themselves as the guardians of the public interest. Feigenbaum (1982, p. 109) quotes a member of the French Parliament: "Who are these men after all, Prince of Petroleum, Duke of Broadcasting Office, Count of French Rail. . . . always of first quality, sometimes more powerful than certain ministers and who have . . . at their disposal, immense apparatuses? To whom are they responsible?" At the same time, if SOEs are not granted any rights or privileges beyond those enjoyed by a similarly situated private firm, they should also be treated equally. If a privately owned airline can diversify into hotels or travel agencies and if SOEs are to be judged by their commercial success, it is difficult to prohibit them from entering into such ancillary businesses. As SOE managers see it restricting their entrance into related business is unfair competition. Ironically, private firms see expansion of SOEs as unfair competition, claiming that the SOE uses its power in the main business or subsidies received from government for its new business to compete against them. A state-owned airline is claimed to enjoy monopoly power. It can use its vast reservation system to direct prospective customers to its hotels. Thus, when El Al Israel Airlines diversified into the hotel business, a strong lobby of the private hotel industry was able to persuade the minister of tourism to seek and obtain a government decision to stop this diversification.

In the United Kingdom, the MMC found that the London Electricity Board's appliance retail shops were losing money and that the board enjoyed the advantage of making up the losses from its main business of electricity supply. The commission felt that this was an anticompetitive practice. It recommended that "a separate and fully detailed profit and loss account should be published as part of the annual accounts" (Monopolies and Mergers Commission, 1983, pp. 35–38).

In many cases of a monopoly, such detailed profit and loss accounts are based on various assumptions about how all sorts of joint costs should be allocated. Transportation or telecommunications companies cross-subsidize their different activities, charging high prices in lucrative operations to cover the losses of losing lines. Such a pricing policy attracts private investors who would like to enter into the profitable lines, which are made even more profitable by the pricing policy. For example, if a telephone SOE subsidizes its local calls from profits made on long-distance calls, giving a hidden subsidy to the domestic callers, private firms attempt to compete on the long-distance lines. Whether or not such competition should be allowed leads us to the problem of "sustainability."

Natural monopoly is consistent with a maximum social welfare as long as a single firm is as efficient as a multiple firm alternative. A single firm will be more efficient than two or more firms if, and only if, costs are subadditive, i.e., if the cost function of its output is such that it can produce that output more cheaply than two or more firms. In the case of firms producing a single product, subadditivity usually means the existence of economies of scale. When a firm produces multiple products, economies of scale are no longer sufficient for subadditivity. We need to measure the economies of scope. Economies of scope exist if a single firm can produce a rate of outputs for each product line cheaper than a combination of two or more specialty firms. Such economies are said to arise from a joint utilization of resources arising, for example, when a given resource is indivisible. Therefore, in any public utility, the crucial question is how separate the utility services are. If cost cannot be separated for each output, production cannot be treated as intended for separate markets, and a single, multiproduct monopolist is more efficient. If an entrant is permitted to produce a subset of products at a lower price, the utility's prices are not sustainable, and such a low price entry reduces consumers' welfare. Several economists have claimed that price discrimination is the best practical outcome for utilities and, therefore, that competition should be prevented (see Panzar and Willig, 1977; Snowberger, 1978). Competition is also resisted because it is likely to undermine reliable service. However, management can control the degree of separability by selecting technologies with a largest element of joint production, and it can cause the accounting system to show a high percentage of joint costs.

Markets are said to be perfectly contestable if there are no barriers to entry and "the potential entrants evaluate the profitability of entry at the incumbent firm's pre-entry prices" (Baumol, Panzar and Willig, 1982, p. 5). The possibility of costless reversible entry and exit creates effective control on incumbent firms. Since entry and exit are easy and costless, such a market is vulnerable to hit-and-run entry and the incumbent cannot reap monopoly profits even if it is the only firm serving the market. In the case of airlines, for example, any city-pair market is characterized by economies of scale, but also by easy entry and exit. If an incumbent airline attempts to achieve monopoly profit, other airlines can easily enter, since capital cost, although substantial, are not sunk cost. Sunk costs, not economies of scale, constitute the entry barrier that confers monopoly powers. In the case of airlines, easy entry and exit barriers mean that regulation is not needed.

In other cases, cross-subsidies are needed to achieve subsidy-free prices. Consider a water utility serving three distinct communities from a common source, at cost of $660. A separate water utility for each community can supply the water for $300, or it can supply any two for $400. From society's point of view, the monopolist utility supplying all three would cost less than any other combination ($300 × 3 = $900, $400 + $300 = $700). However, if the utility charges each community a third of the cost ($660/3 = $220), it is cheaper for any two communities to split off and supply the water at a cost of ($400/2 = $200) than to join the third community. In this case, a natural monopoly is not sustainable in the free marketplace even though it operates efficiently. Sustainability literature is highly technical and abstract and is based on several assumptions, among them that government regulation is virtually costless and economic markets apt, in some cases, to operate very inefficiently or inequitably, if left alone (Faulhaber, 1975; see also Sharkey, 1982). Society is better off if a regulator will intervene. It shows that in some cases, competition will reduce the monopolist's output and force a higher price. Private firms usually refuse to accept these abstract models because they believe that competition is always beneficial.

The problem of scale and joint costs is important also in the case of other firms. Consider a military shipbuilder entering into the construction of civilian ships or an armament manufacturer producing pots and pans. In these cases, it is extremely difficult to allocate all costs fairly. Surely the assurances of military contracts allows the firm a competitive advantage by covering the fixed costs, enabling it to enter the civilian line on a marginal cost basis. But diversification into civilian products reduces dependence on military orders and allows the firm to expand, thus spreading its fixed costs over a higher volume, perhaps even reducing the military procurement costs, and therefore lessening public outlays. Theoretically, the solution is to allow private firms to compete on military orders. However, because of the minimum efficient scale, this solution is not applicable except in very rich countries: very few countries can afford competing shipbuilders, airplane producers or tank manufacturers.

If the military production necessitates a core of production capability at a minimum scale much greater than that needed for this production alone, expansion into civilian products—even on an average cost basis—may allow both consumers and the military lower prices, but the SOE will then create high barriers to entry. In small countries, most SOEs may reduce costs by diversification. A unit supplying computer services to the government may reduce average costs by acquiring more powerful computers and supplying services to private firms, too. A manufacturer of police uniforms may reduce costs by making civilian clothes, and a producer of telephone exchanges may do so by selling PBXs. But from the point of view of the private sector producer, such competition is unfair. The argument is often made that, since SOEs' losses are imposed on the taxpayers, their management should not be allowed to diversify. Whether or not private-sector interests would be able to block diversification moves of SOEs in cases like these depends on their relative power.

Most SOEs are large, capital-intensive firms. Even if their cost of capital is not subsidized, their sheer size may cause barriers to entry. The more successful SOEs are in their business operations, the more private sector competitors feel that the cards are stacked against them. In Singapore, SOEs were very successful in competition with private-sector firms. As a result, a public debate developed on the proper role of government in industry and commerce. The Chinese Chamber of Commerce asked the government to clarify the respective roles of the public and private sectors in economic development. According to Deputy Prime Minister Dr. Goh Keng Swee:

> Concern has been expressed from time to time in business circles about the threatening encroachment of government enterprises. I have explained that the purpose of government entering into business is to promote economic growth and not, except in special cases, to replace private businessmen. These special cases occur, like Singapore Food Industries, when the private sector has clearly failed to provide proper services. [The Singapore Food Industries Private Limited was set up as a result of some private caterers' not being able to provide food supplies efficiently to the ministry of defense.] The dismal failure of private business companies is another example in which government intervention by providing a new management team became unavoidable. Government does not go into business merely for the fun of doing so . . . It is idle to discuss general principles because there is no book of rules which demarcates the respective spheres of private and public enterprises and it is fruitless to argue about where the limit should lie. [In Reddy, 1983, pp. 261–262]

The general rule suggested in Singapore, and in most countries, is that SOEs receive no special privileges. The problem is that it is virtually impossible to determine when an SOE does receive a special privilege and when it suffers from discrimination. Even if SOEs are legally treated exactly like their private-sector counterparts, in practice equality is much harder to achieve. Some private-sector firms would still believe that the competitive success of an SOE is a result of a subtler preferential treatment. Thus, the problem is not the degree of competition but the conditions under which the competition is carried out.

In the case of Yuval, described earlier, Mr. Karniel claimed, when working for Yuval, that he would not use confidential information received in his capacity as a civil servant. However, the very existence of such a conflict of interest makes it appear that the competition is unfair. Civil servants, being human, cannot compartmentalize their knowledge, ignoring what they know when they serve as SOE directors. If a civil servant serves as a director in an

SOE, the competitors of this firm believe that person may prefer the SOE in granting it licenses or procurement orders. Even the fact that the SOE manager has easier access to the minister may be considered unfair competition. If SOE management convinces the minister that a certain private supplier is not reliable and discontinues using those services, this, too, can be interpreted as unfair competition.

SOEs are likely to receive preference even when they do not ask for it. For example, private commercial banks are ready to extend credit to SOEs under terms that they would not be ready to give to a company not owned by the state, assuming the liability is implicitly guaranteed by the government. In at least one instance, a company partly owned by the state went bankrupt. The government's accountant general opposed paying any debts above and beyond the means of the company, clarifying that the SOE was a separate legal entity, not a part of the state. The company's creditors thought differently and applied heavy pressure on cabinet ministers to change the decision. Similarly, it is not always easy to determine whether the government gives preferential treatment to its companies. Private-sector firms often charge that the government gives preferential treatment to its banks over other banks in the granting of funds and the placing of deposits or to other SOEs in procurement. Such allegations are very difficult either to substantiate or prove wrong. Clearly, however, the government in a democratic state is very sensitive to charges of discrimination. As a result, it tends to lean over backward, restricting its SOEs and reducing the discretion of its managers in areas perceived as unfair competition.

SPECIAL RIGHTS AND DUTIES

It is often alleged that SOEs receive special privileges. They do not pay the same taxes, they receive higher subsidies, they are not required to earn profits or pay dividends and they receive purchasing and sales preferences from government. In some countries SOEs are given certain special privileges such as immunity from court claims, preference in the allocation of government funds, better chances to sell their products to the government, cheaper credit, preferences in foreign currency allocation and various concessions or tax reductions. In other countries, SOEs do not enjoy the immunity granted the crown or state, and all laws, including the obligation to pay taxes, apply to them in exactly the same fashion in which they apply to a private firm (see Chapter 2).

Differentiating on the grounds of ownership certainly is sometimes meaningless. State-owned airlines pollute the air to the same degree as privately owned airlines, and a public electric company causes environmental problems no less than a private electric company. From the ecological point of view, the determining factor is the system of production or the technology used, not ownership of the production facilities. In fact, SOEs have exploited their power to refuse compliance with pollution regulations. In Canada, the government proposed stricter air pollution controls to reduce acid rain. The management of Ontario Hydro, which owns a third of all assets of the province's SOEs (Vining, 1983, p. 42), claimed that loss of anticipated power sales in the United States and reduced demand in Ontario makes the air pollution control plan economically unfeasible at this time and deferred for up to 7 years plans for a pollution control project (Sexty, 1983, p. 32). We have also emphasized the many ways by which governments influence profits of private firms. Renault

> [H]as conspired with its private competitors to hold up prices. In Italy, public corporations do the same. In the United Kingdom, the chairman of the publicly owned steel corporation revealed how little has changed when he declared his opposition to competition among subordinate plants: that would be giving profits to the consumers. . . . managers of public enterprises apparently must assimilate themselves to their more numerous private-enterprise colleagues. [Lindblom, 1977, p. 113]

However, SOEs also have fewer special rights and many special duties.

Many SOEs are giant enterprises, very important to the national well-being. The value added of Electricité de France, e.g., represents 1.5 percent and British Electricity Boards comprise 1.7 percent of their respective countries' GDP. Each of the large nationalized firms in the United Kingdom is a huge firm with considerable resources, power and influence on the economy. The five largest—telecommunications, electricity, gas, coal and rail—SOEs control 6.7 percent of the U.K. GDP (Pryke, 1981, p. 2). This concentration leads to escalating conflicts between management and employees, which become conflicts between employees and government. As a result, the government, by its intervention, has lost its ability to act as arbiter. The unions, recognizing that authority has been assumed in practice by government, in effect bypass the board and tacitly negotiate directly with government. In LDCs, larger oil or mining firms such as Brazil's CVRD, Peru's CODELCO, Bolivia's COMIBOL, Indonesia's PERTAMINA or Zambia's ZIMCO, are major foreign exchange earners, huge investors and extremely important employers. In their procurement strategies, SOEs' decisions on domestic versus foreign suppliers, or whether or not to iron out fluctuations in spending levels, are of immense importance to some firms, in particular those depending in a majority of their business on the SOEs (for figures on the U.K. see Harlow 1983). Employment in these firms can be seen as an important source of political patronage, and the wages they pay affect pay-scale in the whole economy.

In a sizable SOE, poorly conceived programs may involve several percentage points of the national investment. As a result, there are many checks, committees and delays in execution that may also affect private firms. Still, because of their size, SOEs do gain access to top-level government officials and can influence policy. They can also use this power to reduce their cost. These larger national firms, according to Jay, are "strong warring baronies . . . [that are] in constant and vicious competition with each other" (1968, p. 38).

When, on the one hand, political power is wielded by self-seeking politicians outside the most advantaged economic sectors, SOEs may be directed to achieve political goals and to redistribute wealth away from strong, commercial private interests. On the other hand, if politics is dominated by those with economic advantage, SOEs will be established and managed to assist those interests and will not be opposed by them (on Kenya, see Dresang and Sharkansky, 1975).

In most countries, the discretion of SOE management in choosing suppliers is limited by the desire to avoid any complaint of unfair treatment. SOEs are often directed to give preferential treatment to local suppliers—in particular, if they are located in depressed regions (on Germany, e.g. see Donges, 1980, p. 193).

Governments normally take great pains to make sure that the prices charged by SOEs should be nondiscriminatory as well as fair and reasonable. This point is important in particular in public utilities or in other SOEs serving a large number of individuals.

Governments also make sure they maintain political distance so that SOE managers rather than political leaders would bear the brunt of public criticism. An SOE provides politicians "with the opportunity to shift the responsibility for difficult or intractable problems onto someone else's shoulders" (Tierney, 1984, p. 78). In Ghana, "if each regime had to shoulder responsibility for every fraud in cocoa trading and every factory that was not earning a profit, the fragile governments would change semiannually" (Pozen, 1972, p. 837).

Wages in SOEs are rarely left to autonomous decisions of management. Mr. Boiteux, CEO of the French EDF, explained why in the Thirteenth Congress of Public and Cooperative Economy:

> [An] undertaking like the EDF is obviously not free to fix its wage levels arbitrarily, if only for the reason that unfortunately the whole civil service and the nationalized industries keep their eyes fixed on EDF wages. We have only to make some slight alteration to our wages and immediately the bush telephone—or indeed, the desk telephone—leads to the same thing being demanded in the entire civil service and all the nationalized industries, and the State has to take a major decision on it. The result is that whatever the written word says, in actual practice wage bargaining is a three-cornered process: it is done by the Government, which fixes wages too low so that it can be sure that demands will not be excessive; by the trade unions,

> *which fix them too high, so as to be sure of getting something; and*
> *by us. We spend our time negotiating first with the State and then*
> *with the trade unions, although in theory we are free to negotiate*
> *our wages with the trade union. [Annals, 1981, p. 175]*

Public disclosure of the SOE's affairs is an important means of ensuring probity and proper management. The deterrence derived from the threat of disclosure is the major reason for the power of an audit. However, this very disclosure may cause SOEs a competitive disadvantage: it is much more difficult to maintain commercial secrecy in SOEs. Indeed, in many countries SOEs were able to avoid even a requirement to publish financial statements. In Argentina, "[s]tatistical reports containing information about investments, sales, and number of employees, have been considered confidential and therefore have not been disclosed to the general public" (Panzoni, 1983, p. 383).

When the European Commission issued directive (80/723/EEC of June 25, 1980) calling for transparency of financial relations between member states and certain SOEs, the U.K., French and Italian governments brought action before the European court seeking to make the directive null and void. The French and Italian governments alleged that the directive "constitutes discrimination between public and private undertakings" (Brothwood, 1981, p. 215). They argued that since the commission has no power to examine the funding provided by the private sector to its enterprises, it should not have such power in relation to SOEs.

The EEC Commission felt a problem arises "where the dual role of the State as both investor and public authority is liable to cause the typical motivations and responsibilities of one and the other to overlap" (10th Report on Competition Policy, 1980, p. 164. For the European Court's decision, see the Twelfth Report on Competition Policy, pp. 151–152.)

SOEs also find more demands are made on management time to answer questions, to appear in Parliament or to spend time with state auditors. SOEs may also be compelled by government to use their funds for the achievement of social purposes or for bailing out ailing firms. Thus, in September 1984, Petronas, Malaysia's state oil company, was forced to rescue Bank Bumiputra, the country's biggest bank, by taking an 87 percent stake in its equity after it was alleged "that members of the bank's Hong Kong subsidiary, Bumiputra Malaysia Finance (BMF), corruptly lent money to the collapsed property empire of Mr. George Tan and to other Chinese-owned companies" and that six former officials of BMF "received money, gifts and loan guarantees from a number of Chinese businessmen" (*The Economist*, January 12, 1985, p. 68). When rescue operations are carried out by SOEs, or when loss-depleted capital of an SOE is replaced, these transfers of public funds are often a clear case of state aid to private business firms.

RULES OF CONDUCT IN AN SOE

When the state uses public funds, the public expects them to be used parsimoniously, that investments will be made with a reasonable degree of caution and that state funds will be efficiently exploited. Citizens also expect that SOE management will treat them according to the principle of natural justice required of the government. Thus, SOEs are expected to act fairly to avoid discrimination and to distribute their work contracts fairly. In the eyes of the public, regardless of the percentage of ownership, an SOE is part of government. One of the many paradoxes regarding SOEs is that the public does not believe SOEs can be efficiently managed, being part of the government, but expects from them much more efficiency, more justice and a higher degree of caution than from a private firm.

Often, once a particular service is provided, the public comes to expect that the service will be continued irrespective of any changes in the economic structure. The curtailment of transportation routes, e.g., causes public outcries and intensive efforts to restore the service. According to Pryke:

> [P]ublic ownership raises expectations. Consumers expect "fair" prices and the provision of unprofitable services, and workers come to believe they have a right to jobs and that wages should be paid regardless of whether they are earned. Both groups believe that the Government will, if necessary, be able to provide the public corporations with money and ask the seemingly unanswerable question of why, since they have been brought into public ownership, the nationalised industries should, like private undertakings, be expected to cover their costs and respond to market forces. [1981, p. 265]

Moreover, no one would object if a private individual employs a lazy cousin in his or her business. SOEs, in contrast, are subject to different rules or conduct. In the words of Galbraith:

> Oddities and inequalities in pay and staffing arrangements are taken for granted in the private firm. Errors in the selection of high personnel are regularly corrected by promoting the individual into a better compensated and more honorific but less important post. Nepotism is not only taken for granted but approved. The son is expected to follow in his father's footsteps; for him to do otherwise is ordinarily taken as a mark of eccentricity or possible feeble madness. It is taken for granted that mistakes will be made in production or investment. What counts is the overall result—and no public outcry arises if there are occasional lapses even in that. The highways and the railway sidings of the U.S., and of other western countries, are replete with monuments to misguided investment. And no one has ever given them a second look. None of these vagaries is vouchsafed to the public enterprise. It must have orderly pay and salary schedules. To

supplement these from the expense account is heinous. Nepotism is a serious offence, for a relative to appear anywhere on the payroll excites suspicion. Mistakes in judgement are not regarded tolerantly. [In Narain, 1980, p. 10]

The rules of conduct should relate to the use of funds and donations; equality; supply of services; fairness in treatment of suppliers, including the obligation to justify the firm's actions and not be arbitrary, regulation to avoid bribes; working conditions and payment level for workers and publicity and transparency of transactions.

Finally, since the demarcation line between the business activities of SOEs and government action are often blurred in the eyes of the public, an SOE is expected not to engage in actions with which the state would not want to be identified. Their ownership status subject SOEs to a greater degree of public scrutiny and a heightened public sensitivity to the way SOEs behave than would be the case for private firms similarly situated. The expectations tend to impinge on managerial freedom in a variety of ways. SOE managers make decisions under uncertainty. Like their counterparts in a private firm, SOE managers can fail or make mistakes because of unforeseen circumstances. Unlike their counterparts in the private sector, however, if the decision turns out to be wrong, they may have to explain it time and again, often years after it was taken when, with 20–20 hindsight, it is easy to see that the decision was wrong. One Indian manager describes his feelings on that question:

Having worked in the private sector for long and having joined the public sector recently, my experience most of the time is that failures occur due to fear, fear of being criticized, fear of being checked and abused; and fear of being abused within four corners of the building or in the press, or by our own people or by audit. A major problem we see is the fear of audit. Every decision we make—an economic decision we make—the immediate question within us or taken up by the financial adviser: beware, there will be an audit, beware there will be CBI on you, beware—even your grandson may be hanged, if you do some mistake. And then it is told so many times that even people who come from the private sector, who were used to making decisions and making four mistakes out of ten, which is rated as very good performance in private sector, are stupefied into not taking decisions. I think, more than anything else, it is the fear of audit which is the greatest ghost standing behind every chief executive or his managers, that they just totally fail to act, or they want 20 signatures, 15 concurrences, by which time, a decision becomes irrelevant to the actual economic situation. [In Narain, 1982, p. 11]

In many SOEs serious flaws were discovered in the ways decisions were reached, in the reporting of managers to their board of directors and the comptrollers, in project planning and equipment purchases, in applying con-

clusions from past experience in the planning of similar activities in the future
or in estimating the size of investments and the outcome of actions. Large
gaps were frequently discovered between planning and implementation, with
unfounded optimism in the planning, lack of caution in the investment of
funds and the absence of an economic investigation of important business
deals. Many SOEs exhibit faulty procedures in commissioning construction
work and establishing projects, in record keeping and inventory control or in
internal auditing.

Quite often, at least a partial reason for failure is that overburdened government representatives forego their power to influence the affairs of the SOE.
In other cases, mistakes are made by the government, and the SOE takes the
brunt of public anger. In India, a large SOE was forced by government to
order machinery from a local supplier, as part of an experiment of being
indigenous. The government overruled the strong objections of the SOE and
its misgivings about the ability of the supplier to produce a quality product.
After installation, the machinery was troublesome. The board of directors
strongly resented the ministry at whose initiative the SOE was compelled to
take the orders, insisting that the ministry take the responsibility. The ministry, for its part, now considered the deal "essentially a commercial matter"
and refused to accept responsibility, writing back to the SOE that it was not
proper for the board to sit in judgment on a government decision and that
bringing the matter on record was "highly objectionable" (Narain, 1982, p.
154).

In Israel, at various times accusations have been made that a small number of auditors and legal advisors enjoy most of the revenue accrued from
employment by SOEs. Various small legal and auditing offices demanded
that SOEs be required to rotate accountants and legal advisors. On May 4,
1969, the Israeli government decided that legal advisors to SOEs are to be
appointed by a committee including three public figures who are not civil
servants and of whom at least one is a professor of law, the director general of
the ministry of justice, director of the Government Companies Authority or
an attorney with a high-level position in the bar association. The committee
was enjoined to work toward "dividing the legal counselling among the largest
possible number of attorneys" (in Aharoni, 1979, p. 191). In 1970, another
public committee was established to choose auditors for SOEs to ensure "a
fair division of jobs among the auditors interested in them in Israel." (*Ibid.*)

Private enterprise regularly makes donations to nonprofit organizations.
In Israel, at least, SOEs are barred from such practices, both to avoid calumny
and because of the belief that SOEs' funds belong to the people. Managerial
discretion is, therefore, restricted in that area. In Italy, since 1974, SOEs are
not allowed to contribute to political parties while private companies were not
restricted from making such contributions (Grassini, in Vernon and Aharoni,
1981, p. 72).

Potential political embarrassment could emanate from routine business
decisions. Private entrepreneurs may give gifts or higher-than-usual commis-

sions. SOEs in Western democracies are looked upon askance if they follow such practices. SOEs are expected to observe strictly ethical norms with regard to everything touching on subjects such as bribes, the payment of higher than ordinary agents' commissions or activities that involve bypassing the law in other countries, even if such activities are permitted there. The Canadian auditor general's report for 1976 questioned so-called refunds payments made by Atomic Energy of Canada Ltd. (AECL) to agents' bank accounts in a foreign country, in connection with the sales of nuclear power plants to Argentina and Korea, an act not forbidden by Canadian law but seen as inappropriate for an SOE. These payments and other financial practices resulted in a review by the Canadian House of Commons Standing Committee on Public Accounts. AECL management was reluctant and uncooperative in testifying. On December 16, 1976, Canada announced new guidelines for Crown corporations involved in international trade, specifying "that all business transactions should be conducted in accordance with the laws of the nations involved and indicated the procedures to be followed when using agents to conduct business in foreign countries" (Sexty, 1983, p. 23).

In July 1977 the House of Commons Standing Committee on Public Accounts issued a report on the business practices of Polymer Corporation: "The practices involved questionable rebates or marketing allowances being remitted after European customers were billed at inflated prices" (Sexty, 1983, p. 24). A number of problems also arose in other countries in connection with the payment of higher than usual agency commissions in foreign sales or actions that could be interpreted as helping the agents evade income tax in their countries.

Undoubtedly, an SOE is more exposed to public scrutiny than a private firm. In Austria, "in the case of business measures which may involve ticklish points of foreign policy, such as investment by an ÖIAG enterprise in South Africa, for example, the Federal Chancellor considered it important that he be informed and consulted at the right time" (Van der Bellen, 1981, p. 62).

Cases of irregularity, bribes or rip-offs obviously embarrass the government, which is, after all, responsible to the nation for the behavior of SOEs. Ministers are accused of too lax controls or in sticking their hands in taxpayers' pockets. Directors are accused of being ineffectual and of being too naive and trusting. When Lufthansa, the German state-owned airline, admitted, in 1981, to paying illegal commissions to German travel agents, the government stepped in. Lufthansa's chairman left "for health reasons," although his term was due to expire in 1984, and the state secretary in the Bonn Transport Ministry was nominated as chairman. The political waves may even cause a fall of the government. In fact, in Norway in 1963, an accident in a state-owned coal mine led to a cabinet crisis.

To conclude, in a mixed economy, where private enterprises and SOEs compete with each other, it is extremely difficult to avoid conflicts and bitterness. Some private business firms benefit from the existence of SOEs, others may lose opportunities for higher profits. In some cases, the entry of an SOE into an industry is designed to increase competition or to increase the amount of information government possesses on the industry (e.g. oil). In many cases, an SOE entry might have unusually wider-ranging consequences for other industries or for society as a whole. The double role of government as a neutral umpire and a producer creates many intractable problems and conflicts. SOEs often complain that the result is more restrictions on their freedom to manage effectively.

RELATIONSHIP BETWEEN THE PRIVATE AND THE GOVERNMENT INVESTOR

The discussion has centered on the state and the private sectors. No less complicated is the relationship between the private investor and the government in a jointly owned company. When the SOE is fully owned, the government may order it not to raise salaries or prices, to invest in a development area, or to undertake any other action it regards as necessary in the public interest. In a joint venture, if such directives are given, the private shareholders may find themselves subject to decisions they do not approve or to orders contrary to their interests.

Viallet (1983) offers a decision-making model for the solution of conflicts of interests between the state shareholders and its private partners on a location decision for a new plant. The model provides the magnitude of a subsidy that will make the private shareholder indifferent as to location. However, it is not easy to apply such a solution in practice.

In the case of Nigeria, Asobie (1983) feels that an SOE entering a management partnership with an MNE is likely to benefit in the short run. In the long run, *"Management in a developing country is, or ought to be, concerned not just with the best way of combining human and material resources to attain goals at minimum cost and maximum speed. It also should deal with the question of whether the goals to be attained are right and whether the benefits will accrue to a large proportion of the general public rather than a small group of elites. Therefore, multinational firms which introduce capitalist institutions, norms and ethics and which transfer the inequities inherent in capitalist mode of production into underdeveloped nations are, by definition, inefficient managers of public enterprises"*, (p. 27).

One possibility is to design a system whereby the private shareholders will be entitled to sell their shares to the government in any instance they believe they cannot accept decisions required in the public interest. But, in such instances it is necessary to fix the price at which the state will purchase the shares, and that is not so simple. Another possibility is to designate that the government is not entitled to act in the public interest in a company in which there are also private shareholders. A third is to view private investors who agree to go into partnership with the government as implicitly accepting the risk of government directives that are contrary to their interests or any other conflicts of interests. A logical extension of this view is that when the government acquires a controlling interest in a company, thus turning it into a SOE, the private shareholders should be permitted to decide whether or not they are interested in such a partnership. Indeed, this is what the Government Company Law of Israel stipulates (Section 9). The solution proposed by the Israeli law does not apply to cases in which the state owns 50 percent or less of the shares. In these cases, it is implicitly assumed that the private investor can control the firm through majority interest.

In reality, governments seem to have been very lenient partners. In many cases, excessive rights were granted to private partners in SOEs. In Israel, the state comptroller's audits of joint ventures revealed that representatives of the state waived their rights to suitable board representation and to a return on state's funds (Douer, 1973). In other cases, the government acquired an interest in a private firm to save it from going under. Government aid was not made dependent on changes in employment and working practices. Government often gives in. Douer (1973) says:

> Theoretically, the private partners of the government corporation or of the government should be anxious about the great power of their partner, a power which may be used for evil or for good. However, in fact, as will also appear below in the review of findings published by State Audit in this sphere, it emerges that the government or government corporation is generally a very convenient partner to undertake joint ventures with; a partner which can make available to the other partners its full financial strength by injecting funds through purchase of shares, giving of loans and guarantees, and offers of grant and support; and at the same time, when disputes arise, not only does this partner not apply all its force to achieve a solution that suits its, but in many cases it does not even insist on its formal and elementary rights. (Douer, 1973, p. 117)

In numerous cases, joint ventures with private-sector entrepreneurs have cost taxpayers a lot of money when promoters persuaded the government to enter into partnership in projects of dubious economic justification. In all these cases, later reports use strong language to attack the government for its incompetence and recklessness with taxpayers' money. Every nation has had some sad experience with slick promoters. Some of these cases were widely publicized: e.g., Bricklin in New Brunswick, DeLorean in the United Kingdom. Others are less known. These experiences sometimes make the government cautious, but then it runs the risk of being accused of delays and procrastination.

In a joint venture, the government can make the firm tackle riskier projects and has a longer time horizon in its investment decisions. If the joint venture firm's shares are traded in the stock exchange, the increased risk may cause the share prices to plummet. At the same time, the assurance of government backing may increase the long-term value of the firm. In the case of CDC in Canada, "the possibility of increased governmental influence on the CDC was perceived as an increased probability of lower profit" (Eckel and Vining, in Stanbury and Thompson, 1982, p. 276). The common shares of the firm have slipped by about eight percent.

In a joint venture, government may insist on a wide distribution of shares, as the Germans did in VEBA and Volkswagen (see Chapter 3). In Canada, the province of British Columbia reduced its holdings in the British Columbia Resources Investment Corporation (BRIC) to less than five percent of the outstanding shares, but provincial legislation stipulates that BRIC may force shareholders to reduce their holdings by selling within 60 days and restricts individual holdings to a maximum of 1 percent and institutions to 3 percent of outstanding shares. The associate membership legislation also precludes shareholders from acting in concert to influence management. Similar provisions can be seen in the case of Alberta Energy Corporation and CDC. Such provisions do not allow private controls, but they reduce public expenditures (see also chapter 9).

Joint ventures between government and private investors are a new phenomenon and not a well researched one. Recently, more joint ventures have been established with MNEs to obtain necessary technology and managerial expertise. The extent and nature of the costs and benefits of such partnerships have not been well studied.

THE TWO FACES OF GOVERNMENT

Government today has two faces: on the one hand, it is a traditional provider of law and order, an administrator of justice and a supplier of essential services such as education, health or welfare. On the other hand, it is a direct producer. The role of the state as a direct producer generates two kinds of reaction, discussed above: private businesspersons attempt to use whatever political influence they have to limit the role of government as a producer, but also to control the public productive apparatus so that its decisions on how public resources are utilized will be made in a way favorable to them. Private businesspersons may create an alliance with the emerging class of SOE managers and technocrats. Such a partnership prefers growth to distribution and benefits to the dominant economic class at the cost of the consumers.

As long as the SOE sector was composed mainly of public utilities, the private sector attempted to get benefits of low cost infrastructure and a reduction in the costs of operations: low-cost delivery of printed matter benefits certain business sectors and the low cost of electricity, water, telex or telephone to business reduces operating costs. In many cases, the market ideology is shared by the private businesspersons and SOE managers, both of which look askance at politicians and civil servants. The SOE sector is used to subsidize business and open bottlenecks that slow economic growth rates (and business profits).

In countries such as Brazil and Venezuela, the accelerated transition from import substitution to export-led industrialization was achieved by an increasing role of capital-intensive SOEs, placing the production of wealth before its distribution with little regard to unemployment. The concentration of economic activities in very few giant SOEs gave rise to a very special kind of new oligarchy: a few dozen SOE CEOs could decide how to invest very large sums of money, and who would benefit. The contest for power has been between business—private and public—and civil servants, not only between private and SOE sectors. The state administration is effectively divided: those who work under Weberian bureaucracy, supplying traditional government services, and those who manage producing enterprises aimed at achieving profits. In between there are the managers of so-called "budget SOEs"—those which provide heavily subsidized services such as public transportation, and are heavily dependent on the government's budget to cover their expenditure.

The private sector in several countries has found that it is better to join the SOE sector than to fight it. Private business firms enter into joint ventures with SOEs, and recommend that the SOE sector should be instilled with entrepreneurial spirit, initiative, innovation and efficiency. They would like to see SOEs autonomous from political intervention. In Venezuela, for example, it was suggested in the mid-1970s that SOEs should be organized by sectors in a series of holding companies (empresas matrices), to be operated under private law. They were to be managed by a national council of sectorial corporations, whose members would be elected by the president of the country. By linking the SOEs directly to the president, it was hoped to avoid mismanagement and corruption associated with political intervention of ministers and civil servants, lending more political weight to SOE managers who are directly connected to the office of greatest political influence. This proposal was not accepted, because of strong opposition raised by the political parties, in particular Action Democratica.

The institutional arrangements by which the SOE sector operates are extremely important, both in terms of the distribution of power within the state, and in terms of the conception of the state itself. A clear division of the traditional and entrepreneurial state can create more economic efficiency and increase the power of entrepreneurs and SOE technocrats. A depoliticization of the management of the SOE sector may increase the commonality of interests of private and SOE managers. The traditional state bureaucracy loses much of its power under such an arrangement and resents it. The larger the size of the producing SOE sector, and the more its managers become experienced and expert, the greater the probability that these managers may form an alliance to achieve more power and control, creating in effect competition not only with private-sector interests, but with the interests of those working for the traditional state. This contest for power may create a restructuring of the state's institutions as important as the breakdown of the feudal system. Such a reform of institutions may reduce or eliminate institutional barriers to economic growth. At the same time, it will completely revamp the political power structure as well as the interactions of private and SOE sectors. The political power of representative government will still be important, but at least as long as the SOEs do not require cash from the treasury, they might gain enormous power and create a new oligarchy. Since the administrative rules of the traditional state are inapplicable to the entrepreneurial state—conflicts and tensions between managers in the two parts of the government seem inevitable, much more so than between private-sector and SOE managers: civil servants would like to be able to control SOEs, to dictate their salary levels, procurement policies, pricing decisions or dividend remittances. SOE managers are reluctant to allow the civil service this power.

Further, if the SOE sector pays much higher salaries than the civil service pay scale, skilled personnel flow from ministries to SOEs, and the government is obliged to move operations to SOEs simply because qualified persons from the civil service are unavailable. A situation of this sort increases the gulf between the two parts of government.

Public administration researchers see the SOEs as an integral part of government. For them accountability is most important and SOEs should not be allowed to bypass the budget laws and formal procedures required before state funds are allocated to different activities. They contend that the SOE "is merely another instrument for accomplishing governmental purposes" (Seidman, 1952, p. 90). For them SOEs "are organized to achieve a public purpose authorized by law" (*Ibid*, p. 93). Others see the SOE "both as a way of reducing government on all levels and as a way of involving the private sector in the service of domestic missions" (Etzioni, 1973, p.322). Political scientists, in contrast, see SOEs as a way for government to *avoid* accountability: to take credit for success but to avoid being blamed for failure (Sharkansky, 1979; Tierney, 1984). In democracies, the political process operates in two different channels, one formal and institutional, through political parties and their representatives in Parliament, and the other informal, through lobbying and consultation with different interest groups that supply information and attempt to influence the bureaucracy and gain access to top decision-makers in government. Economists would like to see SOEs as efficient producers, avoiding any waste. SOEs' activities are based on a contest for power, and their degree of competition with the private sector is a function of the power this sector has. However, if the SOE sector is not effectively removed from internal political struggles, if competent managers are not given enough free rein to achieve results, the economic performance of SOEs will be low.

CONCLUSION

Whether an SOE will be established or a private firm nationalized depends on the power of different actors. As the SOE sector grows and prospers, its managers also gain power. Ideally, private firms and SOEs can operate in harmony to achieve national goals. In reality, they often compete on the allocation of limited resources. The general rule is that the two sectors should be equally treated, but in practice there are enormous difficulties in achieving such equality and especially in convincing everyone that the equality indeed operates. The results are conflicts and tension. Once government gets involved in business, it loses its ability to act as arbiter. At the same time, the use of the SOE is a challenge, not only to private firms but also to government and to the democratic political system. On the one hand, the public sector is expanded and strengthened *vis-à-vis* the private sector. On the other hand, it becomes much harder to govern, and the growth of the SOE sector—paradoxically perhaps—may lead to a weakening of parliamentary control and democratic values.

SOEs, therefore, cannot be equal to their private-sector counterparts. They should jealously follow certain ethical rules of conduct in their relationship with their external coalition and the private sector. SOEs are better placed than private firms to influence public policies. If SOEs establish themselves as independent sources of power, one danger is that they will eventually dominate their formal superiors, who are reluctant to give up the many benefits of having institutions outside the core of government. If the government sees SOEs as political instruments, this may result in inefficiencies. In the case of British Columbia Railroad (BCR), e.g., its

> [m]isadventures have stemmed from the fact that it has been a political tool. . . . For more than twenty years—until the election of Premier William R. Bennett in 1975—the premier of the province served as president of the railway, the board of directors was composed mainly of government representatives, and the general manager of BCR was chosen by the railway's president. . . . concentration of control in the government resulted in an inefficient railway . . . one billion dollars was invested. [Gordon, 1981, p. 120]

Being owned by the state and controlled by ministers, SOEs' management has more opportunities to furnish information in informal consultations and face-to-face communication with ministers. The government is sometimes portrayed as controlling the SOEs, but in reality the managers of the

SOEs, falling between the stools of too many controllers, often gain independent power and have sometimes become the more dominant partners in the contest for power.

If SOEs are left too autonomous, they may expand at the expense of private-sector interests and also the coherence of the state, escaping public accountability. The problem of competition between private and public sectors is not easy to solve. To explore these different questions, we should understand managerial behavior in SOEs.

CHAPTER 8

The Internal Coalition: Can the Manager's Mind Be Nationalized?

INTRODUCTION

In the discussion of the pros and cons of state ownership of enterprises, these enterprises are usually considered to be rational organizations attempting to achieve their prescribed goals. It was naively assumed that once production was nationalized, the ultimate goals of the SOE sector would concur with those of the managers, without any foresight or plan of how the SOEs would function. Emanuel Shinwell, in discussing the National Coal Act, said he "had to start on a clear desk" (Shinwell, 1955, p. 172).

As we have repeatedly stressed, however, organizations are not monolithic entities and have to be managed to achieve their objectives effectively. Top management must decide on alternatives under conditions of uncertainty, initiate actions, motivate subordinates, coordinate different functions and control operations, utilizing limited resources efficiently in a changing environment. The manager may symbolize people's hopes, ambitions, desires and determination: the manager's rational anticipation of responses builds goals and teamwork. Managers also have values, needs and beliefs, which affect goal interpretations.

Management may be hierarchical or form coalitions that influence organizational goals (Cyert and March, 1963; Zalenznik, 1970; Buchanan, 1974; Wamsley and Zald, 1976; Pfeffer and Salancik, 1978; Simon, 1979). Managerial elite values are better predictors of organizational goals than the structural variables of the organization (Hage and Dewar, 1973). Some authors even claim that managerial elite values are actually the organizational policy (Guth and Taguiri, 1965). Since managers' values and orientations are related to the way they manage, the adherence of the SOE chief executives to its *raison d'être* cannot be taken for granted.

The submerging of individual interests for the purpose of achieving organizationally rational action is a theme that has dominated the organization literature since the time of Max Weber. However, it is also well known that individuals do not necessarily act for the benefit of the firm. Managers have discretion in the choice of strategies, product lines, organizational forms and policies. They may use their discretion for staff expansion or to achieve slack or on-the-job leisure (Williamson, 1970, pp. 49–52) or they might opt for a less arduous life (Alchian, 1965).

Moreover, one cannot assume that all decision-makers in the economy work as one to achieve common goals. "The lower in the hierarchy the manager, the greater his incentives to deflect orders . . . and to withhold information. . . . the irony is that while it may be lower-level managers who have the greatest incentive to rely especially on the system of politics, it is the upper managers who are better able to exploit it" (Mintzberg, 1983, p. 127). The relationships, therefore, between managers and state officials controlling them, as well as the positive and negative incentives to managers are of crucial importance.

Nationalization of its physical assets and resources does not automatically guarantee the achievement of an SOE's objectives or secure the cooperation of its executives. Managers are sometimes portrayed as being totally dominated by government controllers, while others see them as being free to achieve their own objectives, having a high degree of autonomy or considerable latitude in setting the direction of the enterprise and being able to co-opt their controllers. Several studies of SOE history suggest that some managers of these enterprises demonstrate concern for economic efficiency and aggressive growth (Dornstein, 1976; Votaw, 1964; Caro, 1974; Trebat, 1983). Managers have criticized what they interpreted as government's encroachment on goals other than economic ones (NEDO, 1976), or attempted to expand into international markets despite government's wishes and policies (Mazzolini, 1979). They characteristically try to keep government at arm's length.

The work of Anastassopoulos (1973) indicates many intermediate positions on a scale where managerial autonomy is partial rather than strong or weak. As we shall see, differences in managerial behavior are a function not only of the job context but also of the background and personal characteristics of the managers, the way they are recruited and their perceptions of their career path.

NATURE OF MANAGERIAL WORK IN SOES

The study of managers and nature of SOE managerial work has been mainly confined to the private sector, and there has not been any major comparative research on SOE general managers. In both cases, studies of individual characteristics of managers as well as other studies (Mintzberg, 1973) are, by and

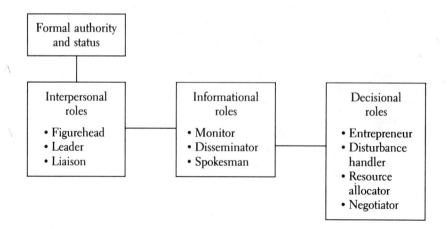

Figure 8.1   The manager's roles

large, purely descriptive and seek to identify patterns in managerial behavior. The most detailed work in this area is that of Mintzberg (1973) who concludes that managerial behavior can be viewed as comprising ten roles (see Figure 8.1). "Formal authority gives rise to the three interpersonal roles, which in turn give rise to three informational roles; these two sets of roles enable the manager to play the four decisional roles" (1973, p. 54).

Studies of Managerial Job Contexts

(e.g., Steuart, 1963, Mintzberg, 1973, Stieglit, 1970, Burns, 1957). Other studies seek to identify factors that make one manageial job context different from another. Among the factors that have been identified are the functions supervised, the job level in the organization, the size of the organization and the characteristics of the particular industry.

From a general manager's perspective, the job context depends on factors both internal (such as functions supervised or size of the organization) and external to the organization. Some of the key external factors are:

The mode of ownership and external control,
The characteristics of the industry in which the organization operates,
The salience of the particular organization in the eyes of the national government and the public.

Other factors being constant, state ownership makes the job context of a general manager in an SOE different from that of the counterpart in a privately owned enterprise in at least four different ways: First, as discussed in Chapter 4, the SOE general manager faces a greater multiplicity of objectives,

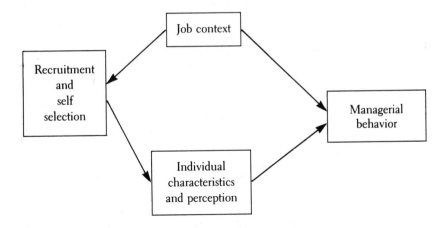

Figure 8.2 Determinants of managerial behavior in SOEs

and diverse claims make it possible to play one claimant against another. Second, the SOE general manager enjoys less managerial discretion than the counterpart in the private sector. This point was partially discussed in Chapters 6 and 7. Third, a greater percentage of the general manager's time is used in interaction with outside bodies. Finally, the SOE general manager enjoys less flexibility in restructuring the organization and in reassigning key subordinates than the counterpart in the private sector. These differences in job context determine managerial behavior, but behavior also depends on methods of recruitment and on individual characteristics and perceptions. Therefore, actual managerial behavior is jointly determined by both variables in the way shown in Figure 8.2.

MANAGEMENT BACKGROUND AND RECRUITMENT

One reason for differences among managers within the SOE sector is their different backgrounds. Some countries recruited SOE managers from the private sector. It is no surprise that these managers share the values and orientations of their private-sector counterparts. In the United Kingdom, e.g., SOE managers often worked in the firm prior to its nationalization or were recruited after a long and successful career in the private sector. Government civil servants, in contrast, come from different backgrounds. They have no business or commercial experience and find it difficult to cope with business management problems. As a result, the relationship between SOE managers and civil servants becomes strained. SOE managers often scorn civil servants and attempt, sometimes publicly, to protect what they see as their prerogatives against governmental interference.

In many other countries, nationalized firms retained the old managers, who had a different outlook from that of the government ministers. A deeply ingrained distrust developed between managers and ministry. Coronel quotes a civil servant in Venezuela as saying, "we don't know everything that is going on in the industry and I have the suspicion that it is in those areas we don't know much about where you are deceiving us" (1983, p. 107).

French managers usually come from a very similar educational and social background to that of the civil servants. Both groups were educated in the elite grandes écoles and are members of the Grand Corps. This common background may have increased the political power of the SOE manager. Indeed "in one well-documented case, the officers of five French state-owned enterprises demonstrated their collective influence by bringing about the dismissal of a French Minister of Industry" (Vernon, 1984, p. 44).

In contrast, many SOE managers in developing countries owe their position to their political or tribal affiliation, not necessarily to their managerial competence. In some cases, positions in SOEs were created to give a job to a politician who lost an election or to a friend of a minister. In these cases, the minister is often the real CEO of the firm, and the officially nominated CEO may be no more than a plant manager, carrying out orders on how the firm should be managed and whose interests are to be guaranteed. In other cases, SOE managers come from civil service backgrounds and see their career path as being within the public sector.

In some countries, SOE managers come from the army and often regard their jobs as temporary. They, as well as the civil service background managers, tend to develop a don't-rock-the-boat syndrome.

Phatak (1969), in an in-depth study of an Indian SOE, found that on average, not more than one employee is either dismissed or laid off per year. Employees in one department admitted that the work assigned to them could be accomplished by half as many employees and in less than half the time taken. One particular employee had been found sleeping on the job several times, yet no disciplinary action had been taken against him. When asked why no corrective action was taken to reduce the number of workers and to punish the employee at fault, the personnel manager said that top management is apathetic. Management does not want to get involved in any disputes with the union because a strike would blemish its now clean record with reference to union-management relations. This apathetic and don't-rock-the-boat attitude, the author observed, has

> [P]ermeated throughout the organization and is unfortunately moulding management practices, policies and politics at all levels— from the board of directors at the apex, right down to workers at the base of the organizational pyramid. The result, in terms of economic and financial performance, is poor. [Phatak, 1969, p. 347]

One reason for apathy is a feeling that the job is temporary since managers change very often with changing regimes or go back to military service after serving as SOE managers for some time. It may also stem from rigid controls or from highly political appointments. In India, the frequent changes of the managers "indicates that managers do not have time to understand the enterprise or to make any real contribution to it" (Narain, 1982, p. 145).

A dramatic illustration of a political appointment for a temporary assignment is that of General Aniline and Film Corporation (GAF). In 1942, certain shares of this company were taken over by the U.S. government because they were the property of nationals of an enemy nation. The U.S. government divested itself of these shares on the open market in March 1965. During the 23 years of confiscation, GAF had eight chief executives and more than sixty directors. Tenure averaged about 5 years, depending on a director's political clout and connections (Vance, 1983, p. 128). The temporary nature of the assignment caused risk aversion and lackadaisical performance. As reported in *Fortune:*

> *The board members were often ill-acquainted with the chemical industry, and tended to feel that conserving the assets the Attorney General had temporarily entrusted to them was their main responsibility. Back in 1953, President Jack Frye confessed to a senatorial committee, "One of the problems of this company is that, due to the ownership situation, the management, the board of directors, and all concerned are extremely cautious about making expenditures. In trying not to make mistakes, they actually move more slowly than do their competitors." [Ross, 1963, p. 125]*

In 1942, GAF sales were $43 million and its net income was $4 million. Dow had $78 million in sales and $9 million in net income, while Monsanto's net sales were $69 million and net income was $5 million. In 1980, Dow grew to $10.6 billion in sales and $805 million in net income. Monsanto's sales for that year were $6.6 billion and $149 million in net income. In contrast, GAF sales were $1.23 billion and it had a $234 million net loss. Perhaps complete rehabilitation after a long period of temporary management is not easily attainable.

Managers who aspire to success and promotion are undoubtedly affected by their perception of the considerations that guide those who appoint and promote them. The criteria used in managers' recruitment are, therefore, very important. Managers can glean what is expected of them from recruitment methods. In the recruitment and promotion of SOEs' managers, some countries stress industrial experience and managerial competence. Others set store by political adroitness and beliefs or loyalty to the supervising minister or tribal affiliation as well as political status.

A common criticism of SOEs is that the managers are too often chosen for their political connections rather than their professional competence. The power to recruit CEOs and board members is used as a key mechanism by the supervising ministers for maintaining control over the enterprise. The history of SOEs in different countries is replete with cases of changing appointments with changing governments, sometimes before the term of the director (or the CEO) has elapsed. In many cases, the political appointment of outsiders as CEOs has adverse effects on the morale of managers inside the SOE.

The system of political appointment may be explicitly recognized, as in the case of the Austrian *Proportz*, dividing board membership according to the strength of the political parties in the coalition government. In other cases, the system operates in the same way but without explicit written agreement. In the single-party system of Zambia, high-level public officials have to demonstrate absolute loyalty and unflinching dedication to the party ideals.

The board "consists of compliant politicians and civil servants" (Ghai in Reddi, 1983, p. 194). The government appoints "political friends of the minister and unsuccessful parliamentary candidates of the ruling party" (*Ibid.*, p. 193). Between 1971 and 1978, ZIMCO's board of directors included all the key ministers, with the President himself as the chairman (p. 216). SOEs "are frequently used as a means of patronage and a source of wealth and power for political and administrative leaders. The managements are either too weak to be able to expose the corruption of the government, or too involved in it to want to" (p. 219). In Italy, the appointments of managers of the major holding companies are blatantly based on party affiliation:

> The Italian Communist party has repeatedly demanded that candidates be selected for top jobs in state industries on professional merits rather than political considerations. But are the communists complaining only because they are out of power, and their members have not been chosen? [Monsen and Walters, 1983, p. 39]

In France, almost all CEOs of the firms nationalized in 1982 were replaced by political appointees who were loyal to the government's lines. In Canada, "[t]he composition of the board [of Ontario Hydro] clearly reflects a more political (which is not to say partisan) approach than would be likely under the same circumstances in a private-sector utility" (Gordon, 1981, p. 23).

In India, CEO recruitment is monitored by the Public Sector Employment Board, which is headed by a member of the planning commission. Its task is to assist the minister in recruiting the 90,000 managers to supervise the two million employees in the SOEs. After reviewing the Indian experience with executive selection, Murthy (1981) notes that one has to analyze the particular needs of the enterprise and recruit individuals whose skills fit those needs. If this task is done by a central selection board, the board must familiarize itself with each enterprise's situation. Murthy further notes that the degree of autonomy of the SOE is critical in this regard: if the ministry has preempted certain key areas of decision-making, the appropriate type of manager might be more the staff or middle manager or, in extremes, even a factory-manager type than a top-manager type. Finding management selection mechanisms that are compatible with enterprise needs, managerial supply and political realities is not an easy task.

People normally join and remain with an organization because of a sense of dedication to an idea or because they seek to accomplish a certain goal. If managers are recruited to manage SOEs on the basis of their ideological beliefs or party loyalty, the policies pursued by them will be different, not because of external controls or pressures but because of response to inner feelings and beliefs. Identification with the goals of the sector (or the government in power) ensures their sensitivity to political wishes and is an extremely effective control mechanism. Unfortunately, political loyalty does not always ensure managerial competence. When the recruitment system is not based on meritocracy, a trade-off is made between managerial competence and loyalty in selecting CEOs.

Since managers are hired by ministers, they can also be fired by them. In many cases, SOE managers were fired or were not reappointed because a minister changed or because they opposed a minister. Although the SOE's independence is stressed, the political limits are often tightly drawn. Political considerations can affect and have affected strategic decisions such as location of factories, levels of employment, pricing policies, capital investments and personnel selection, among others. When SOE managers failed to understand the limits of power, they lost their jobs. In France the government was reticent about giving reasons for its decision to replace Mr. Daniel Deguen, chairman of the Crédit Commercial de France (CCF). According to *The Economist* (June 30, 1984, p. 61) "the outgoing CCF chairman made himself unpopular late last year by protesting against the way state banks were pushed into a rescue package for Creusot-Loire, the heavy engineering group." Mr. Raymond Lévy, chairman of the Usinor Steel Group, won a long debate over the future of the French steel industry:

> But it is no secret that his victory this spring was won against the advice of President Mitterrand's industrial adviser, Mr. Alain Boublil. The industry minister, Mr. Laurent Fabius, supported the rolling-mills project. The Communists, who have four seats in the government, are hostile to job cuts. Mr. Lévy's victory won him a lot of enemies. (The Economist, June 30, 1984, p. 61)

In the U.K., Morrison (1933) placed "considerable reliance on the Minister's civil service advisors, whose tradition of rectitude, incorruptibility and public honesty would make it very difficult for a crooked minister to make crooked appointments" (p. 160). In other countries, the effectiveness of civil servants and legal rules is much weaker. Nkrumah in Ghana, for example, was accused by his opposition of appointing to SOEs "only his cronies from the Convention People's Party (CPP)" (Pozen, 1972, p. 814). This and other allegations were examined by the Jibowu Commission on the operations of the Cocoa Purchasing Company (CPC). "The Commission concluded that the

CPC did in fact use its loan programmes to further the political goals of Nkrumah's party, and that the CPC was an inefficient organization with many corrupt officials" (Pozen, 1972, p. 815). Ghana's Auditor General reported in 1964 that "The primary consideration for the selection of a chairman of a corporation was his party affiliation" and that "the greatest factor that contributed to the heavy losses [of SOEs] was poor management" (in Pozen, 1972, p. 822, fn. 98). It stands to reason that some competent managers simply refuse to manage an SOE and those who do, have to develop a political orientation to be successful. This is not to say that SOE managers lack power and autonomy, only that much time is invested in obtaining discretion, cultivating political support and amassing power. Monsen and Walters (1983) quote an advertisement written by John Elliott, to recruit a chairman for a U.K. SOE:

> [P]erson willing to be pilloried in public, bullied by civil servants and ministers in private, condemned by his employees, paid half what he could receive in the private sector, wanted for a job which he might be allowed to keep for three to five years. No guaranteed extras, although good behavior [may] merit a knighthood if he is polite when visiting Whitehall" (pp. 71, 72).

In other countries, managers cannot even expect a knighthood. They may simply refuse to manage an SOE. This process of self-selection has not yet been studied. Anecdotal evidence suggests that quite a few competent private-sector managers simply refuse to manage an SOE. It stands to reason that this self-selection process is also a function of the available alternatives. In some countries, if one wants to manage a large firm, one has to work for the public sector, unless this manager is kin to an owner. In other countries, opportunities to reach the top for a professional manager are more numerous.

The way managers are recruited also affects their views on job centrality. To those with private-sector backgrounds, their jobs are of central importance in their lives, while others are more interested in other concerns such as maintaining good relations with political leaders or undertaking commitments not related to their job in the SOE. Job centrality is also affected by the degree of autonomy the manager has: the more government intervenes, the less central will be the importance attached by certain SOE managers to their work role.

TYPES OF MANAGERS AND THEIR CAREER PATHS

Different backgrounds and recruitment methods affect the degree of political orientation of SOE management. Zif (1981, 1983) shows that a politically oriented management will be disproportionately likely to seek external support before acting on a new plan, emphasizing sales rather than profit goals and showing an unusual degree of price restraint. Kelly Escobar (1982) uses the term *commissars* to describe managers, sometimes from a civil-service background, who are more comfortable when someone else signs all but the most routine decisions, so that they are off the hook if something goes wrong. These managers look primarily to government and civil-service practices for guidance. They regard their job as one link in a political career. Therefore, they give high priority to the maintenance of good relations with government agencies.

Other managers, often from a business background, are termed *engineers*. They fight for autonomy to pursue their goals by choice, guided by market and business practices, and are profit- and growth-oriented. Using this framework, Kelly Escobar (1982) explained behavioral differences between two similar mineral-based SOEs, one in Brazil and the other in Venezuela. All SOE managers recognize their dependence on government, and this affects their behavior. They must be sensitive to their political environment when resource allocation decisions are made. The second group, however, emphasizes the business orientation, and often act before consulting their controllers (Zif, 1983). Some managers learn that they have to ensure ministerial support, accumulate power and political influence and build themselves independent power bases.

In addition to these two and the military type, three more types of managers are found in SOEs: public entrepreneurs, empire builders and leaders. Public entrepreneurs, unlike the private-sector entrepreneurs, are not motivated by pecuniary gain. They are instead driven by power, glory, prestige and the high need for achievement.

Empire builders derive satisfaction from serving the public rather than private interest and are mainly motivated by the desire to build industrial or other empires of modern capital-intensive enterprises. In many countries these are largely state-owned, and where large-scale activities are not public, they are often in the hands of family groups, where promotion for outsiders is severely limited.

They understand the possibility of procuring power without having an elective position. Some SOE managers think and behave like politicians and are more capable than the ministers to whom they are officially accountable. They explicitly recognize the importance of their organization in state politics and are alert to the weight of public opinion, seeking to shape projects to satisfy various stakeholders. They carefully build power and political clout, often by dispensing small favors to ministers and others. They expect constant pressures from different interest groups, learn to deal with these groups and attend to the media. Some of these empire builders obtain power by controlling information. Others "by monopolizing a technology by hiring all of the country's experts" (Grayson, 1981, p. 253). In state oil firms, in airlines, in energy firms, or in high-technolgoy SOEs, business intricacies yield enormous power to the managers. This power is increased by concealing information (Schvartz, 1974) and by the small size of the controllers' staff. In Australia one minister runs a department with only nine employees, including clerical and secretarial staff that control an SOE with close to 20,000 employees. Another ministry, in charge of overseeing authorities employing some 35,000, has a staff of 30 (Sharkansky, 1979, p. 57).

Robert Moses is an example of an empire builder who was able to seize power and exploit it. He had a genius for working the convoluted and divided city and state units of New York, seeing an opportunity in what others found ungovernable. He was even able to wheedle enormous authority from politicians who distrusted and possibly detested him and to wall off the numerous authorities he chaired against interference from elected officials. A master at making offers that could not be refused, he persuaded private landowners to donate land, mainly because of the fear that an alternative might be worse. He achieved financial independence, exploiting suppliers from one project to build another, accumulating a stable of loyal engineers and administrators in the process (see Caro, 1974; Walsh, 1978).

Finally, some SOE managers are leaders, whose personal magnetism is the basis of their authority and power. Burns identified two basic types of leadership:

> The transactional *and the* transforming. *The relations of most leaders and followers are transactional—leaders approach followers with an eye to exchanging one thing for another: jobs for votes, or subsidies for campaign contributions. . . . The* transforming *leader recognizes and exploits an existing need or demand of a potential follower. But, beyond that, the transforming leader looks for potential motives in followers, seeks to satisfy higher needs, and engages the full person of the follower. The result of transforming leadership is a relationship of mutual stimulation and elevation that converts followers into leaders and may convert leaders into moral agents.* [1978, p. 4]

Transforming leaders may change the organization–environment relationships.

> *Leaders are not a monolithic group. Rather, each individual in this group is, in his own right, a player in a central, competitive game. The name of the game is politics; bargaining along regularized circuits among players positioned hierarchically within the government.* [Allison, 1971, p. 144]

Relationships between CEOs (leaders or managers) and external authority could be hierarchical. In other cases, they are competitive, based largely on a power struggle. The relationships could also be based on *laissez faire*, in which the enterprise receives more autonomy and the external authority is satisfied with minimum compliance with formal directives. Finally, the relationships could be collusive—when managers and controllers cooperate to distort true results and hide inefficiencies to avoid unfavorable attention on both the enterprise and the government. Often, it is not enough to understand formal relationships. One needs to understand the process of interactions among individuals in what might be called a market for power.

One difference between the so-called commissars and military types on the one hand and the engineers, entrepreneurs, empire builders and leaders on the other is their perception of their career paths. Commissars and military types perceive their career in government or in the armed forces. The SOE job is one among other jobs in these sectors. They, therefore, protect themselves and are often conditioned to not making decisions—certainly not without prior clearance and authorization. They do not perceive their lifetime career path as being in management of economic enterprises and, therefore, become apathetic or ask for permission before they act. Engineers and leaders see their promotion opportunities mainly in economic enterprises—in both the public and private sectors. They, therefore, perceive themselves as being constantly evaluated within a national market for managers where alternative job opportunities are traded. If managers are interested in the present value of their earnings, they do not succumb to the temptation of an easy life or of employing only political strategies. Engineers are efficiency-oriented, committed to the public sector, yet contemptuous of the government's bureaucracy. They are mindful of the social objectives of the SOE sector, but believe "the company's affairs should be conducted with the same degree of business acumen [sic] displayed by firms in the private sector" (Trebat, 1983, p. 81). In some countries, as in Brazil, they are also well paid (*Ibid.*, p. 94). Although committed to the objectives of the sector, many of them would not mind if the firm they manage were to be privatized (Aharoni, 1984). They are also willing to move to better jobs in the private sector. Transforming leaders are driven by a vision and can translate it into reality, overcoming numerous obstacles along their path. They, too, would be willing to move between the sectors. The empire builders are motivated mainly by the desire to build empires. Knowing that this is possible for them only in the public sector, they attempt to establish and nurture political power.

Note that the risk to the manager depends on whether or not responsibility is traceable. Whether or not, and to what degree it is, depends on the system design. On the one hand, the use of new and untested technology usually entails high project risk. From the point of view of the SOE manager, success means promotion and prestige, but failure can be regarded as an act of God. On the other hand, the risk of system failure may be very low but the risk to the manager is usually much higher because of the publicity of such a failure. In an electricity-generating firm, e.g., the expected value of lost income resulting from a temporary system failure may be very low. Still, the firm managers may choose to install backup generating capacity to avoid such incidents and the inescapable public outcry. One problem in SOEs is how to make innovation an acceptable risk not only to managers but also to their controllers.

Clearly, different managers will behave differently in the same circumstances, depending on their individual characteristics, background and perceptions of their career paths. The performance of an SOE is not only a function of its external environment or the demands of its controllers, but also of managerial behavior.

POWER AT THE TOP

Managers and directors link the external coalition to the SOE's internal organization. This linking-pin role is especially critical in the case of the CEO. In a private firm, CEOs are depicted in the literature as the most powerful persons in the organization because the owners must rely on the CEOs to manage the organization. The power of CEOs is said to stem not only from their role but also from their ability to distribute rewards and set salaries and other benefits. Their formal power to hire and fire and their possession of a powerful base of special knowledge make CEOs usually the organizations best informed members, and the nerve center of the organization (Mintzberg, 1973). CEOs receive also the so-called soft information that is never documented, and so remains inaccessible to others. They are also said to personify the organization (Long, 1960, p. 211). CEOs in SOEs usually have less authority than those in private firms, and in many cases the CEO is not the manager of the SOE but the president of the country or the sponsoring minister.

The scarcest factor of production for managers is the time at their disposal. Time is the only factor of production that cannot be stockpiled. It is therefore reasonable to assume that managers allocate more time to those factors considered by them more important for the enterprise. However, CEOs' time is often devoured by trivia, more so in SOEs than in private enterprise. They not only represent the firm at ceremonial functions but also escort visiting dignitaries, appear before various investigating and audit commissions and spend time answering questions in Parliament and government ministries and to the press. These figurehead roles cannot be easily delegated since this would entail a high risk of offending various people in powerful positions. Moreover, CEOs may lack confidence in their subordinates because they are rarely allowed to choose their staff.

The more managers feel dependent on decisions reached by civil servants and ministers, the more time they will devote to cultivate political support, leaving less time for the economic management of the firm and for relationships with clients and suppliers. Thus, political orientation is not necessarily based on personality but on the perception the managers have of their role and their degree of dependence on government. In theory, SOEs should be run by competent managers who enjoy autonomy. The reality, however, is different.

Faced with inescapable exposure to political intervention and aware that mere submission to governmental direction does not necessarily reduce the risk of being blamed for errors, managers who see their career in the enterprise sector attempt to develop some measure of security by acquiring a degree of autonomy or increased bargaining power in their relations with the state. Every organization utilizes four basic kinds of resources from the environment: human, financial, physical and informational. Managers are expected to coordinate these resources to achieve certain missions. To this end, they have to carry out certain basic functions including planning; decision-making; organizing; coordinating activities and resources; leading, motivating and managing employees; and controlling, monitoring and evaluating activities. The ability of SOE managers to recruit human resources is almost always constrained by civil-service regulations and limited by political interventions; the ability to tap financial resources is often restricted by the requirement to obtain these funds only from government. Acquisition of major physical assets or diversification is also officially subject to prior approval. However, the managers can control the flow of information to their controllers, using this ability as a major weapon in obtaining more autonomy.

Since a major part of SOE general managers' work is influenced by external bodies and given that they have to coordinate the activities of an organization over which they have only limited control, interpersonal skills and political abilities are more critical for SOE general managers than for their private-sector counterparts. Many SOE managers learned that the trick is to steer clear of trouble. To avoid any political difficulties or clashes, they avoid any discernible harm that is unequivocally traceable to their actions by any strong identifiable group.

Certainly, SOE managers enjoy much more autonomy than their counterparts in the government. Further, some of these managers value social and political objectives more than the private enterprise manager. They also expend much more energy than their private-sector counterparts on the accumulation of power, political influence and a positive public image. They, therefore, have less time to make optimal economic decisions for the organization, and cannot ignore external pressures. The less autonomy government allows its SOEs, the larger the role conflict a manager faces. This role conflict increases frustration, but at the same time, a choice is made between a more internal as opposed to a more external or political role. Given a job context as described here, SOE managers have to decide on the allocation of time between management of the internal organization and of the environment. They also have to choose the degree to which they will attempt to influence the environment or succumb to its pressures. These choices are a function of the managers' background, their values and perception of career path.

One way for managers to achieve more autonomy is to distance themselves from government. This distance is achieved by making the SOEs stand on their own feet as quickly as they possibly can:

> *The less they depend on support out of the public purse—the ideal of being subsidized out of the taxpayer's money is a distasteful one—the more independent and powerful they become. The feudal barons were strong as long as they were sustained by their own local wealth and not dependent on favors bestowed upon them by the king.* [*Frankel, 1966, p. 167*]

The quest for financial independence may lead to a heightened preference for independent foreign sources of funds or for a propensity to select capital-intensive facilities to reduce further needs for out-of-pocket funds and to expansion to foreign markets, taking the firm away from domestic control and giving its management increased power in dealing with its government.

As already mentioned, autonomy is also increased by monopolizing technology. Because of all these reasons, the degree of autonomy evolves with time. Initially, SOEs are dependent on government. With time, in particular when government assistance is not crucial, managers secure much more autonomy. However, if a crisis comes, or a scandal erupts, they lose this hard-won autonomy.

The degree of perceived autonomy also depends on the alternatives available to the manager. Managers can increase autonomy if they are willing to resign unless they get what they want. Successful technocrats, who can move to manage other firms, are able to face with equanimity the loss of their job. Political protégés or commissars cannot afford to take such a risk. Empire builders usually cannot find alternative private-sector appointments allowing them to build empires. They cannot afford a confrontation leading to a possible dismissal. Their desire to remain in power leads them to give in to virulent attacks or to demands of strong politicians. The empire builders also need injections of state funds, and cannot achieve financial independence.

GOAL DISCREPANCY AND AUTONOMY

If managers do not take proactive actions, if they become apathetic, or if they suffer from civil-service mentality, or if they are inept, SOEs can create a series of ill-conceived projects and expend public funds without producing tangible results—either because of sheer incompetence or because of corruption. A good manager is expected to lead, to attempt to achieve results and to innovate. For these ends, management must have autonomy. On the other hand, managerial autonomy has its bounds, for at least three reasons.

First and foremost, SOEs are used to achieve numerous noncommercial goals. Second, to the extent that they need to be financed by the government, they lose autonomy. Third, many SOEs are natural monopolies whose pricing policies are of utmost importance to the national economy as well as to every voter. Governments just could not leave these matters in the hands of the SOE management, and political objectives often predominated strictly business considerations. Unions in these monopolies had a very strong power base and used it to demand and receive higher wage settlements, which were sometimes forced on reluctant managers by ministers with political objectives in mind. The very intervention of the government meant that the SOEs were seen as having a bottomless purse to provide higher wages, lower prices and unneeded employment.

Not all countries of the world safeguard individual citizens against the exercise of power by the executive or separate power among the Parliament, the courts, the bureaucracy and the elected government. Governments often suppress the political forces that are out of power, and thus, public accountability to Parliament is a meaningless term, as is often the case with the exercise of autonomy by the managers of the SOEs.

In many countries in Africa, Asia and Latin America, managers are appointed by the president of the country. These managers, by the nature of things, are totally dependent on the minister. They understand fully that the goals they should pursue are not necessarily those written in the official declarations but those communicated to them *in camera* by the minister. In certain military regimes, managers are appointed for a short period of time, almost as a part of the rotation of military duties. These managers surely are not going to alter the strategy of the enterprise or take a long-term view of its affairs, even if their apathy means high losses. Other types of managers may be able to accumulate power of their own, managing the SOE to achieve goals they see as important.

To the extent that all stakeholders achieve goal congruency, the SOE is directed to achieve the desired goals. What happens if there is a divergence of goals between SOE managers and their controllers? If the manager believes the SOE should achieve only economic goals, the probability of a goal discrepancy is high.

A study of general managers in Israel (Aharoni, 1984) found that they tend, on the whole, to emphasize economic goals such as profits and growth as opposed to political goals—that is, helping the government in power. At the same time, substantial differences were found between the importance of these goals to the managers and their perception of the importance assigned to them by their superiors. As expected, the average goal discrepancy was higher in the SOE sector than in the private sector, was also uniform and was found to affect managers' autonomy.

Anastassopoulos (1973) analyzes managerial autonomy in terms of the rational, the organizational and the political factors. On the rational level, managerial autonomy will be higher the more the SOE competes in the market, the less its activities have public-service characteristics and the higher the degree of expertise required to manage the enterprise, e.g., because of technological complexities. A fourth rational factor is the degree to which the company needs financial assistance from the state and the SOE's economic performance. In general, the less financial assistance is needed and the better the economic performance, the higher the autonomy. However, when the autonomy of an SOE is already very low, poor performance may be a cause for demanding and receiving more autonomy.

The rational factors enumerated here are usually easy to classify and to document. Under organizational factors Anastassopoulos (1973) listed, first, the degree and quality of interaction with state administrators and, second, esprit de corps within the company. The political factors are fourfold: the influence of political leaders, the influence of the company's top management, the degree of congruence between the company's interests and national interests and the inertia of the current situation.

Dependence increases when the SOE relies on government for input factors, when it lacks freedom to utilize and control inputs (e.g., management-controlled salaries) or is constrained by government in output and pricing decisions. Minimal SOE management autonomy diminishes its responsibility for enterprise performance. Efficiency suffers from overconformity with the rules, as in the case of overstaffing to conform with governmental employment goals. Inefficient SOEs are open to criticism, with rising costs causing increasing dependence.

As one example, if an SOE operates in a competitive environment, there is a high probability that its goals will be narrowly defined, not only by the management but also by the government. Governments tend to intervene more when the SOE can build a large slack and when the slack can be used for invisible methods of granting largesse of different kinds to different stakeholders. An enterprise facing strong competition has less slack, its performance can be easily measured relative to its privately owned competitors and, therefore, invisible methods are less possible. In this case, profits become socially legitimized and politically accepted, and the SOE would enjoy a high degree of autonomy.

A neglected area of research is the trade-off between what might be termed *economic* and *political* strategy. The latter involves trading off some dependence by getting government protection against change. There are certainly many instances in which private firms and SOEs chose to use their political clout to get government protection, and in some instances, they used their dependence on one environmental factor to acquire freedom of action on another front (Aharoni, Maimon and Segev, 1978). Thus, SOEs that were not allowed to reduce their labor force exploited this weakness to negotiate with governments for more subsidies and protection thus increasing autonomy and managerial discretion.

MANAGERIAL DISCRETION

Managerial discretion is the most valued of SOE managerial rewards (Aharoni, 1981a), in particular since bonuses are infrequently given. Success brings a manager a high level of discretion, possibilities of future promotion in the same organization or outside the organization, increased mobilty (discretion in selecting a future employer) and alternative opportunities.

Managerial discretion is decision-specific. An SOE manager may have high discretion on expansion of operations for existing product lines but low discretion on diversification into new product lines. Managerial discretion is, therefore, a multidimensional entity, with each dimension relating to a specific but different decision area. The degree of managerial discretion also evolves with time. This can be examined at three different levels.

Formal discretion is the degree of discretion SOE managers have formally and officially (possibly even legally) for particular decisions. *Perceived discretion* is the degree of discretion managers perceive they have over particular decisions. For different decision areas, SOE managers believe their discretion is more or less in line with the rule book: overall, perceived discretion is likely to be less than formal discretion. Finally, SOE managers who, like most individuals, possess limited information-processing capability, may perceive their *actual degree of discretion* incorrectly.

To increase their discretion SOE managers can follow three types of strategies (see Pfeffer and Salancik, 1978). They can avoid control, reduce dependence and control the context of control. First, by avoiding control, the SOE manager does nothing to the environmental context of control but uses various substrategies to prevent this control from becoming constraining. This can be done by balancing various demands by playing one group off another explicitly (Pfeffer and Salancik, 1978, p. 96). Since SOEs are controlled by a variety of government offices and influenced by a plethora of other stakeholders, managers can use the demands of one shareholder to avoid attending to the demands of another. Employment demands justify loans, price control demands justify nonpayment of dividends, and increased wage demands justify higher prices.

Another way of avoiding control is by controlling the expression (but not the generation) of demands. By doing so, SOE management may completely avoid the need for balancing and paying sequential attention to demands. They can

> *manipulate the illusion of satisfaction to avoid the open expression of some demands . . . [or control] the extent to which interest groups have access to communication channels . . .*
>
> [Another] *method for managing demands is to define the request as being satisfied. In this situation, the organization controls the* [definition of] *satisfaction of its interest groups without losing discretion*

*over its behavior . . . The power to control its behavior is enhanced
to the extent that those making the demands are not well equipped
to determine when, or if, they have been met. [Pfeffer and Salancik,
1978, pp. 98 and 99]*

Government-imposed demands result from deliberations and negotiations
with SOE managers who are taking part in the formation of the demands to
which they will be expected to respond. These managers are usually the
professionals on the subject and set the standards and policies. They have a
monopoly on information and latitude in the choice of information for pre-
sentation and the timing of its release. They employ most of the experts on
these subjects. The electricity experts, who are employed by the electricity-
generating firm, know what can be expected or what the various energy-policy
alternatives are. The aviation experts are employed by the airlines, the oil
experts by the oil company, etc. The SOEs employ many more planners,
engineers and other experts than the controlling ministry. When a government considers whether or not to alter a policy, most of the information on
the consequences of such a change may come from the SOE which provides
the controllers with information to support its view. This situation does not
indicate that management avoids supplying information, although this practice is not unknown, or that it willingly distorts it. Belief in one's point of
view suffices for information to justify such a point of view.

The SOE management's expertise enables it to avoid control, more so
when no independent expertise exists. The government ministry or other interest groups lack the quality and quantity of information and experts to evaluate and prove that the SOE's information is incorrect. Consequently, the
SOE's investment plans are often evaluated only by their internal consistency
and plausibility. Even though there may be other possibilities, only this plan
is discussed, and it is extremely difficult for outsiders to offer different
proposals.

Even when monitoring of performance *ex post* shows persistent failure
to achieve the target, the controllers cannot know whether this is because of
overoptimistic forecasts or changing circumstances (for one formal model, see
Rees, 1984). Another way to avoid being influenced is not to possess the
capacity to comply with the demands being made. Thus, both the East African Harbours and East African Posts and Telecommunications have maintained fairly impressive commercial records without responding in radical
ways to political changes (Dresang and Sharkansky, 1975, p. 178). Their
managers have cited technical requirements to excuse their lack of compliance with political demands: because of the long lead time needed to design
and install port or telecommunication facilities, managers could "delay their
responses to specific political demands beyond the point where the politician's
purpose would be served" (*Ibid*, 1978, p. 179).

A second strategy is that of reduction of dependence. Under this strategy,
the context of control remains unchanged, but the SOE manager attempts to

decrease the organization's concrete dependence on external controlling bodies. Running a profitable operation is a major way to reduce organizational dependence. Profitable operations provide an internal source of funds for investment purposes, with managers approaching the ministers less often for additional financing, and as such the minister has less opportunity to control the discretion of these managers. Further, profitable operations provide the media as well as the members of Parliament with less reason to scrutinize them. The following illustration from Kenya appears to be representative of governmental outlook toward profitable versus unprofitable SOEs in virtually all countries:

> In Kenya, the policing of firms that are known to be profitable is done pro forma. In these firms, the financing of new investments is easily obtained from profits or from international credit. The government control tends to concentrate on the problematic cases, where there are financial problems or in cases in which rumors of a scandal are spread in private circles in Nairobi. [Sharkansky, 1975, p. 6]

SOE managers also attempt to diversify their operations to provide lucrative areas that can be used to cross-subsidize losses from other activities without having to go to the government. Further, the uncertainty and instability caused by dependence on one market may be reduced and autonomy increased by geographical and product expansion. Creating subsidiaries abroad reduces the dependence also because many controls do not apply abroad. When a country suffers from a shortage of foreign currency, international operations also allow more latitude. They also enable the SOE to use funds to help political parties or to invite dignitaries to visit the foreign facilities.

The third way managers can increase discretion is by changing the context of control. In some cases, SOE managers have even participated in the process of drafting the legislation that created the SOE they were later to manage (Ramamurti, 1985a). Some of the strategies outlined earlier such as vertical integration and diversification not only serve to reduce dependence within the given context of control but also change the very context of control by redefining the boundaries of the enterprise. SOE autonomy can also be increased by co-optation of the controlling bodies, political lobbying, aligning the media on the side of the SOE, or using other methods of building a separate power base.

These three methods of increasing discretion are somewhat contradictory. Thus, managers attempting to increase discretion by agreeing to avoid reducing the work force need funds to pay their workers, thereby reducing profitability. If an SOE already has low autonomy, its dismal performance may be a cause for increased managerial discretion so that government will not be solely responsible for the bad performance (Anastassopoulos, 1973). The degree of discretion managers enjoy depends on many factors including longevity in command, direct contacts with the prime minister and techno-logical expertise that makes it hard to replace them.

Some SOE managers, mainly the empire builders, were able to amass enormous political power and use it to build new business. Thus, Robert Moses began his career in 1924 in an innocuous organization, the Long Is-land State Park Commission, of which he was the first president. Over the next 44 years of his career, he was instrumental in creating several SOEs and built a power base that made the mayor of New York afraid of him. Enrico Mattei's legendary power has been described. Sir Adam Beck, the first man-ager of Ontario Hydro, ran it for 20 years "as a personal fiefdom":

> He did not hesitate to play off the Ontario legislature against the municipalities, who were in one sense joint owner of the total com-plex, or, when circumstances were different, the municipalities against the legislature. Although he took full advantage of the weight of government, he was much less amenable to public con-straints and accountability. [Gordon, 1981, p. 22]

Ozires Silva of Brazil steered through the government a proposal to de-velop a Brazilian turboprop plane, established EMBRAER and expanded it into a full-line, internationally competitive general aviation enterprise, ex-porting half its production.

SOEs are often monopolies, operating in salient industries. The crucial importance of these SOEs to the economic well-being of the country means they are subject to thorough scrutiny from the media, the Parliament and the government, which theoretically reduces managerial discretion. At the same time, their size, the resources they control and their control of information often give their managers enormous power.

Some observers familiar with SOEs (Robson, 1962 Ch. IV, VI; Hanson 1963, Ch. 7; Clegg and Chester, 1953, Herbert Commission, 1956, paras. 492-9; Narain, 1982.) feel their managers have less discretion than their counterparts in private enterprises, except at the technical level at which man-agerial discretion is equal irrespective of ownership. Others claim that SOE managers enjoy much more discretion. To a large extent, these differences are culture-bound. In addition, they depend not only on the way managers are recruited but mainly on whether the manager relates to a more general market for managers or sees his or her career path to be only in the public sector and therefore bound to be influenced by political patronage.

CONFLICTS

The more managers perceive their roles to be protecting the firm from polit-ical intervention, the greater the probability of an open conflict with their controllers. Although most SOE managers may lose their jobs if they resist the government's directives, many conflicts exist between SOEs' management and their governments, stemming from disagreement about objectives and policies. In some cases, the SOE's interest prevails; in others, the government wins. In still others, a compromise is reached. In Canada, government officials wanted the CDC to bail out the ailing Massey Ferguson, but CDC directors refused (Stanbury and Thompson, 1982, p. 217). Renault stunned the French government by granting its employees a fourth week of holiday, and "several prominent members of government wanted Mr. Dreyfus's head . . . but he was not dismissed. [General de Gaulle] granted him the liberty to succeed" (Anastassopoulos, in Vernon and Aharoni, 1981, p. 111). Conversely, the French government supported the Agency for Energy Savings against the powerful EDF, directing the firm "to immediately stop any publicity favoring the consumption of electricity" (p. 106). An example of a compromise is the U.K. government's granting Inmos money needed for its U.S. investment, while Inmos located a new plant according to government wishes and against its economic judgment.

In Canada, when scrap prices rose in the late 1960s, the management of Sidbec decided to build furnaces that could utilize iron ore pellets instead of scrap. Sidbec could have obtained the 1.5 million tons of pellets it needed either by investing about $50 million in a Brazilian mining company or by mining the iron ore from the Fire Lake deposits on the north shore of the St. Lawrence River. Sidbec's CEO, Jean Paul Gignac:

> [i]nformally consulted Premier Robert Bourassa, members of his Cabinet, and the Leader of the Opposition; they all told him that investing in Brazil was out of the question when iron ore was available on the north shore. The government's decision was also influenced by the plight of Gagnon, a north shore community of 4,000 that "would have disappeared from the face of the map" if Sidbec had not proceeded with the Fire Lake mine. The town's major employer, an iron ore mining company, was, after sixteen years, closing up its operations in the area. [Gordon, 1981, p. 146]

The final cost of the Fire Lake Project was about $630 million. This huge investment left Sidbec with insufficient funds to modernize its more profitable fabricating facilities.

In many cases, investment decisions are based on similar informal, rarely publicized consultations between management and government. Conflicts occur and compromises are reached *in camera*, far from the public eye.

Anastassopoulos (in Vernon and Aharoni, 1981) suggests that the result of the conflict depends on the salience of the issue to the government and the SOE. Of course, if the issue is very salient to the SOE but not to the government, the SOE will show self-confidence. Conversely, if the issue is very important to the government but has low salience for the SOE, the result is submission by the firm. If both the government and the SOE are convinced the decision is essential to their respective goals, the result will be intransigence. Here, "all means of persuasion and action may affect the final issue. . . . Conflict resolution would be better managed if the relationships between state-owned enterprises and government were structured in a set of rules agreed upon and adhered to by both parties" (p. 114). Indeed, the French experimented with the idea of program contracts.

The concept of a program contract for SOEs was first introduced in France in the late 1960s, on the recommendation of the Nora Committee, for increased autonomy for SOEs. In an effort to enhance autonomy, the French government attempted to write a series of contracts between the government and the enterprises. These agreements set up the objectives the enterprises were expected to meet and in return accorded the enterprises freedom to organize and manage their affairs. Even in these contracts, much less freedom was granted for new investments. The first two contracts were negotiated with EDF (electricity) and SNCF (railways). In the case of EDF, the program contract committed the enterprise to carry out an agreed investment program, stay within debt/equity ceilings and realize an eight percent rate of return on investment, five percent rate of growth in total labor productivity and one percent growth in the ratio of net income to sales. In return, EDF was given the liberty to set prices within the average ceiling determined by government. The government also granted the enterprise greater freedom from intervention in its operations, in the use of its earnings and in the autonomy necessary to establish subsidiaries, as well as loan guarantees and compensation for performing specified social obligations.

These contracts, however, had to be abandoned because no one foresaw the oil crisis when they were written. The provisions for revisions built into them were found to be inadequate. The uncertainty and ignorance under which governmental operations are carried out turned out to be an obstinate problem, and commitments have not proved durable under changing economic and political environments. In 1978 and 1979, four more contracts were signed (for a description, see Anastassopoulos, 1980, pp. 161–183) and later abandoned. Since the Mitterrand government came into power in 1982, it has made several major reversals of policies. In 1983 and 1984, ten more contracts were negotiated. Later, facing severe economic problems, the government shifted from a policy of artificial employment boosting subsidized by the state to a modernization program, even at the cost of shedding tens of thousands of workers. SOE managers were put on notice that unless they could achieve profits by the end of 1985, they would be sacked.

These changes in governmental policies certainly affect managerial discretion in SOEs, but it is difficult to imagine a government willing to continue honoring a contract when it feels the need for such major changes. In an uncertain world changes are inevitable—in state-owned as well as in private enterprises—but it might be reasonable to expect that changes would be introduced only after consultation and attempts to reach consensus.

Finally, SOEs are, after all, instruments for the advancement of broader policy objectives, not only commercial undertakings. In the words of the Canadian Privy Council report (1977), each of these corporations "must pursue whatever national objectives are defined by Parliament" (p. 22).

Mr. Boiteux, the CEO of EDF, admits the program contract is not a panacea but feels it has certain advantages. It has

> [T]he merit of obliging the government to tell us in writing what our function is supposed to be . . . I said at the time, rather rudely, that this had merit of transferring control from the rash to the rational. Another thing is that it is a good thing to provide this very proper protection for heads of public undertakings in the exercise of their duty, who were entitled to be judged objectively and not by prejudice. Another advantage . . . is that it gave us an opportunity of thrashing out with our supervising ministers a description of a possible future which, following discussions, became our norm of development . . . In contrast, when later on we had no program contract, we were once again left without any very clear statement of our duties . . . there is no getting away from the very fact that the State or the authorities do not willingly make their directives public. This may be so that they can change them without losing face . . . or because this gives some civil servants the enviable power of knowing what is unknown to the man with responsibility. . . . The second problem . . . was that the decisions on the future development of EDF were continually being revised. . . . When something urgent crops up and we take it to this or that Ministry it has other things to do and has no time to spare for us. [In Annals, 1981, pp. 173–174]

The NEDO report noted, "There is a marked absence of common purpose, trust and understanding between government departments and many of the major nationalized industries. In extreme cases, the result is a continuous covert conflict which occasionally erupts into the public view" (1976, p. 42). When there are no official directives or contracts, these conflicts are solved by a process of negotiation and consultation. To gain more leeway and achieve their goals, SOE managers learn to balance the management of their firms with the management of the environment.

To reiterate, some accounts of SOE managers portray them as very powerful; others see them as apathetic or as instruments of the government. In reality, all these types of managers may be found in SOEs, depending on the perception of the manager as to his or her career path, beliefs and background. Certain managers see themselves as professionals, feel they are evaluated by the market for managers and are ready to hold managerial positions in different sectors of the economy; others perceive their career path to be in the public sector, shifting from government bureaucracy to SOE management. Some are driven into the public service by patriotism, others by "ambition, the wish to command, to be admired, to be famous" (Bismarck, in Jay, 1968, pp. 180–181). Those emphasizing political loyalty are submissive to government wishes, and they may aim for the minimum excusable rather than the maximum possible in terms of economic achievements. Some are extremely ideologically inclined, doing their work in accordance with the standards of the party, and can be trusted to do what is good for the party. Others are feudal barons to whom the government is a menace. They fight each other but unite as one interest group against what they perceive to be government intervention. For them, to quote Jay, "withheld information and unreferred decisions are the bricks that corporation barons build their castles with" (1968, p. 42). Some of them amass political power of their own, others keep the government happy on certain fronts to gain autonomy on others. In responding to political demands, they may choose their high-priority clientèle from a variety of strong groups. They can cite technical reasons as excuses for lack of compliance with political demands. They may also be in a situation where the government in power is controlled by economic groups that prefer economic goals for SOEs.

The autonomy managers have cannot be interpreted by a simple account of the decisions they make. First, managers may perceive themselves to have less autonomy than they do in fact have and, therefore, will refrain from following certain lines of action. Second, the decisions as recorded in official minutes of the board of directors or similar official documents are reached only after a long process of informal negotiations, most of which takes place within cloistered confines and are rarely published. Third, managers may perceive their autonomy to be greater than it is, simply because they never made decisions in a way the government felt was wrong. Managers scout and explore—not unlike boxers in a ring—to find out how far they can go and what is the potential power of the different players in the external coalition. Only when they are mistaken, and a scandal erupts, is the actual limit of their power known.

In most cases, there is an evolution, whereby the power of the managers increases with time. However, sometimes the manager overestimates the degree of autonomy he or she has. In such cases, the manager is replaced or loses autonomy. If the overshooting also meant a political embarrassment or a scandal, the public outcry may mean that the autonomy of all SOE managers will be curtailed. With time, however, the cycle starts again, with new managers gaining more power of their own because of the information they hold and their expertise, and the pendulum swings toward more autonomy.

Not all good managers know how to manage in such a political environment. Some may simply refuse to work for SOEs. Managers used to the culture of a private enterprise find it extremely difficult to work in an SOE. The attributes of private-sector environment, according to Bower (1983, p. 25), are "the power of the purse; the power to hire and fire, the ability to operate out of the corrosive glare of the press, the ability to limit objectives so that they can be achieved, the time to study, organize and act efficiently." Even in private enterprise the increasing intervention and social legislation has fundamentally altered the nature of top management job. Nevertheless, some managers are attracted by the ability to build empires, to ignore short-term costs and quarterly financial statements and to set policy that affects the whole country. These are the effective SOE managers, who also gain their own power base. These managers may also dominate their environment and control the board of directors.

THE BOARD OF DIRECTORS

The term *board of directors* is used for different institutions. In the United Kingdom, the board works full time in the company. In continental Europe (and in Egypt), a two-tier board is legally prescribed: a supervisory board is often staffed with political appointees, but the SOE is run by its executive board. In other countries, board members have full-time occupations elsewhere and do not always come to the meetings.

There are as many opinions on the role of the board of directors as there are on the question of the role of SOEs in society (Robson, 1962, Ch. IX; Seidman, 1952; Acton Society Trust, 1951; Appleby, 1956; Gorwala, 1951; Lord Simon of Wythenshawe, 1957). Since the board is expected to direct the enterprise, the points of view on its role depend on the beliefs on the role of the SOEs. The most extreme of these opinions is that a board is not needed. If the SOE is believed to be mainly a policy tool in the hands of the government, it is sensible to claim that a board is not needed. If a board is legally required, it should be staffed by the minister as chair (and this is the practice in many LDCs and in Canada) and representatives of the minister as members.

The other extreme point of view stresses the autonomy of the SOE and the need to isolate it from political intervention. (e.g. Coronel, 1983; Dimmock, 1949.) The board is expected to act as a buffer between the supervisory ministry (and other ministries) and the SOE top management, representing and protecting the interests of the SOE at higher governmental levels and in broad national planning from too much outside interference. According to this view, the board should be the major organ of controlling the SOE and should be composed of persons with business experience who are not dependent on ministers. Each director should be a trustee of the corporation, not of its shareholders or the minister, and should be allowed to take into consideration other interests only if they are for the good of the company.

These two extreme points of view are reflected in the diametrically opposed recommendations sometimes made about all matters related to the board: composition, nominations, compensation, tenure, reasons for firing directors, loyalty and conflicts of interest.

Neither extreme takes into account the hybrid nature of the SOE. The first sees the SOE only as a government instrument, the second, only as an enterprise selling its output. Some of the believers in the autonomy point of view reconcile the problem of the public interest almost naively by assuming "that there was a partnership of identity of interest between government and corporations and that board members would do what was right in the public interest as a matter of course" (NEDO, 1976, appendix volume, p. 82).

Given this point of view, the board becomes the most important organ in the direction and control of the SOE:

> *Even to the most casual observer it is obvious that the selection of members of the Boards of nationalised industries is a matter of great importance. Unless Board members are skillful, enterprising and able to cooperate harmoniously, the nationalised industries will not be run as efficiently as they should [Acton Society Trust, 1951, p. 1].*

> *The governing board occupies a position of crucial importance in the direction and management of a nationalised industry. The success or failure of a nationalisation is, indeed, likely to depend more on the quality and composition of the boards directing the public corporations than on any other single factor [Robson, 1962, p. 212].*

In Israel the Government Companies Law specified in detail [Section 32(a)] the mandatory functions of the board as the following:

1. *Determine the general policy of the company within the scope of objects, and its financial activities;*
2. *Determine each year*
   a) *the annual budget of the company, the manner of its implementation and the use of the resources at the company's disposal;*
   b) *the company's plan of operations for that year and its long-range plans;*
   c) *the company's establishment of employees and the persons engaged in its service;*
3. *Follow up continuously the implementation of the company's policy, plans and budgets;*
4. *Determine, in accordance with rules prescribed by the Government and with its approval, the pay, social security conditions, benefits, gratuities and other conditions of employment of the general manager, the deputy general manager and the assistant general managers, the departmental managers, the financial manager, the internal controller, the secretary of the company and other office-holders designated in that behalf by the Ministers after consultation with the Authority (all the aforementioned herein collectively referred to as "the senior officials") and of the other employees of the company;*
5. *Approve, on the recommendation of the general manager, the appointment of the senior officials in accordance with the establishment;*

6. Consider the draft financial reports of the company and the comments of the auditors upon them and, after approval of the financial reports, consider each item in respect of which the auditor has expressed a reservation, made an observation or refrained from expressing an opinion;
7. Approve the grant of loans and deposit of moneys which deviate from the ordinary course of the company's business;
8. Consider any matter which the Minister or the Authority have or has requested to be put on the agenda or of which the general manager has given notice under Section 41.

What if, despite basic identity of interests, different persons perceive the situation differently? After all, occupying different roles may be enough reason to perceive a situation differently. Morrison (1933) did not have a convincing answer, except the theory that the activities of the SOEs can be conveniently divided between matters of policy on the one hand and matters of day-to-day administration on the other, and the latter from the sacred private domain of the boards.

The feasibility of making any kind of clear distinction between policy-level and operational decisions has been questioned by many observers. Hannah, e.g., notes:

The supposed division between "general policy" as a matter for the Minister and "detailed execution" as a matter for the Boards—which was implicit in much earlier discussion of the public corporation—proved in practice to be meaningless. . . . a wide range of managerial decision-making was subject to ministerial intervention, while over substantial areas of "general" policy ministerial views made no significant impact. . . . The long, arduous and structured process of conflict over the annual budgets gave the mandarins a chance to probe detailed questions of rural electrification, delays in connecting particular consumers, hire–purchase, finance and other relatively minor areas [1982, p. 58].

Even if a clear distinction between the general (or policy level) and the day-to-day (or operational) was possible, there is little to prevent the minister from exercising informal influence over operational decision-making. As Phatak notes in the case of India:

There is excessive ministerial control over the Public Sector firms. Control is exercised informally through the board of directors. By virtue of the fact that the ministers have the power to appoint or remove the board members, makes the board members "captives" of the appointing ministers. . . . The typical managing director of a Public Sector firm is subject to a continuous barrage of directives from the board members acting on behalf of the various ministries represented on the Board. . . . Ministers thus enjoy authority without the corresponding responsibility, whereas just the opposite is the

> *position of the managing director who is held accountable for all the*
> *actions that follow decisions made in his name by the ministers via*
> *the board members.* [1969, pp. 342–343]

In the United Kingdom, the nationalized industries were expected to be managed, directed and controlled by their independent boards, which were expected to follow good commercial practice. Indeed, most of the directors were recruited from private industry and had considerable business experience.

In many countries, board members represent the environment to management, not vice versa. They were each appointed to be the guardian of the rights of some specific constituent group. They do not necessarily have an appreciation of the industry as a whole or an adequate grasp of its complexities. They do not have time to learn the intricacies of the business and are not interested in devoting the time. Board members who perceive their role as representatives of a constituency measure their effectiveness in terms of the concessions granted to the group they represent. If they represent the farmers on the board of an electricity firm, lower rates to their constituency are a measure of success as a director (Aharoni, 1963). Boards of wholly owned SOEs in Canada have frequently served "as a tool of patronage towards the party faithful" (Langford, 1979, p. 257; see also Peterson, 1977, pp. 156–157).

In India, about 60 percent of the board members are government officials, and many listed as nonofficials are either retired government civil servants, ex-ministers or defeated politicians. These selection criteria create boards of directors that are extremely vulnerable to government interference. The same pattern is found in many other countries.

In describing the boards of parastatals in Africa, Ghai writes:

> *The civil servants who sit on the boards are senior bureaucrats, who*
> *can devote only limited time to the affairs of the parastatals. . . .*
> *Decisions are made more by the circulation of the file, which collects*
> *marginal comments as it winds its way around the corridors; initia-*
> *tive and aggressive policies are shunned in favour of caution and*
> *indecision; and there is undue emphasis on procedure at the expense*
> *of substance. The problem is aggravated by the rules whereby success*
> *is defined and rewarded, for these too travel over from the depart-*
> *ment, so that the important consideration becomes the avoidance of*
> *risk and possible mistake. Promotion comes in due course if nothing*
> *untoward (albeit nothing spectacular either) has happened.* [In
> Reddy, 1983, p. 195–196).

An expert committee nominated in Israel to propose the Government Companies Act suggested the following solution: The SOE should be directed to behave as any private enterprise, unless the government specifically directs it to behave differently. At the same time, it felt that "existing law does not reflect in a proper way the desired dependence between the State as the owner of the controlling shares in an SOE and the board it nominates." (Barak Commission p. 32) The desired dependence, the committee thought, is to allow the state, through its organs, the power to direct the SOE on how it should act to execute the public objectives entrusted to it. This power would ensure not only the performance of the national objectives but also parliamentary control and review on the operations of the SOEs. According to the commission's prescriptions, SOE management should be required to follow a ministerial directive only if it is issued in writing, and the economic cost to the SOE of any social benefit requirements should be identified, assessed and paid back to the SOE in some form of subsidy. The politicians, however, rejected this prescription. Ministers are not allowed today to give written directives. There is little, however, that prevents them from exercising informal influence. Because directors are regarded as representatives of ministries, managers often withhold information from them. Since the representative may have authority in his or her role as a civil servant to approve the SOE's budget or to procure its products, management try to avoid giving this person too detailed data, fearing the information gained will be used in the negotiations on prices paid by the ministry. In some countries, directors receive compensation for their work, and nomination as a director has become a way of conferring patronage or of giving extra income to civil servants or military officers. The directors are invariably senior officials who perceive their roles as conveying the ministry's point of view and monitoring information.

A change of government is often followed by a massive change of SOE directors. Phatak (1969) cites a study according to which, in fifty-three firms studied, 72 percent of the board members had been replaced in a 3-year period by new members; over a 5-year period, 86 percent had been replaced. The average tenure of board members is only 14 months, whereas in the private sector the average tenure is more than six years. In one Indian SOE, Hindustan Machine Tools Ltd., eleven board appointments lasted less than a year (pp. 341–342).

Nevertheless, in some cases, the nomination of directors is made for very long periods. One well-known, albeit vary rare, example is that of the TVA, whose directors are nominated for nine years. They are not attached to any department of the government. Theoretically, their immediate superior is the president of the United States. In practice, however, since the president is a very busy person, the TVA is run by the directors almost independently. The TVA was not very well received by many and has suffered many attacks, lawsuits and a congressional investigation (in 1938 to 1939) into its conduct. It is sometimes described as a branch of the government that does not have to answer to anyone and is a perpetual irritant to conservatives. TVA's unique charter places all power to set rates with the board and has freed this SOE from regulations. It needs approval from Washington, D.C., only when it seeks to extend its borrowing power, as happened several times, but otherwise it is extremely autonomous, with managerial discretion much greater than in other SOEs in Europe or in LDCs. The two major reasons for the autonomy seem to be the long tenure of its very small board of directors and the fact that it generates its revenue from operations.

In most SOEs, top management is neither chosen nor replaced by the board. The board plays two conflicting roles simultaneously. On the one hand, it serves as an agent of the government, representing it to management. On the other hand, it acts as a protector of management against undue government interventions and to insulate SOEs from pernicious external effects.

The level of involvement and effectiveness of the board of directors depends primarily on the distribution of power among three agents: the sponsoring minister, the chairperson and the managing director. Active and powerful ministers may extend their ministerial responsibility over the companies under their control and determine the detailed operations of their companies. Strong chairpersons may have considerable power to perform most of the CEO's tasks. Powerful CEOs may well dominate the board's activities. The control of the SOE is often in the hands of the active managers, who devote all their time to it, while a director devotes very little or no time at all. An entrepreneurial manager takes big risks, and the compensation for his or her labors is advancement, prestige, power or political capital.

CONCLUSION

Managerial behavior is the result of situational and structural factors. One has to combine a study of administrative systems (such as recruitment, performance evaluation, incentives and job context) with key characteristics of important organizational factors (such as motivation, attitudes and perceptions) to understand the way organizations and their members behave. Another important variable is what perception managers have of their career path.

Managers of organizations are human beings, with feelings, aspirations, values, norms and goals. The greater the identity between the goals of the managers and those of the organization they are heading, the greater the probability that these managers will make an effort to create an effective organization. Thus, one determinant of behavior is values and beliefs. Certain SOE managers believe in the values of the public sector, adhere to the ideology of the government or perceive themselves as civil servants or army generals temporarily serving as managers of SOEs. Other managers perceive themselves as professional managers, serving the goals of the firm as they see them, and seeking their remunerations not only in pecuniary gains but also in their evaluations as good managers. Their major problem is "how to manage in a world where there are multiple influences from various levels of governments

. . . and where the corporation and its manager can in turn affect the direction of public policy and government action" (Freeman, 1984, p. 14).

SOE managers may be commissars or military people, both of whom see their career path to be in the public sector; entrepreneurs or empire builders, usually within the public sector, who are motivated by need achievements; engineers, who prefer to run the firm like any private firm, and leaders. Economists recommend using monetary incentives to achieve harmony between owners' goals and management behavior. In an SOE, the incentives used are power, identification with the party and service to the country. All managers see managerial discretion as important, but different types of managers may use different methods to achieve it: the commissars, by following directives of ministries; the entrepreneurs, by ignoring them, and the empire builders, by influencing them and creating their own political base.

The question of legitimacy of the SOE has become an important issue, at least as complex as that of the question of control of the larger U.S. business corporations. It was once believed that the firm should be controlled by its (public and private) owners and that legitimacy is established by a hierarchical chain from owners to the board of directors to the managers and down the organizational pyramid. With time, managers of both large private firms and SOEs came to be regarded as too powerful and the large corporation as too dominating, controlling its own environment. As the significant social consequences of highly concentrated economic power were realized, the call to tame the power of managers intensified. A new design is being sought to ensure accountability to the public without reducing motivation for effective management.

Neil H. Jacoby, in his study on multinational oil, claims:

> Profit-motivated enterprises are better adapted to accept the long risks and to allocate multinational investment than are governments. . . . Private management, disciplined by competition, brings a greater flexibility of operations and adaptability to changing circumstances than would civil servants to management of socialized oil firms. Being prepared to invest in any country, the multinational oil company seeks the most profitable—which is normally the most efficient—way to meet petroleum demands. [1974, p. 282]

However, British Petroleum, ENI and other state oil companies are also "prepared to invest in any country . . . to meet petroleum demands." In fact, Stobaugh tells us that managers of state-owned oil firms refused to respond to ministers, finding more important a tacit agreement on price and markets within their private-sector counterparts (1976, pp. 189–190). When the U.K. government joined other nations in declaring an economic boycott of Rhodesia after it had broken away from the United Kingdom, British Petroleum continued to supply oil to it. "British Government officials claimed that the company took advantage of complex dealings with intermediaries to keep its trade with Rhodesia hidden from its governmental masters" (Sharkansky, 1979, p. 9).

One major difference between SOEs and private firms is that SOEs are a part of a political system, and political intervention might be expected to create differences in managerial behavior, the objectives they try to achieve and other variables like collective bargaining. Another difference is that SOE managers are less motivated by pecuniary gains and more by scope for achievement, power, career opportunities and security. The particular importance of these factors is different among different managers—e.g., commissars valuing security more than others, entrepreneurs wanting achievement, and empire builders seeking political power. Different types of SOE managers also give different weights to the desires of their environment and allocate their time differently among different parties—external and internal.

The SOE is a part of an open system and is far from operating at arm's length from the political system. The SOE is a source of enormous power, and managers who learn how to use this power well actively gain more autonomy. A resourceful SOE manager does not see the government as a source of frustrations and constraints but as a source of opportunities and intelligence and a resource to be used to gain access to political power and establish an independent power base. They "learn to accept and manipulate levers of power in the government and refuse to view their business and regulatory environment as unalterable by them" (Khandwalla, 1984, p. 183).

CHAPTER 9

Privatization and its Alternatives

INTRODUCTION

In the 1950s and 1960s, governments found SOEs to be a convenient means to achieve all sorts of goals. In the 1970s, the growth of state participation in ailing industrial enterprises increased the burden on the state and led to a reevaluation of the role of SOEs. By the end of the 1970s, SOEs had accumulated mountainous losses and increased their borrowing. The problems of SOEs were traced to the influence of politics on corporate management, and the thesis that SOEs are instruments of the state that can be used to achieve numerous economic and noneconomic goals lost many of its supporters in the 1980s. The encouragement of private shareholdings to substitute for state participation was advocated. By the beginning of the 1980s, a tide of privatizations had begun to flow with unusual power in different parts of the world.

SOEs have been sold in the United Kingdom and Canada. Japan sold a part of its share in Nippon Telegraph and Telephone, France and Italy brought some of their SOEs to the stock exchange. Italy sold also its 17 percent equity in the giant chemical enterprise Montedison (*The Economist*, March 24, 1984, p. 72). Israel has sold about 50 of its SOEs since 1968. Mexico promised to privatize 236 of its approximately 550 SOEs to help make up for government income losses caused by the drop in the price of oil. In practice, sales are being made at a slow pace. As of February 1985, there have been only two major groups of transactions: the banks have sold shares in hundreds of firms in which they had bought equity before the 1982 nationalization (and a third of the equity of the banks is now to be offered for sale), and the state-owned Diesel International had sold parts of its operation. By the end of 1985, only 31 out of the 236 have actually gone up for sale (*The Economist*, December 21, 1985, p. 76).

Germany reduced its holdings in VEBA from 44 to 30 percent. Although its minister of finance faced opposition in attempting to sell Lufthansa, he announced a plan to cut federal holdings in Volkswagen from 20 to 14 percent and to sell shares in VIAG and in a state-owned bank (*The Economist*, October 6, 1985, p. 62). Japan announced its intention to sell part of its state-owned airline, and so did Thailand and Turkey. By the end of 1985, minority shares in state-owned airlines were sold by Italy, Malaysia and Singapore. Brazil sold part of PETROBRÃS, announcing its intention to divest 100 SOEs from a list of 520. In Africa, Togo sold a state-owned steel mill to a private buyer, Sudan privatized its airline, and Nigeria announced its intentions to sell certain SOEs. The list of privatizations is growing, and growing even more is the list of announcements of intended sales of SOEs from dozens of countries—both developed and developing.

Stripped of rhetoric, debates on denationalization (or privatization) hinge on the question of how best to channel funds to industry. Shortage of capital is a problem in most countries, and the state's financial burdens are awesome. If government policy is lower budget deficits and smoother funding of companies' cash reserves, selling SOEs' shares is one possibility. Other benefits expected from privatization are mainly increased efficiency because of competition, less political interference, reduced powers of trade unions, expanded range of opportunities for private enterprise and more funds to the government. This lends us to the key issue: would the private sector do a better job of running strategically placed industries? Is denationalization the philosopher's stone?

PRIVATIZATION

The word *privatization* covers a variety of policies. It has come to mean, first, the transfer of ownership: sales to private shareholders of state-owned assets and enterprises; second, introducing or increasing competition or reducing obstacles to it, in the hope of increasing efficiency; third, the encouragement of private provision of services that are currently provided collectively.

Other policies of the government also affect its SOEs. Thus, in the U.K., since November 1983, private suppliers can compete with British Telecom by providing all sorts of attachments to its network. Private long distance coach services compete with British Rail. The government also insists that the National Bus Company be split into small units to prevent its driving out competition from local routes.

Following the successful airline deregulation in the United States, the EEC commission proposed a liberalization of airline fare and a reduction of revenue-sharing agreements among European state-owned airlines. The airlines and their governments did not respond. In September 1985 the EEC transport commissioner said he will use the courts to apply the antitrust clauses of the treaty of Rome if airlines will not respond by June 1986 (*The*

Economist, September 28, 1985, p. 71). In this chapter we shall deal only with political, social and economic forces that accelerate, retard, narrow or enlarge the forces leading to sale of an SOE to the private sector.

Reasons for Privatization

How can the transfer of SOEs to private ownership be justified? To a large extent, the answer to this question is the same as the one dealt with in Chapter 3—namely, what are the origins of SOEs and the motivations for their creation? It has been shown that state ownership can be argued on the grounds of ideology, political power, social structure, economic reasoning and administrative considerations. The same motives are also true for privatization. At one extreme of the ideological spectrum, certain governments are ideologically committed to state ownership of the means of production, or to state ownership of natural resources. In this case, privatization is not seen as a viable alternative. At the other extreme, if one is ideologically committed to the idea that reduction of state power increases wealth, happiness and individual freedom, then one is sure the state should privatize all SOEs.

Since ideology is one reason for state ownership, it comes as no surprise that a change in regime causes a wave of privatization. Thus, the Conservative government in the United Kingdom privatized steel in the 1950s (and the Labour government renationalized in 1967). The Thatcher government, which is ideologically committed to reducing state power, privatized or intends to privatize even state-owned monopolies, believing (despite objective evidence) that a privately owned public utility would be more efficient than a state-owned one. It feels resources are better utilized in the private sector, free of political meddling.

If political considerations are the reason, then privatizations may be a result of changing power of different actors. South Korea's substantial sale of SOEs in the 1980s were also linked to free-enterprise ideology (UNIDO, 1983, p. 10). In Canada, the Conservative government "genuinely believed that there should be less government and that selling some Crown corporations to private buyers would signal in a concerete way their philosophical preferences" (Tupper and Doern, 1981, p. 42). They drew a list of SOEs for sale. When the liberals returned to power in 1980, they put the privatization much lower on their political priority list. Ideological shift, however, is usually insufficient by itself to cause large-scale privatization. In Ghana after Nkrumah's regime was overthrown by a military coup, the government offered for sale 30 SOEs. The SOEs, however, were considered poor risks by the business community and only three were sold (three more became joint stock companies) (Pozen, 1972, p. 824).

In Pakistan the People's party assumed power in December 1971. At that time, the SOE sector comprised 4.2 percent of GDP. In January 1972, the Economic Reforms Order identified ten categories of basic industries that "bear upon the life of every citizen and form the base without which no industrial development in the real sense can take place" (in Jones, 1981c, p.I-4). A series of nationalizations followed: 32 manufacturing units (January 1972); life insurance firms (March 1972); vegetable oil (ghee) factories (September 1972); all banks, petroleum marketing and shipping companies (January 1974) and about 2,000 rice, flour and cotton ginning mills in July 1976. By 1974-75, the SOE sector's share in GDP had reached 7.7 percent. However, in July 1977, the regime was replaced by a military government. The ideological nationalizations of 1972 to 1974 were followed by privatizations of some 2,000 small-scale decentralized units in rice, flour and cotton-ginning mills in September 1977. In September 1978, more SOEs were returned to their original owners (Jones et al., 1982, p. 24).

In Chile the wave of nationalization by the Allende regime was followed by a massive divestment after his fall. The military government that assumed power in 1973 returned 259 firms to the original owners. In addition, 133 SOEs and 21 banks were sold between 1974 and 1982 (Shirley, 1983, p. 57, table 6).

An added incentive for privatization may be an attempt to reduce the public deficit. In Peru, the deteriorating economic situation from 1970 to 1975 caused the overall deficit in the public sector (including SOEs) to grow from 1.4 percent of the GNP to 11.6 percent. The uncoordinated and unplanned expansion of the SOE sector was a major cause of the economic problems:

> By the time the constitutional government was restored in 1980, it was a foregone conclusion that at least some moves towards privatization and denationalization would enjoy support from an important segment of the political spectrum . . . the issue was . . . less charged with political passion than was the case of Argentina, Chile and Uruguay—maybe even less tense than the brief controversy over the state's economic role that erupted in Mexico before Echeverria left office or than the more recent electoral contest in Jamaica. [Glade, in Reddy, 1983, p. 78]

Soaring public-sector deficits have been a major inducement for the sale of SOEs. Thus, the Italian economy in 1985 is suffering the burden of a huge public deficit that could suffocate it. One reaction was attempts to sell non-strategic parts of IRI. It sold several companies and banks and listed another 13 in the stock exchange, retaining a stake in them (*The Economist*, September 14, 1985, p. 23), raising $1.6 billion from 1983 to August 1985 (*ibid*, December 21, 1985, p. 8).

Privatization of SOEs not strictly needed to correct market imperfections or to attend the demands of national security was used in other countries, too, as means of reducing the public sector's borrowing requirements. In the 1960s, SOEs and governments could easily receive funds from the Eurodollar market. In the 1970s, banks—anxious to recycle petrodollars—granted many loans. In the early 1980s, the alarming size of the national debt in many countries caused demands to reduce it.

In the seven largest industrial countries, outstanding debt increased from 40 percent of GNP in 1970 to 51 percent in 1983, and government interest payments rose from 1.9 percent of GNP in 1970 to a forecast 5.2 percent for 1985. Public debt increased in Japan from 12 percent of GNP in 1970 to 67 percent in 1983. In Belgium, for the same period, the rise was from 73 to 116 percent of GNP (*The Economist*, February 2, 1985, p. 65).

Since real interest rates rose in the 1970s and economic growth slowed down, the burden of the public debt became higher. In Latin America, governments have foreign debts they cannot service on time, high inflation and big budget deficits. About 70 percent of Mexico's $96 billion foreign debt has been contracted by the government and its agencies. In Brazil, $65 billion out of a $100 billion foreign debt is owed by SOEs.

The recent explosion of international debt caused multilateral donors, such as the World Bank and the IMF, to focus more sharply on SOEs' economic performance. International authorities are disillusioned with the ability of SOEs to be efficient and are alarmed by the size of their deficits. These institutions have predicated loans on a very strict set of guidelines that include in the 1980s the selling, elimination and rehabilitation of SOEs. Thus, the net losses of the SOE sector in Turkey in 1977 to 1979 were equal to 3.9 percent of GDP. Given the level of the economic problems in Turkey and the near collapse of the state-owned sector, the IMF pressed for fast privatization. The same is true in Latin America and in the Philippines. Within the countries, the increasing need to recycle the debt caused concerns that it may drain capital from private investments. Governments, therefore, are faced with the acute need to cut their structural deficits by cutting spending, raising taxes or selling some state-owned assets. Raising taxes is politically unpalatable, and cutting government spending has proven to be extremely difficult. Selling assets is a much more popular way to raise funds and roll back the frontiers of the state.

The Reagan administration in the United States started in 1985 the so-called Private Sector Initiative (PSI), infusing funds to African countries contingent upon the institution of more liberal economic policies, including the selling of SOEs. Unfortunately, selling the most burdensome SOEs is not an easy task. Such firms may have to be sold at a sizable discount, and even then the prospects for sale are not very propitious.

Most governments, as shown in Chapter 3, nationalize for pragmatic reasons, reacting to *ad hoc* problems. These countries privatize on a discriminating basis. If a government sees in state ownership a pragmatic solution to certain problems, then it should rescind ownership once the original reason for state ownership disappears for one of the following reasons:

1. The stated objectives were achieved;
2. The objectives were revealed as unfeasible;
3. The objectives are no longer essential to the public interest because of revised priorities;

4.   The task was entrusted to other public bodies;
5.   The task can and will be done by nongovernmental bodies.

Another reason for state ownership is the initiation of new activities that the private sector was unwilling to undertake. A number of developing countries including Argentina, Bangladesh, Brazil, Bolivia, Chile, Ghana, Kenya, Malaysia, Mexico, Nepal, the Republic of Korea, Saudi Arabia, Senegal, Singapore, Sri Lanka, Turkey and Thailand have pursued a policy or expressed a desire to sell industrial SOEs to the private sector once the pioneering role of the government has been discharged or because they have fared poorly. This policy is said to enable the government to use its limited financial, managerial and other resources to pioneer new ventures. Thus, President Mobutu in Zaire indigenized foreign business holdings in the mid-1970s, compelling a transfer to private Zairians. The decline in economic activity led President Mobutu to nationalize these firms. This, too, proved unworkable and many assets were sold back to private owners. In other cases, as in the Ivory Coast, government found it impossible to find buyers.

In many countries, the government became the owner of a certain enterprise because it had guaranteed a loan for which the assets of the corporation were collateral. A default on the loan, not any social, political or economic arguments, forced the government to exercise its rights to take over the assets. It seems reasonable to suppose that the government would attempt to sell such an enterprise at the first opportunity. The government may have become an owner because of mismanagement of the previous private owners and its political sensitivity to employment questions, regional development or other political considerations. Here the main objective is to restore the enterprise's economic health; once this is achieved, there is no reason to continue state ownership. In Italy, many firms were acquired by the state-owned GEPI to salvage them. From 1971 to 1980, GEPI intervened in cases involving 58,000 employees. After they were returned to profitable operations, sixty-six firms, involving 16,536 employees, were sold (Fausto, 1982, p. 21). In other cases, the government became a reluctant owner of SOEs because of the inability of the private sector to supply funds or entrepreneurship at crucial junctions of the development process. This was the case, for example, of steel in Brazil (Trebat, 1983, p. 44). If, at a later stage, private enterprise can supply these resources and absorb the risk, privatization is a logical consequence.

Further, some peripheral investments in the portfolio of the state may be sold. Thus, after each wave of nationalization it is found that the nationalized firms have had certain subsidiaries that were unintentionally acquired as part of the deal. In such cases these subsidiaries are divested. This was the case in France after the large number of nationalizations of the Mitterrand government in February 1982. In the United Kingdom, Thomas Cook and Sons, a travel agency, was acquired as part of the assets of the British Railways Company and sold in 1971. Zealous SOE managers may have diversified into fields that are seen as less important for their major mission. Such odd components of the SOE sector are usually the first candidates for privatization. Yet they are a very small portion of the SOE sector in terms of assets and investments. The large SOEs are generally the public utilities; very large, capital-intensive infrastructure firms, often yielding low return on the capital invested, oil and other minerals and firms important for strategic reasons.

It is sometimes argued that "the main aim of privatization is to guide resources to the most highly valued uses" (Beesley and Littlechild, 1983, p. 8). Government ownership, it is argued, means that the enterprise policy reflects short-term political pressures, not attempts for efficiency.

If private enterprises are perceived as being more efficient by definition, then there would not have been a reason for state ownership in the first place. However, it is clear from the evidence presented in Chapter 5 that private ownership does not always mean lower costs. The comparison of SOEs to utopian atomistic competition in friction-free and risk-free markets with full and free information is irrelevant. The sale of large SOEs to private investors will not diminish their size. It is at least unclear whether the visible hand of private firms enjoying monopolistic status or operating in an oligopolistic situation is more efficient than the visible hand of the state.

Privatization of public utilities may cause some additional problems. If one allows competition on the very profitable activities, cross-subsidization practices cannot continue. Whether or not they should is a different matter. Why should express buses subsidize rural bus services or long-distance phone callers subsidize rural telephone services? However, as long as cross-subsidies are used, it is difficult to privatize portions of a public utility. If the whole firm is privatized, shareholders will want a certain guaranteed rate of return on their investment, and prices will have to be raised.

The price the government can get for selling a monopoly is certainly higher than what it would receive if it discontinued the monopoly powers of the SOE. The value of one British Telecom is much greater than that of four competing ones after breaking its monopoly. In fact, the U.K. government offered for sale 51 percent of British Telecom in October 1984 as one company. In this case, at least, the government preferred the higher proceeds from the sale over the economic benefits of increased competition—one indication that the sale was motivated by fiscal policy considerations. When an SOE is large and capital-intensive, operating in heavy industry, private entrepreneurs "accustomed to a quick return on their investments" (Trebat, 1983, p. 69) are not attracted to these firms. The government may find it hard to find buyers, and may be reluctant to sell such important sources of political patronage.

In some countries, e.g., Brazil, the military plays an important role. It "is unlikely, in any foreseeable future, to permit the auctioning off of any state firm in which it had a hand either in establishing or running" (Trebat, 1983, p. 69). In other countries, the populist sentiment may run against selling SOEs that are dependent on the defense budget to purchase its output.

If the capacity of the country to manage its SOEs is insufficient, the execrable performance of some SOEs may raise grave questions about the competency of the SOE sector to manage these firms. The dearth of managerial talent may be a reason for privatization. Indeed, when COROMERCADEO in Venezuela found itself unable to manage its retail outlets without huge losses, it privatized them (Austin, 1984, p. 46). Many SOEs use private distributors to handle wholesaling and retailing. In many cases, however, the claims that private enterprise is more efficient is based more on ideology than on facts. Coal and railroads in Britain "had been suffering from serious mismanagement under private enterprise for about thirty years. They had been going downhill from almost every point of view" (Robson, 1962, p. 222).

One reason given for privatization is the claim that competition has more effect on private enterprise because it has to satisfy the capital markets, while SOE managers feel they can draw on the resources of the state. However, governments bailed out many private firms. The management of any large firm may now feel assured that it can take certain risks because it assumes the government will bail it out. Moreover, the SOE may continue to operate despite losses, but its CEO may be fired. In many cases the government did continue the operations of an SOE despite a heavy drain on the public purse but changed the managers, as the French government did in Renault. Whether the actions against complacent management are greater in the private than in the public sector is an empirical question, on which information is insufficient.

It is sometimes argued that government indulges in less day-to-day interference in the affairs of a corporation if it is privately owned (See, for example, Beesley and Littlechild, 1983). In many cultures, a minister may direct an SOE to employ his or her cousin but may refrain from doing so in a private enterprise (in which the cousin of the owner might become the vice-president). In other cases, nepotism is accepted practice in a private enterprise but is not allowed in an SOE.

When the SOE is divested to a large MNE that can give it access to important markets, better technology and more knowhow, the firm may become more efficient, without increasing the costs to the government. Thus, the Israeli government sold its electronics producer, Tadiran, to GT&E in the hope of getting access to more modern technology and expanded export markets. Most countries, however, are reluctant to allow too many of their domestic firms to be controlled by MNEs. Even Mrs. Thatcher, for whom privatization is a deep-rooted belief, refused to consider an offer from General Motors to acquire the state-owned Jaguar and instead sold the shares of the firm on the London Stock Exchange. To the extent SOEs are less efficient than private enterprises similarly situated, the reasons have to be found in two explanations: lack of transferability of shares and the design of the system. Both may be solved by means other than privatization.

Theoretically, the government may also decide not to interfere in the affairs of SOEs. In fact, a learning process can be observed in the SOE sector: as management of these enterprises becomes more professional and technically competent, governments have learned to allow them more autonomy. If, because of too much interference, better and more qualified managers refuse to work for an SOE, there is a very strong argument for privatization. This, however, is more of a political than an economic argument, and it seems that most cases of privatization were based on political reasons.

Another reason mentioned in Chapter 3 was increasing competitiveness versus foreign owners. SOEs were also created to correct the racial imbalance in entrepreneurship. In Indonesia, SOEs are regarded as a means of extending *pribumi* (indigenous) ownership (Hill, 1982, p. 1016). In Malaysia, SOEs are now being held in trust for the Bumiputras until they are able to buy them from the state. In these cases SOEs can be privatized when the indigenous, or racial, private entrepreneurs are ready to take over. State ownership has also been motivated by security considerations. If SOEs are created for the conduct of a war, they can be disposed of after the war, as was indeed the experience in the United States (see Chapter 2).

Another reason for state ownership has been the belief that SOEs are a potent tool for savings mobilization to generate development financing. Surpluses of SOEs were seen as accruing to the government directly and, therefore, readily accessible to finance capital formation. These savings were also seen as being easier to achieve than reliance on politically unpopular increased taxes.

Experience, however, proved different: instead of mobilizing savings and generating surpluses for the economy as a whole, SOEs persistently ran deficits that had to be financed from the government's general revenues. These disappointing results were sometimes caused by inefficiency and bad management. In some cases the reason the SOE sector was debt-ridden was that it allowed conspicuous consumption of various sorts by a new class of elite bureaucracy. In most cases, the reason has been the tendency of governments to use SOEs as conduits for dispensing invisible subsidies, the size of which is never calculated. Finally, economic development and growth was often achieved by import substitution and was fueled by low-cost subsidies and by denying the SOEs in public utilities the rate structure needed to provide a return on investment and the resources for expansion. If indeed SOEs are not able to sustain themselves, they should be liquidated. If the reason for the losses is low rates, the government may raise the rates and get the extra benefits, which may cause a public backlash and protests. Politically, the government may prefer the sale (see below).

One reason for state ownership has always been the need for revenues. As shown above, SOEs are also *sold* to yield revenues, thus allowing increasing public spending without a commensurate increase in taxes or public debts. Selling SOEs does add to the revenue of government at the time of the sale and, thus, may help it finance other programs. The price, however, is a reduction in the future flow of revenues to the public sector. The capital market may find the equity of an SOE very attractive, but the private buyers are buying a future stream of earnings that will now go to them instead of to the government. If one assumes that firms miraculously become so much more efficient by being in private hands that the government would not have received any yields but the private shareholders would, then there is no such price. However, in most cases even the most ardent believers in the private enterprise system will not argue for such an enormous difference in efficiency between the public and private sectors.

In the United Kingdom, privatization has become not only a major political commitment and the basis for the government's industrial policy but also a prime instrument of fiscal policy. Since 1979 the Thatcher government has not been very successful in cutting spending but was able, in just 5 years, to raise more than £5 billion by selling parts of its SOEs (see Table 9–1). Dozens of other countries announced that they intended to sell state holdings. Whether SOEs will really be sold remains to be seen: in all countries, sales encounter heavy political opposition.

SOEs are often restricted in their investment because they compete for

Table 9.1 The privatization program in the United Kingdom 1979–1984

Year	Status	Net Proceeds (£Millions)
Sales		
1978–1980	5 percent of British Petroleum (October 1979)	276
	25 percent of ICL	37
	Shares in Suez Finance Company and miscellaneous	57
1980–1981	50 percent of Ferranti	55
	100 percent of Fairey	22
	North Sea oil licenses	195
	51 percent of British Aerospace (February 1981)	43
	Miscellaneous and small NEB	91
1981–1982	24 percent of British Sugar (July 1981)	44
	50 percent of Cable and Wireless (October 1981)	182
	100 percent of Amersham International (February 1982)	64
	100 percent of National Freight Consortium (February 1982)	5
	Miscellaneous plus Crown Agent and Forestry Commission land and property sales	199
1982–1983	51 percent of Britoil (first cash call) (November 1982)	334
	49 percent of Associated British Ports (February 1983)	46
	British Rail hotels (March 1983)	51
		(cont.)

Year	Status	Net Proceeds (£Millions)
Sales (*cont.*)		
	Sale of oil licenses, oil stockpiles and miscellaneous (inc. £60 million sterling for International Aeradio)	73
1983–1984	Second cash call for Britoil	293
	7 percent of British Petroleum (September 1983)	543
	25 percent of Cable and Wireless (December 1983)	263
1984–1985	Associated British Ports, remaining 48.5 percent (April 1984)	51
	British Gas onshore oil assets (May 1984)	82
	Jaguar (July 1984)	297
	Sea Link (July 1984)	66
	Enterprise Oil (June 1984)	380
	50.2% of British Telecom (November, 1984)	3,916*
	75% of Inmos	NA
To be Sold (as planned in 1984)		
1984–1985	British Airways	800
1985–1986	British Airports	400
	Royal Ordnance Factories	300
1986–1987	Parts of gas, electricity, plus about £1 billion of smaller enterprises including National Bus, Land Rover, Rolls Royce, Unipart, British Steel profitable businesses, British Nuclear Fuels, Naval war shipbuilding yards	4,700
Local Authority Council House Sales Revenue		
1979–1980		500
1980–1981		800
1981–1982		1,400
1982–1983		1,850
1983–1984		1,700
1984–1985		1,600
1985–1986		1,200

SOURCES: *Financial Times*, February 1984, and *The Economist*, October 19, 1985, p. 42.
NOTES: (1) Total proceeds from SOEs sale until end of 1984 was £7 billion and from sale of council houses and land, £12 billion.

(2) Since date of table, the British government sold the remaining 48 percent of British Aerospace (in May 1985) for £346 million. It also sold (in August 1985) the remaining shares in Britoil for £425 million, and its remaining shares in Cables and Wireless (in December 1985) for £600 million.

(3) Privatization of British Airways was delayed twice. First because the firm faced law suits and again in July 1985 because of uncertainties on aviation agreements with the United States. The government announced its intention of selling the profitable British Gas for £7 billion.

*Gross proceeds
NA = not available

government funds not only according to the rate of return on the investment but also against all kinds of socially justified programs. The dilemma of many governments is how to finance SOEs without adding to the soaring budget deficit. Governments may then prefer to sell the SOE.

There are, however, several political economic reasons for privatization. If a genuine hands-off policy is seen as a contradiction in terms; if state bureaucrats, deprived of personal financial gains, see the benefits only in terms of status and power; if SOE managers are immune to the threat of bankruptcy; if competitive performance cannot be replicated in the SOE sector, then private organizations operate under greater pressure to reduce costs and may be, at least in some cases, more efficient. Even in these cases, efficiency may not be the only consideration. SOEs may be needed to fulfill a public task.

Political contests for power are important in causing state ownership as well as privatization. Privatizations have occurred in some countries as a response to private-sector concerns of growing government involvement. Political opposition may also stall privatization schemes. Mr. Franz Joseph Strauss, Bavarian prime minister and leader of the junior coalition party, opposed the plans of the German finance minister, Mr. Gerhard Stoltenberg, to privatize the 80 percent state-owned Lufthansa. *The Economist* (November 24, 1984, p. 84) suggested that the opposition was motivated by the fear that if the government relaxed its hold, the airline "would no longer be a reliable customer for Airbus." This opposition is said to have stopped the German privatization program.

Professor Romano Prodi, IRI's chairman, reached an agreement on the sale of SME group to Carlo de Benedetti's Buitoni food company. Mr. Craxi, the Socialist prime minister, opposed this specific deal, and two appeals of Mr. Benedetti to courts of law for legal enforcement were rejected. Since then, SME was put on auction, and IRI received other offers, said to be for a higher price. Italy's undersecretary to the prime minister, in a letter to *The Economist*, said on this case, "the prime minister has requested that privatization should be carried out on the open market and not behind closed doors" (*The Economist*, September 28, 1985, p. 6).

Another politically inspired reason to privatize SOEs is the desire to avoid the political repercussions of unpopular decisions. The recognition that certain SOEs must drastically reduce the size of their labor force and increase their prices to avoid being perennial producers of red ink led some governments to consider privatization. While governments recognize that to make a certain firm viable, prices have to be increased and workers have to be fired, they may be reluctant to face the political consequences. From the government's point of view, it is much easier to sell the firm and let the private entrepreneur be the villain. Glade, who studied privatization in Peru, shows that privatization must be seen in the context of a widespread shift in general political forces—and an increasing return to the arguments of *laissez faire*. He concludes:

Privatisation, then, becomes one means, though not the only alternative, for dealing with the fiscal crisis that draws together a variety of contributing factors and undermines the central process of capital formation. Its success, therefore, depends on the likelihood that private management can turn round enterprise operating efficiency sooner, or more completely, than can public management with its rather different set of constraints. Privatisation may also be viewed as a means of transferring to the private sector the onus for unpopular decisions—price increases, the sacking of employees—and hence may be restored to on the ground of political palatability or expediency. [In Reddy, 1983, p. 298]

Opposition to Privatization

Labor unions have been the strongest opponents of privatization schemes. They "have shown their determination to resist the onslaught on their jobs and services and fight the threat of privatisation" (Lord, in Hastings and Levie, 1983, p. 107).

Another interest group that has fought privatization on certain occasions is the managers of the SOEs. Managers, generally, did not oppose being part of the private sector; what they objected to was remaining as managers of SOEs while having to hive off to the private sector some of their more profitable subsidiaries.

In the United Kingdom the 1982 Transport Bill permits the infusion of private capital to the express bus services, National Holidays, and into its property holding. The National Bus Company objected to this sale. In its 1981 annual report, the board made clear it was not opposed to the introduction of private capital into the property portfolio since this led to improvements in their facilities. It was, however, opposed to the hiving off of its National Express (which runs express bus service) and National Holidays subsidiaries, on the ground that it would lose its flexibility and therefore not be able to run the core business in a viable manner. In industries like transportation, it is often feared that private companies would take the profitable parts, leaving the services to remote areas or other losing lines to the SOE. Sales of auxiliary business—such as hotels belonging to British Rail or its hovercraft subsidiary—reduced the profits (and the size) of the SOE.

In the case of the British Electricity Board and British Gas Corporation, the firms own and operate retail appliance shops. Privatization of these shops was seen as forcing an SOE to close down its operations to create a new market for private-sector interests. The British Gas Corporation board argued forcefully that standards of gas installation work would fall if sales passed from that corporation to private retailers. It opposed vigorously the government's decision that it should dispose of all showrooms over a 5-year period. It argued that showrooms are run not only for profits but also to receive payment of bills and give information on tariffs and general advice on appliances, energy and conservation and that synergism is important.

In Japan, management of Japan Airline wants the government to sell its 35 percent stake "so that JAL can be freer from intervention" (*The Economist,* September 28, 1985, p. 72). In Brazil, on the other hand, there is a large reservoir of well-trained professionals from which to recruit SOE managers. These managers feel the firms they manage have to grow in order to maintain a first-rate staff (Trebat, 1983, p. 34) and may oppose the sale of large SOEs if this would affect their career negatively. Further, SOEs create both internal and external constituencies with significant vested interests in their continued operations.

The arguments against privatization were stated in the United Kingdom by the Trade Union Conference in December 1981 as follows:

> The Government is penalising successful public enterprise, because the private sector will buy only profitable assets;
>
> Far from denationalisation helping the funding of public expenditure, as the Government argues, the exchequer loses income from the profitable nationalised industries and is left with the funding of the unprofitable industries;
>
> Denationalisation is unnecessarily disruptive when most industries are in recession;
>
> Denationalisation and liberalisation are likely to break up an industry's network of services, and therefore hit the ability of a nationalised industry to cross-subsidise; and
>
> Liberalisation leads to "*cream-skimming,*" as private companies in such industries as the bus, aviation, and telecommunications industries introduce new services only in the profitable sectors.
> [Hastings and Levie, 1983, p. 15]

CONDITIONS FOR SALE

The sale of a firm is a commercial transaction with all its attendant problems: if the price is too low, the government will be accused of giving away public funds. If it is too high, it is difficult to find buyers.

In many SOEs, losses are high and persistent. These are the enterprises the government always wants to sell and for which it is hardest to find buyers. In cases of unprofitable enterprises that were turned around those who achieve the turnaround often find many reasons not to sell. If the firm is profitable, there are always those who feel that the sale is unwarranted, and "privatization amounts to flogging the family silver to pay the butcher's bill" (*The Economist,* February 23, 1985, p. 74).

The sale of profitable firms gives rise to accusations that the government gives away taxpayers' property. In the case of Canada, Gordon emphasizes, "in returning state-owned companies to the private sector, the government should ensure that taxpayers, who have invested heavily over the years in a particular enterprise, obtain fair value for their investment" (1981, p. 53).

Prospective buyers are often apprehensive that a change of government will cause renationalization. This risk affects their willingness to buy and reduces the price.

In Chile after 1973, "privatization of state enterprises occurred in extremely advantageous conditions for the new owners" (Foxley, 1983, p. 66). Foxley estimated the implicit subsidy for the buyers, on the basis of the market value of assets, "to be equivalent to 30 percent of the firms' net worth and up to 40 percent and 50 percent of the purchase value. The low sale price was influenced by the state's urgency to sell and its doing so in a moment of deep recession and high interest rates, a point at which short-term profitability of the enterprises decreased" (pp. 66-67).

The U.K. government, committed to wide-scale privatization much more than any other country, sold, up to 1985, mainly the profitable firms. Certainly it is easier to find buyers for Jaguar than for British Leyland, British Steel or British Shipyards, not only because they are over-employed but also because of their high debts (British Leyland), the fierce Japanese competition (British Steel) or the world shipping slump (British Shipyards). It is also easier to sell Heathrow airport than to find a buyer for loss-making Prestwick in Scotland. In Asia and Africa, privatization is extremely difficult: Lack of private capital and management skills are serious constraints. Some governments chose instead to demonopolize state activities, as in Madagascar and Sierra Leone (rice authorities) or Mali's cereal marketing board.

Another consideration is making sure that the enterprise can really operate efficiently and profitably as a private firm and that it will not return to public hands because the private entrepreneurs are not able to sustain it. Thus, a government would not want to sell an SOE only to find sometime later that it has to guarantee a loan, subsidize or reacquire the firm. In divesting an SOE, the government is interested in its continuing existence and progress. In some cases, the continuing existence of the firm is possible only if the government is the major customer, like, e.g., in defense-related industries, where the firm is dependent on government procurement. If, after privatization, the firm continues to be dependent on the taxpayers' money, then at least one major objective of the divestiture was not achieved. Even more debatable are cases in which the private buyers insist on guaranteed government orders as a condition of sale, or on guaranteed high tariff protection in the future. One example is Togo's sale of steel mills to a U.S. private investor. Are private profits because of their tariff protection economically justifiable?

In quite a few cases, the alternative to privatization is the use of a private firm as a national champion. John Sheahan argued in the case of Canada that a "hidden crown corporation" (a private firm as a chosen policy instrument), is the only alternative at least in the field of high technology (Tupper and Doern, 1981, p. 43). "Can we prove that there is a difference in performance? In efficiency? In economic and social utility?" (*Ibid.*, p. 43).

Then there is the question of maintaining certain objectives. According to Gordon, if the government still considers applicable the objectives for which an SOE was established:

> [T]hen the terms of sale should ensure that they are not sacrificed by the new ownership status. For example, over the years government spokesmen have emphasized that the Canadian aircraft industry has strategic importance to Canada because of its defense capabilities, its contributions to high technology; and the opportunities it creates for skilled employment and export earnings. The government took over these companies when their existence was threatened. In his memorandum on the two companies, David Golden recommended that their privatization be conditional—that is, that the government require of prospective purchasers assurances relating to prior approval before closure of any facilities, relocation of facilities, maintenance of employment, rationalization of production, and the level of research and development effort. [1981, p. 53]

From the government's point of view, the ideal buyer is one who can offer better management, more market connections, more technologies and more knowhow. Such buyers are not easy to find, however. For some of the stars in the state's portfolio, the only buyers that meet these requirements are large MNEs. Again, the world today is not composed only of millions of small entrepreneurs on whose discretion the invisible hand does not have to rely. The major industries in the world are controlled by a handful of giant firms, many of which are MNEs, operating in an oligopolistic structure. Most governments believe in the *dependencia* argument and are reluctant to allow their firms to be controlled by large MNEs.

A much more sensible alternative seems to be to sell the enterprise to thousands of shareholders in the capital market. Such a policy entails the additional bonus of increasing the size and the efficiency of the capital market. Flotation of SOE shares can develop an active capital market, which helps to reduce the dependence of firms on risk-averse financial institutions. To the extent that the nontransferability of shares is indeed a cause of reduced efficiency in the SOE sector (see Chapter 5), such sales can be very beneficial. They can be carried out in a way that does not relax all possibilities of government control. Such a flotation may be objected to on the ground that it would mean changing the SOE not to a private firm but to an investor-owned and possibly managerially controlled firm. But, then, many investor-owned firms all over the world have demonstrated their enormous viability.

The Federal Republic of Germany followed such a policy of divestiture when it sold Volkswagenwerk, VEBA and other firms. This is also essentially the policy of the Thatcher government. In almost all these cases the government remained either directly or indirectly a major shareholder. Thus, the U.K. government sold less than 50 percent of the shares in British Telecom. In 1985, British Telecom has 1.7 million shareholders that own 12.8 percent of the company (*The Economist*, September 13, 1985, p. 89).

This policy seemed more acceptable than a row over wholesale privatization. Although such a policy has much to commend it in terms of the development of the capital market, it does not necessarily mean total sale of the firm to the private sector. Whether or not less than 50 percent of the shares left in the hands of a government in an SOE is enough to control the firm when the rest of the shares are in the hands of thousands of small shareholders is an empirical question. Most studies on the separation of ownership and control would tend to assume that it is. (See Chapter 5. See also Goldsmith and Parmelee, 1940, Scott, 1979, pp. 52-72, 172).

Attempting to sell shares in the capital market and achieving a wide distribution of these shares are not easy tasks in most countries. Even in the United Kingdom, about half of all financial assets are held by unit trusts, insurance companies and pension funds. Only 7 percent of British adults own shares, compared with 25 percent in the United States. In Africa or Latin America, it is almost impossible to create capital markets with widespread ownership of shares. Some SOEs will remain in the hands of government because their future earnings potential does not make them attractive investments. Others—e.g., public utilities, natural resources or defense-related industries—may remain SOEs because of a combination of economic reasoning and ideological predilections. As Sexty notes in the case of Canada:

> [T]he privatization process will undoubtedly be a slow one. Two difficulties in the process concern the mechanism required to ensure that the corporation will continue to operate in the public interest after the government's divestiture, and the price at which to sell the corporation to private investors especially after years of public subsidization. [1980, p. 376]

Therefore, even if some SOEs are sold to the private sector, alternatives must be found to make the remaining SOEs more efficient.

ALTERNATIVES

There are at least two alternatives to privatization. One is less intervention and petty control by the government. This would allow managers more autonomy to achieve commercial results, instead of spending their time and talent pleading their causes and vying for favors with the government. To make this alternative work and avoid politically dictated interventions as much as possible, the government must be restrained by a constitutional or legal system of checks and balances and unsuccessful SOEs should be divested. A second and related possibility is to distribute shares of SOEs to all taxpayers. Unless one of these alternatives is made operational, state owner-ship may lead to waste and corruption, at least in certain cultures.

Commercialization as an alternative to privatization, requiring the SOE to follow market signals, to be judged on the same footing as private com-mercial firms and to be commercially viable, was suggested in Canada, at least for some of its SOEs. The Air Canada Act of 1977 clearly states that the board of directors is to discharge its responsibilities with "due regard to sound business practices, and in particular the contemplation of profit." (S. 7(2)) Such was also the case with Canadian National and other Canadian SOEs. In the words of the Canadian Privy Council report, "The government wishes to encourage the management of proprietary Crown corporations to operate on a sound commercial basis, to promote their efficiency and maximize the return on the investment to the Canadian taxpayer" (1977, p. 25).

Commercialization was also tried in other countries. In Israel, the Barak Commission proposed a bill that would ensure the SOEs' independence and flexibility and their correct behavior as separate juridical bodies. These objec-tives were reflected in many of the bill's provisions. Thus, it was proposed that the managerial mainspring of the corporation be the board of directors, and the directors must act in the best interests of the corporation, as they perceive them. When these are seen to conflict with external interests, state interests or others, directors should opt for the corporation's interests. If an SOE acts not in pursuance of its own interests but in fulfillment of national goals set by the government, then the government should reimburse the cor-poration for any losses incurred. A number of provisions were proposed to ensure the directors' independence from the state. For instance, a director could be dismissed before the end of the term only by a special majority of the board.

The Barak Commission also proposed to avoid conflicts of interest by barring from appointment as directors ministers, deputy ministers, members of the Knesset (Parliament) and officials whose duties involve them in the affairs of the corporation. A number of proposed provisions sought to ensure the corporation's dependence on the state, government control and compli-ance with guidelines and basic objectives as stated. To ensure legislative su-pervision, it was proposed that funds for the initial investment in a new cor-poration or for further investment in an existing one be duly allocated through the state budget, thus giving the legislature control over allocations needed for the operation of SOEs. Most of these provisions, however, are not in-cluded in the Israeli Government Companies Act of 1975.

In Brazil the government of Getulio Vargas established the first of a new breed of SOEs—the Compahnia Siderurgica Nacional (CSN). CSN was to be independent of state's budget and subsidies. It had to compete with private firms and expected to operate efficiently. This firm and others that proliferated in the 1960s and 1970s enjoyed autonomy and were judged by their profitability. In fact, SOEs in Brazil were found to be too independent. The fact that these firms were mixed enterprises, in which private individuals held minority shares, helped them to be autonomous and commercially oriented.

Proposals for commercialization came also in Sweden (in establishing Stratsförtag) and many other countries. These proposals, even where they were accepted, foundered on the rock of political realities. Government ministers found it extremely difficult to refrain from interference. Commercializations may be more effective if some of the shares are owned by private investors. Indeed, joint ventures between private firms and governments seem to be the most prevalent solution to avoid alteration of goals and policies at the whim of the governing party.

In Africa, many governments turned to foreign MNEs, offering them equity in the enterprise. Even when no equity was offered, the MNE was entrusted with a management contract, allowing it to decide on key policies and most operational decisions. According to Ghai:

> The expansion of the public sector has served to hide the real extent of private, foreign investment in Africa, since it tends to take on a public form, but a realistic analysis of the public sector, and particularly the potential of executive control, must proceed from an examination of numerous agreements and documents which link public enterprises to foreign corporations. [In Reddy, 1983, p. 183]

Ownership matters less than institutional design and the resource allocation process. It is not necessary to privatize SOEs but only to make them more autonomous, more subject to competitive pressures and market discipline. They must be immunized from political interference by choosing the right managers, giving them proper incentives and allowing them to influence results and achieve them. In some countries where corruption is the rule or in others in which governments tend to intervene too much, such a recipe for reform may be seen as utopian. But in many democracies it is possible to achieve such a reform, allow the SOE to be viable (or to be bankrupt) and gain the benefits from their operations. Under the appropriate institutional design, SOEs should not be less efficient than any private enterprise.

If the reason for inefficiency is too little competition and too much intervention, then constitutionally mandated separation of power might be a solution. Reigning and ruling can be separated. The power of the executive branch can be restrained by a system designed with branches of four powers: the legislative, the executive, the courts and the directors of SOEs. Thus, SOEs can be insulated from arbitrary intervention of the government the same way the courts are in democratic states. Monopolies may be split into smaller competitive units, and managers may receive a bonus commensurate with performance. Then, SOEs may behave like any large firm with diffused ownership. The design proposed by the Barak Commission in Israel is one possibility. Such a design, coupled with goal auditing, as discussed in Chapter 4, can simulate a competitive market in ideas, perception of goals and values.

One problem is to avoid resistance to change, commitments to unsuccessful decisions, hindrance to adaptation and innovation and persistence of inefficiency. It is unlikely that governments (or headquarters of large multidivisional private firms) will not be committed to their previous strategic decisions. However, power may serve as a substitute for economic markets. One may view SOEs, both within themselves and as part of a system of state enterprises, as markets in which different individuals attempt to gain power and in which power is the transactions' medium of exchange. Pfeffer and Salancik (1977, p. 23) argued that this view has two implications: making information available to all participants so the market for power and control can work more efficiently and keeping power and control relatively decentralized and diffused so no single organizational actor or set of actors dominates the firm and can therefore institutionalize control and delimit the operation of political contests within the organization.

Such a design is possible in SOEs. A certain amount of conflict is built into the system, with clear limits on the power of each actor. Competing perspectives—economic, social or political—are equally important and should not be subordinated one to another. Goal discrepancies between managers and controllers are, and should be, a fact of life. SOE managers will have more than one boss, with conflicting goals, preventing the concentration of control by a single interest.

A design of this sort may seem to fly in the face of at least some conventional beliefs about unity of command. However, a similar design is used when projects, functions and geographic divisions are organized in a matrix form (Davis and Lawrence, 1977). Governments have already introduced an internal market by purchasing social services from SOEs. In some cases, like Sweden, the government does not have to procure these services from its firms but can tender for the lowest bidder, thus permitting outside supply. By the same token, different ministries may be allowed to purchase innovations or social services. Under such a system, conflict, competition and some degree of power and political activities can be made legitimate and institutionalized.

Conflict is inevitable. It is also potentially productive by bringing into the open different points of view. In a world of uncertainty, need for change and adaptation, a great deal of variation and intrusion of other perspectives is necessary. Complete autonomy, however, does not allow centralization of control and unity of direction. Successful operations need the creation of specific markets for power, allowing experimentation and rewarding risk taking. Such a system does not mean that the center is omnipotent, imposing shadow prices and offering bonuses to get the right response; rather, it means that different actors work together, accepting conflict as a way of life and operating within an elaborate system of checks and balances.

In theory, SOE autonomy needs to be counterbalanced by some central control only if it does not have alternative sources of funds. The experience in the United States clearly indicates that if SOEs are financed by bonds sold in the market, their managers are very commercially oriented and are careful to maintain a high bond rating (see Walsh, 1978; Aharoni, 1983). SOEs are not accountable for results if they cannot go bankrupt, but there is no theoretical reason why governments should not allow SOEs to go bankrupt, or liquidate them.

LIQUIDATION

A SOE may be liquidated either because its objective has been achieved or when it is inherently nonviable. One example would be that of a company established by the State of Israel to plant and develop citrus groves. The company was financed by private individuals who, within the framework of a savings plan, paid in installments toward the final acquisition of a grove. Once the trees began bearing fruit, the individual received title, and the company was liquidated.

Enterprises that have been liquidated for reasons of inherent nonviability include those that were established before an adequate study of the market was made or enterprises that acquired improper equipment or did not have sufficient skilled labor to operate and maintain the equipment. In Peru, e.g., a freeze-drying plant was built, the costs of which exceeded its revenues right from the start of production. After 15 years of losses, liquidation procedures were initiated (Shirley, 1983, p. 54). In Israel, a state-owned company was established to reduce the costs of training air force helicopter pilots. The training was to have been carried out through transportation and agricultural spraying assignments arranged by the firm. The helicopters, however, were found to be unsuitable for spraying activities, and the company was liquidated. Ivory Coast, Zambia and Nigeria closed down SOEs or slashed their staff to a skeleton crew. In many other instances of liquidation, the investments were ill-conceived, the minimum efficient scale was much larger than the demand, the quality of the product was poor or the high level of engineering skills required was unavailable. Changes in the costs of raw materials have also rendered a company nonviable. In cases like these, there is no reason to continue operations when it is evident that a turnaround is impossible. If an SOE is unsuccessful and if better management cannot turn it around, it is better buried. Liquidation is a major force for efficiency. It certainly avoids fiscal drain and allows state resources to be put to more productive use.

CITIZENS AS SHAREHOLDERS

One way to ensure such a design is to distribute shares in the SOEs to all taxpayers. Governments are sometimes reluctant to sell SOEs to private-sector interests for a low price since such a sale may be interpreted as being based on corruption. No such problem would exist if all taxpayers received shares, free of charge, that they could trade in the market. If the taxpayer could trade these shares, the result would be not only build-up of a capital market and wider share ownership but also transferability of shares, with the resulting threats of proxy fights and other controls that mitigate the managers' discretion. Distribution of shares to all taxpayers (or equally to all citizens, if the ideology is one of more equality) is equivalent to a tax cut but with many more benefits. The wider constituency would reduce political pressures to achieve all types of invisible largesse and would reduce the propensity of the government to demand noneconomic goals for political advantages. In Canada at the end of the seventies, the British Columbia government offered *free*, to eligible citizens of the Province who applied for them, eighty percent of its holdings of shares in the British Columbia Resources Investment Corporation to a limit of five per individual (Tupper and Doern, 1981, pp. 42–43). This move was trumpeted as "people's capitalism." In the case of BCRIC, the shares failed to appreciate as much as it had been hoped, and some questionable investments and take-overs caused controversy. This experiment shows that the distribution of the shares by itself is not a panacea. However, it is one way to give SOEs more autonomy.

If the government wants to reduce its domestic national debt, it could exchange shares of SOEs for its bonds. By doing so, it may reduce the interest paid on national debt.

Selling SOEs to the citizens will not only reduce public deficits, it will also relieve the state from the burden of investing additional state funds in these SOEs and the need to borrow funds for this purpose. By achieving transferability of shares and reducing the power of short-term political pressures, the SOEs will also become more efficient. The government has enough power to protect national interests without direct ownership. SOE managers may accept in silence (or in protest) government's impositions because they want to keep their jobs. Under a system of citizen ownership, these managers may be as successful, innovative, effective and expert in leading as any professional manager in the private sector.

When the government creates SOEs, it distributes risk among its taxpayers. These same individuals can hold shares in a private market according to the portfolio they prefer. By giving shares to the taxpayers, welfare will be increased: citizens could allocate risks in ways they prefer, the SOE will have to work for the benefit of its real owners, managers will be subject to the transparency rule of the capital market and to its discipline and individuals who believe they can do a better job may attempt to take over the firm. Shareholders, even if they own small numbers of shares, could ask questions and receive answers in the general assembly meeting.

Competition has long been seen as the way to ensure efficient management and innovation. When competitive markets are not feasible, other markets may be used to achieve the same results. Competitive capital markets could substitute for other forms of competition in keeping management efficient because if management did not employ the firm's assets in an optimal way, the firm's stock price would drop. Entrepreneurs may then gain control of the firm through external takeover or merger and would revitalize the firm.

The proposals above called for the sale or free distribution of all shares— not only a minority position in an SOE. Otherwise, the influence of the government may mean that citizens will lose interest. Such a move for "people's shares" may be effective not only in competitive firms but also in public utilities. In the latter case, there is still the classic problem: how to avoid exploitation of monopoly power. One way to cope with the problem is the setting up of independent regulatory commissions with powers to dictate levels of service, levels of punctuality and levels of consumers' convenience. Thus, the committee may direct a bus SOE to build covers from rain in all stations, or tell a railroad to have dining cars, or the number of standing passengers in trains. (See also Nove, 1973, pp. 121-129.)

SOEs were created to allow the internalization of externalities. Goods are bundles of characteristics that cannot always be separately priced. A supermarket offers free parking because it hopes to attract customers. Failure to supply the service may drive customers away to competitors. By contrast, public utilities may not have competitors. They may, therefore, ignore quality, punctuality, service, choice, and consumers' convenience. As Nove argues:

> Suppose that razor blades are public monopoly, and the operational criterion is the volume of profits, perhaps modified by some sort of output or turnover target. What possible economic interest can the nationalized razor blade firm have in making their blades sharp? Indeed, profit and turnover alike might benefit from blades which have to be thrown away after three shaves (1973, pp. 19-20).

This problem cannot be solved by creating a private monopoly instead of a state-owned one, but only by introducing competition. Competition can be created also among different actors vying for power, including regulatory agencies. Any model of a central direction of the economy means in reality decomposition into competing departments, ministries, and enterprises. This administrative pluralism may be a way to achieve the benefits ascribed to the market. Externalities cannot be eliminated by treating the whole economy as one firm. To be sure, too much fragmentation also causes suboptimal solutions, but in an uncertain world optimality is impossible. Therefore, the solution—imperfect as it may be—is in a market for power with built-in constraints.

CONCLUSION

Since the early 1980s, there has been an increased awareness that losses in SOEs cannot continue forever. Many countries, but mainly the United Kingdom, chose to privatize SOEs. But privatization is not a panacea. Some firms—such as fiscal monopolies or administrators—will never be privatized. Natural monopolies would always be suspect of exploiting their monopoly power, and the amount of implicit subsidy given to the buyers may raise protests. Different institutional processes may be equally or even more effective in making the SOEs' sector an efficient one, allowing conflicts on how efficiency is defined and measured.

Much of the discussion and debate on SOEs is cast in black and white terms: SOEs cannot go bankrupt, they are inefficient, they are prone to petty controls. The market system commits private enterprise managers to pursue partisan efficiency in resource allocation. In contrast, it is claimed that private firms disregard social or national objectives. Americans place a high premium on the concept that society is not more than the sum of the individuals who comprise it. Individuals have inalienable rights and, much less, duties. Other countries believe in the duty of the individual to the community, in dependence and in social obligations. In Japan, these values result in a high degree of cooperation and the sharing of economic power between business and government. Differences in cultural heritage and sociopolitical context are extremely important in discussing state ownership or privatization. If the least government is a better government, then privatization is preferred. If duty to society, self-discipline and harmony of interest are assumed, then other options are possible.

The starting point in making a decision whether or not to sell a firm is an examination of the original reasons and circumstances of the acquisition or establishment of the enterprise. Logically, if those reasons have ceased to exist, there is no point in continuing state ownership, and the government should terminate it. At the same time, state ownership does not necessarily mean inefficiently run enterprises, and not all SOEs can be sold. Problems of social costs, externalities, ways to regulate natural monopolies, national pride and political pressures will not disappear. Therefore, other solutions must be sought. This chapter proposed two related ideas: establishing a market for power and reinforcing it by giving away shares in SOEs to foster the growth of financial markets and give as many people as possible a direct financial stake in the future of the SOEs. These two markets would help SOEs adjust to a new and competitive climate. They will also reduce the possibility of illegitimate use of SOEs for political or personal gain.

CHAPTER 10

International Implications of State-Owned-Enterprise Operations

INTRODUCTION

The system of international institutions and international agreements operating today was hammered out after World War II. To a large extent it was based on the implicit premise that the participants in international trade and investments are private firms, constrained by costs and by the pursuit of profits. The increasing participation of SOEs in the international trade and investment scene raises the question of the validity of that premise. Although some countries imposed more restrictions on international trade than others and although some sectors such as agriculture, oil or shipping and services were carefully screened from international competition, by and large these international agreements have been proved to be propitious for international trade. The rate of growth of international trade has been for most years higher than that of world GNP. Practically all countries have increased their imports sharply relative to the GDP. In the United States, that proportion was 1.2 percent in 1955 but grew to 5.5 percent in 1975 and 8.2 percent in 1983. In the Federal Republic of Germany it went from 3.5 to 9.9 to 26.1 percent. In some small nations, foreign trade is a very high percentage of GDP. In 1983, according to GATT (General Agreement on Tariffs and Trade) figures, imports were about two-thirds of GDP in Belgium, nearly 30 percent in Switzerland, 47 percent in the Netherlands, and 39.6 percent for Portugal (GATT, 1984).

The increased world trade triggered subtler protectionist moves as countries experienced difficulties in adapting to increasing interdependence and changing world markets. Multilateral trade negotiations made substantial progress in limiting the impact of nontariff barriers, but the vague language of agreements and the lack of any agreement on trade in services left many possibilities for action.

Despite official proclamations of their adherence to the principles of trade liberalization and nondiscrimination, governments have attempted to aid their domestic firms as well as to encourage exports and reduce imports. One tool they used in these efforts was SOEs. The increased role of SOEs caused concern that in these enterprises political considerations may take precedence over economic, that they have easier and cheaper access to capital than private enterprise similarly situated, that they are motivated by the desire to avoid unemployment and that they are therefore willing to heed cost considerations. The multiple objectives of SOEs are claimed to be inconsistent with the maintenance of a workable competitive international marketplace. State ownership alone is seen as *prima facie* proof that the SOE behaves differently from private enterprise. They are charged with predatory behavior and are accused of dumping (e.g., Lamont, 1979, Nielsen, 1982, Monsen and Walters, 1983). However, only by understanding the internal workings of state trading enterprises can one establish the extent to which their behavior in the international scene is predatory and the extent to which this behavior is different from that of private firms similarly situated.

We shall start by describing the main changes that have taken place in the international scene since World War II and then the way the system has treated state trading, giving figures on the changing role of state trading in different industries. Based on the evidence, some reactions to the increasing participation of the SOEs in the international trade and investment scene are discussed. Finally, certain hypotheses are proposed about SOE behavior and its consequences to the international system.

INTERNATIONAL BACKGROUND

Economic theory traditionally assumed that the dominant business relations between countries are in the form of free-market-inspired exports and imports carried out by small and individually managed business traders. This assumption of market-determined direction of international transactions has been also one of the basic tenets of the efforts to reduce trade barriers and avoid discrimination through the GATT system. The traditional framework for explaining trade policies since David Ricardo has been the doctrine of comparative advantage and the theory of international trade. In the world of neoclassical economics, direct foreign investment has little place (Kindleberger, 1969), and state trading has no place.

Indeed, until the mid-nineteenth century, international trade was carried out by merchants who purchased their goods from manufacturers and sold them to retailers. However, the building of the railroad and telegraph networks, steamships and cable as well as technological breakthroughs in certain industries allowed substantial scale economies and the maintenance of quality control in both production and retailing. Large firms could achieve cost advantages by mass production and retailing (Chandler, 1962, 1977).

International production almost always followed the building of an export marketing network. By 1914, the value of direct foreign investments by MNEs based in the United States equalled seven percent of the GNP, and that figure was still seven percent in 1966 (Wilkins, 1970, p. 201).

If the transportation revolution of the mid-nineteenth century created the beginning of multinational competition, then the communication and information revolution created the global competition of today. Business firms have responded to the tehnological breakthroughs by global standardization, achieving significant competitive advantages by both cost reductions and high-quality products through value engineering. At the same time, a very large and growing portion of international trade is strongly affected by interventionist policies of the nation-states. Some governments have been able to achieve an impressive transformation of their economies and their social structures by increasing state regulation of economic activities as well as their direct participation in these activities.

These two conflicting trends mean that the assumptions of predominantly market-determined transactions are tenuous and that the theory of international trade is inadequate in explaining international movements of goods, services, capital and technology. Globalization of markets meant an increasing role for the large MNEs that continued to increase their foreign activities and globalized production. Many of the trade activities recorded among nations are not carried out at arm's length but are made within the MNE system. Between 1966 and 1975 the majority-owned affliliates of U.S. firms located in foreign countries originated about one-third of U.S. imports (Helleiner, 1981). MNEs account for about one-third of the exports of the NICs, and in Singapore this share exceeds 90 percent (UNCTC, 1983, pp. 154–155). Moreover, international production has become more important than international trade. MNEs move goods, services and technology across international borders to meet the efficiency needs of their system, not necessarily in response to changes in economic policies, market conditions, the exchange rate or needs and desires in one specific country. Indeed, governments are sometimes described as being impotent in achieving their national goals.

Another large part of international trade does not always react to market forces for reasons of a different sort: governments intervene directly in the market, artificially changing the exchange rate, subsidizing exports, preventing imports and levying tariffs and building various nontariff barriers. It was mainly this situation that was addressed by the elaborate system created after World War II.

Government regulations cause a barrier to globalization. Tariff and nontariff protections, price and interest rate control, quotas, restrictions on dividend and royalty remittances, requirements that a local partner be found, compulsory import deposits, foreign exchange control and multiple exchange rates are designed to protect domestic firms from the competition of the large-scale, cost-effective global firm. A firm may, therefore, decide to adopt a full-blown global strategy. Alternatively, it may opt to rely on government's support and protection against the inroads of the global competitors to remain viable in its home market. Indeed, the poor performance of manufactured exports in Latin America as compared to Asia is said to have resulted largely from the impact of different governmental policies on the behavior of the firms: Latin America's inward-looking development efforts have created high-cost manufacturers that find it extremely difficult to compete in the export markets (Wells, 1983, p. 88). These manufacturers learned to rely on political support rather than on competition in the market to earn their profits.

When experience and a very large scale of operations is the basis of competitive advantages in a global market, firms residing in relatively small countries, having small markets at home, suffering from lack of funds and dependent on banks as a sole source of financing, may be forced out of business. When administrative coordination is preferable to market activities and global corporate strategy is called for, governments may choose to join the game instead of fighting it, creating global firms of their own to ensure that in the Darwinist global survival of the fittest, the country will not fall behind.

Since the 1960s, increasing numbers of governments have opted for export-led growth, both by offering export subsidies and by taking the state-ownership route to compete in world markets. In industries deemed vital to national security, such as armament, aerospace or oil, one finds more global competition between the private-sector MNEs and large SOEs. Governments use their political bargaining power and the taxpayers' money to overcome barriers to entry, and promote exports through quasi-political agreements (Doz, 1976). In industries in which R&D capability is the major differentiating factor in winning or losing competitive wars, governments subsidize the heavy outlays needed to allow their national champions to enter. The nation-state thus competes less through tariff barriers and much more through granting preferential treatment to certain firms, private or state-owned.

The key institutions devoted to the objectives of maintaining open borders, such as GATT, the IMF and the EEC, worked relatively well in maintaining a system of stability and negotiating among them different agreements for the reduction of tariffs and later to the abolition of nontariff barriers. These institutions, however, ignored the importance of the direct operations of government in the market. These transactions may be based on market prices, on barter deals or on *quid pro quo:* one country imports goods from another because the second country gave it aid or imported arms or other goods from that country.

In sum, a significant percentage, sometimes estimated to be as high as

30 percent of total international trade, is based on a variety of government-inspired deals, and a growing portion of international trade and investments is based on direct state trading.

Another portion of international trade does not take place because government protects domestic industry by negotiating voluntary agreements, orderly market arrangements or other neomercantilistic methods. The extent and level of protection is extremely difficult to measure because the exact definition of "protection" is elusive. Trade may be restricted not only by subsidies but also by voluntary export constraints and other hard-to-measure phenomena such as bureaucratic chicanery, bilaterally negotiated restraints or the uncertainty caused by the fear of imposition of new restrictions that reduces investments based on export projection. Despite these caveats, several attempts have been made to estimate the portion of world trade that faces obstacles other than tariffs. Françoise David of the French Ministry of Industry estimated the proportion of world trade so restrained in 1980 to be about 60 percent. Sheila Page, of the National Institute of Economics and Social Research in London, estimated the proportion as 48 percent, and Jan Tumlir guessed it was between 40 and 45 percent total of world trade and around 20 percent of world trade in manufacturing. The difference between these two figures is accounted for by the fact that world trade in oil and agriculture is much more riddled with restrictions than that of manufacturing (Tumlit et al., 1984/5, p. 14). In manufacturing, however, textiles and clothing are securely protected from the low-cost producers of LDCs by the Multifiber Arrangement. Steel is also heavily protected, as are petrochemicals, cars, television sets and ball bearings. Of course, the share of trade not carried out because of protection cannot be included here.

The architects of the world trade system after World War II also ignored international trade in services, which has been steadily growing and in 1980 accounted for approximately 20 percent of world trade. Key services, from telecommunications to shipping, from banking to information supplies, are often protected monopolies, to which the most favored nation (MFN) clause of the GATT does not apply. To be sure, the signatories to the GATT's Government Procurement Code agreed to consider its extension to services, and a commitment was reached at the May 1983 Williamsburg Summit to work toward free trade in services, but practices such as requiring the use of the country's flagships or limiting the right of entry to airlines and telecommunications are common.

We can see that international trade today is far from being free trade. In the specific area of SOEs, governments are said to use these enterprises in the pursuit of their national goals in ways that are regarded as injurious and unfair to the economic interests of other governments. The incidence of such cases seems to be on the increase, generating a potential source of political friction among advanced industrialized societies. To set the stage for a survey of these claims and an analysis of their validity, a short background on the ways the GATT treats SOEs is needed.

GATT AND STATE TRADING

In the second session of the Preparatory Committee of the United Nations Conference on Trade and Employment in June 1947, the delegate of New Zealand advised:

> We should beware of attempting to legislate too precisely to meet the case of State enterprises, not out of any feeling that State enterprises should be put in a privileged position, but rather from the feeling that the first essential of sound legislation is that we should be thoroughly familiar with what we are legislating about. [Bernier, in Kostecky, 1982, p. 245]

Unfortunately, this sound advice has been ignored, and the present GATT measures dealing with state trading are ambiguous, if not an exercise in futility. When the question of state trading was touched on during the negotiations on the GATT agreement, it was decided that the way to deal with it was first to identify the enterprises considered to be involved in these activities and to require regular reports on their activities from the governments. Second, SOEs were expected to behave as if they were private enterprises. They were to "act in a manner consistent with the general principles of nondiscriminatory treatment prescribed by Article I" [GATT, Article XVII (1)(a)] and were required to act according to commercial considerations only, barring in particular the use of quantitative restrictions. Such considerations include "price, quality, availability, marketability, transportation and other conditions of purchase or sale, and . . . adequate opportunity, in accordance with customary business practice, to compete for participation in such purchases or sales" [GATT, Article XVII (1)(b)]. State trading is deemed to exist when a contracting party "establishes or maintains a State enterprise, wherever located, or grants to any enterprise, formally or in effect, exclusive or special privileges" [GATT, Article XVII (1)]. The criterion used implies that state trading may include subsidies or regulation of privately owned firms. However, the terms *state enterprise* and *special privileges* were left undefined and ambiguous, perhaps intentionally. The GATT seems to have accepted that Article XVII does not apply to centrally planned economies (Rueland, 1975, p. 318-323; Baban, 1977, p. 334; Dam, 1970), and Third World countries interpreted this article to apply to developed countries only. Article XVII is also "not intended to include the purchase and sale of services."

The term *commercial considerations* has proved to be less clear than was hoped. Even if the SOE is competitive, its commercial considerations are claimed to be affected by the availability of subsidized sources of capital and other governmental aid. Many SOEs are monopolies, and in these cases the test of commercial considerations is academic. Further, commercial considerations may be interpreted to include ease of procurement and thus to exclude newcomers to international trade.

All in all, neither the rules on commercial considerations nor the reporting requirements exacted in 1955 were very effective. If governments did use SOEs as an invisible method of circumventing the GATT, they could hardly be expected to incriminate themselves by transparency. The contracting parties can always resort to the proviso that "shall not require any contracting party to disclose confidential information which would impede law enforcement or otherwise be contrary to the public interest or would prejudice the legitimate commercial interests of particular enterprises" [GATT, Article XVII, (4)(d)].

Based on an analysis of the existing situation, Bernier concludes:

> [T]hat the existing provisions of the GATT concerning State-trading enterprises have remained so far insignificant. A first serious defect . . . has to do with the limited scope of these provisions: they are presently considered to apply essentially to State-trading enterprises operating in developed countries . . . Secondly, even in the case of enterprises that operate in the context of a market economy, the GATT does not make it clear why and when they must be considered as State-trading enterprises and thereby distinguished from other enterprises. Furthermore, the very idea of requesting such enterprises to act as if they were not state trading enterprises, that is, according to commercial considerations only, appears illusory, and the use of a self-incriminating procedure in order to get information from contracting parties that maintains such entities has not served the situation any better; in fact, it has rarely given any satisfaction. Finally, the attempt to present monopoly margins as essentially equivalent to custom duties has simply not given the results expected. Obviously the time has come to undertake a review of these provisions. [In Kostecky, 1982, pp. 256–257]

Still, in the GATT system, forms of regulation which compromise the independence of enterprise decision-making based on a free market may become suspect (Reuland, 1975, p. 320). Indeed, the GATT vision of free trade not subject to manipulation of national policies and the consequent international division of labor was rejected by Socialist states on ideological grounds. Later, Yugoslavia acceded to GATT in 1966, Poland in 1967, Rumania in 1971, and Hungary in 1973. Cuba and Czechoslovakia were charter members (Reuland, 1955, p. 318). The problems of trade with the socialist countries are not dealt with here. The rules for state trading in a mixed economy were intended to apply only to occasional situations where the state, by virtue of its ownership rights, is able to influence the SOE's decisions (Dam, 1970).

SOES IN INTERNATIONAL TRADE AND INVESTMENTS

At the time the GATT was negotiated, SOEs in mixed economies were mainly confined to natural and fiscal monopolies. These firms could act as barriers to imports, but their participation in the international scene was minimal. Since then, as shown, there has been an explosive growth of state ownership and a surge in state trading and government-to-government deals. It is widely felt that the extensive employment of SOEs has rendered the GATT and similar agreements ineffective, and calls for a review of these provisions have been intensified. Suspicion of SOEs could precipitate strife among the nation-states involved. To understand the issues, it is necessary to analyze the role of SOEs in different industries.

Agriculture

Perhaps the first field in which it has become clear that state trading is not comparable to ordinary commercial activities is agriculture. Gibbon (1952) reports that agricultural state trading monopolies existed in ancient Rome. In more recent times, centralized state trading came about because farmers were able to initiate aid in bad times. The Australian Dairy Products Corporation, a monopolistic state-owned marketing board, started in 1924. This type of governmental agency became more widespread in the 1930s, as a result of the protectionist policies following the depression. In the Scandinavian countries, cooperative organizations created government-sanctioned commodity cartels; in the U.K. dominions, numerous producer-controlled marketing boards were created, and the government granted them compulsory power on domestic pricing, output regulations and foreign trade monopoly. National socialist Germany and fascist Italy created monopolistic state trading enterprises. In the United States, conversely, the initiative to create a government export corporation (the McNarry-Haugen bills from 1924 to 1928) failed.

After World War II, European governments continued a policy to safeguard agricultural produce supplies through governmental bulk purchases and price supports. In the 1960s the United States became one of the most important state traders in international markets by virtue of its trading in grains. McColla and Schmitz estimated for the period 1973 to 1977 that 95 percent of world trade in wheat involved state traders as importers, exporters or both (in Kostecky, 1982, Chapter 3), and Kostecky estimated for all agricultural produce in the mid-1970s that state trading consisted of at least 27 or 28 percent of OECD (Organization for Economic Cooperation and Development) agricultural imports and exports. Kostecky reckons that this figure is an underestimate and that state trading would probably account for 40 to 45 percent of agricultural exports if quasi–state trading arrangements were included (Kostecky, 1982, Chapter 2). State trading by marketing boards consists of most agricultural exports in South Africa and is also very important in

Australia, Canada and New Zealand. It is also important in Austria, Finland, Japan and Norway.

State trading in agriculture in developed countries is justified by the need to achieve price stability, rural employment, guaranteed farmers' revenue, self-sufficiency and regular food supplies. To augment farmers' income, state trading agencies in the developed countries behaved as discriminating monopolists in the exports of products. Export transactions are used to reduce surpluses and are made at much lower than domestic prices.

As an extreme example, government-to-government sales of EEC surplus butter were made at one-third of domestic prices—clearly a case of dumping. One result of the EEC sales was that the New Zealand Dairy Board could not sell its butter in the United Kingdom, although New Zealand dairies produced at about one-third of EEC prices. Since exports are made by SOEs, consumer countries tend to import agricultural produce under rigid state control, too.

Some of the SOEs in agricultural exports have a considerable price-making power: Australia's Wheat Marketing Board has an 11.7 percent share in world exports, and the Canadian Wheat Board has 17.2 percent. The New Zealand Dairy Board controls 20.6 percent of world exports, and the Australian Dairy Corporation has 7.4 percent. The Canadian Wheat Board controls 27.5 percent of world oats exports and 37.2 percent of world barley exports. At the same time Japan's Food Agency procures 9 percent of world wheat imports, 13.3 percent of barley; its Raw Silk Corporation purchases 42.3 percent of the world imports of cocoons and raw silk, while its Tobacco and Salt Public Corporation acquires 7.5 percent of the world's unmanufactured tobacco imports (Kostecky, 1982, pp. 22-54).

Unlike the rich countries, monopolistic marketing boards in developing countries were used mainly to pay lower prices to the growers, and to siphon funds to industrialize. Governments also maintain overvalued exchange rates, which make imported food prices artificially low. As a result, farmers flocked to towns, and those remaining became impoverished. Grain imports into the middle-income developing countries grew from 26 percent of world imports of 109 million tons in 1970 to 36 percent of 1980's 228 million (The Economist, April 14, 1984, p. 14).

Many developing countries depend on one crop as a major source of income and of foreign exchange earnings. In these cases, SOEs are also seen as tools to increase the bargaining power of the country to secure better terms vis-à-vis their trading partners. Experience shows that in agricultural marketing, if the SOE is used as a fiscal agent, farmers may reduce the size of the crop. Ghana's cocoa production, e.g., has fallen from 500,000 tons in 1965 to fewer than 200,000 tons in 1984: the central marketing board pays growers very low prices, and as a result, they grow other crops or smuggle the cocoa to the Ivory Coast and Togo, where they get higher prices and are paid in convertible CFA francs with which they can buy goods Ghana has stopped importing.

A growing number of countries use state-owned marketing boards as a monopolistic buyer of all crops and the sole exporters. Since 1970 agricultural production in industrialized countries has been growing at 1.6 percent per annum, and the number of farmers has fallen by a third. At the same time, the EEC spends billions of dollars on agricultural subsidies, maintaining prices that are 50 percent higher than the world market. *The Economist* calculated that the United States gave each of its 2 million farmers $30,000 (April 14, 1984, p. 23). This world division of labor is maintained largely for political reasons. Developed countries pay their farmers high prices largely because of the political strength of the agricultural lobby. Developing countries tax their farmers to raise funds for industrialization. As a result, since World War II, with the exception of cotton, the export shares of developed countries have increased, and those of developing countries declined.

State trading in agriculture is advocated as the only practical solution for assuring efficient exports and quality control and reaping the benefits of economies of scale, particularly in perishable goods. At the same time, if domestic price stabilization and guaranteed income to farmers is the major objective, then international trade may be based on dumping prices. Further, the monopolistic power of the SOEs may lead to less efficiency within the agency. (See, e.g., Warley, 1963, p. 555).

A monopolistic marketing board can be very effective in restricting imports, without breaking any GATT rules. It can create invisible barriers to trade, which are much more effective than tariffs and quotas, by refusing to import, claiming consumers' tastes and other commercial considerations. It is difficult to counter claims by a tobacco monopoly that it does not import foreign cigarettes because the consumers prefer local tobacco or by an alcohol state monopoly that says consumers prefer local brands of wine. (See Bernier, 1975, pp. 98, 341. See also the European Commission reports on competition.)

Despite the web of government intervention in agriculture, there has never been a serious discussion of the effect of these policies on international trade and division of labor. Since agricultural policies have long been embodied in the political structure of developed market economies, the chance of their fading away is remote. Farmers' lobbies pressure for government support prices and for state subsidies of inputs, transportation and financing. For many countries, agricultural exports are a major foreign exchange earner, and governments want to control these exports. Without modification of internal price fixing, however, very little can be done to regulate distortions in world trade.

Oil

In many LDCs, nationalization was perceived as a weapon to capture benefits previously accrued to MNEs and to end foreign control. Third World governments perceived the world economic order to be designed by the rich, for the rich. Wresting control over key natural resources from foreigners was seen as a major gain for the country. These gains, it was hoped, would enable the government to diversify the nation's economic activities, to generate greater employment opportunities and to promote economic growth. As a result, many oil and mineral resources have been nationalized since the 1960s.

The major energy source apart from oil has been coal. As shown in Chapter 3, much of the coal was moved to state ownership after World War II. Thus, the U.K. NCB controls all local mining, as does Charbonnages de France. Norwegian coal is state owned, and so are coal deposits in Austria, Brazil, India and Mexico. Germany helped create Ruhrkohle. Global economically recoverable coal resources are estimated to be 697.7 million metric tons (Berkowitz, 1979, p. 18). Out of this total, 26.1 percent (182 million metric tons) is located in the United States. Australia, Japan, Belgium and the Federal Republic of Germany account for an additional 9.3 percent. Most of the rest is owned and controlled by SOEs in Eastern and Western Europe, Asia and Africa. It is estimated that SOEs and state-controlled firms (as in Germany) control approximately two-thirds of the world's economically recoverable coal resources. The coal industry has been declining, and most countries protected their local SOEs by forcing other SOEs—mainly in electricity—to purchase local coal at higher than world market prices, thus creating a very potent barrier to international trade.

Until the early 1970s, international oil trade was dominated by MNEs. In 1950, the seven major oil firms owned 98.2 percent of the Western world's crude oil, excluding that in the United States, and other international oil companies owned the rest. Since then the picture has changed dramatically. In 1970 the percentage owned by these seven firms was 68.9, other international oil companies owned 22.7 percent and producing countries' national oil companies owned 8.4 percent. By 1979, the share of the seven firms declined to 23.9 percent, the share of other international oil companies was reduced to 7.4 percent, while the share of national oil companies in producing countries zoomed to 68.7 percent (Levy, 1982, p. 117).

Oil has been recognized as a strategically crucial commodity since the beginning of World War I, and governments sought to avoid reliance on foreign firms for oil. As noted in Chapter 3, the U.K. government acquired in 1914 51 percent of British Petroleum, one of the seven major oil companies, to ensure oil supplies to the navy. France created in 1924 the Compagnie Française des Pétroles (CFP), "to manage the German shares in the Turkish Petroleum Company . . . assigned to France by the San Remo Treaty of 1920 (Zakariya, p. 482). In 1929, the French government owned 35 percent of CFP). Feigenbaum (1985) claims the acquisition of the shares of CFP by the State was, in fact, a bailout" (p. 57). To stimulate domestic refining, France regulated the oil market. Italy created AGIP in 1926 to explore and produce oil abroad. It lost its concessions as a result of the outcome of World War II and, but for the perseverance of Enrico Mattei and the good fortune of gas discovery in Italy, AGIP would have been sold. Argentina established Yacimientos Petroliferos Fiscales de Argentina (YFF) in 1922 and Mexico created Petroleos Mexicanos (PEMEX) in 1938 to manage its nationalized producing areas.

The seven major oil MNEs were able to build formidable barriers to entry. Exploration and refining required large sums of money and technology known only to a few. The MNEs also gradually acquired the know-how of global operations. The U.S. firms had the advantage of learning these skills in the world's largest market, while Royal Dutch Shell and British Petroleum had the good fortune of early oil discovery and access to oil fields in the Middle East. The U.S. firms were at first not allowed to explore in the Middle East, but U.S. government pressures gained them relaxation of these restrictions (Turner, 1978, Chapters 2 and 3). The Achnacarry (or as is) agreement of 1928 was designed to carve out the market among Standard Oil of New Jersey, (now Exxon) Anglo-Persian (now British Petroleum) and Royal Dutch Shell, but with time the four other major U.S. firms also gained access to the market.

Having gained control of upstream supplies, these seven MNEs were also able to achieve downstream control. Transfer pricing left very low margins to refinery operations, leaving the bulk of the profits where entry barriers were highest in the crude production. This policy was fortified until 1975 by certain provision of U.S. tax law (Jenkins and Wright, 1975). The so-called seven sisters dominated international trade in oil, and its price remained relatively low for decades. The seven major firms also controlled the marketing channels. When the National Iranian Oil Company was created in 1951, nationalizing oil in Iran, the marketing power of the seven MNEs was great enough to block the company's ability to sell crude independently.

With time, more national oil companies entered into the picture. Abundant capital was available to governments both from developed countries and from other sources, and a world market in oil technology began to open up. Many countries had new leaders eager to prove their ability to help their country. A generation of young technocrats and politicians trained in industrialized countries was both willing and able to negotiate new conditions, enjoying a familiarity with the intricacies of international trade and the complexities of the international political and economic environment. National oil companies were established in Third World countries mainly to negotiate with foreign oil companies and gather information.

In the 1960s the discovery of oil and gas in the North Sea raised questions about state control of the new resources in both Norway and the United Kingdom. Norway established Statoil as a wholly owned SOE in 1972, and the U.K. government followed this example, creating the British National Oil Company (BNOC) on January 1, 1976. The aim of both was to increase the state's revenues for oil and to ensure more information on and a better understanding of the world's situation. Similar considerations led to the establishment of Petro Canada in 1975 and PETROBRÁS in Brazil in 1953. It seems that the U.K. government did not consider itself sufficiently in control of British Petroleum and therefore created the new company after first exercising its ownership rights through the NCB.

In 1972, Iraq nationalized all properties of the major firms; Venezuela nationalized its oil in 1975; Kuwait National Oil Company took over 100 percent ownership in 1975; Saudi Arabia did so in 1980 and Iranian oil was totally controlled by the National Iranian Oil Company in 1979.

In September 1960, representatives of Iran, Iraq, Kuwait, Saudi Arabia and Venezuela met in Baghdad. They called for stabilization of oil prices and formed the organization of the Petroleum Exporting Countries (OPEC). Quatar joined OPEC in 1961, Indonesia and Libya in 1962, Abu Dhabi (later UAE) in 1967, Algeria in 1971, Ecuador in 1973 and Gabon, after being an associate member since 1973, became a full member in 1975.

In 1970 the Libyan government radically restructured the terms of its agreements with independents, precipitating a rash of contract renegotiations throughout the oil-producing world. The MNEs' revenue per barrel dropped from 80 cents in the early 1950s to 32 cents by 1972, but the growth in the volume of trade allowed continuous profitability despite lower prices offered by independents.

Following the oil crisis, non-oil-exporting countries also established national oil companies. As one example, in the Federal Republic of Germany the state-owned VEBA merged with the privately owned Gelsenberg to create an SOE equal in refining capacity to the largest foreign-owned company in Germany. All in all, more than 100 countries have established state oil companies with mandates to participate in the exploration, production and sale of petroleum. Governments also protected their domestic markets for local refiners, and France, Italy, Germany, Spain, Brazil and India established state-owned refining firms. These changes left oil companies with no option but to supply crude to the state-owned (and protected domestic privately owned) refineries.

In 1973, the seven major oil MNEs still controlled 92 percent of world trade, while direct marketing by producer countries was only 7.9 percent of the total. (It was nil in 1966.) However, the major firms sold 22.5 percent of the world total to independent refineries. The major oil companies sold some refineries and others were nationalized. By 1979, direct marketing by producer countries was 42.2 percent of the world total, and 16.3 percent more was sold by the major firms to independent refineries. The growth of independent refineries and the shortage of oil in the 1970s provided the producing national oil companies with the opportunity to market their crude directly, and this opportunity was seized mainly by the more experienced of these such as those of Iran, Iraq, Kuwait or Venezuela.

The 1979 oil shortage caused the governments of consumer countries to start buying oil directly from the SOEs in producing countries. Neoclassical economists argue that oil and other exhaustible national resources "are basically no different from other factors of production" (Stiglitz, 1979, p. 64).

Governments, however, disagreed. The preponderant place of oil in virtually every national economic sector meant that governments attempted to ensure access to oil supplies, looking at oil as a public good (Smart, 1981). The producing SOEs took advantage of the situation to reduce further the market share of the international MNEs. Petromin, the Saudi Arabian SOE, sold oil to the Danish government on the condition that the latter would not market the oil through existing oil company channels but would establish a state-owned marketing network. By the early 1980s, the seven major MNEs had to purchase 7 percent of their crude oil requirements in the open market. By that time, the structure of international trade in oil was very different, and the power distribution between MNEs, independents and SOEs completely shifted. The seven major MNEs accounted for only 40 percent of refineries that depended on international trade for crude and lost most of their market share to national oil companies upstream.

With increasing government-to-government deals, many of the vertically integrated linkages were completely destroyed, resulting in an increased volatility of crude prices. The loss of a buffer between oil production and its final consumption exposed oil-producing nations to direct pressures of the international markets. The increase in the number of participants in that market and their interests made it difficult for oil producers to maintain pricing disciplines. In addition, the magnitude of direct deals "has given wider latitude to officials from exporting countries, adding to the opportunities for corruption" (Levy, 1982, p. 126). More important, the loss of insulation of the vertical integration made market risks more difficult to manage. The stabilizing role played in the past by the seven major firms has become less important, although these firms still control 40 percent of the international flow of crude oil.

State-owned crude oil producers have been engaged in increasing refining activities, installing new refineries and acquiring existing ones in foreign countries. Still, direct marketing makes it harder for sellers to maintain a stable structure of crude oil prices. As a result, they face heightened uncertainty. In times of glut their export earnings might decline, while when prices increase, nonintegrated refineries are forced to pay higher prices, which may wreak havoc with the economies of countries. The loss of the umbrella shelter provided by the vertically integrated MNEs, with diverse crude oil sources, makes both sellers and buyers more vulnerable to extreme price oscillations. Long-term contracts have proved unreliable in times of major price changes. Many governments in consumer countries responded by increasing government-to-government deals, often through barter agreements to increase the producers' incentives to maintain the contracts. For example, France supplied Iraq with nuclear technology, Japan helped in expanding the Mexican steel industry in exchange for oil and oil trade between Italy and Venezuela has been tied to economic cooperation in industry and agriculture.

The fear of a major cutback in production for reasons such as upheaval in Saudi Arabia or a major oil war is a very important consideration in the unstable and volatile oil world of today. Many countries make strenuous efforts to reduce their dependence on oil imports for fear of a major economic disaster in the event of supply disruptions. The result is heightened government intervention in the energy field and increased operations of national oil companies. These SOEs are seen, first and foremost, as an instrument to secure national energy supplies. As Frankel noted, the oil MNEs "represented a system of global optimization which might have been perfectly justified in itself, yet might conceivably have been deleterious to some individual country or another. No one will accept being optimized out of the system" (1980, p. 5).

For reasons discussed in Chapter 8, the creation of national oil companies did not necessarily mean more government control or even knowledge of the intricacies of the industry. Theoretically, these SOEs are not permitted to operate unfettered by political constraints. In reality, their managers, eager to increase their autonomy, have frequently allied themselves with the major international firms against their government. During the 1973 to 1974 oil crisis, "it was once again evident that oil was too important to be left to oilmen. The old notion of oil companies as the instruments of foreign policy had been turned on its head, as the companies appeared to be making foreign policy" (Sampson, 1976, p. 329). Both U.K. and French oil firms refused to divert deliveries from foreign customers to assure their home country's supply of oil (Sampson, 1976, p. 315). As Stobaugh notes, "BP executives remained adamant, saying the laws and the contracts for delivery written under those laws took priority over instructions from their shareholders" (1976, p. 189). As to France, "although the government had never veered from its original instructions to the companies . . . even the two French companies had also never promised to follow them . . . the CFP allocated its supplies along the same pattern as the majors" (1976, p. 190).

Metal Minerals

Most world production and trade of metal minerals has followed a similar pattern: an increasing share of SOEs and a breakdown of the old oligopolies and their vertical integration. At the beginning of the 1960s only 2.5 percent of the copper capacity in the free world was state owned (Prain, 1975). The four largest privately owned copper MNEs controlled about 50 percent of the mine production of the market economies (Moran, 1974). On December 31, 1966, Joseph Mobutu of Zaire issued a declaration of economic independence, expropriating all assets of Union Minière de Haute Katanga, which controlled virtually all Congolese copper, cobalt, diamond and uranium mining. The assets were transferred to the Société Générale Congolese de Minérals (Gecomin, later Gecamines). In 1969, Zambia took over 51 percent of what was Zambian Anglo American Ltd. and Roan Selection Trust Ltd., and its equity share was increased to just over 60 percent in 1978. All Zambian copper was put under one holding company, ZIMCO. The two separate copper producers were merged in 1982 into Zambia Consolidated Copper Mines Ltd. (ZCCM).

In 1969, Chile nationalized the large copper mines (CODELCO) and completed the takeover in 1971. CODELCO controls nearly 80 percent of Chile's copper output. Peru nationalized in 1974 Cerro de Pasco, subsequently renamed Centromin. A new SOE, Mineroperu, was set up in 1977, and it started production of new copper mines (Cerro Verde). In 1980, Mexico started production in the La Caridad mines, of which the government holds 44 percent. By 1981, 40.5 percent of the Western world's total capacity of copper mining was carried out with significant state ownership, and three of the four largest copper corporations were state owned (CODELCO in Chile, GECAMINES in Zaire and ZIMCO in Zambia). This state ownership is almost exclusively a developing country phenomenon. Outside Africa, Asia, Latin America and Papua New Guinea, significant state ownership in copper mining can be found only in Finland, Spain, Turkey and Yugoslavia. In the subsequent stages of copper processing, the share of SOEs is falling. Thus, while 73 percent of copper mining capacity in developing countries is state owned, it is only 30.6 percent in smelting and 25.9 percent in refining (Radetzki, 1985).

In 1967, the largest copper SOEs established a cartel: the Intergovernmental Council of Copper Exporting Countries Conseil Intergouvernemental des Pays Exportateurs (CIPEC). They attempted a joint reduction in output to influence copper prices, but their dependence on copper for foreign exchange earnings was so strong that it diminished their bargaining power. For example, in 1975 CIPEC decided on a 15 percent production cut from previous years, hoping to reverse the serious fall in copper prices at the end of 1974. Zambia's output was only 3 percent lower than its 1974 level (Radetzki, 1985, p. 165).

The story is repeated for other mineral mines. Guyana completely nationalized bauxite-producing firms in 1971, and Jamaica took over Kaiser's and Reynold's operations in 1977. In 1974, the International Bauxite Association (IBA) came into being.

Several SOEs in Third World countries increased capacity rapidly: Brazil and Guinea are two well-known examples. In 1981, 45 percent of Western world capacity and 71 percent of Third World capacity has significant government ownership. However, analogous to the copper situation, the SOEs' share is substantially lower in alumina refining and aluminum smelting, and most of these facilities are in industrialized countries. By 1980, 24.2 percent of Western world capacity in aluminum refining and 22.8 percent in aluminum smelting had significant state ownership. SOEs that controlled 10 percent or more of Western world capacity in alumina refineries were in Guinea, Jamaica, the Federal Republic of Germany, Italy and Yugoslavia.

The relatively complex technology in aluminum refining enables the MNEs to maintain a firm grip over this stage of production. Smelters moved after the 1973 oil crisis to cheap energy locations, and most of the new smelters were state owned (Bahrain, Dubai, Iran, Turkey, Egypt, South Africa and Venezuela). Also state-owned are smelters in West Germany, Norway and Italy.

In 1981 France nationalized Péchiney-Ugine-Kuhlman, one of the six MNEs in the aluminum industry, controlling (in 1971) 4.9 percent of overall bauxite capacity, 8.2 percent of primary aluminum capacity and 5.9 percent of alumina capacity of the Western world (Rodrik, in Jones et al., 1982, pp. 195-196).

In iron ore, SOEs controlled in 1981 40 percent of the Western world's total and 62 percent of the developing countries' total. This was a result of nationalizations in Mauritania (1974), Peru (1975), Chile (1971), Venezuela (1974), the taking over of LKAB by the Swedish government in 1957 (the government has owned 50 percent of the company's equity since 1907), the expansion of Brazilian Compahnia Vale do Rio Doce (CVRD) and the establishment of the Liberian Lamco Joint Venture and Bong Mining Company in the early 1960s (Vernon and Levy in Jones et al., 1982).

Up to 1952 the only major state-owned tin production was in colonial Indonesia. Bolivia nationalized the three major tin groups in 1952, creating the state-owned COMIBOL with 9 percent of the world market. P.T. Timah, the Indonesian state tin corporation, controlled 80 percent of tin production in Indonesia and 10 percent of the world market, and in Malaysia, 25 percent of tin production is controlled by the 71 percent state-owned Malaysia Mining Corporation. Zaire and Nigeria, holding together 3 percent of Western world output, also acquired large equity stakes in formerly foreign-owned tin mines. Tin smelters, however, are still privately owned, and SOEs did not integrate forward to tin-consuming plants. In 1976, only Indonesia, Bolivia and Zaire had tin-smelting capacity, approximately 6 percent of total world capacity. When the USSR, China and German Democratic Republic were added, SOEs controlled 27.1 percent of world tin-smelting capacity, with private companies accounting for 73 percent. SOEs cannot, therefore, exact strong bargaining power in the market. All in all, state ownership in tin zoomed from practically zero in 1950 to more than 30 percent of Western world production in 1980. Thus, the combination of nationalization and new production by SOEs changed the shape of the major international mineral scene. The same is true for other minerals. Thus, in cobalt, Zaire's SOE accounted for 50 percent of Western world capacity. SOEs operated also in Zambia, Finland and Morocco (Radetzki, 1985; Labysin, Kostecky, 1982, pp. 78-102).

Regarding nickel, however, approximately 85 percent of world production is accounted for by private interests, and no nationalizations have occurred since the Cuban one in 1960. Most of the capacity of lead and zinc is located in industrialized countries, with SOEs controlling only 20 to 25 percent of the overall capacity (Radetzki, 1985).

In sum, SOEs have expanded enormously in the operations of oil and minerals, mostly in developing countries. Apparently this expansion will not continue at the rate of the 1960s and 1970s, which was due mostly to the newly gained political independence of Third World countries and the rectification of perceived colonial ills. Many of these countries are becoming increasingly disillusioned about their ability to manage new expansions in the mineral world on their own. Despite the belief that SOEs have easier access to low-cost capital, most new projects in the mineral field are launched jointly by governments and MNEs. Once governments assert their political independence and economic emancipation, they become more realistic about their ability to manage large-scale enterprises. At the same time, MNEs have learned that there is a great deal to gain from government management contracts.

The most important consequence of the rapid expansion of SOEs in minerals, as in oil, seems to have been a shift from control by a few giant vertically integrated MNEs to more vulnerable national producers. The change in market structure has affected the bargaining power buyers can exert on the producers. The entry of SOEs into the market increased competition among producers by eroding the control of the MNEs over access to sales and technology. Japan has taken advantage of the much reduced cost of ocean transportation, signing long-term agreements for iron ore supplies with Australia. The much weakened vertically integrated chains developed by the U.S. steel firms, a steady decline in the concentration of these industries, and the large number of SOEs reduce the possibility of creating effective cartels.

Bauxite is the only commodity whose price formation the SOEs can influence. The retaliatory power of others in the market still suffices to prevent SOEs from bargaining for significant price increases of other commodities. Few SOEs have demonstrated their ability to develop initiatives or to integrate vertically. Vertical integration is a well-known way to improve stability. Several oil SOEs have attempted this route, e.g., Elf's acquisition of Texas Gulf in 1982. However, an earlier attempt of Elf management to acquire the American firm, Kerr Magee, in 1980, was axed by Raymond Barre, then France's prime minister (see Feigenbaum, 1985, pp. 83-84). Foreign acquisitions by SOEs evoke strong political opposition at home. It is felt that profits should be used to strengthen the domestic economy, or to buy out failing companies to preserve employment (Feigenbaum, 1985, p. 84, Mazzolini, 1979). To the extent that governments do not allow their SOEs to expand internationally, the SOE suffers comparative disadvantage *vis-à-vis* its private competitors.

A country controlling a significant share of the world market production of a commodity may also attempt to manage the market conditions by limiting production. This policy was adopted by India for tea and by OPEC for oil. In the 1980s, however, Chile opted for another policy. From the end of 1974 to 1979 copper prices plummeted and dropped further by about half, in dollar terms, from January 1980 to December 1984. Chile is the world's cheapest producer of copper: CODELCO produces a pound of copper for 40 cents, which is half as much as the U.S. price. In the 1980s, CODELCO expanded production, apparently hoping that low prices would force expensive producers, like the United States, to exit. The U.S. copper producers filed a complaint with the International Trade Commission (ITC), claiming that CODELCO was subsidized by both the Chilean government and soft loans from international lending agencies. The ITC recommended import quotas, but President Reagan overruled this (*The Economist*, December 22, 1984, pp. 69–70). Similar complaints were filed in many cases of declining industries where competition is fierce.

SOES IN MANUFACTURING

Until the 1970s, manufacturing SOEs, except a few, were oriented toward serving local markets. The newly created SOEs, mainly in developing countries, were established as an integral part of an import-substitution policy. In the first stages of operation, they had to master the complex problems of production reliability, and preferred to sell in the protected domestic markets. Even in developed countries, the local demand was generally large enough and governmentally imposed import barriers high enough to lower the propensity of the SOEs to export. The major impact of SOEs during this period was a reduction of the flow of international trade. With time, MNEs established subsidiaries to circumvent import restrictions, and SOEs increased their exports. The reasons for the new trend were different for different industries.

SOEs in Declining and Mature Industries

In the 1970s governments in all countries of the industrial world were faced with a deep recession, two jumps in the oil prices and the resulting balance of payments problems. The rapid industrialization of some developing countries started to bear fruit, and the need for managing transitions in declining industries such as steel, shipbuilding and textiles became acute. Left to unchecked market forces, the adjustment process would have created politically intolerable high unemployment and unacceptable human hardship.

Governments are pressured to ameliorate the social impact of the collapse of large business firms. When a whole industry faces severe financial difficulties or an imminent failure, governments feel they have to take remedial action to reduce the high costs of adjustment: unemployment, shattered careers and destroyed communities. Since the cost of unemployment benefits and welfare payments have to be borne by government, the incentive to maintain employment is greater, and the reaction of some governments has been to save jobs by acquiring the ailing firms. This phenomenon has added to the general suspicion that governments are using their SOEs to export unemployment and to circumvent the restrictions they agreed to honor through the different international agreements of the post–World War II period. The question of state trading has become a major problem on the international agenda and may increase in importance as the problems of adjustment become more acute.

In all industrial countries the steel industry is going through an era of a slow growth in demand, while at the same time many new suppliers have been emerging from Japan and the developing countries. In 1950, the United States clearly dominated the world steel industry, accounting for 57 percent of the free world's raw steel production, but its share dropped to roughly 24 percent in 1981. The EEC's share dropped slightly from 32 percent to 28 percent, while Japan's rose from 3 percent in 1950 to 22 percent in 1981. The rest of the non-Communist world—mainly Brazil, Spain and South Korea—accounted for 8 percent of world production in 1950 and 20 percent in 1981 (Hogan, 1983). The steel firms in all developed countries have found it increasingly more difficult to maintain their market shares.

If markets were left to their own devices, in the long run, basic steel production would shift to developing countries, particularly those with readily available ferrous ore, and would be produced in large integrated coastal plants, operating mainly in Brazil, Venezuela, Argentina and South Korea, and would export the basic steel to developed countries focusing on specialty steels, downstream processing and steel-making equipment. In the medium term, Japan and some of the advanced developing countries would gain market shares, and obsolescent plants in both Europe and the United States would shut down. The division of labor in steel today, however, is not market driven but politically determined. Since governments are concerned with the adjustment costs, and since this concern is accentuated by lobbying of affected interest groups—both producers and labor—governments have made enormous efforts to slow down the adjustment both by subsidizing ambitious programs of modernization and expansion and by protecting local firms from export control.

The reasons for the unmitigated crisis in the United States and European steel industries are manifold. The most important are the following:

The rapid growth of the Japanese steel industry, the world leader in productivity and efficiency. The modern Japanese steel firms employ blast furnaces, which use 30 percent less coke per ton produced than those in the United States. Continuous casting confers another 7 to 8 percent efficiency advantage, and the location of very large plants in coastal areas reduces transportation costs. In 1977, labor productivity

in Japan was 327 tons per wage earner, compared with 249 tons in the
United States, 190 tons in Germany, 239 tons in Italy, 149 tons in
France and 115 tons in British Steel (Stoffaës and Gadonneix, 1980,
p. 414).

The expansion of iron and steel facilities in some developing countries
and in Eastern Europe and China.

The lag of the United States behind the Japanese in the introduction of
technological advances. Lulled into a false feeling of security by increasing demands in the 1960s, big U.S. firms installed basic oxygen
furnaces (BOF) more than a decade after they were used by foreign
competitors.

Reduced demands for steel, both because of inexpensive substitutes (aluminum and plastics) and the reduction in car production.

Reduced ocean transportation costs and rising surface transportation
costs, punishing landlocked U.S. and European producers.

The strategic decisions of governments to protect their domestic industries and retain the old plants despite lagging productivity.

Steel industry output, triggered by constant growth of demand, grew
steadily during the 1960s and the early 1970s. Global production of steel was
340 million tons in 1960, rose to 595 million tons in 1970 and reached a
record output of 709 million in 1974. This continuous growth caused un-
bounded optimism among steelmakers. Few, if any, could see beyond the
euphoria and realize that prosperity would end abruptly in 1975 (Hogan,
1983).

At first, the severe recession faced by the steel industry in 1975 was
thought to be part of a normal business cycle. World steel output in that year
went down to 651 million tons, while OECD countries' output declined from
418 to 341 million tons from 1974 to 1975. Prices deteriorated further later,
but new producers (Australia, Spain, South Korea and Brazil) increased world
capacity. The introduction of new technologies made old plants obsolete. The
reaction of most firms was a vigorous export drive and price cutting to gain
market shares, coupled with pressures on government to protect local industry
against the inroads of imports.

In 1978 and 1979, world steel production was respectively 717.2 and
747.5 million tons. Socialist countries produced 34.6 and 33.3 percent respectively of the total, SOEs in market economy countries produced 14.2 and
15.2 percent and private enterprises in market economy countries were responsible for 51.2 and 51.5 percent respectively. Nearly half the steel production, therefore, was state owned. In contrast, as early as 1950, 77 percent of
the world's steel output was in private hands (Hogan, 1983, p. 227).

In 1965, of the EEC countries, only Ireland, Italy and Germany had
state-owned steel firms, covering respectively 100 percent, 60 percent and 40
percent of output. The only other European state-owned steel plants operated

in Austria. In 1967, the United Kingdom renationalized almost its entire steel industry. By 1981, state-owned steel was 76 percent of production in the United Kingdom, 70 percent in France, 57 percent in Belgium, 60 percent in Italy, 100 percent in Ireland, 30 percent in Denmark and 30 percent in the Netherlands. Sweden also nationalized the industry in the last decade as a response to its troubles, and Spain built new capacity. Further, some of the new steel plants in the developing countries have been created by governments and were therefore state owned originally. Among the emerging suppliers, steel firms in Chile, Iran, South Korea, Peru, Saudi Arabia, Libya, Tunisia, Algeria, Morocco and China will be entirely state owned by 1988, and in Venezuela, Turkey, Argentina, Brazil, Spain and Mexico the majority will be state owned. Private steel production still exists in Brazil (35 percent of total output) and in small shares in Mexico and Argentina (the largest steel producer, Somise, is state owned). These countries built capacity in excess of anticipated market growth, achieving economies of scale and encouraging exports to gain foreign currency. The shift to more state ownership is also a result of the growth of steel production in the USSR and in the Eastern European Communist countries.

Private ownership still dominates in the United States, Japan, Luxembourg and Germany. These countries also gave their industries heavy financial support to allow them to start (Japan) or reduce or to avert the social hardships of the adjustment. The result has been a bewildering array of trade control measures, subsidies, guarantees of loans and equity and cartel arrangements to aid domestic industry.

One question raised by this situation is what are the differences, if any, between government aid and government ownership? Another is the consequences of the different support systems to the autonomy of the firm. Thus, it might be argued that the very act of nationalization eliminated the powerful lobby of the business managers and owners and thus altered the political coalition and modified the outcomes. A different hypothesis is that the policy clashes that characterized government–business relations have been internalized into the government apparatus. In Chapter 2, I argued that an efficient method of effecting change and reducing the size of the employment is moving the firm into state ownership. The need to grant the firms direct subsidies often entails governmental or parliamentary approval for the additional budget needed. A government that succumbs to political pressures and bails a company out finds it difficult to continue to pay subsidies year in and year out. Helping a firm through tariff protection is a one-shot deal that does not need annual budget appropriations.

A comparison of private and state-owned steel firms may give us a better idea as to the most efficient adjustment method from both the economic and the social point of view. If indeed a private firm is more likely to be aided by tariff protection or subtler methods like a trigger price mechanism (TPM) and an SOE by direct governmental subsidies, then it may well be that the propensity of the firms to decline will be higher under state ownership than under private ownership. This seeming paradox is explained by the changing visibility of the aid to the industry as well as the changing structure of the political coalition.

In 1965, the French government negotiated the Steel Plan with the private industrialists. Two major poles of concentration were created (Usinor in the north and Sacilor-Sollac in Lorraine). The two private firms received government funds to erect two large integrated steel plants with modern technologies, close to the coast. While the new modern plants were erected with public aid, old plants were retained, and the labor force was not reduced. Annual production increased from 17 million metric tons in 1960 to 27 million in 1974. The labor force remained exactly the same—158,000 employees—but productivity increased by 40 percent. In 1975, the inroads of competition from the new producers and the antidumping quotas introduced by the United States caused prices to collapse and production to fall by 20 percent. Assuming the recession to be short-lived, the labor force was still not reduced. In 1977, a new plan was worked out that reduced the labor force by 20,000, initiated a financial moratorium and assistance and closed obsolete plants. In 1978, the steel companies were effectively nationalized. The two steel firms absorbed almost half of all French subsidies (Fr5.5 billion out of a total of Fr12.85 billion—less than half of what these SOEs wanted), and their losses in 1983 reached Fr9 billion ($1 billion). Between the peak of 1974 and the end of 1981, steel employment in France declined from 197,800 to 97,500. The French government required the firms to balance their books by 1985, knock steel production down and reduce employemnt by another 35,000 (Stoffaës and Gadonneix, 1980).

British Steel, the world's third largest steel producer, creates a sea of red ink. It embarked on an ambitious modernization program in the early 1970s to reduce its costs in anticipation of a demand increase that did not materialize. In the meantime, imports grew from 5 to 20 percent of the U.K. market. Despite the huge losses between 1974 and 1978, British Steel was prevented from closing works and reducing employment at the rate required by market conditions. Still, employment in the U.K. steel industry was reduced by 31 percent from 1960 to 1980. Between 1974 and December 1981, steel employment in the United Kingdom fell from 194,300 to 88,300 (Hogan, 1983, p. 51).

In the United States, "[s]teelmen attribute their misfortunes to unfair trade practices, heavy-handed government interference, and high labor costs" (Lawrence and Dyer, 1983, p. 72). They constantly charged that foreign producers were dumping steel in the United States and were able to win some such cases and to receive different protections like the TPM, introduced in March 1978. The steel crisis and the specter of rising imports caused the management and the unions to sign in 1973

> [T]he Experimental Negotiating Agreement (ENA), which granted
> the steelworkers annual wage increases of three percent plus cost-of-
> living adjustment (plus a bonus at the first signing). In exchange,
> workers pledged not to strike and to lend support to lobbying efforts
> against imports. . . . as a result, steel workers' real wages rose well
> in excess of productivity improvements. Between 1973 and 1979
> wages in the mills rose 119 percent, compared with a 63 percent rise
> in the consumer price index. At the same time, the rate of produc-
> tivity improvement slowed down alarmingly. Since 1962 it has
> grown by only two percent per annum. [Lawrence and Dyer, 1983,
> p. 75]

Because marginal operations were closed, the labor force in the U.S. steel industry between 1960 and 1979 dropped by 25 percent from 450,000 to 340,000 (Lawrence and Dyer, 1983, p. 76)—less than in the United Kingdom where government prevented British Steel from reducing the labor force! In the predominantly private German steel industry, employment was 232,000 at the peak of 1974 and was reduced to 186,700 by December 1981. The only exception is Italy, where employment for the same period increased from 95,700 to 97,500 (Hogan, 1983, p. 51).

The picture is certainly more complicated and is composed of many variables, including unfettered optimism, the impact of the EEC plans (Davignon plan) for the rationalization of European steel (that allowed construction of new plants only if producers involved agree to dismantle old plants of equivalent size) and management inertia. The short cases presented, however, do not show that state ownership necessarily means more government aid or freezing employment. On the contrary, British and French SOEs reduced employment more than privately held U.S. and German firms.

However, there is a strong preconceived notion that SOEs are the servants of their governments, abiding by all their commands, and these governments seek to increase foreign exchange earnings and maintain employment by exporting the products of their SOEs at all costs, which has a disrupting effect on the international markets and places privately owned firms at a distinct disadvantage. The U.S. administration has been under growing protectionist pressure from carbon steel management and labor beginning in 1975 and reaching a peak in 1977. In 1978, immediately following the introduction of the TPM, employment in the U.S. steel industry increased, and capacity utilization reached 85 percent. Lobbyists for the industry continued to demand protection against imports.

As the value of the dollar climbed against the yen, the trigger price was lowered in dollar terms. At the same time, the fall of European currencies vis-à-vis the yen and the U.S. dollar made European exports more profitable at the trigger price levels. U.S. Steel made it clear that the U.S. industry would revive antidumping suits against European firms should substantial

TPM concessions be made. On December 1981, the U.S. Secretary of Commerce, Malcolm Baldridge, and Viscount Étienne Davignon of the EEC agreed "to try to achieve peace by amending the TPM" (*The Economist*, December 19, 1981, p. 32. See also Dielman, 1981). However, on January 11, 1982, seven U.S. steel producers, including U.S. Steel, Bethlehem Steel and Jones & Laughlin Steel, charged "that foreign producers, mostly from Western Europe, had chiseled their way into a 19 percent import share of the U.S. market by selling government subsidized steel to American buyers" (*Time*, June 21, 1982, p. 50). As a result of the U.S. steel firm's antidumping suit, the Commerce Department ruled that the European SOEs were indeed subsidized, a ruling that required punitive action (see discussion following). On October 21, 1982, Secretary of Commerce Baldridge reached an agreement with Viscount Davignon that limited steel imports from Europe to the United States for 3 years, and the U.S. industry withdrew the suits. Clearly, SOEs competing with the declining U.S. industries can expect aggressive industry and government responses to their activities. Indeed, in 1984 President Reagan decided to impose new restrictions on imports of steel.

Whether or not policies to resist or delay adjustments are justifiable, these policies are widespread. Deprived by GATT of using tariff increases, governments have turned to other means of achieving the same objective of blocking changes in international trade flows. Governments used subsidies, nontariff barriers, import restrictions or "voluntary" exchange restrictions. It is not obvious that distortions to trade flows affecting private firms are less serious than those achieved through SOEs. To the extent that distortions are intended to maintain employment and real wages, the use of SOEs may reduce the level of subsidy, since profits do not have to be taken into account. From a political point of view, the visible aid through SOEs may be reduced faster than invisible protection.

SOEs in High-Technology Fields

The major private firms in the aerospace field are in the United States. Canada nationalized this industry, Brazil created Embraer, the Europeans created Airbus Industrie and the British, French, German, Spanish, Italian and Israeli aerospace firms are state owned.

Export of high-technology items is based on the creation of distribution channels, as well as after sale services. SOEs do not seem to have any comparative advantage when the products are intended for the mass consumers' markets. However, SOEs were successful in selling large-scale one-shot deals, in particular when the ability to offer financing at preferential terms or the willingness to accept barter arrangements as payments for the exports are important. Indeed, several SOEs were able to reach agreements on large-scale engineering projects. Interbrás, a subsidiary of Brazilian Petrobrás "has undertaken to promote the exports of a wide spectrum of Brazilian goods, including goods from private sources" (Vernon, 1981, p. 110). Airbus Industrie dominates today certain markets, e.g., in Asia. In 1985, it succeeded in taking the Indian market away from Boeing (*The Economist*, September 28, 1985, p. 75). Embraer has clearly demonstrated its ability to compete in the U.S. commuter aircraft market, penetrating mainly the niche of a mid-sized commuter aircraft (Sarathy, 1985).

SOEs are signing an increasing number of collaboration accords with United States and Japanese high-technology firms to gain access to new technology. Bull, the French state computer group, acquired a 10 percent stake in Ridge Computers of California in 1984 in exchange for taking the U.S. firm's high-performance industrial and scientific computer into its product range. Other French SOEs signed similar agreements with U.S. firms. Thus, Matra agreed on joint development and sales with Datapoint for the French office-automation market. Rhône Poulenc has formed a joint venture with Siltec for the manufacturing of silicone wafers, and another French SOE (Tecs: Software) collaborated with Rank Xerox on the development of artificial intelligence systems. SNECMA entered into joint venture with General Electric to develop the CFM 56 engine.

SOES IN SERVICES

SOEs are becoming increasingly important in services, too. Almost all countries of the world, with the glaring exception of the United States, operate state-owned airlines. In many countries, commercial banks are state owned. When banks are ranked in terms of assets less *contra* accounts, state-owned banks account for 23.0 percent of the assets held by the top fifty banks in the world in 1983 (23.7 percent in 1974) (calculated from *The Banker*, Top 300, 1976, 1979 and 1984 issues).

Banks, including state-owned banks, have expanded their operations abroad, opening subsidiaries and participating in international finance. Governments have reacted by restricting foreign banks' entry, but these restrictions apply to private as well as state-owned banks.

Both airlines and banks, as well as shipping, are increasingly important in carrying out international trade in services. There is a very interesting difference among these services: state-owned airlines are often charged with predatory behavior and are said to compete without any regard to costs. Banks, in contrast, are rarely accused of similar practices. Perhaps all banks, irrespective of ownership, have their arms twisted to help companies when the national interest is seen to be at stake. Experience shows that a government can control bank credit and manipulate the interest rate without owning financial institutions. Central bank lending and regulations can be dominated by government. As in other cases, the distinction is not based on ownership but on control and the means by which politics and economics are bridged.

Government may own the banks to dictate allocative choices, but it can achieve the same results by negotiations with interest groups at financial institutions (as in Germany). As Zysman argues:

> First, a credit-based price-administered financial system is an instrument of state intervention which blurs the lines in the market between public and private sectors. . . . Second, financial systems with extensive and efficient capital markets both limit the channels of state action and generate opposition to intervention. . . . Third, institution-led or bank-dominated capital markets create the conditions for negotiated adjustment. [1983, pp. 93–94]

In shipping, between 1971 and 1976, Soviet merchant marine increased the value of liner cargoes it carried to the United States nearly 45-fold. In 1978, the Soviets captured 13.8 percent market share in the Gulf Coast–Far East route, 5.8 percent in the Pacific Coast–Far East route and 9.3 percent of the Atlantic, Gulf, Pacific to Indonesia, Malaysia and Singapore market. It was alleged that the Soviet rates were 16.16 percent below the conference rates. The United States responded by enacting the Ocean Shipping Act of 1978.

> The major theme throughout the development of the Act was that state-controlled economy firms could lower rates with virtual impunity, because they were not bound by the same rules as those applicable to market economy firms, i.e., whereas the latter are required to cover costs in the long-run, the former may not be so restricted [Ellsworth et al., 1983, p. 483].

The provisions of the law are similar to the Antidumping Act of 1921: if the rates of a controlled carrier are found to be unreasonably low and are causing injury to a domestic firm, the competition is declared predatory.

MULTINATIONAL SOES

The voluminous literature on MNEs refer to their firms as privately owned. Certainly, writers on the topic knew that firms like British Petroleum or Renault are state owned, but these facts, to the extent they are noted, were seen as aberrations. More recently, SOEs have initiated or acquired subsidiaries in other countries in Europe, Latin America, Africa and the United States. Thus, Renault acquired a minority interest in American Motors Corporation, increasing its share in 1980 from 4.7 to 46.4 percent of the equity of that corporation; Elf-Aquitaine acquired 63.1 percent of Texas Gulf Inc. Canadian SOEs have also acquired subsidiaries beyond their national boundaries.

State-owned MNEs are particularly important in the petroleum sector. These firms went abroad to secure raw material supplies, assured markets for their oil and, sometimes, upstream investments. The state-owned MNEs in this group include firms from both industrialized countries (ENI in Italy, Elf-Aquitaine and CFP in France and British Petroleum) and developing countries such as PEROBRÃS in Brazil, PERTAMINA in Indonesia and PEMEX in Mexico, YPF in Argentina or PETROVEN in Venezuela.

Other SOEs went abroad to secure a critical resource such as copper or iron. Thus, the Brazilian Compahnia Vale do Rio Doce has acquired a coal mine in British Columbia and Pemex has acquired an affiliate in Spain (Wells, 1983, pp. 130–131 lists more examples) or to achieve economies of scale in production and marketing. The automobile industry, e.g., has become global, and the SOEs such as Volkswagen, B.L. (formerly British Leyland) or Renault are as much MNEs as Ford Motor Company or Toyota. SOEs went multinational also to protect existing export markets that were threatened by import substitution policies of the host government (Kumar, 1981) or acquired subsidiaries in the EEC and the United States to assure access to these markets without paying duties. In some cases, governments of several nations agreed to undertake jointly an economic activity each one of them alone could not handle. One famous case is that of Airbus Industrie, a joint venture of a number of European governments. Other examples are found in developing countries (Kumar and McLeod, 1981).

Despite the wide publicity of SOE investments, they have remained less than 5 percent of all foreign direct investments in the United States. The International Trade Administration (U.S. Department of Commerce, March 1983) identified only 147 cases of foreign government-owned or controlled direct investments in the United States made during 1974 to 1981, of which 124 were completed. The ITC list included also U.S. affiliates and subsidiaries of the five major international groups nationalized in France in 1982. Still, with each major acquisition by an SOE, waves of alarm were created and pressures have been growing to reconsider the international rules of the game.

The most complete study of multinational SOEs was carried out by Anastassopoulos *et al.*, (1985). They analyze what they term "public multinationals," "public enterprises or the way to multinationalization" and "engineering firms."

The authors divide these firms according to the propensity of the SOE to internationalize its activity on the one hand and the propensity of the government to interfere on the other hand. Thus, PEMEX is seen as a firm with a minimum propensity for multinational operation and a high level of government's propensity to intervene. Firms of this sort are called "pillars of development." Péchiney, Rhône Poulenc, DSM or Salzgitter have a high propensity to be MNEs and low government intervention. These are "multinationals quasi-private." Firms such as PETROBRÃS or YPF are seen as having medium propensity to be an MNE and a high level of government intervention. These are called "instruments of foreign policy" (1985, pp. 206-227).

THE PERCEIVED THREAT FROM SOES

The growth of new types of SOEs has been perceived by some U.S. commentators to be a threat to the U.S. position in world markets (Lamont, 1979, Nielsen, 1982, Monsen and Walters, 1983). It is alleged that these firms commonly have easier access to capital, often at subsidized rates: that governments underwrite their risks and that they receive preferential treatment in taxes, are exempt from import regulations, are free from government regulation, receive preference in governmental purchases and see their cost of capital as equal to zero. Further, SOEs may sell their products at lower prices overseas. An SOE is alleged to attempt to maximize employment. For all these reasons, SOEs are alleged to tend to increase exports by lowering prices, even below marginal costs, especially if the SOE has easier and cheaper sources of capital than private enterprises similarly situated and if it is expected to earn foreign currency. As a result, SOEs are alleged to have become a source of unfair competition.

These considerations are cited as *prima facie* proof that some specific restrictions on SOE exports, as well as international agreements on their market behavior in general, are long overdue.

There are mounting pressures for the international surveillance of SOEs, for the forced curtailment of their international activities and for the imposition of countervailing duties on SOEs' exports. On June 25, 1980, e.g., the EEC adopted a directive (80/723/EEC) "requiring member states to provide information on financing arrangements for SOEs and semi-public enterprises with a cumulative turnover of greater than 280 million pounds over the last two years." (Wyles, *Financial Times*, October 4, 1980). That certain governments—notably Italy and France—refused to supply the required information was seen by U.S. businesspeople as a sign that these governments have transactions they prefer to hide.

The erosion of U.S. hegemony since World War II has lessened the country's tolerance for foreign competition. The United States enacted the Trade Agreement Act of 1979, which expanded the scope of subsidies deemed countervailable, under Section 303 of the Tariff Act of 1930—that is, cases in which the U.S. government imposes countervailing duties to offset the competitive advantage gained by products subsidized by a foreign government. GATT rules prohibit export subsidies. The U.S. law included for the first time within its ambit domestic subsidies—subsidies given to exporters and nonexporters alike—that benefit exports to the United States. The 1979 Trade Agreement Act defined "subsidy," among other things, to include "the provision of capital, loans, or loan guarantees on terms inconsistent with commercial considerations" (19 U.S.C. §1677(5)(B)(Supp. V, 1981). Under the new law, several U.S. carbon steel manufacturers filed petitions for countervailing duties against the major steel producers in Western Europe, alleging, among other things, the existence of widespread and pervasive government subsidization. One of these alleged subsidies was participation of government in the equity of the firms.

Both in its preliminary and in its final countervailing duty determination of June 10, and of August 24, 1982, the U.S. Commerce Department determined government equity funding to be a countervailable subsidy. It thus made it a key component of the countervailing duty margins for SOEs in Belgium, France, Italy, Luxembourg, and the United Kingdom. Government participation in the equity of SOEs was seen as a subsidy if the funds were provided on terms "inconsistent with commercial considerations." Equity participation was deemed inconsistent with commercial considerations if the firm was uncreditworthy from the standpoint of an investor at the time the investment was made. Essentially, the Commerce Department's approach was that if an SOE loses, it is uncreditworthy. In this case, as related earlier, a political agreement was reached, and the U.S. steel firms withdrew their suits.

The Commerce Department decision obviously had enormous ramifications on the exports of SOEs to the United States (for details and analysis, see Barshefsky, Mattice and Martin, 1983). It essentially means that the United States may impose countervailing duties on SOEs because a government increased equity participation in any firm that showed losses. The U.S. Trade and Tariff Act of 1984 declared the U.S. policy of seeking to liberalize world trade in services, giving the president authority to retaliate or impose restrictions on services. It also allows consideration of upstream subsidies, such as the pricing of fuel below cost to produce final products for exports at lower costs, in countervailing duty investigations.

There have also been charges of excessive and predatory competition by state-owned airlines, especially in the North Atlantic market (Lowenfeld, 1975). These state-owned airlines have been accused not only of receiving indirect subsidies but also of seeking nonprofit goals.

In the aerospace industry, Embraer offered long-term credit to its buyers. Fairchild, its major competitor, petitioned the U.S. International Trade Commission to impose countervailing duties on the imports of the Bandeirante plane, charging Embraer with unfair trade practices, and mainly of offering below-market rates of financing. The ITC "estimated that the net result of the lower interest was a discount on the price of the Bandeirante of between 9 percent and 20 percent" (Sarathy, 1985, p. 70). Embraer, however, was able to convince the ITC that the plane had a comparative advantage in terms of reliability and delivery as well as a better engine and versatility. The ITC ruled that predatory financing was not the sole reason for the Bandeirante's success and Fairchild's petition was denied. However, the lengthy legal battle involved in such complaints is costly and increases the uncertainty of prospective buyers.

The United States has thus introduced a string of "trade restrictions administered on a contingent basis by complex bureaucracies exercising a considerable degree of discretion" (Barry Eichengreen and Hans van der Ven in

Baldwin and Kreuger, 1984, p. 68). The United States fought what it saw as dumping since it enacted the Antidumping Act of 1916. Since 1921, Congress required the imposition of antidumping duty if imports are sold for less than "face value." As markets have grown increasingly integrated, various amendments to the act since 1954 made it easier to impose antidumping duties and shortened the required time limit within which an antidumping determination should be charged. SOEs are seen as subject to national political forces, and therefore more suspect of dumping.

CONSEQUENCES OF SOES OPERATIONS IN THE INTERNATIONAL ARENA

Many of the sweeping allegations of unfair competition by SOEs refer to one small subset of these enterprises: those acquired by the government or kept operating to save them from bankruptcy to preserve employment. However, the possible effects of increasing state ownership on variables such as supply, cost, prices and investment are very different, depending on the basic economic nature of the industry, which affects the degree of autonomy of the SOEs and the degree of dependence on its controllers.

Fiscal monopolies may not allow imports equal treatment, as in the case of alcohol or cigarette monopolies. In the case of state-owned fiscal monopolies, it is easy enough to claim that they do not restrict imports but that the imported products are simply not in demand. Of course, a product that is not offered for sale may not be in demand.

Fiscal monopolies were ruled to be contradictory also to the international commitments embodied in the terms of the Treaty of Rome, which established the EEC. According to Article 37 of the treaty, member states must allow free movements of goods after the end of the transition period. Fiscal monopolies, or as the EEC calls them, "state monopolies of a commercial character," were considered by the European Commission to violate Article 37 because they were given exclusive rights. In 1965, the European Court of Justice ruled that Article 37 requires the abolition of the exclusive right of a state monopoly of a commercial character to import from other states. The court also considered the imposition of the countervailing charges on imported products or of taxes on imported products different from those imposed on the national products as being discriminatory and, therefore, incompatible with Article 37.

As a result of the commission's action, almost all fiscal monopolies within the EEC have been eliminated. Others were forced to adapt their rules of conduct to comply with the rules of competition. Thus, the French cigarette, potash fertilizer and alcohol industries have been the subject of several complaints and a European Court of Justice's rulings, as the various Reports on Competition show every year. Italy failed to harmonize tobacco taxes and was censured by the Court of Justice (*The Economist*, July 7, 1984, p. 50).

In the case of natural resources, the major consequence of increasing state ownership has been the breakdown of vertical integration. The efforts of SOEs to achieve stability and raise prices by the creation of cartels were not successful and "so called long-term contracts have proved perishable in practice" (Vernon, 1981, p. 151). These contracts were abrogated when price changes made them unprofitable to one of the partners. SOEs—e.g., in Saudi Arabia—also discriminated in favor of state-owned buyers at the expense of private ones, but state-to-state deals proved vulnerable not only to commercial hazards but also to political disputes. Thus, CFP in France terminated its contract for expensive Mexican oil in July 1981. In this case, Mexico retaliated by breaking off all economic relations with France, and considerable arm-twisting from the government "led CFP managers to return to the Mexican well" (Feigenbaum, 1985, p. 85). Iraq, too, broke off agreements with France for the sale of oil. "Iran and India suspended long-term arrangements for the sale of iron ore, and Jamaica, Trinidad-Tobago and Mexico abandoned a long-debated project for a joint operation in bauxite, alumina and aluminum (Vernon, 1985, p. 142).

In large-scale capital-intensive industries such as minerals, steel, chemicals or fertilizers, fixed costs are high and variable costs low. A combination of such a cost structure and a tendency to look at labor as a fixed cost may increase the propensity to cut prices as demand declines. But this tendency is not necessarily different because of ownership. The freedom of private firms to fire workers is much more circumscribed in the 1980s than it was in the 1960s. At the same time, governments fighting swelling budget deficits are much more reluctant to allow SOEs to suffer losses in the 1980s than they were in the 1960s.

In global industries such as car manufacturing or oil, the industry develops an oligopolistic price stability. Newcomers—state-owned or private firms—may not follow industry practice and will be disposed to cut prices to gain a foothold. However, the more well established the firms become, the more they share a common interest for mutual forbearance and the less the tendency to change existing price structures.

Some SOEs are heavily subsidized, but so are private firms. Renault was given subsidized government funds to acquire Berliet, a private competitor, but "government funds were made available at the same time, on a much larger scale, to enable the number two private automobile producer, Peugeot, to acquire the other private French firm, Citroën" (Sheahan, in Shepherd, 1976, p. 138).

In some cases, SOEs receive special subsidies to compensate them for carrying out special social services. In many cases, however, the same subsidies are offered to private firms if they are willing to pursue the same social goals.

There is another difficulty in analyzing the incidence of subsidies. If subsidies to SOEs or even increased equity are deemed countervailable, as in the U.S. case cited earlier, governments may decide to break SOEs down into two separate corporate entities, one owning the inefficient plants, receiving high subsidies and supplying the domestic market, and the other owning the most efficient plants and exporting.

Strange analyzed trends in protectionism in developed and developing countries in three declining industries—steel, shipbuilding and textiles:

> *One last conclusion seems fairly strongly supported by the evidence: the trend away from the market economy . . . towards the greater involvement of the state in business and the greater dependence of business on government. In each of the three sectors considered and in many others as well, there has been a noticeable increase in the involvement of European and American governments in economic matters supposedly belonging to the private sector.* [1979, p. 332]

Ganz (1977) analyzed the nature and extent of state assistance to private industry in the United Kingdom. The numerous examples Ganz provides makes it clear that SOEs are not alone in receiving extensive state support, especially when the going gets difficult.

Car manufacturers, who are large employers, tend to shop among governments to get the best package of incentives and subsidies for setting up new factories. When Ford Motor Company wanted to set up a new auto assembly plant in Europe several European countries including France, Austria, Ireland, Spain, Germany and Portugal, vied with one another to attract Ford to their respective nations. France, one of the prime candidates, is believed to have offered Ford the equivalent of between $370 million and $440 million in a financial package if it would set up the plant in Lorraine, an economically depressed area where laid-off steelworkers were mounting violent pressure on the government. Austria, the other contender, introduced a law providing the necessary financial means for the proposed Ford project which is estimated to include subsidies and tax benefits amounting to $285 million. Here again, the offers were announced and pursued by the Austrian chancellor. Renault and Peugeot-Citroën teamed up in opposing the French government's incentives to the Ford Motor Company and came up with a counterproposal, involving the creation of 9,400 jobs (Aharoni, 1980, pp. 18–19).

U.S. states are extremely active in encouraging employment by seeking major investments. When Volkswagen announced its intention to build a facility in the United States, an intensive competition was begun among the states to attract the plant and its thousands of new jobs. Pennsylvania won the competition with a multimillion dollar package that included "low-cost loans, tax relief, and highway and rail improvements, totalling as high as $65 million by some estimates" (Kline, 1983, p. 65). Nissan's $300 million truck assembly plant, expected to mean over 2,000 jobs and a payroll of $40 million, brought offers from thirty-nine states, and Tennessee won.

Whether or not such subsidies are economically rational, they are certainly granted to both private and public firms. Investment subsidies and incentives provided by states to achieve noneconomic goals are sought and received by both SOEs and private firms. Increased competition is opposed as much by private firms as by an SOE.

One important difference remains: state ownership is an invisible method of achieving preferential treatment, despite international agreements. Thus, when a government resorts to using all sorts of bilateral agreements, it might prefer to use SOEs, which it sees as more pliant. When MNEs are faced with competition of import-substituting SOEs, they may team up with the SOE through joint venture or licensing. For the MNE, such a strategy is a way to fend off competition in the local market. Since it is prevented from direct access, it will choose the joint venture route.

In service industries, as mentioned earlier, privately owned U.S. airlines have often alleged that state-owned European airlines play by different rules and have dumped capacity in the North Atlantic market and slashed prices below cost, thereby making it impossible for U.S. carriers to earn fair rates of return. However, a study by Pustay (1979) has shown that there is no evidence that competition in the North Atlantic passenger market is excessive, unfair or predatory. He has shown that the behavior of state-owned European carriers is consistent with the profit maximization motive and that little empirical evidence supports the theory that they seek nonprofit goals such as maximization of employment or foreign exchange.

State-owned banks and other financial institutions seem to be often very independent of their governments. State-owned insurance firms may have a higher propensity to get international reinsurance business. As to shipping, firms enjoy government protection, giving preference to national flagships irrespective of ownership.

How different are state-owned MNEs from those that are privately owned? In many ways, large-scale MNEs of the private sector exhibit most of the characteristics of the SOEs: both operate in an oligopolistic market structure, and in both cases one can discern problems of goal conflict between the owners and the managers (and between managers of different levels or different units); therefore, the need exists for an incentive structure to induce managers to behave in a desired way. Both have complex, hierarchical, highly bureaucratic decision structures and difficulties in measuring and rewarding individual performance. To the extent that managers perceive themselves as a part of a general market for managers, and to the extent that there is a free flow of managers between the private and the public sectors in any given country, these managers will face the same issues in the same way. This is so, first, because they behave in both cases as professional managers and, second, because the market will evaluate their performance as managers.

There are certainly more similarities than differences between investor-owned MNEs and large multinational SOEs. Not only do they operate in the same markets and in the same market structure, but also they are both subject to public and governmental pressures. Both may be called to pursue social goals or support political aspirations of the government.

There are, however, at least three areas in which differences may be found. First, *ceteris paribus*, governments may be more influential in avoiding the internationalization of an SOE and, to a lesser extent, the further geographical expansion of an existing one. Second, there may be some differences in the way managers are recruited and, therefore, in their behavior. Third, differences may be caused by the international experiences of different firms.

SOEs differ from private MNEs because they are subject to direct government control. The government as an owner is sometimes more reluctant to allow its enterprises to take the international route (Mazzolini, 1979). It can also encourage direct foreign investments to enable the firm to secure important raw materials, to stabilize its markets or because of political reasons. Mazzolini reminds us that the original idea for building a Renault plant in Canada came when General de Gaulle was pursuing his policy of encouraging Quebec's autonomy. He suggests that the idea "apparently came from the General himself in view of establishing tangible ties between the two countries" (1979, p. 337).

Further, to the extent that managerial recruitment in SOEs is influenced by party affiliation and political patronage, they may behave differently (see Chapter 8).

The major difference between SOEs and other MNEs is the degree of experience in the international field. Only a handful of large SOEs have been MNEs for a few decades. More of them entered the field only recently, and their lack of experience may explain some of the variance in their behavior. Thus, when nationalization broke the ownership link in vertically integrated firms in petroleum, copper, iron ore and bauxite, it did not remove in any way the desire of the newly created SOE and the MNE whose mines were nationalized for stability of the market. However, SOEs are still groping for ways to achieve this stability (Vernon and Levy, Rodrik, both in Jones *et al.*, 1982).

The new and inexperienced SOEs are still involved in a transition process toward maturity, which may have temporarily led to lower outputs and higher prices in minerals and to disruptions of the oligopolistic structure. As the SOEs gain experience, they learn to operate skillfully and to use their expertise to achieve autonomy from their controllers. Most research on MNEs was on those firms whose headquarters are in the United States, Europe and Japan. Most interest in SOEs has concentrated among development economists, who have been studying the LDCs. However, some of the most powerful SOEs in the world are based in Europe, Canada, or the United States. They are often very efficient and behave very much like private firms. Two ironies are of interest. First, the governments often complain that SOEs are profit-seekers and powerful and that they ignore government directives.

Second, most of the arguments put forward several years ago by economists from LDCs against the MNEs from the private sector are now promulgated against the multinational SOEs. Perhaps much of the opposition to the growth of SOEs is simply an attempt to maintain the balance of oligopolistic industry against structural changes caused by the entry of newcomers. It is not clear that the welfare of citizens is threatened by the influx of SOEs into such oligopolistic industries.

SOEs also have certain competitive advantages. They can use credit underwritten by government, they enjoy a near-monopoly situation in the domestic market, they may take a leisurely approach to market development, "with several years of losses being sustained by the state treasury's deep pockets" (Sarathy, 1985, p. 75). They are also saddled with many drawbacks, as suggested above. The major problem, however, is that "forms of regulation which compromise the independence of enterprise decision-making based on a free market may become suspect" (Reuland, 1975, p. 320). This problem arises when a government uses ownership rights *or* subsidies. Of course, subsidies are not confined to SOEs, and their existence promises to be a major issue in trade discussions in the 1980s.

CONCLUSION

The increasing importance of the government as a regulator and an entrepreneur and the growth of the large MNEs, coupled with major technological changes and shifts in consumers' tastes, have created an economic order totally different than the one assumed to exist only a few decades ago. Many markets have become global. In these global markets, a significant percentage of the flow of international exports and of technology is intrafirm trade of large industrial MNEs and government-to-government and intrafirm SOE trade. These shares are both growing.

Governments are not bystanders or neutral referees. Two points must be strongly stressed. First, governments can use their power to change the rules of the game and the competitive scene. The changes created by governments have been studied mainly when they led to protectionism. Governments increasingly help SOEs to become competitors in the global scene. Since differences exist between these firms and other MNEs, understanding these differences is extremely important. Second, the desire of managers—in the private and public sectors—to assure the success of their enterprises and to achieve stability in the face of environmental changes has created strong pressures for continued growth of MNE operations. Decisions on prices, outputs, deliveries, wages and unemployment are reached less and less in the market. They are made by managers, coordinating current demand and allocating resources for the future. These managers operate in an environment of strong governmental influence. To be successful, they have to take into account governmental policies and desires. Enterprises—and the government—are not monolithic maximizers. They are hierarchies in which different coalitions of interest groups operate, on the basis of power as much as on that of economic rules.

The actors on the global chessboard are not only private firms but also SOEs and governments. The decision-making process may be different when these different key actors are considered, although the structure may be the same. In some countries, the belief has been that harmonious interactions between the state and the private sector are possible. Others attempt to cut sharply the economic role of the state. The evolution of an interventionist state and global markets can be understood only if interdisciplinary research by both economists and political scientists addresses this issue. Attempts to negotiate international agreements of these issues would require not only mutual tolerance on the part of the negotiators but also a better understanding of the role, magnitude and growth of these operations, the behavioral characteristics and the consequences of operation of SOEs in the international arena.

CHAPTER 11

A Contingency Model of State-Owned Enterprise Behavior

INTRODUCTION

With the dramatic growth of SOE involvement in both domestic and international transactions has come an increasing interest in their behavior. The behavior of a private firm, operating in a world in which the government's role is largely limited to the maintenance of law and order and the preservation of the institutional system, is certainly different from that of an SOE. The real question, however, is to what extent the SOE is different from the real-life, large business firms, operating in an oligopolistic market and accommodating themselves to the risks and opportunities created in an era of increasing government responsibility for the management of the economy.

SOEs may be viewed from at least three angles. First, the *macro* picture: what is the role of the SOEs as a group and what are the aggregate results of their operations? Second, the *external elements*: the relations between SOEs and their governments and between themselves and private investors. Third, *the inner workings* of SOEs: how is strategy determined and implemented? Who makes which decisions? This book deals with all three levels, emphasizing the importance of management of the SOEs as a major variable explaining their behavior. The SOE is analyzed as one institution in a political economy. As Zysman (1983) notes:

> [A]*lthough traditionally viewed as different means of coordinating activities, political commands and market prices in fact melt together in the actual workings of the advanced economies. . . . Market positions are a source of political power and government choices shape the operations of the market. Thus any analysis must begin from the understanding that there are no markets apart from politics, that markets were in fact, political creations and that political life is entangled with the workings of markets and institutions.* [1983, pp. 17, 18]

Whatever the original reason for their creation, once established the SOEs have a life of their own. To understand SOEs performance, they cannot be viewed in isolation. They must be seen in the context of a more general system of which they are a part: that of the political economy of a country. At the same time, it is impossible to understand the performance of SEOs without an awareness of the administrative problems involved and the decision-making process, the measures used to control these enterprises and the degree of discretion allowed to the managers.

The purpose of this concluding chapter is twofold: first, to suggest the major variables that affect the performance of SOEs in different countries and their evolution; second, to summarize proposals for institutional means for making SOEs accountable to the public and effective in making strategic choices.

SOME COMMON PROBLEMS

All SOEs face some common problems, including objectives, control, pricing, information and financing (Floyd, 1984). They also face several managerial problems. SOEs are expected to steer their operations to achieve the goals of their owners—namely, the citizens of the country—who are assumed to be interested in many goals, not only in profits. These goals are ambiguous, ill-defined and even conflicting, and trade-offs among them are rarely quantified, often allowing managers to avoid accountability. To many observers, SOEs are by definition expected to achieve broader goals than private firms. Profitability is seen as one of many goals but certainly not the most important one. Sen makes this point succinctly:

> *Private firms, by and large, maximize profits, and if profit maximization were the right objective for the public sector also, there may remain no compelling reason for nationalizing industries and setting up a public sector. The decision to set up a public sector is, therefore, congruent with the decision not to maximize profits. To create a public sector and then to ask it to do what the private sector would have done is like going to a cinema to try to sleep rather than to see the movie. [1970, p. 16]*

Others would disagree. To them SOEs are important as a tool to generate public savings by the most efficient method, and it is the distribution of these savings that makes SOEs different from private enterprise. Providing direction for SOEs is extraordinarily difficult in an environment suffused with ambiguity. Rigorous economic criteria become impossible to apply.

A major reason for different opinions on SOEs' performance is the divergence of views about the reasons for their operations: are they tools of government? are they instruments of ministers to achieve political goals? are they independent business enterprises, different from private firms only in the distribution of their systems, or are they social institutions, expected to create harmonious labor relations, or to cater to the needs of different stakeholders? These different points of view have never been reconciled. In daily life, SOE managers learn that they have to take into account different points of view about their *raison d'être*.

Yet without clearly defined objectives, it is hard, if not impossible, to pin down what the SOE manager is expected to achieve. The problems of SOE managers faced with conflicting directions and becoming part of a power struggle were analyzed in Chapter 4.

In different countries and at different times, governments have used a variety of methods to communicate their priorities and have taken various approaches to the control of the SOEs, oscillating from one extreme to another.

When the State's business activities were limited in scope, these activities were carried out within the framework of government departments. This set-up allowed close and uninterrupted supervision, at the price of being inflexible, leading to "unnecessary delays and a general inability to respond to consumer needs promptly" (Seidman, 1968, p. 156). With the growth of the interventionist state, governments realized that the nature of their business activities was fundamentally different from their role as an administrator and a regulator. Their assumption of new economic functions compelled the governments to create a new kind of institution to be granted a considerable amount of autonomy. It was recognized that an SOE must be able to arrive at and implement decisions on its own responsibility. The result of this recognition was the formation of the first statutory corporations in England and the United States before World War I and the creation of SOEs in Europe and Latin America. The pendulum swung to the other extreme, characterized by almost no government control.

Gradually, it was felt that the State was losing control over the SOEs, and that no public supervision was exercised over SOEs that were amassing a great deal of power. The pendulum swung back to its former position. In the United States the earlier framework of Government companies was abandoned and the Government Corporation Control Act was passed in 1945, while in Canada and Turkey, Government supervision was greatly intensified. The U.S. National Academy of Public Administration (1981, Vol. 1) criticized the Government Corporation Control Act because its classification of companies as wholly owned or mixed disregarded the potential impact of corporate operations on U.S. Treasury (p. 11).

Despite the proliferation of SOEs in the 1960s and 1970s, the right balance between control and supervision on the one hand, and autonomy and flexibility of business operations on the other, has not yet been found. In many cases, the problem is that legal control is reduced to a mere sham. The real control is political and informal. Inefficient control systems, according to

Gelinas (1978) may be "more harmful than no control at all" (p. 23). Carey-Jones (1974) correctly notes: "the greater the desire to limit political intervention by ministers, through using quasi-autonomous forms, the greater is the ability of the minister to intervene without being held to account for his intervention. This makes quasi-autonomous forms very attractive to ministers, since through them they achieve power without responsibility" (p. 44).

Governments often interfere too much in the operational details of the SOEs and too little in their strategic directives. The problems of control were discussed in Chapter 6. Other factors are the level at which the enterprise operates (some are at the municipal level, others are at the level of central government) and their organization—from a department in the government subject to annual parliamentary (or congressional) appropriations and working under the rules and regulations of the governmental civil service, to a statutory organization created by a special law to the creation of an SOE (or a subsidiary of one) by the purchase of all or a controlling portion of the shares of a private corporation.

Another method of control that has been advocated very often is to let SOEs compete either against other SOEs or against private enterprises. Allowing SOEs to compete against private enterprises creates different types of problems, which were discussed in Chapter 7.

The issue of pricing inputs and outputs in SOEs is a major problem economists have attempted to solve. The first best solution for such enterprises, if they are monopolies, is to price their outputs equal to marginal costs. Since unit cost falls as output rises, the marginal cost of production is below unit cost, and marginal cost pricing would result in a loss. Therefore, if the SOE charges economically efficient prices, it will need a subsidy to cover its costs, and this subsidy will have to be covered by taxation, creating distortions of its own. The distortion effect of taxation can be reduced by using Ramsey's rule—that is, taxing goods with inelastic demands so that demand will not be affected. Problems of pricing have been adequately covered by many economics textbooks (e.g., Webb, 1976; Bös, 1981) and they were touched on in Chapter 5. These problems are also related to the measurement of SOE performance and effectiveness. Pricing ensures efficiency in organizing scarce resources to produce goods and services for sale, but SOEs are expected to achieve other goals, too. SOEs have been used to control inflation; to help increasing output, income, exports and employment; to accelerate industrialization; to rectify imbalances between income groups and between regions or to forestall foreign ownership. In developing countries, SOEs were an important training ground for indigenous managers and other professional staff.

The market economy model defines inefficiency in a narrow economic sense. It is also based on a system of rewards for individuals who are so-called "economic men." Inefficiency can also be defined in terms of underconsumption of certain goods, e.g., education or housing, and overconsumption of others. Human motivation is seen as based on the need for achievement and for opportunities.

Even if one accepts the inadequacy of prices as indicators of social needs, it must be acknowledged that political processes or bureaucracy, with its tendency toward uniformity and the consequent lack of creativity and innovation, is not an ideal substitute. The problem is that an alternative system for economic markets is not well developed. The lack of such an alternative means that the evaluation of SOEs performance is fraught with difficulties.

To manage its SOEs the government needs sufficient information on them. Information is also crucial in establishing trust because the cultural gap between senior civil servants and businesspeople is wide. The fear of establishing a nationwide precedent hampers many negotiations between government and SOEs, and more information may help.

The financing problem is also as yet unresolved. Should SOEs enjoy preferential access to public funds? When and to what extent should the government use surpluses from SOEs to finance its regular budget? What is the optimal debt/equity ratio for an SOE? Should the government finance loss-ridden SOEs and, if so, for how long? The fiscal burden caused by SOEs' losses is increasingly recognized as a problem. Less attention has been paid to the problem of the impact of starving the SOEs from funds on the incentives of their managers or on resource allocation. Littlechild (1983a, p. 246) has shown that telephone penetration is significantly more responsive to per capita GDP and to population density in private systems than in government-owned systems. He found no difference in responsiveness between government departments and SOEs. It is, therefore, conceivable that governments tend to ration funds for telephone system expansion.

These considerations lead us to the political role of SOEs as bodies working on the fringes of the state, used to reduce visible budget allocations, or to distribute largesse to different stakeholders. Indeed, the major problems of SOEs are related to politics: who controls the SOEs? In whose interest are they managed? Textbooks preach the virtues of keeping the income-generating SOE outside the realm of politics and free of political pressures. However, ministers do intervene, and managers may become complacent, inward-looking, inbred and amateur, or alternatively, they may enter the political game, accumulating power.

The relationships between SOE managers and their controllers also change with time. The SOE goes through an evolution, gaining with time more power for the managerial class. Although ownership is collective, decisions are made by individuals, who become what Djilas (1957) called the "new class": those having control of the means of production. We discussed this question—inasmuch as it related to control—in Chapter 6, while the behavior of managers was discussed in Chapter 8.

There is an enormous amount of literature on SOEs in single countries and the beginnings of more comparative work. Despite many gaps in our knowledge about the internal workings of these firms, enough is known to suggest the basic contours for a contingency theory of SOEs, explaining possible differences between SOEs and private firms and among different types of SOEs in a democratic state. Such a theory should explain the reasons for the creation of SOEs, their operations, their performance, the distribution of their surplus, and the reasons for their expansion or contraction. Questions of origins were discussed in Chapter 3, those of contraction in Chapter 9, while some reasons for expansions were analyzed in Chapter 8. It should be clear by now that, despite bureaucratic abhorrence of diversity, SOEs are not a single discrete group of institutions.

VARIABLES AFFECTING SOES' BEHAVIOR

A common feature of many assessments of performance is that they tend to view the SOE in isolation, detached from the private sector, and from the alternatives governments have, such as subsidies or regulations. To understand the way SOEs operate, it is crucial to differentiate between variables inherent to ownership and other differences within the SOE sector group. The extent to which differences are found between SOEs and private firms similarly situated depends mainly on five variables:

> The ideology and culture of the country on the role of government and the individual that affect conception of law and public authority, legal and political traditions and the measures used by governments in attempting to manage the economy.
> The political milieu in which these enterprises operate.
> The historical processes of industrialization.
> The expectations and political power of different stakeholders, workers, controllers, consumers and managers that affect control procedures. These are partially a function of culture but also of other variables like the ability of consumers to choose between suppliers.
> The orientation of the managers, which may stem from different personal background, recruitment methods or career paths.

Other intervening variables—the level of bureaucratization or the rewards and incentive structure e.g.,—may affect managerial behavior in an SOE.

Ideology and Culture

While most SOEs become state-owned for pragmatic reasons, ideological and cultural differences are extremely important in determining the way SOEs are managed and controlled and the differences between them and private enterprises.

Ideology provides a map of what is proper and possible in political and economic life (Apter, 1964). Ideology and world views affect the way events are interpreted and endow experience with meaning. They also affect the degree to which government interferes in the economy. World views also become entrenched in a bureaucracy's recruitment and socialization procedures (Armstrong, 1973), and bureaucracies express the cultural values of the societies from which they emerge (Crozier, 1964). To be sure, when procedures and organizations change, the attitudes of those working in them shift as well (Zysman, 1977, Chapter 6). Still, ideas and world views explain institutional arrangements in politics, economies and bureaucracies.

In the United States, the ideology and norms are based on Locke's natural laws of individualism, property rights, competition, limited government and scientific specialization and fragmentation (Lodge, 1974, 1975). Lodge believes these ideas are in the process of changing. Among the changes is the recognition that the role of government is inevitably expanding and that federal planning is needed. He adds, in the case of electric power:

> But this does not mean that these companies should be nationalized. . . . The companies must realize what government, and only government, can and must do: plan the allocation of resources and make the critical judgments of costs of benefits. To do this it must interfere with authority and coherence. [1974, p. 72]

Thus, even in Lodge's view, the holding of property is a natural and absolute right, although "community need to satisfy consumer desire is replacing competition as a means for controlling the use of property" and "rights of membership are overshadowing property rights" (1974, pp. 65, 66). The law is dominated by an adversary process rather than partnership, and the ideal is an individualistic, stubborn independence. Society is no more than the sum of individuals who comprise it, and individuals enjoy inalienable rights but very little in terms of duties to the country. Societal relationships are based on competition as the major social control mechanism and as the means for resolving conflicts.

The government is of laws and not of people. Individuals should not be subject to the whims of other individuals but to the rule of objective and fair law. Politics in the United States is also a process of competition among special interest groups, and private property is a sacred notion, both for tangible and intangible forms of property. Government is a source of intangible properties or entitlements (Reich, 1964). This power of government creates the potential for abuse of bureaucratic authority and, in the American view, must be controlled by a powerful system of checks and balances, to ensure public accountability.

Even in the United States, some observers have called for the creation of federal SOEs. Lamont (1979) sees this solution as part of a policy of reciprocity against what he terms *state enterprise capitalism* that "means marshalling all the nation-state's resources and the talent to enable the nation-state to compete better in the world market" (p. 193). However, most Americans are skeptical of the ability of their government to manage business enterprises. When the U.S. government establishes enterprises, they are expected to be run as government bureaus: the Ramspeck Act of 1940 makes all employees of U.S.-owned government corporations Federal civil servants (unless exempt like TVA employees), and the Government Corporation Act of 1945 treats these enterprises as standard Federal agencies, subject to governmental budgeting and auditing requirements. There is a strong reluctance to grant autonomy to SOEs, at least at a federal level (Seidman, 1952, 1959, 1983b, Moe, 1979). Autonomous managers with independent political power are perceived as mandarins (Walsh, 1978. For a different view, see Etzioni, 1973).

The United Kingdom shares with the United States the same legal and political traditions concerning individual rights. The United Kingdom, however, does not have, at least not to the same extent as the United States, a tradition of a rugged pioneer. Instead, its social system is largely based on the class structure and a civil service career is a duty of the aristrocracy (Tuchmann, 1966).

The Morrisonian tradition in the United Kingdom is to allow SOEs wide latitude and avoid excessive control or interference. The U.K. culture has proved extremely resilient to change of ownership: managers of the firms came mainly from the private sector, workers continued to be alienated (and perhaps even more militant in their collective bargaining behavior) and civil service controllers had little understanding of the industry. This has caused not only an intellectual muddle but also antagonism, mistrust and confrontation between employees and SOE managers and between the managers and the civil servants. This gap between civil servants and industrial leaders is even greater in the United States. Vogel (1982a) points out the many informal ways of achieving social responsibility in the United Kingdom and contrasts them with the strict and elaborate legalistic system in the United States. Civil servants lack technical competence and business judgment. The lack of informal mechanisms for elite collaboration and for the achievement of consensus leads to a reliance on official channels, laws and regulations. However, compared to continental Europe, there is much less consensus and more public confrontations.

The result has been piecemeal solutions to perennial problems. In addition, governments in the United Kingdom have been plagued by ideological instability (Grant, 1982), and the many oscillations of policies have caused confusion for the managers of SOEs. Sir Peter Parker, chairman of British Railways, puts the problem succinctly: "Nothing erodes morale more than not knowing what winning means, not having targets clear. That problem has long bedevilled the relationship between government and public industry" in

(Redwood and Hatch, 1982, p. 6). Managers perceive civil servants as short-sighted and their requirements as unreasonable.

In India, closely modeled on the British tradition, the distrust between civil servants and SOE managers is even greater. Murthy (1981) argues that only a collaborative process of learning on the part of both the government and SOEs would avoid endemic conflict between SOEs and their controllers. Indian bureaucracy, notes Heginbotham (1975), has a heterogeneous cultural context, with conflicts between traditional and modern, Indian and Western, that influence the meanings attached to organizational processes.

In many other countries, the concept of the state as a benevolent public power acting in the name of the common good is much stronger. The rights of the individual are seen less as a natural law and more as a product of recognition by the state. The state is expected to serve its citizens, but good citizenship means the precedence of public obligations over the private needs of selfish individuals (Dyson, 1980). In such a culture, governmental controls and restrictions of property rights are not limited to SOEs. Thus, wage or price controls may be imposed on all large firms. Therefore, it is necessary to study the environment to find out whether or not different rules apply to the public and the private sector.

Medieval conceptions of harmony and the common goal are a significant strand of the Iberian culture ethos in many Latin American countries. The role of the state in these countries, Stepan (1978) argues, is based on what he terms "organic statism", that is "a normative model of the relations between state and society" (Stepan, 1978, p. 6). In Latin America (and Spain), interest groups have not been at liberty to combine, dissolve and recombine freely in accordance with their interests. Rather, they were chartered by the state according to the state's interest. In Israel, "CEOs of industrial enterprises perceive their role environment similarly regardless of sector affiliation" (Lachman, 1985, p. 676), largely because government agencies and its policies influence private firms as much as they do SOEs.

In Germany and Austria, order is highly valued, and individuals accept readily the concept of the corporation as an association of interests. Workers and capitalists are social partners who should collaborate to achieve social goals. Firms should also collaborate, emphasizing common interests and dividing the markets through cartel arrangements (Braunthal, 1965). The German board of directors is divided accordingly, into a supervising board composed of representatives of workers and owners (Aufsichstrat) and an executive board (Vorstand). Representatives of banks are a majority of the members of the Aufsichstrat. Moreover, while the 1883 British Bankruptcy Act makes the interest of the creditors a major reference point of the receiver (and the shareholders in a going concern), the German (and the French) law is based on the notion of the corporation as a community of interests. Its continued existence and survival is of utmost importance to safeguard customers, workers and other stakeholders. Therefore, a corporation can gain an immediate moratorium by proposing a court-supervised settlement with the creditors. The French laws go even further: if the saving of the corporation is in the national interest, a court-appointed administrator may prepare and execute a plan for its reorganization even without the approval of its creditors.

SOEs in Germany and Austria are said to be managed with very little governmental guidance or interference. However, the firms in these countries are enmeshed within a complex web of institutional interests that bind different interests. This creates a closed social network that allows informal information to flow and that binds decision-makers in government and SOEs. In such a system, there is much less need for official intervention since many problems are solved unofficially, secretly and collaboratively. Communication channels do not have to be established; they are an integral part of the social fabric.

In France, the state role is that of a strategist, allowing it direct and detailed intervention in business affairs (Baum, 1958). France does not enjoy the same belief in order and collaborative industrial relations as Germany, but a French firm does not have to be state owned to accept readily the right of government to direct it and chart for it strategic missions. Private authority is regulated in the interests of consistency, equity and the common welfare, although this tendency is somewhat tempered by the revolutionary tradition of resistance to authority. The state responsibility for economic growth is accepted by all (Cohen, 1977). The elite has a common background, based on education in the *grandes écoles* and membership in the *grand corps* (Aubert *et al.*, 1984). They rotate between governmental position, SOE management and the private sectors *(pantouflage)*. The tradition and the ideology is that of the *dirigiste* state, meaning that state intervention and leadership are accepted and even expected in both private and public sectors. The network of French bodies of control over SOEs will be seen as bewildering to someone accustomed to a different culture, but the problems of communication between SOE managers and their controllers are much less severe than in the United Kingdom.

Italy shares with Germany and France much of the basic beliefs about individuals and the state. Its political structure, however, has traditionally been weak and replete with patronage politics. Although legally the authority of the state is extremely important, some of its SOE managers have enormous autonomous political power.

In many developing countries, corruption is an accepted norm, and SOEs may be managed for the self-interest of their managers, their controllers or both (see Bates, 1981). In addition, the administrative capacity of government is weak, making it difficult to control the many enterprises. Furthermore, SOEs may enjoy extralegal autonomy because of the fragmented nature of the government. The SOEs are controlled by the office of the president and by a plethora of other ministries, a situation that allows entrepreneurial corporate managers to play one governmental body against another. The collapse of governmental institutions in many countries may also affect the autonomy of the SOEs.

Studies such as those by Crozier (1964) on France and Abegglen (1958) on Japan suggest that traditional features of the society and culture carry over into many organizations, including the SOEs. Hofstede (1980) identified four dimensions that distinguish national cultures: power distance, uncertainty avoidance, individualism and masculinity. The first dimension reflects the extent to which power and inequalities are valued as legitimate (high for India or Mexico, low for Austria or Israel). Uncertainty avoidance relates to cultural preferences for stability, formal rules, expertise and orderliness (Japan, Portugal), contrasted to cultural acceptance of informality, risk-taking and ambiguity. Individualism is high in the United States, the United Kingdom and Australia, while strong group identification and loyalty are important in Venezuela and Pakistan. Masculinity includes male assertiveness, high independence and task performance (Austria, Japan) in contrast to values placed on interdependence and quality of life (the Netherlands, Sweden).

These cultural differences have significant implications for all organizations—private and state owned. Thus, in individualistic cultures it may be harder to achieve consensus by mutual adjustment than in countries in which high value is placed on collective responsibility. Trust and common goals may be easier to achieve in Japan than in the United Kingdom. In other cultures, result orientation is much weaker than in the United States. Indian culture values planning and staff role (Heginbotham, 1975). Other cultures may emphasize aid to members of the same tribe at the expense of more efficiency.

Nations are held together by ideology and organization design (Schurmann, 1969, p. 1). When the ideology is that of a strong state, people see the government as an independent variable and believe that it is its right to give orders. A manager who upsets a minister may simultaneously thwart his own career. Managers may then either comply with all requests or attempt to cover their tracks. Further, the greater the impact of the state on economic activities, the wider its tendency to consult on policy with all sorts of interest groups. The selection of the groups that have access to this policy process is of crucial importance (La Palombara, 1964, pp. 258-270).

Clearly, when the state is only a mediator among interest groups, or when it is captured by a strong private sector, the role of SOEs will be smaller than when the state acquires an independent power because of ideology, because warring classes balance each other, or because of revolution and an elite response to crisis, causing a restructure of the relationships among sectors and between sectors and the state.

One variable that is strongly affected by ideology and culture is the belief in homogeneity. When the state is strong, there is a marked tendency to achieve homogeneity. There are attempts to equalize salaries, incentives and working conditions across the whole public sector. SOEs are expected to have working conditions comparable to government departments, and surplus funds may be moved from a profitable SOE to the general government budget. If diversity is emphasized, different SOEs may have different salary structures. They may not be required to use local goods and services unless the suppliers are competitive. SOEs are also used less as a source of political patronage, or to supply employment for the party loyals.

The Political Milieu

A significant part of the theory of SOEs has been written on socialist countries of a command economy type. In this model, the firm management has very little autonomy, and a central planning board decides on specific output goals. In the Oscar-Lange version of market socialism, each firm has much autonomy, but its investment decisions are usually based on the decisions of a central planning board. The focus of this book is on SOEs operating in a mixed economy, side by side or even in competition with private enterprises to which their performance may be compared. In these mixed economies, there are still other important differences in the political milieu. Some of them are democracies, in which different political parties propose to the voter candidates for political leadership. Others are dictatorial regimes, attempting to achieve different goals. In a democracy, it is often assumed that the behavior of political leaders is significantly influenced by their desire to be re-elected. If the major goal of a government is indeed to be re-elected, one may assume that it will use all the resources it controls, including the SOEs, to achieve this goal. Therefore, the SOEs' policies will be subject to political influence. Governmental political intervention tends to increase the greater the visibility of the SOE's tasks to the public at large (Tierney, 1984, p. 86), the nearer are the elections and as a function of macroeconomic conditions: a government that suffers acute budgetary deficits will behave differently toward its SOEs than a government whose resources are less limited.

In many countries, governments do not have to worry about re-election; political forces that are out of power are suppressed. Debates on public issues or a free press do not exist, and even operational details of the SOEs are unconditionally dictated by the government in power. The distinctions between party, government and enterprise are blurred, and the SOEs are pulled back to the orbit of government. Unlike the situation in certain democracies, the right of the government to direct the enterprise is not circumscribed by separate power centers, and the party in power is able to exploit SOEs for partisan purposes. Managers are appointed and dismissed at will by the minister, who often appoints political friends or unsuccessful parliamentary candidates (on Ghana, e.g., see Pozen, 1976). In the single-party system of Zambia, "the requirement that high-level public officials demonstrate absolute loyalty and unflinching dedication to the party ideals tends also to be functionally captivating to the freedom of action of the members within the system, which includes public enterprise managers" (Simwinga, in: Austin, 1983, p. 12). Institutional systems cannot be transferred from one environment to another because their success is closely related to the environment in which they operate (Hanson, 1965, p. 336).

Another difference among countries is in the respect given to the rule of law. In some countries, citizens are law-abiding, and public servants have compliant and passive attitudes. In others, aggressive managers and civil servants pay less attention to the letter of the law, ignoring it in their pursuit of power. When the law is taken seriously, SOEs may be used to escape the rules designed to curb favoritism and patronage or to tailor programs to serve a particular interest group, avoiding the requirement for equivalent service to the whole population. When the law is ignored, differences between government, SOEs and private enterprises are less important.

Pozen (1976) contrasts the instrumental and symbolic views of the role of SOEs laws. Instrumentalists measure the success of the law in terms of the degree to which the law is implemented, symbolists in terms of the degree to which it is accepted. According to Pozen (1976), "the covert objectives and latent functions of many laws are symbolic despite the instrumental character of the state's official goals for these laws" (p. 163).

Frank (in Ranis, 1971, p. 170) compared the performance of SOEs in Ghana, Nigeria and Uganda. The performance was best in Uganda, which at that time was the least politicized of the countries studied. He concluded that the political milieu was by far the most important determinant of economic efficiency. In Ghana, the policies of IDC have been left to be formulated by the firm's foreign experts. Research on different firms in Ghana revealed a similar disinterest in general policy.

Rather than being a cohesive unit, government frequently is an uneasy coalition of disparate elements, dependent on ambiguity for its survival. Government is often a plethora of ministries or even a series of feudal estates belonging to different parties. The agency of the government that is empowered to control the SOEs varies under different regimes. In almost no case are conflicts on goals resolved or trade-offs clearly stated. This is so not only because information is unavailable but also because ambiguity may serve the self-interest of different actors. When goals are in conflict, a clear-cut resolution or the setting of priorities may not be the optimal solution to all actors. Actors will then rather resort to a quasi-resolution of conflicts, defer the exact definition of the problem or use log rolling but will avoid an open confrontation, even though confrontation may be needed to resolve the conflict and elicit exact guidelines to the enterprise. In other cases, a strong president may act as if all SOEs are part of a personal portfolio.

The political milieu also affects the power setting, consisting of those actors who can exert an immediate influence on the organization or on which the organization exerts an immediate influence, including those who hold the formal authority to regulate the resources or acitivities of the enterprise, or to audit, evaluate, inspect or report on the SOE's compliance with standards, as well as constituents, clients, allies and adversaries.

The role of SOEs is different in different political milieu. In turn, the political milieu itself is undergoing change under the pressures and tensions of development. In an industrialized state, in which respect for the law is high, and contending social forces are stable, SOE managers know intuitively what is expected of them. When the political machine is controlled by a powerful private sector, there are strong pressures for a smaller-sized SOE sector, but also for improved performance of existing SOEs. At the same time, SOE managers cater to the demands of the politically strong consumers, and to the wishes of the economically powerful private sector for low-cost services. Several studies on Canada and the United States, cited in Chapter 5, corroborate this view (e.g., Peltzman, 1971; Gordon, 1981). In a developing country, SOEs may have grown as a reaction to an attempt of a colonial power to topple the regime, as in the case of Nasser's Egypt (O'Brien, 1966). Since political forces are in flux, and a new alignment may seize power, managers may take an apathetic attitude, with deleterious effect on SOEs' performance. If SOEs were created to take power away from old colonial powers and exogenous entrepreneurs (Asians in Africa, Chinese in Indonesia), their management may be weak. More generally, the performance of SOEs crucially depends on the resolution of conflict among contending political forces.

> "Where this remains in contention, uncertainty and conflict govern the operation of public enterprise. This is reflected in its capacity to generate surpluses and in conflicts over the distribution of these surpluses" (Sobhan, 1979, p. 29).

If there is a political consensus SOEs may serve as an engine for the generation of surpluses. If political power is not in the hands of those having economic interests, SOEs are often used for party building, diverting resources to the improvement of the lifestyle of the bureaucracy.

Once the SOE sector grows, its managers may become more powerful politically. They "equate their own power and lifestyle with the growth and prosperity of the sector" (Sobhan, 1979, p. 31). In such a case, government may attempt to restrict the freedom of SOEs to mobilize external resources. Autonomy is maximized when all political forces have a stake in improved performance of SOEs. However, civil servants may fear they lose their domination over SOEs, and attempt to restrict this autonomy (Compare to Coronel, 1983). If SOEs are large and profitable, a *clientela* relationship often develops. A *clientela* relationship thrives because both sides of the relationship can and do derive clear cut advantages from it (La Palombara, 1964, p. 266). Electricity SOEs and their Ministry, or national oil companies or airlines and their controllers, often develop such relationships. The ministry aids the SOE in political battles because it wants to see the sector developed and because its expertise is needed to an important degree: the ministry may become "colonized" by the SOE (Richardson, 1981, p. 41). The imbalance in expertise means that the controlling authority does not possess the ability to exercise effective control. The congruence of interests means that they are not anxious to exercise control: "the interests of controller and controlled may coincide" (*Ibid.*, p. 40).

While the impact of the political milieu on SOEs is usually recognized, the political impact of SOEs has been largely ignored. There is mounting evidence that SOEs are an important political institution, gaining more and more power as they grow and as the size of the SOE sector in the country increases.

Historical Processes of Industrialization

Gerschenkron (1962) proposes that the historical timing of a country's industrialization defines the economic tasks the society must accomplish and the social, financial and technical resources that must be mobilized—and, therefore, the policies needed for industrialization to be successful. In the United Kingdom, textiles were the leading growth engine for industrialization. An individual entrepreneur could mobilize the limited funds needed to start up a textile firm. In Germany it was steel. The mass work force and the large sums of money needed for this industry meant that financial institutions and government had to play an active role, if industrialization were to become a workable solution. Further, early industrialists had a competitive advantage over newcomers in military and economic power. Newcomers need a greater rate of development to amass the strength needed to compete with the entrenched countries and gain a significant market share. This need for speed again meant more government initiative. Latecomers to the industrial scene would thus develop different relations with government, and the government would have bigger entrepreneurial roles and much more influence over the economy.

In the newly developed countries, government initiative was crucial in achieving industrialization. To mobilize and organize resources for export-led strategies, government intervention was essential. In the industrialized countries, government had to enter because of the political problems of adjustment. All this meant more state ownership. However, the stronger the political power of the entrenched private-sector interests, and the greater the ideology of private property, the less the government was able to amass political agreement to state ownership and the greater the differences between SOEs and private firms.

Many of those who claim that government intervention, and certainly ownership, is destructive call for such intervention when a large firm with a sizeable employment faces imminent collapse or threatened closure of a major plant or when a whole sector or region has a problem of decline. In many cases, the result has been an extension of the SOE sector. One major difference between SOEs and private firms, therefore, is that many of the SOEs were created or expanded to socialize capitalists' losses.

An intractable and pervasive issue on the political agenda of the 1970s in most industrialized countries has been the need for adjustment. The first major adjustment from agriculture to industry could often be achieved by market forces. Governments could "purchase the political aquiescence of the farm block with subsidies and price support" (Zysman, 1983, p. 23). The new adjustments needed a release of labor from declining industries to new ones. However, the mismatch of skills between the industries made this process more difficult. Governments were expected to ease the wrenching dislocations in the labor force and to protect employment and have responded in two directions. On the one hand, they bowed to voices calling on it for relief, at least to those firms with a high level of employment, and on the other hand, they have attempted to replace protectionist policies by facilitating positive adjustment—relocating the labor force in new technologies and industries—both by retraining and by fostering the development of new technologies and new industries. Governments often created SOEs to achieve both these goals.

Subsidies and government interventions have been shown to increase x-inefficiency (Martin and Page, 1983) and to cause bad macroeconomic performance in terms of inflation, growth rates, return on investment and the savings rate (Balassa, 1984, pp. 10-12). However, governmental intervention and subsidies may be achieved by a variety of tools, and using SOEs is only one of them. I argued in Chapters 2 and 10 that the use of SOEs to reduce adjustment may be less costly to the economy. In an open economy and a democratic regime, the more visible the aid given through SOEs, the less strong the political alignment demanding the aid, and more of the aid is given to labor without having to compensate owners too; again, the alternative to an SOE is not an idealized "free" or "contestable" market, in which firms have to meet the market test or go out of business. The alternative is often a regulated firm or oligopoly of large and politically powerful private firms.

Another variable may be the traditions of economic management of pre-colonial past. (French étatisme as opposed to British laissez faire). This factor may become less important with time (Pozen, 1972).

Gerschenkron's (1962) argument can thus be seen to predict that SOEs will grow because of development gaps and absence of alternative actors able to mobilize domestic resources. Alternatively, the demand for SOEs activities can grow because a large middle class depends on the activities of the state for its economic well-being. The political power of different demands depends on the ability of stakeholders to gain access to the policy formation process.

Expectations and Political Power of Stakeholders

The basic direction of policy in any country is governed by a shift in the relative power and political interests of the members of the coalition comprising a country's elite. In countries in which private business interests dominate, SOEs will be directed to subsidize strong political interests, and SOE managers will find it extremely difficult to diversify into profitable lines of business in direct competition with entrenched private business interests. In these countries, SOEs will be loss-ridden or at least less profitable than private firms similarly situated. Baer and co-workers (1976) raise questions about the degree to which the state sector in Brazil reflects disproportionate influence by a group called the military-industrialists.

To understand the behavior of SOEs, one has to learn who gains from their operations, who controls the political machinery and can manipulate it advantageously and who can participate in politics and define the terms under which such participation is possible. Since the pattern of influence is often based on institutional links between state bureaucracy and interest groups, which participate in the policymaking process, a change in these institutional arrangements is a powerful force in reshaping political interests and the conflicts between them and, thereby, in affecting the performance of SOEs.

Moreover, with the expansion of the SOE sector, the managers of SOEs become an interest group on their own, strongly influencing government action. In the United Kingdom, e.g., the establishment of the parliamentary SCNI enabled managers of the industries to speak openly about their problems and to resist government's pressures (Coombes, 1966, Chapters 5 and 6). Lunch meetings of the chairmen of the major nationalized industries were used to coordinate policies, and in 1978, a formal system was established by the creation of the Nationalised Industries Chairmen Group (NICG), with a director to coordinate and carry on the affairs of the group. European SOEs created a lobbying organization in the EEC (CEEP), and in all countries, representatives of SOEs meet regularly with government ministers and sometimes have confrontations with them in public. SOE managers are seen sometimes—mainly by neo-Marxists—as managerial oligarchies, rustling up support to achieve their goals, or as instruments of the capitalist state. The power of managers is sometimes said to be restricted because they are appointed by the minister and owe him or her their allegiance. However, the minister may find it hard to replace a recalcitrant manager if this manager is known to be very effective. Sir Denis Rooke, e.g., was appointed in 1981 for a second term as the chairman of British Gas, even though he fought the government's attempts to privatize the firm's retail gas appliances.

In some countries, a consensus is reached between different stakeholders that SOEs are to be used to increase wealth available for redistribution. In others, each group wants more for itself. Unions tend to use their political influence and involve ministers in negotiations. Often government has to be involved because actions taken by one SOE invariably have repercussions in other SOEs. The intensity of these demands increases the lower the level of employment in that region and the more crucial the work of the employees. Even though each firm is a separate legal entity, there is much more comparison of salaries and other working conditions within the whole sector.

Creditors of SOEs tend to regard their loans as safer than comparable loans to private firms because they feel that the government will not allow its firms to default on their loans; there are fewer demands for information, securities and, perhaps, a lower rate of interest. As a result, banks tend to give an SOE much more credit in relation to its equity capital or other norms of bank lending.

Orientation of Management

Managerial behavior was shown in Chapter 8 to be a function of the background and selection of managers, their beliefs and their perceptions of career paths. They beliefs are based not only on ideology, but also on the available alternatives for promotion. Managers are the link-pin between the organization and its environment and their behavior is a crucial determinant of SOEs' performance. Most studies of management of SOEs "are more concerned with constitutions, policies and structures than with management processes" (Baker, 1969, p. 17). However, it is the process of decision-making and strategy formation that is crucial for performance.

The less developed a country is, the more difficulties it may encounter in finding competent managers to run the SOEs, executives in governments to control them and accountants and auditors to give them information or to check on them. When performance of SOEs in these countries is discussed, it is important to avoid the fallacy of attributing any inefficiencies or differences in outcomes between these firms and private sector firms in industrial countries to the vagaries of public ownership. It has to be shown that these problems are not inherent in the level of development or in some cultural attributes.

For instance, it is often said that many SOEs in certain countries are inefficient because their managers are corrupt. As *The Economist* said in a lead article on February 4, 1984, Nigeria is riddled with corruption from top to toe: "The minister may take his million dollar kickback for the international contract; the marriage registrar takes the soiled five naira note" (p. 13). However, it is difficult to say where patronage ends and corruption begins. It is also difficult to make the assumption that corruption is limited to the SOEs alone. One should also note that in many countries political alliances are built around clan relations and monetary benefits, not necessarily around ideological proclivities. Are SOEs expected to behave differently from the private sector? Unfortunately, in some cases, the corruptly obtained contract that leads to a shoddy factory or overpriced products is accepted as a way of life, in particular when bribes are taken not for personal enrichment but to help the party, tribe or clan. Where corruption has clawed its way to the very top and where power is unchallenged, it is extraordinarily difficult to cut out corruption in SOEs or elsewhere. Corruption of both the political and economic elite will certainly affect the behavior of the enterprise sector—state owned or otherwise.

Management is often assumed to be concerned only with implementation of specifications and performance, coordinating the different functions in the organization in getting the job done. Given such a portrait of management, someone else, higher in the hierarchy, should give directions, spell out objectives, surveying the situation and choosing the course to be steered between several possibilities, with many possible consequences. But most managment is not so apathetic. It symbolizes hopes, desires, ambitions and determination of the internal coalitions, and attempts to gain discretion. An SOE is not necessarily an inert, passive entity guided mainly by the hand of external controllers. The capacity, opportunity and incentives for action of managers in SOEs vary for different cultures and under different political regimes.

Some writers see SOEs managers as "feudal barons" (e.g., Jay 1968, Feigenbaum 1985; Walsh, 1978). Others see the managers as striving "to keep the government happy with the company's *political* performance" (Monsen and Walters, 1983, p. 53). This writer believes that managerial orientation is an independent variable, different in different SOEs. Managers, as shown in Chapter 8, can play one stakeholder off against another and attempt to achieve a higher level of discretion. In many cases, it is hard to tell whether the government bureaucracy controls its SOEs or vice versa. In West Africa, the financial resources of the marketing board both on current and capital accounts exceeds those of the West African government. The major Austrian state-owned banks are vast empires that the government needs to obtain funds. Most national oil companies have enormous power and may even control political power. PERTAMINA, for example, "has become the single most important economic and political entity in Indonesia; its capacity for stimulating and controlling the Indonesian economy has already become legendary" (Fabrikant, 1975, pp. 527-528). Its manager felt "that what is good for PERTAMINA is necessarily good for the country" (*Ibid.*, p. 528).

The stereotypical image of the SOE is an organization totally hemmed in by rules, regulations, restrictions and precedents imposed on it by a rule-conscious external bureaucracy. It is seen as rigid, unable to dismiss tenured employees, forced to retain archaic structures mandated by law, held to antiquated rule books and accounting practices because they are used in other parts of the government, continuing to produce a product even when there is no longer a demand for it because to discontinue it would cause politically unacceptable unemployment. It is perceived as a heavily bureaucratized organization in which employees are motivated either by the job security attached to governmental employment or by the excessive wages permitted by an organization that is not held accountable by market criteria. While there may be elements of truth in this image in some cases, SOEs do not always fit this stereotype. The operation of an SOE depends on the interaction of its environment with critical internal operations and conditions, decision-making, control and coordination, motivation, communication, leadership and change, and mainly the managers it is able to recruit. These managers, if they are highly capable, push for expansion to satisfy their ambition.

In most countries, capital markets do not play an important role in allocating investable resources. Instead, the generation of capital depends largely on financial intermediaries and the government. In some cases, the government creates SOEs. In others, it affects economic behavior by regulation. The performance of SOEs in the 1980s can be compared, not to that of an ideal model in a world of perfect competition but to the available alternatives.

One way of learning about organizations and their behavior is by carefully studying how specific decisions are made. Research on specific decisions (such as the sale of state-owned enterprises, nomination of a new general manager, conflicts between SOE managers and government), or specific turning points (like a change of government) may reveal a wealth of information on SOEs and their relationship to the environment in which they operate and explain their behavior according to the variables enumerated earlier. SOE behavior also changes with time, mainly because the relationships with the environment evolve through learning and adaptation. Managers can employ two very different methods to deal with conflicting pressures: "Change conflicting pressures to reinforce desired performance, or change structure and process mechanism to reconcile conflicting pressures" (Brown, 1983, p. 67). Both may imporve performance.

Managers of SOEs try to achieve more political power than managers of privately owned firms. They are less concerned about the consequences of risky decisions. Private businesspersons, for their part, demand from SOEs more services for less pay and oppose any direct competition by SOEs.

DIFFERENCES WITHIN SOES

While all SOEs face certain common problems, they are also very heterogeneous. Any enterprise, irrespective of ownership, has to respond to its environment, and different SOEs face different environments. The major variables that cause differences within the SOE group are in the structure of the markets in which they operate; the degree of professionalism of the managers; the interface between them and their controllers in government, including the degree of dependence on government for funds; their size and age, their importance to the country, and their major mission.

Market Structure

How does market structure influence SOEs? Competition determines potential comparative advantage but also affects the degree of intervention of the government: the tendency of the governments to call on the enterprise to achieve all sorts of goals will be greater when the costs of these goals can be hidden or cross-subsidized. To the extent that the firm competes in the market and does not generate enough funds to cross-subsidize, the government may demand fewer social goals. Governments fully understand the limits imposed by markets on the performance of enterprises even though it may take them some time to realize all the costs. If the market in which the SOE operates is competitive, then any demands for achieving noneconomic goals reduce the ability of the SOE to compete. Moreover, since the results can be easily compared to those of private enterprises similarly situated, the ability to dispense largesse invisibly is curtailed. In this case, profits become socially legitimized and politically accepted. The SOE enjoys a high degree of autonomy, and the government makes fewer demands on it to achieve noneconomic goals.

Conversely, an SOE operating as a monopoly in an area of important public service, such as the electricity or telephone systems, will be subject to strong pressures to increase its slack and to use a variety of invisible methods to better the conditions for certain groups of its customers. Further, the government will tend to interfere in most of its strategic, pricing and even some of its operating decisions, attempting to achieve other goals. This will lead to politicized behavior of both the controlled and their controllers. If the firm is financially dependent on government and subject to closed hierarchical control, the external coalition will dominate. If the firm is financially independent, the internal coalition may prevail, and the firm may break away from government control.

Some SOEs are expected to generate very high rates of profits and are used mainly as a tax agency—national lotteries are one example. Others are expected to cover their costs, and still others have limited external revenue sources and are supported by the government for the majority of the funds they need, while other SOEs are allowed or even encouraged to tap debts from the private capital market. This spectrum of product/market diversity is important in understanding the behavior of these firms.

Competition may also be stimulated. In Nicaragua, "by creating parallel public marketing channels in commercialization and distribution, the state stimulated production and consumption of basic foods" (Austin, Fox and Kruger, 1985, p. 33). In Brazil, the rivalry among state-owned electricity firms for funds and the conflict of interest among them forced them to be more efficient (Tendler, 1968, p. 141), despite the existence of "camaraderie among state power-interests, based on the common cause of state capitalism or dislike of the foreign utility" (*Ibid.*, p. 145).

If government wants to use competition as a sanction against complacent managers, it should allow SOEs to go bankrupt if they do not meet the test of the market. If the firm is a monopoly, the private firm has both shareholders and workers squabbling over the spoils of monopoly. In an SOE, on the other hand, the spoils may be used for political benefits. A possible solution is to allow competition *for* the monopoly.

Managerial Professionalism

In some countries, firms were nationalized as going concerns after they had operated for a long time under private ownership with many decades of successful management traditions and distinctive organizational culture, led by professional managers who were fiercely loyal to the organization and had a strong *esprit de corps.* In these cases, there was in the firm a cadre of professional managers and an ethos and culture of the firm, and these managers attempted to operate the firm the way it had been in the past (Coronel, 1983). In other cases, the private managers left or the SOEs inherited inadequate patterns of administration. This is said to be the case for the telephones which are managed in many countries as a government department attached to the Post Office. In some cases, managers were ebullient and self-confident. In others, there were no indigenous managers, and a major role of the SOEs was that of a training ground for new managers. In fact, one of the greatest achievements of the SOEs in many African countries has been that they trained managers, admittedly at a high cost to the nation. (Training managers takes a long time, and there are very few short cuts.)

Killick (in UNIDO, 1983) analyzed industrial SOE performance in four African countries (Ghana, Senegal, Tanzania and Zambia). He found that of the six performance variables (finance, productivity, balance of payments, employment, distributional effect and Africanization), only one—Africanization—was positive (*Ibid.*, pp. 1–2).

Size and Age of Firms

The more government attempts to control the enterprises, the more it might cause detrimental effects. Public administration is often characterized by delays, committees and slow response, which are not very helpful for commercial operations. Often, government tinkering with the activities of the enterprise causes apathy. In other cases, it creates conflicts and fights for power. This pattern of relationship changes with the size and age of the SOE. The bigger the SOE and the longer it has been in operation, the greater the political power of its managers. These managers often develop their own culture, controlling the SOEs like feudal barons. New SOEs tend to be more subservient to government than older, more established ones. Small SOEs may sometimes escape control because they are perceived by civil servants as not being important enough to warrant an investment of time.

Interface Between Controlled and Controllers

Top managers can alter the flow of funds by altering the design of measurement, rewards or organizational structure to encourage their subordinates to produce the results they want. They can also use their power to influence the government to allocate more funds to the operations and are able to encourage, counsel, cajole or demand the performance they want from their subordinates if they have the power to reward and punish. Finally, they can become involved in the substance of decisions. The same alternatives are open to governments, too. However, as in a private firm, the capacity of the government as top managers to influence the flow from operations varies inversely with the product/market diversity. The more the diversity, the less the influence (Lorsch and Allen, 1973). Managers resent and resist government involvement in the substance of operating issues. Meddling and interference can be as demotivating in a public as in a large private organization.

Governments typically lack information about the operations of the SOEs. This problem is solved in many countries by appointing representatives of the different government ministries to the board of directors. The result, however, is that these civil servants see the board as an interministerial committee to decide on governmental policy, and they attempt to bring the point of view of the ministry to the board instead of being independent trustees of the interest of the enterprise.

Importance to Country

Important or *essential* industries are rather imprecise words. First, differences of opinion may exist about what is important. Second, a company may be both important and dependent on the government (e.g., if the government is a monopsonistic buyer of its product), important but not dependent (a very large firm like a national oil company) or dependent but not important (a small firm whose sole customer is the government). An industry is important to the government if (1) it produces a relatively large share of GNP or is a large employer; (2) its prices affect the cost structure of major industries in the economy (such as electricity, railroads or water); (3) it is considered highly prestigious such as aerospace or electronics; (4) a large percentage of its production is considered essential for defense; (5) it is a large-scale exporter.

Dependence on government may be caused by (1) a high percentage of sales to government, (2) strong foreign competition, (3) a supply of public goods that is subsidized and (4) being a declining industry. The more important an industry (or a single SOE) is, the more the government attempts to dictate its strategic decisions. The more dependent the company is, the easier it is for the government to dictate its strategy.

Mission

The classification of SOEs according to form of organization, legal status, status of employees (civil servants or non-civil servants) are less important than the major missions that materially affect their behavior. Some of these SOEs are expected to create national wealth, others, to distribute existing wealth.

Fiscal monopolies are similar in many respects to a tax agency. Public utilities "always have certain conditions and fixed objectives to which they are bound, however much their individual managers might like to be imaginative and adaptable" (Baker, 1969, p. 24). Competitive SOEs, on the other hand, can develop new products or services and drop others, enter new markets and withdraw from them. The products they sell are not part of an indivisible network. Still, even a public utility has a lot of discretion: postal deliveries in remote areas, the avoidance of power on cold days, the provision of bus shelters to keep rain off passengers, may or may not be supplied. They all "require investments which will usually not seem to pay" (Nove, 1973, p. 109).

After half a century of operations of large, private corporations, the persistence of the belief that SOEs should be compared to an idealized private firm is not very helpful. It is hard to question the validity of statements that SOEs ought to be assessed on the basis of their net contribution to social welfare, but large private firms are also expected to be socially responsible, and in both cases the measurement of social benefits is faced with insurmountable difficulties.

Some SOEs were created because of administrative convenience and "as a means for escaping personnel and financial controls and excluding expenditures from the budget" (Seidman, 1983b, p. 65). These SOEs are actually not very different from any government department. They get their financing from annual budget appropriations. In this case it is more appropriate to discuss differences between SOEs and government than between SOEs and private-sector enterprises. Widespread use of SOEs to achieve administrative tasks of the government may result in loss of prestige of the civil service. SOEs may drain away from the civil service the most ambitious and most talented personnel.

EVOLUTION OF THE RELATIONSHIPS BETWEEN SOES AND THE STATE

All SOEs change with time. They are created to achieve certain gaols and to satisfy certain extraneous norms. With time, they grow and their managers institutionalize their own norms, playing a game of power with the environment, reducing their dependence on the state, reducing the probability of government intervention and enhancing their autonomy. The constant interaction between the SOEs and other state organs improves information, communication and civil servant understanding of the needs of the SOE. In turn, the managers gain a clearer view of the constraints they face. They also strike bargains and commit themselves to future courses of action—often before seeking approval. With time, what Mintzberg (1983) terms the "dominated" situation, with the SOE as an instrument, moves to what he calls "the closed system"—an autonomous SOE.

A strong dictator may not allow a closed system to evolve by continuing to dictate policies even at the cost of reduced motivation of managers. In most cases, however, successful SOE managers gain more power, achieve more autonomy and decide on goals. Hafsi (1981) has shown that SOEs move in their strategy-making process through a life cycle of the state–SOE relationship from cooperation to confrontation to autonomy. In Hafsi's terms, the autonomous SOE develops its own rules, procedures and communication channels, reducing the power of the external coalition and becoming less subservient to the environment. Anastassopoulos (1973), building on Allison's (1971) framework, has speculated on the rational, organizational and political factors impinging on autonomy, which were enumerated in Chapter 8. Anastassopoulos, however, does not tell us how these factors (and the autonomy profile) change. He implies that the change is exogenous, following changes in the variables he lists.

Although SOEs cannot pursue policies that are blatantly contrary to government's preferences, we have seen that quite often, because of the expertise it has and the information it holds, the SOE can dominate the generation of such preferences. The state technocratic managers may control not only the resources of the SOE but also the strategic choices, even persuading government to change internal and foreign policy to fit the SOE's needs, co-opting their controllers in the process.

When SOE managers exaggerate their power, playing their hand in a way that causes a scandal to erupt, they may lose all power. The pendulum swings back to more control. Thus, ENI was accused of behaving too much like a private oil firm and being a tool of the Christian Democratic party. Since 1970, ENI has been subject to price control and is no longer left alone to work out its destiny. The heady period of expansion under Mattei is over. This situation occurred partly because ENI lost its assured cash basis and partly because of the loss of its CEO's political power. The government adopted a parsimonious financial policy, resulting in a low capital base, and ENI had to comply with its directives. PERTAMINA's management lost its power because of a scandal, and the manager of Elf-Aquitaine was fired (Fabrikant, 1976, Feigenbaum, 1985).

Even the most powerful SOE manager has to take into account the potential power of the political parties in power. If this is not done, the manager may lose his or her job. The new manager will again start the cycle, moving from subservience to autonomous positions. These power struggles often take time and energy, diverting attention from the efficient management of the business to the need for cultivating political support and creating an independent power base. However, an SOE "cannot work properly if society does not want it to work and does not believe it is doing any good" (Baker, 1969, p. 31).

POSSIBLE LINES OF ACTION

To the extent that SOEs are less efficient than private enterprises, they become a burden on the government purse since their losses must be covered from other governmental revenue sources or by increasing invisible taxes—that is, charging more for the services of the SOE or protecting it from foreign competition. In any case, the citizens of the country bear the brunt of the additional economic burden. Therefore, ways to increase efficiency and managerial effectiveness in SOEs are of paramount importance.

One solution is to avoid state ownership, moving all possible services to private hands. The prospects and problems of this approach were discussed in Chapter 9.

A second approach, often recommended by economists, is designing different rules of behavior for SOEs. This approach envisages a combination of change in the external environment in which SOEs operate and a change in their internal incentive structure. External efficiency may be improved by the introduction of competition or by the introduction of Demsetz auctions on the rights to manage SOEs. * The internal environment may be improved by granting managers of enterprises more autonomy and making governmental intervention in the affairs of the enterprises illegal (NEDO, 1976).

Another approach is to design a set of specific instructions to make the SOE a welfare maximizer (Drèze and Marchand, 1976; Finsinger and Vogelsang, 1982) by means of an incentive system that aligns the interest of managers with the fulfillment of specified objectives. Economists recommend that SOE goals should be identical to those of private enterprise to avoid a situation where poor commercial performance can be ascribed to the achievement of poorly specified and multiple social goals and a shift from instrumental to politicized behavior. Others believe that goals should be negotiated. As Ferrario puts it, "a state enterprise can be a tool for government intervention, but each project has to be negotiated so that the core identity and the mission of the organization and its technical capabilities are not destructively affected" (1978, p. 238).

---

* Demsetz (1968) proposed that a natural monopoly would be run as a government franchise. The franchise is to be put up periodically for auction. At the beginning of each period, the franchise is awarded to the bidder prepared to make the best bid—not necessarily to the firm that won the previous bid.

Since SOEs are expected to achieve socially optimal goals, it is often proposed that their performance should be monitored by adjusting accounting profit measures—e.g., for subsidy or tax payments. The possibility of mechanisms to compensate the SOEs for the costs of social obligations is also explored. We have seen that such schemes are very difficult to implement. The major problem with this approach seems to be that it assumes what economists call rational behavior by both politicians and managers of the SOEs. Most of the problems of SOEs, however, stem not from lack of a theoretical framework or rules of conduct but from the difficulty of enforcing such rules in a real-life political regime.

Politicians who instruct SOEs to avoid price rises to combat inflation may give such an instruction because they do not understand the economic ramifications of their commands. At least equally likely is the probability that the politicians realize the long-run ramifications of such an instruction but have a short time-horizon. A politician facing an upcoming election may decide that winning the election is much more important than the long-run consequences of a certain policy decision. To hope that politicians will not indulge in these practices is to assume that they will cease to be politicians.

The voluminous literature on the political business cycle shows that politicians do behave differently immediately before and after elections. The very nature of the political process means that one cannot expect SOEs to be totally immune from political intervention or politicians to commit what they may perceive as political suicide by not responding to the demands of a variety of interest groups. When IRI was instructed to build a steel plant in Calabria, the criterion applied was not long-term welfare maximization but an expedient response to riots of hungry workers demanding jobs. When SOE managers in Africa were replaced by Africans, or when Malaysia preferred Malaysian to Chinese workers, they consciously preferred a political claim to the generation of more resources for distribution.

Many social scientists seem to feel that the best society is one driven, guided and managed by intellectuals who share some basic understanding of normative solutions and the criteria for these solutions. These experts are informed and wise and can therefore run the system—or the country—if not by the people, then for them. They disregard human fallibility as well as the limited ability of the human brain. They, therefore, feel they can construct a comprehensive theory of right and wrong, based on an infallible criterion of correctness. The leader or the expert is assumed to know best what is good for his or her fellow citizens and can advise other human beings on how to behave, what to do and how to solve problems. In the Communist systems, this belief means that the planner does not need the vast amount of information required to understand the preferences of millions of consumers: he or she knows what is best for the consumers and plans accordingly. Marx, Lenin and Mao designed comprehensive theories of right and wrong and of social change, which were based on the belief that conflicts are wrong and that harmony of all possible interests is both achievable and can be accomplished by the great leader. The same belief, albeit stemming from totally different basic ideological roots, is manifested in many attempts to create enterprises whose management is based on idealism, cutting any direct link between an individual's contribution to production and the real income from which he or she benefits, like in the Israeli kibbutz or in some attempts to create utopian societies. Plato, Rousseau and Hegel, on the philosophical front, also believed in the possibility of harmonious relations. Other philosophers such as Aristotle, Hobbes and Kant saw human relationships as based on conflict rather than harmony. Market relationships are not based on harmony, benevolence or "great, glorious and correct" solutions by the party. As Dahl says, "The key characteristic of a democracy is the continuing responsiveness of the government to the preferences of its citizens" (1971, pp. 1–2).

How can a government respond to the preferences of its citizens? These preferences are not always known, and if they are, they are conflicting! The economist's answer, at least as far as SOEs are concerned, is that the citizens' preferences may be determined by their willingness to pay. In reality, however, one of the government's problems is that citizens tend to demand services and assume that others will pay for them!

Economists may attempt to reach a solution that is as near as possible to what they believe would be achieved in a perfect market or at least a so-called second best solution. These solutions assume that knowing the answer, even if the answer is based on many simplifying assumptions and on certain values embedded in the assumptions, may be enough for the solution to be chosen and carried out.

Political scientists believe in a model of interactive processes in which checks and balances, committees and negotiations take place. In this model, there is no analytically right solution. One muddles through. It is recognized that problems do not have solutions and that any solution will raise new problems (Lindblom, 1977). What is important to the political scientist is the interaction mechanism or the patterns by which decisions are made, compromises achieved and commitments for the future accumulated.

The establishment and operations of an SOE are likely to add to the work load of the ministers and the administration, who must comprehend the problems of the SOEs and spend time understanding the results of their operations, discussing problems and so on. Since in most countries civil servants do not have any business experience, and many of them never set foot outside the civil service, it is not very easy for them to comprehend industrial or commercial strategic problems, even though they are doing their best. In most LDCs, where the shortage of experienced administrators is acute, the ability of the administration to control the SOEs is questionable. In some cases they may not even try.

In a world characterized by uncertainty, high costs of information, lack of knowledge of the set of social preferences, busy government officials whose precious time has to be devoted to hundreds of tasks and governments too fragmented to make explicit their social preferences, alternative approaches must be sought to improve interaction between management of SOEs and government. Incentives, compensation or performance contracts like those attempted in France proved disappointing in inducing SOE managers to pursue instrumental patterns of behavior. These devices are extremely costly to negotiate, and it is almost impossible to cover the gamut of alternative outcomes or to avoid politicizing the negotiation process.

As shown in Chapter 4, the preoccupation with goal clarification is not very fruitful. The formidable informational requirements and the inevitable uncertainty make such tools ineffective. In many cases, controllers can end up dominated by the controlled. The mode of organization whereby an enterprise can most efficiently achieve its goals is contingent on the specific environment in which it is active (Lawrence and Lorsch, 1967) for SOEs as for a private enterprise. The less routine the operations of SOEs, the greater the need for organic (that is, informal and decentralized) division of work (Burns and Stalker, 1961). One major problem in these cases is the wide gap in perception and ways of thinking between SOEs managers and their government controllers which leads to external conflicts.

Beesley and Evans (in Vernon and Aharoni, 1981) suggested initiating an evolutionary process of learning, starting with simple decision rules. As the government and the enterprise learn more about the side effects resulting from these decision rules, these rules might be made more complex and the prescription more complicated. They feel that given the paucity of information and behavior, such a simple decision rule may be the beginning of a process through which an SOE and its government will learn more of each other's problems and how to cooperate. As parties attempt to direct the evolution of their relationship, Beesley and Evans hope, uncertainty will be reduced and mutual trust will increase. As coordination around this decision rule evolves, the rules prescribing enterprise behavior can be made increasingly complex.

Beesley and Evans (in Vernon and Aharoni, 1981) stress that their decision rule is a transitional learning tool. However, single decision criterion are often adopted in *ad hoc* attempts to direct SOEs toward socially desired directions. Such an approach violates a basic premise of economics—the trade-off: achievement of a specified goal cannot be presumed socially desirable until opportunity costs are considered. Only if gains exceed losses has social welfare increased.

Thus, partial criteria may prove more destructive than no criteria. Only those adaptations that focus on procedures rather than outcomes avoid this pitfall. Beesley and Evans suggest one possible avenue, but their approach, emphasizing evolution in interface communication, implicitly presumes ability to achieve harmony and an unchanging institutional structure (see also Murthy, 1981). While no pragmatic managerial prescription can presuppose radical institutional (and thus political) change, some adaptations of institutions and procedures may be possible in a given political environment.

The reality of life in the public sector is that there are many conflicts, points of view and demands of different interest groups for a variety of lines of action. The system of checks and balances may mean that many have veto power over decisions, and a change in policy is extremely difficult to effect. Paradoxically, people look for solutions that are based on rational action, on planning of the whole system. They also look for depoliticization of the system and for experts to supply answers. Basically, the same way that the party knows best, the planner knows best. These experts are expected to work for an objective public interest to find optimal and correct solutions. An early example, at the beginning of the twentieth century, was the Progressive movement in the United States, which advocated good government and preached for an expert city manager who would reach the right solutions for the city rather than political accommodation of warring interests. Today, many observers would like to see SOEs managed by competent, expert professional managers who, again, would reach the right solutions. The managers of SOEs would agree to this line of reasoning. They would argue that the efficiency of SOEs can and should be judged by objective criteria, not by political or personal whims. Further, they would argue that if managers are not allowed to exercise their professional skills, it will be hard, if not impossible, to recruit good managers to manage the state's business.

In an SOE, commercial problems become political issues and sometimes liabilities. SOEs are always vulnerable to political pressures and to concessions to privileged groups. In a democracy, the concentration of SOEs under strict governmental control is one major cause of problems. First, it raises the expectation that the government will always subsidize the firm. The results are that the consumers expect the enterprises to supply them with services at low prices and to provide these services even if they are unprofitable. Gordon (1981) notes "One dubious belief—that there was a social advantage in having utilities financed by low-cost, government backed borrowing" (p. 44). Workers in SOEs persist in their belief that there is no limit to how much they should receive in wages and fringe benefits or to the extent of the job security to which they are entitled. Industry expects an SOE to supply it with procurement orders at prices that are higher than those prevailing in the world market.

These expectations evolve not simply because the firm is state-owned but because of the structure of the SOEs and their relationships to government. Workers see demands for a meaningful and secure job as totally justified. They have been working in the firm for so many years, doing a very good job; they were disciplined; they crawled into the mine, flew the airplane or drove the bus or did whatever other job faithfully. It is not their fault that the world has changed and that prices of coal went down or that IATA (International Air Travel Association) is no longer an effective cartel. From the workers' point of view, the firm was nationalized in the first place so the workers in it would be more satisfied and less subject to the vicissitudes of the capitalist world. So they fight against changes, strike and even rebel. If government ministers, interested in votes, then help them, they learn that next time there is no reason to negotiate with the management or the board, who are perceived as not having enough authority or are not acting as guardians of the national interest. Once expectations have been proved to be right, they may increase but certainly do not diminish. Once a government subsidizes its SOEs, demands for further subsidization would have no end.

How can these problems be alleviated? First, we have to understand their causes. These problems are the result of political intervention coupled with control structures that allow this intervention and that forbid the enterprises to use any alternative ways to get their funds. Today, one certainly sees political intervention in private enterprises, too. Governments have been attempting to maintain employment by helping private enterprise. Still, the range of discretion of the SOEs is much more limited.

Inefficiency of SOEs is not necessarily the result of ownership. The abysmal record of SOEs has been the result of the structure of their control and processes of their management, including their relations with the government. Private enterprise management, too, when it feels it can rely on the government to bail it out, may become less responsible and run its operations less efficiently, paying much less attention to industrial relations or better marketing. The records of ENI under Mattei, IRI in the 1950s and many of the U.K. nationalized industries until the mid-1960s, when there was less political interference, show that the problem of inefficiency is not an inherent problem of state ownership.

The reliance on analysis and the belief that the higher one is in the hierarchy, the more one has the correct answers have not always turned out to be true. Marx believed that once property is not owned by private capitalists, the administration would be quite simple, and this led him to the doctrine of the withering away of the state. The reality, of course, is different. One problem with SOEs, then, is the belief that some central organization somehow will know the answers better.

All transactions are carried out within a social and legal structure. The authority to make decisions is also rooted in the institutional and legal arrangements. Organizational decision-making does not always follow the legal prescriptions, and the actual authority of different actors may be different from that prescribed. But there is a promise in applying concepts of organizational design to the problems of guiding and controlling SOEs.

Indeed, one possible solution to the problem is to adapt institutional arrangements to influence the process of decision-making regarding SOEs rather than concentrating on the outcomes of the decisions and the ideal measurement of performance. What adaptations of institutional and procedures—in a given political context—are both feasible and could help secure a constructive evolution of the relationship between enterprise and government?

What kind of institutional design may make the SOEs more efficient? A simple solution is to let each of these enterprises be managed in a system that is as near as possible to that existing in a market exchange economy. That means, first, imposing rules to constrain government officials from commanding the enterprises or from interfering in its operating affairs. This system means that the managers would be constitutionally liberated and allowed to use their judgment in achieving the best interest of the enterprise. Second, and more important, it means creating competition within the public sector (see Chapter 9).

State ownership does not necessarily mean strict government control. If the government, for whatever reason, wants a certain enterprise to achieve a certain goal, it should pay for any additional marginal costs of carrying out the directive. Such a system would force management to look for least-cost solutions. In addition, it would force the consumers, workers and other stakeholders to realize the costs and the necessity for the government to foot the bill for the additional costs involved. Most important, governments should be ready to shut down mismanaged SOEs or dispose of them, instead of continuously pouring funds into them.

Compensation is not based only on economic rationale; managers will bargain for higher compensation, and the system will become politicized. Perhaps a system of auctions for achieving national objectives could be developed that would be open to private firms as well as SOEs. For example, if the government wants to get additional employment in a certain region, it might call for bids, giving the contract to the firm that bids the least cost per additional employee. If the government cannot find someone to agree to do a job it wants done, it can, with parliamentary approval, create another enterprise to do the job. That is essentially what the Italian government did in creating GEPI. The government may also use the threat of creating such an enterprise as part of its bargaining with the SOE management.

Under such a system, who will elect the directors and the managers? The answer is that the system would not be much different from that prevailing in large investor-owned private business with diffused ownership: the directors may be elected for a long period, and then others will be elected. The TVA was to be managed by three directors, appointed for 3, 6 and 9 years, and afterward for the full 9 years. This way Roosevelt ensured not only a long-term point of view of the directors but also that no president, even in a two-term administration, would be able to replace all three directors. The board was to select all other executives and was not bound by civil service regulations. A variation on that scheme would be that the directors would be elected for a long tenure but allowed to fire a fellow director by a majority vote. A minister might be allowed to give a written order to the directors, and one such written order could be to fire a director.

Autonomy and full decentralization are essential because the government cannot possibly make all the decisions, lacking as it does the necessary information and time. Autonomy is necessary, first and foremost, so that SOEs may attract good managers. Many of the present managers of SOEs would fear the new responsibilities that would be thrust on them. The world in which government can be blamed for inefficiency and the continued existence of the enterprise is externally guaranteed is very congenial to those managers who do not want to bear too much risk. Many civil servants whose careers are based on the power to direct SOEs may also be against such a reform. Such managerial and bureaucratic resistance was also apparent in the USSR when price reforms were proposed (Nove, 1964, p. 62; Schurmann, 1969, pp. 195ff; Katz, 1972, pp. 193 and 201).

Another important part of such a system might be to allow SOEs access to the capital markets but without government guarantees. The citizens of the country would be able to acquire shares in the SOEs, resulting in more diffused ownership and greater control of the capital market over the operations of the firms (see Chapter 9).

Such a system might allow the SOEs to pursue partisan efficiency in their operations, while the profits would still belong to the nation. At the same time, the danger exists that SOE managers would operate without due regard to other national goals such as plant location, finding new technologies or earning foreign exchange. The government could bargain for the achievement of these goals, paying as it goes for their additional costs from the appropriate budget. This would entail another advantage—namely, that the real costs of different governmental programs would be registered in the appropriate budgets and national accounts.

Power is an important feature in SOEs, and the selection of managers in these enterprises should take this point of view into account. The values, beliefs, attitudes and ideology of different managers and different civil servants can be heterogeneous; SOEs do not enjoy the legitimacy to operate solely as profit maximizers and do not have the legitimacy to operate as a government bureaucracy, dispensing largesse without regard for commercial considerations. SOE managers, by the nature of their job, not only have to safeguard scarce resources but also ensure public support by catering to the diverse demands made on them. They must recognize that their operations and decisions affect the interests of many groups, each of which promotes a different set of goals. They have power because they control information and because, assuming they are good managers, they are hard to find and difficult to replace. Government controllers should also have power to represent some aspects of the public interest and to control the state's resources.

Is such a system feasible? Theoretically, yes; politically, maybe. It is to be hoped that governments will recognize that the use of resources for patronage can impede the generation of more resources for distribution. The government civil servants may feel that they are too dependent on the goodwill of the SOE managers. There is indeed such a danger. These managers should be allowed to refuse government orders unless they are adequately compensated for carrying them out. At first thought, such an idea may sound ridiculous since the owners in a private business certainly can give the enterprise an order. Again, the real owners are the citizens of the country, not the civil servants or the politicians in power. Policymaking under such a system will mean much more internal negotiations and the need for much more mutual adjustment. Such a structure, one should hope, would lead to much better performance and certainly to more checks and balances.

Some may feel that the additional checks and balances envisaged will reduce efficiency rather than increase it. Certainly, if all problems had easily recognizable solutions, if they were within the limited cognitive capacity and if all persons had the incentives to behave in the most efficient way, then other structures, less complex, would have been adequate. The history of the SOEs, as analyzed in this book, seems to show that these conditions are lacking. If states want to maintain an effective SOE sector, this sector should be regarded as an independent one, not less so than the judicial system.

It may well be that such a system is feasible only in more stable states with long traditions of governance and in which SOEs have created internal and external constituents with significant vested interests in their survival. With time, a system of relationship among the different sectors of government can be developed also in Asian and African new countries. In these countries, in particular, it is more important to have an efficient SOE sector than to engage in futile attempts at privatization.

CONCLUSION

Economies of the Western world have been mixed for many years. The precise balance of the mix and the tools to be used in achieving this balance have been subject to an acute debate. Part of the debate has centered on the role of SOEs, and on their performance. A comparison based on relative profitability of the private sector and SOEs show the first to be far superior. Comparisons based on relative cost efficiency, or on effectiveness, yield different results. In the 1980s, the role of vote-seeking politicians and bureaucrats is far better understood, and their tendency to place extensive demands on the valuable time of top management executives recognized.

Differences among enterprises may stem not only from differences of ownership but also from environmental factors such as differences in relationship with the government or in the level of international activity, market structure, technology, scale and rates of growth. The differences may also stem from the way in which managers are recruited. It may be that managers in different sectors or in different firms are differently motivated because of different personal backgrounds or as a result of different ideological beliefs.

Managerial behavior in the SOEs can be explained as a joint function of the following: first, the ownership; second, the environment; third, the sociopolitical background, work experience and ideological beliefs of the managers, as well as their orientation.

In the 1980s, SOEs will face several intractable problems. They will confront the need to adapt to a changing environment and shifting international political economy. They will continue to face tensions between the calls for efficiency, the demands for equity and the pressures for achieving politically dictated goals. Governments will be alarmed by the proliferation of those firms, and attempt to control them better. Questions such as who should approve the creation of an SOE, the establishment of a subsidiary, the appointments of directors and managers, and corporate plans and budget? How can Parliament effectively scrutinize their operations? Should SOEs be compensated for carrying out social or public policy functions? and, most important, who benefits and who should benefit from their operations?, will continue to be of importance. SOEs function in a contradictory world. They are expected to do what they are told, but to be innovative, to be government instruments, but also businesslike, to achieve national goals, but also to be autonomous and profitable, to promote change, but also to secure and preserve jobs. These contradictions are built into the very hybrid nature of an SOE. They are seen as accountable not only for efficiency, but also for equity, stability and redistribution.

Feigenbaum(1985), in concluding his case study of French petroleum policy and the role of the national oil firms, asks "can one conceive of a state at war with itself?" (p.141). As long as different persons have different conceptions of the public interest, the answer must be positive. Conflicts are inevitable, frictions are part of life, and harmony has proven to be an impossible dream. Trade-offs between efficiency and equity, or between political demands and economic requirements are not easily found. This book could not seek to solve these problems, but I hope it has clarified what they are.

BIBLIOGRAPHY

BOOKS, ARTICLES AND GOVERNMENT DOCUMENTS

Abegglen, James C., 1958, *The Japanese Factory: Aspects of its Social Organization* (New York: Free Press).

Aberbach, Joel, Robert D. Putnam, and B. A. Rockman, 1981, *Bureaucrats and Politicians in Western Democracies* (Cambridge, Mass.: Harvard University Press).

Acton Society Trust, 1950, *Accountability to Parliament*, Nationalised Industry Series No. 1 (Claygate: Acton Society Trust).

Acton Society Trust, 1951, *The Men on the Boards: A Study of the Composition of the Boards of Nationalised Industry*, Nationalised Industry Series No. 4 (Claygate: Acton Society Trust).

Adar, Zvi, and Yair Aharoni, 1980, "Risk-Sharing by Managers of State-Owned Enterprises" (Paper presented at the Second BAPEG Conference, Cambridge, Mass., April).

Administrative Staff College, 1963, *The Accountability of Public Corporations* (Henley on the Thames: Administrative Staff College).

Aguilar, Francis J., 1967, *Scanning the Business Environment* (New York: Macmillan).

Aharoni, Yair, 1963, *The Functions and Roles of Directors* (Tel Aviv: Israel Institute of Productivity) (Hebrew).

Aharoni, Yair, 1976, "The Role of the Public Sector in the Face of Economic Crisis," *Annals of Public and Co-operative Economy* 47, no. 3–4: 301–324.

Aharoni, Yair, 1977, *Markets, Planning and Development: The Private and Public Sectors in Economic Development* (Cambridge, Mass.: Ballinger).

Aharoni, Yair, 1979, *State-Owned Enterprises in Israel and Abroad* (Tel Aviv: Gomeh), (Hebrew).

Aharoni, Yair, 1980, "The State-Owned Enterprise as a Competitor in the World Markets," *Columbia Journal of World Business* 15, no. 1: 14–22.

Aharoni, Yair, 1981a, *The No-Risk Society* (Chatham, N. J.: Chatham House Publishers).

Aharoni, Yair, 1981b, "Performance Evaluation of State-Owned Enterprises: A Process Perspective," *Management Science* 27, no. 11: 1340–1347.

Aharoni, Yair, 1981c, "Managerial Discretion in State-Owned Enterprises," in Raymond Vernon and Yair Aharoni, eds., *State-Owned Enterprise in the Western Economies* (London: Croom Helm).

Aharoni, Yair, 1982, "State-Owned Enterprise: An Agent without a Principal," in Leroy P. Jones, ed., *Public Enterprise in Less-Developed Countries* (New York: Cambridge University Press), 67–76.

Aharoni, Yair, 1983a, "Comprehensive Audit of Management Performance in U.S. State-Owned Enterprises," *Annals of Public and Co-operative Economy* 54, no. 1: 73–92.

Aharoni, Yair, 1983b, "State-Owned Enterprises' Performance and Innovation Ability—Implications for System Design" (Paper presented at a conference sponsored by the Institute for Advanced Studies in Administration and the Latin American Council Schools of Administration, Caracas, Venezuela, November).

Aharoni, Yair, 1984, *Managers in the State, Histadrut and Private Sectors in Israel: A Comparative Study,* Research Report 53/84 (Tel Aviv: Israel Institute of Business Research, September).

Aharoni, Yair, and Ran Lachman, 1982, "Can the Manager's Mind be Nationalized?" *Organization Studies* 3, no. 1: 33–46.

Aharoni, Yair, Zvi Maimon and Eli Segev, 1978, "Performance and Autonomy in Organizations: Determining Dominant Environmental Components," *Management Science* 24, no. 9: 949–959.

Aharoni, Yair, Zvi Maimon and Eli Segev, 1981, "Interrelationships between Environmental Dependencies: A Basis for Tradeoffs to Increase Autonomy," *Strategic Management Journal* 2, no. 2: 197–208.

Ahlbrandt, Roger, S., Jr., 1973, "Efficiency in the Provision of Fire Services," *Public Choice* 16 (Fall): 1–15.

Ahmed, Zia, ed., 1982, *Financial Profitability and Losses in Public Enterprises of Developing Countries* (Ljubljana: I.C.P.E.).

Aitken, Hugh G.J., ed., 1959, *The State and Economic Growth* (New York: Social Science Research Council).

Alchian, Armen A., 1961, "Some Economics of Property Rights," RAND Corporation Study, P-2316 (Santa Monica: RAND Corporation).

Alchian, Armen A., 1965, "Some Economics of Property Rights," *Politico* 30 (December): 816–829.

Alchian, Armen A., 1977, *Economic Forces at Work* (Indianapolis: The Liberty Fund).

Alchian, Armen A., and Harold Demsetz, 1972, "Production, Information Costs and Economic Organization," *American Economic Review* 62, no. 5: 777–795.

Aldcroft, Derek H., 1968, *British Railways in Transition* (London: Macmillan).

Aldrich, Howard E., 1979, *Organizations and Environment* (Englewood Cliffs, N.J.: Prentice-Hall).

Aldrich, Howard E. and Jeffrey Pfeffer, 1976, "Environments of Organizations," in Alex Inkeles, ed., *Annual Review of Sociology,* 2 (Palo Alto, Calif.: Annual Reviews), pp. 79–105.

Allison, Graham T., 1971, *The Essence of Decision: Explaining the Cuban Missile Crisis* (Boston, Mass.: Little, Brown).

Anastassopoulos, Jean-Pierre, 1973, "The Strategic Autonomy of Government-Controlled Enterprises Operating in a Competitive Economy," (Ph.D. dissertation, Graduate School of Business, Columbia University, New York).

Anastassopoulos, Jean-Pierre, 1980, *La Stratégie des Entreprises Publiques* (Paris: Dalloz).

Anastassopoulos, Jean-Pierre, 1981, "The French Experience: Conflicts with Government," in Raymond Vernon and Yair Aharoni, eds., *State-Owned Enterprise in the Western Economies* (London: Croom Helm).

Anastassopoulos, Jean-Pierre, Georges Blanc and Pierre Dussauge, 1985, *Les Multi-nationales Publiques* (Paris: P.U.F.).

Andrlik, Erich, 1983, "The Organized Society: A Study of Neo-Corporalist Relations in Austria's Steel and Metal Processing Industry" (Ph.D. dissertation, MIT, Cambridge, Mass.).

Annals of Public and Co-operative Economy, 1981, "Public and Co-operative Enterprises: Autonomy, Controls, Participation" (Report on the Proceedings of the Thirteenth International Congress on Public and Co-operative Economy, Lisbon, June 2–4, 1980), *Annals of Public and Co-operative Economy* 52: 1–2.

Appelby, Paul, 1956, *Re-examination of India's Administrative System with Special Reference to Administration of Government's Industrial and Commercial Enterprises* (New Delhi: Government of India, Secretary of the Cabinet).

Apter, David E., 1964, "Introduction: Ideology and Discontent, " in David E. Apter, ed., *Ideology and Discontent* (New York: Free Press), 15–46.

Argyris, Chris, and Donald Schön, 1978, *Organizational Learning: A Theory of Action Perspective* (Boston: Addison-Wesley).

Armstrong, John R., 1973, *The European Administrative Elite* (Princeton, N.J.: Princeton University Press).

Arrow, Kenneth J., and R.L. Lind, 1970, "Uncertainty and the Evaluation of Public Investment Decisions," *American Economic Review* 60, no. 3: 364–378.

Asian Center for Development Administration, 1976, *Approaches to Public Enterprise Policy in Asia: Investment, Prices and Returns Criteria* (Kuala Lumpur, September).

Ashley, C.A., and R.G.H. Smails, 1965, *Canadian Crown Corporations: Some Aspects of Their Administration and Control* (New York: St. Martins).

Asobie, H.A., 1983, "The Influences of Multinational Corporations on the Management of Public Enterprises in Nigeria," *Africa Development* 7, no. 1: 5–30.

Atkinson, Anthony, and Joseph Stiglitz, 1980, *Lectures on Public Economics* (New York: McGraw-Hill Economics Handbook Service).

Aubert, Nicole, Bernard Ramanantsoa and Roland Reitter, 1984, "Nationalization, Managerial Power and Societal Change: A Field Study in France, 1982–1983" (Research paper prepared for the Harvard Business School Seventy-Fifth Anniversary Colloquium on Leadership, March 4–9).

Austin, James E., 1983, *"State-Owned Enterprises at the Micro Level: Managerial Issues,"* Working Paper HBS 83–30 (Boston, Mass.: Harvard Business School).

Austin, James E., 1984, *State-Owned Enterprises: The Other Visible Hand* (Boston, Mass.: Harvard Business School, Working Paper).

Austin, James E., and Michael J. Buckley, 1983, *"Food Marketing SOEs: Mexico vs. Venezuela,"* Working Paper 84–31 (Boston: Harvard Business School).

Austin, James E., Jonathan Fox and Walter Kruger, 1985, "The Role of the Revolutionary State in the Nicaraguan Food System," *World Development* 13, no. 1: 15–40.

Australian Royal Commission on Australian Government Administration, 1975, *Report and Appendix*, 4 vols. (Canberra: Australia Government Publishing Services).

Averch, Harvey, and Leland L. Johnson, 1962, "Behavior of the Firm under Regulatory Constraint," *American Economic Review* 52, no. 5: 1052–1069.

Baban, Roy, 1977, "State Trading and the GATT," *Journal of World Trade Law* 11, no. 4: 334–353.

Baer, Werner, and Adolfo Figueroa, 1980, "The Impact of Increased State Participation in the Economy on the Distribution of Income: Some Reflections Based on the Cases of Brazil and Peru" (Paper presented at the Second BAPEG Conference, Cambridge, Mass., April).

Baer, Werner, Isaac Kerstenetsky and Annibal V. Villela, 1973, "The Changing Role of the State in the Brazilian Economy," World Development 1, no. 11: 23–34.

Baer, Werner, Thomas Trebat, and Richard Newfarmer, 1976, "State Capitalism and Economic Development: The Case of Brazil" (Paper prepared for the Conference on Implementation in Latin America's Public Sector: Translating Policy into Reality; University of Texas, Austin, April).

Bailey, Elizabeth E., and John C. Malone, 1970, "Resource Allocation and the Regulated Firm," Bell Journal of Economics and Management Science 1, no. 1: 129–142.

Bain, Joe S., Richard S. Caves and Julius Margolis, 1966, Northern California's Water Industry (Baltimore: The Johns Hopkins University Press).

Baker, R.J.S., 1969, "Organization Theory and the Public Sector," Journal of Management Studies 6 (February): 15–32.

Balassa, Bela, 1984, "External Shocks and Policy Responses in Sub-Saharan Africa, 1973–78," Finance and Development 21, no. 1: 10–12.

Baldwin, John R., 1975, The Regulatory Agency and the Public Corporation: The Canadian Air Transport Industry (Cambridge, Mass.: Ballinger).

Baldwin, Robert E., and Anne O. Krueger, eds., 1984, The Structure and Evolution of Recent U.S. Trade Policy (Chicago: University of Chicago Press for the National Bureau of Economic Research).

Balinky, Alexander, et al., 1967, Planning and the Market in the U.S.S.R: The 1960's (New Brunswick, N.J.: Rutgers University Press).

Balls, Herbert R., 1953, "The Financial Control and Accountability of Canadian Crown Corporations," Public Administration 31: 127–144.

Balls, Herbert R., 1970, "Improving Performance of Public Enterprises through Financial Management and Control," Canadian Public Administration 13, no. 1: 100–123.

Barak Commission, 1970, "Report of the Committee for the Preparation of a Government Corporations Act" (Jerusalem: The Hebrew University of Jerusalem, Faculty of Law, Institute for Legislative Research and Comparative Law; Hebrew).

Baran, Paul, and Paul M. Sweezy, 1968, Monopoly Capital (New York: Penguin).

Barnard, Chester, 1938, The Function of the Executive (Cambridge, Mass.: Harvard University Press).

Barshefsky, Charlene, Alice L. Mattice and William L. Martin II, 1983, "Government Equity Participation in State-Owned Enterprises: An Analysis of the Carbon Steel Countervailing Duty Cases," Law and Policy in International Business 14, no. 4: 1101–1158.

Bates, Robert H., 1981, Markets and States in Tropical Africa (Berkeley: University of California Press).

Baum, Warren C., 1958, The French Economy and the State (Princeton, N.J.: Princeton University Press).

Baumol, William J., 1959, Business Behavior, Value and Growth (New York: Macmillan).

Baumol, William J., 1977, "On the Proper Cost Tests for Natural Monopoly in a Multiproduct Industry," American Economic Review 67, no. 5: 809–822.

Baumol, William J., ed., 1980, *Public and Private Enterprise in a Mixed Economy*, Proceedings of a Conference held by the International Economic Association in Mexico City (New York: St. Martin's Press).

Baumol, William, J., 1984, "Toward a Theory of Public Enterprise," *Atlantic Economic Journal* 12, no. 1: 13–20.

Baumol, William J., Elizabeth E. Bailey, and Robert D. Willig, 1977, "Weak Invisible-Hand Theorems on the Sustainability of Multiproduct Natural Monopoly," *American Economic Review* 67, no. 3: 350–365.

Baumol, William J., and David F. Bradford, 1970, "Optimal Departures from Marginal Cost Pricing," *American Economic Review* 60, no. 3: 265–283.

Baumol, William J., John C. Panzar and Robert D. Willig, 1982, *Contestable Markets and the Theory of Industry Structure* (New York: Harcourt, Brace Jovanovich).

Baylis, B.T., 1980, "Competition and Industrial Policy," in A.M. El-Agraa, ed., *The Economics of the European Community* (Oxford: Philip Allan) pp. 113–133.

Beer, Stafford, 1959, *Cybernetics and Management* (New York: John Wiley & Sons).

Beesley, Michael, and Stephen Littlechild, 1983, "Privatisation: Principles, Problems and Priorities," *Lloyds Bank Review*, 149: 1–20.

Bennett, Douglas, and Kenneth Sharpe, 1980, "The State as Banker and Entrepreneur: The Last-Resort Character of the Mexican State's Economic Intervention 1917–1976," *Comparative Politics* 12, no. 2: 165–189.

Bennet, James T., and Manuel H. Johnson, 1979, "Public versus Private Provision of Collective Goods and Services: Garbage Collection Revisited," *Public Choice* 34: 55–63.

Bergson, Abram, 1968, *Planning and Productivity under Soviet Socialism* (New York: Columbia University Press).

Bergson, Abram, 1973, "On Monopoly Welfare Losses," *American Economic Review* 63, no. 5: 853–870.

Bergson, Abram, 1978, "Managerial Risks and Rewards in Public Enterprises," *Journal of Comparative Economics* 2, no. 3: 211–225.

Bergson, Abram, 1984, "Income Inequality under Soviet Socialism," *Journal of Economic Literature* 22, no. 3: 1052–1099.

Berkowitz, N., 1979, *An Introduction to Coal Technology* (New York: Academic Press).

Berle, Adolph, A., Jr., 1959, *Power without Property* (New York: Harcourt Brace and World).

Berle, Adolph A., Jr., and Gardiner C. Means, 1932, *The Modern Corporation and Private Property* (New York: Macmillan) (rev. ed., 1968).

Berliner, Joseph S., 1976, *The Innovative Decision in Soviet Industry* (Cambridge, Mass.: MIT Press).

Bernier, Ivan, 1975, "Le GATT et Le Problème du Commerce d'État dans les Pays à Economie de Marché: Le Cas des Monopoles Provinciaux des Alcools au Canada," *Canadian Yearbook of International Law* 13: 98–155.

Bhambhri, Chander Prakash, 1960, *Parliamentary Control over State Enterprise in India* (Delhi: Metropolitan Books).

Bilky, Warren J., 1973, "Empirical Evidence Regarding Business Goals," in James L. Cochrane and Milan Zeleny, eds., *Multiple-Criteria Decision Making* (Columbia: University of South Carolina Press), 613–634.

Bizaguet, Armand, *et al.*, 1971, *L'Evolution des Entreprises Publiques dans La*

Communaute Européenne au Cours des Dernières Années (Bruxelles: CEEP, May).

Blair, John M., 1976, *The Control of Oil* (New York: Pantheon Books).

Blair, John P., 1976, "The Politics of Government Pricing: Political Influences on Rate Structures of Publicly Owned Electric Utilities," *American Journal of Economics and Sociology* 35, no. 1: 31–36.

Blankart, Charles B., 1979, "Bureaucratic Problems in Public Choice: Why Do Public Goods Still Remain Public?" in R.W. Roskamp, ed., *Public Finance and Public Choice* (Paris: Cujas Publishers), 155–167.

Boneo, Haracio, 1981, "Political Regimes and Public Enterprises in Argentina," Technical Papers Series 31/1981 (Austin: Office of Public Sector Studies, Institute of Latin American Studies, University of Texas).

Boneo, Haracio, 1983, *Governmental Control over Public Enterprises in Latin America* (Ljubljana, Yugoslavia: ICPE)

Bonnefous, Edouard, 1977, *Rapport Sur Le Contrôle des Enterprises Publiques en 1976*, Senat no. 421, Session Extraordinaire, Paris.

Borcherding, Thomas E., Warner W. Pommerehne and Friedrich Schneider, 1982, "Comparing the Efficiency of Private and Public Production: The Evidence from Five Countries," *Zeitschrift für Nationalökonomie*, Suppl. 2, pp. 127–156.

Bös, Dieter, 1978, "Cost of Living Indices and Public Pricing," *Economica* 45: 59–69.

Bös, Dieter, 1981, *Economic Theory of Public Enterprise* (Berlin: Springer-Verlag).

Bostock, Mark, and Charles Harvey, 1972, *Economic Independence and Zambia Copper: A Case Study of Foreign Investment* (New York: Praeger).

Bower, Joseph L., 1977, "Effective Public Management," *Harvard Business Review* 55, no. 2: (March-April), 131–140.

Bower, Joseph L., 1983, *The Two Faces of Management: An American Approach to Leadership in Business and Politics* (Boston: Houghton Mifflin).

Boyne, George, 1984, "The Privatisation of Public Housing," *Political Quarterly* 55, no. 2: 180–187.

Bracewell-Milner, Barry, 1982, "Nationalised Industries: The Public Interest in Private Financing," *Director* 34: 47–49.

Braunthal, Gerald, 1965, *The Federation of German Industry in Politics* (Ithaca, N.Y.: Cornell University Press).

Brittan, Samuel, 1984, "The Politics and Economics of Privatisation," *Political Quarterly* 55, no. 2: 109–128.

Broadway, Frank, 1969, *State Intervention in British Industry 1964–68* (London: Kaye & Ward).

Brothwood, M., 1981, "The Commission Directive on Transparency of Financial Relations between Member States and Public Undertakings," *Common Market Law Review* 18, no. 2: 207–218.

Brown, L. David, 1983, "Toward a Theory of Public Enterprise Organization," Mimeographed report to the World Bank, March.

Bruggink, Thomas H., 1982, "Public versus Regulated Private Enterprise in the Municipal Water Industry: A Comparison of Operating Costs," *Quarterly Review of Economics and Business* 22, no. 1: 111–125.

Buchanan, Bruce, 1974, "Government, Managers, Business Executives and Organizational Commitment," *Public Administration Review* 34, no. 4: 339–347.

Burns, James MacGregor, 1978, *Leadership* (New York: Harper & Row).

Burns, Tom, 1957, "Management in Action," *Operational Research Quarterly* 8, no. 2: 45–60.

Burns, Tom, and G.M. Stalker, 1961, *The Management of Innovation*, second edition (London: Tavistock).

Cameron, David R., 1978, "The Expansion of the Public Economy: A Comparative Analysis," *American Political Science Review* 72, no. 4: 1243–1261.

Cameron, Kim, 1980, "Critical Questions in Assessing Organizational Effectiveness," *Organizational Dynamics* 9, no. 2 (Autumn), 66–80.

Campbell, John P., 1976, "Contributions Research Can Make in Understanding Organizational Effectiveness," *Organization and Administrative Sciences* 7, no. 1–2: 29–45.

Campbell, John P., Marvin D. Dunnette, Edward E. Lawler III and Karl E. Weick, Jr., 1970, *Managerial Behavior, Performance, and Effectiveness* (New York: McGraw-Hill).

Canada, Auditor General of Canada, 1976, *Report of the Auditor General of Canada to the House of Commons for the Fiscal Year Ended March 31, 1976*, Ottawa, Cat. no. FAl–1976.

Canada, Privy Council Office, 1977, "Crown Corporations: Direction, Control and Accountability—Government of Canada's Proposals," Cat. no. CP 32-39/1977 (Ottawa).

Capon, Noel, 1981, "Marketing Strategy Differences between State and Privately Owned Corporations: An Exploratory Analysis," *Journal of Marketing* 45, no. 2: 11–18.

Carey-Jones, N.S., S.M. Patankar and M.J. Boodhoo, 1974, *Politics, Public Enterprise and the Industrial Development Agency* (London: Croom Helm).

Carlson, Sune, 1951, *Executive Behavior* (Stockholm: Strombergs).

Carlsson, Bö, 1984, "Public Industrial Enterprises in Sweden: Searching for a Viable Structure," Mimeographed paper for the World Bank (Case Western Reserve University).

Caro, Robert A., 1974, *The Power Broker: Robert Moses and the Fall of New York* (New York: A.A Knopf).

Carsberg, Bryan and Stephen Lumby (1984), *Privatizing British Airport Authority: Policies, Prospects, Procedures* (London: Public Money).

Causey, Margaret Cameron, 1984, "Public Enterprise in Algeria: Law as a Bridge between Ideology and Reality," *Public Administration and Development* 4, no. 2: 155–169.

Caves, Douglas W., and Laurits R. Christensen, 1980, "The Relative Efficiency of Public and Private Firms in a Competitive Environment: The Case of Canadian Railroads," *Journal of Political Economy* 88, no. 5: 958–976.

Centre Européen de L'Entreprise Publique (CEEP), 1978, *L'Enterprise Publique dans la Communauté Economique Européenne* (Brusselles: CEEP).

Centre Européen de L'Entreprise Publique, 1981, L'Entreprise Publique dans la Communauté Economique Européenne (Brussels: CEEP).

Chambers, David, 1984, "Plans as Promises: What Does Corporate Planning Mean in a Publicly Owned Corporation?" *Public Administration* (London) 62: 35–49.

Chandler, Alfred D., Jr., 1962, *Strategy and Structure: Chapters in the History of the American Industrial Enterprise* (Cambridge, Mass.: MIT Press).

Chandler, Alfred D., Jr., 1977, *The Visible Hand: The Managerial Revolution in American Business* (Cambridge, Mass.: The Belknap Press).

Chandler, Marsha A., 1982, "State Enterprise and Partisanship in Provincial Politics," *Canadian Journal of Political Science* (Ontario) 15, no. 4: 711–740.

Chao, Hung-Po, 1983, "Peak-Load Pricing and Capacity Planning with Demand and Supply Uncertainty," *Bell Journal of Economics* 14, 1: 179–190.

Chenot, Bernard, 1959, *Les Entreprises Nationalisées* (Paris: P.U.F.).

Chester, Daniel Norman, 1951, *The Nationalised Industries (An Analysis of the Statutory Provisions)* (London: Allen & Unwin Ltd., for the Royal Institute of Public Administration).

Chester, Daniel Norman, 1958, "Boards and Parliaments," *Public Administration* 36: 87–92.

Chester, Sir Daniel Norman, 1975, *The Nationalisation of British Industry 1945–51* (London: HMSO).

Chevalier, François), 1979, *Les Entreprises Publiques en France* (Paris: Documentation Française).

Child, John, 1972, "Organizational Structure, Environment and Performance: The Role of Strategic Choice," *Sociology* 6: 1–22.

Chiplin, Brian, and Mike Wright, 1982, "Competition Policy and State Enterprise in the U.K.," *Antitrust Bulletin* 27: 921–956.

Choksi, Armeane M., 1979, *State Intervention in the Industrialization of Developing Countries: Selected Issues*, Staff Working Papers no. 341 (Washington, D.C.: World Bank).

Churchill, Neil, 1962, "The Effects of an Audit" (Ph.D. dissertation, University of Michigan).

Churchill, Neil, and William W. Cooper, 1964, "Effects of Auditing Records," in William W. Cooper, H.J. Leavitt and M.W. Shelley, eds., *New Perspectives in Organization Research* (New York: John Wiley & Sons), 250–275.

Clegg, Hugh Armstrong, 1951, *Industrial Democracy and Nationalisation* (Oxford: Basil Blackwell).

Clegg, Hugh Armstrong, and Theodore Edward Chester, 1953, *The Future of Nationalization* (Oxford: Basil Blackwell).

Cline, William, 1982, *Exports of Manufacturers from Developing Countries: Performance and Prospects for Market Process* (Washington, D.C.: Brookings Institution).

Coase, Ronald H., 1937, "The Nature of the Firm," *Economica* 4: 386–405.

Coates, David, 1980, *Labour in Power?* (London: Longmans).

Cockerill, Anthony, 1980, "Steel," in Peter J. Johnson, ed., *The Structure of British Industry* (New York: Nicholas Publisher), 131–153.

Cohen, Morris R., and Ernest Nagel, 1934, *An Introduction to Logic and Scientific Method* (New York: Harcourt, Brace & World).

Cohen, Stephen G., 1977, *Modern Capitalist Planning: The French Model* (Berkeley: University of California Press).

Commission of the European Communities, 1980, *Tenth Report on Competition Policy* (Brussels and Luxembourg).

Commission on the European Communities (1982), *Twelfth Report on Competition Policy* (Brussels and Luxembourg).

Commission on the European Communities (1983), *Thirteenth Report on Competition Policy* (Brussels and Luxembourg).

Commission on the European Communities (1984), *Fourteenth Report on Competition Policy* (Brussels and Luxembourg).

Committee on Public Accounts, 1977–1978, *8th Report* (London).

Commonwealth Secretariat, 1976, "The Role and Management of Public Enterprises," Report of a seminar in Jamaica (London).

Commonwealth Secretariat, 1978a, "Performance Evaluation of Public Enterprises," Report of a seminar in Botswana (London).

Commonwealth Secretariat, 1978b, "Issues in Public Enterprise Development," Report on the Pan Commonwealth Seminar in New Delhi (London).

Commonwealth Secretariat, 1979a, *Issues in Public Enterprise Development* (London).

Commonwealth Secretariat, 1979b, *Performance Evaluation of Public Enterprises* (London).

Coombes, David, 1966, *The Member of Parliament and the Administration: The Case of the Select Committee on Nationalised Industries* (London: Allen & Unwin).

Coombes, David, 1971, *State Enterprise: Business or Politics* (London: Allen & Unwin).

Coronel, Gustavo, 1983, *The Nationalization of the Venezuelan Oil Industry: From Technocratic Success to Political Failure* (Lexington, Mass.: D.C. Heath, Lexington Books).

Cowling, Keith, and Dennis C. Mueller, 1978, "The Social Costs of Monopoly Power," *Economic Journal* 88: 727–748.

Cowling, Keith, and Dennis C. Mueller, 1981, "The Social Costs of Monopoly Revisited," *The Economic Journal* 91: 721–725.

Crain, Mark W., and Asghar Zardkoohi, 1978, "A Test of the Property Rights Theory of the Firm: Water Utilities in the United States," *Journal of Law and Economics* 21: 395–408.

Crain, Mark W., and Asghar Zardkoohi, 1980, "Public Sector Expansion: Stagnant Technology or Attenuated Property Rights?" *Southern Economic Journal* 46, no. 4: 1069–1082.

Crew, Michael A., ed., 1979, *Problems in Public Utility Economics and Regulation* (Lexington, Mass.: D.C. Heath, Lexington Books).

Crosland, C.A.R., 1952, "The Transition from Capitalism," in Richard Crossman, ed., *New Fabian Essays* (London: Turnstile Press), 33–68.

Crosland, C.A.R., 1956, *The Future of Socialism* (London: Jonathan Cape).

Crossman, Richard, 1976, *The Diaries of a Cabinet Minister* (New York: Holt, Rinehart & Winston).

Crozier, Michael, 1964, *The Bureaucratic Phenomenon* (Chicago: University of Chicago Press).

Crozier, Michel, and E. Friedberg, 1977, *L'Acteur et le Système* (Paris: Editions de Seuil).

Cunningham, Simon, 1981, *The Copper Industry in Zambia: Foreign Mining Companies in a Developing Country* (New York: Praeger).

Cyert, Richard M., and James G. March, 1963, *A Behavioral Theory of the Firm* (Englewood Cliffs, N.J.: Prentice-Hall).

Dahl, Robert A., 1971, *Polyarchy* (New Haven, Conn.: Yale University Press).

Dahrendorf, Ralf, 1959, *Class and Class Conflict in Industrial Society* (Stanford, Calif.: Stanford University Press).

Dam, Kenneth W., 1970, *The GATT Law and International Economic Organization* (Chicago: University of Chicago Press).

Daniels, R.W., 1977, "The Regulation and Control of Public Utility Prices: British Experience 1960–1975," in Alexis P. Jacquemin and Henry W. de Jong, eds., *Welfare Aspects of Industrial Markets* (Leiden: Martinus Nijhoff), pp. 367–400.

Das, N., 1966, *The Public Sector in India* (New York: Asia Publishing House).

Davenport, E.H., and Sidney Russell Cooke, 1923, *The Oil Trust and Anglo American Relations* (London: 1976 reprint published by Hyperion, Westport, Conn.).

Davies, David G., 1971, "The Efficiency of Public versus Private Firms: The Case of Australia's Two Airlines," *Journal of Law and Economics* 14, no. 1: 149–65.

Davies, David G., 1977, "Property Rights and Economic Efficiency: The Australian Airlines Revisited," *Journal of Law and Economics* 20, no. 1: 223–226.

Davies, David G., 1981, "Property Rights and Economic Behavior in Private and Government Enterprises: The Case of Australia's Banking System," *Research in Law and Economics* 3: 111–142.

Davies, J.R., and W.M. McInnes, 1982, "The Efficiency and the Accountability of UK Nationalised Industries," *Accounting and Business Research* 13, no. 49: 29–41.

Davis, Stanley M., and Paul R. Lawrence, 1977, *Matrix* (Reading, Mass.: Addison-Wesley).

Deaglio, M., 1966, *Private Enterprise and Public Emulation* (London: Institute of Economic Affairs).

De Alessi, Louis, 1969, "Implications of Property Rights for Government Investment Choices," *American Economic Review* 59, no. 1: 13–24.

De Alessi, Louis, 1973, "Private Property and Dispersion of Ownership in Large Corporations," *Journal of Finance* 28, no. 4: 839–851.

De Alessi, Louis, 1974a, "An Economic Analysis of Government Ownership and Regulation: Theory and the Evidence from the Electric Power Industry," *Public Choice* 19: 1–42.

De Alessi, Louis, 1974b, "Managerial Tenure under Private and Government Ownership in the Electric Power Industry," *Journal of Political Economy* 82, no. 3: 645–653.

De Alessi, Louis, 1975, "Some Effects of Ownership on the Wholesale Prices of Electric Power," *Economic Inquiry* 13, no. 4: 526–538.

De Alessi, Louis, 1977, "Ownership and Peak-Load Pricing in the Electric Power Industry," *Quarterly Review of Economics and Business* 17, no. 4: 7–26.

De Alessi, Louis, 1980, "The Economics of Property Rights: A Review of the Evidence," *Research in Law and Economics* 2: 1–47.

De Bandt, Jacques, 1983, "La Gestion du Secteur Public et du Système Productif," *Revue d'Economie Politique* (Paris), 93, no. 5: 704–713.

Delapierre, Michael, et al., 1983, *Nationalisations et Internationalisation: Stratégies des Multinationales Françaises dans la Crise* (Paris: Mespéro-La Decouverte).

Delion, André G., 1968, *L'Etat et les Entreprises Publique* (Paris: Sirey).

Demsetz, Harold, 1967, "Toward a Theory of Property Rights," *American Economic Review* 57, no. 2: 347–359.

Demsetz, Harold, 1968, "Why Regulate Utilities?" *Journal of Law and Economics* 11: 55–65.

Demsetz, Harold, 1983, "The Structure of Ownership and the Theory of the Firm," *Journal of Law and Economics* 26: 375–390.

Dholakia, Bakul H., 1978, "Relative Performance of Public and Private Manufacturing Enterprises in India: Total Factor Productivity Approach," *Economic and Political Weekly Review of Management*, Feb. 25, pp. M.4–M.10.

Diamond, Peter A., and Jan A. Mirrlees, 1971a, "Optimal Taxation and Public Production, Part I: Production Efficiency," *American Economic Review* 61, no. 1: 8–27.

Diamond, Peter A., and Jan A. Mirrlees, 1971b, "Optimal Taxation and Public Production, Part II: Tax Rules," *American Economic Review* 61, no. 3: 261–278.

Diamond, William, 1957, *Development Banks* (Baltimore, Md.: John Hopkins Press).

Dickinson, James M., 1983, "State and Economy in the Arab Middle East: Some Theoretical and Empirical Observations," *Arab Studies Quarterly* 5: 22–50.

Dielmann, Heinz J., 1981, "U.S. Response to Foreign Steel: Returning to Trigger Prices," *Columbia Journal of World Business* 16, no. 3: 32–42.

Dimock, Marshall E., 1949, "Government Corporations," *American Political Science Review* 43, no. 6: 1145–1164.

Dimock, Marshall, E., 1971, *Business and Government*, 4th ed. (New York: Holt, Rinehart & Winston).

Diskin, Ehud, 1980, "The Attitude towards Risk in Israeli Private and Public Enterprises" (Ph.D. dissertation: Hebrew University).

Djilas, Milovan, 1957, *The New Class* (New York: Praeger).

Donges, Juergen B., 1980, "Industrial Policies in West Germany's Not So Market-Oriented Economy," *World Economy* 3, no. 2: 185–204.

Dornstein, Miriam, 1976, "Managerial Theories of Social Responsibility and Goal Orientation of Top-Level Managers in State-Owned Enterprises," *Journal of Behavioral Economics* 5, no. 2: 65–92.

Downs, Anthony, 1967, *Inside Bureaucracy* (Boston: Little, Brown).

Doz, Yves L., 1976, "National Policies and Multinational Management" (DBA dissertation: Harvard Business School).

Doz, Yves L., 1980, "Multinational Strategy and Structure in Government Controlled Business," *Columbia Journal of World Business* 15, no. 3: 14–25.

Dresang, Dennis L., and Ira Sharkansky, 1973, "Public Corporations in Single-Country and Regional Settings: Kenya and the East African Community," *International Organization* 27, no. 3: 303–328.

Dresang, Dennis L., and Ira Sharkansky, 1975, "Sequences of Change and the Political Economy of Public Corporations: Kenya," *Journal of Politics* 37, no. 1: 163–186.

Drew, Elizabeth, 1983, *Politics and Money: The New Road to Corruption* (New York: Macmillan).

Dreyfus, Pierre, 1977, *La Liberté de Réussir* (Paris: Jean Claude Simoen). Republished 1981, as *Une Nationalisation Réussie: Renault* (Paris: Fayard).

Drèze, Jacques H., 1964, "Some Postwar Contributions of French Economists to Theory and Public Policy," *American Economic Review* 54, part 2 (Suppl.): 1–64.

Drèze, Jacques H., 1980, "Public Goods with Exclusion," *Journal of Public Economics* 13, no. 1: 5–24.

Drèze, Jacques H., and Maurice Marchand, 1976, "Pricing, Spending and Gambling Rules for Nonprofit Organizations," in R.E. Grieson, ed., *Public and Urban Economics—Essays in Honor of William S. Vickrey* (Lexington, Mass.: D.C. Heath, Lexington Books), pp. 59–89.

nomics—Essays in Honor of William S. Vickrey (Lexington, Mass.: D.C. Heath, Lexington Books), pp. 59–89.

Drucker, Peter, 1954, *The Practice of Management* (New York: Harper & Brothers).

Drucker, Peter, 1974, *Management: Tasks, Responsibilities, Practices* (New York: Harper & Row).

Dubois, Pierre, 1974, *La Mort de l'Etat-Patron* (Paris: Edition Ouvrières).

Dudley, Geoffrey, 1979, "Pluralism, Policy-Making and Implementation: The Evolution of the British Steel Corporation's Development Strategy," *Public Administration* 57: 253–270.

Due, John F., 1981, "Railroads: An Endangered Species and the Possibility of a Fatal Mistake," *Quarterly Review of Economics and Business* 21, no. 1: 58–76.

Dunn, James A., Jr., 1977, "Railroad Policies in Europe and the United States: The Impact of Ideology, Institutions, and Social Conditions," *Public Policy* 25, no. 2: 205–240.

Dupont-Fauville, A., 1983, "Nationalization of the Banks in France: A Preliminary Evaluation," *Three Banks Review*, no. 139, 32–41.

Duvall, Raymond D., and John R. Freeman, 1981, "The State and Dependent Capitalism," *International Studies Quarterly* 25, no. 1: 99–118.

Dyson, Kenneth, 1980, *The State Tradition in Western Europe* (Oxford: Oxford University Press).

Dyson, Kenneth, and Stephen Wilks, 1983, *Industrial Crisis: A Comparative Study of the State and Industry* (New York: St. Martin's Press).

Eckstein, Alexander, ed., 1971, *Comparison of Economic Systems* (Berkeley: University of California Press).

Eilon, Samuel, 1971, "Goals and Constraints," *Journal of Management Studies* 8, no. 3: 292–303.

Einaudi, Mario, Maurice Bye and Ernesto Rossi, 1955, *Nationalization in France and Italy* (Ithaca, N.Y.: Cornell University Press).

Ellman, Michael, 1979, *Socialist Planning* (London: Cambridge University Press).

Ellsworth, Robert A., Austin L. Schmitt and John A. Zerby, 1981, "Regulating the Rate Practices of State-Controlled Shipping Companies: The Development and Implementation of the Ocean Shipping Act of 1978," *Journal of Maritime Law and Commerce* 12, no. 4: 467–484.

Eltis, Walter, 1979, "The True Deficits of Public Corporations," *Lloyds Bank Review*, no. 131: pp. 1–20.

Ennis, R.W., 1967, *Accountability in Government Departments: Public Corporations and Public Companies* (London: Layon Grant and Green).

Epstein, Edwin M., 1969, *The Corporation in American Politics* (Englewood Cliffs, N.J.: Prentice Hall).

Epstein, Edwin M., 1973, "Dimensions of Corporate Power: Part I," *California Management Review* 16, no. 2: 9–23.

Epstein, Edwin M., 1974, "Dimensions of Corporate Power: Part II," *California Management Review* 16, no. 4: 32–47.

Epstein, Edwin M., 1976, "The Social Role of Business Enterprise in Britain: An American Perspective: Part I," *Journal of Management Studies* 13, no. 3: 213–233.

Epstein, Edwin M., 1977, "The Social Role of Business Enterprises in Britain: An American Perspective: Part II," *Journal of Management Studies* 14, no. 3: 281–316.

Etzioni, Amitai, 1973, "The Third Sector and Domestic Missions," *Public Administration Review* 33, no. 4: 314–323.

Eutsler, Roland B., 1939, "Public and Private Ownership of Water Supply Utilities," *Annals of American Academy of Political and Social Science* 201: 89–95.

Evans, Peter, 1977, "Multinationals, State-Owned Corporations, and the Transformation of Imperialism: A Brazilian Case Study," *Economic Development and Cultural Change* 26, no. 1: 43–64.

Evans, Peter, 1979, *Dependent Development, The Alliance of Multinationals, State and Local Capital in Brazil* (Princeton, N.J.: Princeton University Press).

Ezra, Derek J., 1973, "Strategy in Public Industrial Enterprises," *Journal of General Management* 1, no. 1: 13–15.

Fabrikant, Robert, 1975, "PERTAMINA: A Legal and Financial Analysis of a National Oil Company in a Developing Country," *Texas International Law Journal* 10, no. 3: 495–536.

Fabrikant, Robert, 1976, "PERTAMINA: A National Oil Company in a Developing Country," in International Legal Center, ed., *Law and Public Enterprise in Asia* (New York: Praeger), pp. 192–246.

Fama, Eugene, F., 1980, "Agency Problems and the Theory of the Firm," *Journal of Political Economy* 88, no. 2: 288–307.

Faulhaber, Gerald R., 1975, "Cross-Subsidization: Pricing in Public Enterprises," *American Economic Review* 65, no. 5: 966–977.

Fausto, Domenicantonio, 1982, "The Finance of Italian Public Enterprise," *Annals of Public and Co-operative Economy* 53, no. 1: 3–23.

Feibel, C., and A.A Walters, 1980, *Ownership and Efficiency in Urban Buses*, Staff Working paper 427/1980 (Washington, D.C.: World Bank).

Feigenbaum, Harvey B., 1982, "Public Enterprise in Comparative Perspective," *Comparative Politics* 15, no. 1: 101–122.

Feigenbaum, Harvey B., 1985, *The Politics of Public Enterprise: Oil and the French State* (Princeton, N.J.: Princeton University Press).

Fernandes, Praxi, ed., 1978, *Financing of Public Enterprises in Developing Countries* (Ljubljana: ICPE).

Fernandes, Praxi, ed., 1979, *Control Systems for Public Enterprises in Developing Countries* (Ljubljana: ICPE).

Fernandes, Praxi, 1980, "Management Culture—Changing Public Policies and Management," *Public Enterprise* 1, no. 1, pp. 11–18.

Fernandes, Praxi, 1981, *Public Enterprises and the Bottom Line: Some Reflections on the Why and How of Profits and Losses in Public Enterprises in Developing Countries* (Ljubljana: ICPE).

Fernandes, Praxi, and Pavle Sicherl, eds., 1981, *Seeking the Personality of Public Enterprises: An Enquiry into the Concept, Definition and Classification of Public Enterprises* (Ljubljana: ICPE).

Ferrario, Mario C., 1978, "Strategic Management in State Enterprises" (DBA dissertation: Harvard Business School).

Ferrier, Ronald W., 1982, *General History of British Petroleum Company: The Developing Years, 1901–1932* (Cambridge: Cambridge University Press).

Finsinger, Jörg, 1983a, "Competition, Ownership and Control in Markets with Imperfect Information," in Finsinger, Jörg, ed., *Public Sector Economics* (Berlin: International Institute of Management), pp. 111–133.

Finsinger, Jörg, 1983b, *Economic Analysis of Regulated Markets* (London: Macmillan).

Finsinger, Jorg, and Ingo Vogelsang, 1982, "Performance Indices for Public Enterprises," in Leroy P. Jones, *et al.*, ed., *Public Enterprises in Less Developed Countries* (Cambridge: Cambridge University Press), pp. 281–296.

Fisher, Peter S., 1982, "Alternative Institutional Structures for State and Local Government Ownership of Railroads," *Logistics and Transportation Review* 18, no. 3: 235–254.

Floyd, Robert H., 1978, "Some Aspects of Income Taxation of Public Enterprises," *International Monetary Fund Staff Papers* 25, no. 4: 301–342.

Floyd, Robert H., 1979, "Income Taxation of State Trading Enterprises" (paper presented at the International Conference of the Centre for International Business Studies, École des Hautes Études Commercials de Montreal, April).

Floyd, Robert H., 1984, "Some Topical Issues Concerning Public Enterprises." in *Public Enterprise in Mixed Economies: Some Macroeconomic Aspects* (Washington, D.C.: International Monetary Fund), pp. 1–34.

Foreman-Peck, James, and Michael Waterson, 1985, "The Comparative Efficiency of Public and Private Enterprise in Britain: Electricity Generation between the World Wars," *Economic Journal*, 95 Suppl.: 83–95.

Foster, Christopher D., 1971, *Politics, Finance and the Role of Economics: An Essay on the Control of Public Enterprises* (London: Allen & Unwin).

Fox, J. Roland, 1974, *Arming America* (Boston, Mass.: Harvard Business School).

Foxley, Alejandro, 1983, *Latin-American Experiments in Neoconservative Economics* (Berkeley: University of California Press).

Frankel, Paul H., 1966, *Mattei: Oil and Power Politics* (London: Faber and Faber and New York: Praeger).

Frankel, Paul H., 1980, "The Rationale of National Oil Companies," in *State Petroleum Enterprises in Developing Countries*, UN Center for Natural Resources, Energy and Transport (New York: Pergamon), pp. 3–7.

Freeman, John R., 1982, "State Entrepreneurship and Dependent Developments," *American Journal of Political Science* 26, no. 1: 90–112.

Freeman, John R., and Raymond D. Duvall, 1984, "International Economic Relations and the Entrepreneurial State," *Economic Development and Cultural Change* 32, no. 2: 373–400.

Freeman, R. Edwards, 1984, *Strategic Management: A Stakeholder Approach* (Marshfield, Mass.: Pitman).

Frieden, Jeff, 1981, "Third World Indebted Industrialization: International Finance and State Capitalism in Mexico, Brazil, Algeria and South Korea," *International Organization* 35, no. 3: 407–431.

Friedman, Milton, 1962, *Capitalism and Freedom* (Chicago: University of Chicago Press).

Friedman, Milton, and Rose Friedman, 1980, *Free to Choose: A Personal Statement* (New York: Harcourt Brace Jovanovich).

Friedmann, Wolfgang G., ed., 1954, *The Public Corporation: A Comparative Symposium* (Toronto: Carswell Co).

Friedmann, Wolfgang G., ed., 1974, *Public and Private Enterprise in Mixed Economies* (New York: Columbia University Press).

Friedmann, Wolfgang G., and J.F. Garner, eds., 1970, *Government Enterprises, A Comparative Study* (New York: Columbia University Press).

Fubara, Bedford A., 1984, "Strategy Formulation and Political Intervention in State-Owned Companies in LDCs," *RVB Newsletter and Research Papers* 4, no. 1: 7–17.

Funkhouser, Richard, and Paul W. MacAvoy, 1979, "A Sample of Observations on Comparative Prices in Public and Private Enterprises," *Journal of Public Economics* 11, no. 3: 353–368.

Furubotn, Eirik G., and Svetozar Pejovich, 1972, "Property Rights and Economic Theory: A Survey of Recent Literature," *Journal of Economic Literature* 10: 1137–1162.

Furubotn, Eirik G., and Svetozar Prejovich, eds., 1974, *The Economics of Property Rights* (Cambridge, Mass.: Ballinger).

Gaitskell, Hugh T.N., 1956, *Socialism and Nationalisation*, Fabian Tract. No. 300.

Galbraith, John Kenneth, 1967, *The New Industrial State* (Boston: Houghton Mifflin).

Galbraith, John Kenneth, 1975, *Money: Where it Came, Where it Went* (Boston: Houghton Mifflin).

Galbraith, John Kenneth, 1976, "The Economic Problems of the Left," *The New Statesman* (February 20), p. 218.

Gantt, Andrew H., and Guiseppe Dutto, 1968, "Financial Performance of Government-Owned Corporations in Less Developed Countries," *IMF Staff Papers* 15, no. 1: 102–148.

Ganz, Gabriele, 1977, *Government and Industry: The Provision of Financial Assistance to Industry and Its Control* (Abington, Oxon: Professional Books).

Garner, John Francis, 1963, *Administrative Law* (London: Butterworth).

Garner, Maurice R., 1976, *Relationships of Government and Public Enterprises in France, West Germany and Sweden* (London: National Economic Department Office).

Gellerson, Mark W., and Shawna P. Grosskopf, 1980, "Public Utility Pricing, Investment and Reliability under Uncertainty: A Review," *Public Finance Quarterly* 8, no. 4: 477–492.

General Agreement on Tariffs and Trade, 1984, *International Trade 1983/84* (Geneva: GATT).

Gelinas, André, ed., 1978, *Public Enterprise and the Public Interest* (Toronto: Institute of Public Administration of Canada).

Georgiou, Petro, 1973, "The Goal Paradigm and Notes towards a Center Paradigm," *Administrative Science Quarterly* 18, no. 3: 291–310.

Gerschenkron, Alexander, 1962, *Economic Backwardness in Historical Perspective* (Cambridge, Mass.: Harvard University Press).

Ghai, Yash, ed., 1977, *Law in the Political Economy of Public Enterprise: African Perspectives* (New York: International Legal Center).

Gibbon, Edward, 1952, *Rise and Fall of the Roman Empire* (New York: The Viking Press).

Gillis, Malcolm, 1977, "Efficiency in State Enterprises: Selected Cases in Mining from Asia and Latin America," HIID Development Discussion Paper no. 27.

Gillis, Malcolm, 1980, "The Role of State Enterprises in Economic Development," *Social Research* 47, no. 2: 248–289.

Gillis, Malcolm *et al.*, 1980, "Public Enterprise Finance: Towards a Synthesis," Development Discussion Paper 101 (Cambridge, Mass.: Harvard University, Harvard Institute for International Development).

Gillis, Malcolm, and Ignatius Peprah, 1981/1982, "State-Owned Enterprises in Developing Countries," *Wharton Magazine* 6, no. 2: 32–40.

Gillis, Malcolm, 1982, "Allocative and X-Efficiency in State-Owned Mining Enterprises: Comparisons between Bolivia and Indonesia," *Journal of Comparative Economics* 6, no. 1: 1–23.

Gilmour, Ian, 1978, *Inside Right: A Study of Conservatism* (London: Quartet Books).

Goldsmith, R.W. and R.L. Parmelee, 1940, *The Distribution of Ownership in the 200 Largest Nonfinancial Corporations* (Monographs of the Temporary National Economic Committee, Number 29, Washington: Government Printing Office for U.S. Senate).

Goodermote, Dean, and Richard B. Mancke, 1983, "Nationalizing Oil in the 1970s," *The Energy Journal* 4, no. 4: 67–80.

Goodman, Richard Allen, 1984, "A Comparison of Industrial Policies in Five Nations: Brazil, France, Germany, Israel and the Netherlands," in Richard Allan Goodman and Julian P. Morote, eds., *Planning for National Technology Policy* (New York: Praeger), pp. 138–154.

Gordon, Marsha, 1981, *Government in Business* (Montreal: C.D. Howe Institute).

Gordon, Robert A., 1945, *Business Leadership in the Large Corporation* (Berkeley: University of California Press).

Gorwala, A.D., 1951, *Report on the Efficient Conduct of State Enterprises* (New Delhi: Government of India Planning Commission).

Government of India, 1956, "Industrial Policy Resolution of 1956," in *Second Five-Year Plan* (New Delhi: Central Statistical Organization).

Grant, Wyn, 1982, *Political Economy and Industrial Policy* (London: Butterworth).

Gray, Clive S., 1984, "Toward a Conceptual Framework for Macroeconomic Evaluation of Public Enterprise Performance in Mixed Economies," in *Public Enterprise in Mixed Economies: Some Macroeconomic Aspects* (Washington, D.C.: International Monetary Fund), pp. 35–109.

Grayson, Leslie E., 1981, *National Oil Companies* (New York: John Wiley & Sons).

Green, Reginald H., 1977, "Historical, Decision-Taking, Firm and Sectoral Dimensions of Public Sector Enterprise: Some Aspects of and Angles of Attack for Research," in Yash Ghai, ed., *Law and the Political Economy of Public Enterprise: An African Perspective* (New York: International Legal Center), pp. 92–124.

Gregory, Paul, and Gert Leptin, 1977, "Similar Societies under Differing Economic Systems: The Case of the Two Germanys," *Soviet Studies* 29, no. 4: 519–542.

Gresh, Hani, 1975, "Enterprises Publiques et la Création de Filiales," *Economie et Statistique* 65 (March): 29–43.

Grieve-Smith, John, 1981, "Strategy—The Key to Planning in the Public Corporation," *Long-Range Planning* 14, no. 6: 24–31.

Grieve-Smith, John, 1984, *Strategic Planning in Nationalised Industries* (London: Macmillan).

Grunwald, Oskar, 1980, "Steel and State in Austria," *Annals of Public and Co-operative Economy* 51, no. 4: 477–491.

Guesnerie, R., 1980, "Second-Best Pricing Rules in the Boiteux Tradition: Derivation, Review and Discussion," *Journal of Public Economies* 13, no. 1: 51–80.

Guth, William D., and Renato Taguiri, 1965, "Personal Values and Corporate Strategy," *Harvard Business Review* 43, no. 5: 123–132.

Haar, Ernst, 1981, "Public Enterprises and their Employees: The Case of the German Federal Railways," *Annals of Public and Cooperative Economy* 52, no. 1–2: 145–155.

Hafsi, Taieb, 1981, "The Strategic Decision-Making Process in SOEs," (DBA dissertation: Harvard University).

Hafsi, Taieb, 1984, *Enterprises Publiques et Politique Industriel* (Paris: McGraw-Hill).

Hage, Jerald, and Michael Aiken, 1970, *Social Change in Complex Organizations* (New York: Random House).

Hage, Jerald, and R. Dewar, 1973, "Elite Values vs. Organizational Structure in Predicting Innovation," *Administrative Science Quarterly* 18, no. 3: 279–290.

Hall, Peter A., 1984, "Socialism in One Country," in Philip Cerny and Martin Schain, eds., *Socialism, the State and Public Policy in France* (London: Frances Pinter), pp. 81–107.

Hamilton, Neil W., and Peter R. Hamilton, 1981, *Governance of Public Enterprises: A Case Study of Urban Mass Transit* (Lexington, Mass.: D.C. Heath).

Handoussa, Heba Ahmad, 1980, "The Impact of Economic Liberalization on the Performance of Egypt's Public Sector Industry" (Paper presented at the Second BAPEG Conference, April), Cambridge, Mass.

Hannah, Leslie, 1976, *The Rise of the Corporate Economy: The British Experience* (Baltimore: The Johns Hopkins University Press).

Hannah, Leslie, 1979, *Electricity before Nationalisation* (London: Macmillan).

Hannah, Leslie, 1982, *Engineers, Managers and Politicians: Electricity Supply Industry in Britain from 1948 to the Present* (London: Macmillan).

Hannan, Michael T., and John H. Freeman, 1977, "The Population Ecology of Organizations," *American Journal of Sociology* 82, no. 5: 929–964.

Hanson, Albert H., ed., 1955, *Public Enterprise: A Study of Its Organization and Management in Various Countries* (Brussels: International Institute of Administration Services).

Hanson, Albert H., 1961, *Parliament and Public Ownership* (Oxford: Casell for the Hansard Society).

Hanson, Albert H., 1962. *Managerial Problems in Public Enterprise* (London: Asia Publishing House).

Hanson, Albert H., ed., 1963, *Nationalisation—A Book of Readings* (London: Allen & Unwin for Royal Institute of Public Administration).

Hanson, Albert H., 1965, *Public Enterprise and Economic Development*, 2nd ed. (London: Routledge and Kegan Paul).

Harberger, Arnold C., 1954, "Monopoly and Resource Allocation," *American Economic Review* 44: 77–87.

Harlow, Christopher, 1977, *Innovation and Productivity under Nationalisation: The First Thirty Years* (London: Political & Economic Planning, Allen & Unwin).

Harlow, Christopher, 1983, *Commercial Interdependence: Public Corporations and Private Industry* (London: Policy Studies Institute, November).

Harrell, Thomas W., 1961, *Manager's Performance and Personality* (Cincinnati: Southwestern Publishing Co).

Harris, D.J., and B.C.L. Davies, 1981, "Corporate Planning as a Control System in United Kingdom Nationalised Industries," *Long-Range Planning* 14, no. 1: 15–22.

Harris, Richard G., and Elmer G. Wiens, 1980, "Government Enterprise: An Instrument for the Internal Regulation of Industry," *Canadian Journal of Economics* 13, no. 1: 125–132.

Hastings, Sue, and Hugo Levie, eds., 1983, *Privatisation?* (Oxford: Spokesman Books).

Hatfield, Michael, 1978, *The House the Left Built: Inside Labour Policy-Making 1970–75* (London: Victor Gollancz).

Hayward, Keith (1983), *Government and British Aerospace* (Manchester: Manchester University Press).

Heath, Milton S., 1950, "Public Railroad Construction and the Development of Private Enterprise in the South before 1861," *Journal of Economic History* 10 (Suppl.): 40–53.

Hector, Gary, 1984, "The Nationalization of Continental Illinois," *Fortune* 110, no. 4 (August 20): 125–128.

Hee, Park Chung, 1970, *Our Nation's Path* (Seoul: Hollym).

Heginbotham, Stanley J., 1975, *Cultures in Conflict: The Four Faces of Indian Bureaucracy* (New York: Columbia University Press).

Hellenier, G.K., 1981, "Intra-firm Trade and the Developing Countries: An Assessment of the Data," in Robin Murray, ed., *Multinationals beyond the Market* (New York: John Wiley & Sons), pp. 31–57.

Heller, Peter S., and Allan A. Tait, 1984, "Government Employment and Pay: Some International Comparisons," Washington, D.C.: International Monetary Fund Occasional Paper no. 24, revised.

Hellman, Richard, 1972, *Government Competition in the Electric Utility Industry* (New York: Praeger).

Herbert Commission, 1956, *Report of the Committee into the Electricity Supply Industry*, Cmnd 9672 HMSO.

Hibbard, Benjamin H., 1939, *A History of Public Lands Policies* (New York: P. Smith).

Hill, Forest G., 1951, "Government Engineering Aid to Railroads before the Civil War," *Journal of Economic History* 11 no. 3: 235–246.

Hill, Hal, 1982, "State Enterprises in Competitive Industry: An Indonesian Case Study," *World Development* 10, no. 11: 1015–1023.

Hill, Roy, 1979, "Petroven under Pressure," *International Management* 34, no. 1: 14–17.

Hindley, Brian, ed., 1983, *State Investment Companies in Western Europe* (London: Macmillan, for Trade Policy Research Center).

Hirsch, Werner, Z., 1965, "Cost Functions of an Urban Government Service: Refuse Collection," *Review of Economics and Statistics* 47, no. 1: 87–92.

Hirshleifer, Jack, James C. DeHaven, and Jerome W. Milliman, 1960, *Water Supply: Economics, Technology and Policy* (Chicago: University of Chicago Press).

Hirshleifer, Jack, and David L. Shapiro, 1970, "The Treatment of Risk and Uncertainty," in Robert H. Haveman and Julius Margolis, eds., *Public Expenditure and Policy Analysis* (Chicago: Markham Publishing Company), pp. 291–313.

Hirschman, Albert O., 1970, *Exit, Voice and Loyalty* (Cambridge, Mass.: Harvard University Press).

Hochmuth, Milton S., 1979, "The SOE as a Tool for Implementing Foreign Policy" (Paper presented at the State-Owned Enterprise Conference, March). Harvard Business School, Boston, Mass.

Hodgetts, J.E., 1950, "The Public Corporation in Canada," *Public Administration* 28: 283–294.

Hofstede, Geert H., 1968, *The Game of Budget Control* (New York: Barnes and Noble).

Hofstede, Geert H., 1980, *Culture's Consequences: International Differences in Work-Related Values* (Beverly Hills, Calif.: Sage).

Hogan, William T., 1983, *World Steel in the 1980s: A Case of Survival* (Lexington, Mass.: D.C. Heath, Lexington Books).

Holland, Stuart, ed., 1972, *The State as Entrepreneur: New Dimensions for Public Enterprise* (London: Weidenfeld and Nicholson).

Holland, Stuart, 1974, "Europe's New Public Enterprise," in Raymond Vernon, ed., *Big Business and the State: Changing Relations in Western Europe* (London: Macmillan) pp. 25–42.

Holland, Stuart, 1975, *The Socialist Challenge* (London: Quartet Books).

Holland, Stuart, ed., 1978, *Beyond Capitalist Planning* (London: Blackwell).

Holter, Darryl, 1982 "Mineworkers and Nationalization in France: Insights into the Concept of State Theory," *Politics and Society* 11: no. 1: 29–49.

Hoos, Sidney, ed., 1979, *Agricultural Marketing Boards—An International Perspective* (Cambridge, Mass.: Ballinger).

Hope, Kempe R., 1982, "Improving Public Enterprise Management in Developing Countries," *Journal of General Management* 7, no. 3: 72–85.

Horn, Richard J., ed., 1981, *Studies in the Management of Government Enterprise* (Boston: Kluwer).

Hubbard, Preston J., 1961, *Origins of the TVA* (New York: W.W. Norton).

Hundred Group, 1981, "The Financing of State-Owned Industries" (Report by the Hundred Group of Chartered Accountants, December). London: The Hundred Group.

Iacocca, Lee, with William Novak, 1984, *Iacocca: An Autobiography* (New York: Bantam Books).

India, Bureau of Public Enterprises, 1978, *Annual Report on the Working of Industrial and Commercial Undertakings of the Central Government 1962–77*, Vol. 1 (New Delhi).

Indian Institute of Public Administration, 1957, "Administrative Problem of State Enterprises in India" (Report of Seminar, New Delhi, December).

Innis, Harold A., 1923, *A History of the Canadian Pacific Railway* (Toronto: McClelland and Stewart).

International Legal Center, 1976, *Law and Public Enterprise in Asia* (New York: Praeger Special Studies in Economic Development).

Iqbal, Zafar, 1982, *Financial Interrelationships between Public Authorities and Public Enterprises: The Pakistan Experience* (Ljubljana: ICPE).

Irvine, A.G., 1971, "The Delegation of Authority to Crown Corporations," *Canadian Public Administration* 14: 556–579.

Israel, Government Companies Law, 57357-1975, *Sefer Ha-Chukkim* 770, p. 162–183 in English version.

Israel, Ministry of Finance, 1985, *Report of Government Corporations and on Government Investment in Shares as of March 31, 1984*, Report no. 23 (Jerusalem).

Israel, State Comptroller, 1972, *Reports on Auditing of SOEs*. Jerusalem: State Comptroller.

Israel, State Comptroller *Annual Report*: Various Years. Jerusalem: State Comptroller.

Izraeli, Dov, and Jehiel Zif, 1977, *Societal Marketing Boards* (New York: John Wiley & Sons).

Jackson, Raymond, 1969, "Regulation and Electric Utility Rate Levels," *Land Economics* 45, no. 3: 372–376.

Jacoby, Neil H., 1974, *Multinational Oil* (New York: Macmillan).

Jacquemin, Alexis P., and Henry W. De Jong, 1977, *European Industrial Organization* (New York: John Wiley & Sons).

James, Estelle, Egon Neuberger, and Robert Willis, 1979, "On Managerial Rewards and Self-Selection: Risk Taking in Public Enterprises. A comment on A. Bergson 'Managerial Risks and Rewards in Public Enterprises,'" *Journal of Comparative Economics* 3, no. 4: 395–406.

Jay, Anthony, 1968, *Management and Machiavelli* (New York: Bantam).

Jenkins, Clive, 1976, *Power at the Top: A Critical Survey of the Nationalized Industries* (Westport, Conn.: Greenwald Press).

Jenkins, Glenn P., and B.D. Wright, 1975, "Taxation of Income of Multinational Corporations: The Case of the United States Petroleum Industry," *Review of Economics and Statistics* 57, no. 1: 1–11.

Jensen, Michael C., and William H. Meckling, 1976, "Theory of the Firm: Managerial Behavior, Agency Costs and Ownership Structure," *Journal of Financial Economics* 3, no. 4: 305–360.

Jones, Leroy P., 1975, *Public Enterprise and Economic Development* (Seoul: Korea Development Institute).

Jones, Leroy P., 1981a, "Public Enterprises for Whom?: Some Perverse Distributional Consequences of Public Operations" (Paper presented at OECD Conference on Problems and Policies of Industrialization in Opening Economies, Istanbul, August).

Jones, Leroy P., 1981b, "Toward a Performance Evaluation Methodology for Public Enterprise" (Paper presented at the United Nations Conference on Economic Performance of Public Enterprise, Islamabad, Pakistan, November).

Jones, Leroy P., 1981c, *Efficiency of Public Manufacturing Enterprises in Pakistan*, Prepared for Pakistan Ministry of Production and Pakistan Division, World Bank.

Jones, Leroy P., and Sakong Il, 1976, *A Social Accounting System for Public Enterprises*, Working Paper (Seoul: Korea Development Institute).

Jones, Leroy P., and Ingo Vogelsang, 1982, *The Effect of Markets on Public Enterprise Conduct and Vice Versa* (Ljubljana: International Centre for Public Enterprises, October).

Jones, Leroy P., *et al.*, eds., 1982, *Public Enterprise in Less-Developed Countries* (New York: Cambridge University Press).

Jordan, William A., 1979a, "Airline Performance under Regulation: Canada vs. the United States," in R.O. Zerbe, Jr., ed., *Research in Law and Economics* 1 (Greenwich, Conn.: JAI Press), pp. 35–79.

Jordan, William A., 1979b, "Comparisons of American and Canadian Airline Regulation," in G.B. Reschenthaler and B. Roberts, eds., *Perspectives on Canadian Airline Regulation* (Montreal: Institute for Research on Public Policy).

Kahn, Alfred E., 1970, *The Economics of Regulation: Principles and Institutions* (New York: John Wiley & Sons).

Kamerschen, David R., 1966, "An Estimation of the Welfare Losses from Monopoly in the American Economy," *Western Economic Journal* 4, no. 3: 221–236.

Kania, John J., and John R. McKean, 1976, "Ownership, Control and the Contemporary Corporation: A General Behavior Analysis," *Kyklos* 29, no. 2: 272–291.

Kania, John J., and John R. McKean, 1978, "Ownership, Control and the Contemporary Corporation: A Reply," *Kyklos* 31, no. 3: 497–499.

Katz, Abraham, 1972, *The Politics of Economic Reform in the Soviet Union* (New York: Praeger).

Katzarov, Konstantin, 1964, *The Theory of Nationalization* (Hague: Martinus Nijhoff).

Katzenstein, Peter J., 1984, *Corporatism and Change: Austria, Switzerland and the Politics of Industry* (Ithaca, N.Y.: Cornell University Press).

Kay, J.A., 1983, "A General Equilibrium Approach to the Measurement of Monopoly Welfare Loss," *International Journal of Industrial Organization* 1: 317–331.

Kay, J.A., and Z.A. Silberston, 1984, "The New Industrial Policy: Privatisation and Competition," *Midland Bank Review* (Spring), pp. 8–16.

Kelf-Cohen, Reuben, 1958, *Nationalisation in Britain—The End of a Dogma* (London: St. Martin's Press).

Kelf-Cohen, Reuben, 1969, *Twenty Years of Nationalisation: The British Experience* (New York: St. Martin's Press).

Kelf-Cohen, Reuben, 1974, *British Nationalisation 1945–1973* (New York: St. Martin's Press).

Kemper, Peter, and John M. Quigley, 1976, *The Economics of Refuse Collection* (Cambridge, Mass: Ballinger).

Keyser, William, and Ralph Windle, eds., 1978, *Public Enterprise in the EEC*, 7 Volumes (Alphen aan den Rijn, the Netherlands: Sijthoff and Noordkoff).

Khandwalla, Pradip N., 1984, "Some Lessons for the Management of Public Enterprises," *International Studies of Management and Organization* 14, no. 2–3: 167–196.

Killick, Tony, 1978, *Development Economics in Action* (New York: St. Martin's Press).

Kim Kwan S., 1981, "Enterprise Performances in the Public and Private Sectors: Tanzanian Experience, 1970–75," *Journal of Developing Areas* 15, no. 3: 471–484.

Kindleberger, Charles P., 1969, *American Business Abroad: Six Lectures on Direct Investment* (New Haven, Conn.: Yale University Press).

Kirzner, Israel M., 1973, *Competition and Entrepreneurship* (Chicago: University of Chicago Press).

Kitchen, Harry M., 1976, "A Statistical Estimation of an Operating Cost Function

56–76.

Klapp, Merrie G., 1982, "The State—Landlord or Entrepreneur?" *International Organization* 36, no. 3: 575–607.

Klein, Rudolf, 1976, "The Politics of Public Expenditure: American Theory and British Practice," *British Journal of Political Science* 6, no. 4: 401–432.

Kline, John M., 1983, *State Government Influences in U.S. International Economic Policy* (Lexington, Mass.: D.C. Heath).

Knight, Arthur, 1982, "The Control of the Nationalized Industries," *Political Quarterly* 53, no. 1: 24–34.

Kobrin, Stephen J., 1980, "Foreign Enterprise and Forced Divestment in the LDCs," *International Organization* 34, no. 1: 65–88.

Koenig, Christian, 1985, *The State-SOE Relationship* (Unpublished manuscript, Boston, Mass.).

Kostecky, Maciej H., ed., 1982, *State Trading in International Markets; Theory and Practice of Industrialized and Developing Countries* (New York: St. Martin's Press).

Kumar, Krishna and Maxwell G. McLeod, 1981, *Multinationals from Developing Countries* (Lexington, MA: Lexington Books).

Kurth, Wilhelm, 1980, "Textile and Clothing: A National and International Issue" (Paper presented at the International Symposium on Industrial Policies for the 1980s, Madrid, May).

Lachman, Ran, 1985, "Public and Private-Sector Differences: CEOs' Perceptions Of Their Role Environments," *Academy of Management Journal* 28, no. 3: 671–680.

Lacina, Ferdinand, 1977, "The Development of the Austrian Public Sector since World War II," Series Number 7, Office of Public Sector Studies, Institute of Latin American Studies, University of Texas at Austin.

Lal, Deepak, 1980, "Public Enterprises," in John Cody, Helen Hughes and David Wall, eds., *Policies for Industrial Progress in Developing Countries* (New York: Oxford University Press for the World Bank), 211–234.

Lall, Sanjaya, 1983, *The New Multinationals: The Spread of the Third World Enterprise* (New York: John Wiley & Son).

Lall, Sanjaya and Paul Streeten, 1977, *Foreign Investment, Transnationals and Developing Countries* (London: Macmillan).

Lamont, Douglas F., 1979, *Foreign State Enterprise, A Threat to American Business* (New York: Basic Books).

Lange, Oscar and F.M. Taylor, 1938, *On Economic Theory of Socialism* (Minneapolis: University of Minnesota Press).

Langer, Edmond, 1964, "Nationalizations in Austria," *Annals of Public and Co-operative Economy* 35, no. 2–3: 115–163.

Langford, John, 1979, "Crown Corporations as Instruments of Public Policy," in G. Bruce Doern and Peter Aucoin, eds., *Public Policy in Canada* (Toronto: Macmillan), pp. 239–275.

Langford, John W., 1982, "Public Corporations in the 1980's: Moving from Rhetoric to Analysis," *Canadian Public Administration* (Toronto) 25, no. 4: 619–637.

Lanier, J. Michael, 1976, "Historical Development of Municipal Water Systems in the United States," *American Water Works Association Journal* 68: 173–180.

La Palombara, Joseph, 1964, *Interest Groups in Italian Politics* (Princeton, N.J.: Princeton University Press).

Larner, Robert J., 1966, "Ownership and Control in the 200 Largest Nonfinancial

Corporations, 1929 and 1963," *American Economic Review* 56, no. 4, part 1: 777–787.

Larner, Robert J., 1970, *Management Control and the Large Corporation* (New York: Dunellen).

Laski, Harold, 1948, *The American Democracy* (New York: Viking Press).

Lauterbach, Albert, 1985, "The Austrian Public Sector in International Perspective: A Socio-Historic Evaluation," in Alfred H. Saulniers, ed., *Economic and Political Roles of the State in Latin America* (Office of Public Sector Studies, Institute of Latin American Studies, University of Texas at Austin), pp. 61–72.

Lawrence, Paul R., and David Dyer, 1983, *Renewing American Industry* (New York: Free Press).

Lawrence, Paul R., and Jay W. Lorsch, 1967, *Organization and Environment: Managing Differentiation and Integration* (Cambridge, Mass.: Harvard University Press).

Leeman, Wayne A., 1962, *The Price of Middle East Oil* (Ithaca, N.Y.: Cornell University Press).

Leff, Nathaniel H., 1979, "Entrepreneurship and Economic Development: The Problem Revisited," *Journal of Economic Literature* 17, no. 1: 46–64.

Leibenstein, Harvey, 1966, "Allocative Efficiency vs. X-Efficiency," *American Economic Review* 56, no. 3: 392–415.

Leibenstein, Harvey, 1976, *Beyond Economic Man* (Cambridge, Mass.: Harvard University Press).

Leibenstein, Harvey, 1978, "On the Basic Proposition of X-Efficiency Theory," *American Economic Review* 68, no. 2: 328–334.

Leland, Hayne E., and Robert A. Meyer, 1976, "Monopoly Pricing Structures with Imperfect Discrimination," *Bell Journal of Economics* 7, no. 2: 449–462.

Le Pors, Anicet, 1977, *Les Béquilles du Capital* (Paris: Seuil).

Lescuyer, Georges, 1962, *Le Contrôle de l'État sur les Entreprises Nationalisées* (Paris: R. Picon et R. Durand-Anzias).

Levine, Herbert S., 1983, "On the Nature and Location of Entrepreneurial Activity in Centrally Planned Economies: The Soviet Case," in J. Ronen, ed., *Entrepreneurship* (Lexington, Mass.: D.C. Heath, Lexington Books), pp. 235–267.

Levitt, Theodore, 1973, *The Third Sector, New Tactics for a Responsive Society* (New York: American Management).

Levitt, Theodore, 1983, *The Marketing Imagination* (New York: The Free Press).

Levy, Brian D., 1982, "World Oil Marketing in Transition," *International Organization* 36, no. 1: 113–133.

Levy, Brian D., 1983, "The Industrial Economics of Entrepreneurship and Dependent Development" (Ph.D. dissertation: Harvard University).

Levy, Brian D., 1985, "A Theory of Public Enterprise Behavior," Williams College, Mimeographed, Williamstown, Mass.

Levy, Victor, 1981, "On Estimating Efficiency Differentials between the Public and Private Sectors in a Developing Economy—Iraq," *Journal of Comparative Economics* 5, no. 3: 235–250.

Lewis, Ben W., 1965, "Comparative Economic Systems: Nationalized Industry; British Nationalization and American Private Enterprise: Some Parallels and Contrasts," *American Economic Review* 55, no. 2: 50–64.

Lewis, Edward G., 1957, "Parliamentary Control of Nationalized Industry in France," *American Political Science Review* 51, no. 3: 669–683.

Lewis, Vivian, 1980, "France's Nationalised Banks—A Whiff of Reprivatisation," *The Banker* 130, no. 653 (July): 43–50.

Lewis, Vivian, 1981, "French Banks after Nationalisation," *The Banker* 131, no. 670 (December): 25–27.

Lewis, Vivian, 1983, "Is There Life after Nationalisation—Part Two?" *The Banker* 133, no. 694 (December): 41–45.

Likierman, Andrew, 1979, "The Financial and Economic Framework for Nationalised Industries," *Lloyds Bank Review*, number 134 (October), pp. 16–32.

Lindblom, Charles E., 1977, *Politics and Markets: The World's Political Economic Systems* (New York: Basic Books).

Lindsay, Cotton M., 1976, "A Theory of Government Enterprise," *Journal of Political Economy* 84, no. 5: 1061–1077.

Lipsey, R.G., and K. Lancaster, 1956/1957, "The General Theory of Second Best," *Review of Economic Studies* 24: 11–32.

Lipsky, Seth, ed., 1978, *The Billion Dollar Bubble* (Hong Kong: Dow Jones, Asia).

Little, Ian M.D., and James A. Mirrlees, 1974, *Project Appraisal and Planning for Developing Countries* (New York: Basic Books).

Littlechild, Stephen, C., 1983a, "The Structure of Telephone Tariffs," *International Journal of Industrial Organization* 1, no. 4: 365–377.

Littlechild, Stephen C., 1983b, "The Effect of Ownership on Telephone Penetration," *Telecommunications Policy*, no. 3: 246–247.

Lockwood, William W., 1965, *The State and Economic Enterprise in Japan* (Princeton, N.J.: Princeton University Press).

Lodge, George Cabot, 1974, "Business and the Changing Society," *Harvard Business Review* 52, no. 2 (March-April): 59–72.

Lodge, George Cabot, 1975, *The New American Ideology* (New York: A.A. Knopf).

Long, Norton, 1960, "The Corporation, Its Satellites and the Local Community," in Edward S. Mason, ed: *The Corporation in Modern Society* (Cambridge, Mass.: Harvard University Press), 202–217.

Lorsch, Jay W., and Stephen A. Allen III, 1973, *Managing Diversity and Interdependence* (Boston: Division of Research, Harvard Business School).

Lowenfeld, Andreas F., 1975, "A New Take-Off for International Air Transport," *Foreign Affairs* 54, no. 1: 36–50.

Lowitt, Richard, 1971, *George W. Norris: The Persistence of a Progressive* (Urbana, Ill.: Illinois University Press).

Lumby, Stephen, 1981, "New Ways of Financing Nationalised Industries," *Lloyds Bank Review*, no. 141 (July), 34–44.

Maccoby, Michael, 1976, *The Gamesman* (New York: Simon & Schuster).

Mace, Myles L., 1971, *Directors, Myth and Reality* (Boston: Division of Research, Harvard Business School).

Madden, C., 1977, "Forces Which Influence Ethical Behavior," in C. Walton, ed., *The Ethics of Corporate Conduct* (Englewood Cliffs, N.J.: Prentice-Hall), pp. 31–78.

Maniatis, George C., 1968, "Managerial Autonomy vs. State Control in Public Enterprises: Fact and Artifact," *Annals of Public and Co-operative Economy* 39, no. 4: 513–530.

Manifesto Group of the Parliamentary Labour Party, 1977, *What We Must Do: A Democratic Socialist Approach to Britain's Crisis* (London).

Mann, Patrick C., 1970, "Publicly Owned Electric Utility Profits and Resource Allocation," *Land Economics* 46, no. 4: 478–484.

Mann, Patrick C., 1974, "User Power and Electricity Rates," *Journal of Law and Economics* 17, no. 2: 433–443.

Mann, Patrick C., 1979, "Public Ownership in Water Service" (Paper presented at the State-Owned Enterprises Conference, Harvard Business School, Boston, Mass., March).

Mann, Patrick C., and John L. Mikesell, 1971, "Tax Payments and Electric Utility Prices," *Southern Economic Journal* 38, no. 1: 69–78.

Mann, Patrick, C., and John L. Mikesell, 1976, "Ownership and Water-System Operation," *Water Resources Bulletin* 12: 995–1004.

Mann, Patrick C., and Edmond J. Siefried, 1972, "Pricing in the Case of Publicly Owned Electric Utilities," *Quarterly Review of Economics and Business* 12, no. 2: 77–89.

Manne, Henry G., 1965, "Mergers and the Market for Corporate Control," *Journal of Political Economy* 73, no. 2: 110–120.

Marks, M., 1980, "State and Private Enterprise," *Business Economist* 11, no. 2: 5–15.

Marris, Robin, 1964, *The Economic Theory of Managerial Capitalism* (London: Macmillan).

Martin, John P., and John M. Page, Jr., 1983, "The Impact of Subsidies on x-Efficiency in LDC Industry: Theory and an Empirical Test," *The Review of Economics and Statistics* 65, no. 4: 608–617.

Mascarenhas, R.C., 1982, *Public Enterprises in New Zealand* (Wellington: New Zealand Institute of Public Administration, Government Printing Office).

Mathijsen, Pierre, 1972, "State Aid, State Monopolies, and Public Enterprises in the Common Market," *Law and Contemporary Problems* 37, no. 2: 376–391.

Maunder, Peter, ed., 1979, *Government Intervention in the Developed Economy* (New York: Praeger).

Maurer, John G., 1971, *Readings in Organization Theory: Open-System Approaches* (New York: Random House).

May, Annabelle, 1979, "Concorde—Bird of Harmony or Political Albatross: An Examination in the Context of British Foreign Policy," *International Organization* 33, no. 4: 481–508.

Mazzolini, Renato, 1979, *Government Controlled Enterprises* (London: Wiley).

McCraw, Thomas K., 1975, "Regulation in America: A Review Article," *Business History Review* 49, no. 2: 159–183.

McCraw, Thomas K., 1980, "Regulatory Agencies," in *Encyclopedia of American History*, vol. 2: Glenn Porter, ed.

McCready, Gerald B., 1977, *Profile Canada: Social and Economic Projections* (Georgetown, Ontario: Irwin-Dorsey).

McEachern, William A., 1975, *Control, Compensation and Performance in the Large Corporation* (Lexington, Mass.: D.C. Heath).

McEachern, William A., 1976, "Corporate Control and Risk," *Economic Inquiry* 14, no. 2: 270–278.

McEachern, William A., 1978, "Ownership, Control and the Contemporary Corporation: A Comment," *Kyklos* 31, no. 3: 491–496.

McKenna, Thomas Joseph, 1982, "AMTRAK and the Tennessee Valley Authority: A Case of Government Corporations and Autonomy" (Ph.D dissertation: Fordham University).

McLachlan, Sany, 1983, *The National Freight Buy-Out* (Basingstoke: Macmillan Press).

Melman, Seymour, 1970, *Pentagon Capitalism* (New York: McGraw-Hill).

Melman, Seymour, 1974, *The Permanent War Economy* (New York: Simon & Schuster).

Menon, Krishnagopal, 1982, "Financial Reporting by SOEs" (Ph.D. dissertation: Pennsylvania State University).

Menzies, Hugh D., 1979, "U.S. Companies in Unequal Combat," *Fortune*, 99, no. 7 (April 9), 104–110.

Mestmacker, Ernst-Joachim, 1967, "State-Trading Monopolies in the European Economic Community," *Vanderbilt Law Review* 20, no. 2: 321–353.

Meyer, John R., and William B. Tye, 1979, "State-Owned Enterprises and Predatory Competition in International Markets: International Airlines as a Case Study" (Paper presented at the State-Owned Enterprises Conference, March, Harvard Business School, Boston, Mass.).

Meyer, Robert A., 1975, "Publicly Owned versus Privately Owned Utilities: A Policy Choice," *Review of Economics and Statistics* 57, no. 4: 391–399.

Miller, Donald B. (1977), *Personal Vitality* (Boston: Addison-Wesley).

Miller, Jeffrey, and Peter Murrel (1979), "The Problem of Equity in Determining Managerial Rewards in Public Enterprises. A Comment on A. Bergson, Managerial Risks and Rewards in Public Enterprises," *Journal of Comparative Economics* 3: no. 4: 407–415.

Miliband, Ralph, 1969, *The State and Capitalist Society: The Analysis of the Western System of Power* (London: Weidenfeld & Nicholson).

Minns, Richard, and J. Thornley, 1978, *State Shareholding* (London: Macmillan).

Mintzberg, Henry, 1973, *The Nature of Managerial Work* (New York: Harper & Row).

Mintzberg, Henry, 1983, *Power in and Around Organizations* (Englewood Cliffs, N.J.: Prentice-Hall).

Mirrlees, James A., 1976, "Optimal Tax Theory: A Synthesis," *Journal of Public Economics* 6, no. 4: 327–358.

Mishan, Ezra J., 1962, "Second Thoughts on Second Best," *Oxford Economic Papers* 13, no. 3: 205–217.

Mitchell, Bridger M., and Paul K. Kleindorfer, eds., 1980, *Regulated Industries and Public Enterprises: European and United States Perspectives* (Lexington, Mass.: D.C. Heath).

Mitchell, Bridger M., and Willard G. Manning, 1978, *Peak-Load Pricing* (Cambridge, Mass.: Ballinger).

Moe, Ronald C., 1979, "Government Corporations and the Erosion of Accountability: The Case of the Proposed Energy Security Corporation," *Public Administration Review* 39, no. 6: 566–571.

Mohring, Herbert, 1970, "The Peak-Load Problem with Increasing Returns and Pricing Constraints," *American Economic Review* 60, no. 4: 693–705.

Mohring, Herbert., 1972, "Optimization and Scale Economies in Urban Bus Transportation," *American Economic Review* 62, no. 4: 591–604.

Monnier, Lionel, 1978, *Capitaux Publics et Stratégie de l'Etat* (Paris: Rouen University).

Monopolies and Mergers Commission, 1980, *British Railways Board: London and South East Commuter Services*, Cmnd. 8046 (London: HMSO).

Monopolies and Mergers Commission, 1983, *London Electricity Board*, Cmd. 8812 (London, HMSO).

Monsen, R. Joseph, 1969, "Ownership and Management: The Effect of Separation on Performance," *Business Horizons* 12: (August), pp. 45–52.

Monsen, R. Joseph, and Kenneth D. Walters, 1979, "A Theory of State-Owned Firms in a Democracy" (Paper presented at the State-Owned Enterprises Conference, Harvard Business School, Boston, Mass., March).

Monsen, R. Joseph, and Kenneth D. Walters, 1980, "State-Owned Firms: A Review of the Data and Issues," in Lee Preston, ed., *Research in Corporate Social Performance and Policy*, vol. 2, Greenwich, Ct., JAI Press, pp. 125–156.

Monsen, R. Joseph, and Kenneth D. Walters, 1983, *Nationalized Companies: A Threat to American Business* (New York: McGraw-Hill).

Moore, John, R., ed., 1967, *The Economic Impact of TVA* (Knoxville: The University of Tennessee Press).

Moore, Thomas G., 1970, "The Effectiveness of Regulation of Electric Utility Prices," *Southern Economic Journal* 36, no. 4: 365–375.

Moran, Theodore H., 1974, *Multinational Corporations and the Politics of Dependence: Copper in Chile* (Princeton: Princeton University Press).

Morandiere, Leon J., and Maurice Bye, eds., 1948, *Les Nationalisations en France et a l'Étranger* (Paris: PUF).

Morgan, W. Douglas, 1977, "Investor Owned versus Publicly Owned Water Agencies: An Evaluation of the Property Rights Theory of the Firm," *Water Resources Bulletin* 13: 775–781.

Morris, Charles R., 1980, *The Cost of Good Intentions; New York City and the Liberal Experiment 1960–1975* (New York: W.W. Norton).

Morrison, Herbert Stanley, 1933, *Socialisation and Transport* (London: Counstable).

Moses Committee, 1965, *Report of the Committee on Management of State Enterprises* (Jerusalem, December); Hebrew.

Mueller, Denis C., 1979, *Public Choice* (Cambridge: Cambridge University Press).

Muller, Jürgen, 1979, "The Political Economy of Efficient Pricing Rules by SOEs" (Paper presented at the State-Owned Enterprises Conference, Harvard Business School, Boston, Mass., March).

Murray, Michael A., 1975, "Comparing Public and Private Management: An Exploratory Essay," *Public Administration Review* 35, no. 4: 364–371.

Murthy, K.R.S., 1980, "Strategic Management of Public Enterprises: A Framework for Analysis" (Paper presented at BAPEG Conference on Public Enteprises in LDCs, April, Cambridge, Mass.).

Murthy, K.R.S., 1981, "Control Environment of Public Enterprises in India: An Evolutionary Perspective," Report of the World Bank (October).

Musolf, Lloyd D., 1959, *Public Ownership and Accountability: The Canadian Experience* (Cambridge, Mass.: Harvard University Press).

Musolf, Lloyd D., 1972, *Mixed Enterprise: A Developmental Perspective* (Lexington, Mass.: D.C. Heath, Lexington Books).

Musolf, Lloyd D., and Harold Seidman, 1980, "The Blurred Boundaries of Public Administration," *Public Administration Review* 40, no. 2: 124–30.

Musolf, Lloyd, D., 1983, *Uncle Sam's Private, Profit-Seeking Corporations* (Farnborough: Gower).

Narain, Laxmi, 1979, "Public Enterprise in India—An Overview," *Annals of Public and Co-operative Economy* 50, no. 4: 59–79.

Narain, Laxmi, 1980, *Principles and Practices of Public Enterprise Management* (New Delhi: S. Chand & Co.).

Narain, Laxmi, 1981, *Organization Structure in Large Public Enterprises* (Jawahar Nagar, Delhi: S. Balwant for Ajanta Publications).

Narain, Laxmi, 1982, *Autonomy of Public Enterprises* (New Delhi: Scope).

Nash, Chris, 1985, "Paying Subsidy to British Rail: How to Get Value for Money," *Public Money* 5, no. 1: 35–40.

National Academy of Public Administration, 1981, *Report on Government Corporations*, 2 vols. (Washington, D.C.: National Academy of Public Administration).

National Economic Development Office (NEDO), 1976, *A Study of U.K. Nationalised Industries* (London: HMSO).

Nelson, Richard R., ed., 1982, *Government and Technical Progress: A Cross-Industry Analysis* (New York: Pergamon Press).

Neuberg, Leland Gerson, 1977, "Two Issues in the Municipal Ownership of Electric Power Distribution Systems," *Bell Journal of Economics* 8, no. 1: 303–323.

Neustadt, Richard E., 1960, *Presidential Power* (New York: John Wiley & Sons).

Nielsen, Richard P., 1981, "Competitive Advantages of State-Owned and Controlled Business," *Management International Review* 21, no. 3: 56–66.

Nielsen, Richard P., 1982, "Government-Owned Businesses: Market Presence, Competitive Advantages and Rationales for Their Support by the State," *American Journal of Economics and Sociology* 41, no. 1: 17–27.

Nigro, Flexi, and Lloyd Nigro, 1977, *Modern Public Administration*, 4th ed. (New York: Harper & Row).

Niskanen, William A., ed., 1971, *Bureaucracy and Representative Government* (Chicago: Aldine-Atherton).

Nora, Simon, 1967, Group de Travail du Comité Interministériel des Entreprises Publiques, *Rapport sur les Entreprises Publiques* (Paris: La Documentation Française).

Noreng, Øystein, 1980, *The Oil Industry and Government Strategy in the North Sea* (London: Croom Helm).

Normanton, E. Leslie, 1966, *The Accountability and Audit of Governments* (Manchester: Manchester University Press).

Nove, Alec, 1964, *Economic Rationality and Soviet Politics* (New York: Praeger).

Nove, Alec, 1973, *Efficiency Criteria for Nationalised Industries: A Study of the Misapplication of Micro-Economic Theory* (London: Allen & Unwin).

Nove, Alec, 1981, "Public Enterprises: Performance Evaluation," monograph (Ljubljana: ICPE).

Nunnenkamp, Peter, 1981, "The Efficiency of State-Owned Enterprises in the Manufacturing Industry of Taiwan," *Academia Economic Papers* 9, no. 2: 87–124.

Nyman, Steve, and Aubrey Silberston, 1977, "The Ownership and Control of Industry," in Alexis P. Jacquemin and Henry W. De Jong, *Welfare Aspects of Industrial Markets* (Leiden: Nijhoff), pp. 43–72.

O'Brien, Patrick, 1966, *The Revolution in Egypt's Economic System: from private enterprise to socialism 1952–1965* (London, Oxford University Press).

O'Connor, James, 1973, *The Fiscal Crisis of the State* (New York: St. Martin's Press).

Offe, Claus, 1972, "Advanced Capitalism and the Welfare State," *Politics and Society* 2, no. 4: 479–488.

Ohashi, T.M., T.P. Roth and Z.A. Spinaler, eds., 1980, *Privatization: Theory and Practice: Distributing Shares in Private and Public Enterprises* (Vancouver: Fraser Institute).

Ollig, Gerhard, 1980, "Steel and State in Germany," *Annals of Public and Co-operative Economy* 51, no. 4: 423–438.

Olson, Mancur, 1965, *The Logic of Collective Action: Public Goods and the Theory of Groups* (Cambridge, Mass.: Harvard University Press).

Olson, Mancur, 1982, *The Rise and Decline of Nations* (New Haven, Conn.: Yale University Press).

Otter, Casten von, 1984, "The Welfare State—The Public-Sector Efficiency and Neo-Conservative Critique," *Economic and Industrial Democracy* 5, no. 2: 249–260.

Palmer, John, 1972, "The Separation of Ownership from Control in Large U.S. Industrial Corporations," *Quarterly Review of Economics and Business* 12, no. 3: 55–62.

Panzar, John C., and Robert D. Willig, 1977, "Free Entry and the Sustainability of Natural Monopoly," *Bell Journal of Economics* 8, no. 1: 1–22.

Panzoni, Erico E., 1983, "Background, Nature and Problems of the Public Sector in Argentina Economy," *Annals of Public and Co-operative Economy* 54, no. 3: 377–386.

Papandreou, Andreas G., 1952, "Some Basic Problems in the Theory of the Firm," in Bernard Francis Haley, ed., *Survey of Contemporary Economics*, Vol. 2 (Homewood, Ill.: Irwin), pp. 183–219.

Parsons, Talcott, 1956, "Suggestions for a Sociological Approach to the Theory of Organizations," *Administrative Science Quarterly*, no. 1: 63–85.

Parsons, Talcott, 1960, *Structure and Process in Modern Societies* (New York: Free Press).

Pashigian, B. Peter, 1976, "Consequences and Causes of Public Ownership of Urban Transit Facilities," *Journal of Political Economy* 84, no. 6: 1239–1259.

Peltzmann, Sam, 1971, "Pricing in Public and Private Enterprises: Electric Utilities in the United States," *Journal of Law and Economics* 14, no. 1: 109–147.

Penrose, Edith T., 1952, "Biological Analogies in the Theory of the Firm," *American Economic Review* 42, no. 5: 804–819.

Perroux, François, 1955, "Note sur la Notion de Pôle de Croissance," *Economie Appliquée*, 8, nos. 1–2: 307–320.

Pescatrice, Donn R., and John M. Trapani III, 1980, "The Performance and Objectives of Public and Private Utilities Operating in the United States," *Journal of Public Economics* 13, no. 2: 259–276.

Peterson, Susan, assisted by Morris Heath, 1977, *Canadian Directorship Practices: A Critical Self-Examination* (Ottawa, The Conference Board in Canada).

Pfeffer, Jeffrey, and Gerald R. Salancik, 1977, "Organization Design: The Case for the Colonial Model of Organizations," *Organizational Dynamics* 6, no. 2: 15–29.

Pfeffer, Jeffrey, and Gerald R. Salancik, 1978, *The External Control of Organizations: A Resource Dependence Perspective* (New York: Harper & Row).

Phatak, Arvind, 1969, "Governmental Interference and Management Problems of Public-Sector Firms," *Annals of Public and Co-operative Economy* 40, no. 3: 337–350.

Philip, George, 1982, *Oil and Politics in Latin America: Nationalist Movements and State Companies*, Latin American Studies no. 40 (Cambridge: Cambridge University Press).

Pick, Pedro J., 1983, "Managing State-Owned Enterprises More Effectively: The Venezuelan Case," *Annals of Public and Co-operative Economy* 54, no. 3: 387–396.

Pierce, Harry H., 1953, *Railroads of New York: A Study of Government Aid, 1826-1875* (Cambridge, Mass.: Harvard University Press).

Pillai, Phillip N., 1983, *State Enterprise in Singapore: Legal Importation and Development* (Singapore: Singapore University Press).

Pletcher, David M., 1958, *Rails, Mines and Progress: Seven American Promoters in Mexico, 1867–1911* (Ithaca, N.Y.: Cornell University Press).

Pliatzky, Leo, 1982, *Getting and Spending: Public Expenditure, Employment and Inflation* (Oxford: Basil Blackwell).

Pondy, Louis R., 1969, "Effects of Size, Complexity and Ownership in Administrative Intensity," *Administrative Science Quarterly*, 14, pp. 47–60.

Poole, R.W., Jr., 1983, "Objections to Privatization," *Policy Review*, vol. 24 (Spring), pp. 105–119.

Posner, Michael V., and Richard Pryke, 1966, *New Public Enterprise*, Fabian Research Series no. 254 (London: Fabian Society).

Posner, Michael V., and S.J. Woolf, 1967, *Italian Public Enterprise* (Cambridge, Mass.: Harvard University Press).

Powell, Fred W., 1921, *The Railroads of Mexico* (Boston: Stratford).

Pozen, Robert C., 1972, "Public Corporations in Ghana: A Case Study in Legal Importation," *Wisconsin Law Review*, 1972, no. 3: 802–844.

Pozen, Robert C., 1976, *Legal Choices for State Enterprises in the Third World* (New York: New York University Press).

Prain, R., 1975, *Copper, the Anatomy of an Industry* (London: Mining Journal Books Ltd.).

Prakash, Om, 1963, *The Theory and Working of State Corporations with Special Reference to India* (New York: Praeger).

Prichard, J. Robert S., ed., 1983, *Crown Corporations in Canada: The Calculus of Instrument Choice* (Toronto: Butterworth).

Priest, George L., 1975, "The History of Postal Monopoly in the United States," *Journal of Law and Economics* 18, no. 1: 33–80.

Primaux, Walter, J., Jr., 1975, "A Re-examination of the Monopoly Market Structure for Electric Utilities," in Almarin Philips, ed., *Promoting Competition in Regulated Markets* (Washington, D.C.: Brookings Institution), 175–200.

Primaux, Walter J., 1977, "An Assessment of X-Efficiency Gained Through Competition," *Review of Economics and Statistics* 59, no. 1: 105–108.

Primaux, Walter J., Jr., 1978, "Rate Base Methods and Realized Rates of Return," *Economic Inquiry* 16, no. 1: 95–107.

Pryke, Richard, 1971, *Public Enterprises in Practice: The British Experience of Nationalisation over Two Decades* (London: MacGibbon and Kee).

Pryke, Richard, 1981, *The Nationalised Industries: Policies and Performance Since 1968* (Oxford: Martin Robertson).

Pryor, Frederick L., 1970, "The Extent and Pattern of Public Ownership in Developed Economies," *Weltwirtschaftliches Archiv* 104, no. 2: 159–188.

Pustay, Michael W., 1979, "The Transatlantic Airline Market: Exploring the Myths of Excessive, Unfair and Predatory Competition," *Quarterly Review of Economics and Business* 19, no. 2: 47–63.

Radetzki, Marian, 1985, *State Mineral Enterprises: An Investigation into Their Impact on International Mineral Markets* (Baltimore: The Johns Hopkins University Press) (citations are from 1983 draft).

Radetzki, Marian, and Carl Van Duyne, 1984, "The Response of Mining Investment to a Decline in Economic Growth: The Case of Copper in the 1970s," *Journal of Development Economics* 15, nos. 1–2–3: 19–46.

Ramamurti, Ravi, 1982, "Strategic Behavior and Effectiveness of SOEs in High-Technology Industries: A Comparative Study in the Heavy Engineering Industry in India" (DBA dissertation: Harvard University).

Ramamurti, Ravi, 1985a, "A Profile of the Public Entrepreneur" (Paper presented at the Forty-Fifth Annual Meeting of the Academy of Management, San Diego, August).

Ramamurti, Ravi, 1985b, "State-Owned Enterprises and Profits: An Empirical Study in an LDC" (Paper presented at the Forty-Fifth Annual Meeting of the Academy of Management, San Diego, August).

Ramanadham, V.V., 1981, *Parliament and Public Enterprise: Some Basic Concerns* (Ljubljana: ICPE).

Ramanadham, V.V., ed., 1984a, *Public Enterprise and the Developing World* (London: Croom Helm).

Ramanadham, V.V., 1984b, *The Nature of Public Enterprise* (London: Cromm Helm).

Ramsey, Frank, 1927, "A Contribution to the Theory of Taxation," *Economic Journal* 37: 47–61.

Randall, Maury R., 1978, "Government Purchases and the Rate of Return on Capital," *Quarterly Review of Economics and Business* 18, no. 4: 69–79.

Ranis, Gustav, ed., 1971, *Government and Economic Development* (New Haven, Conn.: Yale University Press).

Reddy, Ram G., 1983, *Government and Public Enterprise: Essays in Honour of V.V. Ramanadham* (London: Frank Cass).

Redwood, John, 1980, *Public Enterprise in Crisis: The Future of the Nationalised Industries* (Oxford: Basil Blackwell).

Redwood, John 1984, *Going for Broke: Gambling with Taxpayers' Money* (Oxford: Basil Blackwell).

Redwood, John, and John Hatch, 1981, *Value for Money Audits* (London: Center for Policy Studies).

Redwood, John, and John Hatch, 1982, *Controlling Public Industries* (Oxford: Basil Blackwell).

Reed, P.W., 1973, *The Economics of Public Enterprise* (London: Butterworth).

Rees, Ray, 1968, "Second-Best Rules for Public Enterprise Pricing," *Economica* 35: 260–273.

Rees, Ray, 1976, *Public Enterprise Economics* (London: Weidenfeld and Nicholson).

Rees, Ray, 1984, "The Public Enterprise Game," *Economic Journal* 94 (Suppl.): 109–123.

Reich, Charles, 1964, "The New Property," *Yale Law Journal* 73, no. 5: 733–787.

Reid, Graham, and Allen Kevin, 1970, *Nationalised Industries* (Harmondsworth: Penguin).

Reith (Lord), 1956, "Public Corporations: Need to Examine Control and Structure," *Public Administration* 34: 351–354.

Republic of Kenya, Ministry of Economic Planning and Development, 1979, *Economic Survey* (Nairobi: Government Printer).

Reuland, James M., 1975, "GATT and State-Trading Countries," *Journal of World Trade Law* 9, no. 3: 318–339.

Reynolds, Lloyd G., 1983, "The Spread of Economic Growth to the Third World," *Journal of Economic Literature* 21, no. 3: 941–980.

Richards, Max, 1978, *Organizational Goal Structures* (St. Paul, Minn.: West).

Richardson, J.J., 1981, "Problems of Controlling Public-Sector Agencies: The Case of Norwegian Oil Policy," *Political Studies* 29, no. 1: 35–50.

Riggs, Fred W., 1964, *Administration in Developing Countries: The Theory of Prismatic Society* (Boston: Houghton, Mifflin).

Roberts, David R., 1959, *Executive Compensation* (Glencoe, Ill.: Free Press).

Roberts, Marc J., 1975, "An Evolutionary and Institutional View of the Behavior of Public and Private Companies," *American Economic Review* 65, no. 2: 415–427.

Robson, William A., 1962, *Nationalised Industry and Public Ownership*, 2nd ed. (London: Allen & Unwin).

Robson, William A., 1969, "Ministerial Control of the Nationalized Industries," *Political Quarterly* 40: 103–112, 494–496.

Robson, William A., 1977, "The Control of Nationalised Industries," *National Westminster Bank Quarterly Review* (November), pp. 6–16.

Rodrik, Dani, 1979, "The Bauxite Aluminum Study—State-Owned Enterprises in the Industry" (mimeographed, Harvard University).

Roll, Lord, of Ipsden, ed., 1982, *The Mixed Economy*, Proceedings of Section F (Economics) of the British Association for the Advancement of Science, Salford 1980 (London: Macmillan).

Roman, Zoltan, 1981, *Government Control and Performance Evaluation of Public Enterprises in the Hungarian Industry* (Ljubljana: ICPE).

Ross, Irwin, 1963, "General Aniline Goes Private," *Fortune* 63: no. 3, September, pp. 127–156.

Sales, Armand, 1972, "A Firm and the Control of Its Environment," *International Studies of Management and Organization* 2, no. 3: 230–257.

Sampson, Anthony, 1976, *The Seven Sisters: The Great Oil Companies and the World They Shaped* (New York: Bantam).

Sapolsky, Harvey M., 1972, *The Polaris System Development* (Cambridge, Mass.: Harvard University Press).

Saraceno, Pasquale, 1962, "Public Enterprise in the Market Economy," in A. Winsemius and J.A. Pincus, eds., *Methods of Industrial Development* (Paris: OECD).

Saraceno, Pasquale, 1977, "The Italian System of State-Held Enterprises," *Journal of International Law and Economics* 11, no. 3: 407–446.

Sarathy, Ravi, 1985, "High-Technology Exports from Newly Industrialized Countries: The Brazilian Commuter Aircraft Industry," *California Management Review* 27, no. 2: 60–84.

Saulniers, Alfred, 1980, "State Trading Organization: A Bias Decision Model and Applications" (Paper presented at the Second BAPEG Conference, Cambridge, Mass., April).

Savas, Emanuel S., 1977a, "Policy Analysis for Local Government: Public vs. Private Refuse Collection," *Policy Analysis* 3, no. 1: 49–74.

Savas, Emanuel S., 1977b, *Evaluating the Organization and Efficiency of Solid Waste Collection* (Lexington, Mass.: D.C. Heath, Lexington Books).

Savas, Emanuel S., 1979, "Public vs. Private Refuse Collection: A Critical Review of the Evidence," *Journal of Urban Analysis* 6: 1–13.

Savas, Emanuel S., 1982, *Privatizing the Public Sector* (Chatham, N.J.: Chatham House Publishers).

Scherer, Charles R., 1977, *Estimating Electric Power System Marginal Costs* (New York: Elsevier).

Scherer, Frederick M., 1980, *Industrial Market Structure and Economic Performance*, 2nd ed. (Chicago: Rand McNally).

Schnitzer, Martin, 1972, *East and West Germany: A Comparative Economic Analysis* (New York: Praeger).

Schurmann, Franz, 1969, *Ideology and Organization in Communist China*, 2nd ed. (Berkeley: University of California Press).

Schvartz, Julien, rapporteur, 1974, Rapport sur les Sociétés Pétrollères Opérant en France," Commission d'Enquête Parliamentaire, Assemblée Nationale (Paris: Documentation Française).

Schwartzman, David, 1960, "The Burden of Monopoly," *Journal of Political Economy* 68: 627–630.

Scott, John, 1979, *Corporations, Classes and Capitalism* (London: Hutchinson & Co.).

Sèrre, H., ed., 1975, *Les Entreprises Publiques* (Paris: Edition Sociales).

Seidman, Harold, 1952, "The Theory of the Autonomous Government Corporation: A Critical Appraisal," *Public Administration Review* 12, no. 2: 89–96.

Seidman, Harold, 1954, "The Government Corporation: Organization and Control," *Public Administration Review* 14, no. 3: 183–192.

Seidman, Harold, 1959, "The Government Corporation in the United States," *Public Administration* (London) 37: 103–114.

Seidman, Harold, 1968, "Organizational Relationship and the Control of Public Enterprises," in U.N. *Organization and Administration of Public Enterprises, Selected Papers*, ST/TAO/M/36 (New York: United Nations), pp. 156–168.

Seidman, Harold, 1980, *Politics, Position, and Power: The Dynamics of Federal Organization*, 3rd ed. (New York: Oxford University Press).

Seidman, Harold, 1983a, "Public Enterprises in the United States," *Annals of Public and Co-operative Economy* 54, no. 1: 3–18.

Seidman, Harold, 1983b, "Public Enterprise Autonomy: Need for a New Theory," *Revue Internationale des Sciences Administratives* 49, no. 1, pp. 65–72.

Select Committee on Nationalised Industries, *Ministerial Control of the Nationalized*

Industries, first Report; session 1967–1968, Vol. 1, par. 40 (London: HMSO).

Select Committee on Nationalized Industries, *Reorganizing the Electricity Supply Industry*, ninth report; session 1977–1978 (28 September 1978). (London: HMSO).

Self, Peter, 1977, *Administrative Theory and Politics*, 2nd ed. (London: Allen & Unwin).

Selznick, Philip, 1949, *TVA and the Grass Roots* (Berkeley: University of California Press).

Sen, Anmartya, 1970, "Profit Maximization and the Public Sector," mimeographed, Memorial Lecture, Kerala University, India.

Servan-Schreiber, Jean Jacques, 1967, *Le Défi Américain* (Paris: Danoel).

Sexty, Robert W., 1980, "Autonomy Strategies of Government-Owned Business Corporations in Canada," *Strategic Management Journal* 1, no. 4: 371–384.

Sexty, Robert W., 1983, "The Accountability Dilemma in Canadian Public Enterprises: Social versus Commercial Responsiveness," *Annals of Public and Co-operative Economy* 54, no. 1: 19–34.

Shackleton, J.R., 1984, "Privatization: The Case Examined," *National Westminster Bank Quarterly Review* (May), pp. 59–73.

Shafer, Michael, 1983, "Capturing the Mineral Multinationals: Advantage or Disadvantage?" *International Organization* 37, no. 1: 93–119.

Shakaw, Don M., 1983, "Disequilibrium Processes in the Market for Electricity: The Case of Municipal Ownership," *Energy Journal*, 4, no. 2: 159–164.

Shanks, Michael, ed., 1963, *The Lessons of Public Enterprise* (London: Jonathan Cape).

Shapiro, David L., and Robert B. Shelton, 1981, "Public Ownership and Natural Resource Utilization," in Richard J. Horn, ed., *Studies in the Management of Government Enterprise* (The Hague: Martinus Nijhoff), pp. 96–108.

Sharkansky, Ira, 1975, "The Use of Government Corporation as a Tool for Economic Development—Opportunities and Problems," *Organization and Administration* (Hebrew), 21, no. 131–132: 4–11.

Sharkansky, Ira, 1979, *Whither the State? Politics and Public Enterprise in Three Countries* (Chatham, N.J.: Chatham House Publishers).

Sharkey, William W., 1982, *The Theory of Natural Monopoly* (New York: Cambridge University Press).

Sheehan, Robert, 1967, "Proprietor in the World of Big Business," *Fortune* 75: (June) 178–183.

Shelton, John, 1967, "Allocative Efficiency v. 'X-Efficiency': Comment," *American Economic Review* 57, no. 5: 1252–1258.

Shepherd, William G., ed., 1965, *Economic Performance under Public Ownership, British Fuel and Power* (New Haven, Conn.: Yale University Press).

Shepherd, William G., ed., 1976, *Public Enterprise: Economic Analysis of Theory and Practice* (Lexington, Mass.: D.C. Heath).

Shepherd, William G., 1979, *The Economics of Industrial Organization* (Englewood Cliffs, N.J.: Prentice-Hall).

Shinwell, Emanuel, 1955, *Conflict without Malice* (London: Odhams Press).

Shirley, Mary M., 1983, *Managing State-Owned Enterprises*, Staff Working Paper 577 (Washington, D.C.: World Bank).

Shonfield, Andrew, 1965, *Modern Capitalism: The Changing Balance of Public and Private Power* (London: Oxford University Press).

Short, R. Peter, 1984, "The Role of Public Enterprises: An International Statistical Comparison," in *Public Enterprises in Mixed Economies: Some Macroeconomic Aspects* (Washington, D.C.: International Monetary Fund), pp. 110–196.

Silver, Morris, 1980, *Affluence, Altruism, and Atrophy: The Decline of Welfare States* (New York: New York University Press).

Silver, Morris, 1983, *Prophets and Markets: The Political Economy of Ancient Israel* (Boston: Kluwer-Nijhoff).

Simon, Herbert A., 1959, "Theories of Decision-Making in Economics and Behavioral Science," *American Economic Review* 49, no. 3: 253–283.

Simon, Herbert A., 1964, "On the Concept of Organizational Goal," *Administrative Science Quarterly* 9: 1–22.

Simon, Herbert A., 1978, "How to Decide What to Do?" *Bell Journal of Economics* 9, no. 2: 494–507.

Simon, Herbert A., 1979, "Rational Decision-Making in Business Organizations," *American Economic Review* 69, no. 4: 495–513.

Simon of Wythenshawe, Lord, 1957, *The Boards of Nationalised Industries* (London: Longmans).

Simonnot, Philippe, 1975, *Le Pouvoir Monétaire* (Paris: Seghers).

Simwinga, George Kalenga, 1977, "Corporate Autonomy and Government Control: A Study of Three State Enterprises under a National Planned Developing Economy—INDECO RDC and NCCM of Zambia" (Ph.D dissertation: University of Pittsburgh).

Sloman, Martyn, 1978, *Socializing Public Ownership* (London: Macmillan).

Smart, Ian, 1981, "Energy and the Public Good," *International Journal* 36, no. 2: 255–272.

Smith, Adam, 1937, *The Wealth of Nations* (New York: Modern Library).

Smith, Bruce L.R., ed., 1975, *The New Political Economy: The Public Use of the Private Sector* (London: Macmillan).

Smith, Bruce L.R., and D.C. Hague, 1971, *The Dilemma of Accountability in Modern Government (Independence versus Control)* (London: Macmillan).

Smith, H.L., 1944, *Airways* (New York: A.A. Knopf).

Smith, Peter S., 1972, "Petrobrás: The Politicizing of a State Company, 1953–1964," *Business History Review* 46, no. 2: 182–201.

Snowberger, Vinson C., 1978, "Sustainability Theory: Its Implications for Governmental Preservation of a Regulated Monopoly," *Quarterly Review of Economics and Business* 18, no. 4: 81–89.

Sobhan, Rehman, 1979, "Public Enterprises and the Nature of the State," *Development and Change* 10, no. 1: 23–40.

Sobhan, Rehman, and Ahmed Muzaffer, 1980, *Public Enterprise in an Intermediate Regime: A Study in the Political Economy on Bangladesh* (Dacca: Bangladesh Institute of Development Studies).

Spann, Robert M., 1977, "Public versus Private Provision of Governmental Services," in Thomas E. Borcherding, ed., *Budgets and Bureaucrats: The Sources of Government Growth* (Durham, N.C.: Duke University Press), pp. 71–89.

Stanbury, W.T., and Fred Thompson, eds., 1982, *Managing Public Enterprises* (New York: Praeger).

Stano, Miron, 1975, "Executive Ownership Interests and Corporate Performance," *Southern Economic Journal* 42, no. 2: 272–278.

Starbuck, William H., and John M. Dutton, 1973, "Designing Adaptive Organizations," *Journal of Business Policy* 3, no. 4: 21–28.

"State in the Market, The," 1978, *The Economist*, December 30, pp. 37–58.

State of New York, Temporary State Commission on Coordination of State Activities, 1956, *Staff Report on Public Authorities under New York State* (Albany, N.Y.: Williams Press).

Steers, Richard M., 1975, "Problems in the Measurement of Organizational Effectiveness," *Administrative Science Quarterly* 20, no. 4: 546–558.

Stefani, Giorgio, 1981, "Control Mechanisms of Public Enterprises," *Annals of Public and Co-operative Economy* 52, nos. 1–2: 49–71.

Steiner, George A., 1969, *Top Management Planning* (New York: Macmillan).

Stepan, Alfred, 1978, *The State and Society: Peru in Comparative Perspective* (Princeton, N.J.: Princeton University Press).

Stewart, Rosemary, 1963, *The Reality of Management* (London: Heinemann).

Stieglitz, Harold, 1970, "The Chief Executive's Job and the Size of the Company," *The Conference Board Record* 7: 38–40.

Stiglitz, Joseph E., 1979, "A Neo-Classical Analysis of the Economics of Natural Resources" in Kerry V. Smith (ed.) *Scarcity and Growth Reconsidered* (Baltimore, Md.: The Johns Hopkins University Press), pp. 36–66.

Stobaugh, Robert B., 1976, "The Oil Companies in the Crisis," in Raymond Vernon, ed., *The Oil Crisis* (New York: W.W Norton), pp. 179–202.

Stoffaës, Christian, and P. Gadonneix, 1980, "Steel and State in France," *Annals of Public and Co-operative Economy* 51, no. 4: 405–422.

Stoffaës, Christian, and Jacques Victorri, 1977, *Nationalisations* (Paris: Flammarion).

Strange, Susan, 1979, "The Management of Surplus Capacity: Or How Does Theory Stand Up to Protectionism 1970s Style?" *International Organization* 33, no. 3: 303–332.

Su, Hu Yao, 1982, "The World Bank and Development Finance Companies," *Journal of General Management* 7, no. 1: 46–57.

Tendler, Judith, 1968, *Electric Power in Brazil: Entrepreneurship in the Public Sector* (Cambridge, Mass.: Harvard University Press).

Thimm, Alfred L., 1976, "Decision-Making at Volkswagen 1972–1975," *Columbia Journal of World Business* 11, no. 1: 94–103.

Thoburn, John, 1981, *Multinationals, Mining and Development: A Study of the Tin Industry* (London: Gower).

Thompson, James D., 1967, *Organizations in Action* (New York: McGraw Hill).

Thompson, James D., and William J. McEwen, 1958, "Organizational Goals and Environment: Goal-Setting as an Interaction Process," *American Sociological Review* 23, no. 1: 23–31.

Thomson, Leslie R., 1938, *The Canadian Railway Problem* (Toronto: Macmillan).

Thornhill, W., 1968, *The Nationalized Industries: An Introduction* (London: Nelson).

Tierney, John T., 1981, *Postal Reorganization: Managing the Public's Business* (Boston: Auburn House Publishing Co.).

Tierney, John T., 1984, "Government Corporations and Managing the Public's Business," *Political Science Quarterly* 99, no. 1: 73–92.

Timsit, Gerald, 1983, "Les Relations entre l'État et les Entreprises Publiques," *Revue Administrative* (Paris) 36: 9–14.

Tivey, Leonard, ed., 1973, *The Nationalised Industries Since 1960: A Book of Readings* (London: Allen & Unwin).

Tivey, Leonard, 1982, "Nationalized Industries as Organized Interests," *Public Administration* 60, no. 1: 42–55.

Topik, Steven, 1979, "The Evolution of Economic Role of the Brazilian State," *Journal of Latin American Studies* 11, no. 2: 325–342.

Tornblom, Lars, 1977, "The Swedish State Company Limited: Statsforëtag AB: Its Role in the Swedish Economy," *Annals of Public and Co-operative Economy* 48, no. 4: 451–461.

Trebat, Thomas J., 1983, *Brazil's State-Owned Enterprises: A Case Study of the State as Entrepreneur* (New York: Cambridge University Press).

Tuchman, Barbara, 1966, *The Proud Tower: A Portrait of the World before the War 1890–1914* (London: Hamish Hamilton).

Tucker, B.G., 1974, "Planning for State Business," *Journal of General Management* 1, no. 3: 63–68.

Tumlir, Jan, Anne Kreuger, and Robert Lighthizer, 1984, "Competing in a Changing World: Three Views," *Economic Impact*, no. 48: 13–21.

Tupper, Allan, and Bruce Doern, eds., 1981, *Public Corporations and Public Policy in Canada* (Montreal: Institute for Research in Public Policy).

Turner, D.W., 1976, "Strategic Planning in the British Airports Authority," *Journal of General Management* 3, no. 3: 12–22.

Turner, Louis, 1978, *Oil Companies in the International System* (London: Allen & Unwin for the Royal Institute of International Affairs).

Turvey, Ralph, 1971, *Economic Analysis and Public Enterprises* (London: Allen & Unwin).

United Nations, 1958, *Management of Industrial Enterprise in Underdeveloped Countries*, E/3143 ST/ECA/58 (New York: United Nations).

United Nations, 1959, *Economic Survey of Europe*, Prepared by the Secretariat of the Economic Commission of Europe, Geneva (New York: United Nations).

United Nations, 1968, *A System of National Accounts and Supporting Tables*, E:69 (New York: United Nations).

United Nations, 1984, *Performance Evaluation of Public Enterprises in Developing Countries: Criteria and Institutions*, TCD/SEM 84/5 (New York: United Nations).

United Nations, Center on Transnational Corporations (UNCTC), 1983, *Transnational Corporations in World Development, Third Survey* (New York: UNCTC).

United Nations, Department of Economic and Social Affairs, 1968, *Organization and Administration of Public Enterprises*, Selected papers (New York: United Nations).

United Nations, Department of Economic and Social Affairs, 1973, *Measures for Improving Performance of Public Enterprise in Developing Countries* (New York: United Nations).

United Nations, Industrial Development Organization (UNIDO), 1983, *The Changing Role of Public Industrial Sector in Development*, v. 83–56863 (Vienna: UNIDO).

United States, Comptroller General, 1981, *Standards for Audit of Government Or-*

ganizations, Programs, Activities and Functions, rev. ed. (Washington, D.C.: U.S. General Accounting Office).

United States, Department of Commerce, International Trade Administration, 1983, *Direct Investment in the United States by Foreign Government-Owned Companies, 1974–1981* (Washington, D.C., March).

United States, International Trade Commission, 1978, A *Survey and Analysis of Government Ownership in Market Economy Countries: A Study of Steel, Automobiles and Iron Ore* (Washington, D.C.: Government Printing Office).

U.S. Civil Aviation Board, 1975, *Government Ownership, Subsidy and Economic Assistance in International Aviation* (Washington, D.C.).

Vance, Stanley C., 1983, *Corporate Leadership: Boards, Directors and Strategy* (New York: McGraw-Hill).

Van der Bellen, Alexander, 1981, "The Control of Public Enterprises: The Case of Austria," *Annals of Public and Co-operative Economy* 52, no. 1–2: 73–100.

Vaughn, Garrett A., and Janet M. Rives, 1981, "Ownership Form, the Output Rate and the Demand for Inputs: The Case of Electric Utilities," *Applied Economics* 14, no. 3: 305–314.

Vernon, Raymond, ed., 1974, *Big Business and the State: Changing Relation in Western Europe* (London: Macmillan).

Vernon, Raymond, 1979, "The International Aspects of State-Owned Enterprises," *Journal of International Business Studies* 10, no. 3: 7–15.

Vernon, Raymond, 1981, "SOEs in Latin American Exports," *Quarterly Review of Economics and Business* 21, no. 2: 98–114.

Vernon, Raymond, 1984, "Linking Managers with Ministers: Dilemma of the State-Owned Enterprise," *Journal of Policy Analysis and Management* 4, no. 1: 39–55.

Vernon, Raymond, 1985, "Uncertainty in the Resource Industries: The Special Role of State-Owned Enterprises," in Raymond Vernon, *Exploring the Global Economy: Emerging Issues in Trade and Investment* (Lanham, Md.: University Press of America).

Vernon, Raymond, and Yair Aharoni, eds., 1981, *State-Owned Enterprise in the Western Economies* (London: Croom Helm).

Viallet, Claude, 1983, "Resolution of Conflicts in the Ownership of a Firm: The Case of Mixed Firms," *Annals of Public and Co-operative Economy* 54, no. 3: 255–270.

Villajero, Dan, 1961–1962, "Stock Ownership and the Control of Corporations," *New University Thought* 2: 33–77 and 3: 47–65.

Vining, Aidan R., 1983, "Provincial Ownership of Government Enterprises in Canada," *Annals of Public and Co-operative Economy* 54, no. 1: 35–56.

Vogel, David, 1982a, "Corporate Responsibility and the Market Ethos: A Comparison of Great Britain and the United States" (Paper prepared for the Forty-Second Annual Meeting of the Academy of Management, New York).

Vogel, David, 1982b, "The Power of Business in America: A Reappraisal," *British Journal of Political Science* 13: 19–43.

Votaw, Dow, 1964, *The Six-Legged Dog: Mattei and ENI—A Study in Power* (Berkeley: University of California Press).

Wallace, Richard L., 1967, "Cost and Revenue Associated with Increased Sales of TVA Power," *Southern Economic Journal* 33, no. 4: 526–534.

Wallace, Richard L., and Paul E. Junk, 1970, "Economic Inefficiency of Small Municipal Electric Generating Systems," *Land Economics* 46, no. 1: 98–104.

Walsh, Annmarie Hauck, 1978, *The Public's Business: The Politics and Practices of Government Corporations* (Cambridge, Mass.: MIT Press).

Walstedt, Bertil, 1980, *State Manufacturing Enterprises in a Mixed Economy: The Turkish Case* (Baltimore: The Johns Hopkins University Press).

Walters, Kenneth D., and R. Joseph Monsen, 1979, "State-Owned Business Abroad: New Competitive Threat," *Harvard Business Review* 57, no. 2 (March–April): 160–170.

Wamsley, L. Garry, and Mayer N. Zald, 1976, *The Political Economy of Public Organizations* (Bloomington: Indiana University Press).

Warley T.K., 1963, "The Future Role of Marketing Organizations," *Journal of Agricultural Economics* 15, no. 4: 550–566.

Warwick, Donald P., 1980, "A Transactional Approach to the Public Enterprise" (Paper presented at the Second BAPEG Conference, April, Cambridge, Mass.).

Webb, Michael Gordon, 1973, *The Economics of Nationalized Industries—A Theoretical Approach* (London: Thomas Nelson and Sons).

Webb, Michael Gordon, 1976, *Pricing Policies for Public Enterprises* (London: Macmillan).

Webb, Sidney, and Beatrice, 1920, *A Constitution for the Socialist Commonwealth of Great Britain* (London: Longmans).

Weidenbaum, Murray L., 1974, *The Economics of Peacetime Defense* (New York: Praeger).

Wells, Louis T., Jr., 1973, "Economic Man and Engineering Man," *Public Policy* 21, no. 3: 319–342.

Wells, Louis T., Jr., 1983, *Third World Multinationals: The Rise of Foreign Investment from Developing Countries* (Cambridge, Mass.: MIT Press).

Welsh, Frank, 1982, *The Profit of the State: Nationalised Industries and Public Enterprises* (London: Temple Smith).

Wheatcroft, S.F., 1973/1974, "Integrating British Airways," *Journal of General Management* 1, no. 2: 23–36.

White Paper, 1961, *The Financial and Economic Obligations of the Nationalised Industries*, Cmd. 1337 (London: HMSO, April).

White Paper, 1965, *Steel Nationalisation*, Cmd. 2651 (London: HMSO, April).

White Paper, 1967, *Nationalised Industries: A Review of Economic and Financial Objectives*, Cmd. 3437 (London: HMSO, November).

White Paper, 1978, *The Nationalised Industries*, Cmd. 7131 (London: HMSO, March).

Whitfield, Dexter, 1983, *Making it Public: Evidence and Action against Privatisation* (London: Pluto Press).

Wilkins, Mira, 1970, *Emergence of Multinational Enterprise: American Business Abroad from the Colonial Era to 1914* (Cambridge, Mass.: Harvard University Press).

Williams, M.L., 1975, "The Extent and Significance of the Nationalisation of Foreign-Owned Assets in Developing Countries, 1956–72," *Oxford Economic Papers* 27, no. 2: 260–273.

Williamson, Oliver E., 1964, *The Economics of Discretionary Behavior: Managerial Objectives in a Theory of the Firm* (Englewood Cliffs, N.J.: Prentice-Hall).

Williamson, Oliver E., 1970, *Corporate Control and Business Behavior: An Inquiry into the Effects of Organization Form on Enterprise Behavior* (Englewood Cliffs, N.J.: Prentice-Hall).

Williamson, Oliver E., 1975, *Markets and Hierarchies—Analysis and Antitrust Implications* (New York: Free Press).

Wilson, Ernest, 1984, "Contested Terrain: A Comparative and Theoretical Reassessment of State-Owned Enterprises in Africa," *Journal of Comparative and Commonwealth Studies* 22, no. 1: 4–27.

Wilson, Harold, 1979, *Final Term* (London: Weidenfeld and Nicholson).

Wionczek, Miguel, 1964, "Electric Power," in Raymond Vernon, ed., *Public Policy and Private Enterprise in Mexico* (Cambridge, Mass.: Harvard University Press), pp. 19–110.

Worcester, Dean A., 1973, "New Estimates of the Welfare Loss to Monopoly, United States: 1959–69," *Southern Economic Journal* 40, no. 2: 234–245.

World Bank, 1977, *Zambia, the Basic Economic Report* Annex 2: *The Parastatal Sector* (Washington, D.C.: mimeographed report no. 15866–ZA).

World Bank, 1981, *Accelerated Development in Sub-Saharan Africa* (Washington, D.C.: World Bank).

World Bank, 1983, *Work Development Report 1983* (New York: Oxford University Press).

World Bank, 1984, *World Development Report 1984* (New York: Oxford University Press).

Yoshitake, Kiohiko, 1974, *An Introduction to Public Enterprise in Japan* (London: Sage).

Yuchtman, Ephraim, and Stanley E. Seashore, 1967, "A System Resource Approach to Organizational Effectiveness," *American Sociological Review* 32, no. 6: 891–903.

Yunker, James A., 1975, "Economic Performance of Public and Private Enterprise: The Case of U.S. Electric Utilities," *Journal of Economics and Business* 28, no. 1: 60–67.

Zakariya, Hasan S., 1978, "State Petroleum Companies," *Journal of World Trade Law* 12, no. 6: 481–500.

Zaleznik, Abraham, 1970, "Power and Politics in Organizational Life," *Harvard Business Review* 48, no. 3 (May–June): 47–60.

Zaleznik, Abraham, 1977, "Managers and Leaders: Are They Different?" *Harvard Business Review* 55, no. 3: 67–78.

Zaleznik, Abraham, 1979, "Power and Leadership in State-Owned Enterprises" (Paper delivered at a conference on State-Owned Enterprises in Industrialized Countries, Harvard University, Graduate School of Business Administration, Boston, Mass., 26–28 March).

Zardkoohi, Asghar, and Alain Sheer, 1984, "Public versus Private Liquor Retailing: An Investigation into the Behavior of the State Governments," *Southern Economic Journal* 50, no. 4: 1058–1076.

Zeitlin, Maurice, 1974, "Corporate Ownership and Control: The Large Corporation and the Capitalist Clan," *American Journal of Sociology* 79, no. 5: 1073–1119.

Zif, Jehiel, 1981, "Managerial Strategic Behavior in State-Owned Enterprises—Business and Political Orientations," *Management Science* 27, no. 11: 1326–1339.

Zif, Jehiel, 1983, "Explanatory Concepts of Managerial Strategic Behavior in SOEs: A Multinational Study," *Journal of International Business Studies* 14, no. 1: 35–46.

Zysman, John, 1977, *Political Strategies for Industrial Order: State, Market and Industry in France* (Berkeley: University of California Press).

Zysman, John, 1983, *Governments, Markets and Growth: Financial Systems and the Politics of Industrial Change* (Ithaca, N.Y.: Cornell University Press).

NEWSPAPERS, TRADE JOURNALS

The Banker, London
Business Week, New York
The Economist, London
Euromoney, London
The Financial Times, London
Fortune, New York
Institutional Investor, New York
The New York Times, New York
The Wall Street Journal, New York

Subject Index

British South American Airways. *See* United
Kingdom.
British Steel Company. *See* United
Kingdom.
British Waterways Board, 98
budget deficit, 326
budgetary burden, 178
budgetary difficulties, 229–230
Budgetary Procedure Act of 1959, 12
Bull and Ridge Computers, 365
Bumiputas, 323
Bumiputa Malaysia Finance, 270
Burma, 17, 19, 97, 181
  telephone, 109

Canada, 1, 2, 19, 20, 51, 60, 72, 92–94, 95,
    108, 112, 118, 111–142, 144–147, 180,
    205–206, 250, 303, 307, 310, 315, 317,
    318–330, 331, 336, 348, 366, 374, 379,
    390
  Air Canada Act of 1977, 332
  Air Canada, 144, 159, 256
  aircraft industry in, 330
  airlines, 204
  Alberta Energy Corporation, 277
  alcohol, 96
  Atomic Energy of Canada Ltd., 159
  auditor general, 274
  Auditor General Act, 250
  banks, 112
  British Columbia Hydro, 36
  British Columbia Railroad (BCR), 280
  British Columbia Resources Investment
    Corporation, 277, 336
  board of directors, 307, 310
  Canadian Cellulose Company Limited,
    122–123
  Canadian Development Corporation
    (CDC), 94, 105, 114, 115, 148, 277, 303
  Canadian National Railways, 78, 117,
    205–206, 332
  Canadian Northern Railroad, 78
  Canadian Pacific Air, 204
  Canadian Pacific Railroad, 78, 205–206
  Canadian Wheat Board, 93, 348
  coal, 25
  Eldorado Nuclear, Ltd., 93, 261
  electricity, 93, 108, 104
  Federal Combines Act, 261
  grain, 348
  Hydro Quebec, 36, 108, 198
  hydroelectric power, 108
  insurance, 94
  Newfoundland Light and Power, 198
  oil, 351
  Ontario Hydro, 36, 93, 268, 302
  Petro Canada, 351
  Petrocan, 105

Polysar Limited, 393
Potash Corporation of Saskatchewan, 105
  and privatization, 329–330
Privy Council report, 131
railroads, 77–78, 205, 206
Sidbee, 204, 303
telephone, 107, 109
transportation, 94
Uranium Canada, Ltd., 261
World War II, 93
Cape Province, South African Iron and
  Steel Corporation, 103
capitalism, 45
Capon, Noel, 61
car manufacturing, 24, 371, 372
career paths, 293
CEEP, 6, 13, 393
Cefis, 116
Central Electricity Generating Board
  (CEGB). *See* United Kingdom.
Chad, 109
Chamberlain, Joseph, 109
checks and balances, 278–279
Chesapeake and Delaware Canal, 98
Chiarelli Commission, 245
Chile, 19, 20, 27, 97, 112, 180, 181, 189,
    262, 318, 320, 329
  Allende regime, 262, 318
  CODELCO, 133, 255, 358
  copper, 133, 355, 358
  CORFO, 112
  credit institutions, 112
  iron, 356
  steel, 361
China, 356
  steel, 360, 361
  tin, 356
Chrysler Corporation, 9, 44, 114
Churchill, Winston, 100
Civil Aviation Act, 1971, 135
Coal Industry Nationalization Act of 1946,
    53
coal, 2, 3, 96, 138, 322, 350
coalition
  external, 153, 154–155, 223–224
  internal, 153, 154
cobalt, 356
cocoa, 97–98
  marketing, 256
CODELCO. *See* Chile.
Colbert, 96
Colombia, 30, 60, 181
commanding heights, 101
commercial-type enterprises, 218
commercialization, 144–145, 147, 332–335
  as an alternative to privatization, 332–333
commissars, 291
Commodity Credit Corporation, 52

Author Index

471